THE
ILLUSTRATOR
IN AMERICA 1860-2000

Illustration by Howard Pyle
The Mysterious Chest, **Harper's Monthly,** December, 1908.

Dean Cornwell, *The Race of the Natchez and the Robert E. Lee,* painted for **True** magazine.

THE
ILLUSTRATOR
IN AMERICA 1860-2000
by Walt Reed

THE SOCIETY OF ILLUSTRATORS, NEW YORK

Charles Santore, advertisement for Hunt Manufacturing Co.

THE ILLUSTRATOR IN AMERICA 1860-2000

ISBN 0-942604-80-6, Society of Illustrators
ISBN 0-8230-2523-3, Watson-Guptill

Library of Congress Catalog Card Number 00 133287

Book and Cover designed by Illustration House, Inc.

Distributors to the trade in the United States and Canada:
Watson-Guptill Publications
1515 Broadway
New York, New York 10036

Distributed throughout the rest of the world by:
Harper Collins International
10 East 53rd Street
New York, New York 10019

ACKNOWLEDGEMENTS

No less than before, credit is owed to all those who were of assistance in the preparation of the first and second editions of this book. For this edition, the following individuals or institutions should be thanked for making helpful contributions in bringing the history up to date:

To the many cooperating illustrators, magazine and book publishers, museums, and private collectors for permissions to reproduce artworks.

Also, to the following individuals:
Terrence Brown, Director, Society of Illustrators, for initiating the sponsorship of this publication and following through with the Society's support.
Gerald McConnell, Publication Chairman of the Society, for his expert hands-on coordination which helped to keep the book on schedule and production details under control.
Arpi Ermoyan, whose careful editing removed many inconsistencies in format, spelling, and syntax and added insight from her long association with the Society.
Vincent DiFate, expertise with science fiction art and contemporary illustration.
Jill Bossert, advice on the "new" illustrators movement.
Frederic Taraba, supplier of facts and dates when needed.
Harry Katz, Library of Congress, for access to original Civil War art, especially by the Waud brothers.

And, for those involved in production:
Lyn German - basic layout and early decades;
Ellen Feigen - scanning and layouts;
Melissa Watson - SoHo Reprographics;
Lisa Green, for her skill with color and whose diligent efforts in many ways kept the book on schedule;
My wife, Mary Reed, who typed the manuscript;
Jenny Bonilla, who typed the bibliography;
Jim Pratzon - photography;

And finally, to my son, Roger, whose editing and helpful tightening up of the text, along with myriad pertinent suggestions, has made a significant improvement to the completed book.

It should also be noted that many deserving illustrators could not be included here due only to constraints of space and those omissions do not represent any less respect and admiration for their works.

— Walt Reed

Published by:
The Society of Illustrators, Inc.
128 East 63rd Street
New York, New York 10021
Fax: (212) 838-2561, Phone (212) 838-2560

Printed in Hong Kong.

CONTENTS

Assault of The Second Louisiana (Colored) Regiment on the Confederate Works at Fort Hudson, May 27th, 1863. Francis H.Schell, Wood Engraving.

INTRODUCTION TO THE THIRD EDITION

It is a privilege to have the opportunity to do a third edition of The Illustrator in America. With it comes the use of color throughout, enough more pages to expand the history back to the decade of the Civil War, and to update entries to the twenty-first century. Almost all of the artists are represented by new examples, particularly to make use of color, and new biographies have been added in each of the decades, bringing the total number to 647.

Beginning with the first edition in 1966, which covered the period of 1900-1960s, it was still possible to obtain biographical information directly — either verbally or by questionnaires — for a majority of the included artists who were then living. The questionnaires provided a trove of primary data such as the first published appearance of an artist's work. In covering the careers of the earlier deceased artists, it was necessary to rely on authoritative books or papers, but this was only sometimes possible. Standard encyclopedic art references were cross-checked to verify accuracy of facts and dates, as were newspaper obituaries. Since illustrators were often not recorded in the standard biographical dictionaries of artists, however, it was also necessary to consult many of the contemporary periodicals for their random, often brief, commentaries on artists who may have been featured within an issue.

Thus, the information is an amalgam from many sources, which we do not attempt to pinpoint. The bibliography at the back of this volume lists many of these sources, but it is by no means complete or exhaustive. It also lists useful sources in addition to those actually used, to provide more complete information for those who may wish to do further study. The same methods of gathering information were continued through the present volume.

For the second edition of the Illustrator in America: 1880-1980, published in 1984, the advent of the Golden Age of American Illustration was chosen as a logical beginning, and it allowed the book to span a century.

For this current edition, we are reaching further back. Prior to the Civil War, illustration was mostly limited to crude wood cuts and copper engravings printed in publications of small circulation, or as paintings seen only by patrons of museums or exhibitions. The invention of lithography made the production of larger editions of images possible and it, as well as the improvement in techniques of wood engraving, came together by the time of the Civil War, when a mass audience was anxious for word and picture of the events of that conflict. This radical enlargement of audience and improvements in the reproduction of illustration is an appropriate starting place for this record.

We've retained the organization of the biographies alphabetically by decade, as browsing reveals each artist's professional context in any particular era. An attempt has been made to place each artist in the decade in which he or she first came into professional prominence.

Many illustrators fraternized at the art clubs in major cities, and some considered themselves students or followers of another artist even when there was no personal contact, since magazines provided a periodical "gallery" through which they could become

thoroughly familiar with each other's work. The chart (pages 10 & 11) diagrams in broad strokes some of the progressive influences that have shaped American illustration over the last 150 years.

The artwork selected for each illustrator has been drawn from many quarters. Whenever possible, pictures have been reproduced directly from the original drawings or paintings, with the cooperation of many owners, public and private, as credited. It is estimated that less than a tenth of all published pictures still exist, however. Since they were considered to have no further function once reproduced, many pictures were given away by the publishers or were simply destroyed if not retrieved by the artist. Too many artists did not bother; the pictures could not be used again, they took up space, and they had little monetary value. Artists sometimes exchanged pictures with fellow illustrators, those who admired each other's work, or would give them away to fans who asked for them. Some even painted new pictures over their old ones. Estate tax consequences also prompted some artists to destroy their works to avoid a burden on their survivors.

For many illustrators, therefore, their careers survive largely on the printed page, and it has been necessary to reproduce their work from such reproductions. Thanks to the sophistication of today's scanning and printing technology, the disparity in quality between re-screened reproductions and those from the original art has been greatly minimized and in many cases, the recycled images look better than the first time they were reproduced. This is even true when the originals have survived. Until recently,

halftone printing could not capture a broad range of values, and for reasons of economy, full color paintings were often reproduced in black and white only, or in black and one second primary color. We can now present those pictures here for the first time the way the artists painted them.

As with the last update, a new generation of current illustrators is also presented. The turn of the millenium is again a period of great change. The marketplaces for illustration have continued to shift and shake out as old magazines failed and new publications were launched. Just as the inventions of lithography, halftones, and television had great impact on illustration, the computer is causing radical changes in the publishing industry, as well as on the very working methods of illustrators today.

Many hitherto impossible effects can be created and utilized to produce radical new forms of illustration that do not even require paper or canvas, but can go from computer screen via digitized disc to the printing press. However, the pioneering illustrator using the computer faces the problem of losing his or her individual identity through the software's predispositions, much as earlier illustrators' individual styles were lost due to the limitations of the wood engraving process.

It is the beginning of an exciting new period, only introduced here. Does it herald the end of the creation of unique, original works of illustrative art? Posterity must await yet a fourth edition to see how the field further evolves.

"The Bloody Massacre Perpetrated in King Street, Boston, on March 5, 1770, by a party of the 29th Reg't." An early illustration engraved by Paul Revere. Hand colored and distributed to an outraged populace, it played a large role in arousing public support for the American Revolution. This version of the event was shamelessly plagiarized from the original version made by Henry Pelham (1749-1806) and was published by Revere a week earlier under his own name.

Mr. Richard Mather by John Foster (1648-1681). Woodcut, America's First Print. By permision of the Houghton Library, Harvard University.

A Buffalo Chase by George Catlin circa 1830. Such paintings were exhibited widely in the Eastern States and in Europe, where they presented Native American culture to fascinated audiences.

PREFACE - ORIGINS OF AMERICAN ILLUSTRATION

Of necessity, the earliest illustrations grew out of the primitive conditions of a frontier country. Cut off from the sophistication of the arts in Europe, many early American artists trained themselves, and improvised methods for inscribing printing plates of wood or of copper. Early books, broadsides, newspapers and magazines reflected this crude technique, and it was at least another 150 years after John Foster before European standards of training and technology could be challenged.

Though backward, Americans had a rich mine of subject matter to exploit. There is also a sense that these primitive but talented American artists could present their observations more honestly than with the interfering gloss of technical facility. A good example is George Catlin, whose portraits and paintings of native life could be seen only in traveling exhibitions. Their reproduction in color would have to wait decades until the invention of new printing methods.

In both Europe and America, limitations to the reproduction of the art was the major barrier to accurate, printed translation of the original drawings or paintings.

The invention of printing with movable type in the sixteenth century had a profound influence on the form of this art. Earlier hand-penned texts could be illustrated (or "illuminated") with elaborate full-color, painted imagery, but audiences were limited to the elite since each book was highly precious. While the new audience for printed texts grew explosively, the printing technology imposed severe restrictions on illustrators. Their means of expression was abruptly limited by the requirements of the printing process. Images became reduced to those that could be cut into wood or metal plates mounted into forms with the movable type, which were then inked and pressed firmly onto sheets of paper.

Over the next four centuries, artists (and printers) gradually improved and refined their crafts, gaining increased freedom of expression in the process, and raising the engraving quality to remarkable levels of interpretive artistry. It was not until the combination of photography with halftone engraving at the end of the nineteenth century, however, that the artists began to see reproduction of their works with fidelity to their original drawings or paintings.

Freed from their dependence on the middlemen engravers to interpret tonal works into line plates (which had removed most of the distinguishing hallmarks of an individual artist's technique), illustrators could begin to display their personal virtuosity. The combination of high-speed rotary plate presses, ever-improving quality of halftone engraving and an enlarging audience by the 1890s brought about a Golden Age of Illustration. By World War I, Americans had overcome their sense of cultural inferiority to Europe, and American illustrators were greatly respected. The best artists of that era were attracted to this mode of expression and vigorously competed in pursuit of the huge readership of nationally distributed magazines, books and newspapers, which eventually dwarfed that of Europe.

This book traces the progress of that combined evolution of technology and artistry in America from 1860 to 2000.

CURRIER & IVES

Produced indigenous art based on sensational news events, such as shipwrecks and fires which followed the historical chapbook and broadside tradition.

THE CIVIL WAR

Provided a powerful need for more news and pictures. It gave rise to the "special artists" who pictured the progress of the war for publications such as *Frank Leslie's* and *Harper's Weeklies.*

PERIODICAL STAFFS

Were created with on-the-job training by publishers which provided a source of talent through a "bull pen" of artists.

EUROPEAN SCHOOLS

Were considered far superior to American schools; academies in Italy, Germany, France, and England provided a post-graduate training for American artists.

Several forces brought the **GOLDEN AGE** of American Illustration to flower. Edwin Austin Abbey, A.B. Frost, Charles Dana Gibson, Frederic Remington, and Howard Pyle were setting high standards for excellence. Half-tone printing was greatly improved and permitted reproduction of the art in full color.

The Ashcan school was quickly eclipsed by **THE ARMORY SHOW** of 1913. Although too radical for its time, especially for illustration, its influence would appeal to avant-garde painters and the socialist artists for **THE MASSES**. Wallace Morgan, Frederic Gruger, and Henry Raleigh continued a reportorial style.

Illustrators were active during **WORLD WAR I** on battlefields and the home front.

J.C. LEYENDECKER

and F.X. Leyendecker kept the European influence alive. Robert Henri was also an important teacher. Walter Biggs added an impressionist "Fine Arts" tie to commercial illustration.

| 1860 | 1870 | 1880 | 1890 | 1900 | 1910 | 1920 |

EUROPEAN INFLUENCES

Came from illustrations printed in periodicals from England, France, and Germany. British artists were especially studied and influenced American artists who adapted their pictorial conventions to domestic ones.

AMERICAN SCHOOLS

As artists returned from European academies, many passed on their training through teaching or by example. Private art schools such as the Eric Pape School of Art in Boston and the Howard Pyle School in Wilmington, Delaware, had major influences on illustration.

The staffs of newspapers in the '90s were also producing **ARTIST-REPORTERS** who then graduated to the magazines, including a group from Philadelphia: John Sloan, William Glackens, and Everett Shinn who would become members of the "Eight" or **"ASHCAN SCHOOL"**. Their exhibition on February 3rd, 1908, created a sensation.

Many of **PYLE'S STUDENTS** carried on The Pyle School philosophy in their work by teaching, most notably **HARVEY DUNN** who taught another generation of illustrators. Several of Pyle's women students, including Jessie Willcox Smith and Elizabeth Shippen Green, also made important artistic contributions.

"Moderne" art consisted of many new infusions of art, but it was **JOHN HELD JR.** who best symbolized the Jazz Age. **ART DECO** came from Europe, represented largely through *Vogue* and *Vanity Fair* magazines.

AMERICAN ADVERTISING

centered in Chicago, was influenced by **HADDON SUNDBLOM**.

CURRENTS OF AMERICAN

Like all of the arts, illustration should be seen in context with its time. Most illustrations are created and shaped within the prevailing cultural forces. Occasionally some artists will strike out in new, original ways, counter to their times, and thereby create a new idiom to be followed by others.

If an analogy is made of time as a river with tributaries flowing into it at intervals, it makes a convenient metaphor for the history of American Illustration. Not that the river has always flowed evenly: there were many currents and cross-currents, eddies and backwaters.

The GREAT DEPRESSION forced many cutbacks in budgets for magazine art. New markets were sought in motion picture art, calendar art, and especially in the PULP MAGAZINES Many artists survived only through the assistance of the Works Progress Administration (WPA).

Illustration was now big business. *The Saturday Evening Post* cover was the apex showcase. THE POSTWAR BOOM, prosperity, big advertising budgets and pent-up consumer desires for housing and consumer goods created a strong demand for fiction and for advertising art. Photography was now seriously competing in the advertising field.

An unforeseen threat in the form of TELEVISION began to erode the century-old success of the family magazines, as advertising budgets were siphoned off to reach a public that preferred the new medium. Even fiction, the mainstay of illustrators, drew more viewers to TV than readers to magazines.

An emerging market in covers for PAPERBACK BOOKS provided assignments for many artists. *Sports Illustrated* and other specialty magazines began to replace the old-line publications. Illustrators were now encouraged to do more EXPERIMENTATION. Led by Austin Briggs, Bernie Fuchs and Bob Peak, illustration became more innovative.

Many illustrators created their own outlets by painting sports, military, Westerns, or science fiction subjects for a newly developed "print" market of signed reproductions. Artists were also needed in courtrooms as TV coverage was still excluded. A "NEW" ILLUSTRATORS school gathers momentum.

1930   1940   1950   1960   1970   1980   1990   2000

The end of the Depression was hastened by the onset of WORLD WAR II and the re-arming of Europe. The art outlook became more literal with an emphasis on the realism of weaponry depicted. *Collier's* illustrators established a look similar to the pre-war German artist Ludwig Hohlwein.

AL PARKER was setting the pace for a new school of illustration. Large studios were formed to supply the talent. COOPER STUDIO was the best.

THE FAMOUS ARTISTS SCHOOL trained thousands of artists under the tutelage of Albert Dorne, Norman Rockwell, Austin Briggs, Robert Fawcett, and other faculty members.

The Saturday Evening Post, Collier's, Liberty, Woman's Home Companion and *American* magazines collapsed. An enterprising group exemplified by ROBERT WEAVER, MILTON GLASER, and artists of the PUSH PIN STUDIO helped to create a bridge to a new art style.

This was the culminating decade of a century-and-a-half of the traditional role of the magazine. By now most of the old magazines were dead. Publications became more and more specialized. Even comic books came into their own, some with excellent artwork. The AIR BRUSH was resurrected to create a "new" look.

Illustrators looked for a fresh idiom to keep relevant. Many quickly adapted their talents to COMPUTER TECHNOLOGY, composing pictures and utilizing painting programs that could produce effects impossible by hand. Pictures could go from the computer screen via disc to publication without the need for a brush, paint, or canvas — a brave new world indeed!

ILLUSTRATION 1860-2000

This chart attempts to record the major artistic influences that have entered the stream of American Illustration over the past century-and-a-half beginning with the Civil War era and arriving at the present time.

Although the emphasis here is on American Illustration, the artistic influences have been international almost from the very beginning. It is the outlook that is American more than the artistic techniques of expression. We have recorded the various influences at their points of entry and their consequent manifestations in the careers of many of the major illustrators who adapted and enriched them through their own contributions.

1860–1870

Currier & Ives
    George Henry Durrie
    Frances Palmer
    Charles Parsons
Theodore R. Davis
Felix Octavius Carr Darley
Edwin Forbes
Edward Lamson Henry
Winslow Homer
Eastman Johnson
Moran family
    Edward
    Thomas
    Peter

Thomas Nast
Allen Carter Redwood
Francis H. Schell
William Henry Shelton
William Ludwell Sheppard
Xanthus Russell Smith
Arthur Fitzwilliam Tait
Elihu Vedder
Thomas Worth
Alfred Rudolph Waud
William Waud

Felix O. C. Darley (1822-1888) Bank-note design. *Zoave Trooper,* American Bank Note Company, 1862. Collection of Murray Tinkelman.

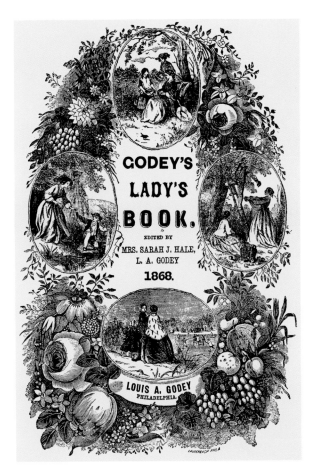

Artist Unknown, cover design for ***Godey's Lady's Book***, 1868.

THE DECADE 1860-1870

At the beginning of this decade, illustration was still mostly a home-grown art form, evolving out of local needs. There was little demand for pictures in newspapers and magazines, except drawings for manufactured products, politician's portraits or occasionally, designs for currency or stock certificates might be commissioned. An illustrator's art training was largely by on-the-job apprenticeship, often through the craft of wood engraving or lithography in the art department of a printer or publisher.

The Civil War changed all this dramatically. There was an immediate great public need for more pictures to illustrate the momentous events of enlisting and training troops, military maneuvering and battles, defeats and victories, and portraits of opposing politicians and military leaders.

Newspapers and magazines such as *Leslie's Illustrated News, The New York Illustrated News* and *Harper's Weekly* added artist-reporters to their staffs and assigned them to draw pictures at the sites of the war's events. These sketches were then dispatched to the publishers for translation onto wood blocks by engravers in the art departments. It was a slow process; cutting a wood engraving could take many days. For panoramic scenes of battle, several artists would usually be employed, each cutting a sectional block of the whole scene. The blocks were then bolted together with a master engraver cutting the meshing lines, and printed as a unit. Weeks could thus elapse between the event and its publication. More engravers were apprenticed and trained to speed up the process and to keep up with increasing demand. *Leslie's* alone was receiving some 20 to 40 sketches from their field artists every day, from which the most newsworthy subjects were selected to be engraved.

Photography was yet in its infancy; the equipment was cumbersome and exposure times too slow for action. Also, the ability to reproduce it was still in the hands of the wood engraver. Its greater influence would await the development of halftone engraving two decades later.

Illustrators such as Winslow Homer, Theodore R. Davis, Edward Forbes and Alfred Waud developed their artistic skills as war correspondents. Homer's field work was limited to a few months of the Peninsula Campaign, but in that time he accumulated a large number of studies which he was to draw upon for many major paintings long after the war. Other artists covered the action for varying assignments — some for the entire war. Most shared the life of the troops, carrying sketch pads rather than rifles, easily hobnobbing with officers as well as regular soldiers and selecting a vantage point to best present the action. Their dedication produced a vital record of that terrible conflict from the viewpoints of both North and South.

Following the war, some artists continued to make careers of it, producing illustrations for published personal reminiscences by officers or historians, particularly for ***The Century*** magazine in the 1880s. However, there was much else to record of the fast-changing postwar period, including the Southern Reconstruction and the Frontier West as it was being "civilized" by a flood of immigrants and discharged veterans from both North and South.

Magazines were beginning to publish some literary material as well as articles of science, travel, and art, and would commission illustrations for them. Henceforth pictures would play an increasing role in all publishing as a complement to the printed text.

Fanny Palmer, *"The 'Lightning Express' Trains Leaving the Junction"*

CURRIER & IVES

As publishers of popular prints, the firm of Currier and Ives was an illustration factory which exploited the newly-invented process of lithography as a means of reproduction. A drawing on a porous stone surface with a wax-based pencil or brush could be inked and printed in large numbers (the open areas of stone when wet would not accept the ink and thus not print). After pulling the black plate, the prints were painted in watercolors by a battery of ladies at a long work table, each confined to completing a single color or area and passing it on to the next. A supervising artist maintained quality control and applied the finishing touches as needed. The relative ease and speed of the process also made it cheap to produce. A catastrophic shipwreck or a major fire could be represented within a day or two of the event and the prints hawked on the streets by the hundreds, like newspaper "Extras." Much of this art was done from imagination, far removed from the event depicted.

In between such events, the firm produced popular prints for the home with titles such as *"The Lover's Quarrel," "The Soldier's Return,"* or *"Steamboat Race on the Mississippi."* Despite their limitations, the Currier and Ives firm did make important contributions to the history of American illustration by documenting the lives and events of their day. As they succeeded financially, they used more talented artists who could present their subjects more accurately and the major events of the period were recorded with more authenticity. The artists presented on these two pages represent a sampling of the best from the unrecorded number of talents who produced over 7,000 picture subjects.

The founder of the firm was Nathaniel Currier, an ambitious young lithographer, who opened his shop in lower Manhattan in 1834. As the business prospered, he invited James Merritt Ives, who was then the bookkeeper and an amateur artist (and his son-in-law), to become a partner in 1857.

Their dynamic association produced an unending stream of pictorial dramatizations of American life and events for several decades until the firm finally closed in 1907.

F. Palmer

FRANCES "FANNY" FLORA BOND PALMER (1812-1876) was the person most closely identified with the Currier and Ives art staff. She was a genteel, but poor, recent immigrant from England (her husband was an alcoholic "gentleman," who didn't work), and found employment as an artist to support a large family by the only means she had, based on her ladies private school art training. Although she created many popular subjects, her specialty was in establishing backgrounds or settings for various tableaux. She also planned the color schemes and supervised the coloring process. It is sometimes difficult to identify her images, which were translated by the lithographer from her sketches and variously used in collaboration with other artists. Her signature often was either inconspicuous or omitted entirely. Palmer was also credited with improvements in the lithographic crayon which was manufactured by Charles Currier and used throughout the lithographic trade.

Charles Parsons, *Central Park, Winter*

PARSONS

CHARLES PARSONS, A.N.A. (1821-1910) had a long career as a lithographer, as a marine painter, and in 1863 joined Harper and Brothers where he became revered as the art director who nurtured the talents of Edwin Austin Abbey, A B. Frost, Charles Reinhart, Howard Pyle, and many others.

Parsons was born in Rowlands Castle, Havent, England, and came to America as a child. At the age of 12, he was apprenticed to the Endicott Company Lithography department and eventually became its Art Director. Currier and Ives was an Endicott client for whom Parsons made many originals of railroads, landscapes, and marine subjects. He also translated the paintings of other artists for them. Parsons became an associate of the National Academy of Design and was a member of the American Watercolor Society.

G. H. DURRIE

GEORGE HENRY DURRIE (1820-1863) was known as the "Snowman" for his many winter scenes. His specialty was New England farm pictures which provide an excellent record of rural life in the mid-nineteenth century. Born in New Haven, Connecticut, he studied under Nathaniel Jocelyn, and after a brief period as a portrait painter, turned to landscapes. His winter subjects were particularly well suited to reproduction by lithography, and his carefully recorded details of nature and foliage added authenticity to his depictions. Among his more popular prints were "Autumn in New England — Cider Making," "Winter in the Country — Getting Ice," and "Winter Morning — Feeding the Chickens." The New York Public Library includes several of Durrie's paintings in its collection.

George Durrie, *Home to Thanksgiving*

The Field of Battle at Champion's Hill.

Artist's "note" for scene above. Both from **How a Battle is Sketched.**

An Incident, Battle of New Hope Church. Bad Fix for a Confederate Sharp Shooter.
Davis himself experienced a similar "adventure" when he was exposed to enemy fire
while sketching a battle from the vantage point of a tall tree.

THEODORE R. DAVIS (1840-1894) had a long and diversified career as an artist-reporter and illustrator. One of the younger (21 years old) such "specials" for **Harper's Weekly,** he covered more areas of the fighting than any other artist, including a junket in the South in 1861. Traveling in company with a British journalist, Davis passed himself off as an artist for the **Illustrated London News** and gained much valuable information about Southern weaponry, uniforms and tactics for use in his later **Harper's** pictures.

Davis's enterprising abilities often landed him at the center of key actions, especially during his travels with General Grant's staff and the campaign at Vicksburg. His artistic skills were best shown in his great attention to details in documenting personnel

and place, much of it necessarily added to the hurried notes made during intense action. Twice wounded, and with his horse shot from under him, Davis was respected for his bravery and found a welcome among the military wherever he went.

After the war, he continued his reportorial work for **Harper's**, recording the Reconstruction in the South and traveling extensively in the Far West, newly opened to homesteading Army veterans. Generally known as "Theo," Davis used the pseudonym "Croquis" for his work published in **The New York Evening Mail** in 1868. In the 1880s, he served as a consultant on the cyclorama paintings projects for the Missionary Ridge and Atlanta murals. He wrote and illustrated a treatise entitled "How a Battle is Sketched" for **St. Nicholas** magazine in July, 1889.

FELIX OCTAVIUS CARR DARLEY, N.A. (1822-1888) can well be considered America's first important illustrator. Self-taught, he created an immense volume of work over a long career. Beginning as a staff artist with a Philadelphia publisher, he learned to take on a wide variety of subjects. Later in New York, his work was reproduced by many book publishers, *Harper's Weekly,* and other magazines. Among the important authors whose books he illustrated were Irving, Hawthorne, Longfellow, Poe and Cooper. He also wrote and illustrated his own book, *Sketches Abroad with Pen and Pencil,* published in 1869. An important project was the illustrating of *Our Country, A Household History,* containing over 500 illustrations in four volumes by Benson Lossing, printed in 1890. He also created designs for bank notes and exhibited at the National Academy, becoming a member in 1852. Darley was the first of a new American school of illustrators which was to successfully challenge the dominance of English and Continental illustration during the mid-nineteenth century.

F. O. C. Darley, *Civil War Veteran's Tale,* pencil and grey washes, circa 1865.

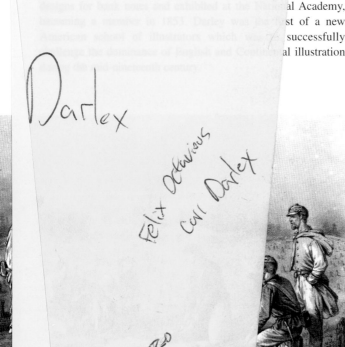

Edwin Forbes, *Pickets Trading Between the Lines,* pencil and Chinese white. Library of Congress Collection.

EDWIN FORBES (1839-1895) was a student of Arthur Fitzwilliam Tait and joined the staff of ***Leslie's Illustrated*** newspaper as a war artist in 1861 at age 22. One of the youngest, he was also one of the few artists who covered the entire war, attached to the Army of the Potomac. Although his focus was usually on the daily life of the soldiers, he was also at the scene of many of the important battles and recorded the sweep of action with accurate authority. Here he shows a lull in the action when cautious overtures were made between pickets to trade coffee, tobacco or the latest news. Among his noteworthy pictures were the *"Second Battle of Bull Run," "Hooker's Charge at Antietam,"* and *"Meeting Jackson's Flank Attack, Chancellorsville."*

Many of his pencil sketches became the basis for his major work after the war in a series of detailed etchings. These were published as ***Life Studies of the Great Army,*** in 1876, and ***Thirty Years After: An Artist's Story of the Great War,*** in 1890. Forbes also illustrated three children's books of military history, one on the career of General William T. Sherman written by his wife, Ida B. Forbes. A large collection of the artist's works was acquired by the Library of Congress in 1919.

Edwin Forbes, *The Advance of the Calvary Skirmish Lines,* oil on canvas, private collection. (This subject was also interpreted by Forbes as an etching)

Snap the Whip, **Harper's Weekly,** September 20, 1873, published by wood engraving.

Snap the Whip, 1872. Collection of the Butler Institute of American Art, Youngstown, Ohio.

Skirmish in the Wilderness, 1864. Collection of the New Britain (Ct.) Museum of American Art. Harriet Russell Stanley Fund.

WINSLOW HOMER, N.A. (1836-1910) drew from an early age and absorbed his knowledge of art from many sources. At nineteen he was employed by a Boston lithography firm and at twenty-one left to work on his own. His earliest illustrations were done for **Ballou's Pictorial** magazine followed by an association with **Harper's** publishers in New York. He continued with **Harper's** for the next sixteen years, illustrating a wide variety of subjects. During part of this time he was sent by **Harper's Weekly** as a special correspondent to cover the outbreak of the Civil War. Attached to the Army of the Potomac, he filled his sketchbooks with informal studies of uniforms, weapons, and the daily activities of the individual soldiers. While he did not continue his field reportage beyond a few months (October 1861 – May 1862), his experiences and the material collected provided him with authentic knowledge that enabled him to paint some of the finest pictures of the Civil War.

He also began to branch out in his subject matter for **Harper's** and to paint genre scenes of boating, hunting and fishing, farm life, and the sea.

Most of his pictures were reproduced in black and white, primarily by wood engravings, and the public was slow to recognize his talents, though halftone engravings of works after the 1880s gave greater fidelity to Homer's artistry. As he began to exhibit his paintings, the critics started to notice (if not to accept him seriously). His later watercolors in the 1870s brought him more public and financial success. He always maintained an independent course and in his later years he tended to be a recluse.

Certainly his artistic contributions by now have been recognized for their uniquely American roots and they helped to bridge that imagined gulf between story-telling illustration and "pure" art. Homer's works are held in many major museums, with a large collection of his Civil War drawings at the Cooper-Hewitt Museum in New York.

The Baggage Guard, 1865. Published in ***The Century,*** 1887.

19

E. L. Henry, *Early Days of Rapid Transit,* Delaware and Hudson Railway Company.

EL Henry

EDWARD LAMSON HENRY, N.A. (1841-1919) His birthplace was Charleston, S.C. but he was orphaned at an early age and raised by relatives in New York City. Showing a proclivity for art, he began to study at fourteen with Walter M. Oddie and in 1858 attended the Pennsylvania Academy of the Fine Arts. In 1860, he furthered his studies in Paris under Gustave Courbet and Charles Gleyre and traveled in Italy. It was as a fully trained artist that he returned to the U.S. in 1863 to face the Civil War. He served as a captain's clerk on a supply ship under the Quartermaster General's Department and recorded many war-time scenes on the James and Potomac rivers. This experience was probably responsible for his specialization in depicting various forms of transportation throughout his subsequent career. His paintings of every subject are characteristically highly detailed with their emphasis on accuracy, whether of contemporary subjects or recreations of an earlier era.

Henry made three more trips abroad, to France and England, eventually settling in Cragsmoor, N.Y. as one of the founders of that art colony. His was a long and successful career, in which he achieved many awards and he is represented in many major American museum collections.

E. J.

Like many of his contemporaries, EASTMAN JOHNSON, N.A. (1824-1906) got his start as an apprentice lithographer — first at Bufford's firm in Boston — later he worked in other New England firms and in Washington, D.C. To further his art, he attended the German Academy in Düsseldorf studying with Emanuel Leutze and went on to Rome, Paris, and the Hague (known there as the "American Rembrandt"). He returned to the U.S. in 1855 and began his career as a genre painter specializing in Native American subjects in the Midwest, southern African-Americans, and scenes of rural life including his well-known *The Kentucky Home, The Pension Agent* and *Husking Bee.* In his latter years, he was in great demand as a portraitist, and he painted many of the leading politicians of that era, including Daniel Webster and Presidents John Quincy Adams, Benjamin Harrison, Chester Arthur, and Grover Cleveland. His exhibited works won many awards in the U.S., Paris, and London, and he is represented in The Metropolitan Museum of Art, the Corcoran Gallery, The White House, the Capitol building at Albany and many other institutions. One of his paintings, *The Wounded Drummer Boy,* based on an incident at Antietam, was exhibited at the National Academy and immediately became a public favorite.

Eastman Johnson, *The Boy Lincoln,* 1868. Collection of the University of Michigan.

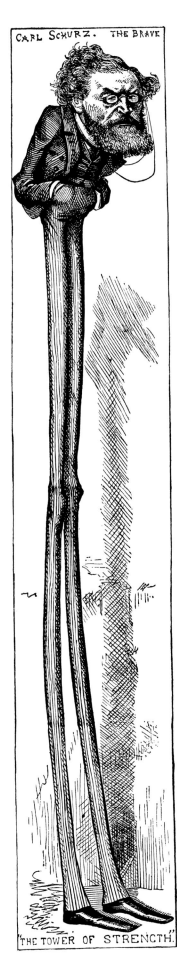

CARL SCHURZ. THE BRAVE

'THE TOWER OF STRENGTH'.

"Let us Prey." The Tweed gang at bay as a group of vultures waiting for the storm to blow over. ***Harper's Weekly,*** September 23, 1871.

Th: Nast. x

Not all of Nast's targets were corrupt ones. Carl Schurz, later Secretary of the Interior under President Rutherford B. Hayes, was a "victim" singled out because he was of a political persuasion opposite to Nast's. Horace Greeley was another target, who by contending against Ulysses S. Grant for the Republican presidential nomination, was made the subject of Nast's concentrated ridicule.

THOMAS NAST (1840-1902), whose work as a political cartoonist and caricaturist had an immense influence on American politics, was born in Bavaria and died in Guyaquil, Ecuador, while serving as the American consul-general. With a precocious art talent, he made his first professional illustration for *Frank Leslie's Illustrated Newspaper* at the age of fifteen. Later assignments included trips abroad to England, Sicily and Calabria, following Garibaldi's army. In 1861 he returned to America and soon became a staff member of Harper's, producing many war-related illustrations for *Harper's Weekly.* President Lincoln considered Nast one of the most influential recruiters for the Northern cause.

One of his assignments at Harper's art department was to translate the special artists' hurried drawings from the battlefield into finished drawings for the wood engravers. Nast sometimes signed his own name to these drawings, thereby obtaining an unmerited reputation as a war artist and the strong resentment of the "specials" who were risking their lives to make the drawings.

It was following the war, however, during the reign of the Tammany political machine in New York, that Nast developed his own effective style in attacking the corruption of Boss Tweed and his ring, eventually forcing them out of office.

Nast was the first to personify our Santa Claus image when he created illustrations based on Clement Moore's "The Night Before Christmas," making him a combination of the "jolly old elf" described, with the German Pelz-Nicol of his own childhood. The symbols of the Republican elephant, the Democratic donkey and Uncle Sam were among many of Nast's pictorial inventions.

Edward Moran, *The Unveiling of the Statue of Liberty ("Liberty Enlightning")*, 1886.
The J. Clarence Davies Collection, Museum of the City of New York.

THE MORAN FAMILY

In the 1860's, the Morans were a prominent family of artists, at least a dozen of whom were important enough to be known as the "Twelve Apostles." Among them were painters, etchers, lithographers, photographers, and illustrators. Many of them were also gifted musicians and married into musical families. It was a rich artistic environment that nurtured potential talents of both men and women members, that otherwise might not have flourished. Mary Nimmo Moran (1842-1899), the wife of Thomas, was an accomplished etcher represented in the print collection of the Library of Congress.

Edward Moran

The founder of the family art dynasty in America, EDWARD MORAN (1829-1901) came up the hard way. Born in Lancashire, England, he was the eldest of fourteen children. His was a family of weavers who emigrated to America when he was a child. Edward was always more interested in drawing. After a series of unrelated jobs, including house painting, one of his employers gave him a letter of introduction to a Philadelphia artist, James Hamilton. This exposed him to the art world and he learned to draw on stone to earn money as a lithographer. He also began to paint in oils and soon was able to start exhibiting and selling. His pictures represented a departure from the prevailing academic Germanic style and attracted public attention that he exploited with his colorful personality into a long, successful career as a genre painter. His sons, LEON (1864-1941), and PERCY (1862-1941) were also popular illustrators and painters who carried on the family name.

Peter Moran, *Federal Cavalry Camp at Dawn,* oil on panel, 5" x 20", illustration for ***History of the 9th New York Cavalry, Poland Center,*** 1901.

PETER MORAN (1841-1914) was brought to Maryland from England at the age of three. He, too, gravitated to art and studied with his brothers Edward and Thomas. He became a prominent etcher exhibiting at the Centennial Exposition in Philadelphia in 1876 and had a one-man show at the National Academy in 1877, thereafter exhibiting widely and was the recipient of many awards. He was also a painter of landscapes and animals and went West before Thomas in 1864. In 1879 and 1880, he accompanied his brother to the Tetons, New Mexico and Arizona. His works are represented in the Amon Carter Museum, Parrish Art Museum, the Metropolitan Museum of Art and the New York Public Library.

Big Springs in Yellowstone Park, 1872. Private Collection.

Ӽ'ORAN.

THOMAS MORAN, N.A. (1837-1926) The most industrious and eventually the most illustrious of the Moran family, Thomas was from the same Lancashire, England, birthplace as his brothers, coming to the United States in 1844. He also studied with James Hamilton in Philadelphia as well as under his older brother, Edward, and in London, Paris and Italy. While he did some illustrating, his fame is based on his large, panoramic landscape paintings of the Grand Canyon, Yosemite, and other monumental sites in the West. He accompanied the U.S. Geological Survey of Yellowstone with photographer W. H. Jackson and traveled through many of the national parks. Mount Moran is named for him. His paintings are in many museum collections including The National Gallery of Art, The Department of the Interior Museum, The Thomas Gilcrease Institute of American History and Art, The Metropolitan Museum of Art, The Museum of Fine Arts in Boston, and his painting "The Three Tetons" has hung in the White House Oval Office.

Moran's initialed signature, following his first visit to the Yellowstone area in 1871, incorporated a "Y" in the center which stood for "Yellowstone" and indicated his commitment to the campaign to make Yellowstone the first National Park.

Baby Glacier 3 miles below Big Cañon, Stickeen River, Alaska. By contrast with his huge paintings, Moran's illustrations were very small, almost at reproduction size and drawn with a lithographic pencil on a pebbled surface, in a method similar to the lithography he had practiced early in his career.

Cobb's and Kershaw's Troops Behind the Stone Wall, Marye's Heights, Fredericksburg, May, 1863.

A.C. Redwood

Unlike many of the artists who illustrated the action of the Civil War from the sketches sent to the publishers, ALLEN CARTER REDWOOD (1834-1922), was an active participant. He enlisted in 1861 and served in the 55th regiment of the Army of Northern Virginia. Captured at the second battle of Bull Run, he was later exchanged and advanced in rank to Major.

After the hostilities were over, many memoirs and histories of the war were published, and Redwood's artistic services provided an authentic documentation from the Southern side. Redwood also illustrated many other subjects in the postwar years for **The Century, Harper's**, and other magazine and book publishers.

Fighting with hand grenades at the siege of Vicksburg, July 13, 1863. Woodcut based on sketch by Schell published in **The Soldier in our Civil War**.

Frank H. Schell

FRANCIS H. SCHELL (1834-1909) had been a lithographer in Philadelphia prior to the Civil War. In 1861, he joined the roster of **Frank Leslie's Illustrated News** staff as a special artist and during the course of the conflict over 200 of his pictures were published by **Leslie's.** His pictures were wide ranging, covering the Peninsula campaign, Antietam, and the Battle of Belmont.

Schell returned after the war to become the head of **Leslie's** art department. He next resumed his lithography career starting a thirty-year partnership with his friend Thomas Hogan. Together they produced many Civil War subjects relying on wartime sketches, rendered in pen and ink and in large watercolors. Many of these jointly produced pictures were of naval battles based on field sketches by Henry Walke and were included in the comprehensive **Battles and Leaders of the Civil War**.

W. H. Shelton, *General Duke Searching for Tracks,* from "A Romance of Morgan's Rough Riders", **The Century,** January, 1891.

W. L. Sheppard, *Citizens of Richmond taking refuge in Capital Square during the conflagration following upon the evacuation, April 3, 1865.* "Grant's Last Campaign," **The Century.**

WILLIAM HENRY SHELTON (1840-1932) studied at the Art Students League. As a Union artilleryman commanding a center section of Battery D at the Battle of the Wilderness, he was wounded in the leg, taken prisoner and sent deep into the South. Over the next several months, he made several escape attempts, finally making it back to the Union lines on the day of Lincoln's second inauguration. Shelton's first-hand account of the adventures of his capture and escape, titled "A Hard Road to Travel out of Dixie," was published by **The Century** magazine in October, 1890.

After the war, he continued to illustrate for **Harper's, Leslie's,** and **The New York Ledger.** He was one of the founders of the Salmagundi Club and served as its librarian; he helped to acquire its art collection. He also held the position of curator at the Jumel Mansion in New York City. His history of the Salmagundi Club was published in 1926.

We owe much to WILLIAM LUDWELL SHEPPARD (1833-1912) for his artistic coverage of the Southern side of the Civil War. From Virginia, Sheppard was a trained artist, having studied in New York and Paris. At 29, he joined the Richmond Howitzers in the Army of Northern Virginia, reaching the rank of engineering officer. All of his spare time was spent in recording the lives of his fellow soldiers in drawings and paintings. Many of these are included in the collection of the Confederate Museum in Richmond and were published in **Battles and Leaders of the Civil War.**

Sheppard continued his artistic career after the war as a painter and book illustrator. And as a sculptor, he was commissioned to do the Soldiers and Sailors Monument in Richmond, Virginia. Sheppard was given the unique compliment by a former Union officer of the 29th Pennsylvania who purchased three of the artist's paintings of the Chancellorsville Campaign in which his troops had been involved.

Xanthus Smith, *Battle between The Monitor and Merrimac.* Courtesy of the Wiscasset Bay Gallery, Wiscasset, Maine.

XANTHUS RUSSELL SMITH (1839-1929) was the son of landscape painter Russell Smith. A medical student at the University of Pennsylvania, Smith switched to art, attending the Pennsylvania Academy of the Fine Arts and the Royal Academy in London before enlisting in the Union Navy at the age of 22. His duties as Captain's clerk and later as a staff aide gave him the opportunity to make the sketches and studies which were the basis of many postwar paintings. He served aboard the flagship Wabash, at Port Royal and Fort Pulaski and accompanied Admiral Farragut's squadron, running the gauntlet of Confederate forts along the Mississippi and breaking through to Mobile Bay. While many of his wartime sketches were in pen and ink, after the war he produced several panoramic oils of both land and sea actions. His works are in collections at the Boston Museum of Fine Arts, Mariner's Museum, Delaware Historical Society, Colby College and the Pennsylvania Academy of the Fine Arts.

ARTHUR FITZWILLIAM TAIT, N.A. (1819-1905) was never employed directly by Currier & Ives, but many of his paintings were reproduced by them, and his were some of their most popular and successful lithographs. He is best remembered for his pictures of trapping, hunting, and outdoor life in the West which were purchased by collectors and art dealers who then arranged for their lithographic reproduction. Tait painted some of his early pictures of Native Americans from reference in the New York Public Library, but later he scrupulously painted from first-hand observation, both in the Far West and from his Adirondacks camp.

The artist, who was born in England and studied art at night school there, came to the U.S. as a young man and quickly gravitated to American subjects of outdoor life. He became a member of the National Academy in 1858. Some of his paintings were also made in collaboration with J.M. Hart and Louis Maurer.

A. F. Tait, *Life on the Prairie – The Buffalo Hunt,* published by Currier and Ives, 1862.

Head of a young woman, pastel.

Cover design for *The Century* magazine, February, 1882.

ELIHU VEDDER, N.A. (1836-1923) Of Dutch ancestry, Vedder was born in New York, and his artistic talents were precocious. At the age of twenty, he went to Europe to study, staying for four years. On his return to the United States, he quickly established himself as an illustrator and a painter. He became a full member of the National Academy by the age of twenty-seven, the youngest painter so elected. In 1867, he returned to Europe and settled permanently in Italy, with periodic visits to America.

Among his murals are a mosaic in the Library of Congress and a commission for the Walker Art Gallery at Bowdoin College. His best known illustrations were done for the *Rubaiyat of Omar Khayam* in 1884. He also wrote poetry, and his autobiography, *The Digressions of Vedder,* was published in 1910.

THOMAS WORTH (1834-1917) was largely self-taught and one of the most popular of all the artists who worked for Currier and Ives. His outlook was usually humorous and kindly, but reflecting the temper of the times, was overtly racist in his "Darktown" series.

Worth was an enthusiastic hunter, fisherman and a connoisseur of fine horses. Many of his illustrations pictured trotting matches and famous thoroughbreds. Worth was also a regular contributor to *Harper's* magazines and he was an exhibitor at the National Academy of Design in 1874.

A Native American porter greets Christopher Columbus upon his arrival in the New World. Watercolor commemorating the landing for The Pan American Exposition of 1897.

A. R. Waud, *Custer's Division retiring from Mount Jackson in the Shenandoah Valley, October 7, 1864.* *"Burning and destroying the enemy's supplies."* Rough sketch of the action. Alfred Waud Collection of the Library of Congress

Wood engraving, finished rendering redone from the above sketch for publication in ***Battles and Leaders of the Civil War.***

As a "special artist," ALFRED RUDOLPH WAUD (1828-1891) covered the Civil War, first for **The New York Illustrated News** and then for **Harper's Weekly.** Assigned to the Army of the Potomac, he made drawings and wrote dispatches during the whole conflict from the Yorktown campaign and the first battle of Bull Run to the surrender of Lee at Appomattox in 1865. "Alf" Waud won the confidence of officers and enlisted men alike, and he was able to freely cover events wherever the action was.

His drawings (which were translated into woodcuts back at the publishers) were trustworthy because he accurately drew what he saw. In one case, his drawing of a battlefield made from a perch in a tree while under fire from Confederate sharpshooters, was used by the Union general in planning a counterattack.

Waud was born in England and was trained at the School of Design of the Royal Academy. He came to the U.S. in the fifties where he worked as a newspaper artist in Boston and New York. He and his younger brother, William, both became artist correspondents at the outset of the war, although their assignments often took them in different directions.

Following the war, Waud continued as a **Harper's** artist, traveling through the South and then the frontier West. As a freelance artist, he contributed pictures to **Picturesque America** and later **Battles and Leaders of the Civil War,** published by The Century Company in 1884-1888. A large collection of the artist's work is held in the Waud Collection at the Library of Congress in Washington, D.C.

WILLIAM WAUD (ca. 1830-1878) was born in England like his brother Alfred, but trained as an architect. He became an assistant to Sir Joseph Paxton in the construction of the Crystal Palace for the Great Exhibition in 1851. Soon afterward, he joined Alfred in America. First employed by **Frank Leslie's Illustrated Newspaper** as the war approached, he covered assignments in the South, including the inauguration of Jefferson Davis as President of the Confederacy. He was on hand to record the bombardment of Fort Sumter which initiated the hostilities, scoring a scoop for **Leslie's.** After the declaration of war, he was limited to Northern campaigns. He later accompanied Admiral Farragut's fleet in the expedition against New Orleans, as it fought its way through the Southern forts on the Mississippi. In 1864, he left **Leslie's** for **Harper's,** and covered the Petersburg campaign in company with his brother. Later assignments included General Sherman's invasion of the Carolinas and after the assassination of President Lincoln in 1865, he followed the funeral train at its various stops enroute to burial in Springfield, Illinois. Like his brother, William was an excellent writer, and his dispatches were often published along with his drawings. Many of his works are also included in the Waud collection at the Library of Congress.

William Waud, *Signaling by Torches across the James River*, October, 1864. **Harper's Weekly**, November 12, 1864. The William Waud Collection of The Library of Congress

1870–1880

Edwin Howland Blashfield
Milton J. Burns
Frederick Stuart Church
Julian O. Davidson
Harry Fenn
Mary Hallock Foote
Paul Frenzeny
Charles S. Graham
Howard Helmick
Francis Davis Millet
Henry Siddons Mowbray

Charles Stanley Reinhart
Henry Sandham
Walter Shirlaw
Francis Hopkinson Smith
Isaac Walton Taber
Jules Tavernier
Thure de Thulstrup
Edwin Lord Weeks
Michael Angelo Woolf
Rufus Fairchild Zogbaum

John Everett Millais (1829-1896). *Good Words,* 1863.

James McNeill Whistler (1834-1903). *Once A Week,* 1862.

Frederick Sandys (1832-1904). *Once A Week,* 1862.

Charles Samuel Keene (1823-1891). *Punch's Almanack,* 1869.

THE DECADE 1870-1880

If American artists were of necessity still insular at this time, they were not entirely ignorant of the work being published in Europe.

The strongest outside influence on American illustration at this time was the group of British artists who had undergone a renaissance in the 1860s, inspired by the Pre-Raphaelite circle. Their works, which ran the gamut from humor to the most serious themes, were pictured on the pages of magazines such as *Once A Week, Cornhill Magazine, Good Words,* and *The Graphic.* Imported to America, these and other publications were eagerly studied by American artists who emulated the compositions and pictorial devices of the artists they admired.

Building upon the pioneering improvements in wood engraving by Thomas Bewick (1753-1828), British wood engravers as represented by the Dalziel Brothers were then amongst the finest in the world. They presented the works of the illustrators to the best effect then possible, and the engravers' contribution to the plates was recognized with a credit equal to that of the artist.

Among the many influences on American illustrators were Arthur Boyd Houghton, John Everett Millais, Frederick Sandys, Fred Walker, George John Pinwell, and Charles Keene. These influences were not always at long distance or secondhand. Several British artists visited America, particularly to cover the Civil War as correspondents for British publications and mingled freely with their American counterparts. Arthur Boyd Houghton traveled through the then-wild West in 1870 and made many illustrations of his adventures for the *Graphic,* some of which were also published in American magazines such as *Every*

Saturday and *Harper's Weekly.*

Other European artists played influential roles, including Daniel Vierge of Spain, J.L.E. Meissonier and Gustave Doré of France, and Adolf Menzel of Germany, all of whom were master practitioners of pen and ink.

Since American art schools were not yet able to provide the advanced art training available in Europe, some ambitious students took advanced study in the academies of Düsseldorf, Munich, Rome, London, or Paris. The Ecole des Beaux Arts and the Academie Julian in Paris were particular magnets. For a short while the American expatriate James McNeill Whistler also taught classes in Paris.

Upon conclusion of this post-graduate training, most students who entered the field of illustration quickly found work with the best American publications.

At this time, the major publishers such as Harper's and Scribner's, formed their own staffs of artists and engravers who were learning by practical experience how to create effective illustrations based upon almost any theme required. This was a valuable training ground and many artists found this route to success including Charles Reinhart, John White Alexander, A.B. Frost, Theodore R. Davis, and Frederick S. Church.

Many of these same illustrators periodically augmented their practical training with selective study in art school evening classes or took a sabbatical leave to attend a European academy for a year or two. Some contributed to foreign publications during their stays abroad and learned by fraternizing with fellow illustrators.

31

(left) E. H. Blashfield, *The Angel with The Flaming Sword,* **The Century,** September 1893.

(right) E. H. Blashfield, *The Boston People Watching From the Housetops, Firing at Bunker Hill.* Painted in 1882. Collection of The Home Insurance Company.

MILTON J. BURNS (1853-1933) was an artist-sailor and virtually all of his work as an illustrator was concerned with the sea or ships. His dual career was instigated by chance — as a 16-year-old, he signed on to a whaling ship, which had been chartered by William Bradford, the famous painter of the Arctic. The ship, "Panther," spent several months off Greenland and Burns had the opportunity to observe Bradford at work and to learn the ropes as a sailor. After the return trip, Burns enrolled at the National Academy School, later transferring to the Art Students League under J. G. Brown. He soon found work as an illustrator. The authenticity of his pictures was obvious, covering yacht racing, shipwrecks, and fishing expeditions on assignment for nearly every magazine that needed nautical expertise. These ranged from **St. Nicholas** and **Harper's Young People** to **Scribner's** and **Harper's Monthly.**

Burns was a founder of the Salmagundi Club and friend of Winslow Homer, Edwin Austin Abbey and Frederic Remington. He married the daughter of Civil War artist Alfred Waud.

He sailed often to the Grand Banks off Newfoundland and to the North Sea; he had a studio boat, "Sarah," which was moored on the Hudson River.

Milton Burns, *A Marine Artist's Studio in New York,* from **Scribner's Monthly,** January, 1880, gives a good picture of a marine painter (probably himself) at work.

EDWIN HOWLAND BLASHFIELD, N.A. (1848-1936) had a long career, distinguished by virtually every American artistic honor attainable. Blashfield was a meticulous technician in his work; he studied with Leon Bonnat in Paris following his earlier training at the Pennsylvania Academy of the Fine Arts.

President of the National Academy and the National Institute of Arts and Letters, he became most famous as the dean of American mural painters. His decorations were commissioned for court houses, capitol buildings and churches across the country, including Essex County, New Jersey; Baltimore, Md.; Cleveland, Ohio; Detroit, Mich.; St. Paul, Minn.; Pierre, So. Dakota; and the Library of Congress in Washington, D.C. He exhibited at the Paris Salon from 1874-79, '81 and '92. For several of these same years his work was also shown at the Royal Academy in London. His paintings won gold medals or other awards in the St. Louis Exposition in 1904, as well as at exhibitions in Paris. He served as co-editor of an edition of Vasari's **Lives of the Painters** and wrote **Mural Painting in America** in 1914.

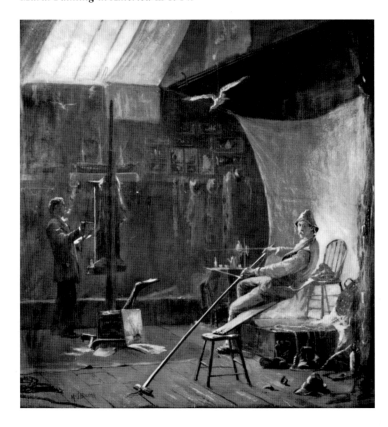

CHURCH FREDERICK STUART CHURCH, N.A. (1842-1924) was born in Grand Rapids, Michigan. He volunteered in the Civil War and took part in many engagements, including Sherman's march to the sea. After discharge, he studied art with Walter Shirlaw at the Chicago Academy of Design. He went to New York for further study at the National Academy of Design; several years later he was elected a full member of the Academy. In 1875, he was one of the founders of the Art Students League. His work is represented in the Metropolitan Museum of Art, the National Gallery in Washington, D.C., the City Art Museum of St. Louis, the Grand Rapids Public Library, and the Brandywine River Museum at Chadds Ford, Pennsylvania.

His forté was allegorical subject matter, and he found an enthusiastic public reception for his whimsical illustrations, etchings and paintings for exhibition. Along with A. B, Frost and E. W. Kemble, he was also an early illustrator for the "Uncle Remus" stories of Joel Chandler Harris.

F. S. Church, *The Chafing Dish,* 1897. Collection of Hitoshi Kimura.

J.O. DAVIDSON

JULIAN O. DAVIDSON (1853-1893) was a specialist in naval illustration, and the editors of **The Century** relied on him heavily to depict the highlights of action by navies of both North and South. Since it was much more difficult to have artists' direct records of these events, it was necessary to reconstruct them from eyewitness accounts or amateur sketches. Davidson was an expert in this, making renditions in opaque watercolor for translation to woodcuts. Many of these were reproduced in **Battles and Leaders** *of the Civil War, Harper's Weekly* and **St. Nicholas**. Born in Cumberland, Maryland, Davidson studied with Mauritz de Haas, a marine painter, and regularly exhibited his paintings at the National Academy of Design and the Salmagundi Club. His work is held in the Franklin Delano Roosevelt Library at Hyde Park, New York, and the Dossin Great Lakes Museum in Detroit. Davidson kept his studio at the Nyack Boat Club and was himself a champion-class sculler.

J. O. Davidson, *The Encounter of The Monitor and The Merrimac at Short Range,* **Century War Book,** 1894

Harry Fenn, *Confederate Fortifications at Manassas Junction,* from **Battles and Leaders of the Civil War.**

 HARRY FENN (1838-1911) was born in Richmond, Surrey, England, and received his early art training as an apprentice with the Dalziel brothers who ran the famous wood engraving firm.

After completing his term, he took a vacation journey to Canada and at nineteen, a side trip to America to see Niagara Falls. He stayed to work in the States for the rest of his career, interrupted only by a trip to study further in Italy. In 1870, he took on a major project for D. Appleton publishers to travel extensively throughout the country and illustrate **Picturesque America.** This was followed by several similar volumes, including **Picturesque Europe** and **Picturesque Palestine, Sinai and Europe** as well as illustration work for **Harper's Monthly** and other magazines.

Fenn was also a major contributor to Century's **Battles and Leaders of the Civil War** project in the 1880s.

MARY HALLOCK FOOTE (1847-1938) was from Quaker stock and raised in a liberal family, which fostered her artistic inclinations. Despite the prevailing attitudes against women in the profession, she was determined to be an artist and, after graduation from the Cooper Union Institute of Design for Women, began her career as a wood engraver. She soon was given book and magazine illustration assignments and was at the beginning of a successful career when she married a young mining engineer, Arthur De Went Foote, in 1876.

Her husband's career came first, and she lived for many years in various primitive mining towns in Colorado, Idaho and California. Despite the hardships of makeshift living and raising three children, she wrote sixteen novels, and when her husband was ruined in a business failure, resumed her illustrating career to support the family. Many of her pictures were published by **Scribner's** and **The Century** magazines. She also painted for exhibition, showing at the Columbian World's Fair in Chicago in 1893, and participated in the Armory Show in 1913; her painting, *The Old Lady,* was purchased by the Art Institute of Chicago. A number of her originals are included in the Cabinet of American Illustration at the Library of Congress. Her reminiscences, edited by Rodman Paul, were published by the Huntington Library in 1972 as **A Victorian Gentlewoman in the Far West**.

Mary Hallock Foote, *The Maiden was happy, sorting her sketching blocks,* **The Century,** 1896.

Paul Frenzeny, *Indians by a Riverbank,* ca. 1873-1874.
Photo courtesy of Spanierman Gallery, LLC, New York, NY.

P. FRENZENY.

A French native, PAUL FRENZENY (ca. 1840-1902) served in the French cavalry in Mexico in the mid-1860s, and thus was an accomplished rider. He came to the U.S., and drew well enough to find employment with *Harper's Weekly*, his first illustrations being published in 1868. Frenzeny was teamed by *Harper's* with Jules Tavernier on several assignments before their joint trip from the Atlantic to the Pacific coasts in 1873 and 1874. From their excursion came many excellent records of pioneer life, as they traveled by rail, stagecoach, and horseback into remote areas of the western territories. Frenzeny made later trips on his own into Central America, Nevada and California. He settled in San Francisco for five years, worked freelance for *Leslie's Weekly* and *Harper's*, and illustrated *Fifty Years on the Trail; A True Story of Western Life,* by Harrington O'Reilly in 1889.

His works are represented in several public collections including the Boston Museum of Fine Arts and the Denver Public Library.

CHARLES GRAHAM (1852-1911) was born in Rock Island, Illinois, in what was then the West. His first employment was with the Northern Pacific Railroad as a topographer for a surveying party extending the rails westward into Montana and Idaho. Here he got to know the frontier at first hand. Although never formally trained as an artist, Graham sketched regularly and worked in a succession of art-related jobs that developed his skills, beginning with work as a scenic artist in theaters in Chicago and in New York. He was eventually hired on the art staff at *Harper's* and contributed regularly to the *Weekly* for the next fifteen years. Branching out in the '90s, he became a freelance illustrator for the *New York Herald, Collier's, The Century, Leslie's Weekly* and other publishers. Of his later pictures, some of the best included his documentation of the Chicago Columbian World's Fair from 1891 through 1893, as he served as the official artist of the Exposition. After 1900, Graham left illustration to paint in oils for exhibition, concentrating on English and Dutch scenic subjects.

Charles Graham, *A Hunter's Shack in the Rocky Mountains,* **Harper's Weekly.**

Howard Helmick, *Bounced on a Pillion behind the liveried Footman.*
Illustration for "By The Waters of the Chesapeake," **The Century,** December, 1893.

H.Helmick

HOWARD HELMICK (1845-1907) spent much of his working career abroad. From Zanesville, Ohio, he pursued his advanced studies in Paris at the Ecole des Beaux Arts under Cabanel. With the advent of the Franco-Prussian war he and many students removed to England. Following a stay in London, he found his way to Ireland and a rich mine of picture material in recording the lives of Irish peasants at work.

In spite of his sophisticated training, Helmick was more interested in rural life than that of the cities and on his return to America continued to focus on that subject matter; many of his pictures were of the South with themes of African-American life.

Helmick's works were reproduced by **The Century, Scribner's**, and other publications, and he was an active etcher. At the end of his career he taught at Georgetown University.

F. D. Millet

FRANCIS DAVIS MILLET, N.A. (1846-1912) went down with the S.S. Titanic, ending an illustrious career. Born in Mattapoisett, Massachusetts, he studied at the Royal Academy of Arts in Antwerp. During the Russo-Turkish War of 1877, he became a special correspondent for the **London Daily News** and was decorated by the Roumanian and Russian governments. He was also a correspondent for the **London Times** in Manila during the Spanish-American War.

In 1893, Millet was director of decorations at the Chicago Columbian Exposition. He also served as vice-chairman of the Federal Committee of Fine Arts, was executive officer of the American Academy in Rome and was a founder of the American Federation of Arts.

A National Academician, Millet exhibited regularly there. He painted a number of portraits, including one of Mark Twain, and several murals.

A Cozy Corner, published by **St. Nicholas Magazine,** December 1892.
Collection of the Metropolitan Museum of Art, gift of George I. Seney, 1887.
Photograph ©1992 The Metropolitan Museum of Art.

H·SIDDONS MOWBRAY·

HENRY SIDDONS MOWBRAY, N.A. (1858-1928) Born Henry Siddons in Alexandria, Egypt, he was adopted by his aunt and Professor George Mowbray after the death of his parents when he was but four years old. Growing up in North Adams, Massachussetts, he was attracted to art early on. After a short stint at West Point, he attended art school in Paris under Bonnat and became a friend of Gérôme. He joined the prevalent Classical and Orientalist movements, first exhibiting at the Salon in 1880.

Upon his return to the U.S., his refined technique and rich color quickly earned him membership in the National Academy and contacts with the leading architecture firm of McKim, Mead and White to decorate their new buildings, churches, and for the "White City" at the World's Fair in 1893.

Among his special mural commissions were the residence of F. W. Vanderbilt, J. P. Morgan's library, the Appellate Court House, and the ceiling of the University Club in New York. He was appointed as a painter-member of the National Commission of Fine Arts by President Woodrow Wilson in 1921.

While Mowbray's work as an illustrator was limited, it was distinguished by idealized subject matter and poetic conceptions.

H. S. Mowbray, illustration for "Silence," by Mary E. Wilkins, *Harper's Monthly,* July, 1893.

C·S·REINHART

CHARLES STANLEY REINHART, A.N.A. (1844-1896) was one of the select group of young artists who were to launch the Golden Age of American Illustration. Under the tutelage of Charles Parsons, head of the art department of Harper & Brothers in the 1870s, the group included E. A. Abbey, Robert Blum, A. B. Frost and Howard Pyle. Reinhart was the senior member, having begun his association as early as 1871, after his art studies in Paris and Munich. He was an expert draftsman in pen and ink, employing fine lines in modeling forms. His gouache illustrations suffered from the translation to wood engravings, but indicate his good control of values. Reinhart was also an active exhibitor, winning a medal at the Paris Exposition in 1889, and the Temple Gold Medal from the Pennsylvania Academy of the Fine Arts in 1888.

Illustration for "Dolly Varden," 1890.
Collection of Albert B. Roberts.

Hy Sandham, *"Clearing of under-currents"* illustration for "Hydraulic Mining in California," **The Century**, January, 1883.

Known as "Hy," HENRY SANDHAM (1842-1912) was a Canadian, born in Montreal, who divided his career between Canada, the United States, and England. He studied art under Otto Reinhard Jacobi and John A. Fraser. He also divided his career between painting for exhibtion and illustrating for magazines and books. He was a regular contributor to **The Century** magazine, and illustrated **Picturesque Canada**, **Lenore** by Edgar Allen Poe and **Ramona** by Helen Hunt Jackson.

Sandham was a charter member of the Royal Canadian Academy of Fine Arts in 1879 and exhibited in the Royal Academy in London, at the Salon in Paris, in Boston, and at the Philadelphia Centennial Exposition, winning numerous medals. His work is also represented in the collection of the National Gallery of Canada.

WALTER SHIRLAW (1838-1909) arrived in America from Paisley, Scotland, at the age of two or three, and did not finish grammar school. He was apprenticed at age twelve to a five-year term with the Western Bank Note Company in Chicago as an engraver. His aspirations were more highly artistic, and in 1870 he had earned enough to spend some six years at the Munich Academy. Upon his return to America, it took some time to make a living as a painter. Twice he visited the Frontier West, in 1869 for six months in the Rocky Mountains, and in 1890, he was one of six artists commissioned as special agents to survey the Indian tribes in Montana and Wyoming. His western paintings are more noted for their spirit and action than for detail, but they serve as a valuable resource of that era.

Shirlaw eventually was involved with almost every aspect of the arts, as a genre painter, portraitist, muralist, illustrator, engraver, and etcher. He was an instructor at the Art Institute of Chicago and at the Art Students League of New York and was a founder and the first president of the Society of American Artists. A frequent exhibitor at the National Academy of Design, he also showed at the Chicago World's Fair in 1893. His work illustrated articles and fiction in many magazines, including **St. Nicholas, Harper's, Scribner's,** and **The Century.**

Walter Shirlaw, *A Sonnet,* watercolor for exhibition.

The above illustration accompanied Hopkinson Smith's article, "The Parthenon by way of Papendrecht" in *Scribner's Magazine* of April, 1909.

F. Hopkinson Smith

Born in Baltimore Maryland, FRANCIS HOPKINSON SMITH (1838-1915) was a many-talented, self-taught artist and writer. Trained as a naval engineer, he was involved with construction on the base of the Statue of Liberty and several breakwater projects. Attracted to art and artists, however, he learned to master watercolor and eventually won many honors in this medium. Many of his travel articles were illustrated by his on-the-spot watercolors. Smith became an intimate with many members of the

Tile Club, including Abbey, Homer, Reinhart, and Frost, and later compiled a five-part volume, *American Illustrators,* published in 1894. Among his many works of fiction were the best-selling *Fortunes of Oliver Horn,* and *Colonel Carter of Cartersville.*

Smith's affiliations included the Philadelphia Art Club, the Cincinnati Art Club, the American Watercolor Society (he was its treasurer from 1873-78), the Century Association, and New York's Society of Illustrators.

Taber *"Weary hours, Andersonville Prison,"* **Battles and Leaders of the Civil War.**

 Born in New Bedford, Massachussetts, ISAAC WALTON TABER (1857-1933) was a pupil at the Cooper Union Art School of New York. His nearly 250 illustrations far outnumber those of the other artists who worked on the monumental project **Battles and Leaders of the Civil War**, and it is probable that he was a Century staff artist since he was also a regular contributor to the monthly. His best skill was as a renderer in pen and ink and most of his work was translated or composed from photographic reference. Taber also contributed to **Scribner's Monthly** and **St. Nicholas** magazines. He is recorded as a member of the Salmagundi Club and is represented in the Society of Illustrators Museum of American Illustration.

I. W. Taber *"Working at the tunnel,"* illustration for "Colonel Rose's tunnel at Libbey Prison," by Frank E. Moran, **The Century,** March, 1888.

Jules Tavenier, Main Street in Wichita, Kansas, in 1873, signed only by Tavernier. Courtesy of Witchita-Sedgwick County Historical Museum.

JULES TAVERNIER

JULES TAVERNIER (1844-1889) was born in France and trained under Felix Barrias prior to his participation in the Franco-Prussian War. Emigrating to America in 1871, he found employment as an illustrator for *Harper's Weekly* and the *New York Graphic.* In 1873, he was commissioned by *Harper's Weekly* along with another French-born artist, Paul Frenzeny, to travel across the American continent, recording the frontier life. As described by the editor of *Harper's,* "They will make long excursions on horseback into regions where railroads have not yet penetrated, where even the hardy squatter, the pioneer of civilization, has not yet erected his rude log cabin . . . "

This was a period not only of migration and settlement onto homesteads, but also one of intense speculation in land. Migrants laid out towns with the hope that stage or railroad lines would make them viable. Some, like Witchita, Kansas, as pictured by Tavernier in 1873, made it. Others, like the nameless settlement (perhaps Zorah, Barton County, Kansas) pictured in the same year by Frenzeny and Tavernier, did not, and were abandoned to the wolves and coyotes.

Busted, from *Harper's Weekly,* October, 1873.

Land Office in Sedgwick County, Kansas, October, 1873. Depicted jointly by Frenzeny and Tavernier for *Harper's Weekly.*

FRENZENY-TAVERNIER

Because the artists worked jointly and both signed their names to the work, it is often difficult to differentiate between them, particularly after reproduction by wood engraving. Tavernier was believed to be stronger in concept and picture composition, Frenzeny in the rendering and detail.

Both artists continued their illustration careers after their successful cross-country assignment. Tavernier settled in San Francisco, but adopting a self-indulgent, Bohemian life style that eventually was his undoing, escaped his debtors only by shipping off to an exile in Hawaii. After his death, a monument was erected in his memory by his San Francisco friends and fellow artists.

Battle of Antietam, reproduced by Louis Prang as a chromolithograph in the 1880s.

THURE DE THULSTRUP (1848-1930) was a Swedish subject, born in Stockholm. A graduate of the Swedish military academy, he fought with the French Army during the Franco-Prussian War of 1870-71. He studied art in Paris in 1872 and shortly after emigrating to the United States in 1873, he attended the newly organized Art Students League in New York. His first illustrations were made for the old **Daily Graphic** of New York; later he became a staff artist for Frank Leslie's periodicals. By 1881, he was a regular contributor to **Harper's** magazine, then to **The Century, Scribner's, Cosmopolitan,** and other leading magazines, covering many major historical events including the Spanish-American War and the funeral of President U. S. Grant.

His work is forthright and without frills, whether rendered in pen and ink, black and white gouache, or in full color. His careful observance of fact and a strong compositional sense gave him the versatility to depict any subject convincingly, but he was especially authoritative with horses and military subjects.

Field Artillery in Action, from **Harper's Pictorial History of the War With Spain,** Harper and Brothers, 1899.

Here Thulstrup depicts the latest modes of transportation, 1895

Although EDWIN LORD WEEKS (1849-1903) was born in Boston, his training and painting career was decidedly international. His focus was on the countries of the Middle East and North Africa including Jerusalem, Egypt, and Tangiers, as a part of the Orientalist interest of the French academics. Indeed, Weeks was trained in Paris at the Ecole des Beaux Arts under Bonnât and Gérôme and his work reflected that training.

In addition to his illustrations for travel articles in *The Century* and other magazines, Weeks exhibited in Buffalo, Boston, Philadelphia, and throughout Europe, winning prizes in London, Paris, Berlin, Munich, Dresden, Bavaria, and at the Pan-American Exposition in Buffalo in 1901.

His book, *From the Black Sea Through Persia and India,* was decorated with colorful illustrations of his experiences in the exotic princely palaces and bazaars as well as his travels in the desert with nomads and their camel transport.

Before a Mosque was painted in 1893 when the artist first visited India.

MICHAEL ANGELO WOOLF (1837-1899) was born in London, and came to the U.S. as an infant. Although he returned to Europe to study art in Paris and Munich, his artistic specialty became the depiction of American city slum kids. "Woolf's Waifs," which combined pathos and humor, became a favorite feature in *The Ladies' Home Journal*, *Life*, and other publications. Woolf must have had a direct influence on R. F. Outcault's later creation of the Yellow Kid of "Hogan's Alley," credited as being the first American newspaper comic page.

At a time when immigrants were surging into America and generally meeting with ridicule for their as-yet-unassimilated speech and customs, Woolf was remarkably sympathetic, especially in his drawings of the homeless children of the streets. By focussing on their plight, his efforts paralleled those of Jacob Riis, who crusaded for the improvement of working and living conditions of the shamelessly exploited new immigrants. Woolf made the children come alive and deserving of admiration for their plucky good humor in the face of poverty and neglect.

Michael Angelo Wolfe, *"The Paradise Park Dramatic Club gave the poisoning scene from Hamlet at their last entertainment."* **Life**, April 21, 1892.

*Painting the Town Red, **Harper's Weekly,** 1886. In this illustration and others, Zogbaum vies with Remington and Russell in presenting the wild and wooly West.*

R.F. Zogbaum

RUFUS FAIRCHILD ZOGBAUM (1849-1925) was a lifelong student of and expert in the depiction of battle scenes. He wrote and illustrated a book entitled **Horse, Foot, and Dragoons,** published by Harper and Brothers, as well as several scholarly articles for **Scribner's,** including "From Port to Port with the White Squadron" in the October, 1890 issue. He specialized in American war illustrations: of the Civil War, the skirmishes with Native Americans, and the Spanish-American War. In his pictures, there is an originality of approach and authenticity of detail that mark him as a master. Zogbaum also made trips to the West in the 1880s, which resulted in several early depictions of cowboy life, published by Harper's. Unfortunately, the great bulk of his work pre-dated halftone engraving and was reproduced by the cruder method of wood engraving.

He painted the "First Minnesota Regiment at the Battle of Gettysburg" as a mural at the State Capitol in St. Paul, Minnesota, and the "Battle of Lake Erie" for the Federal Building in Cleveland, Ohio.

*"The White Squadron in Mid-Ocean," **Scribner's** magazine, September, 1890.*
From "With Uncle Sam's Blue Jackets Afloat," written and illustrated by Zogbaum.

1880–1890

Edwin Austin Abbey

Otto Henry Bacher

Daniel Carter Beard

Reginald Bathurst Birch

Robert Frederick Blum

Clifford Carleton

J. Andre Castaigne

Benjamin West Clinedinst

Kenyon Cox

Henry F. Farney

Arthur Burdett Frost

William Gilbert Gaul

Childe Hassam

Elizabeth B. Humphrey

Maud Humphrey (Bogart)

Max Francis Klepper

Louis Loeb

Will Hicok Low

Willard Leroy Metcalf

Henry Alexander Ogden

Joseph Pennell

Edward Henry Potthast

Howard Pyle

William Allen Rogers

William Thomas Smedley

Albert E. Sterner

Thomas Starling Sullivant

William Ladd Taylor

William Francis Ver Beck

Thomas Dart Walker

Edwin Austin Abbey, exhibition program cover.

Howard Pyle, *Otto of the Silver Hand.*

A.B. Frost, *The Tar Baby,* from **Uncle Remus.**

THE DECADE 1880-1890

The decade of the 1880s was one of great changes in printing and publishing, which had a major impact on illustration itself. A photo process for the production of line art made it possible to reproduce the lines of pen and ink exactly as drawn – no longer requiring their translation by wood engraving. This process would be accompanied at the end of the decade by the invention of halftone engraving. This revolutionary process for translating tonal pictures into a pattern of tiny, varied dots permitted a more faithful representation of the original painting than ever before possible through wood engraving. The new engravings could be made more quickly and were far less costly. Publishers were therefore able to increase the number and quality of pictures. At the same time improvements in presses made printing much faster and less expensive. With improved publication at lower cost the numbers of subscribers also increased rapidly. Magazines entered upon a prosperous era, paying higher rates for manuscripts and attracting the most talented artists with generous payments.

Among the artists who best exemplified this beginning of the Golden Age was Edwin Austin Abbey. Having risen through the staff ranks at **Harper's** and developing an exquisite technique in pen and ink, he set such a lofty standard in his interpretation of Shakespeare, Goldsmith, and Herrick that his work, in turn, became an inspiration to the English illustrators. Abbey, sent by **Harper's** to England in 1878 to research settings for his illustrations for **The Quiet Life,** by Austin Dobson, chose to remain in England for the rest of his career surrounded by the authentic settings and costumes available only there. However, he continued to work for **Harper's** and his work was reproduced in their publications for many subsequent years.

A new chromolithographic printing process was also introduced at this time using lithographic stones. Although short-lived, it was also capable of printing color, even earlier than the halftone engraving process. It was cumbersome, however, and its use was generally limited to short-run printing of calendars, advertising, and trade cards. The magazine **Puck**, founded in 1877 as a humorous German language weekly, also made use of this process for its covers and a centerfold in color. **Truth** followed suit as did another humorous rival magazine, **Judge** in 1881. **Life** magazine was established in 1883 featuring social satire.

As yet, there were few compartments in American art. Nearly every artist who had the ability was drawn to illustrating for publication. It was well-paying and prestigious. Many painters divided their efforts between the gallery and magazine pages. However, it was difficult to earn a living by "Exhibition Art" alone. Americans who collected art bought it in Europe, as they were not yet convinced of the merit of native talent. It would be long into the future before Homer, Sloane, Glackens, and others would find sufficient financial acceptence to follow their personal artistic destinies. Until then, the publisher would still be the principal artistic patron.

King Lear, Cordelia's Farewell, Act 1, Scene 1. Collection of The Metropolitan Museum of Art.

A Measure, from **The Decameron,** 1904.
The Kelly Collection of American Illustration.

EDWIN AUSTIN ABBEY, N.A., R.A. (1852-1911) was both illustrator and artist in the fullest sense. His work, beginning with small black-and-white illustrations for the old **Harper's** magazine, and culminating in the huge mural decorations for the Boston Public Library and the State Capitol in Harrisburg, Pennsylvania, was done with extraordinary artistic dedication.

Abbey's drive for authenticity was legendary among his fellow illustrators and eventually led him to live in England where the original props and costuming required for his historical illustrations were still to be found.

Many of his later illustrations were rendered in watercolor or in oils for reproduction in full color, but he continued to use pen and ink as a serious art medium. The brilliant draftsmanship of his pen-and-ink drawings for the plays of Shakespeare has never been surpassed.

Abbey was born in Philadelphia and attended the Pennsylvania Academy of the Fine Arts. His first employment at nineteen was with the art staff at Harper and Brothers, where he worked alongside Charles S. Reinhart, A.B. Frost, John White Alexander, and Howard Pyle. A full record of his life and work is contained in the two-volume **Edwin Austin Abbey** by E.V. Lucas, published in 1921.

A permanent collection of his drawings, paintings, and pastels is retained in the Edwin Austin Abbey collection at Yale University in New Haven, Connecticut.

In 1994, a major exhibition of Abbey's works on his Shakespearean subjects entitled "Unfaded Pageant," was held at the Miriam and Dr. Wallach Art Gallery at Columbia University; it drew upon collections at Yale University, the Corcoran Gallery of Art, and the Folger Shakespearean Library, both of Washington, D.C.

"Will Had Her to the Wine," from "Phillada" ***Harper's Monthly***, July, 1887.

"His House Was Known to All the Vagrant Train," ***Harper's Monthly***, March, 1902.

OTTO HENRY BACHER (1856-1909) A.N.A. was a native of Cleveland, Ohio, and had his early art training in Cincinnati. Like most ambitious young artists of his era, he then looked to Europe for further training. He studied with Boulanger, Corolus-Duran, Lefebvre, Duveneck and Whistler in Paris. Whistler considered him one of his favorite pupils, and with a joint interest in etching, Bacher accompanied Whistler on his sketching jaunts. Bacher published his book, **With Whistler in Venice**, in 1907. In addition to his prints, Bacher was an excellent illustrator, working for **The Century, Scribner's, McClure's, St. Nicholas** and other magazines, and was one of the founding members of the Society of Illustrators in 1901. In that same year, his work won a prize at the Pan-American Exposition in Buffalo, and a medal at the Louisiana Purchase Expo in 1904. He is considered an early American Impressionist in oils and was included in recent exhibits at the Whitney Museum of American Art and the National Gallery of Art in Washington, D.C. His work is included in the Cleveland Museum of Art and a large collection of his etchings is in the Print Collection of the Library of Congress.

Illustration for *"When Polly Takes the Air"*, *The Century,* September, 1893.

Today, DANIEL CARTER BEARD (1850-1941) is better remembered as one of the founders of the Boy Scouts of America, in 1910, with which he was completely involved for the latter part of his life. Mt. Beard, located near Mt. McKinley, was named in his honor.

Born in Cincinnati, Ohio, son of James Henry Beard, a National Academician, he studied at the Art Students League with John Sartain and J. C. Beckwith. His high sense of humor made him an ideal candidate to illustrate Mark Twain's **A Connecticut Yankee in King Arthur's Court**, and he was a regular contributor to **St. Nicholas Magazine.** He also wrote and illustrated books on animals and outdoor life as well as the **American Boy's Handy Book.** Active in the Society of Illustrators, he served as its president in 1914.

"Great Scott! But There Was a Sensation," illustration for **A Connecticut Yankee in King Arthur's Court**, 1889.

The Ameya or *Itinerant Candy Vender.* Collection of The Metropolitan Museum of Art.
This picture won Blum his election as a full National Academician in 1893 — at that time its youngest member.

ROBERT FREDERICK BLUM, N.A. (1857-1903) was a masterful performer in pen and ink. In his technique there is evidence of the influence of Fortuny, the Spanish master, but the soundness of draftsmanship and form were his own.

Blum was born in Cincinnati, Ohio, and was apprenticed to a lithographer's shop in 1871. He studied nights at the McMicken Art School of Design in Cincinnati, later attended the Pennsylvania Academy of the Fine Arts in Philadelphia. Blum made many trips abroad, and the majority of his pictures are of foreign subjects. In 1890, he traveled to Japan accompanying the writer, Sir Edwin Arnold, to illustrate his book, **Japonica.** While in Japan, he produced some of his finest drawings and paintings.

REGINALD BATHURST BIRCH (1856-1943) was known as "the children's Gibson" because of the great number of pen-and-ink illustrations for children's stories and fairy tales he did for **St. Nicholas** magazine.

His drawings give the appearance of great spontaneity and directness resulting from his practice of using models only for his preliminary sketches and rendering the finished drawings freely from them.

Although Birch also illustrated for **The Century** magazine, **Harper's, McClure's, Scribner's, Collier's,** the old **Life, Youth's Companion,** and nearly 200 books, his best known illustrations were done for **Little Lord Fauntleroy,** by Frances Hodgson Burnett in 1886. These were responsible for a whole generation of Victorian boys' being forced to wear black velvet suits, lace collars and curls, patterned after Birch's prototype.

Birch was born in England, grew up in San Francisco, and studied at the Art Academy in Munich, Germany.

Blum was at home in every medium from pencil, pen and ink, pastel, etching watercolor and oils, but with less emphasis on technique than on ethereal mood. In the last phase of his career, he painted a series of mural decorations in Mendelssohn Hall in New York.

The Dragon & the Dragoon, **St. Nicholas** magazine, July, 1895.

*"The Unwelcome Before-Breakfast Caller," **The Society of Illustrators Annual**, 1911.*

C. Carleton.

CLIFFORD CARLETON (1867-1946) was born in Brooklyn, New York, and studied at the Art Students League under H. Siddons Mowbray. Carlton was at his best with rural subjects, such as the watercolor painting reproduced here. He produced a great amount of work and illustrated for most of the leading magazines of his day, including the old *Life, Harper's Weekly, Harper's Bazar,* and *Scribner's.* Books he illustrated include: *Pembroke* by Mary Wilkins, *People We Pass* by Julian Ralph, and *Their Wedding Journey* by William Dean Howells.

A. Castaigne.

J. ANDRE CASTAIGNE (1861-1930) came to America in 1890 with the thorough training of the French Academy. Born in Angoulème in the Bordeaux region, he studied successively at the Academie Suisse and at the Ecole des Beaux Arts under Cabanel and Gérôme. After graduation, he won early honors in the Paris Salon and one of his pictures was purchased for the French government. A portrait commission brought him to Baltimore, and he soon became a part of the art community as an instructor at the Charcoal Club.

The Century magazine offered him the opportunity to illustrate a manuscript, and this contact led to his association with that publication for many years. His work was also published by *Scribner's, McClure's,* and *Harper's* magazines. Among his reportorial illustrations were for the Chicago World's Fair in 1893 and the Pan American Exposition in Buffalo in 1901. Castaigne was also active in French and English publications *L'Illustration* and *The London Graphic*, while continuing his long association with *The Century* and other American publishers.

For his other role, as a portraitist, he was awarded the Legion d'Honneur.

This painting of immigrants in steerage from 1913 is similar to illustrations the artist produced in black and white for his own articles about the immigrant experience published in *The Century* in the 1890s. Private Collection.

B. WEST CLINEDINST

BENJAMIN WEST CLINEDINST, N.A. (1859-1931) was one of the original ten founders of the Society of Illustrators in New York in 1901. He was born in Woodstock, Virginia, and studied at the Ecole des Beaux Arts in Paris where he was a pupil of Cabanel and Bonnât. In addition to his illustrations for many magazines and books, he painted portaits of several national figures including President Theodore Roosevelt and Admiral Peary.

From 1903-05, he was art editor of *Leslie's Weekly.* He exhibited widely and was elected to membership in the National Academy in 1898. The last years of his life were devoted to painting and teaching of illustration at Cooper Union in New York.

•KENYON COX•

The son of a Civil War general who later became governor of Ohio, KENYON COX, N.A. (1856-1919) was a sickly child who survived two major operations and was confined to his bed from the age of nine to thirteen. During that time he resolved to become an artist. Enrolled first in the McMicken Art School in Cincinnati, he progressed to the Pennsylvania Academy of the Fine Arts and thence to several years of study in Paris under numerous French masters, including Carolus Duran, Cabanel, Bouguereau, LeFebre and Gérôme.

He returned to the United States to pursue a varied career as illustrator, portraitist, muralist, author, and landscape painter, as well as a teacher at the Art Students League. With all of these diversions, his output as an illustrator was limited but distinguished by his classical sense of beauty and structure.

B. W. Clinedinst, ca. 1900. Collection of Marcello Bruno.

1.697"

51

"Blow Sammy, blow. He's a comin' by gum!," "Smoking Him Out," **Charles Scribner's Sons,** 1903.

Self-caricature – painting on location.

"Brer Rabbit ax 'im if he'll do er a favor for one er his 'ol time fren's," "Impty-Umpty and the Blacksmith," **Metropolitan** magazine.

A. *Congressman's Day of Reckoning,* **Collier's,** 1903; watercolor.
This image was also issued as a print. Full caption, from margin of art reads: *#4
"Congressman Hookemsneerey meets a committee of his constituents on his return from
the City."*
Collection of Ilene and Steven Berman.

A. B. FROST.

ARTHUR BURDETT FROST (1851-1928) was our best
illustrator of rural America. He usually treated his characters with
humor, and in his drawings there was a directness and honesty
which showed his sympathetic understanding of his subjects. His
sound draughtsmanship was combined with an intimate
knowledge of nature. the details in his picture are always very
specific, as though drawn on the spot, and so artfully chosen and
placed as to carry out the picture's idea in a natural and entirely
convincing manner.

He may be best remembered now, however, for his charming
illustrations for the Uncle Remus tales by Joel Chandler Harris. In
the preface and dedication by Harris for the 1896 edition, he wrote
of Frost "..you have conveyed into their quaint antics the
illumination of your own inimitable humor, which as true to our
sun and soil as it is to the spirit and essence of the matter...The
book was mine, but now you have made it yours, both sap and
pith..."

Frost was apprenticed as a wood engraver and gravitated to
work as a lithographer. His first success came with his
illustrations for *Out of the Hurly-Burly* by Max Adler. He became
a member of the Harper's Brothers art staff alongside Abbey and
Pyle, studied with Thomas Eakins and William Merritt Chase. The
Frost family also sojourned in France for a long period of study
for Frost and his two sons.

"Smoke got sociable ways 'aint't it?" "A Golden Wedding," **Harper's Monthly,** 1884.

The Captive, Collection of the Cincinnati Art Museum; gift of Mrs. Benjamin E. Tate and Julius Fleischmann in memory of their father Julius Fleischmann.

HENRY F. FARNY (1847-1916) was the son of a prominent Republican refugee from France and his early years, 1853-1859, were spent in the wilderness of western Pennsylvania. There he made his first contact with the Seneca tribe, with whom he became friendly. The family eventually moved by raft downriver to the more civilized city of Cincinnati where Farny became apprenticed to a lithography firm. Needing further art training, he saved enough to go abroad to Rome, Vienna, Munich and Düsseldorf on two successive trips, sporadically working to support his classroom studies. On his return to the United States, he began to illustrate for Cincinnati publishers as well as for Harper's.

He also became drawn to and specialized in Native American subject matter, and in 1881 made the first of many visits to the West, recording the contrasts in white and native interaction. Many of these drawings and paintings were published in **Harper's Weekly** and **The Century** magazine which sent Farny and a reporter on the trips. There Farny met and drew Sitting Bull; later he introduced the famous warrior to General Grant. President Theodore Roosevelt was a personal admirer of Farny's work.

After 1890, Farny concentrated on easel painting, relying on his large collection of tribal costumes, artifacts, photos and sketches for reference. The accuracy and artistry of his work combine to make him one of our major painters of the Old West.

Nest of Rattlesnakes, 1894. Photo courtesy Spanierman Gallery, LLC New York, N.Y.

Federal troops reading a message at fireside. Collection of Don Stivers.

Gilbert Gaul-

WILLIAM GILBERT GAUL, N.A. (1855-1919) specialized in military subjects to which he gave a feeling of great authenticity. His characters were not paintings of polished, costumed models, but of real people revealed by carefully observed gestures. The uniforms look lived-in, powder stained, torn or patched. Like Matthew Brady's photos, the effect is one of raw honesty to which he added the drama of lifelike action.

Gaul was born in Jersey City, New Jersey, and was educated at the Claverack Military Academy. He studied art in New York City under painter J. G. Brown. His illustrations appeared regularly in **Harper's Monthly** and other magazines.

He won a Gold Medal from the American Art Association in 1881 for his painting, *Hold the Line at All Hazards. Charging the Battery* won a medal at the Paris Exposition in 1889.

Indian Boy By The Fire.
Collection of the Eiteljorg Museum of American Indians and Western Art.

Childe Hassam pen and ink illustration for *The New York Commercial Advertiser.*

Although he later became one of America's eminent Impressionist painters, CHILDE HASSAM, N.A. (1859-1935) was interested in drawing at an early age and participated in nearly every phase of American art, including a long career as a working illustrator for magazine and book publishers. Among his clients were *Wide Awake, St. Nicholas, The Century, Scribner's,* and *Harper's*; his book credits include *Youth in Twelve Centuries, Ballads of Romance and History,* and *An Island Garden.*

Hassam had started out in a wood engraving firm making newspaper drawings and studying at the Boston Art Club in the evening. He also studied with the Boston painter Ignatz M. Gaugengigl. From 1886 through 1889, he was in Paris attending the Academie Julian, but came under the influence of the Barbizon and Impressionist schools and adopted their approach. This marked a new direction in his style and after returning to the U.S., devoted the remainder of his life to painting in the Impressionist idiom. He won innumerable honors and awards, and is represented in many major museum collections.

ELIZABETH B. HUMPHREY (pre 1850-circa 1890) was a staff illustrator for Louis Prang and Company and most of her work was reproduced by the chromolithographic process. A versatile artist, she had an excellent training at the Cooper Union School of Design, and studied with Worthington Whittridge. In addition to her many greeting cards and gift book products for Prang, she painted landscapes, figures and still life subjects for exhibition. Four of her pictures were reproduced in *Beyond the Mississippi* in 1867, and she also made a number of paintings and drawings on a later trip to California. After her death, Prang published a book, *Child Life*, as a memorial record, reproducing many of the subjects she had produced in her long association with them.

Elizabeth B. Humphrey, *"Come bring the holly, let's be jolly."*
Prang design reproduced both with and without decorative border.
Collection of The Hallmark Archives, Hallmark Cards, Inc.

The typical Maud Humphrey subject, here playing the role of a visiting doctor.

Master Humphrey de Forest Bogart at the age of seven weeks, drawn by his mother for a valentine.

MAUD HUMPHREY (BOGART) (circa 1865-1940) was not related to Elizabeth Humphrey, although she may well have been influenced by her since she also designed artwork for Louis Prang and Company. Maud went on to illustrate for Frederick A. Stokes Co., *Harper's* magazine, and *The Century*. In 1898, she married Dr. Belmont Bogart, and her son was the model for many beautiful children before he grew up to be the famous actor Humphrey Bogart.

Maud had studied at the Art Students League and in Paris under Whistler. She was an active exhibitor with the American Watercolor Society and was a member of the Boston Art Club and New York Watercolor Society. She and her sister Mabel also produced two miniature books for Frederick Stokes Company. In later years, she was the art director for *The Delineator* magazine.

MAX FRANCIS KLEPPER (1861-1907) was brought to America from Germany by his parents in 1876, and was apprenticed to a lithography firm in Chicago. Later, he returned to study at the Royal Academy in Munich for four years. Back in New York, he began to illustrate for major magazines such as *Harper's, Scribner's* and *The Century.* He was expert in depicting animals of all kinds, particularly horses, which are featured in many of his illustrations of action in the Civil and Spanish-American wars. He exhibited at the Art Institute of Chicago in 1891.

Max Klepper, *Light Artillery Drill of U.S. Regulars at Port Tampa, Florida-* "Halt!" *Harper's Weekly*, May 28, 1898. Collection of Jean S. and Frederic A. Scharf.

Louis Loeb, *"Forbear the song is too sweet."* from *"Cantator."*

— LOUIS · LOEB —

LOUIS LOEB, N.A. (1866-1909) was born in Cleveland, Ohio, of German immigrant parents. Because of his early interest in art, he was apprenticed at thirteen to a lithography house. He saved up to go to New York to attend the Art Students League; his instructor there was George DeForrest Brush. Like the majority of illustrators of his day, Loeb received his advanced art training abroad. He studied under Gérôme in Paris and exhibited in the Paris Salon in 1895 and 1897 before returning to the States. As an illustrator, his work appeared in *The Century, Harper's Monthly* and other publications. He was a founding member of the Society of Illustrators.

Loeb was also an active etcher and painter for exhibition, winning a number of awards, including the Hallgarten prize of the National Academy of Design in 1902, the Carnegie prize in 1905, and the Society of Washington Artists prize in 1906. He was elected a full member of the National Academy in 1906.

WILL HICKOCK LOW (1853-1932) like many other ambitious artists of his generation had to look to Europe for advanced training. Paris was the magnet for many, and he chose the Ecôle des Beaux Arts. There, over a period of five years, he studied with Gérôme and Carolus-Duran. Although he had done some limited illustration earlier, upon his return to the U.S. he was able to find full employment as an illustrator for *The Century, Harper's, McClure's,* and *Scribner's* magazines as well as for books and posters. The Waldorf-Astoria Hotel commissioned him to paint their mural decorations, a project he shared with Edwin Blashfield. Like Blashfield, John LaFarge, and Elihu Vedder, Low shared an interest in reviving classical subjects and motifs.

He taught for several years at the Cooper Union Art School, the National Academy of Design and at the Art Institute of Chicago. He wrote of his experiences as the author of *A Chronicle of Friendships* in 1908, and *A Painter's Progress* in 1910.

Advertising poster for *Scribner's Fiction Number* circa 1895;

WILLARD LEROY METCALF (1858-1925) first made his mark
as an artist with the publication of his illustrations for **Harper's** on
the Zuni Indians in 1885. He had studied at the Lowell Institute
and Boston Museum of Fine Arts School, but lived in the
Southwest during the years 1881-1883. Feeling the need for more
advanced training, he then moved to Paris to study at the
Academie Julian, where he remained for six years.

Upon his return to the States, he embarked on a long, diverse
career as an illustrator, painter and teacher. His paintings
consistently won him prizes, and he is represented in many private
and public collections, including the National Gallery of Art, the
Pennsylvania Academy of the Fine Arts, the Detroit Art Institute,
the St. Louis Museum, the Albright Knox Gallery in Buffalo, and
many others. His best known works are his landscapes which
were painted around the Old Lyme Colony in Connecticut and in
Cornish, New Hamphshire.

For several years he conducted classes at the Cooper Union
Art School in New York.

W. L. Metcalf, "Her Dying Words," by Thomas Bailey Aldrich, **Scribner's Magazine,** August, 1893. Collection of Irwin and Rita Silver.

HENRY A. OGDEN (1856-1936) had an all-consuming interest
in military subjects and was particularly an authority on uniforms
and colonial costumes. He was both author and illustrator of
several books on those topics, including **Our Army, The Boy's
Book of Famous Regiments,** and **Our Flag.** He was
commissioned by the U.S. Government to compile a pictorial
history of army uniforms covering 1774-1907, and his work is
represented in **The Pageant of America.**

Ogden began his career as a staff artist for **Frank Leslie's
Illustrated Newspaper**. After eight years, he joined the New York
staff of the Strobridge Lithograph company of Cincinnati.
Periodically, he sharpened his skills by attendance at The
Brooklyn Academy of Design, The Art Students League, and the
National Academy of Design. Ogden became a member of the
Society of Illustrators in 1911.

H. A. Ogden, *Raising the Stars and Stripes,* American Lithograph Company, 1904.

The South Transept Portal of Rouen Cathedral.
Lithograph published in **The Century** magazine.

"Lifting Workmen out of the Gatum Lock," from a series of lithographs, "Building the Panama Canal," **The Century** February, 1912.

"Turner's Last Dwelling-Place," from "Old Chelsea" 1884.

JOSEPH PENNELL, N.A. (1860-1926) was a pictorial reporter interested chiefly in architectural subjects. He ranged the world on assignments for **The Century**, **McClure's**, and **Harper's** magazines, sending back exquisite etchings, pen-and-ink drawings or lithographs of cathedrals, plazas, street scenes, and palaces at a time when only the rich could go abroad. He also skillfully depicted the panoramic aspects of major construction or engineering projects — the Locks at Niagara Falls, the construction of the Panama Canal and the war production efforts in Britain, France and America during World War I.

He was a friend and great admirer of James McNeill Whistler, whose biography he wrote. He also wrote a number of books, including **Joseph Pennell's Pictures of the Wonder of Work,** his highly opinionated chronicle of his profession, **Adventures of an Illustrator,** and the perennial favorite, **Pen Drawing and Pen Draughtsmen,** which stayed in print through several editions. He also wrote and illustrated books on travel subjects, many in collaboration with his wife, Elizabeth Robins Pennell, such as **Our House, and London Out of Our Windows** and **Play in Provence.**

E. Potthast

EDWARD HENRY POTTHAST, N.A. (1857-1927) is an important figure in American Impressionist painting, noted especially for his brilliantly colorful beach scenes with bathers. The latter part of his life was involved with painting for exhibition, and he was elected to full membership in the National Academy in 1906. He also had a distinguished career as an illustrator; many of his subjects were African-Americans, which he depicted with great integrity.

Potthast was born in Cincinnati, the son of a cabinet maker. He studied at the McMicken School of Design and found his first work as an apprentice lithographer. With his earnings, he went to Antwerp for study at the Academy. Later he attended schools in Paris and Munich. After returning to Cincinnati, he resumed his lithography employment, but also began to find work as an illustrator for *Scribner's* and ***The Century***. Eventually he moved to New York and became an active participant in New York art shows as a member of the American Watercolor Society, the Salmagundi Club, and the Allied Artists of America. There he won many medals and awards.

The Family of Rose Ann, Washerwoman, ***The Century,*** January 1902. Collection of Irwin and Rita Silver.

At the Seashore, a typical impressionist painting by Potthast, set at the New York area beaches.

"Walking the Plank," for "Buccaneers and Marooners of the Spanish Main," by Howard Pyle, **Harper's Monthly.**

"How The Declaration Was Received in Connecticut," **Harper's Monthly.**

H. Pyle.

The illustrations of HOWARD PYLE, N.A. (1853-1911) are as exciting now as they were over a century ago, while pictures by many of his contemporaries look dated and mannered today.

Several special qualities combined to make Pyle America's foremost illustrator. Pyle was interested in pictures, first of all, as drama. As a young man his initial visit to a theatrical performance had made a great impression on him and influenced his point of view from then on. In his illustrations, Pyle sought to dramatize themes with universal appeal. The pictures portrayed basic human emotions: the ruthlessness of pirate greed, raw grief in the break-up of Lee's army after Appomattox, smug pride, humble petition.

Pyle's concept of a picture was never trite. He deliberately looked for new ways to tell a story and involved himself in his subject so thoroughly that each picture makes the reader an eye-witness to a vivid experience.

Pyle developed his compositions to present the picture idea in the strongest possible terms; his pictures are fascinating to analyze. No area of a picture is wasted; each makes its contribution, through placement, line, tone, or color, to the whole story. Through the details, the viewer's eye is purposefully led toward the focal center.

Pyle wrote, as well as illustrated, many books himself. He did original research on the obscure subject of the buccaneers in the New World. It is from **Howard Pyle's Book of Pirates** that our present-day concept of pirates has come. His **Men of Iron**, **The Story of King Arthur and His Knights**, **The Merry Adventures of Robin Hood**, and others, are still read today.

As a teacher, Pyle attracted a large number of students, and inspired them as much by his idealism as by the high standards he set for picture-making. Over the years, he taught at the Drexel Institute in Philadelphia, lectured at the Art Students League in New York, and eventually conducted special classes for gifted students at Wilmington, Delaware, and during the summer, at Chadds Ford, Pennsylvania. He did not charge for his teaching and in fact, built a set of studios for the students to work in. N.C. Wyeth, Harvey Dunn, Stanley Arthurs, Jessie Willcox Smith and Frank Schoonover were among the beneficiaries of this instruction, and passed along to others Pyle's unique approach as they in turn became illustrators and teachers.

At a time when it was customary and fashionable to study in Europe, Pyle had a strong conviction that students should seek their training and inspiration in America. Many of Pyles's greatest pictures came from his intense and loyal interest in Americana. His renditions of the Revolutionary War period and of Civil War subjects have since become standard pictures in history books, among them Woodrow Wilson's **History of the American People** and James Truslow Adams's **History of the United States**.

After Pyle's death, his students collected many of his original paintings as a nucleus for the present comprehensive collection of his work in the Delaware Art Museum. An excellent biography was written by Henry C. Pitz and published in 1975.

"An Attack on a Galleon," "The Fate of a Treasure Town," by Howard Pyle, **Harper's Monthly,** December 1905. Collection of Delaware Art Museum.

"The Nation Makers," *Collier's Weekly,* June 2, 1906. Collection of the Brandywine River Museum.

W. A. Rogers, *A Holiday in a Logging Camp,* ***Harper's Weekly,*** January 8, 1898.

WILLIAM ALLEN ROGERS (1854-1931) took over the political cartoon cover of ***Harper's Weekly*** after Thomas Nast left, and for many years his pen was at the service of the editorial policy of that magazine. While his cartoons never quite approached Nast's in power, his ideas were strongly presented and his drawings somewhat more skillful.

Rogers was born in Springfield, Ohio, and by the age of fourteen was drawing cartoons for a midwestern newspaper. He soon gravitated to the East and began to work as an apprentice in the art department of Harper's under the supervision of Charles Parsons. There he developed the skills to take on every kind of assignment, eventually becoming a "special artist" for ***Harper's Weekly.*** It was when on an assignment for them to Minneapolis to cover the visit there of President Rutherford Hayes that he seized a proffered opportunity to visit the frontier Northwest. Although the trip was not at all authorized, he came back with such an abundance of colorful sketches, that it resulted in many articles which he both wrote and illustrated, and his being AWOL was forgiven.

Rogers was a member of The Century Association and the Society of Illustrators. He wrote an autobiography, ***A World Worthwhile***, which was published in 1922.

Off to School, ***Thirty Favorite Paintings,*** P.F. Collier and Son, 1908.

WILLIAM THOMAS SMEDLEY, N.A. (1858-1920) was born in West Chester, Pennsylvania, received his art education at the Pennsylvania Academy of the Fine Arts in Philadelphia, and later studied with Jean Paul Laurens in Paris.

He began his career in the early 1880s as a pen-and-ink artist for Harper and Brothers; later, after halftone engraving was introduced, he changed to working in gouache.

As a free lance artist, he was an active contributor to most of the major magazines, including ***Scribner's, Harper's,*** and ***The Ladies' Home Journal.*** He also illustrated many books for authors such as William Dean Howells and Henry James.

An active painter, Smedley was a member of the American Watercolor Society, the National Association of Portrait Painters, and the National Institute of Arts and Letters. He won many awards, including the Evans Prize, A.W.C.S. 1890; the Proctor Prize, National Academy of Design, 1906; and the Carnegie Prize, National Academy of Design, 1916. His work is also represented in the National Gallery of Art, Washington, D.C.

Albert Sterner

ALBERT E. STERNER, N.A. (1863-1946) was a versatile performer in many media, including pen and ink, watercolor, oils, lithography, pastel, etching, monotype, crayon, red chalk and charcoal.

Born in London, Sterner studied on a scholarship at the Birmingham Art Institute. He came to America at seventeen to start his career working as a scene painter, then went on to lithography and drawing for engravers on wood blocks.

By 1885, Sterner had moved to New York and begun illustrating for the old **Life, St. Nicholas,** and **Harper's** magazines. Sterner became art editor for **Munsey's Weekly** and later a staff member of **The Century** magazine. He also taught at the Art Students League, the school of the National Academy of Design, and the New York School of Applied Design for Women. During his long career he also received commissions to paint portraits of members of socially prominent families, including the Vanderbilts, the Lamonts, and the Whitneys.

Sterner was president of the Society of Illustrators in 1907 and 1908 and was elected a full member of the National Academy of Design in 1934.

Cover design for **Jugend**. Exhibited at The New-York Historical Society, "200 Years of American Illustration," 1976.

Thomas Sullivant

THOMAS STARLING SULLIVANT (1854-1926) was not an illustrator of serious subjects, yet his humorous drawings were so skillfully done that no survey of American illustration would be complete without them. He was born in Columbus, Ohio, and studied at the Pennsylvania Academy of the Fine Arts. His work reveals him as a master draftsman even though he chose to distort the facts rather than to record them literally.

Sullivant's drawings of animals of all kinds are a delightful combination of an intimate knowledge of their anatomy with calculated exaggeration, through which he imparts human qualities to them. An excellent collection of his early artwork appeared in **Fables for the Times**, by H. W. Phillips, and his work appeared regularly in the old **Life** magazine.

Noah loading up the Ark, from **Life** magazine, is Sullivant at his best. Collection of Ricardo Martinez.

The Passing of the Farm, from **The Ladies' Home Journal**, 1901.

W. L. TAYLOR -

WILLIAM LADD TAYLOR (1854-1926) had a thorough art education in art schools in Boston, New York, and with Boulanger and Lefebvre in Paris.

Taylor returned to settle in Boston and to record a long series of subjects, usually of an historical or regional nature. His interest in antiques and in recreating the era of their use was reflected in an excellent series of paintings of nineteenth century scenes in New England. Other series included *Old Southern Days, Home Scenes,* and *Frontier Scenes,* the latter painted during the course of an illness and a year's stay in Colorado.

For many years these pictures were a regular feature as full-color, full-page reproductions in **The Ladies' Home Journal**, and reprints of the pictures for framing were very popular. A large number of the pictures were also compiled in a book, **Our Home and Country,** published by Moffat, Yard and Company in 1908.

A comprehensive exhibition of the artist's work was shown at the Wellesley Historical Society in 1999.

A Rocky Mountain Mining Camp, from **Our Home and Country.**

Frank Ver Beck, Bears gathering honey surrounded by swarming bees.

WILLIAM FRANCIS VER BECK (1858-1933) was born in Belmont County, Ohio. He was famous for his comic bears and other animals produced as illustrations for children's stories. Many were collaborations with author Albert Bigelow Paine for a series of books about "The Arkansaw Bear," a combination of song and story. Ver Beck also wrote and illustrated his own *Ver Beck's Book of Bears, The Donkey Child,* a "Little Black Sambo" series and *The Little Cat Who Journeyed to St. Ives.* Frank also produced a popular comic strip featuring bears and was a designer of the Ver Beck earthenware models.

T. DART WALKER (1869-1914) distinguished himself as a "special artist" and journalist for *Harper's Weekly*, recording events of the Spanish-American War. Attached to General Miles's forces, he documented many events including the advance on Guayana in Puerto Rico and the postwar peace negotiations. Earlier, he had pictured the construction and opening of the World's Columbian Exposition held in Chicago in 1893.

Born in Goshen, Indiana, Walker landed his first art job as a staff artist for the publishing firm of Harper Brothers and over the years he also illustrated for *Harper's Monthly* and *Harper's Young People.* Walker pursued an additional career as an exhibiting painter of portraits and marine subjects.

T. Dart Walker, "*Assistant Naval-Constructor Hobson's Heroic Exploit in Blowing up the Collier* Merrimac *at the Entrance to Santiago Harbor.*" **Harper's Pictorial History of the War with Spain**, Harper & Brothers, 1899

1890–1900

Vernon Howe Bailey
Will H. Bradley
Alfred Laurens Brennan
Walter Appleton Clark
Will Crawford
Frank Vincent DuMond
George Wharton Edwards
Jean Léon Gerome Ferris
Charles Dana Gibson
Walter Granville-Smith
Jules Guérin
Jay Hambidge

Edward Winsor Kemble
Henry McCarter
Peter Sheaf Newell
Eric Pape
Edward Penfield
Victor Semon Perard
Frederic Sackrider Remington
Alice Barber Stephens
George Edmund Varian
Albert Beck Wenzell
Irving Ramsey Wiles

Frederic Remington covered the Spanish-American War.

Charles Dana Gibson "A Love Song"

Edward Windsor Kemble, stereotypical portrait.

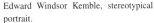

Edward Penfield, *Harper's Monthly*, 1897.

THE DECADE 1890-1900

While no official designation exists, there is general agreement among historians in the field that the decade of the nineties marked the flowering of a "Golden Age of Illustration," which ended with the disruptions and cultural shifts of World War I.

A fortuitous combination of elements came together in publishing, printing technology and the arts, to stimulate this productive period. The major publishing houses were now equipped with high-speed rotary presses, able to keep up with rapidly growing lists of subscribers. The price of paper dropped. Wood engravings were more and more giving way to the new halftone process which was able to represent the artists' work with much greater fidelity to the original drawing or painting.

Some of America's greatest talents in the field had emerged by this time, including Pyle, Frost, Abbey, Kemble and Gibson. Frederic Remington's pictures of cowpokes and Indian wars brought him great admiration from a public eager to follow events in the "taming" of the West. A. B. Frost's paintings of fishing and hunting were full of the authentic detail that delighted sportsmen, and Howard Pyle's pictures of knights and chivalry attracted the readers of romance and adventure. These artists were joined by the newly-trained graduates from the European art academies who readily found their niches in the best magazines. Eric Pape, A. B. Wenzell and Arthur I. Keller could paint historical pageantry as well as the contemporary social scene with panache. Jules Guérin drew beautiful renderings of exotic sites and American architecture. Robert Blum traveled to Japan and returned to present lively intimate drawings and watercolors of Japanese life.

The social satire magazine *Life* launched the immensely successful career of Charles Dana Gibson. The handsome young men in his drawings were smooth-shaven, and that influence

effectively ended the era of mutton chops and other beards. "The Gibson Girl" was admired for her spectacular wholesome beauty, and young women everywhere emulated her. Her image appeared on spoons, banners, and pillows. She, and her creator Gibson became stars of popular culture.

American illustrators were exposed to many movements and influences. The French poster artists Toulouse-Lautrec, Jules Chéret and Alphonse Mucha, as well as the British "Beggerstaff Brothers," stimulated an American Poster movement led by Edward Penfield, Ethel Reed and Will Bradley. British illustration had a second wave of brilliance; Aubrey Beardsley and Phil May particularly, attracted adherents in America.

The gaslight decade saw newspapers at war for circulation and public opinion, as they became the nation's primary reading matter. The "Special artists" formed the staff employed to draw news events either on the spot, or from verbal descriptions, under tight deadlines. Newspapers suddenly filled with reportorial drawings and the first comic strips, causing the market for illustrators to mushroom. Most of the members of "The Eight" learned both their draftsmanship and preference for common-folk subjects from this rigorous training.

The decade ended with the Spanish-American War, precipitated in no small part by the ambitions of newspapermen William Randolph Hearst and his rival Joseph Pulitzer. Their sensational headlines sold more papers and were used to provoke an outraged demand for war. Hearst employed Frederic Remington as an artist-correspondent; other papers and magazines enlisted Glackens, Luks, Christy, Zogbaum and Reuterdahl. They presented the action by land and sea with patriotic fervor and authenticity of detail.

WILL H BRADLEY ✳

WILL H. BRADLEY (1868-1962) began his career as a printer's devil on a local newspaper in Ishpeming, Michigan, initiating a lifelong fascination with type and printing. He moved to Chicago in 1886 to launch his career as an illustrator, working in pen-and-ink for *The Inland Printer* and *Frank Leslie's Illustrated Newspaper.*

Greatly influenced by William Morris of the Arts and Crafts movement in England, Bradley incorporated Morris's theories in his work, along with the influences of Aubrey Beardsley and other Art Nouveau artists. One of the first Americans to produce posters, he had a major influence on that art in the United States.

A multi-talented artist, Bradley organized his own publishing firm, the Wayside Press; designed type faces; wrote and illustrated stories in his magazine, *Bradley, His Book;* was a design consultant for several advertising agencies and corporations, ran an art service; and served as art director for *Collier's Weekly, Good Housekeeping, Success,* and *Metropolitan* magazines. In 1915, he was employed by William Randolph Hearst as art supervisor for *Hearst's International* and other Hearst magazines, and also for several Hearst-produced motion pictures. He later wrote and directed his own film, *Mangold*.

Advertising illustration for the Overman Wheel Company, 1895.

"Standing Full before the Royal Target she said, 'I am the Empress!" **St. Nicholas,** April, 1886.

ALFRED LAURENS BRENNAN (1853-1921) was born in Louisville, Kentucky, and was one of the major talents in the use of pen and ink in his day. To the apparent influence of the Spanish master Fortuny, he added his own technical virtuosity and an unconventional point of view which makes his work always arresting and intriguing.

Like Fortuny, he made telling use of pure blacks and pure whites

which effectively set off the intermediate values and fine detail. His elaborate compositions prevented his being as prolific as many of his contemporaries, but his work appeared regularly in publications such as *Harper's, The Century,* and *St. Nicholas* magazines. He also illustrated several children's books, each distinguished by his individuality of conception.

Early newspaper illustration for the **Boston Herald.**

Vernon Howe Bailey

VERNON HOWE BAILEY (1874-1953) began his art career at fifteen on the newspaper staff of the **Philadelphia Times** in 1892 after brief study at The Pennsylvania Museum of Art school. Two years later he worked for the **Boston Herald** primarily covering news events, such as fires, courtroom trials and political rallies.

He was sent to London by the **Herald** in 1901 to picture the coronation of King Edward VII. During his extensive stay, he also recorded many of the old quarters of London, which were published by British papers as well. He thus began a new career as an international traveler and his work was subsequently published by **Scribner's, McClure's, Harper's, The Century, Metropolitan,** and **Everybody's** magazines. In 1926 he published a portfolio of drawings and watercolors of **Little Known Towns of Spain.** In 1928, he spent a year at the invitation of Pope Pius XI recording the interiors of Vatican City and the Palace with its art treasures. Returning to New York, Bailey took on an even larger project of making, in pen and ink, **Intimate Sketches of New York**, for the **New York Sun** and later, **Sketches of New York Suburbs.** During both World War I and World War II, Bailey was assigned by the U. S. Government to record the war preparations by the Navy in shipyards, munitions factories and at sea. Many of these works are now in the Smithsonian Institution in Washington, D.C.

Walter Appleton Clark

The life of WALTER APPLETON CLARK (1876-1906) was cut tragically short by complicatons following a bout with typhoid fever, but even in that time he established himself as a mature and versatile artist.

While Clark was still a student at the Art Students League, one of his drawings on the classroom wall was seen by the art editor of **Scribner's** magazine. This led to his first commission as an illustrator. He thus fortunately began his career very early and worked industriously for the remaining ten years of his life.

He took on a wide variety of subjects and had a faculty for executing each assignment in an original and dramatic way. In addition to his illustrations for magazines and books, he also produced a series of large oils for a mural project based on the **Canterbury Tales.** These were published in book form in 1904 by Fox Duffield & Co. and one appeared as a cover for **Scribner's** magazine in 1905.

Wandering on from one air to another...
This illustration won the Silver Medal in the "Exposition Universelle de 1900."

WILL CRAWFORD (1869-1944), a staff artist for the **New York World,** had a special flair for humor. With thorough mastery of his pen, he loved to contrive very elaborate situations based on actual historical incidents, poking fun at or exposing what really happened. He did a number of these illustrations, called "Historic Bits," for the old *Life* magazine at the turn of the century. He was also a pungent political cartoonist and appeared regularly in *Puck* magazine, often with a full-color, double-page spread.

Crawford spent some time in Indian territory and was an authority on the American frontier. He was also a good friend of the Western illustrator, Charles Russell, and it is apparent that Russell improved his own pen-and-ink technique through Crawford's example. Among the books Crawford illustrated were **Long Remember** and **Romance of Rosy Ridge** by MacKinlay Kantor, as well as works by Owen Wister.

Crawford, who was born in Washington, D.C., began drawing for the old **Newark Call** (N.J.) while still in his teens and later also illustrated for **Puck, Munsey's** and **St. Nicholas.**

Will Crawford, The Moqui Snake Dance, *Life* magazine, January 9,1902.

FRANK VINCENT DuMOND, N. A. (1865-1951) had a great influence on illustration through his classes at the Art Students League where, like the anatomy teacher, George Bridgman, he was a fixture for many years. He also taught at the Traphagen School of Design, Pratt Institute and took students to study and paint in southern France.

Probably not many of his students, particularly in his later years, quite realized how good he was as a practicing artist. His training was in the tradition of the French Academy where he studied with Benjamin Constant, Boulanger and Lefebvre in Paris. His early illustrations for *The Century*, *Scribner's,* and *Harper's Monthly* were spectacularly beautiful. Among his outstanding works were the illustrations for Mark Twain's *Personal Recollections of Joan of Arc*. His paintings received a long list of awards including a Silver Medal from the Paris Salon in 1890; Gold Medal in 1896; and two Silver Medals in the Pan American Exposition in Buffalo, 1901. He also produced several murals.

A retrospective exhibition of his work was presented at the Florence Griswold Museum in Old Lyme, Connecticut, in 1990.

Frank Vincent DuMond, *Nativity,* Collection of N. Robert Cestone.

GEORGE WHARTON EDWARDS, A. N. A. (1869-1950) was an international traveler who both wrote about and painted a record of his journeys in Belgium, Holland, France, Spain and England. Holland was a particular favorite where he spent three years and produced many paintings and illustrations for his books, **Holland Today,** and **Marken and its People.**

Edwards was born in Greenwich, Connecticut, and studied art in Paris with Eugene Feyten and Cancale. He exhibited his paintings in both the U.S. and in Europe and was the recipient of many awards and medals including the Legion d'Honneur in France, and Knight Chevalier, Order de la Couronne, Belge. Among his American affiliations were the American Watercolor Society, the National Institute of Arts and Letters, The Allied Artists of America, and the Painters and Sculptors Gallery Association in New York.

George Wharton Edwards, *A Zeeland Interior,* illustration for **Holland Today,** published in 1919.

JEAN LÉON GEROME FERRIS (1863-1930) was steeped in art from birth. He was named for the French Academician, Gérôme. His mother was from the Moran family, a sister to Edward, Peter and Thomas. His father was a successful painter and etcher. Ferris studied under his father and at the Pennsylvania Academy of the Fine Arts. This was followed by study at the Académie Julian in Paris under Gérôme and Bouguereau. Encouraged to do historical paintings, he began a lifelong portrayal of American history, particularly of the colonial era and the Revolutionary War. Many of his subjects centered on George Washington's life.

Ferris was always striving for accuracy. Many of his props were careful scale models and costumes were carefully researched. His prized palette had once been owned by Gilbert Stuart.

For many years Ferris's paintings were reproduced in **The Ladies' Home Journal** and as covers for **The Literary Digest.** Much of his work was displayed in Independence Hall in Philadelphia and in the Smithsonian Institution. In 1985 a comprehensive retrospective exhibition of the artist's work was assembled through the Lauren Rogers Museum of Art in Laurel, Mississippi.

Jean Léon Gerome Ferris, *Writing the Declaration of Independence, 1776.*

73

The Greatest Game in the World — His Move, published by **Collier's Weekly,** 1903.

The Hunt Ball.

"Picturesque America, Anywhere along the coast," Life Publishing Co., 1906.

Postage stamp commemorating the Gibson Girl.

CHARLES DANA GIBSON, N. A. (1867-1944) could draw a pretty face. His drawings of women were so beautiful, so gracious, that it was the highest compliment to a young woman to say that she looked like a Gibson Girl. She was depicted on the stage; her likenesses were printed on pillow covers, painted on chinaware, and molded on silver spoons. The Gibson Girl, although aloof and refined, was everyone's ideal sweetheart.

The popularity of Gibson's art was based on much more than a pretty girl. First, he was a master-draftsman with pen and ink. He used a pen point almost as a brush, "painting" in his values with sure capability.

Not that his sureness of technique was an overnight acquisition. John Ames Mitchell, art editor of the old *Life* magazine, who bought Gibson's first drawing, related that he "detected beneath the outer badness of these drawings peculiarities rarely discovered in the efforts of a beginner . . . his faults were good, able-bodied faults that held their heads up and looked you in the eye. No dodging of the difficult points, no tricks, no uncertainty, no slurring of outlines . . . there was always courage and honesty in whatever he undertook." Gibson's later virtuosity was developed through many years of solid application

and gradual refinement.

Most important, he was a commentator on the social life and mores of his day, with a satiric but gentle point of view. His people, like "Mr. Pipp," were those with whom everyone, rich or poor, could identify. This happy combination of abilities made Gibson the highest paid illustrator of his time. In 1904 Gibson accepted a contract from *Collier's Weekly* for $100,000 for one hundred illustrations over a period of four years, a contract, incidentally, that repaid *Collier's* many times over in increased circulation.

During World War I, Gibson, as president of the Society of Illustrators, formed and became the head of the Division of Pictorial Publicity under the Federal Committee of Public Information. He recruited the top illustrators of the day to design posters, billboards, and other publicity for the war effort.

After the war, Gibson became owner and editor of the old *Life,* a step which greatly curtailed his own drawing output. By the early 'thirties, he had retired to paint exclusively. In his long career, however, Gibson had compiled a warm and eloquent pictorial record of his era.

WALTER GRANVILLE-SMITH, N. A. (1870-1938) pursued dual careers as illustrator and painter; eventually, he devoted full time to painting for exhibition. Active in affairs of the Salmagundi Club and the National Academy, he was elected to full membership in the latter in 1915. Granville-Smith's paintings are represented in numerous museums and private collections including the Smithsonian, the Butler Art Institute, the Fort Worth Museum, and the Toledo Museum of Art.

He was born in Granville, New York, and studied at the Art Students League as well as abroad. His illustrations were generally of a humorous or light-hearted turn, and he did many covers and illustrations for *Truth* magazine as well as for *The Ladies' Home Journal, The Century* magazine, and others.

Walter Granville-Smith, advertising illustration for Ivory Soap, ca. 1900. The Charles Martignette Collection.

JULES GUÉRIN, N.A. (1866-1946) was an architectural draftsman who also illustrated and painted. He specialized in architectural illustrations in which the figures were usually subordinate to the setting. His panoramic view, usually featuring a man-made structure (ranging from the Pyramids to a colonial church) was presented in a very carefully designed and well-ordered composition. His use of color was particularly effective, usually a bold statement, yet with very subtle modulations. His work was reproduced with many travel articles, often in collaboration with the author Robert Hitchens, and serialized in *The Century.*

Guérin was born in St. Louis, Missouri, and received his art training in Paris where he studied under Benjamin Constant and Jean-Paul Laurens. He exhibited at the Paris Exposition in 1900 and the Pan-American Exposition in Buffalo in 1901, received a Silver Medal at the St. Louis Exposition in 1904, and was elected a member of the National Academy in 1931.

Guérin was also a muralist; he decorated the Pennsylvania Railroad station in New York, but best known are his friezes in the Lincoln Memorial in Washington, D.C.

Jules Guérin, *Men of Galilee,* for *From Nazareth to Jerusalem* by Robert Hitchens, *The Century* magazine, May 1910.

JAY HAMBIDGE

JAY HAMBIDGE (1867-1924) was born in Ontario, Canada, the eldest of nine children. After running away from home, he landed in Council Bluffs, Iowa, becoming a surveyor's helper. He next worked for the **Kansas City Star** in the lowly position of a printer's devil. After a ten-year apprenticeship, he moved on to the **New York Herald** and began to study nights at the Art Students League. Among his teachers were William Chase and Walter Appleton Clark.

His interest in Greek antiquities led Hambidge to visit Greece in 1900 where he drew many of the ruins and studied the classical designs. He became aware of some constant proportions and his analysis of their principles led him to publish them in a book titled **Dynamic Symmetry** in 1917. His idea was that these proportions, used in particular arrangements, could be universally applied to achieve beauty. This publication created controversy but also made many converts, and other artists, such as George Bellows and Robert Henri, used the principles in composing their pictures. Hambidge taught and lectured extensively to promote his theories, and found their acceptance at Yale and Harvard Universities.

Hambidge continued his own illustration career and was a prolific contributor to **The Century, Collier's, St. Nicholas, Harper's Monthly, Scribner's,** and **McClure's.**

Jay Hambidge, *A Gypsy Fortune Teller,* illustration for "The American Gypsy," by Riley M. Fletcher Berry, **The Century** magazine, August, 1910.

KEMBLE

EDWARD WINDSOR KEMBLE (1861-1933) was a self-taught artist whose work reveals a strong sense of humor and an acute observation of character. His outlook was similar to that of A. B. Frost, and like Frost, he illustrated many of the Uncle Remus stories by Joel Chandler Harris.

Kemble illustrated several other famous books, including Mark Twain's **Huckleberry Finn,** and **Puddin' Head Wilson,** Harriet Beecher Stowe's **Uncle Tom's Cabin,** and Washington Irving's **Knickerbocker History of New York.** His humor made him an effective political cartoonist as well. He had special rapport with African-American characters, and drew them alternatively with great empathy or with the most outrageous of stereotypes.

Edward Kemble, *In the Quarters,* **The Century** magazine.

Henry McCarter, cover illustration for *Outing* magazine.

HENRY McCARTER

HENRY McCARTER (1865-1943) occupied a special niche with his work — midway between the traditional approach to illustration and painting for exhibition. His talents lent themselves best to the interpretation of poetry, and although he illustrated some fiction and travel subjects, verse was his specialty. His illustrations for "Claire de Lune" and "Le Piano" by Verlaine were outstanding.

McCarter studied at the Pennsylvania Academy of the Fine Arts under Thomas Eakins, and later in Paris with Puvis de Chavannes. His illustrations were published by *The Century*, *Scribner's*, *Harper's Monthly*, *Collier's* and other magazines. The artist was also an excellent teacher, lecturing at the Art Students League and taught for many years at the Pennsylvania Academy in Philadelphia.

Peter Newell

PETER SHEAF NEWELL (1862-1924) demonstrated a great sense of humor in his work, and the art editors of several magazines kept him busy exercising it. *Harper's Monthly* used his work regularly for their feature, "The Editor's Drawer." He also illustrated several books by humorist John Kendricks Bangs, and other authors; particularly effective were his interpretations of Lewis Carroll's *Alice in Wonderland.* He wrote and illustrated a number of his own novelty books as well: *The Hole Book, The Slant Book, The Rocket Book* and *Peter Newell's Pictures and Rhymes* all were popular successes.

Newell was largely self-taught with but three months' instruction at the Art Students League.

Peter Newell

Trial scene from *The Scarlet Letter*.

'Oh King,' he said, 'the ears of the god are open,' Illustration for ***The Fair God,*** by Lew Wallace, Houghton Mifflin & Co., 1898.

Christened Frederick Moritz Pape, ERIC PAPE (1870-1938) was born in San Francisco, California, and received his art education in New York and Paris. A gifted student, he enrolled in the Ecole des Beaux Arts, studying under Gérôme, Delance, and Laurens, followed by training with Rodin and Whistler. Pape quickly became a successful exhibitor with works accepted by the Paris Salon Champs de Mars in 1890, and in subsequent years in Munich and at the World's Columbian Exhibition in 1893. He also held one-man shows in the Detroit Museum of Art, the Cincinnati Art Museum, the Pennsylvania Academy of the Fine Arts, the Boston Arts Club and the National Academy. Pape was also an active illustrator, and had works commissioned for most of the important magazines, including ***McClure's, Scribner's, Cosmopolitan, Collier's, The Saturday Evening Post*** and ***Life*** as well as by many book publishers.

Pape is best remembered for his epic series of illustrations for the immensely popular book, ***The Fair God*** by General Lew Wallace, about the conquest of Mexico. Pape spent several months in Mexico to prepare himself for the three hundred illustrations produced. Several other book assignments followed, including ***The Arabian Nights, The Legend of Sleepy Hollow, The Scarlet Letter, Rip Van Winkle*** and ***Notre Dame de Paris.***

He founded the Eric Pape School of Art in 1897 in Boston (where N. C. Wyeth was one of his students), and later taught in New York City and in Salisbury, Connecticut. Pape, whose first wife was an actress, was also active in the theatre as a scenic designer, and was a longtime member of the Players Club in New York City, where he was sponsored by Mark Twain.

Illustration for Victor Hugo's ***Notre Dame de Paris,*** Ives Washburn, 1928. Collection of Charles Collins.

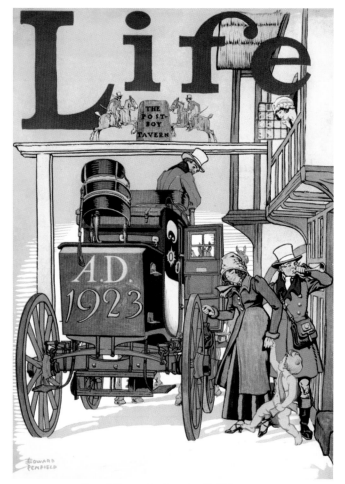

Cover, *Life* magazine, December 28, 1922.

Cover design for Hart, Shaffner & Marx, ca. 1910.

Poster design for R.H. Russell & Son.

In the City of Amsterdam, from *Holland Sketches, Scibner's,* 1907.

EDWARD PENFIELD (1866-1925) produced some of America's finest posters. His clean style and large silhouetted shapes resulted from much careful preliminary refinement and elimination of detail. Horses and coaches were a favorite subject with him, as typified by this picture of the colnial Post Road. A notable series of his illustrations were contained in his book, *Holland Sketches,* published by Scribner's in 1907. Another was a series of calendar illustrations based on the 1843 "Old Farmer's Almanac" and redrawn in 1918 for the Beck Engraving Company.

Penfield had a profound influence on American illustration through his own work, in his post as art director for *Harper's* magazines, and through his teaching at the Art Students League. He was president of the Society of Illustrators in 1921 and 1922 and was elected to the Illustrators' Hall of Fame in 1998.

This typical coaching picture displays Penfield's expertise and love for the subject.

VICTOR SEMON PERARD (1870-1957) was born in Paris and received his early art training at the Ecole des Beaux Arts where he studied with Gérôme. Additionally, he studied at the National Academy of Design and at the Art Students League in New York. To further his knowledge of anatomy, he also attended the New York University Medical College. Following this preparation, he entered the field of illustration, working for *Scribner's, Harper's Weekly* and *The Century* as well as several book publishers. A gifted teacher, Perard lectured on anatomy and taught at the Traphagen School of Art and at the Woman's Art Department at Cooper Union from 1914 to 1932. He reached a larger audience of students, however, through his many art instruction books, including *How to Draw*, *Drawing Horses* and many others, some twenty in total. An active member of the Society of Illustrators and Salmagundi Clubs, he exhibited widely and is represented in many museum collections, including the Metropolitan Museum of Art, The Library of Congress, the Cooper Union Art School, the New-York Historical Society, and the National Gallery of Art.

Victor Perard, *South Street, New York, 1906.*
Collection of the New-York Historical Society.

Sincerity and good taste, as well as technical excellence, make the illustrations of ALICE BARBER STEPHENS (1858-1932) a pleasure to look at. The early discipline of her work as a wood engraver for *Scribner's* was in some measure responsible for her fine draftsmanship. She was most successful in quiet settings, with humble subjects. Among her best is a series of pictures of old men and women, inmates of the Philadelphia almshouse.

She was trained at the Pennsylvania Academy of Fine Arts under Thomas Eakins, and at the Philadelphia School of Design for Women, where she later taught portrait and life classes.

Among her many awards were the Mary Smith prize, from the Pennsylvania Academy of the Fine Arts, in 1890; Bronze Medal, Atlanta Exposition, in 1895; and a Gold Medal in London, 1902.

ce Barber Stephens, *Madge and Her Wood-Engraving, Harper's Young People,* March 7, 1893.

The Sentinel, P.F. Collier & Son, 1909. Collection of the Frederick Remington Art Museum, Ogdensburg, New York.

Questionable Companionship, Collection of the Buffalo Bill Historical Center, Cody, Wyoming.

Titled *The Last Stand* when first reproduced in 1900, this painting is now known as *The Intruders.*

Frederic Remington ✗

FREDERIC SACKRIDER REMINGTON, A.N.A. (1861-1909) was a huge, hearty man who loved adventure and hard work equally. After a brief period of training in art at Yale University, he departed with the romantic idea of striking it rich in the West of the 1880's.

Remington arrived on the scene during the final period of the old lawless West. Today, we are the richer for the record of those picturesque days in the prodigious outpouring of drawings, paintings, and bronzes, his vigorous talent has left with us.

If his earliest work was somewhat crude, and had to be re-drawn for publication by a staff artist for **Harper's Monthly**, the authenticity of his subject matter won him immediate recognition; as his technical ability improved, he was given assignments as a reporter-artist, not only in the West, but also in other parts of the world.

In 1898, he accompanied the Fifth Corps to Cuba as a war correspondent where he made many notable paintings and drawings of the action of the war with Spain. His painting *Charge of the Rough Riders at San Juan Hill,* helped enhance Theodore Roosevelt's reputation as a soldier and boosted his subsequent political career. The two men had become personal friends, and Remington later illustrated several of Roosevelt's books and magazine articles.

Remington loved horses. He made a lifelong study of horses and knew at first hand the several strains of the western broncos, their peculiarities and strengths. His article "Horses of the Plain" was published by **The Century** magazine in 1889. His own suggested epitaph: "He Knew the Horse " was well earned.

After his death, a Remington Memorial Museum was established in his home town of Ogdensburg, New York. Here are to be found some of the finest of his paintings and bronzes. His Indian Collection, together with his studio effects, are preserved in the Whitney Gallery of Western Art in Cody, Wyoming. Collections of his work are also included in the Amon Carter Museum, in Fort Worth, Texas, and in the Thomas Gilcrease Museum in Tulsa, Oklahoma.

News From the Front, drawing from **Done in the Open,** P.F. Collier & Son Publishers, 1902.

George Varian, *The Prince's Vision.*

IRVING RAMSEY WILES, N. A. (1862-1948) was taught by his artist father, Lemuel M. Wiles, attended classes at the Art Students League where he studied with William Merritt Chase, and then went abroad to complete his studies at the Académie Julian in Paris.

When he returned to America, he found an immediate reception for his pictures. He was a painting virtuoso, particularly in transparent watercolor, which suited itself perfectly for reproduction in the magazines. He also entered New York exhibitions and won many prizes; he became a member of the American Watercolor Society, the Society of American Artists, and was elected a full member of the National Academy in 1897. In the latter part of his life, he concentrated on portraiture, but also painted genre and landscape subjects.

GEORGE EDMUND VARIAN (1865-1923) had the distinction, along with Vulcanologist Professor Angelo Heilprin and reporter August Jaccaci, to witness and record the eruption of the volcano at Mt. Pele, Martinique, in May of 1902, narrowly escaping death from one of the many subsequent eruptions. The report and pictures were published by *McClure's* magazine in that August. The rest of Varian's career, if less adventuresome, was long and productive. He illustrated for most of the major magazines of the day, including *McClure's*, *Scribner's*, *St. Nicholas*, and *The Century*.

Varian was born in England and came to America in his youth. He studied at the Brooklyn Artists Guild and at the Art Students League, and exhibited at the Paris Salon in 1907. His many memberships included the Brooklyn Art Club and the Salmagundi Club in New York.

The convalescent, 1890.
Exhibited at the 23rd annual of the American Watercolor Society.

Idle Conversation. The Kelly Collection of American Illustration.

ALBERT BECK WENZELL (1864-1917) was born in Detroit, Michigan, and was sent to study art first in Munich and then in Paris, where he stayed for seven years. Upon his return to America, he became the acknowledged master of fashionable society and drawing-room subjects. He was the appropriate illustrator for Edith Wharton's **House of Mirth,** and a regular contributor to **The Ladies Home Journal, Harper's Monthly, The Century, Cosmopolitan, Associated Sunday Magazines,** and **The Saturday Evening Post.** Wenzell was also published regularly in **Die Fliegende Blätter,** a German satirical journal.

His paintings were done with much "technique," in oils or gouache. Much of his work was reproduced in black and white, although the oils were often painted and reproduced in full color. If his preoccupation with the rendering of the sheen of a silk dress or a starched shirt sometimes competes with the message of his pictures, he did, nevertheless, leave us an historic record of the settings and costumes of fashionable society at the turn of the century and set a high artistic standard.

He was awarded a Silver Medal at both the Pan-American Exposition at Buffalo in 1901, and the St. Louis Exposition in 1904.

Two volumes of his paintings were published by P. F. Collier, **Vanity Fair** and **The Passing Show.** Wenzell was one of the founders of the Society of Illustrators and became its second president in 1902.

Woman regarding the Crowns of Europe, 1892.

1900–1910

John Wolcott Adams

Sydney Adamson

Stanley Massey Arthurs

Edmund M. Ashe

Clifford Warren Ashley

William James Aylward

Anna Whelan Betts

Ethel Franklin Betts (Bains)

Harold Matthews Brett

Walter Harrison Cady

William Vincent Cahill

John Cecil Clay

Joseph Clement Coll

J. M. Condé

Fanny Young Corey (Cooney)

Harry Grant Dart

Arthur G. Dove

Harvey Dunn

Thomas Fogarty

George Gibbs

Charles Allan Gilbert

William J. Glackens

Philip R. Goodwin

Elizabeth Shippen Green

Thomas King Hanna

Charlotte Harding

George Matthews Harding

Lucius Wolcott Hitchcock

Gayle Porter Hoskins

Henry Hutt

Oliver Kemp

B. Cory Kilvert

Walt Kuhn

Orson Byron Lowell

Winsor McCay

Guernsey Moore

Francis Louis Mora

Thornton Oakley

Violet Oakley

Frederick Maxfield Parrish

Clara Elsene Peck

Henry Jarvis Peck

Ernest Clifford Peixotto

Herman Pfeifer

Charles M. Relyea

Henry Reuterdahl

Charles Marion Russell

Charles Nicolas Sarka

Remington Schuyler

Frank Earle Schoonover

Everett Shinn

Florence Scovel Shinn

John French Sloan

Dan Smith

Howard Everett Smith

Jessie Willcox Smith

Frederic Dorr Steele

Sarah S. Stilwell (Weber)

Fred Strothmann

Frank Walter Taylor

Harry Everett Townsend

Allan Tupper True

John Scott Williams

George Hand Wright

Newell Convers Wyeth

Frederick Coffay Yohn

N.C. Wyeth, *The Moose Hunters,* **Scribner's Monthly.**

William Glackens, *Shopping on the Lower East Side,* line drawing, newspaper style.

Jessie Willcox Smith, *Gathering Greens,* from Bryn Mawr College calendar, 1902.

THE DECADE 1900-1910

This was the era when all of the elements that engendered illustration's "Golden Age" came together. Howard Pyle was at the height of his creative powers. Edwin Austin Abbey was still contributing his beautiful pen and inks to **Harper's Monthly,** and he had also painted a spectacular series of murals on the "Quest for the Holy Grail" for the Boston Public Library which was completed in 1895.

It was the revolution of color printing that was as much required for the success of the art as the artists themselves. Pyle and Abbey, indeed many of the great black-and-white artists, were now painting in full color, the reproduction of which had been denied them for most of their careers. Once halftone printing could reproduce black-and-white artwork with previously unattainable fidelity, the next logical step was the imposition of four halftone plates inked with red, yellow, blue, and black, and the effect of a full color painting could be printed. New presses would make it economically feasible to include at least a few color reproductions in an issue of a magazine or at least the frontispiece of a book. Artists, art editors, engravers and printers all collaborated to bring about this letterpress breakthrough, and the results soon became extraordinarily good. **Harper's, Scribner's, McClure's,** and **The Century,** which were all literary magazines publishing the finest authors and scientists, were doing their editorial best to provide the high standards that complemented this golden period. Being an illustrator was no stigma; in fact, it was an honor for artists to have their work reproduced in the magazines, and nearly all of America's best painters at some time provided illustrations for them.

Harper's Weekly had long dominated the field with an emphasis on news and current events. Now other weekly publications competed by broadening the mix of news, science, and fiction. **The Saturday Evening Post**, resurrected in 1897 under Cyrus Curtis, became a major competitor, as did its rival **Collier's Weekly**, founded in 1888. These new publications were joined by other monthly magazines: Frank Munsey succeeded in taking on the established "Big Four" by successfully opening up his pages to advertising and selling his magazine for less than its cost of production by means of the advertising subsidy. As a result, he had to lower the standards to a broader, common denominator in order to attract more readers. This new economic base of advertising was impossible for the other publishers to ignore, however, and it increasingly became a compromising element in the magazine makeup over the following decades.

Other new magazines, such as **American Magazine, McCall's, Peterson's, Woman's Home Companion,** and **Metropolitan** found responsive subscribers, and niche magazines such as **Outing, The Delineator, All-Story Magazine, Vogue** and others were launched. This meant a huge increase in openings for illustrators and the need for new talents. Many artists who started in newspaper art departments graduated to the national magazines. Among them were Joseph Clement Coll, Frederic R. Gruger, Everett Shinn, William Glackens and Henry Raleigh, who brought their self-assured ability to draw anything required, in a convincing documentary style. They added a new look and vitality to the roster of illustrators.

The older artists were also attracting capable disciples. James Montgomery Flagg took on the vigorous pen-and-ink style of Gibson, adding his own talents in color. From his base in Wilmington, Delaware, Howard Pyle was starting to graduate an extraordinary, select group of students, both men and women, who would come to dominate this and the next decade through their "Pyle School" illustrations. N.C. Wyeth, Harvey Dunn, Frank Schoonover, and Stanley Arthurs followed their master's lead. Pyle's women students also came on to develop their own decorative styles, among them Jessie Willcox Smith, Elizabeth Shippen Green, Violet Oakley, Sarah S. Stillwell and Ellen Thompson. Henceforth, women would play an increased role in the magazines, particularly those oriented to family audiences.

John Wolcott Adams, *The Prize Fight* combines pen and ink with watercolor. Date and place of publication unknown.

JOHN WOLCOTT ADAMS (1874-1925) was born in Worcester, Massachusetts, a descendant of two illustrious United States presidents. He studied at the Art Museum in Boston, the Art Students League in New York, and with Howard Pyle.

His illustrations appeared in *Scribner's, The Century, The Delineator* and other magazines, usually as pen-and-ink drawings to accompany old songs, poetry and historical incidents. His style and subject matter were closely patterned after that of Pyle.

Adams was also interested in the theatre, and designed the stage settings for one of Walter Hampden's productions, "The Jolly Roger," at the National Theatre. He was a member of The Players, The Dutch Treat Club and the Society of Illustrators.

In 1998, a collection of his work was exhibited by the Brandywine River Museum entitled "John Wolcott Adams: American History in Miniature."

SYDNEY ADAMSON was born in Dundee, Scotland, and received his art training in England. Active in English and Scottish art circles, he exhibited at the Royal Academy and in Edinburgh.

A world traveler, he wrote articles about his adventures accompanied by his own illustrations, which were published in American magazines such as *The Century, Harper's Monthly, Scribner's* and *Success.*

His brother, also an illustrator, had a more popular public following under the pseudonym of Penrhyn Stanlaws.

"The Bazaars are scenes of bewilderment and joy." Adamson wrote and illustrated "Within the Walls of Fez" for *Harper's Monthly,* July, 1912.

S. M. Arthurs

STANLEY MASSEY ARTHURS (1877-1950) was a student of Howard Pyle and one who was very close to him personally. Arthurs devoted his career to depicting American historical subjects, painting a series of events from earliest Colonial times through the Civil War era.

After Pyle's death, Arthurs occupied his studio and set for himself the same high standards Pyle had taught. Every detail of his pictures was painstakingly researched, and he immersed himself as thoroughly as possible in the mood and character of his picture subjects.

Arthurs' use of color was rich and varied and he produced a valuable contribution to the American historical record. Many of his pictures are reproduced in James Truslow Adams' *History of the United States,* in the 15-volume *Pageant of America* edited by Ralph H. Gabriel, and in *The American Historical Scene* published in 1935.

Arthurs also painted a number of murals, including the *Landing of DeVries* at Delaware College and *The Crusaders* at the State Capitol in Dover, Delaware.

Changing Horses from "On the Old Boston Post Road" written and illustrated by Arthurs. **Scribner's Magazine,** November, 1908.

Edmund Ashe, *Forty Miles to Falmouth,* **Munsey's Magazine,** June, 1907.

One of the earliest members of the Society of Illustrators (he joined in the first month), EDMUND M. ASHE (1867-1941) was a founder of the Silvermine Guild in Norwalk, Connecticut. Along with fellow illustrator George Wright, he also formed the nucleus of the well-known Westport artists colony in Connecticut, which attracted many prominent illustrators to the area.

During Theodore Roosevelt's administration, Ashe was an artist-correspondent at the White House and was able to secure several scoops through his personal friendship with the president.

In addition to his illustrations for a variety of magazine titles, he taught for many years. In the early 1900s, he instructed at the Art Students League; later at the Carnegie Institute of Technology from 1920 to 1939.

89

Clifford Warren Ashley, "*Lancing a Whale,*" illustration for **She Blows! And Sparm at That!** by William John Hopkins. Houghton Mifflin Co., 1922.

C W Ashley

A student of Howard Pyle, CLIFFORD WARREN ASHLEY (1881-1947) came by his interest in the sea naturally. He was born in New Bedford, Massachusetts, the center of the early whaling industry, and specialized in illustrations of fishing and whaling subjects.

Ashley was also the author and illustrator of several books relating to seafaring, including **The Yankee Whaler** and **The Ashley Book of Knots,** an 11-year project, with some 7,000 drawings and diagrams, and the definitive work on the subject.

Ashley is represented by paintings in the Brooklyn Museum; the Whaling Museum in New Bedford; the Canajoharie (New York) Museum; Massachusetts Institute of Technology; the Delaware Art Museum in Wilmington; and the Mariner's Museum, Newport News, Virginia.

W. J. Aylward

WILLIAM JAMES AYLWARD (1875-1956) was born in Milwaukee, Wisconsin, but like Ashley, his greatest interest was in the sea and related nautical subjects. He, too, was a student of Howard Pyle.

Aylward's interest embraced more of the history of seafaring, however, and he both illustrated and wrote articles describing the earlier days of sailing. He also illustrated Jack London's **Sea Wolf,** Jules Verne's **Twenty Thousand Leagues under the Sea** and other books on naval or marine subjects.

Aylward belonged to many art societies and exhibited widely, winning the Shaw purchase prize at the Salmagundi Club in 1911; the Beck prize, Philadelphia Watercolor Club in 1912; the Salmagundi prize for Illustration in 1914. He was also an official artist with the A.E.F during World War I. Many of those drawings and paintings are in the collection of the Smithsonian Institution.

William James Aylward, "*Nemo remained motionless as if petrified in mute ecstacy,*" **20,000 Leagues Under the Sea,** by Jules Verne, Charles Scribner's Sons, 1925. The Kelly Collection of American Illustration.

Anna Whelan Betts, *The Easter Bonnet.*

ANNA WHELAN BETTS was born in Philadelphia and went to school there, studying at the Pennsylvania Academy of the Fine Arts under Robert Vonnoh. She then attended Howard Pyle's classes, first at Drexel Institute and later in Wilmington, Delaware. Through Pyle's contacts, she and several fellow students were commissioned to illustrate a serial story for *Collier's* magazine. After its publication, she found assignments from other magazines as well, and over the years worked for *St. Nicholas, Harper's Monthly, The Ladies' Home Journal* and *The Century* magazine. Her work was characterized by its great beauty and sensitivity.

In mid-career, she developed eye trouble and had to give up illustrating to save her sight. Instead she became associated with the Solebury School in New Hope, Pennsylvania, as a director and as its art teacher, a post she held for another twenty years.

ETHEL·FRANKLIN·BETTS·

ETHEL FRANKLIN BETTS (BAINS) was the sister of Anna Whelan Betts and, like her, studied with Howard Pyle at the Drexel Institute classes of illustration in Philadelphia. After Pyle established his own school in Wilmington, Delaware, she and her sister moved there to participate.

She soon found commissions for book illustrations which included several collections of poems by James Whitcomb Riley, *Favorite Nursery Rhymes, The Complete Mother Goose,* and *Fairy Tales from Grimm.* She also illustrated mostly child-oriented stories, for *St. Nicholas, McClure's* and *Collier's Weekly.* Betts exhibited her paintings regularly in the Philadelphia area and won a Bronze Medal at the Panama-Pacific International Exposition in 1915.

Ethel Franklin Betts, illustration for *A Little Princess,* by Frances Hodgson Burnett, Charles Scribner's Sons, 1905.

Harold Matthews Brett, *Major André making caricatures of American officers,* for "Two Romantic Figures of the American Revolution," **The Century**, November, 1910.

HARRISON·CADY

WALTER HARRISON CADY (1877-1970) was a self-taught artist whose inspiration was nature and wildlife. Born in Gardner, Massachusetts, he went to New York at eighteen with his savings of thirteen dollars and some sample pen-and-ink drawings. His first published work was for **Truth** magazine, followed by free-lance sales to many publications including **St. Nicholas, Puck, Life, Judge, The Saturday Evening Post, Boys' Life** and **The Ladies' Home Journal.**

Other associations included the children's book publishers McLoughlin Brothers, and a stint as an editorial artist for the **Brooklyn Eagle.** In 1913, he found his true metier in a long association with Thornton Burgess, author of **Old Mother West Wind** and **Bedtime Stories** featuring Peter Rabbit, Jimmy Skunk, and other humanized animals in countless benign adventures. Cady also produced a syndicated Peter Rabbit comic strip for over twenty years.

Cady had other less-known aspects of his career. For years, he contributed political cartoons to **Life** magazine which were anything but benign — particularly during World War I. These drawings were very large and intricately detailed in pen and ink, and gave vent to his conservative views in a serious, and sometimes quite dark mien. He was also an etcher, painted in oils and water colors, and exhibited at the Salmagundi Club, the Allied Artists, the Society of American Etchers and the National Academy of Design, winning the Palmer Memorial Prize in the 1945 Annual.

Harold Matthews Brett

HAROLD MATTHEWS BRETT (1880-1955) grew up in Brookline, Massachusetts, and studied at the School of the Museum of Fine Arts in Boston under Philip Hall and Frank Benson. Later he moved to New York to study at the Art Students League with Walter Appleton Clark, H. Siddons Mowbray and Kenyon Cox. Although by then a well-trained artist, Brett went to Wilmington, Delaware, in 1906, to study further under Howard Pyle.

He was soon thereafter able to make his professional debut in **Harper's Weekly,** and his work began to appear in most of the national magazines. Brett moved back to Chatham on Cape Cod and for several years was associated with the Fenway School of Illustration in Boston. Brett particularly liked to do New England subjects with an historical setting; he did a series of portraits of Cape Cod sea captains. Eventually he specialized in portraiture, maintaining studios in New York City and Chatham.

Harrison Cady, *Animal Picnic.* Collection of John Snyder.

W·V·CAHILL

WILLIAM VINCENT CAHILL (1878-1924) was one of the peripheral group of students who moved to the Wilmington area in order to obtain occasional critiques of their work from Howard Pyle. Cahill came in 1907 and also studied the next summer with N. C. Wyeth and Howard E. Smith at Chadds Ford. Since he had previously been trained at the Art Students League and by Birge Harrison, he was somewhat out of sync with the Pyle philosophy. He was artistically very competent however, both in advertising and story illustration. Cahill maintained studios in New York and Boston. In 1914 he relocated to California and teamed up with John Hibbard Rich to open a school for illustration and painting.

Cahill later joined the faculty of the University of Kansas as professor of drawing and painting. Cahill was also an active exhibitor, who won numerous prizes and medals. His works are in the municipal collection in Phoenix, Arizona, and in the Museum of History, Science and Art in Los Angeles.

William Cahill, *"Frost Pictures,"* advertising illustration for Cream of Wheat, 1911. Courtesy Nabisco, Inc.

John Clay, *Life* magazine cover, April 8, 1909

JOHN CECIL CLAY (1875-1930) was born in Ronceverte, West Virginia, descended from an old southern family. He studied at the Art Students League under H. Siddons Mowbray as he pursued a career as an illustrator. His strength was in drawing and his graphic style was well suited to the design of magazine covers. Among his long-running showcases were ***Frank Leslie's Popular Monthly*** and the covers of *Life* magazine, featuring pretty young women. As a footnote, when ready to retire, he sold a family heirloom, a document signed by Button Gwinnet of Georgia, who was one of the rarest signators of the Declaration of Independence, from a document of a family ancestor, setting a then-record price for an autograph.

Cover illustration in watercolor and first chapter heading in pen and ink for *Sir Nigel,* by Arthur Conan Doyle.
Published by the *Associated Sunday Magazines,* December 3, 1905.

JOSEPH CLEMENT COLL (1881-1921) was perhaps America's greatest virtuoso in the use of pen and ink. He commanded an awesome technical dexterity. He employed his pen point as freely as a paint brush, showed it capable of the finest subtlety as well as the boldest slashes of black. As an illustrator, he also made masterful use of the white areas of his pictures, incorporating them to create a full spectrum of values.

His skill had been acquired through careful study of his predecessors, particularly Vierge, and the demanding pressure of deadlines in his earlier employment as a newspaper sketch-artist.

This technical skill was coupled with a vivid and unusual imagination which he displayed best in illustrations with exotic settings or for mystery stories by such authors as A. Conan Doyle and Sax Rohmer.

Coll illustrated several books and his work appeared in many periodicals, including *Associated Sunday Magazine*, *Collier's* and *Everybody's*, up to the time of his sudden death at the age of forty while his talents were at their height.

This Coll illustration for **The White Peacock** by Sax Rohmer was one of the popular "Fu Manchu" stories published by *Collier's* magazine in the teens and early twenties. It appeared on March 6, 1915.

J. M. Condé, "Mr. Possum's Motorcar," by Albert Bigelow Paine. Published in *Harper's Monthly*, April, 1916.

While J. M. CONDÉ (active circa 1890s-1910s) is little remembered today, he was one of the early interpreters of the Uncle Remus stories of Joel Chandler Harris. He subsequently made a career of illustrating similar subject matter featuring animated woodland creatures for books by Albert Bigelow Paine, such as *When Jack Rabbit was a Little Boy* and the *Hollow Tree and Deep Woods Book*. Some of his most charming pen-and-ink drawings were published in *The Jumping Kangaroo and the Apple Butter Cat* by John W. Harrington. Condé's pen line, which was crisp and lively, was a perfect complement to his subjects and he obviously empathized with the individual characters he so lovingly created.

F Y CORY FANNY YOUNG CORY (COONEY) (1877-1972) was born in Waukegan, Illinois, and moved East to attend the Art Students League and the Metropolitan School of Art. Fanny was the niece of newspaper cartoonist, J. Campbell Cory, who helped her make her professional debut.

As an illustrator, her special forté was children. Her drawings were generally in line or line and wash and usually had a humorous tilt. Her work appeared in *The Century* magazine, *Harper's, The Bee* and *St. Nicholas,* as well as a number of books including *The Memoirs of a Baby,* by Josephine Daskam, *The Master Key*, by L. Frank Baum, and *Alice in Wonderland* by Lewis Carroll.

Cory took a hiatus from her career in 1904 upon her marriage to Fred Cooney, and the couple moved to a Montana ranch. After raising three children, she resumed her art career and began a long stint as a newspaper cartoonist for King Features, producing a "Little Miss Muffet" strip and another feature "Sonny Sayings" which ran for thirty-six years, until her retirement in 1956. She was named "Mother of the Year" by the state of Montana in 1951.

Fanny Cory, *Baby Really Needs Rest, But It's Hard On the Birdies to Give Up Their Nest,* ca.1927, The *Fairy* series by F.Y. Cory. © F.Y. Cory Publishers, Inc. 1977, Robert G. Dodgson, President.

Harry Dart, *"Going into Action," **Harper's Weekly,*** July 20, 1907.

HARRY GRANT DART. Unlike many illustrators who graduated from newspaper art departments to the more lucrative magazine markets, HARRY GRANT DART (1869-1938) continued to work in both fields. Beginning with the ***Boston Herald,*** he was sent to Cuba in 1898 by the ***New York World*** to cover the Spanish-American War as an artist-correspondent. Later, he became art editor of the ***World*** with a staff of artists under him.

He carried on a simultaneous free-lance career as an illustrator for ***Harper's Weekly, Life, Judge*** and other magazines. He was especially intrigued by the future of flight and concocted large, complex pictures of fanciful flying machines and future cities, all in perfect perspective with convincing detail.

Dart was a member of the Players Club and the Society of Illustrators.

ARTHUR G. DOVE (1880-1946) had an enigmatic artistic career. In his early years, he was a successful illustrator with a decidedly light, humorous touch. Yet, he also found a fascination with the idea of reducing subjects to their abstract meaning after a sojourn in Paris in 1907 through 1909. His early such experiments were exhibited with Albert Stieglitz's "291" gallery in 1910 and 1911.

Making the break from illustration was not, however, financially feasible, although he received subsidies from Stieglitz and Henry Raleigh, who admired his artistic ambitions. He tried to paint, and farm part time but could not support his family. The rest of his life was a financial struggle; his "extractions" were ahead even of the abstraction movement in Europe, and he had no defined niche in American art. Only after his death has a belated recognition been given for his pioneering work, and his works are now honored in the Museum of Modern Art, in the Phillips Memorial Gallery and many other private and public collections.

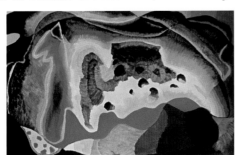

Arthur Dove, *U.S. 1940,* Courtesy of Terry Dintenfass Gallery.

"The Tie that Binds," by George Frederick, ***American Magazine,*** August, 1906.

Dakota Woman. One of many paintings documenting Dunn's South Dakota heritage, mostly painted during the 1940s. Collection of South Dakota Memorial Art Center, Brookings. ©1960 by The Friends of the Middle Border, Mitchell South Dakota.

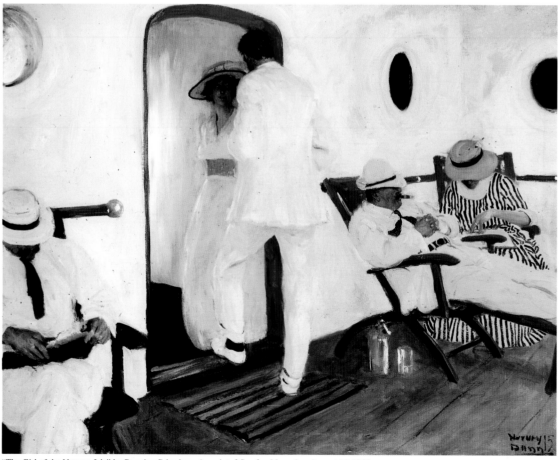

"The Girl of the Nutmeg Isle" by Beatrice Grimshaw, *Associated Sunday Magazine,* August 15, 1915.

Illustration for *The Calf Path* by Kennett Harris. February 17, 1912, ***The Saturday Evening Post.*** The Kelly Collection of American Illustration.

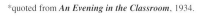

HARVEY DUNN, N.A. (1884-1952) was a large, powerful man who paid for his art schooling by "sod-busting," plowing under the thick, virgin, prairie grass for his home-steading neighbors of the Red Stone Valley of South Dakota.

From the Art Institute of Chicago, he was invited by Howard Pyle to study at Chadds Ford. Of all Pyle's students, Dunn was most deeply imbued with his philosophy, and as a teacher passed it along together with his own ideas, his straight-forward honesty and intolerance of pretense. Among his students were Dean Cornwell, Harold Von Schmidt, Amos Sewell, Lee Gustavson, Mario Cooper, Saul Tepper, and numerous others.

Dunn's pictures, like the man, were forceful, yet combined great sensitivity with brilliant use of color. During World War I, Dunn was commissioned a Captain as an official war artist with the A.E.F. His experiences under fire produced many striking documentary drawings and paintings, now part of the archives of the Smithsonian Institution.

From notes taken during one of his classroom criticisms, the following fittingly describes his credo:

"Art is a universal language, and it is so because it is the expression of the feelings of man. Any man can look at a true work of art and feel kin to it and with him who made it – for he has the same number of heartbeats a minute, comes into the world to face the same joys, sorrows, and anticipations, the same hopes and fears. A vastly different vision may arise in the consciousness at the mention of a word, but our feelings are the same. By this you may know that the Brotherhood of Man *is*."*

*quoted from ***An Evening in the Classroom***, 1934.

Cover, ***The American Legion Magazine,*** July, 1928

Thomas Fogarty, *Cabaret performers,* date and place of publication unknown.

George Gibbs, magazine cover, *Woman in Lace,* pastel on paper.
Collection of Mr. and Mrs. Jeffrey Moores.

THOMAS FOGARTY

THOMAS FOGARTY (1873-1938) painted his illustrations from his own nostalgia for an earlier era, and editors regularly assigned him fiction with an historic basis.

Fogarty did much illustration in many media but was at his best with simple homespun subjects in pen and ink or wash and crayon, as exemplified by his interpretive pictures for the David Grayson books. He also illustrated *The Making of an American,* by Jacob Riis and *On Fortune's Road,* by Will Payne.

For many years he was a famous teacher at the Art Students League; among his pupils were Walter Biggs, McClelland Barclay, and Norman Rockwell.

GEORGE GIBBS (1870-1942) was a native of New Orleans and planned a career in the Navy, attending the Naval Academy for three years. He developed a preference for art, and changed to the Corcoran School of Art in Washington, D.C., followed by classes at the Art Students League in New York.

To support his studies, he sold real estate and worked as a newspaper reporter. He later capitalized on these experiences, both in writing and illustrating, producing some fifty novels and many screen plays for films. He both wrote and illustrated *Pike and Cutlass, Hero Tales of Our Navy* in 1900 and illustrated the novels of many other authors, while several of his books and magazine stories were illustrated by other artists. His work was published in a wide range of magazines, including *Scribner's, McClure's, Harper's, Cosmopolitan, Redbook, Collier's,* and *The Saturday Evening Post.* Gibbs lived in Rosemont, Pennsylvania, and was an active member of the Philadelphia Alliance, the Philadelphia Art Club and also served as president of the Franklin Gun Club.

C. A. Gilbert, Young woman holding hand mirror, 1899.
Collection of Delaware Art Museum.

CHARLES ALLAN GILBERT (1873-1929) chose art as a career after discovering his talent while sketching during a childhood as an invalid. Following training at the Art Students League, he went to Paris where his teachers were Constant and Laurens. He returned to the U.S. to begin a very successful illustration career, with a special aptitude for the portrayal of beautiful young women. Their portraits were included in several gift books and published as prints and postcards. Among his books and portfolios were *In Beauty's Realm, A Portfolio of Heads, Cameo Heads, Heads in Color,* and *Women of Fiction.* He also illustrated books about famous actresses, including impersonator Olga Nethersole, also *Julia Marlow in Barbara Frietchie,* and *Maude Adams in The Little Minister.* His many magazine appearances included *The Ladies' Home Journal, Vogue, Life, Woman's Home Companion, Scribner's Magazine* and *Vanity Fair.* Gilbert also invented and patented a process of combining animated drawing with live actors for motion pictures.

WILLIAM J. GLACKENS, N.A. (1870-1938) began his career in the 1890s as a newspaper artist in Philadelphia. John Sloan, Frederic R. Gruger, and Everett Shinn were his co-workers; together they covered fires, riots, parades, and public ceremonies. Glackens's rapid facility made him the expert in sketching crowds.

McClure's magazine sent him to Cuba as an artist-correspondent during the war with Spain, but even before the success of these drawings he had entered the field of magazine illustration.

Hard work preceded the apparent ease of his drawings. He would sketch an action or pose of a figure over and over until he knew it thoroughly. Then, discarding the sketches, he would be able to put down the essence of the pose with a deceptive economy of means.

Glackens had been early attracted to the work of Manet and Renoir and adopted the Impressionist approach in his own fine art work. Gradually, his interest shifted entirely to painting. He became one of The Eight, that famous and controversial group of painters who exhibited independently of the National Academy in 1908, and who gave a new impetus and direction to American art.

William Glackens, Washington Square, New York, cover for **Collier's** magazine, April 16, 1910. Collection of Arthur G. Altschul.

101

A typical Goodwin oil, *Fording a Stream,* 1911.

Philip R. Goodwin

PHILIP R. GOODWIN (1881-1935) of Norwich, Connecticut, was a student at the Rhode Island School of Design, the Art Students League in New York, and the Drexel Institute of Philadelphia, where he studied with Howard Pyle. His work exhibits much of Pyle's earnestness and discipline but is restricted almost entirely to subjects of hunting and fishing. One of Goodwin's early assignments was to illustrate **The Call of the Wild** by Jack London, which brought him to national attention. He also became a close friend of Charles Russell and helped him to improve his color.

Goodwin's pictures were published in Harper's magazines, **Outing, Scribner's** and **Everybody's,** in addition to calendar subjects for Brown & Bigelow and advertising for Winchester Arms and the Marlin Firearms Company. He also illustrated **African Game Trails** for Theodore Roosevelt.

Elizabeth Shippen Green

ELIZABETH SHIPPEN GREEN (1871-1954), later Mrs. Huger Elliot, was born in Philadelphia and studied at the Pennsylvania Academy of the Fine Arts with Robert Vonnoh and Thomas Eakins. She also studied with Howard Pyle at the Drexel Institute where she met Jessie Willcox Smith and Violet Oakley. The three became close friends and shared studios for many years.

Although Elizabeth did some early illustrations for **The Ladies' Home Journal** and **The Saturday Evening Post,** as well as a number of books, for many years she was under exclusive contract with **Harper's Monthly.** Her sensitive work is also decorative, with rounded edges and hand-hewn lines, similar in concept to that of stained glass windows. In a time when magazines used color very sparingly, a large percentage of her illustration work was reproduced in full color, which she handled brilliantly. Because she worked in a bold outline, her pictures reproduced equally well in color or in black and white.

Elizabeth Shippen Green, *The Love Match,* by Justus Miles Forman, **Harper's Monthly,** August, 1907.

-T- K- HANNA-

The illustrations of THOMAS KING HANNA (1872-1951) are strong and straightforward, yet very skillful. He did not rely on a stylish "technique," as did some of his contemporaries, to cover weaknesses in drawing or composition.

He was at home with both historical costume scenes and contemporary subjects such as the one reproduced here.

Born in Kansas City, Missouri, Hanna studied at Yale University and at the Art Students League in New York under Kenyon Cox, Irving Wiles and Charles S. Reinhart.

After a long career in illustration for magazines such as *Harper's, Scribner's, Life, American, Liberty, The Saturday Evening Post,* and *Woman's Home Companion,* he turned to painting and exhibited actively. One of his paintings is in the National Gallery of Art in Sydney, Australia.

Thomas Hanna, illustration for "And Angels Came," by Anne O'Hagan, *Harper's Monthly,* 1905.

Charlotte Harding, "An Exchange of Confidences," by Elsworth Kelley. *Harper's Monthly,* August, 1903. Collection of Robert T. and Susan K. Horvath.

G. Harding.

CHARLOTTE HARDING (1873-1951), later Mrs. James A. Brown, was a student at the Philadelphia School of Design for Women, The Pennsylvania Academy of the Fine Arts, and of Howard Pyle at Drexel Institute. She also received encouragement and help from Alice Barber Stephens, with whom she shared a studio in Philadelphia.

Pyle's influence in her compositions is clearly apparent, but she had her own strong decorative sense as shown in her use of linear shapes and flattened tonal areas. Her work evinces her special sympathy and understanding of children who were her favorite subjects.

Charlotte Harding was awarded a Silver Medal at the St. Louis Exposition in 1904 and at the Panama Pacific Exposition at San Francisco in 1915.

Toward the end of her life, without the prospect of gallery or museum exhibitions, Harding burned the great majority of her drawings.

GEORGE HARDING

GEORGE MATTHEWS HARDING, N.A. (1882-1959) was the
younger brother of Charlotte Harding, and through her work,
became interested in illustration. With her influence, he was
admitted to Howard Pyle's illustration classes in Wilmington. He
later spent several months studying and sketching the life of
Newfoundland fishing families. With this background, he returned
home to find a market for his work with **The Saturday Evening
Post** and other major magazines.

He was one of eight official artists sent overseas with the
A.E.F. during World War I, with roving assignments to document
the war in drawings and paintings. In his drawings he was
concerned more with the effect of war on the men themselves than
with portraying panoramic scenes of battlefields or ruins. These
are now part of the permanent collection of the Smithsonian
Institution in Washington, D.C.

A world traveler, Harding was sent with writer Norman
Duncan on a trip through the Middle East, Southwest Asia,
Australia and China to do a series of illustrated stories about their
travels.

Harding subsequently taught illustration at the Pennsylvania
Academy of the Fine Arts; he exhibited regularly and painted
several murals.

George Harding, *"Native Boats Gather about Eager to Barter,"* from "Shipmates of
the Coral Sea" by Norman Duncan, ***Harper's Monthly Magazine,*** February, 1915.

Lucius Hitchcock, charcoal illustration for "The Plagiarist" by Georgia Wood Pangborn.
Harper's Monthly, January, 1909.

LUCIUS WOLCOTT HITCHCOCK

LUCIUS WOLCOTT HITCHCOCK (1868-1942) painted in the
academic tradition of the Laurens and Colarossi School of Paris
where he studied with Lefebvre and Constant. His pictures were
extremely well painted, and he was especially effective in
presenting the social elite. His work appeared in most of the major
magazines, including ***Scribner's, Harper's Monthly*** and
Woman's Home Companion.

Hitchcock was also a teacher at the Buffalo Society of Artists
and the Buffalo Art Students League. Later he taught at the
William Chase School at New York.

He was one of the early members of the Society of
Illustrators; he also joined the Salmagundi Club and the New
Rochelle Art Association. His awards were many, including a
Silver Medal for Illustration in Paris in 1900, a Silver Medal for
Illustration and a Bronze for Painting at the St. Louis Exposition
in 1904.

Gayle Hoskins, Hunter dismounted, stalking antelope, a late work dated 1946.
Collection of Gary Blakeslee.

Gayle Hoskins

GAYLE PORTER HOSKINS (1887-1962) was raised a
Westerner, having been moved from his birthplace in Brazil,
Indiana, to Denver when he was only five. Growing up there gave
him a chance to ride and work with horses and he served with
Troop C of the Colorado State Cavalry for three years. A strong
interest in drawing led to his first art job at fourteen doing
cartoons for the *Denver Post.* When his family moved to Chicago
in 1904, Hoskins enrolled at the Chicago Art Institute. Howard
Pyle visited the school in 1907; he was impressed and invited
Hoskins to study further with him in Wilmington. This advanced
training helped to launch his long and successful illustration
career. Although his story assignments varied, he became best
known for his outdoor and Western subjects. As the Pulp
magazines evolved, Hoskins' work was especially well suited to
the requirements of the Western covers and he was associated with
the publishers Street & Smith for many years.

Hoskins enjoyed teaching and was a founding member of the
Wilmington Society of the Fine Arts. Along with Frank
Schoonover, he was active in the Wilmington Sketch Club.

HENRY - HUTT -

In a day when the illustrators set the fashion, no artist was more
influential in depicting the stylish, up-to-date woman than
HENRY HUTT (1875-1950). After the passage of a century, the
subtle detail and good taste of Hutt's illustrations is still apparent.

Hutt was born in Chicago, Illinois, and studied at the
Chicago Art Institute. He sold his first picture to the old *Life*
magazine at the age of sixteen, and thereafter illustrated for most
of the magazines of his day.

Published by the Century Company, *The Henry Hutt Picture
Book*, a volume containing more than eighty of his illustrations,
was a popular gift book in 1908.

Henry Hutt, cover, *Collier's* magazine, April 12, 1902.

Oliver Kemp, *Bass — A Critical Moment*. One of a suite of four fishing paintings titled *Days A Fishing* published by **Scribner's** magazine, June, 1909.

Like several other Pyle students, OLIVER KEMP (1887-1934) gravitated toward outdoor subject matter that paralleled his personal interests in fishing, camping, and hunting. It was these subjects that made him an early and popular painter of covers for **The Saturday Evening Post, Outing, Collier's, Redbook** and **Good Housekeeping** as well as for interior illustratons. He also wrote several books about the wilderness.

While his study with Pyle was part-time and limited to critiques, Kemp was also given instruction by Jean-Léon Gérôme, James McNeal Whistler, William M. Chase, John Singer Sargeant and Edwin Austin Abbey. Kemp later became a teacher and director of the School of Industrial Arts in Trenton, New Jersey.

B-CORY KILVERT

BENJAMIN SAYRE CORY KILVERT (1879-1946) was the son of the mayor of his birthplace: Hamilton, Ontario, in Canada. Kilvert migrated to New York at attend classes at the Art Students League. Among his teachers were George Bridgman and Robert Henri. He found early employment as a staff artist for the **New York World** and later, **Collier's** magazine. He also began to submit humorous artwork to **Life, Punch, Judge** and **St. Nicholas** magazines and illustrated several children's books.

During World War I, Kilvert served with the Canadian Expeditionary Force, based in London, devising techniques for camouflage. He also developed an interest in map making and created several mural-sized pictorial maps, including one for the Pinehurst Country Club in North Carolina.

Kilvert complemented his illustration career with rural landscape paintings of the Catskill Mountains, street scenes in Charleston, South Carolina, marine paintings in the Biddeford, Maine area, and New York City skylines. He was a member of the American Watercolor Society and the Salmagundi Club in New York where he regularly exhibited.

B. Cory Kilvert, *Little Children Should Love One Another*, 1906.

WALT KUHN (1877-1949) is not well remembered for his career as a cartoonist and illustrator. Beginning at five dollars a week salary as a cartoonist on a San Francisco newspaper, he eventually gravitated to the *New York Sun.* His featured drawings of animals and comical birds were very popular and were later collected in book form, entitled *A Little Bird Told Me,* published by Life. Even after he left cartooning, the feature was continued by Paul Bransom and other artists.

Kuhn's later career was as an American painter and he had a prominent role in the avant-garde movement, serving as secretary for the Armory Show in 1913 and successfully exhibiting his portraits of circus and vaudeville performers and still-life paintings.

Kuhn had studied at the Academy Colarossi in Paris, the Munich Academy and in Holland, Spain, and Italy. He himself taught at the New York School of Art in 1908 and 1909, and the Art Students League in 1926 and 1927. His work is to be found in many private and museum collections, including the Whitney Museum of American Art, the Detroit Institute of Art, the Addison Gallery of Americn Art and the Los Angeles Museum of Art.

ORSON BYRON LOWELL (1871-1956) was the son of the landscape painter, Milton H. Lowell, and his father encouraged his early efforts by expecting him to draw something every day. He attended the Art Institute of Chicago classes in 1887, remaining as a student and then as an instructor until 1893, when he moved to New York to enter the illustration field.

He found immediate success there and worked for most of the top magazines, including *The Century, Scribner's, McClure's,* the Harper's publications, *Puck, Judge, Collier's,* and the Curtis magazines in Philadelphia. He also illustrated many books. In 1907 he became a member of the *Life* staff and was a prolific contributor for many years, often featured with humorous centerfold double-spread pen and inks.

Lowell maintained studios in New York and in New Rochelle, and was a member of the Society of Illustrators, the Players, the Dutch Treat Club, the Cliff Dwellers (of Chicago), and the New Rochelle Art Association.

"He: Charming! Delightful! What a sympathetic touch! Please play something longer – and rather loud," Life magazine, ca. 1910.
Shown at Orson Lowell travelling exhibition, 1911.
The Kelly Collection of American Illustration.

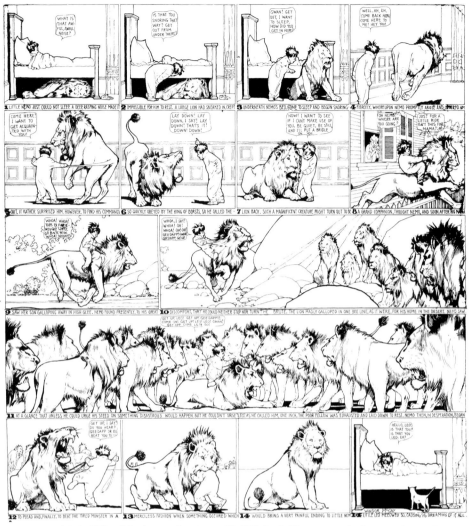

A typical "Nemo" Sunday page from January 28, 1906. Atypical however, was the discovery of a pasted over earlier version of the final panels, shown above, in which Nemo was actually devoured by the lion!

A "Gertie the Dinosaur" drawing, one of thousands McCay drew for his pioneering animated feature.

Music sheet cover for the Little Nemo Broadway Play.

Replacement panel with a more benign finale.

WINSOR McCAY (1871-1934) possessed a unique imagination that found its perfect expression in a Sunday comic page for **The New York Herald,** "Little Nemo in Slumberland," which began in 1905 and was an immediate success. In it, Little Nemo is summoned by the King of Slumberland into a series of fantastic adventures made believable only by McCay's beautifully drawn settings. These evolved into increasingly dangerous situations from which Nemo, modelled after the artist's son, was saved only by awakening in the last panel. The feature continued under changes of title and publisher and some interruptions until 1914.

Simultaneously, McCay was a popular performer on the vaudeville circuit giving chalk talks and lectures, as well as drawing other features, "Little Sammy Sneeze," "The Dream of the Rarebit Fiend" and "A Pilgrim's Progress." In 1908, a musical based on "Little Nemo" with music by Victor Herbert was produced on Broadway and toured successfully for two seasons.

McCay also invested an immense amount of his energy in experimenting with animation and producing his first major animated film, "Gertie, the Dinosaur," in 1914 with ideas that are still basic to the present industry.

As a contracted employee of William Randolph Hearst, McCay was finally ordered to give up his Nemo strip and vaudeville appearances to do editorial cartoons at the behest of Hearst's editor, Arthur Brisbane. McCay dutifully produced carefully drawn though often uninspired editorial drawings supporting Hearst's isolationism prior to World War I until his contract ran out. In the mid-twenties, Nemo was revived for four years by the **New York Herald Tribune.** McCay also worked on other animated films including **The Sinking of the Lusitania, Bug Vaudeville,** and **Flip's Circus.** He continued working actively until the time of his death.

Guernsey Moore, *Collier's* cover, circa 1905.
Collection Delaware Art Museum.

Guernsey Moore

Although he worked for *Collier's* magazine, *The Ladies' Home Journal,* and other publications, GUERNSEY MOORE (1874-1925) is most closely identified with *The Saturday Evening Post.* He produced some of their earliest covers, beginning in 1900, totaling more than forty by 1924. During part of that time he also served as art director for the *Post.*

Moore was born in Germantown, Pa., and studied at the Pennsylvania Academy of the Fine Arts. Working in opaque watercolor, he developed a poster-like style that was ideal for magazine covers because of its strong carrying power.

F. Luis Mora.

FRANCIS LUIS MORA, N.A. (1874-1940) was born in Montevideo, Uruguay, the son of a Spanish sculptor, and was brought to the United States as a youngster. His art training was from his father, the Museum of Fine Arts in Boston under Frank Benson and Edmund Tarbell, and at the Art Students League in New York under H. Siddons Mowbray. He started illustrating in 1892 and eventually worked for most of the leading magazines including *The Ladies' Home Journal, The Century, Harper's Monthly,* and *Hearst's International.*

At the same time, he began the first of a series of mural paintings with commissions in 1900 for the Lynn (Mass.) Public Library, followed by decorations for the Missouri State building at the St. Louis Exposition in 1904, a decorative panel for the Red Cross headquarters in Washington, D.C. and for the Orpheum Theater in Los Angeles.

Mora also painted many notables' portraits, including president Warren G. Harding and Andrew Carnegie. His work was exhibited in numerous shows and won him honors and medals from the Philadelphia Art Club, the first Hallgarten Prize from the National Academy of Design in 1905, a Silver Medal at the International Fine Arts Exposition in Buenos Aires in 1910 and two Gold Medals at the San Francisco Exposition in 1915. He was a member of many art associations including the American Watercolor Society, the National Academy and the Society of Illustrators.

F. Luis Mora, illustration for "The White Umbrella," by Chester Bailey Fernald, *The Ladies' Home Journal,* September, 1919.

The Answer to Tyndal's Prayer.   *The Martyrdom of Anne Askew*
Violet Oakley, two panels from the Governor's Reception Room, Capitol Building,
State of Pennsylvania. Published in **The Century,** June, 1905 and in **The Holy
Experiment** privately printed in 1922.

Thornton Oakley, *News Vendor on Broadway,* 1905.

V. Oakley

VIOLET OAKLEY (1874-1961) came from a family of artists:
two grandfathers were members of the National Academy, and she
was always encouraged in her own artistic efforts. She attended
classes at the Art Students League and spent several months in
England and France where she was a pupil of Edmund Aman-
Jean. She returned to the States to enroll in the Pennsylvania
Academy of the Fine Arts, studying under Cecilia Beaux, then
switched to Drexel to study with Howard Pyle. While Pyle helped
her to gain illustration assignments, she preferred to work in
stained glass and at a larger, decorative scale.

Pyle's encouragement was the beginning of her long career
as a designer of stained glass windows and murals. Her largest
commission was for the murals in the Governor's Reception
Room in the new Capitol building in Harrisburg, Pennsylvania.
Edwin Austin Abbey, who was painting another, larger portion of
the mural decorations, died in 1911, and Oakley completed his
commission as well, taking another nineteen years to finish.

When the League of Nations was being formed in 1927,
Oakley spent several months in Geneva, Switzerland, recording
the sessions and making portraits of the participants. Her work
won her many awards and an honorary degree of Doctor of Laws
from the Drexel Institute in 1948.

T Oakley -

This painting by THORNTON OAKLEY (1881-1953) is
emblematic of the artist's strong, carefully composed pictures. His
style was particularly appropriate for industrial subjects and the
theme of men at work with heavy machinery. He both wrote and
illustrated for many magazines, including **The Century, Collier's,
Scribner's,** and **Harper's Monthly.**

Oakley studied architecture at the University of
Pennsylvania; he also studied illustration with Howard Pyle.
Throughout his career, he both illustrated and painted for
exhibition. His work is represented in many major museums in the
United States and abroad. During World War II he painted a series
of forty-eight pictures of "American Industries Geared For War,"
and related subjects, for the **National Geographic** magazine,
published in 1942, 1943 and 1945.

Oakley also taught and lectured about art; for some twenty
years he served as head of the Department of Illustration at the
Philadelphia Museum School of Industrial Art.

Clara Elsene Peck, illustration for "Queen Christmas," by Carolyn Wells, published by *The Ladies' Home Journal,* December, 1920.

Clara Elsene Peck

CLARA ELSENE PECK (1883-1968) specialized in drawing women and children as an illustrator. Her pictures are decorative in composition and sensitive in rendering. They were particularly appropriate to articles she illustrated in the women's magazines on such subjects as education, child psychology, and the expectant mother. She also illustrated fiction in magazines and books, did advertising campaigns for Procter & Gamble, the Aeolian Company, Metropolitan Life and others.

For a time, she was married to artist John Scott Williams and their styles merged during that period, permitting their occasional collaboration on pictures which they signed jointly. On her own, she beautifully illustrated and designed several books, including *In the Border Country* by Josephine Daskam Bacon, *A Lady of King Arthur's Court* and *Shakespeare's Sweetheart* by Sarah Hawks Sterling.

Peck was born in Allegan, Michigan, acquired her art education at the Minneapolis School of Fine Arts, the Philadelphia Academy of the Fine Arts and with the painter William M. Chase. She was a member of the American Watercolor Society, exhibited extensively and won many awards.

Henry J. Peck

HENRY JARVIS PECK (1880-1964) grew up in Warren, Rhode Island, and studied at the Rhode Island School of Design, as well as the Eric Pape Art School in Boston where he became acquainted with N. C. Wyeth and Clifford Ashley. In 1901, Peck was accepted as a student of Howard Pyle. After three years, he began his career as an illustrator sharing a studio in Wilmington with Ashley. He was particularly good at rural and New England marine subjects, and occasionally wrote articles and short stories accompanied by his own illustrations. An excellent violinist, Peck also played in the Wilmington orchestra. Several Pyle school graduates founded an artists' colony "Naamans-on-Delaware" in the teens and Peck was an active member.

His work was published in *The Saturday Evening Post, Harper's Weekly, Outing, The Century, Scribner's Monthly, Collier's, Redbook, Pearson's* and other magazines.

Henry Jarvis Peck, *"The Tortoise and the Hare."*

*Land of Make Believe, **Scribner's Magazine,** August, 1912.*
"Let's pretend the parting hour never more shall find us," for "Make Believe," by Rosamund Marriott Watson.

The Rubaiyat, 1916. Illustration for Crane's Chocolates.

The Lantern Bearers, **Collier's Weekly** cover, December 10, 1910.

"La Palazzima" Villa Gori Siena from **Italian Villas and Their Gardens,** by Edith Wharton, published by The Century Company, 1904.
Collection of the Society of Illustrators Museum of American Illustration.

Throughout his long lifetime, FREDERICK MAXFIELD PARRISH, N.A. (1870-1966) created and painted a world of his own. As a child, he made careful drawings of figures, cutting around their outlines and mounting the silhouetted shapes. This emphasis on flat shapes was later carried over into many of his magazine covers and mural decorations, in which the figures were superimposed against highly detailed backgrounds.

Parrish's subject matter, too, seemed to have originated with his childhood interests in fairy tales, giants, castles and other make-believe. His most successful illustrations were made for such books as Eugene Field's **Poems of Childhood** and Kenneth Grahame's **Golden Age** and **Dream Days.** He visited the same well for advertising art and mural subjects. His 30-foot wall decoration depicting "Old King Cole," painted for the old Knickerbocker Hotel, was later reinstalled in the St. Regis Hotel in New York. Other subjects included "The Pied Piper," for the Sheraton-Palace Hotel in San Francisco and "Sing a Song of Sixpence," in the Hotel Sherman in Chicago.

He was a sumptuous, rich colorist, noted especially for his luminous "Parrish blue" skies. Reproductions of his cover designs or illustrations were saved and framed by tens of thousands of families. Like "The Dinkey Bird," his most popular pictures were idylls of young girls in archaic dress, or no dress, amid dramatic landscapes and classical architecture. His mass appeal also made Parrish a favorite Brown & Bigelow calendar illustrator when he turned to pure, idealized landscapes for several subsequent decades.

A Man of Letters, **Life** cover, January 5, 1922.

The Market Place, Ragusa, from "Impressions of Dalmatia," written and illustrated by Peixotto, ***Scribner's Magazine,*** July, 1906.

ERNEST CLIFFORD PEIXOTTO, A.N.A. (1869-1940) was born in San Francisco and received his art education in Paris as a student of Constant, Lefebvre and Coucet. Peixotto exhibited and won awards at the Paris Salon in 1895 and the World's Columbian Exposition in 1893. He was also a writer and world traveler. His articles, combined with his illustrations, were published in ***Harper's Monthly, Scribner's Magazine*** and other periodicals.

Peixotto also painted several murals, including *La Morte d'Arthur,* for the Cleveland Public Library. During World War I, Peixotto was one of the group of eight artists sent to the war front with the Allied Expeditionary Force, and he became an expert in the design and use of camouflage. Much of his war reportage is in the collection of the Smithsonian Institution.

HERMAN PFEIFER (1874-1931) was a pupil of Howard Pyle, studying with him in Wilmington in 1903 and 1904. His illustrations are marked by their unembellished, straightforward presentations, making them solidly believable, with but little of the romantic drama of Pyle's approach.

Pfeifer was a regular contributor to most of the national magazines, including ***The Ladies' Home Journal, Woman's Home Companion, American Magazine, Redbook, Scribner's Magazine*** and ***Associated Sunday Magazine,*** from 1905 through the 1920s. He also did some advertising illustration for various clients, such as Procter & Gamble's Ivory Soap.

Herman Pfeifer, illustration for "A Gentle Knight of Old Brandenburg," by Charles Major; ***Associated Sunday Magazine,*** May 16, 1909.

CHARLES M. RELYEA (1863-1932) was so versatile and prolific that he is not readily identifiable with a particular style or theme, and art editors gave him a wide variety of manuscripts to illustrate. Born in Albany, New York, Relyea attended the Pennsylvania Academy of the Fine Arts and studied there with Thomas Eakins. He also attended the Art Students League in New York where his teacher was Frank Vincent DuMond. Relyea afterward studied in Paris. Upon his return to the U.S., he illustrated for virtually every magazine, including *Munsey's Magazine, The Century, St. Nicholas, Life* and *The Ladies' Home Journal.*

Relyea was a member of the Artists Guild, The Players Club, the Salmagundi Club and the Allied Artists of America.

HENRY REUTERDAHL (1871-1925) was a master painter of ships and the sea. His early pictures were literal and factually accurate, but in his later pictures, his knowledgeability allowed him a heightened impressionistic approach in the manipulation of the elements of weather, sea and ships, with a brilliance of color appropriate for his ageless, primal subject.

During the Spanish-American War, he served as an artist-correspondent. He also accompanied the American Fleet on several voyages including one through the Straits of Magellan in 1907, and another to the Mediterranean in 1913. As a Lieutenant Commander during World War I, he was artistic adviser to the United States Navy Recruiting Bureau in New York and made paintings for many of the Navy's most effective and dramatic posters.

He is represented in the collections of the National Museum in Washington, D.C.; the Naval Academy at Annapolis, Maryland; the Naval War College in Newport; and in the Toledo Museum.

Charles Relyea, illustration for "The Sunday Husbands," by Eleanor Hallowell Abbott; *Munsey's* magazine, April, 1907.

Henry Reuterdahl, *American Destroyer Patrol along the Atlantic,* from ***Art and the Great War*** by Albert Eugene Gallatin, 1919. The Kelly Collection of American Illustration.

The Water Hole. Reproduced as a special supplement for the August, 1926 number of **Country Life** magazine.

Russell became an excellent draftsman with pen and ink, thanks in great part to the tutelage of his friend, Will Crawford, a master of the medium.

"The Last Laugh." Here Russell empathizes with the wolf in one of his many bronzes.

In without Knocking was based on an incident involving Russell's cowhand friends who related the story to him and which Russell painted from memory a quarter of a century later. Reprinted with permission of and copyrighted by Brown & Bigelow, St. Paul, Minnesota.

The life and career of CHARLES MARION RUSSELL (1864-1926) has a number of singular parallels with that of Frederic Remington. They were both largely self-taught, both spent their early years living the rugged frontier life of the West, and both recorded, in drawings, paintings, and sculpture, the panorama of a vanishing era. Yet they pursued their goals separately. Remington had early success but died young. Russell struggled for several years before gaining a national reputation, and had a relatively long career.

Russell was the more compassionate observer of the natives' side of the "civilizing" of the West. His open-hearted, direct manner led Indians to trust him instinctively. He lived with the Blackfeet in Alberta for several months, learning the language and making many drawings and paintings. For a while he seriously considered becoming a "squaw man" himself.

Most of Russell's early pictures were made for himself or to give away to friends, until the economic necessities of marriage forced his wife to find a market for them. Within a few years, Russell's paintings and bronzes commanded high prices, and today his original works are eagerly sought by collectors and museums. Among the museums with good collections of his pictures are the Historical Society of Montana in Helena and the Trigg-Russell Gallery at Great Falls. One of his finest paintings is a mural, almost 25 x 12 feet, entitled *Lewis and Clark meeting the Flathead Indians at Ross's Hole,* in the Montana State Capitol.

In the inscription is Russell's approximation of the spelling of the name of his friend, "Lex" Godillot, who had been a Mountie in Canada.

117

CHARLES NICOLAS SARKA (1879-1960) had a chronic wanderlust which, if it interfered with the volume of work he might have done, nevertheless gave him a first-hand knowledge of the exotic subjects of his pictures.

He traveled to many remote areas, from Tahiti and the South Seas to North Africa and the hill tribes of Morocco, paying his expenses on the way with his brush. Thomas "Pop" Hart was one of his traveling companions. His credo was: "This was my art school: to travel and paint; to paint and travel."

Sarka first illustrated for newspapers in Chicago, San Francisco and New York. By 1904, he was working for *Judge* and *Cosmopolitan* and later added most of the other major magazines.

He was a fluent watercolorist and a life member of the American Watercolor Society, but his early work was in line, and the mastery of his pen-and-ink drawings is brilliant, full of tonal subtleties, rich in texture.

Charles Sarka, *The Realist.*
First Nymph: *Do you think he sees us?*
Second Nymph: *I'm afraid not; he's a realist.*

Remington Schuyler, *The Disputed Trail,* painted for *The Century*, August, 1911.

REMINGTON SCHUYLER

REMINGTON SCHUYLER (1884-1955) was an expert on Native American Indian lore, lecturing, painting and writing extensively on the subject. He was active for over thirty years in the Boy Scouts, wrote some of the Merit Badge requirements, illustrated for *Boys' Life* magazine and served in volunteer roles from Scout Master to Vice President of Council. He also illustrated many books, including *Daniel Boone, Wilderness Scout* by Stewart Edward White, *Indian Hunting Grounds* and *Great White Buffalo.* Other illustrations were published in *Life, St. Nicholas* and *The Century* magazines.

Resourceful and self-reliant during the Depression years, he painted many covers for pulp magazines, did some WPA murals and sometimes bartered his paintings for haircuts, meals and dental work.

Schuyler, who was related through his mother to Frederic Remington, was a student of art at Washington University in St. Louis, Missouri, the Art Students League with Bridgman, the Académie Julian in Paris and, briefly, with Howard Pyle. In addition to his illustrating, he was active in local theatre in Pelham Manor, N.Y. and Westport, Connecticut. He taught for six years as Artist-in-Residence and Associate Professor at Missouri Valley College in Marshall, Missouri.

"There was always on guard one who sat and watched the Gulf." From "In the Haunts of Jean Lafitte," written and illustrated by Schoonover; published by **Harper's Monthly,** December, 1911.

Frank E. Schoonover

FRANK EARLE SCHOONOVER (1877-1972) owed much to Howard Pyle's belief that an illustrator should thoroughly immerse himself in his subjects, painting those things he knows best. After studying with Pyle at the Drexel Institute, in Wilmington and at Chadds Ford, Pennsylvania, Schoonover began to receive assignments to cover Indian and frontier subjects. In order to qualify himself properly, he made two trips to the Hudson Bay country, first in 1903 by snowshoe and dog team, and in 1911 by canoe, observing the life and customs of the Indians. Over the years he did a great number of excellent, authoritative illustrations based on these expeditions.

Similarly, he made field trips to other locations, such as the Mississippi Bayou country for a book he both wrote and illustrated: *Lafitte, the Pirate of the Gulf*.

Over his long and productive life, Schoonover illustrated for many magazines and books, designed stained glass windows, taught at the John Herron Art Institute and at his own studio, and painted many landscapes of the neighboring Brandywine and Delaware River valleys.

Drummer Boy, painted by Schoonover circa 1899, while he was still a student of Howard Pyle, unpublished; Collection of the Brandywine River Museum, Margaret I. Handy Memorial Fund.

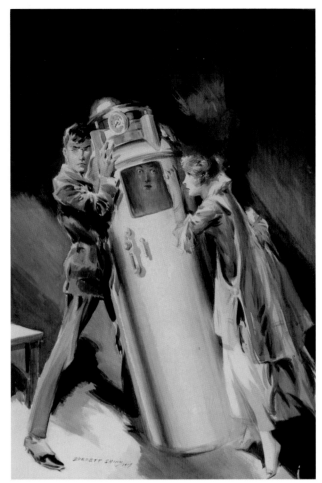

Everett Shinn, *The Messiah of the Cylinder,* an early science fiction story; cover illustration for *Everybody's,* June, 1917, watercolor.
Collection of Glynn Crain.

Florence Shinn, *"Puttin on 'Henry' seemed to bring the Lion right into the Family."*
Illustration for "Miss Clegg's Adopted," *The Century* magazine, July, 1904.

Everett Shinn, *Fourteenth Street at Christmas Time,* pastel and gouache; comprehensive sketch for *Harper's Monthly,* 1904.
Collection of The Library of Congress, Washington, D.C.

EVERETT SHINN

As one of "The Eight," EVERETT SHINN, N.A. (1876-1953) made a lively contribution to American art both in the gallery and on the printed page.

His milieu was New York, Broadway, the theatre, and colorful public gatherings. His immense artistic facility was always evident, developed in his early career as a newspaper illustrator which demanded rapid, on-the-scene drawings for immediate deadlines. An individual of great enthusiasms and many interests, Shinn was also an accomplished inventor, playwright, and actor. He took on illustration commissions sporadically throughout his career, mostly when he needed money, working for *The Century, McClure's* and *Hearst's International* as well as several book projects in the 1930s, such as *The Mystery of Edwin Drood,* and *Rip van Winkle.*

A mural, done for the residence of his friend, Clyde Fitch,led to a large number of other such projects, including those of the Belasco Theatre, the Oak Room of the Plaza Hotel in New York, and a 22 x 44-foot mural for the Trenton, New Jersey City Hall.

Shinn is represented in many collections and museums, including the Metropolitan Museum of Art, the Whitney Museum of American Art, and the Phillips Memorial Gallery.

Florence Scovel Shinn

FLORENCE SCOVEL SHINN (1869-1940) was already a successful illustrator before her marriage to Everett Shinn. They had met as classmates at the Pennsylvania Academy of the Fine Arts. Their marriage lasted fourteen years, and though divorced because of his philandering, they remained friends.

Her illustrations, usually in pen and ink, and with a humorous, light touch, were used in *The Century* magazine to accompany a regular feature, the "Editor's Drawer." She also worked for *Harper's Bazar, Truth, Life,* and did a number of book commissions, including *Mrs. Wiggs of the Cabbage Patch* and the sequel, *Lovey Mary,* by Alice Hegan Rice.

In the latter part of her life, she wrote a number of books having a religious and philosophical outlook and lectured on the subject at Carnegie Hall and the New York Unity Society.

DAN SMITH

DAN SMITH (1865-1934) was born of Danish parentage in Ivigtut, Greenland. He came to America as a child, and later went to Copenhagen where he studied at the Public Arts Institute. Subsequently, he returned to the United States and studied further at the Pennsylvania Academy of the Fine Arts.

Smith found his first work as a member of the art staff of *Leslie's Weekly*; at the time of the Spanish-American War, he joined the Hearst organization.

Through drawing for newspapers, Smith developed a remarkable dry-brush technique that made him the star attraction for many years in the Sunday supplement of the old *New York World.* His drawings were syndicated and distributed throughout the country. During this time, he also illustrated for the national magazines and exhibited his etchings and oils.

Typical illustration demonstrating Dan Smith's masterful control of dry brush and lively sense of design.

"His Desk – We bought the desk together," **Harper's Monthly,** 1911. Exhibited at the Howard E. Smith Retrospective, Montgomery Gallery 1986.

HOWARD SMITH

HOWARD EVERETT SMITH, N.A. (1885-1970) was a New Englander, born in West Windham, New Hampshire. After attending the Art Students League in New York with classes under George Bridgman, he transferred to the Howard Pyle school in Wilmington, Delaware. He later attended advanced classes with Edmund Tarbell at the Boston Museum School of Fine Arts.

He was very soon able to have his work published, making early appearances in *Harper's Weekly* and *Harper's Monthly.* His illustrations were also published in *Scribner's Magazine* and in *The Ladies' Home Journal,* as well as in a number of books including *The Children's Longfellow* and *The Beginning of the American People.*

Smith was especially interested in Impressionism, and in 1911 won the Paige Traveling Scholarship from the Museum School for two years' study and travel in Europe. With income from his illustrations, he extended his study for another year. After his return in 1914, he became an instructor at the Rhode Island School of Design. In addition to landscapes, he also painted a number of portraits and worked with lithography. In his later years, Smith moved to California to become an active participant in the Carmel Art Association, exhibiting and winning many awards.

Hot Cross Buns, **Good Housekeeping** magazine, 1916.

"Noah's Ark," illustration for **The Bed-Time Book** by Helen Hay Whitney; Duffield and Company, 1907.

JESSIE WILLCOX SMITH

JESSIE WILLCOX SMITH (1863-1935) never married, but throughout her long career, specialized in drawing and painting mothers, babies and children. Her training was acquired at the School of Design for Women, the Pennsylvania Academy of the Fine Arts with Thomas Eakins, and at the Drexel Institute under Howard Pyle.

She had begun as a kindergarten teacher but turned to an art career with the stimulus and assistance of Howard Pyle. Some of her best-known illustrations were for books: *Little Women*, *Heidi*, *A Book of Old Stories* and Robert Louis Stevenson's *A Child's Garden of Verses*. She also painted a great many illustrations for magazines such as **Collier's** and **McClure's**, and did nearly 200 covers for **Good Housekeeping**. For several years, she shared house and studio with two other Pyle students, Elizabeth Shippen Green and Violet Oakley. Working in close proximity they also strongly influenced each other's work as well as that of several other Pyle-school women. This relationship is told in **The Red Rose Girls** by Alice Carter. Smith painted and exhibited widely, receiving many awards, including a Silver Medal at the 1915 Panama-Pacific Exposition in San Francisco. She was also commissioned to paint many portraits of children.

Two other biographies, **Jessie Willcox Smith** by S. Michael Schnessel, and **Jessie Willcox Smith American Illustrator** by Edward D. Nudelman (who also contributed **A Bibliography)** have been published.

John Sloan, cover illustration for *Collier's* magazine, January 2, 1904, in which he replicates a pen-and-ink illustration by his colleague, Charles Dana Gibson.

JOHN FRENCH SLOAN (1871-1951) worked for the *Philadelphia Press* as a young newspaper artist, together with William Glackens, George Luks and Everett Shinn, all of whom studied at the Pennsylvania Academy of the Fine Arts. They subsequently became members of "The Eight," but for some years continued to paint for exhibitions at the same time they were illustrating for the magazines.

Sloan came to New York in 1905 and became interested in recording city life and the social upheaval as he saw it around him. He became famous for his illustrations on this subject for the radical magazines, *The Masses, The Call,* and *Progressive Women.* He also contributed to *McClure's, Collier's,* and *Cosmopolitan.*

He later devoted himself exclusively to painting, etching, and lithography, and is represented in many major collections and museums, including the Museum of Fine Arts, Boston, and the Metropolitan Museum of Art in New York City.

For several years, Sloan taught at the Art Students League in New York. He was elected president in 1918 of the Society of Independent Artists, a position he held for the rest of his life. Sloan summarized much of his painting philosophy in his book, *Gist of Art,* published by American Artists Group in 1939. A comprehensive collection of his work was donated by Helen Farr Sloan to the Delaware Art Museum in 1978.

Wake of the Ferry, painted by Sloan in 1907, was issued as a United States postage stamp in 1971. © USPS.

FREDERIC DORR STEELE (1873-1944) was a prolific illustrator for *The Century* magazine, *McClure's, Scribner's* and other publications, but he is best remembered for his unique portrayal of Arthur Conan Doyle's *Sherlock Holmes.* He had illustrated all but four of the last thirty-three Holmes stories and was working on an anthology of the whole series for the Limited Editions Club at the time of his death. Steele's drawings were almost always made in line, with either a pencil on a textured paper or in dry-brush. Benday screens were often used for tonal effects in these illustrations.

Steele also illustrated the works of many other famous authors, including Mark Twain, Richard Harding Davis, F. R. Stockton, Rudyard Kipling, Booth Tarkington, O. Henry, Joseph Conrad and Arnold Bennett.

Born in a lumber camp near Marquette, Michigan, Steele studied at the National Academy of Design and at the Art Students League in New York where he also later taught illustration.

He became a member of the Society of Illustrators in 1902 and was awarded a Bronze Medal at the St. Louis Exposition in 1904. He was also the first living illustrator to be honored by inclusion in the Cabinet of American Illustration at the Library of Congress.

Frederic Steele, "A Reminiscence of Sherlock Holmes" by Arthur Conan Doyle, for the cover of *Collier's* magazine, April 30, 1904.

Fred Strothmann, "What the Pug Knew," Editor's Drawer, *Harper's Monthly,* March, 1919.
Collection of Stanley Kulza.

Strothmann.

FRED STROTHMANN (1879-1958) originally wanted to be a portrait painter. He was a pupil of Carl Hecker, and studied in New York, Berlin and Paris. However, his natural inclination was more for humor, and he gradually shifted to illustration with a decidedly comic slant. As he put it, *"It was at the suggestion of those whose portraits I tried to paint that I went in for funny pictures."*

Strothmann was a regular contributor to ***Harper's Monthly, Life, The Century, Hearst's International,*** and other magazines, as well as illustrator for many books and articles by authors such as Ellis Parker Butler, Ring Lardner, Mark Twain (***Extracts from Adam's Diary***), and Carolyn Wells.

J. Walter Taylor

FRANK WALTER TAYLOR (1874-1921) worked almost exclusively with charcoal which he employed with a full tonal range from the white of the paper to rich blacks. His pictures give us an intimate view of social life of the times.

Taylor was born in Philadelphia, the son of Frank H. Taylor who had been a Civil War artist/correspondent and newspaper artist. He was instructed by his father and also studied at the Pennsylvania Academy of the Fine Arts. There he was awarded a traveling scholarship which enabled him to study in Paris. Upon his return to America, he worked as an illustrator for numerous magazines and also contributed a number of his own short stories. He was awarded a Medal of Honor for Illustration at the Panama Pacific International Exposition in 1915.

Frank Taylor, illustration for *Harper's Monthly,* 1915.

During World War I, Captain Townsend spent some time in France with the fledgling U. S. Air Service, recording activities of the 147th Squadron of the First Pursuit Group in a series of drawings like the above.

Allen True, *The Mountain Pony has the Climbing Ability of the Goat* for "The Mountain Pony," ***Outing*** magazine, circa 1906-07.

Although HARRY EVERETT TOWNSEND (1879-1941) painted and exhibited in full-color oils, some of his best work was done in black and white, including his drawings in line for ***Adventure*** magazine.

Townsend was born in Camp Grove, Illinois, and attended school at the Art Institute of Chicago. In 1900 he was invited to study with Howard Pyle in Wilmington, Delaware, and stayed there until 1904. Moving to New York, he was soon illustrating for the leading magazines.

In 1917, Townsend was commissioned as a Captain with the A.E.F. and assigned to record the war. These drawings and paintings are now in the Smithsonian Institution.

Active in art circles, Townsend was a member of the Society of Illustrators, the Allied Artists' Association, the Salmagundi Club, the Architectural League of New York, the Brooklyn Society of Etchers, the Westport Artists, the Darien Guild of Seven Arts, the Silvermine Guild, and others. He was awarded the Shaw Prize for illustration at the Salmagundi Club in 1920.

ALLEN TRUE ALLEN TUPPER TRUE (1881-1955) was a Westerner born in Colorado Springs, Colorado, and his lifelong interests as an artist centered on frontier themes. After two years of study at the University of Denver, he moved to Washington, D.C. to attend the Corcoran School of Art. As one of the fortunate applicants to be accepted, True studied under Howard Pyle from 1902 to 1906. He then launched his illustration career with assignments from ***Outing, Scribner's, Collier's, The Saturday Evening Post*** and other periodicals, but soon gravitated to mural painting. Beginning in the 1910s, True became an assistant to the British muralist Frank Brangwyn. He assisted Brangwyn with the decorations for the Panama-Pacific Exposition in 1915 and the murals for the dome of the Missouri State Capitol. True went on to paint many other murals on his own, including the Wyoming State Capitol, the Montana National Bank, the Mountain States Telephone Building, the Billings Public Library, and the Greek Theater Civic Center in Denver. The artist was a member of the Mural Painters Society of America, the Authors Club in London, and the Cactus Club of Denver, Colorado.

"Hands Up," from "The Story of Montana" published by ***McClure's*** magazine, August, 1906. Collection of Valley National Bank, Phoenix, AZ.

"I am Sir Launcelot du Lake" from ***The Boy's King Arthur,*** Charles Scribner's Sons, New York, 1917. Collection of Andrew Sordoni.

Endpapers, ***Treasure Island,*** Charles Scribner's Sons, New York, 1911. Collection of The Brandywine River Museum. Purchased in memory of Hope Montgomery Scott.

"The Rakish Brigantine," *Scribner's,* August, 1914.

N·C·WYETH

NEWELL CONVERS WYETH, N.A. (1882-1945) had a huge zest for life. He carried this enthusiasm through a great number of paintings, more than 3,000 illustrations, numerous vast murals, and many still-life and landscape paintings.

Howard Pyle was his teacher and idol. At first, Wyeth emulated Pyle's approach as nearly as possible, painting much of the same kind of subject matter — medieval life, pirates, Americana. To this he added his own dramatic picture concepts and rich, decorative color. Outstanding in this phase of his work were the more than twenty-five books he illustrated for Charles Scribner's Sons' Classics series. The popularity of these books is such that, even after decades, many of them are still in print.

He came to resent the constraints of illustration, and after painting in oils for many years, Wyeth turned to the egg tempera medium and began to paint more for exhibitions. He also encouraged an interest in the arts in his children, giving them every opportunity for self-expression. His daughters, Henriette and Caroline, were both accomplished painters; Ann, a composer; and his son, Andrew, is famous as a painter. His grandson, Jamie, is also an excellent painter.

At the time of his tragic death in a railway crossing accident, N. C. Wyeth was one of America's best loved illustrators.

The October, 1965, issue of *American Heritage* contains an article by Henry C. Pitz about the career of Wyeth and his family, and a biography by David Michaelis was published in 1998.

127

SARAH S. STILWELL WEBER

SARAH S. STILWELL WEBER (1878-1939) was fortunate as a student to attend the Drexel Institute in Philadelphia at the time Howard Pyle conducted his illustration class there (1894-1900). She also attended his summer classes at Chadds Ford, Pennsylvania.

Although Pyle's influence is clearly evident in her work, her point of view was often highly imaginative and exotic; she did fairy tales about or for children particularly well. Her pictures were well adapted to books, and in addition to such magazines as *Harper's Bazar, Collier's, St. Nicholas* and *The Saturday Evening Post,* she illustrated a number of children's books. She also wrote and illustrated a song book, *The Musical Tree.*

Stilwell also worked in collaboration with Howard Pyle in illustrating his *The Angel and The Child* in sensitive pen-and-ink drawings, as well as with Katherine Pyle (Howard Pyle's sister) illustrating her book *Childhood* and verse published in *Harper's Bazar.* Among her many advertising clients were Wamsutta Mills, Kiddie-Kar, Fleishman's Yeast, H-O Oats, Scranton Lace Company, Rit Dyes, and Williams' Talc Powder.

Sarah Stilwell Weber, *Collier's* cover, March 17, 1906.
The Kelly Collection of American Illustration.

J. Scott Williams.

JOHN SCOTT WILLIAMS, N.A. (1877-1976) was born in England, and studied composition with Fred Richardson at the Art Institute of Chicago. His first illustrations were done as early as 1905 for *The Saturday Evening Post*. In subsequent years, he did work for more than 20 different American magazines. From 1927 to 1934, he also contributed covers regularly for the magazine section of the *New York Herald Tribune.*

Williams later became a designer and painter of mural decorations including those for the Indiana State Library and Historical Building, for Johns Hopkins University and a huge (72-by-28-foot) ferro-porcelain enamel mural for the main concourse of the Union Terminal in Cleveland, Ohio.

John Scott Williams, *Early Traders of the East Indies,* 1918. Collection of John Cleater.

The son of a blacksmith, GEORGE HAND WRIGHT, N.A. (1873-1951) always retained a sympathy for rustic subjects and working people in his illustrations for *The Century, Scribner's, Harper's, The Saturday Evening Post* and other publications. He researched his pictorial material as a reporter, filling innumerable sketch books and making his finished illustrations from these on-the-spot drawings. In fact, many of his sketches were reproduced directly in the magazines as reportorial coverage for accompanying articles. He made no distinction in approach between these commissioned illustrations and the fine arts prints, etchings or pastels to which he restricted himself in his later years.

Wright studied at the Spring Garden Institute and the Pennsylvania Academy of the Fine Arts in Philadelphia. He was a member of the Westport Artists, The Salmagundi Club, the Dutch Treat Club and the Society of American Etchers. Wright served as president of the Society of Illustrators in 1926 and 1927.

F. C. YOHN

FREDERICK COFFAY YOHN (1875-1933) is most noted for his illustrations of historical and battle subjects. He did many reportorial paintings of the War with Spain in 1898, of both the Cuban and Philippine phases of the conflict. He also painted a fine series of historical illustrations to accompany Henry Cabot Lodge's "The Story of the Revolution," published by *Scribner's* magazine. His painting of the Surrender of Fort Sackville to George Rogers Clark in 1779 was the subject of a commemorative U.S. postage stamp in 1929.

Yohn was born in Indianapolis, attended the Indianapolis Art School and the Art Students League in New York where he studied under H. Siddons Mowbray. At nineteen, he made his first illustrations for Harper's periodicals. This was followed by a long

"The Drum-Beat of the Town," by Nelson Lloyd. *The Majesty of the Law,* illustration from the artist's sketch book for *Scribner's Magazine,* November, 1909.

career in illustration with most of the major magazines.

Yohn was one of the founders of the Society of Illustrators, and a collection of his work is in the Cabinet of American Illustration at the Library of Congress in Washington, D.C.

F. C. Yohn, *General Herkimer Directing the Battle of Oriskany,* Utica Public Library.

1910–1920

Victor C. Anderson

George Wesley Bellows

Wladyslaw Theodor Benda

Walter Biggs

Ernest Leonard Blumenschein

Franklin Booth

Paul Bransom

George Brehm

Worth Brehm

Arthur William Brown

Charles Livingston Bull

Charles Shepard Chapman

Howard Chandler Christy

Lafayette Maynard Dixon

Helen Dryden

Walter Jack Duncan

William Herbert Dunton

Charles Buckles Falls

Harrison Fisher

James Montgomery Flagg

Will Frederick Foster

Dan Sayre Groesbeck

Frederic Rodrigo Gruger

William Ely Hill

Arthur Ignatius Keller

Robert L. Lambdin

Frank Xavier Leyendecker

Joseph Christian Leyendecker

Walt Louderback

Angus Peter MacDonall

Charles Davis Mitchell

Wallace Morgan

Harold James Mowat

Rose Cecil O'Neill (Wilson)

Coles Phillips

George Wolfe Plank

William Andrew (Willy) Pogany

Norman Mills Price

Henry Patrick Raleigh

Penrhyn Stanlaws (Adamson)

Frank Stick

Adolph Treidler

John Alonzo Williams

Edward Arthur Wilson

The automobile replaces the horse. *Popular Magazine* cover, June, 1909, by Joseph Christian Leyendecker.

Recruiting poster by James Montgomery Flagg.

"Class War in Colorado," by John Sloan, *The Masses* cover, June, 1914.

THE DECADE 1910-1920

The relationship between the magazines and their readers was remarkably close. Many publications had a "Letters" section for exchanges between editors and the public. Editors vented their views both by direct articles and by an opinionated stable of editorial writers. *McClure's* became (in)famous for its hard-hitting articles exposing unsanitary conditions in the meat packing industry, the monopolistic practices of the Standard Oil Company, and other "muckraking" stories that aroused the citizenry as Thomas Nast had done earlier, and which resulted in national legislative reforms.

On a personal level, readers were quick to report any inconsistencies between the authors' narratives and the illustrators' interpretations thereof. An illustrator was entirely responsible for accuracy, and was answerable to the editor for any errors. A heroine's description in the manuscript could not be pictorially mismatched without triggering scores of protesting letters. More serious factual mistakes could terminate the artist's employment.

At the same time, the relationship between illustrators and art editors was still generally collegial out of mutual respect. Many illustrators had become famous personages to the readers. They rated a byline along with the authors, and to an observant public, each had a recognizable individuality that attracted partisan readers. Some illustrators — particularly those who drew the prettiest women — had fan clubs whose members wrote letters, met regularly, and aped the fashions depicted by their idols.

Established illustrators could now command significant fees for their work, and living expenses were very low, especially before Federal Income Tax. Jessie Willcox Smith's friends called her "the Mint"; the Leyendecker brothers built a chateau in New Rochelle; Rose O'Neill became a wealthy mega-star when she spun off her Kewpie character in dolls, ads, and a comic strip.

Illustrators who had hitherto maintained the academic practice of drawing or painting only from the model, began to be tempted by the time-saving (and cost-saving) practice of posing and photographing the models, giving them many more optional poses available to work from. It was an easy next step to use a Baloptican or pantograph to trace off the photo onto the drawing board or canvas. For years, the offending illustrators kept their photos hidden or the Baloptican in a closet, until the practices became to widely employed that there was no longer need for any subterfuge.

Meanwhile, a rebellion was brewing in the National Academy establishment and a younger radical group of painters was rejecting the classical viewpoint in favor of a more realistic look at the contemporary world. Centered around Robert Henri, these members formed their own association and, known as "The Eight," held an exhibit in 1908 that brought them ridicule as the "Ashcan School." Members such as Everett Shinn, William Glackens and John Sloan continued to illustrate. A committed Socialist, Sloan also contributed his work to *The Masses.* Though the Ashcan artists helped organize it, The Armory Show of 1913 exhibited the more radical cubists of Europe, and the art world began to split into factions of avant-garde, mainstream, and commercial, ending the monolithic art exhibitions of the past.

World War I came late in the decade for the U.S., but it was an intense, patriotic period. The artists not volunteering to fight were keen to contribute to the war effort in the form of posters, billboards, and public painting demonstrations to raise money for the sale of war bonds. Chaired by Charles Dana Gibson, the Committee of Public Information's Division of Pictorial Publicity met regularly to assign the artists' projects. A group of eight prominent illustrators, including Harry Townsend, Harvey Dunn, W. J. Aylward, Ernest Peixotto, Walter Jack Duncan and Wallace Morgan, were commissioned as captains in the Engineers Reserve Corps and sent directly to the Western Front to record the war at first hand. Their paintings and drawings were sent back to the U.S. to encourage further support for the war effort. If not as propagandistic as the military might have liked, these drawings and paintings are now preserved in the Smithsonian Institution and provide an invaluable record of that great conflict.

Victor Anderson, *Circus Pageant*. This opening parade is an outstanding example of Anderson's many paintings of the circus and its performers. Collection of Woodward A. Warwick, Jr.

VICTOR C. ANDERSON
(1882-1937)

was the son of the Hudson River School painter, Frank Anderson. Although his father died when he was only eight, Victor drew and painted from an early age and by the time he attended Pratt Institute in Brooklyn, he was advanced enough to go directly into life drawing class. In the summer he studied with Birge Harrison in Woodstock, New York.

His illustrations soon appeared regularly in the old *Life* magazine, usually of homespun, rural subjects with a whimsical edge, and he was a contributor of their covers and the double center spreads for many years. He also appeared in *Woman's Home Companion, The Ladies' Home Journal, American Magazine, Collier's Weekly, Country Gentlemen, Woman's World* and many other magazines. Anderson also illustrated two children's books, *Tommy Trot's Visit to Santa Claus* and the *Moonbeam Wish Book.*

During these same years, Anderson was painting landscapes for exhibition; he showed at the National Academy, the Salmagundi Club and the Grand Central Galleries in New York,

W.T. Benda

WLADYSLAW THEODOR BENDA (1873-1948) is mostly remembered today because of his beautiful character masks. These creations, uniquely his, occupied much of his career and were adopted for theatre and dance performances around the world.

Benda himself had an international background. He was born in Poznan, Poland, and drew from his earliest years. After a false start in civil engineering at the Krakow College of Technology, he switched to the Academy of Art. Following further studies in Vienna, he came to the United States and began his career as an illustrator.

It was the era of the Pretty Girl on magazine covers, and the "Benda Girl" joined the rest, but she stood out as intriguingly exotic among the American types with her elongated eyes. Her success kept Benda busy working for most of the magazines, from *The Saturday Evening Post* to *The Shriner* for many years.

Benda became an American citizen but was always proud of his Polish heritage and contributed several poster designs for recruiting Polish patriots during World War I.

An example of Benda's exotic beauties; this work combines charcoal and watercolor.

George W. Bellows, illustration for "Men like Gods" published by *Hearst's International*, November, 1922.

Q.W. Bellows.

GEORGE WESLEY BELLOWS, N.A. (1882-1925) exploited a wide variety of artistic experiences in a relatively short lifetime. Born in Columbus, Ohio, he had divided loyalties between art and sport. At the end of his college days at Ohio State, he turned down an offer to play professional baseball and migrated to New York to study under Robert Henri. Henri's teaching was philosophical as much as academic and he encouraged Bellows' own diversity of artistic interests. While still in Henri's painting class, Bellows had a painting accepted for exhibition in the National Academy Annual and he subsequently became a regular exhibitor and consistent prize winner there and in other major shows. Bellows was also involved in lithography; several subjects featured his interest in boxing. During World War I, he produced a series of propagandistic lithographs protesting German war atrocities and the execution of Nurse Edith Cavell who had aided the escape of wounded Allied soldiers.

Bellows was also an active illustrator as an adjunct to the rest of his art career, describing it "as art of quite as high a type as the portrait, landscape or more abstract subject..." In his work Bellows focussed on "the atmosphere of time, and place and character, rather than a photographic portrait." Bellows was a regular contributor to **The Century** magazine and **Hearst's International** and also illustrated **The House of La Milleause.** Bellows was an avid follower of Jay Hambidge's theory of "Dynamic Symmetry" and employed its principles in many of his pictures.

E · L · BLUMENSCHEIN

ERNEST LEONARD BLUMENSCHEIN, N.A. (1874-1960) was among the group of artists who settled early in or near Taos, New Mexico, attracted by the Indian life and picturesque color. Blumenschein painted many award-winning pictures there, and he is represented in several museum collections by his Native American subjects.

This Taos period came comparatively late in his life; earlier he had had an active career as an illustrator in the East. Born in Pittsburgh, Pennsylvania, he had attended the Cincinnati Art Academy and the Art Students League in New York. Later he studied with Constant, Laurens and Collin in Paris. Blumenschein was a very versatile and competent painter with a fresh, unusual viewpoint. Although he worked realistically, there was always strong design underlying his pictures.

For many years, Blumenschein divided his time between New York and New Mexico, eventually settling permanently in Taos.

E. L. Blumenschein, interpretation for MacDowell's "The Indian Suite" for the Steinway Collection, 1918.

Advertising illustration for International Silver, which received an award in the *Fourth Advertising Art Annual*, 1925.
Collection of Houshyar Kashani.

Gospel singing. *Cosmopolitan* magazine, circa 1932.
Collection of Pamela M. and Joseph B. Wright.

WALTER BIGGS, N.A. (1886-1968) represented the South at its best, both as a gentleman and as an artist who painted the South with sensitive artistry and poetic nostalgia.

Biggs was born in Elliston, Virginia, and spent his boyhood there. He arrived in New York to study art at the Chase School, later renamed the New York School of Art. Among his teachers were Edward Penfield, Lucius Hitchcock and Robert Henri. Henri was an especially inspiring teacher who instilled in the students a real desire to work. Biggs was in an unusual class which included Clifton Webb, Eugene Speicher, Edward Hopper, George Bellows, Guy Pene Dubois, Rockwell Kent and W. T. Benda, all of whom became famous in their respective ways.

Biggs himself became a famous illustrator and teacher at the Art Students League and the Grand Central School of Art in New York. His illustrations over the years appeared in *Harper's, Scribner's, The Century, The Ladies' Home Journal, Woman's Home Companion, Good Housekeeping, Cosmopolitan, McCall's,* and others.

He exhibited regularly at the National Academy, the Salmagundi Club, the American Watercolor Society and the Philadelphia Watercolor Society, winning many awards. In 1963, the Society of Illustrators elected him to the Hall of Fame, "For distinguished achievement in the art of illustration." In 1986, the Virginia Watercolor Society arranged a comprehensive retrospective exhibition of Biggs's work at Roanoke College in Virginia.

The House of Rimmon, **Scribner's Magazine.**

As a farm boy near Carmel, Indiana, FRANKLIN BOOTH (1874-1948) wanted to be an artist and so studied pictures in all of the books and magazines available. Most of the reproductions at that time were printed from steel or wood engravings. Mistakenly believing that the drawings were made with pen and ink, he painstakingly copied their character line by line. This was eventually to become the basis for his unique line technique.

Booth described his working methods in the **Professional Art Quarterly** in 1934, "...In doing a drawing it has been my custom first, of course, to lay in my entire conception with the pencil. This penciled sketch is not a completed thing, but a generalization. Parts of this I then draw in more fully and follow immediately with the pen. My drawings are usually somewhat involved and a completed pencil drawing to begin with would, in place, become smudged and lost in the process of inking in other parts. So I proceed and complete a part or section at a time and follow through, in this way, to the outer edges of my drawing. At times in the making of my drawings, in one section or more, a completed picture will be seen in the midst of white paper and penciled suggestions.

"By this method, also, the general relationship of values of the whole drawing, at the start, can be established in one small part. This becomes the guide. The point, therefore, of the beginning of a picture will usually be a place where a section of the darkest dark, the grays and the highest whites appear together."

In an introduction to Robert Frank's 1925 book **Franklin Booth**, a selection of sixty of Booth's drawings, Earnest Elmo Calkins wrote: "Mr. Booth has done more than almost any one man to break down the barrier between the pure art of decoration as applied to the book or magazine page and the same art applied to the advertising page. Anything undertaken by him is approached in the same creative spirit and executed with the same sure touch... His two great qualities are his dexterity with his pen

Date and place of publication unknown.

135

Paul Bransom

PAUL BRANSOM (1885-1979) began drawing animals from early childhood. He was born in Washington, D.C., and after leaving school at thirteen, became an apprentice draftsman assisting with mechanical drawings for patents. This rigorous discipline in drawing, combined with his free-time sketching at the National Zoo, engendered his habit of making a careful analysis and recording of the individual characteristics of each animal he drew. His work later led him to New York, and the chance to take over a vacancy at the *New York Evening Journal* doing a comic strip, "The Latest News from Bugville." He credited Walt Kuhn and T. S. Sullivant (both of whom did animal cartoon subjects then) with having most influenced his career, and "...of course, the greatest of all animal illustrators, Charles Livingston Bull."

During this time he haunted the Bronx Zoo to such a degree that he was permitted to set up a studio at the Lion House. His goal was to draw and paint animals for the magazines. The work in his portfolio so impressed the editor of *The Saturday Evening Post* that he bought, on the spot, four pictures for covers and several other drawings.

Paul Bransom had a long and distinguished career. He illustrated nearly fifty books on wildlife subjects, including Jack London's *Call of the Wild,* and hundreds of stories and articles for almost all of the mainstream magazines. He also painted for exhibition and taught summer classes at an outdoor art school at Jackson Hole, Wyoming.

Paul Bransom, *Escaping Muskrats,* date and place of publication unknown.

Charles Livingston Bull

CHARLES LIVINGSTON BULL (1874-1932) learned about animals almost literally from the inside out. His first job, at sixteen, at Ward's Museum in Rochester, New York, consisted of scraping out the inner linings of animal pelts preparatory to their being mounted. Later, he became an accomplished taxidermist and worked for the National Museum in Washington, D.C., as an expert on the anatomy of birds and animals.

Bull studied at the Philadelphia Art School and continued to focus on animals in the course of his training, soon becoming one of the foremost animal illustrators. Both his taxidermy and paintings were greatly admired by President Theodore Roosevelt for whom he mounted several specimens now in the National Museum. Bull's artwork was also influenced by the Japanese Ukiyo-e woodblock artists, and his compositions reflect that admiration.

For many years, Bull lived directly opposite the Bronx Zoo in New York in order to be able to sketch from living models. A lover of the outdoors, he also made numerous field trips into Mexico and Central and South America where he studied wildlife in its natural habitat. One of his books, *Under the Roof of the Jungle,* is a collection of illustrations and short stories of animal life in the Guiana wilds based on his explorations there. Bull was active in bird-banding for the United States Biological Survey and particularly interested in the plight of the American eagle. To arouse public interest in their preservation, he made many drawings and posters for pictorial publicity. Bull was elected into the Hall of Fame of the Society of Illustrators in 2000.

Charles Livingston Bull, "The Stork of the Woods" by C. William Beebe, *The Century* magazine, July, 1911. Collection of Kathy and David Dunham.

THE SATURDAY EVENING POST

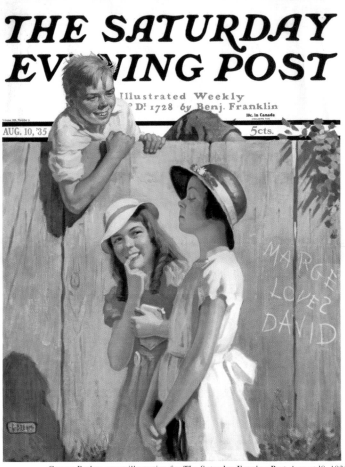

Illustrated Weekly
? D! 1728 by Benj. Franklin

AUG. 10, '35

5cts.

George Brehm, cover illustration for *The Saturday Evening Post,* August 10, 1935. © 1935, 1963 The Curtis Publishing Company.

Both GEORGE BREHM (1878-1966) and his younger brother Worth, had the ability to illustrate stories about children, particularly boys, sympathetically and convincingly. Perhaps this insight developed from their small-town Hoosier upbringing.

George studied at the Art Students League in New York with Twachtman, DuMond, and Bridgman, but did his first illustration for the *Reader's Magazine*, published by the Bobbs-Merrill Company near his home in Indianapolis. On the strength of this work, he obtained an assignment from *The Delineator* in New York, and his career was launched. Over the years, he illustrated a variety of mainstream magazines; his most memorable pictures were done for *The Saturday Evening Post* for story series by Booth Tarkington, Octavius Roy Cohen, and M. G. Chute.

It was a source of pride to Brehm that the *Post* never required him to submit preliminary sketches, although he made many of them for himself before embarking on a finished picture.

WORTH BREHM

WORTH BREHM (1883-1928) became interested in art through his brother George. He prepared a series of sample drawings in Indiana, brought them to New York, and *Outing* magazine bought them all. Publication of these pictures led Harper's to commission him to illustrate *The Adventures of Tom Sawyer* and *Huckleberry Finn.*

He later did general illustration for many magazines; the best known were for the Penrod stories by Booth Tarkington in *Cosmopolitan.* While Brehm had a good color sense, he seldom had the opportunity to use it, since printing in color was still sparingly used because of the cost. Worth usually worked in charcoal. He was never at a loss for models, and regularly used the neighboring children for his characters, sometimes dressing them in period clothing, as befitted the story.

Brehm's work was always in demand from magazines and advertisers until his untimely death at age 44.

Worth Brehm, frontispiece illustration for *The Adventures of Huckleberry Finn* by Mark Twain, Harper & Brothers, 1912.

137

Arthur William Brown, illustration for "Oh Annice!" by Alexine Heyland, published by *Woman's Home Companion,* June, 1918.

"Yankee lawyer, Ephraim Tutt" was made famous by Brown in a long series of stories by Arthur Train; this one was published in *The Saturday Evening Post* ©1938, 1966 by the Curtis Publishing Co.

ARTHUR WILLIAM BROWN (1881-1966) had one of the longest and most prolific careers of any American illustrator. Born in Canada, he landed his first job as a chalk-plate artist on the local Hamilton, Ontario, *Spectator* at the age of fifteen. After four years of this, he saved enough money to go to New York where he studied at the Art Students League under Walter Appleton Clark.

Brown's first chance at magazine illustration came when a friend was assigned to write a circus article for *The Saturday Evening Post.* "Brownie" took a chance that he could make acceptable accompanying drawings and spent six weeks traveling with the circus. The *Post* was pleased with the result and the published illustrations became the first of a long and popular association which lasted over forty years.

During this time, he had the opportunity to collaborate with many famous authors, including O. Henry, F. Scott Fitzgerald, Booth Tarkington, and Sinclair Lewis. In the early stages of their careers, Frederic March, John Barrymore, and Joan Blondell all posed for him.

Brown was a long-standing active member of the Society of Illustrators. He was its president from 1944 to 1947, and in 1964 was unanimously voted into the Illustrators Hall of Fame.

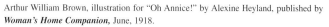

Charles Chapman, "Redwoods," published by *The Ladies' Home Journal*, May, 1921.

CHARLES SHEPARD CHAPMAN, N.A. (1879-1962) was an illustrator and painter whose compositions convey a feeling of spaciousness and dignity. The effect is partly achieved through his use of scale, but subject matter also contributed. He was interested in the beauty of nature, especially in forest subjects, painted with much imagination and experimentation in textural and color effects.

Chapman was born in Morristown, New York, and attended the New York School of Art, studying under William Merritt Chase and Walter Appleton Clark. He and Harvey Dunn conducted a school of illustration in Leonia, New Jersey, for several years in the 1910s. He also taught at the Art Students League, exhibited regularly and won many awards. His painting, "In the Deep Wood," was purchased by the Metropolitan Museum of Art in New York.

Howard Chandler Christy, *The American Girl,* from **Liberty Belles**
©1912, The Bobbs, Merrill Company.

Howard Chandler Christy .

HOWARD CHANDLER CHRISTY (1873-1952) had a long, colorful and varied career. He had made his early reputation when he accompanied the United States troops to Cuba during the Spanish-American War, and articles illustrated by his drawings were published by **Scribner's** and **Leslie's Weekly**. One picture for **Scribner's**, the "Soldier's Dream" [of his girl] became famous, and from then on, he specialized in drawing and painting beautiful "Christy Girls" for **McClure's** and other magazines.

Christy's painting technique was sumptuous, and he was in great demand as a portraitist. Among the notables he painted were President and Mrs. Calvin Coolidge, Secretary of State Charles Evans Hughes, Amelia Earhart, Lawrence Tibbett, Mrs. William Randolph Hearst, and Benito Mussolini.

Christy was also a popular teacher and at various times instructed at Cooper Union, the Chase School, New York School of Art and the Art Students League.

In later years, he painted several murals, including his well-known decorative nudes for the Café des Artistes in New York City. His most famous mural is a 20- by 30-foot canvas, "The Signing of the Constitution," which hangs in the rotunda of the Capitol in Washington, D. C. He was elected to the Society of Illustrators Hall of Fame in 1980.

HELEN DRYDEN

The career of HELEN DRYDEN (1887 - date unknown) is most closely linked with **Vogue** magazine, the publication she was so long associated with and for which her cover art helped to define its look in the 1910s and 1920s. Her sources of inspiration were eclectic, based on influences as wide-ranging as Art Nouveau, Aubrey Beardsley, children's books from the turn of the century, the primitive Italian painters, and Japanese prints. Although she was affiliated with the American **Vogue,** her covers were regularly also published on the London and Paris editions.

Dryden's subjects were rich and sensuous in color, witty and lighthearted, but also with a haughty air of elegance. The longevity of her career with **Vogue** (almost from its beginning, from 1911 to 1923) was due in great part to her adaptability. She was able to sense and stay at the forefront of the latest artistic trends as well as to interpret the latest nuances of fashion changes. (Credit should also be given to the **Vogue** publisher Condé Nast and art director Heyworth Campbell for giving her so much freedom of expression.)

Dryden was born in Baltimore and studied at the Pennsylvania Academy of the Fine Arts. Her first artwork was advertising done for Strathmore papers, followed by fashion advertising and costume design. In the later twenties, she left **Vogue** and worked for a wide variety of advertising and fashion clients, including Stehli Silks, Galey and Lord, Knox Hats, Kayser stockings and in addition to covers for **The Delineator** magazine. She was involved with redesigning the Studebaker auto in 1937. Dryden was a member of the Society of Illustrators, the Artists Guild, and the Society of Independent Artists.

Helen Dryden, V*ogue* cover, December, 1922 (London edition).
Collection of the Delaware Art Museum.

Maynard Dixon, "The Road Agent" by
Stewart Edward White, *Collier's Weekly*
magazine, circa 1912.

LAFAYETTE MAYNARD DIXON (1875-1946) was born into a family of ranchers in Madera County, California. His own predilections were toward drawing, not ranching, but his subjects throughout most of his artistic career were nearly always of the West and its inhabitants. Dixon was essentially self-taught and learned most from studying nature and from his artist friends, such as Edward Borein and Xavier Martinez.

The authenticity of his pictures brought him ready work from *Harper's Weekly*, *Sunset*, *McClure's*, *Collier's*, *Scribner's*, and other magazines, and also from book publishers. Dixon moved East to work as an illustrator in New York during the years 1907 to 1912. Dixon was not at home with romanticized fiction of the West, however, and decided to return to California where he embarked on a series of murals for the Mark Hopkins Hotel in San Francisco, the State Library in Sacramento, two murals for Pacific Mail steamships and many other projects. He also began to paint for exhibition, and joined a group of like-minded artists, the "Painters of the West."

His mural projects had a major effect in the direction of his painting style which became increasingly more stylized and geometric, but rooted in the basic elements of the earth and sky. Dixon married the photographer Dorothy Lange, and both were involved in labor and social conflict causes. During the Depression, his controversial "Forgotten Man" paintings won him support but no sales. He eventually returned to more universal themes and today his paintings are highly prized and included in many major museum collections. Dixon was elected into the Hall of Fame of the Society of Illustrators in 1997.

Walter Jack Duncan, *"The Bride repairs to the wedding seated behind her future Lord,"* from "In Shakespeare's America" by William Aspenwall Bradley, published in *Harper's Monthly*, August, 1915.

WALTER JACK DUNCAN (1881-1941) came from Indianapolis to study at the Art Students League in New York. His first work was for *The Century* magazine in 1903. *Scribner's* sent him on assignment to England in 1905, and he subsequently worked for *McClure's, Harper's* and other major publishers. In 1917, he was one of the artists commissioned as officers in the Engineer Corps, who went overseas with the A.E.F. to record the fighting at the Front.

Duncan specialized in pen-and-ink, which he employed with great directness and skill. The directness resulted from his very careful and thoroughly worked out preliminary studies. He had been attracted to line drawing because of its harmony with the text of the printed page and his interest in both books and writing. Most of his best friends were writers, among them Christopher Morley, for whom he illustrated several books, including *Tales from a Rolltop Desk, Pipefuls,* and *Plum Pudding.* Duncan himself wrote and illustrated a scholarly book entitled *First Aid to Pictorial Composition,* published in 1939 by Harper's.

W. Herbert Dunton, *Ready for the Kill*, Hunting Deer, Wyoming, 1907. Collection of William and Dorothy Harmson.

W. Herbert Dunton

WILLIAM HERBERT DUNTON (1878-1936), who was born in August, Maine, studied at the Cowles Art School in Boston and the Art Students League of New York under Andreas M. Anderson, Joseph De Camp, Frank Vincent DuMond, William Ladd Taylor, E. L. Blumenschein, and Leon Gaspard. This thorough training is evident in his accomplished and well-composed illustrations for *Harper's*, *Scribner's*, *Everybody's*, and other magazines. His subject matter was spirited, usually of the West or other outdoor scenes, and his use of color was effectively keyed to the mood.

Dunton settled permanently in Taos, New Mexico, in 1921. In addition to his illustrations, he also painted and exhibited widely, received a Gold Medal in Nashville, Tennessee, in 1927, and won many other awards. He is represented in the collections of the Peoria Society of Applied Arts (Illinois), the Witte Memorial Museum, San Antonio, Texas, the Museum of New Mexico in Santa Fe, and by murals in the Missouri State Capitol, Jefferson City, and in the White House, Washington, D.C.

Falls

CHARLES BUCKLES FALLS (1874-1960) approached illustration primarily as a designer. Realism in his pictures was always tempered by a strong sense of decoration. This quality was first exemplified in the fine posters he made for many of the old vaudeville theatres in New York, now collectors' items.

In 1918, he designed a famous "Books Wanted" poster for the Armed Forces, which provoked an enthusiastic flow of books to the training camps and gained him an international reputation.

His pictures were ideally suited for books. As a personal project, he created an ABC book for his daughter, then three years old, comprised of colored woodcuts. After publication, this book became a classic of its kind.

Falls's long career included much illustration for advertising, magazine covers, and editorial art for fiction and articles. In addition, he taught at the Art Students League in New York and produced his own woodcuts and paintings. He executed numerous mural commissions, among them a series of historical portraits for the ceiling of the New York State Office Building at Albany.

Falls made two trips to Haiti where he found the native culture a great stimulus for woodcuts, drawings, and paintings, as represented here.

141

"Gathering Honey," published in *Scribner's*, 1907, also *The Harrison Fisher Book*, 1908, and *Pictures In Color*, 1910.

"Oh! Promise Me" (Robin Adair).
The Saturday Evening Post cover, January 15, 1910.

HARRISON FISHER (1875-1934) showed an early interest in drawing, and from the age of six was instructed by his father, Hugh Antoine Fisher, a landscape painter. When his family moved from Brooklyn to San Francisco, Harrison studied there at the Mark Hopkins Institute of Art. At sixteen, Fisher had begun to make drawings for the *San Francisco Call* and later for the *Examiner.*

Soon after returning to New York, Fisher sold two sketches to *Puck* magazine, which also hired him as a staff artist. He soon became noted for his ability to draw beautiful women, and his Fisher Girl became a rival to those of Gibson and Christy. The American Girl was a favorite theme for magazines then, and Fisher provided cover illustrations for most of them. For many years, he was under an exclusive contract to paint the covers for *Cosmopolitan,* but eventually he restricted himself to portraiture, including many actresses and theatrical personalities. In 1997, he was inducted into the Hall of Fame of the Society of Illustrators.

The Ladies' Home Journal cover, February, 1913.

142

Angry Uncle Sam with empty treasury. **Judge Magazine** cover, April 24, 1920. Flagg was most often his own model for Uncle Sam.
Collection of Irwin and Rita Silver.

Young woman in kimono, a typical Flagg pen-and-ink illustration, date and place of publication unknown.

The Fencer, Collection of the Lotus Club in New York where it is affectionately known as "Puss in Boots."

JAMES MONTGOMERY FLAGG (1877-1960) lived with gusto. He epitomized the public concept of the handsome, bohemian artist, surrounded by beautiful models, dashing off pictures with sheer exuberance of talent. In Flagg's case, this was nearly true. He worked rapidly and easily in all media and with any subject matter. Humor and satire were his special forté. Early in his career he did a cartoon feature entitled "Nervy Nat," and for many years he illustrated the zany characters of the P. G. Wodehouse stories and created the prototypical interpretation of the valet, "Jeeves." His rapid portrait studies and incisive caricatures were prized by many prominent sitters.

For over thirty years he turned out an immense amount of work, including many posters during World War I. Probably his best known illustration was the famous "I Want You" Uncle Sam recruiting poster. Over four million copies of this were printed and distributed throughout the country.

Flagg was a painter of serious portraits, too. He exhibited in the Paris salon of 1900, at the National Academy of Design, and the New York Watercolor Club. He was elected to the Society of Illustrators Hall of Fame in 1980.

Will F. Foster, *The Explanation*, circa 1920s.
Collection of Charlaine and Richard Voorhies.

WILL FREDERICK FOSTER, A.N.A. (1882-1953) first had ambitions to be a violinist, but after seeing a painting by Albert Beck Wenzell, changed his goal from music to art. His first art instruction was under Frank Duveneck and Joseph Henry Sharp at the Cincinnati Art Academy. His studies were then continued at the Art Students League and the New York School of Art with Robert Henri and William Merritt Chase. He was able to support himself and to gain practical experience by painting theatrical backgrounds for the Lee Lash Studios at Union Square.

In 1903, he sold his first illustration to *Life* magazine in a style which very closely resembled that of Wenzell, with great emphasis on technique in depicting high society. Gaining popular appeal, Foster was soon illustrating for almost all the major magazines, which included *Collier's*, *Cosmopolitan*, *Everybody's*, *The Delineator*, *The Saturday Evening Post*, *Associated Sunday Magazine*, *Harper's Monthly*, *Munsey's*, *Harper's Bazar*, *Red Book*, and *Liberty.*

During World War I, Foster served in France, with his own ambulance, as a member of the American Volunteer Motor Ambulance Corps.

On his return, Foster resumed his illustration career, but moved to Chicago where he also taught at the Art Institute. He then began to paint for exhibition and became an Associate in the National Academy of Design. Eventually, Foster settled in Los Angeles and a painting career which included work with Willy Pogany on a mural project at the Hearst estate in Wyntoon, California. Foster was made an honorary lifetime member of the California Art Club, and taught many students who went on to successful careers. An excellent biography of the artist, *William Frederick Foster, A.N.A.* by Phyllis Settecase Barton was published by Richlane Publishing in 1987.

DAN SAYRE GROESBECK (1879-1950) had a theatrical flair in his work that made him a natural for his long affiliation with the Hollywood film industry as a movie poster artist. Among his most memorable projects were *The Buccaneer* for Cecil B. DeMille, *The Good Earth*, *Gone with the Wind*, and a series of portraits of the stars of the epic movie *For Whom the Bell Tolls*, which included Ingrid Bergman and Gary Cooper.

Groesbeck started his career as artist and reporter for a newspaper in Los Angeles and he illustrated many of O'Henry's newspaper stories. He soon worked as a magazine illustrator as well, with assignments from *Harper's Weekly* magazine*, The Century, Success, Everybody's, Liberty, McClure's, Collier's, The Literary Digest*, and *Cosmopolitan.*

Groesbeck also illustrated many books, including Jack London's *The Strength of the Strong*. Among his other artistic projects were printmaking and a huge mural in the Santa Barbara Courthouse.

'"My mamma won't let me talk to show-boat folks,"' illustration for "Show Boat" by
Edna Ferber, published by **Woman's Home Companion**, April 1926.

The Father, published by the **Woman's Home Companion**, August, 1928.

FREDERIC RODRIGO GRUGER (1871-1953) wrote on the
subject of Illustration for the Encyclopedia Britannica, describing
the illustrator's role as follows:

"...Illustration may become a great art, but to become a great
art, it must be creative. It cannot hope to compete with the camera
in the reporting of facts. It has no business with the outer shell of
things at all. It deals with the spirit. Dealing with the
psychological aspects is a great opportunity and a serious
handicap. Presupposing a pictorial presentation of the relations of
people, the telling of a story is inevitable. A great and simple
story, akin to truth, or a poor and trivial one, akin to meagre facts,
may be told about the same incident—depending upon the insight,
the vision of the artist. The nature of the story portrayed is the
measure of the artist who portrays it..."

Gruger demonstrated this insight and vision in his work. His
pictures were always concerned with the larger themes, and
although the original drawings were actually quite small, they
appear monumental in scale. In an era when color was limited and
expensive to reproduce, the majority of Gruger's illustrations
were rendered in black and white.

He worked in a medium developed out of his earlier
reportorial work for the **Philadelphia Ledger.** The drawing was
made with Wolff pencil, rubbed with a stump or eraser, often over
an underlying wash. This combination produced a full range of
values, particularly a rich, velvety black. The board he drew on
was an inexpensive cardboard used by newspapers for mounting
silver prints. It had a receptive, soft surface, and became known
as "Gruger board" among the illustrators who adopted it.

Gruger graduated to **The Century** magazine and worked
subsequently for most other publishers and many advertisers, but
was most closely identified through his 40-year-long career with
The Saturday Evening Post. In 1981, he was elected into the
Society of Illustrators Hall of Fame.

A typical Hill satirical drawing from "Among Us Mortals."

WILLIAM ELY HILL (1887-1962) was born in Binghamton, New York. He attended Amherst College and contributed to the college newspaper. After selling some of his sketches to the old *Life* magazine, he decided to become a professional cartoonist. He freelanced from 1910 to 1917, being published in *Puck, McClure's, Metropolitan* and other magazines. He began a weekly series of sketches of human foibles with sly commentary for the *New York Tribune Magazine* in April 1916, entitled "Among Us Mortals." The page was immediately popular, and published in book form within the year; eventually the feature was syndicated to newspapers throughout the country, with a different theme each week. At its height, the page was published in over 50 papers nationwide with a combined circulation of over 15 million. It continued for 42 years until his eventual retirement in 1960. Hill also illustrated the book cover for F. Scott Fitzgerald's *The Beautiful and Damned* in 1922. A large collection of the artist's work is in the archives of the Dallas Public Library in Texas.

Psychology students are familiar with a Hill drawing, "My wife/My mother-in-law," which is reproduced in textbooks as a classic example of perceptual ambiguity.

W. E. Hill, *The Retort Brutal: "Here in this gallery are portraits of some of my ancestors" "Humph! They evidently looked on Eugenics as a joke!"* Cover design for *Puck,* March 26, 1913.

Robert Lambdin, illustration "For the Sake of Phyllis," by Shirley L. Seifert, *The Ladies' Home Journal,* November 1920. Collection of Diane and Jordan Berman.

ROBERT L. LAMBDIN (1886-1981) was one of the many illustrators who came out of the training school of the newspaper art departments. Born in Dighton, Kansas, he studied for a year at the Read Art School in Denver. His first job was with the *Rocky Mountain News*; he then worked for the *Denver-Republican,* and eventually the *Kansas City Star,* where he became an illustrator of feature stories.

From this training ground, Lambdin came to New York in 1917, and obtained his first story manuscript from the old *Green Book* magazine. In subsequent years, he illustrated for nearly all the major magazines, took on advertising commissions, and illustrated many books.

Much of Lambdin's early work was done in pen and ink, following the style of J. C. Coll, and he continued illustrating for the Sax Rohmer stories for *Collier's Weekly* after Coll's death in 1921. As line drawing went out of vogue, he worked in watercolor washes and oils.

A member of the National Society of Mural Painters, Lambdin painted a series of murals in New York City, for the Post Office in Bridgeport, and for several schools and banks in other Connecticut locations.

Vignetted illustration for *Hills of Han,* by Samuel Merwin, The Bobbs-Merrill Company, 1919.

Coney Island, 1919, place of publication not known.

Life on a Riverboat, representative of Louderback's later experimental style.

Walt Louderback

The brushwork of WALT LOUDERBACK (1887-1941) was broad and direct, with few subtleties. Yet for all his sledge-hammer technique, romanticism permeated his pictures. His characters and their emotions seemed heroic, larger than life. For the reader, the vicarious thrill of participating in the adventure was thereby heightened as well.

Louderback was born in Valparaiso, Indiana, and studied at the Art Institute of Chicago. He lived in Europe for some time in the 'twenties, delivering his pictures by ship. He was a regular contributor to **Hearst's International**, **Cosmopolitan**, and **Good Housekeeping**. A painter as well as an illustrator, he experimented with a stylized Cubist-influenced approach. He was awarded the Daughters of Indiana Purchase prize and given a special honorable mention at the Hoosier Salon in 1933.

Ichabod Crane Romancing, from **The Legend of Sleepy Hollow,** The Bobbs-Merrill Company, 1906.
Sanford Low Memorial Collection, The New Britain Museum of American Art.

"How Happy Could I be With Either." Date and place of publication unknown.

A first response to the work of ARTHUR IGNATIUS KELLER (1866-1924) is one of admiration for the brilliant facility of his technique. His preliminary studies, especially, show a mastery of drawing itself, the result of his long training both at the National Academy of Design and with Loefftz in Munich. The studies are not a stolid assimilation of facts, however, but rather a poetic exploration of the forms, freely and directly made from the model for his own use in the finished illustrations.

An original sense of interpretation and poetry is carried further in his compositions, often crowded with figures, but controlled through passages of light or accents of carefully placed tones rendered with an impression of great spontaneity.

Some of Keller's finest illustrations were painted for Washington Irving's **The Legend of Sleepy Hollow,** and his work accompanied stories by major authors including Bret Harte, Rupert Hughes, and J. P. Marquand. An important collection of his pictures is included in the Cabinet of Illustration in the Library of Congress and he is represented in the New Britain (Connecticut) Museum of American Art. In 1989, Keller was inducted into the Society of Illustrators Hall of Fame.

Women conversing over tea. Unpublished watercolor.

149

Born in Germany, FRANK XAVIER LEYENDECKER (1877-1924) was very competent, but was always overshadowed by his older brother. Frank's work was more sensitive, and highly detailed, but it never matched the assurance and dramatic poster quality of Joseph's. Frank also painted covers for leading publications such as **The Saturday Evening Post**, **Vogue**, and notably, **Collier's**. He later designed stained-glass windows.

The two brothers never married, and worked together in a large studio estate in New Rochelle. The fascinating story of their personal lives is related in Norman Rockwell's book, **My Adventures as an Illustrator.**

JOSEPH CHRISTIAN LEYENDECKER (1874-1951) was born in Montabaur, Germany, and came to America at the age of eight. Showing an early interest in painting, he got his first job at 16 in a Chicago engraving house on the strength of some large pictures he had painted on kitchen oilcloth. In the evenings after work, he studied under Vanderpoel at the Chicago Art Institute, and saved for five years to be able to go to France to attend the Académie Julian in Paris.

Upon his return, as a thoroughly trained artist with immense technical facility, Leyendecker had no difficulty in obtaining top commissions for advertising illustrations and cover designs for the leading publications. His first **Post** cover was done in 1899, and he did well over 300 more during the next 40 years. Among the most famous of these was his annual New Year Baby series.

His advertising illustrations made his clients famous. The Arrow Collar Man was a byword for the debonair, handsome male, and women wrote thousands of love letters to him in care of Cluett Peabody & Company. His illustrations for Kuppenheimer Clothes were equally successful in promoting an image of suited elegance. He was elected to the Society of Illustrators Hall of Fame in 1977.

A major retrospective exhibition of Leyendecker's work was mounted at the Norman Rockwell Museum in Stockbridge, Massachusetts, in 1997-98.

Cover for **The Bookman**, 1902. The Kelly Collection of American Illustration.

A. Unpublished poster illustration: Men at forge. "Save Coal; Keep the War Fires Burning." U.S. Fuel Administration, ca. 1917. Leyendecker submitted this poster design during World War I, with the typical caption of that time; the design was, however, not published. The artist later re-submitted the painting as a World War II poster, after overpainting it with the slogan, "Work for Victory," in stencil-style letters suitable for the 1940s. The work was not reproduced for the latter war either. The overpaint was later removed and the original design recovered.

B. Magazine cover, © **The Saturday Evening Post,** December 22, 1923. © 1923, 1951 by The Curtis Publishing Co.

C. Magazine cover, The First Aeroplane Ride, **Collier's Weekly,** August 28, 1909. The Kelly Collection of American Illustration.

D. Magazine cover, The Brass Ring, **The Saturday Evening Post,** September 6, 1930. © 1930, 1958 by The Curtis Publishing Co.

E. Magazine cover, Automobile Number, **Collier's Weekly,** January 6, 1917.

A

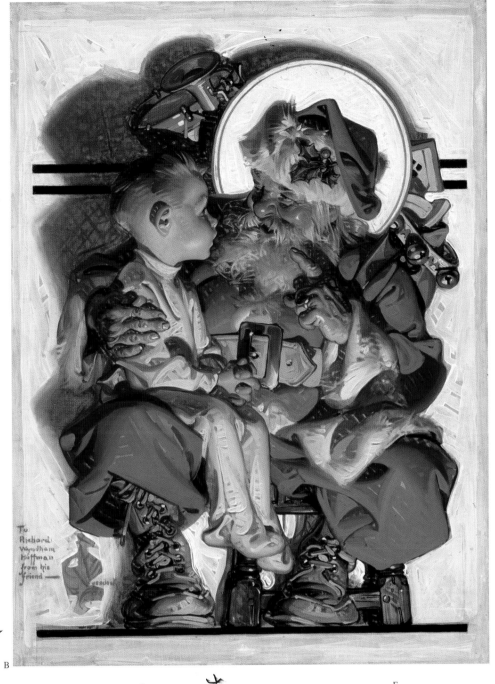

B

C

D

E

151

ANGUS MAC DONALL

ANGUS PETER MacDONALL (1876-1927) came from St. Louis, and was one of the early group of artists who settled in Westport, Connecticut, to make it a famous art colony. MacDonall was especially popular with fellow-illustrators because of his three beautiful daughters who were in great demand as models.

MacDonall illustrated for many magazines, including *Scribner's, Harper's, American,* and *The Ladies' Home Journal.* For several years, he provided a regular double-spread illustration of human interest or social commentary for the old *Life* magazine.

CHARLES D. MITCHELL

CHARLES DAVIS MITCHELL (1887-1940) had great drawing facility, and most of his illustrations were done in a technique somewhat similar to that of his friends, Arthur William Brown and Harold Mowat.

Mitchell drew very attractive young women, successfully adapting their changes in style and taste over three decades. His work appeared regularly in *McCall's*, *Redbook*, *Good Housekeeping*, *Cosmopolitan*, *Pictorial Review*, *The Delineator*, *The Saturday Evening Post*, *The Ladies' Home Journal*, and other magazines.

Originally from Wilmington, Delaware, Mitchell had his studio in Philadelphia, and was a member of the Artists Guild of New York, and the Art Club in Philadelphia.

Cover illustration for *The Saturday Evening Post,* February 28, 1920.

C. D. Mitchell, illustration for "Beauty's Promise" by Kathleen Norris, *Liberty* magazine, May 1, 1926.
Reprinted by permission of Liberty Library Corporation. © 1926, 1954 Liberty Weekly, Inc.

Wallace Morgan, *The Final Examination,* cover for *Life* magazine, Commencement Number, June 4, 1925.

WMORGAN —

At the turn of the century, WALLACE MORGAN, N.A. (1873-1948), went through the tough school of the newspaper artist as did his friends Glackens, Shinn, and Sloan. Forced to draw a constant variety of subjects under pressure, on-the-spot or from memory, he emerged with such facility that he never needed models in his later work. His finished renderings were attempted directly, without preliminary sketches. If difficulties arose, he'd abandon the drawing for a new try. This was the secret of his inimitable spontaneity.

Morgan viewed the human comedy with warmth, wisdom, and humor laced with irony. He traveled across the country with Julian Street, sketching while Street wrote *Abroad at Home*. This ran serially in *Collier's* and was published in 1914 by The Century Company.

Morgan was one of the official artists assigned to the A.E.F. during World War I. His quick sketching was especially useful for documenting life in the trenches, as it was for his swift, salty portraits of top brass. This special flavor made his style a natural for illustrating the P. G. Wodehouse stories which ran in *The Saturday Evening Post* and other magazines.

Morgan taught at the Art Students League at intervals, from 1905 to 1929. He was made an honorary member of the League, a rare honor reserved for such greats as Bellows, Pyle, Henri, DuMond, and a few others. He was elected a full member of the National Academy in 1947, and received an award from the National Institute of Arts & Letters.

Morgan's clubs included The Players, the Century Club, and the Dutch Treat Club; he was president of the Society of Illustrators from 1929 to 1936. In January, 1949, a memorial exhibition of Wallace's drawings was given at the Society, of which he was honorary president at the time of his death.

MOWAT.

HAROLD JAMES MOWAT (1879-1949) always preferred to work in black and white, obscuring many of the details, highlighting others out of an overall tonality. In this method, he shared the approach of a number of fellow artists: Henry Raleigh, Arthur William Brown, and especially Frederic R. Gruger.

Mowat was born in Montreal, Canada, and received his art education at the New York School of Art. His first illustrations were made for the *American Magazine*. He lavished so much time and expense in models' fees on his work that he barely broke even. This kind of conscientiousness made him a relatively slow worker throughout his career, and he never became as popular with the public as did many of his more facile co-workers. However, other illustrators respected him and acknowledged his dedication. He illustrated for most of the top publications, including *The Saturday Evening Post, The Ladies' Home Journal, McCall's, Woman's Home Companion,* and *Redbook*.

Describing his work, Mowat said, "My medium is a piece of white paper and a black pencil. Sometimes a bit of dirt from the floor. When at work, I'm at it from early morning until far into the night. I haven't known the meaning of true peace of mind for years, but I infinitely prefer the uncertainties and struggles of the illustrator to any other game on earth."

Harold James Mowat, illustration for "With a Modern Leading Lady" by Fanny Kilbourne; *The Saturday Evening Post,* July 9, 1927. © 1927, 1955 by the Curtis Publishing Co.

Rose O'Neill, illustration for "Baby's First Christmas," by Margaret G. Hayes, *Harper's Bazar*, December, 1910.

The familiar and pleasing legacy of ROSE CECIL O'NEILL (WILSON) (1875-1944) is the Kewpie doll. The dolls were patterned after her drawings of Kewpies — fanciful, elf-like babies who solved all sorts of problems in a bumbling, good natured way. Her drawings and stories were immensely popular for over two decades, appearing first in *The Ladies' Home Journal,* then as a special feature in *Good Housekeeping* magazine. The dolls were sold all over the world.

A self-trained artist, Rose O'Neill became nationally known as an illustrator at nineteen. Her pictures appeared in *Puck, Truth,* the old *Life, McClure's,* and *Harper's*. She was also a novelist and poet, a member of the Societé des Beaux Arts in Paris, and the Society of Illustrators in New York, which elected her into its Hall of Fame in 1999.

GEORGE WOLFE PLANK (1883 - no date) had a strong influence on a very specialized segment of the field of illustration, both in America and in Europe, through his covers for *Vogue* magazine. His own influences appear to have been quite eclectic, drawing upon European sources, such as Alphonse Mucha, Gustav Klimt and contemporary poster artists.

Unlike other *Vogue* artists, his covers relied less on specific fashions than on a timeless dramatic effect of costume combined with fantasy. In fact, one of his earliest covers (of 1911), depicting a woman riding a peacock, could be repeated in 1918 without appearing dated. Plank continued to be a dominant force for *Vogue* up through 1927, sharing the covers with a handful of other artists, such as Helen Dryden, Georges LePape, and F. X. Leyendecker. Plank insisted on, and received, complete freedom in his designs for Condé Nast, who nurtured the independent and expatriate artist with advances and praise. Later, as British and Paris editions were established, additional artistic influences gained ascendancy, challenging Plank's dominance and taking the covers into a more radically "moderne" direction. It is a credit to his great versatility and artistry, however, that he was able to continue so long in a field marked by fickle and frequent changeability.

George W. Plank, cover for *Vogue*, April 15, 1915.

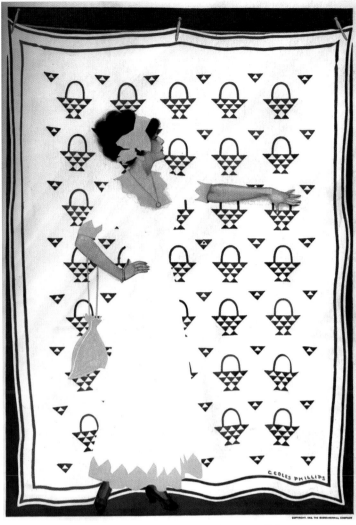

Illustration from *A Young Man's Fancy*, The Bobbs-Merrill Company, 1912.

Advertising illustration for Holeproof Hosiery Company, 1921.

C. COLES
PHILLIPS

The "Fadeaway Girl" was the particular hallmark of COLES PHILLIPS (1880-1927): he pictured fashionably beautiful young women, using the device of tying the figure into the background by either color, value, or pattern. This approach produced an intriguing poster-like effect of great simplicity; actually it was based on the most careful preliminary planning of shapes to carry out the illusion of the full figure.

Phillips was born in Springfield, Ohio, and had his first pictures reproduced as a student contributor to the *Kenyon College Monthly* magazine. Upon graduation, he tackled a New York career, first as a solicitor for an advertising agency. Later he formed his own studio of artists, including the young Edward Hopper. After further study at the Chase Art School, he decided to launch his art career. His first effort was sold to the old *Life* magazine as a double-page spread. When *Life* began to use color on its covers, the "Fadeaway Girl" made her initial appearance and was an instant success. For many years thereafter, she appeared in a variety of guises, but was always a patrician beauty.

Phillips prided himself on being a good businessman-artist. His pictures, both for covers and for advertising campaigns including Holeproof Hosiery and Community Plate Silverware, were the product of a meticulous, cerebral craftsman.

Cover for *The Saturday Evening Post*, October 2, 1920.
Collection of the Delaware Art Museum.

WILLIAM ANDREW (WILLY) POGANY (1882-1955) was a native of Hungary and his first studies in Budapest and Paris were in engineering. Success in caricaturing led him to pursue an art career, first in London and then in America. His influences were the Oriental artists and illuminated books, and much of his career was devoted to book illustration.

Among his many successes were **The Rubaiyat**, **The Kasidah**, **The Children's Book of Northern Myths**, **The Witch's Kitchen**, **The Frenzied Prince**, **Sonnets from the Portuguese**, **Fairy Flowers**, **Forty-Four Turkish Fairy Tales**, **Tales of the Persian Genii**, **A Treasury of Verse for Little Children**, **Stories to Tell the Littlest Ones**, **Hungarian Fairy Book**, and **Gulliver's Travels**. He also painted murals, did etchings, designed stage settings, exhibited widely, and was a favorite in Hearst's magazines.

Two illustrations by Willy Pogany from **The Tale of Lohengrin** (G. G. Harrap & Co., London, 1913), which he completely designed and lavishly illustrated.

Penrhyn Stanlaws, cover illustration for the **Metropolitan Magazine,** February, 1914.

PENRHYN STANLAWS (PENRHYN STANLEY ADAMSON) (1877-1957) was the younger brother of illustrator Sydney Adamson and changed his name to avoid a confusion of identity. Actually, their work was too dissimilar to have caused any problem. Penrhyn was completely absorbed in the presentation of pretty girls and did so with great success. Their beautiful faces appeared on many magazines, including **The Saturday Evening Post**, **Associated Sunday Magazine**, **Hearst's International**, and **The Metropolitan** magazine.

Another contribution to the arts was his construction of a studio building, the Hotel des Artistes, at 1 West 67th Street in New York, which is now a famous landmark for having housed so many prominent artists over the intervening years.

Stanlaws wrote plays for theater and movies, and he spent the latter part of his career in Hollywood.

The Battle of the Frigate United States and the Macedonian, **True** magazine, November, 1947. Collection of Robert Klatt.

NORMAN MILLS PRICE (1877-1951) never fully received the popular recognition that his work deserved. Because he was so intently interested in historical subjects, he restricted his work to these almost exclusively.

The dedication and artistry he brought to his work, however, was especially appreciated and respected by a select group — his fellow-illustrators. His painstaking research into every detail made each picture an authentic documentary, but the detail was never allowed to detract from the dramatic concept of the illustration itself. Although Price made effective use of tone and color, his pen-and-ink drawings were especially effective, exhibiting a full range of values and textural effects.

Price was born in Canada, studied art there and in London and Paris. By 1912, he had established himself in New York and had begun to work for American publications. Some of his most successful illustrations were done for a long series of historical novels by Robert W. Chambers for **Liberty** magazine. He was a charter member of the Guild of Free-Lance Artists, and honorary president of the Society of Illustrators at the time of his death.

Slave Auction, Society of Illustrators Thirty-seventh annual exhibition catalog, 1939.

Illustration for "The Return of Virtue," **Collier's** magazine, September 9, 1950.

A

A. Illustration for "Easy to Kill," by Agatha Christie, **The Saturday Evening Post,** November 19, 1938, ©1938, 1966 by the Curtis Publishing Company.
B. Advertising illustration for Maxwell House Coffee, 1926. Collection of Mr. and Mrs. James Cheek.
C. Couple meeting at a party. Publication and date unkown.
D. Group looking out to sea. Publication and date unkown.

B

RALEIGH

HENRY PATRICK RALEIGH (1880-1944) was one of the most prolific of all our illustrators. In spite of this, he consistently maintained high quality and good taste in all his work. His renderings in black and white, or line combined with wash or colored inks, were ideally suited to the printed page.

In his illustrations, he was able to translate the mood and setting of the story with easy versatility. His pictures look as though they flowed from pen or brush. He was probably at his best with society subjects and for many years depicted the ultimate in fashionable society for his series of Maxwell House Coffee advertisements.

Raleigh was born in Portland, Oregon; he later moved to San Francisco, and left school at the age of twelve to help support his mother and sisters. Befriended by the head of the coffee firm for which he worked as a clerk, Raleigh was sent to Hopkins Academy, a San Francisco art school, for two years.

At 17 he got a job in the art department of the **San Francisco Bulletin**, where he learned to make drawings for the chalk-plate process. As an artist-reporter, he was later sent on assignments to sketch newsworthy subjects such as fires, floods, or corpses at the city morgue.

By the age of 19, Raleigh was working for the **San Francisco Examiner** as one of its highest paid artists. His work attracted the attention of William Randolph Hearst, who sent him to New York to work for the **Journal.** He next went to the **New York World,** doing special features three days a week. This experience served as a base for his entry into the magazine field.

Raleigh was also a serious etcher and produced many fine plates, but these were seldom exhibited. Among his many awards were the Shaw Prize for Illustration at the Salmagundi Club in 1916 and the Gold Medal for Advertising Art in America in 1926. He was elected to the Society of Illustrators Hall of Fame in 1982.

C   D

Typical example of Stick's covers of *Sports Afield* and other outdoors magazines. Collection of the Delaware Art Museum, Copeland Memorial Fund, 1974.

FRANK STICK

FRANK STICK (1884-1966) came from a frontier background; he was born in the Dakota Territories. Early on, he became an ardent sportsman. He was also ambitious to become an artist and moved to Chicago to enroll in the Art Institute. From there, he applied for an opening in the Howard Pyle School in Wilmington and was accepted against long odds. After graduation, he and fellow-Dakotan Harvey Dunn shared a studio in Wilmington.

He naturally gravitated to hunting and fishing subjects, and his first professional work was painted for outdoor magazines, prints, and calendars, featuring camping, wild animals, hunting, rifles, and fishing tackle. He also wrote and illustrated his own articles for *St. Nicholas*, *Field & Stream*, and other magazines.

Fishing was his particular favorite. He co-authored and illustrated a book on surf fishing, and illustrated several fishing books by Zane Grey; as friends, they often fished together. This specialty led Stick to a long-term project of painting specimens of some 300 East Coast fresh- and salt-water fish. A resulting book, *An Artist's Catch*, was published posthumously by his son. Stick was also a conservationist and activist on behalf of the Wright Brothers Memorial at Kitty Hawk, the Cape Hatteras National Seashore Recreational area, and for the establishment of the Roanoke Island National Park. He was also active in public affairs and was elected mayor of Interlacken, New Jersey, in the 1920s.

ADOLPH TREIDLER

ADOLPH TREIDLER (1886-1981) was born in Westcliffe, Colorado; he studied at the California School of Design in San Francisco and with Robert Henri in New York. He first illustrated for *McClure's* magazine in 1908, then made pictures or cover designs for *Harper's*, *The Century*, *Scribner's*, *Collier's*, *The Saturday Evening Post*, *Woman's Home Companion*, and many national advertisers.

Posters were his particular specialty. During World War I, Treidler designed numerous Liberty Loan and recruiting posters, and was Chairman of the Pictorial Publicity Committee for the Society of Illustrators during World War II.

His travel subjects were especially effective. For many years, he painted posters for the Bermuda Tourist Offices, and the Furness Bermuda and French Lines, and through these associations traveled the world over.

Treidler was a member of the Art Directors Club, a charter member of the Artists Guild, and life member of the Society of Illustrators which elected him into its Hall of Fame in 1999.

Adolph Treidler, cover illustration for *Tavern Topics*, January, 1920.

John Alonzo Williams

John Alonzo Williams, illustration for "Home Sweet Home" by Sophie Kerr, published in the **Woman's Home Companion.**

JOHN ALONZO WILLIAMS, N.A. (1869-1951) painted in watercolor throughout his career. Since most illustrations were reproduced in black and white in his era, a large portion of his work was done in wash, usually transparent. This example in color was published later in his career, but is typical of his style.

Williams studied at the Art Students League and the Metropolitan Museum of Art school. During the same years he was illustrating, he also painted regularly for exhibition. In addition to his membership in the Society of Illustrators, he was also a member of the Artists Guild, the Salmagundi Club, the American Watercolor Society and the New York Watercolor Club. He was elected a full member of the National Academy in 1947.

E. A. Wilson, advertisement for "La Salle," the Cadillac Motor Car Co., 1927.

Faw

EDWARD ARTHUR WILSON, A.N.A. (1886-1970) was elected to the Society of Illustrators Hall of Fame in 1962 in recognition of his long and distinguished career as an illustrator. He was born in Glasgow, Scotland, spent his childhood in Rotterdam, Holland, and later came to America where he studied at the Chicago Art Institute, and with Howard Pyle in Wilmington, Delaware.

Wilson's first commissions were for advertising, and he was most active in this field for many years. During the 1920s and '30s, he won many awards and honorable mentions in annual exhibitions of the Art Directors Club in New York. Notable among the campaigns he contributed to were La Salle, Cadillac, Coral Gables Corporation, and Victrola. He also illustrated for most of the major magazines during this period.

His first book illustrations were done as woodcuts for a collection of sea chanteys, entitled **Iron Men and Wooden Ships**. It was a labor of love as well as a great artistic success. He had always been most interested in nautical subjects and this book established his reputation as an authority. Over the next several years, he illustrated **Full and By,** a collection of drinking songs, **The Pirate's Treasure,** which he also wrote, **Robinson Crusoe, Two Years Before the Mast,** and **Treasure Island**. Altogether, he illustrated well over sixty books, many of them for the Limited Editions Club and The Heritage Press.

After his death, a large collection of Wilson's originals was donated to the University of Oregon Library.

HOME FOR CHRISTMAS

Colored wood block print for **Iron Men and Wooden Ships.** It was this image, designed as a Christmas greeting in 1921, that started Wilson on his new career as a book illustrator.

1920–1930

Samuel Nelson Abbott
Rolf Armstrong
Maginel Wright (Enright) Barney
Ralph Barton
Arthur Ernst Becher
Maurice L. Bower
Charles Edward Chambers
James Alfred (Rene) Clarke
Thomas Maitland Cleland
Lee Conrey
Fred Cooper
Dean Cornwell
Miguel Covarrubias
Charles Defeo
Erte (Romain De Tirtoff)
Walter H. Everett
Maud Tousey Fangel
Clark Fay
Nancy Fay
Laurence Fellows
Anton Otto Fischer
John Richard Flanagan
Ernest Fuhr
Arthur D. Fuller
Robert Graef
Gordon Hope Grant
William Heaslip
John Held Jr.
Albin Henning
Guy Hoff
Frank B. Hoffman
Lynn Bogue Hunt

Walter Beach Humphrey
Rea Irvin
Lyle Justis
William Henry Dethlef Koerner
Robert Lawson
William Andrew Loomis
Louise Patterson Marsh
Neysa Moran McMein
Harry Morse Meyers
William Oberhardt
Russell Patterson
Herbert T. Paus
James Moore Preston
May Wilson Preston
William Meade Prince
Ellen Bernard Thompson (Pyle)
Grant Tyson Reynard
Norman Rockwell
Tony Sarg
John E. Sheridan
J. Allen St. John
Frank Street
Donald Teague
Earle Grantham Teale
Saul Tepper
Leslie Thrasher
Raeburn L. Van Buren
John Vassos
Loran Frederick Wilford
Charles David Williams
Edgar Franklin Wittmack

Norman Rockwell represented America's idealized vision of its rural and small town past. *The Buggy Ride,* cover for ***The Saturday Evening Post,*** September 19, 1925; Printed by permission of the Norman Rockwell Family Trust.

Teaching an Old Dog New Tricks
John Held's "flappers" and "sugar daddies" kicked up their heels and ridiculed the past. *Life* magazine cover, February 18, 1926.

THE DECADE 1920-1930

Illustrators of the '20s faced a fast-changing society that wanted no part of the past. The young doughboys returning after World War I were not interested in the League of Nations or in going back to the farms from which they came. They were a restless vanguard of a population rapidly shifting from a rural and small town America into an urban social structure. Henry Ford was adding to the mobility by making cars that almost everyone could afford. Real estate agents were plotting out lots in Florida and California and selling them to absentee speculators.

Prohibition, passed while the troops were away at war, was increasingly flouted. Speakeasies, bootleggers, and rum-runners flourished. The collegiate crowd adopted the defiant attitudes of the veterans, carrying them several steps further. Young women enthusiastically joined the rebellion. Shingled hair, shortened skirts and rolled down stockings or garters were hallmarks of the "Flapper" that John Held Jr. immortalized in his popular stylized drawings. Rudolph Valentino in his movie role as "The Sheik" made them all yearn to be Shebas. Young men pomaded their hair in emulation and played their roles in plus-fours or bell-bottomed trousers; a hip flask and a coonskin coat completed the attire.

The market for illustration boomed along with the rest of the post-war economy. The great expansion of advertising in magazines needed artists to picture the products or to portray the people using them. Color printing was becoming increasingly affordable. The market for escapist fiction was immense, and some of America's best short story writers and novelists, like F. Scott Fitzgerald, J. P. Marquand, Edna Ferber, and Ernest Hemingway were being published in the family magazines, ably illustrated by Dean Cornwell, Walter Biggs, Charles Chambers, James Montgomery Flagg, and many others, who shared by-lines with the authors and were celebrities themselves.

Norman Rockwell, whose showcase was the cover of ***The Saturday Evening Post,*** was captivating the public by recording the past that was rapidly disappearing and idealizing it with a respectability that it never quite had. His humor was universal and timeless however, and loved by everyone but the art critics, who ignored everything but the European avant-garde. Rockwell himself took a hiatus to Paris and tried to become "au courant," but ***The Saturday Evening Post*** quickly nipped that in the bud, and he continued his natural inclination to see the best in us with camera-like clarity.

The Rockwell and J. C. Leyendecker anecdotal magazine covers were being alternated with Pretty Girl creations of Howard Chandler Christy, Coles Phillips's "Fadeaway Girls" and Harrison Fisher's beauties. Neysa McMein of the Algonquin Round Table crowd also held open house in her own capacious studio where celebrities like Alexander Wolcott, Harpo Marx and Jascha Heifetz could kibbitz while she created cover girls in pastel for *McCall's* and other magazines.

The New Yorker, founded in 1925, attracted an audience among the urban intelligentsia, and presented a fresh look through its covers by Rea Irvin, Constantin Alajalov, and Peter Arno. Other magazines like ***Vanity Fair, Smart Set*** and ***College Humor,*** had found sophisticated partisan subscribers and new artists to illustrate their contents. The talents of Miguel Covarrubias, Ralph Barton, Anne Fish and Russell Patterson combined witty intelligence and satire expressed in unconventional, simplified line drawings.

Many of the mainstream illustrators were still an effective force. Harvey Dunn returned from his stint with the A.E.F., and resumed his great influence as artist and teacher, thus extending the Howard Pyle tradition. Most illustrators had all the work they could handle and there was plenty of room for newcomers.

Advertising, then centered in the Midwest, developed a strong, identifiable Chicago style through artists such as Frederic Mizen, Philip Lyford and Haddon Sundblom. They had their eyes on the virtuoso, *alla prima* painters in Europe, such as Anders Zorn, and John Singer Sargent.

With all of these influences intermixed, it was a wide open period of plenty — in art, ideas and money. Very few sages foresaw its end in a crash at the close of the decade.

S.N.
ABBOTT

The life and work of SAMUEL NELSON ABBOTT (1874-1953) would be better remembered today except for the artist's own modesty and sense of loyalty. Born in Illinois, he had saved up enough to study in Paris under Laurens and Constant. Upon his return to the United States, he was given his first assignment to design the cover and fashion illustrations of a catalog for the Hart, Schaffner & Marx clothing manufacturers. This began a collaboration that generated twenty-five years of full color style booklets. Though such advertising work was rarely signed, his work was identifiable by other illustrators, designers and agencies and greatly admired. According to Peter Helck, Abbott rejected offers for any other commercial illustration assignments out of deference to his first employer, although he did some editorial illustration and cover paintings for *The Ladies' Home Journal, The Saturday Evening Post* and *Collier's.* His fine sense of design and color deserve much greater recognition.

Samuel Nelson Abbott, cover illustration for *The Ladies Home Journal,* November, 1920.

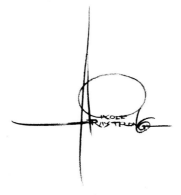

The flamboyant signature of ROLF ARMSTRONG (1890-1960) accompanied hundreds of equally spectacular portrayals of beautiful models and movie stars, glamorized to the ultimate degree. For many years his covers appeared on *Photoplay, College Humor* and *Metropolitan Magazine;* his girls also advertised products such as hosiery, underwear, lipstick and phonograph machines. But his greatest success was in the calendar field; Brown & Bigelow printed his subjects by the million for many years.

Armstrong's success was based on solid training—three years under John Vanderpoel at the Art Institue of Chicago and further study under Robert Henri in New York. To pay for his education, he gave boxing and baseball lessons — he was a good athlete — and worked at many other odd jobs.

Early on, Armstrong discovered pastel and learned to exploit its special qualities in depicting flesh under complex lighting arrangements which contributed an exotic flavor to his beauties.

Rolf Armstrong, *Paris Nude,* a huge 84"x 48" painting done by Armstrong in France in 1919-1921. Collection of Jim Steranko.

MAGINEL WRIGHT BARNEY

MAGINEL WRIGHT ENRIGHT — later BARNEY — (1881-1966) was the youngest of three children; the eldest, Frank Lloyd Wright, always encouraged his sister's talent for drawing and painting. When her school days were over, she attended the Chicago Art Institute. Then she worked for several years at an advertising agency before her marriage to Walter J. Enright, another young artist. They soon came to New York where, eventually, both became successful illustrators.

Maginel's earliest published efforts were pictures for some fantasies by one Laura L. Bancroft, later unveiled as that "Wizard of Oz," L. Frank Baum. Maginel illustrated juvenile classics — *Heidi, Hans Brinker of the Silver Skates* — and innumerable fairy tales. She was largely responsible for revolutionizing the quality of illustration in children's readers (until then fairly insipid) and over the years painted cover designs and illustrations for many magazines: *McClure's*, *Everybody's*, *Woman's Home Companion*, *The Ladies' Home Journal*, *Woman's World*, and others.

When work became scarce during the Depression, she took up "painting in wood," landscapes, and flower pictures. There were two exhibitions of these at the Marie Sterner Gallery and one at the Sagittarius Gallery, in New York.

In 1965, she published her childhood reminiscences in a book, *The Valley of the God-Almighty Joneses*.

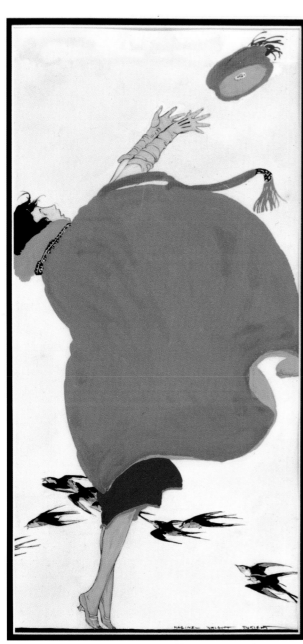

Maginel Barney, cover design, *Woman's World.*

RALPH BARTON (1891-1931) was multi-talented: an artist, cartoonist, and drama critic. Born in Kansas City, Missouri, he was drawn to the sophisticated New York City scene. After studying art in Paris, he made Manhattan his artistic base, with intermittent sojourns to France. His early work appeared in *Judge* and *Puck* magazines, followed by *Cosmopolitan*, *Vanity Fair*, *Smart Set*, and the old *Life* magazine for which he also served as drama editor.

Barton had a very stylized and decorative approach, usually satiric, drawn in thin lines and flat tone or color. This was an ideal technique for books, and he illustrated for many authors, such as Anita Loos's *Gentlemen Prefer Blondes* (1925) and *But Gentlemen Marry Brunettes* (1928), Heywood Broun's *Nonsensorship* and Balzac's *Droll Stories.* At the height of his career, he took his own life following the breakup of his stormy marriage to actress Carlotta Monterey.

Ralph Barton, *Vive Priape*, unpublished.

·ARTHUR·E·
·BECHER·

ARTHUR ERNST BECHER (1877-1960) was born in Germany, and brought by his parents to Milwaukee at the age of eight. After high school, he worked for a lithography firm and studied art with local teachers. He also joined a local sketch club whose members included Carl Sandburg, Herman Pfeifer, William Aylward and Edward Steichen, under the tutelege of Louis Mayer. Becher, Aylward and Pfeifer all later became students of Howard Pyle; Becher enrolled in the Wilmington school in 1902 and 1903. In 1908, in London on assignment by *Appleton's* magazine, he took advantage of the opportunity to go to Germany where he studied further under Otto Strutzel in Munich.

Becher contributed illustrations regularly to magazines such as **The Ladies' Home Journal**, **Scribner's**, **McCall's**, and **Pictorial Review**, and many of his pictures had an allegorical theme or accompanied poetry. Although much of his work was done with carbon or charcoal pencil, he was a good colorist and worked in oils at a large scale. He also painted landscapes and exhibited them occasionally; he was a member of the Society of Illustrators, the Artists Guild and the Salmagundi Club.

Arthur Becher, *Courtier watching Woman at Mirror.* Painted in Munich, 1908. Collection of R. MacIntyre.

MAURICE LINCOLN BOWER (1889-1980) was born in Ohio and like most youngsters who become artists, began to draw at a very early age. His family moved to Philadelphia, and Bower went through high school there and for a year at Pennsylvania State University. Learning about the classes being taught by Pyle alumnus Walter Everett, he switched to the School of Industrial Art in Philadelphia. While still a student, he began to be published in **St. Nicholas** magazine. Contracts totaling four years' work for the Hearst Syndicate followed.

Bower had always wanted to live and work in Paris, and when offered the opportunity by the McCall Corporation to do so, he accepted at once. For five years, he spent the spring and summer in Paris and the fall and winter in Philadelphia; this wonderful life ended with the stock market crash. He continued to work for most of the major magazines and painted several **Saturday Evening Post** covers in the 1930s. In his early work, Bower worked in charcoal, often on toned paper with chalk highlights. Later his pictures became more realistic and literal as he switched to oils.

Maurice Bower, *"Hereabouts, if a man and a woman are seen twice together in public, the murder is out,"* from "Keeping the Peace," by Gouverneur Morris, **Cosmopolitan** magazine, April, 1924.

C. E. Chambers

CHARLES EDWARD CHAMBERS (1883-1941) was born in Ottumwa, Iowa, studied at the Chicago Art Institute, and later at the Art Students League in New York with George Bridgman.

His illustrations were extremely skillful, marked by subtlety of value and color. He early learned to adapt his method of painting for the best possible reproduction, and to insure fidelity of printing, he often followed the assignments through to the hands of the engraver who made the plates.

Chambers divided his time almost equally between editorial and advertising assignments. Among his advertising commissions was an outstanding series of portraits of musicians for Steinway & Sons. His distinctive illustrations for billboards, notably for Chesterfield and Palmolive Soap, set high standards for that field.

He painted a dramatic series of cover designs for **Redbook**, worked under exclusive contract for **Cosmopolitan** magazine for several years, and illustrated such authors as Pearl Buck, Louis Bromfield, Faith Baldwin, and W. Somerset Maugham.

Among his numerous awards was the second Altman Prize at the National Academy of Design exhibition in 1931 for his portrait of watercolorist and fellow-illustrator John Alonzo Williams.

Charles Chambers, illustration for "The Price of Love" by Arnold Bennett, serialized in **Harper's Monthly** magazine, 1913-14.

René Clark, cover illustration for **Woman's Home Companion,** April, 1926.

R.C.

RENÉ CLARKE (1886-1969) began life in Eustis, Florida, as James Alfred Clarke. He grew up in Springfield, Massachusetts, studied art briefly at the Connecticut League of Art Students in Hartford, Connecticut. While working on a number of printing and advertising jobs, he came under the influence of the French illustrator René Vincent. Later, he joined the advertising firm of Calkins & Holden, Inc., where he talked so much about his friend that the name René became transferred to him, and remained.

Although Clarke did some editorial illustration for **Woman's Home Companion, Collier's, McCall's,** and **Judge,** the greater part of his work was concerned with advertising. His drawings and high-key watercolor designs for such clients as Wesson Oil, Snowdrift, Crane Paper Company and the Hartford Fire Insurance Company, were distinguished by artful simplicity and elegant taste.

His work was awarded four gold medals and numerous other awards from 1920 to 1950 in annual Art Directors Club exhibits. As art director, and later president, of Calkins & Holden, he had a considerable and constructive influence in maintaining high artistic standards in the field of advertising art.

167

Thomas Cleland, "The Programme," illustration for the West Virginia Pulp and Paper Co., 1926.

THOMAS MAITLAND CLELAND (1880-1964) achieved three or four distinguished reputations. He was known to one group of people as the foremost decorative designer in America; to another, as a great printer; to still another as a great typographer. T. M. Cleland was not only an illustrator, he was a master in the world of graphic arts. Describing Cleland at a dinner in his honor at the Grolier Club, host George Macy said, "When he accepts a commission, every detail of it bears the touch of his genius."

At 16, Cleland became a printer's apprentice; at 20, he had designed a typeface with ornaments and gone into the printing business for himself. For two years prior to World War I, he was art director of **McClure's** magazine.

Combining printing with designing and illustrating, Cleland was one of the first to make institutional advertising a high art. His clients included Locomobile, Cadillac and Rolls-Royce. One notable project was the "Grammar of Color" which he wrote, designed and printed for the Strathmore Paper Company in 1914.

His sojourns in Paris confirmed his preoccupation with 18th-century subjects. His first commission for the Limited Editions Club was a two-volume **Tristram Shandy**; he spent three years on a masterful interpretation with more than 62 color drawings. Two Fielding books followed—**Jonathan Wilde** and **Tom Jones** — which related text and illustrations in the finest tradition of the art of printing.

Cleland was a member of The Players, the Century Club, the Coffee House Club, the Architectural League of New York, and the American Institute of Graphic Arts.

Lee Conrey, "Visitors to a Mayan Temple," **American Weekly,** date unknown. Collection of Barry Klugerman.

LEE F. CONREY (1881- unknown) was a legendary master of the drybrush technique, oftentimes with added watercolor washes. Little has been found about the details of his life, but publicly, he was well-known to the readers of **The American Weekly**, the Sunday supplement section of Hearst's newspapers. Generally, his assignment was to produce a sensationalized version of the latest scandal, or homicide, or a lurid exposé of other human foibles.

Conrey seemed to do this with complete acceptance, taking it in stride, but occasionally he was able to find subjects more worthy of his obviously great talents. Even so, the frequency of his deadlines precluded sufficient research time or posing of models, and one must be somewhat skeptical of the veracity of the information presented in some of his pictures. His great skill and stylish renditions are to be admired nonetheless.

An Oregonian by birth, FREDERICK GOSS COOPER (1883-1961) migrated to San Francisco because of an early inclination toward art. His intended studies at the Mark Hopkins Art Institute lasted but one day, and instead he landed a tedious but instructive job of making drawings of farm equipment and hardware for a 1400 page catalog. By its end he was ready for virtually anything!

A move to New York led to his introduction to Charles Dana Gibson and to J. A. Mitchell, publisher of the old *Life* magazine. Cooper's spot drawings became a lively feature there, and his affiliation with *Life* lasted for some thirty years. Another long-term relationship was formed with the New York Edison Company, beginning with free-lance work; eventually his illustrations became their official hallmark, both for the corporate image and the *Edison Weekly* magazine. He produced their newspaper ads, flyers, billboards, letterheads, and calendars for over three decades. In addition to those accounts, Cooper free-lanced for *Collier's*, *The Subway Sun*, Wrigley's Gum and other clients.

Cooper had an abiding interest in lettering which played a key part in many of his picture designs, sometimes taking them over. Although the typeface, "Cooper Black" by Oswald Cooper is often misattributed to Frederick, he designed several of his own alphabets, often manipulated to suit the needs of his designs. He wrote and designed a treatise on the "Art of the Monogram" which was not published during his lifetime, but incorporated into *The Lettering and Graphic Design of F. G. Cooper* by Leslie Cabarga, published by the Art Direction Book Company in 1996.

Advertising poster for Bull Durham, ca. 1928.

COVARRUBIAS

MIGUEL COVARRUBIAS (1904-1957) was a multi-talent in the arts who followed several diverse pursuits. His reputation rests on the witty and devastating caricatures he produced in the 1920s for the *New York World, Vanity Fair, Life, Time, Holiday, McCall's, Fortune,* and other publications. These included improbable pairings of celebrities such as Mussolini and Huey Long, or renditions of his fellow cartoonists John Held Jr. and Ralph Barton.

Born in Mexico City, Covarrubias came to New York on a Mexican Government scholarship. His art found a ready audience and he pursued illustration and caricature work until the 1930s when he was commissioned to paint murals for projects in Mexico City and San Francisco. Winning a Guggenheim fellowship permitted him a long stay in the South Seas, which culminated in his illustrated book *The Island of Bali*, published in 1937.

His interests in Mexican culture led him to studies in archaelogy and anthropology, particularly centered on the Olmec culture. Many of the objects unearthed in the excavations under his direction are now housed in a special wing at the Archaeological Museum of Mexico named in his honor.

Other arts affiliations included the Directorship of Department of Dance of the National Institute of Fine Arts, the Board of Directors of Popular Arts and Industries; he also served as an adviser to the Secretary General of the United Nations.

Sally Rand vs. Martha Graham, *Vanity Fair*.

A

B

A. Story illustration from "The River's End," by James Oliver Curwood, *Good Housekeeping,* 1919. The Kelly Collection of American Illusration.

B. *Her face reflected the radiance of the rising sun...,* from "The Valley of the Silent Men," by James Oliver Curwood, *Good Housekeeping,* 1919.

C. Illustration for "A Black Angel," *Red Book* magazine, August, 1917. Private Collection, Courtesy of Berry-Hill Galleries, Inc.

D. Book illustration,"House of Nazareth," *City of the Great King,* by William Lyon Phelps, *Cosmopolitan Book Corporation,* 1926.

E. Mississippi Riverboat, *True* magazine cover.

C

DEAN CORNWELL

DEAN CORNWELL, N.A. (1892-1960) was a brilliant, left-handed painter who dominated the illustration field for many years. As a student of Harvey Dunn, he inherited much of the teachings of Howard Pyle and later studied under Frank Brangwyn, the British muralist. To these influences Cornwell added his own monumental style, both intricate and bold.

Cornwell was an untiring worker who made a great many preliminary studies and trial compositions before attempting a final painting in oils. These drawings have great interest by themselves for the beauty of their draftsmanship.

Prolific and in great demand, he illustrated for a wide variety of magazines and advertisers, but found time as well to paint many important murals. Notable among them were those for the Los Angeles Public Library, The General Motors mural at the 1939 World's Fair in New York, The Tennessee State Office Building, the Eastern Airlines building in Rockefeller Center, and the Raleigh Room at the Hotel Warwick in New York City.

Dean was president of the Society of Illustrators from 1922-1926 and was elected to its Hall of Fame in 1959. He taught illustration at the Art Students League in New York, and by example created a "Cornwell School."

E

D

Charles DeFeo, Bandito's arm being bandaged.

Charles De Feo

CHARLES GRAND DeFEO (1892-1978) was never a formal student at the Pyle School, but was accepted as an apprentice when he was not yet 16. His job was to clean Pyle's palette and brushes and, among other duties, take Pyle's pet poodle for a walk! He completed his art studies at the Pennsylvania Academy, The Art Students League and in the art colony of Provincetown, Massachusetts.

While he did some general story illustrations for *Cosmopolitan*, *Liberty*, *McCall's*, and other national magazines, DeFeo's primary focus was on sports and adventure, including many cover designs for the Pulp magazines. In his work, DeFeo painted decoratively with great emphasis on the arrangement of

negative and positive shapes, while amalgamating the diverse influences of his teachers Harvey Dunn, Frank Vincent DuMond and Charles Hawthorne.

Defeo taught at the Grand Central School of Art and was a member of both the American Watercolor Society and The Salmagundi Club in New York.

ROMAIN DE TIRTOFF (1892-1990) created his nom-de-brosse, "ERTÉ", from the french pronunciation of his initials. Born in St. Petersburg, the son of a Russian admiral, Erté was interested in art from childhood. After studying painting under Ilya Repin, he moved to Paris in 1912, and quickly became caught up in the fashion world. Joining the House of Poiret, he developed an intuitive sense of the unlimited possibilities of dress, and applied his fantasies to fashion, costume design for theatre, opera, the film industry and musical comedy.

Embarking on his own career, he illustrated his ideas in highly decorative and imaginative paintings that helped define the new Art Deco look. In 1915, he signed a ten-year exclusive contract to do all the covers for *Harper's Bazar* (later renewed for another ten years), and continued to design costumes for international clients from Hollywood to the Folies Bergère in Paris. He became involved with every part of production from set designs to costumes and accessories even to shoes, umbrellas, mirrors and floral arrangements. He helped create the spectacular effects for the George White Scandals, the Ziegfeld Follies, and several movies with Louis B. Mayer. Among his later projects were the design of a ballet for television and the creation of sets and costumes for Rossini's Barber of Seville in 1945. In 1967, an exhibition of 170 of his works was entirely bought out by the New York Metropolitan Museum of Art. His autobiography was published in his eighties, and he continued producing up until his death at 98.

Erté, cover design for *Harper's Bazar*, January, 1918.

Walter Everett, *Couple in Garden*, **Good Housekeeping** magazine, date of publication unlnown. The Kelly Collection of American Illustration.

WALTER H. EVERETT (1880-1946) lived on a farm in southern New Jersey and, as an art student, used to bicycle from home to the Wilmington ferry, cross the Delaware, and ride up to Howard Pyle's composition class on Franklin Street. He also worked his way through the School of Industrial Arts in Philadelphia, where he later taught illustration for many years.

Everett developed a highly personal approach to illustration. His later paintings were almost like posters, with flattened shapes and unmodeled forms, relying largely on color and value changes to delineate the objects. Unfortunately, most of his pictures were reproduced only in black and white, but those which did appear in color, particularly in **The Ladies' Home Journal,** were brilliant and impressionistic.

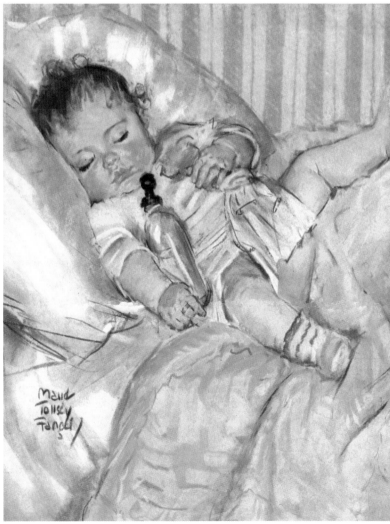

MAUD TOUSEY FANGEL (1881-1968) had a special knack for drawing and painting babies that was both artistic and extremely appealing. Because she always insisted on drawing directly from life, each of her babies was a specific individual and her pictures reveal extra insight and understanding of infant characteristics that could only have been gained in this way. Much of her work was done in pastels, appropriate to her subjects in range of color and textures.

For many years, she was very productive as a cover designer for **The Ladies' Home Journal, McCall's, Woman's Home Companion** and many other magazines, as well as an illustrator for national advertising by the Cream of Wheat Corporation, Swift & Company, Squibbs Cod Liver Oil and other products for children.

Born in Boston, Fangel attended the Massachusetts Normal Art School, Cooper Union and the Art Students League in New York. She also executed many portraits in addition to her published illustrations.

Maud Tousey Fangel, *The High Cost of Babies,* illustration for **The Ladies' Home Journal,** October, 1923.

173

Clark Fay, illustration for "Scratch 'im Cow-Punch!" by Courtney Ryley Cooper. Published in *The Country Gentleman*, September, 1928.

CLARK FAY (1894-1956) traveled East from Denver, Colorado, to study illustration with N. C. Wyeth and Harvey Dunn. Most influenced by Dunn, Fay's work is bold and direct, with emphasis placed on the broad picture concept.

Fay's success came early. He illustrated for *The Saturday Evening Post*, *The Delineator*, and other major publications for several years. Fay was an ardent polo player and captained the polo team of the Fairfield County Hunt Club in Connecticut. After divorcing his wife, he moved abroad to the village of Chamant, outside Paris; later he lived in London, where he continued to pursue his career in illustration.

NANCY FAY

NANCY FAY (1893-1930) was the first wife of Clark Fay and enjoyed a successful career along with her husband, while raising two children. As a couple, they took an active part in the social life of the early Westport, Connecticut art colony. Her humorous and spirited work was freely drawn in compressed carbon pencil and watercolor washes; it appeared regularly in *The Ladies' Home Journal*, *Woman's Home Companion* and other women's magazines in the 1920s.

Nancy Fay, advertisement for Atwater Kent Radio, November, 1925.

Laurence Fellows, illustration for "Embracing Opportunity" by J. A. Waldron. *Judge,* circa 1914.

LAURENCE FELLOWS (1885-1964) is probably best remembered for his outstanding series of Kelly-Springfield Tire advertisements in the 1920s. The drawings were in black-and-white, with large areas of white space and an economy of line; they combined good taste with a restrained sense of humor.

Fellows was a native of Ardmore, Pennsylvania, and studied at the Pennsylvania Academy of the Fine Arts. This was followed by a stay in England and France where he continued his studies. By the 'twenties, he had returned to America, and contributed a great many humorous drawings for *Judge* and the old *Life* magazines.

His technique was ideally suited to fashion illustration; his work also appeared regularly in *Vanity Fair*, *Apparel Arts*, and *Esquire*.

JOHN RICHARD FLANAGAN (1895-1964) carried on the tradition of Joseph Clement Coll in his pen-and-ink technique. For many years, he was type-cast with the same kind of subject matter in his illustrations for the "Dr. Fu Manchu" stories by Sax Rohmer for *Collier's* magazine. His renderings were much more controlled than Coll's, but as demonstrated here, he also used a richly varied pattern of textures and values in his paintings.

Flanagan was born in Sydney, Australia, and apprenticed to a lithographer at the age of 12. At the same time he enrolled in art school. When he completed his art training, he came to the United States, where he obtained his first assignment from *Every Week* magazine to illustrate a story with a Chinese background. This and subsequent stories established him as an authority on the Orient, although he did not visit there until many years later on an assignment for the French Line.

Actually, Flanagan did a wide variety of illustration, in full color as well as with pen and ink or scratchboard. In later years, he designed stained-glass windows and also served as an instructor at the York Academy of Arts in York, Pennsylvania, from 1954 until the time of his death.

John Flanagan, *Uldine and Huldbrand* from **Merlin's Isle — Relics from an Enchanted World.** Collection of Barry Klugerman.

ANTON OTTO FISCHER

The marine paintings by ANTON OTTO FISCHER (1881-1962) are as authoritative as only a working sailor could make them. Born in Munich, Germany but orphaned as a boy, Fischer ran away to sea at 16 and spent eight years before the mast on a variety of sailing ships. Paid off in New York, he stayed to apply for American citizenship and to teach seamanship on the school ship, "St. Mary's." He later served as a hand on racing yachts on Long Island Sound and worked as a model and handyman for the illustrator A. B. Frost. When he had saved enough money, he spent two years at the Academie Julian in Paris under Laurens.

Returning to the United States, Fischer sold his first picture to *Harper's Weekly* in 1908, around the time he moved to Wilmington to receive critiques from Pyle. *Everybody's* magazine sent him the first of several Jack London stories. In 1910, he began a 48-year association with *The Saturday Evening Post*, which included illustrating seialized characters such as Peter B. Kyne's "Cappy Ricks," Norman Reilly Raines's "Tugoat Annie," Guy Gilpatrick's "Glencannon," as well as serials for Kenneth Roberts and Nordoff and Hall.

In 1942, he was given the rank of Lieutenant Commander as "Artist Laureate" for the United States Coast Guard and was assigned North Atlantic convoy duty on the Coast Guard cutter "Campbell" during the winter of 1943. The "Campbell" was disabled during a successful attack on a German U-boat, and Fischer's dramatic paintings of this experience were published by *Life* magazine. The pictures are now in the Coast Guard Academy at New London, Connecticut.

In 1947, Fischer wrote and illustrated a book about his earlier sailing years, entitled *Fo'c'sle Days,* published by Charles Scribner's Sons.

Full-rigged ship on high seas, 1922.

A Burning Tanker, painted by Fischer as a Lt. Commander, USCGR while on convoy escort duty aboard the Coast Guard cutter "Campbell" during World War II. Published by *Life* magazine, July 5, 1943.

Ernest Fuhr, illustration for "Authentic Stuff" by Laurie York Erskine, *American Boy-Youth's Companion*, June, 1930.

ERNEST FUHR (1874-1933), a pupil of William Chase, also studied in Paris, but was most influenced by the point of view of Frederic R. Gruger.

The majority of Fuhr's illustrations were in black-and-white, and although he depicted a wide range of story backgrounds, he was at his best with small-town and rural subjects. His characters were never glamorous or fashionable; they were ordinary people presented plainly, and, therefore, convincingly.

He began his career as a newspaper artist for the *New York Herald* and the *New York World* and for many years was associated with *The Saturday Evening Post*. His work also appeared in numerous other publications, including the juvenile magazines *Youth's Companion* and *American Boy*. Fuhr was a member of the Artists Guild and the Society of Illustrators.

Arthur Fuller, story illustration dated 1919. Date and place of publication unknown.

ARTHUR D. FULLER (1889-1966), an ardent sportsman all his life, was identified with hunting and fishing pictures for the major part of his career. The accuracy of detail in his covers and story illustrations for *Field & Stream* won him a large following among sharp-eyed and critical readers for many years.

Earlier in his work, Fuller had illustrated more general subject matter for nearly all of the major magazines, including *Green Book,* where he started, *Redbook, The Saturday Evening Post, Collier's, The Ladies' Home Journal, Cosmopolitan, The American Legion* and *McCall's.*

Fuller was born in Exeter, New Hampshire, and was educated at Harvard, the Fenway School of Illustration in Boston ,and the Chicago Academy of Fine Arts; he also studied with Harvey Dunn, whose influence is clearly evident. Fuller was a member of the Animal Artists Society, the Salmagundi Club, the Westport Artists, and the Society of Illustrators in New York.

Gordon Grant, *The Whaler "Wanderer,"* published by the Seamen's Bank for Savings.

Gordon Grant

GORDON HOPE GRANT, N.A. (1875-1962) was born in San Francisco. His father sent him to school in Scotland in order to maintain ancestral ties. The voyage of four-and-a-half months,from San Francisco, was made around the Horn in a full-rigged Glasgow sailing vessel. Grant's life-long interest in the sea began with this early experience. After graduation from school in Fifeshire, he studied art in London at the Heatherly and Lambeth Schools.

On his return to America, Grant served on the Mexican border with the Seventh Regiment National Guard and as a war correspondent, contributed pictures to newspapers in New York and San Francisco. Early in his career, he illustrated a great variety of subject matter, but as his reputation grew, he restricted himself to nautical subjects.

His painting of the "U. S. S. Constitution" was used by the Navy Department to raise funds for the preservation of "Old Ironsides;" the picture was hung in the President's office in the White House. Grant is represented in many collections, including the Metropolitan Museum of Art, the Library of Congress, the Annapolis Naval Academy, the IBM collection, and the New Britain Museum of American Art. He also painted a mural for the Post Office in Kennebunkport, Maine.

Grant illustrated a number of books, was both author and illustrator of **Ships under Sail** in 1942, **The Secret Voyage** in 1943, and other marine stories.

Robert A. Graef

ROBERT A. GRAEF (ca. 1878-1951) has come to be recognized as one of the more important artists specializing in the science-fiction genre in its early days.

Born and raised in Brooklyn, N.Y., Graef studied at Pratt Institute in 1896, then did freelance illustration for **Boy's Life** and **The Delineator** magazines, among others. These were straightforward, somewhat staid conceptions, which he produced alongside his more lurid Pulp work. He began working for the **Munsey** magazines, especially **The Argosy,** in the late 1920s. By the 1930s, he had developed his mature artistic style and was capable of great design, subtle modelling and robust anatomy on deadline. Graef generally preferred to work in watercolor — gouache and dry-brush — rather than in oil.

For **The Argosy,** Graef painted covers for Abraham Merritt's and Otis Adelbert Kline's memorable stories, including the latter's "Maza of the Moon" (1929) and "Planet of Peril" (1929); he also depicted "Zorro." Animals were a specialty of Graef's, which made him popular with his editors for the depiction of fantastical creatures.

Robert Graef, cover design for *Argosy* magazine, Feb. 24, 1934, illustrating "The War of the Purple Gas" by Murray Leinster.

William Heaslip, *Lincoln Beachey Flying the Falls,* in 1911.

HEASLIP

WILLIAM HEASLIP (1898-1970) was born in Toronto, Canada, and as a boy, he decided to become an artist. He was apprenticed to a lithographer at fifty cents a week (the amount to be raised fifty cents semi-annually for five years!)

World War I provided an opportunity for him to enlist in the Royal Flying Corps, and he became interested in flying and depicting aviation subjects from that time on.

After the war, Heaslip came to New York to study at the Art Students League and the National Academy of Design where he won the Suydam Medal. He soon thereafter broke into the magazines, and his illustrations appeared in **The Saturday Evening Post, Collier's, Boy's Life** and many other national publications.

Albin Henning

ALBIN HENNING (1886-1943) is best remembered for his spirited illustrations of World War I; after the war, he visited the battlefields to check the authenticity of his work.

His special forté was adventure, and in addition to illustration for major magazines such as **The Saturday Evening Post** and **The Country Gentleman,** he did many assignments for **Boy's Life** and **The American Boy**, with subjects ranging from the French Foreign Legion to polar exploration.

Henning was born in Oberdorla, Germany, but was reared in St. Paul, Minnesota. He studied at the Art Institute of Chicago and with Harvey Dunn at the Grand Central School of Art in New York City.

Albin Henning, cover for **The American Boy**, May, 1935, depicting Admiral Byrd in Antarctica.

Here Henning's war story illustration conveys the realism of an on-the-spot sketch.

179

A

B

C

John Held Jr

More than anyone else, JOHN HELD JR. (1889-1958) expressed in his pictures the brash spirit of the 'twenties with his famous flappers and collegiate capers, bootleg gin, jazz bands, and necking parties. His highly stylized drawings are brittle and delicate, yet entirely appropriate to the artificiality of the era.

As a youth, Held had made a number of linoleum cuts styled after the early, crude, wood engravings. Harold Ross, the *New Yorker* editor, encouraged Held to develop this earlier approach; it became a very popular feature, usually as a vehicle for satirical parody of the Victorian era.

All of Held's work was tremendously successful throughout the twenties and appeared copiously in the old *Life, Judge, Liberty, College Humor, Cosmopolitan,* and the *New Yorker*, as well as by myriad advertisers, some of whom reportedly were willing to write him blank checks for his services.

Once the Depression descended, such frivolity was no longer appropriate, and Held quietly turned to the more serious career of breeding and sculpting horses, and switched to bronze, ceramic and wrought iron. He was artist in residence at Harvard in 1940 and at the University of Georgia in 1941. In 1986-1989, a national tour of "John Held's America — Flappers, the Jazz Age and Beyond" was arranged by the Smithsonian Institution Traveling Exhibition Service.

A. "Telling her folks: she quit her job and is going out to be somebody." *McClure's.*
B. World War I-vintage cartoon of "Julian and Julienne."
C. Typical Held linoleum cut, reproduced from *The Works of John Held Jr.,* published by Ives Washburn in 1931.
D. Cover illustration for *McClure's* magazine, August, 1927.
E. "Roaring Twenties" postage stamp issued May 28, 1998.
F. One of a series of Manhattan cityscape watercolors painted in the mid-1930s.

D

E

F

Guy Hoff

Born in Rochester, New York, GUY HOFF (1889-1962) was trained at the Art School of the Albright Gallery in Buffalo, and the Art Students League in New York City.

His first commercial illustrations were done for the Niagara Lithograph Company in Buffalo. In New York, he designed program covers for the Shubert Theatres and then sold his first magazine cover to *Smart Set,* which put him on the national scene. Over the years, in addition to work for *Smart Set, Pictorial Review, The Saturday Evening Post* and other magazines, he also did advertising illustrations for Procter & Gamble, Lux, and Ivory Soap. His last commercial work was done in 1938; after that he concentrated on pastels and paintings for exhibition.

Guy Hoff, cover illustration for *Smart Set,* 1920's.

Walter Beach Humphrey, *His Majesty, the Janitor,* cover painting for *The Saturday Evening Post,* January 13, 1923. © by the Curtis Publishing Company, 1923, 1951.

WALTER · BEACH · HUMPHREY

WALTER BEACH HUMPHREY (1892-1966) specialized in painting magazine covers and he eventually did work for almost all of them, beginning with small-circulation publications such as *The Zenith*, *Elks*, *Peoples' Popular Monthly*, *Argosy*, and the YMCA's *Association Men*, and progressing to the major weekly magazines: *Collier's*, *The Saturday Evening Post*, and *Liberty.*

Born in Elkhorn, Wisconsin, Humphrey studied at Dartmouth and the Art Students League under Frank DuMond. He spent two years painting murals for the student dining room of his Dartmouth alma mater, unveiled in 1939, which later became the center of a heated controversy. Based on a mythological Indian theme, it aroused the ire of the Native American students who were first admitted in 1970 and saw no humor in Humphrey's interpretation of the college drinking song or white cheerleaders in headdresses. The murals were shuttered.

The rest of Humphrey's career was less sensational. He was an active member of the New Rochelle Art Association and taught at the Albert Leonard High School in New Rochelle and at the Phoenix Art Institute in New York City.

Hoffman's dry-brush drawings, as typified by this vignette for the *American* magazine, inspired countless imitators among Pulp magazine illustrators who found the technique ideally suited to reproduction in line.

Hoffman

The father of FRANK B. HOFFMAN (1888-1958) raced horses in New Orleans, and young Frank spent all of his spare time working and sketching around the stables.

Through the interest of a family friend from Chicago who admired Frank's drawing of horses and other animals, he was given a job on the old *Chicago American* newspaper. There he had an opportunity to draw a great variety of subjects, from opera to prize-fights; he eventually became head of the art department. Meanwhile, he acquired a more formal art training by studying privately with J. Wellington Reynolds for five years.

In 1916, having been rejected for military service because of an eye defect, Hoffman went West to paint, and eventually was drawn to the art colony in Taos, New Mexico. His bold, broad brush-work and striking color attracted the attention of advertisers. He painted for national campaigns for many corporations, including Great Northern Railroad, General Motors, General Electric, and others. This was followed by illustrations for leading national magazines for which he specialized in Western subjects. His ranch in New Mexico was convenient for keeping live models, not only of cow ponies and thoroughbred horses, but also longhorn steers, several breeds of dogs, eagles, a bear, and burros.

From 1940 on, Hoffman was under exclusive contract to Brown & Bigelow and painted over 150 canvases of the West which were used as calendar subjects.

L. B. Hunt, *A Sharp Skinned Hawk and American Woodcock,* illustration for an article by T. Gilbert Pearson, "Can We Save our Game Birds?" — one of a series of paintings related to the protection of threatened species.

REA IRVIN (1881-1972) was born in San Francisco and studied art at the Mark Hopkins Art Institute, but he is best known as the quintessential New Yorker artist. He created the portrait of "Eustice Tilly" for the first issue of the magazine, and the same cover was run for many years on the anniversary issue.

Irvin also served as the New Yorker's first art editor for some twenty-one years and contributed many other covers himself. His art was clean and spare, usually with an outline that carried the form, and the color was applied without much tonal modelling — the perfect technique for a poster or a magazine cover.

Prior to his affiliation with *The New Yorker*, Irvin was a regular contributor to the old *Life* magazine, doing both covers and inside illustrations.

LYNN BOGUE HUNT

LYNN BOGUE HUNT (1878-1960) painted pictures of wildlife almost exclusively. Although he occasionally included human figures in his illustrations, he felt more at home with animals, fish, or birds, which he painted with authority and dramatic color.

Born in Honeoye Falls, New York, Hunt became interested in wildlife at an early age. He studied the anatomy of birds and animals, and learned taxidermy. Some of Hunt's first illustrations were done for *Outing* magazine. He subsequently worked for a wide range of publications and manufacturers of arms and ammunition, but for many years was closely identified with *Field & Stream* magazine.

Drawing by Rea Irvin. Copyright © 1925, 1953 *The New Yorker* Magazine, Inc. Reprinted by permission.

LYLE JUSTIS

In this lively illustration, LYLE JUSTIS (1892-1960) displays his unique approach to pen drawing. Self-taught, Justis evolved a method of developing his drawings and compositions by means of a series of warm-up work sheets, covered with exploratory characters and poses. They were done without preliminary penciling-in or any prior planning. With these drawings as a guide, he was able to retain much free informality and vigor in his finished renderings. As an illustrator, Justis was at his best with historical subjects crowded with figures, especially rough frontier types, his jagged pen line perfectly adapted to reproduce their roistering gusto.

Justis was born in Manchester, Virginia, and obtained his first art work designing sheet music covers. Eventually, he illustrated for many books, magazines, advertising campaigns and motion pictures. For many years, he was an active member of the Sketch Club and the Pen and Pencil Club of Philadelphia; his pictures won several awards in exhibitions of the Philadelphia Art Directors Club.

Lyle Justis, illustration for *Treasure Island* © 1930 by Carl J. H. Anderson Illustrated Editions, Inc.

Vignette for "The Long Rifle—Indian Country" by Stewart Edward White. Published by *The Saturday Evening Post*, March 14, 1931. © 1931, 1959 by The Curtis Publishing Company.

Cover illustration for *The Saturday Evening Post*, October 24, 1931. © 1931, 1959 by The Curtis Publishing Company.

W. H. D
Koerner

WILLIAM HENRY DETHLEF KOERNER (1878-1938) came from Clinton, Iowa. His first art job, when he was 15, was with the *Chicago Tribune*, where he later became assistant art editor. After a brief stint as the art editor of a Midwest magazine and an attempt to freelance in New York, he realized his need for further study.

By this time Howard Pyle was no longer carrying on his school, but Koerner went to Wilmington where Pyle gave him special help. Pyle's pupils — Dunn, Wyeth, Arthurs, and Schoonover — were in the area and provided helpful criticism.

With this background, Koerner was able to achieve his ambition to become an illustrator. He was identified with *The Saturday Evening Post* for most of his long career, specializing in western and outdoor subjects. He also illustrated several books, including *Covered Wagon,* and *North of 36,* by Emerson Hough.

Illustration for "Ranchero Mantanza" by Stewart Edward White. Published by *The Saturday Evening Post*. © 1931, 1959 by The Curtis Publishing Company. Collection of Ruth Koerner Oliver.

Robert Lawson, 1921. Place of publication unknown.

ROBERT LAWSON (1891-1957) was a versatile artist who successfully tried many avenues of expression. He illustrated more than forty books by other authors, wrote and illustrated another seventeen books of his own, including **Ben and Me,** and **Rabbit Hill.** The most famous of his books, **The Story of Ferdinand the Bull,** written by his friend, Monro Leaf, was later made into an animated film by Walt Disney. Among his book honors were the Caldecott Medal in 1941 and the Newberry Medal in 1945; he was the first to be awarded both. It is less well known that he was also active as an illustrator for magazines such as **Everybody's**, **This Week**, **The Designer**, **The Delineator**, **Pictorial Review**, **The Ladies' Home Journal**, and **Harper's Monthly**, where he specialized in stories of fantasy and fairy tales. He was also active in etching, using similar imaginative subjects. One of his plates won the John Taylor Arms Prize of the Society of American Etchers.

Born in New York, Lawson was raised in Montclair, New Jersey. He attended school at the New York School of Fine and Applied Art. During World War I, he served in the camouflage section of the 40th Engineers at the Front (where he shared a dugout with the etcher Kerr Eby). Lawson was one of the early and active members of the art colony in Westport, Connecticut.

ANDREW LOOMIS

As a youngster, WILLIAM ANDREW LOOMIS (1892-1959) loved to draw pictures, but it was a visit to the nearby studio of Howard Chandler Christy that made him decide to seek for himself an artist's career.

Loomis was born in Syracuse, New York, and grew up in Zanesville, Ohio. At 19, he went to New York to attend the Art Students League, where he studied under George Bridgman and Frank Vincent DuMond.

In 1915, he got a job in Chicago with the art organization of Charles Daniel Frey; he also attended classes at the Chicago Art Institute. This was interrupted in 1917 when he enlisted in the Army and served 20 months, half of them in France.

After the war, Loomis returned to Chicago to work at the Charles Everett Johnson advertising art studio, then for Bertch and Cooper. He finally opened his own studio as a free-lance artist. Equally at home in either editorial or advertising illustration, Loomis had a long career in both and also painted many twenty-four-sheet poster advertisements.

This broad experience especially qualified him as a teacher at the American Academy of Art in Chicago. Countless other art students who could not study with him personally have benefited from his several art books, including **Fun with a Pencil, Figure Drawing for All It's Worth,** and **Creative Illustration,** published by The Viking Press. In 1999 Loomis was inducted into the Society of Illustrators' Hall of Fame.

Andrew Loomis, cover painting for **This Week** magazine, April 18, 1937.

Lucile Patterson, cover design for *Every Week* magazine, October 23, 1916.

Lucile Patterson Marsh

LUCILE PATTERSON (MARSH) (1890-unknown) was born in Rapid City, South Dakota. She studied at the Art Institute of Chicago and was awarded an American Traveling Scholarship by the Institute in 1913.

She then migrated from Chicago to Greenwich Village in New York City, to pursue a career of depicting children for covers of many national magazines and advertisers of child-related products. She also illustrated books, including the **Gates School Reader.**

Marsh's work is marked by a strong sense of design and imaginative poster shapes, in contrast to that of many of her more conventional contemporaries.

McMein

NEYSA MORAN McMEIN (1890-1949) — later Mrs. John Baragwanath — wanted, as a girl in Quincy, Illinois, to be a musician. Although she changed her mind and attended the Art Institute of Chicago, she paid her way through school by writing music and playing piano in a ten-cent store.

During World War I, she went to France under the auspices of the YMCA, and entertained the troups with her singing and piano accompaniment to showings of Winsor McCay's animated film "Gertie the Dinosaur".

She painted her first *McCall's* magazine cover in 1923, and for many years made pastel portraits of beautiful or notable young women for *McCall's* monthly issues, as well as occasional covers for the **Woman's Home Companion, McClure's, Photoplay,** and **The Saturday Evening Post.** She also regularly contributed her drawings for the annual **New York Times'** Hundred Neediest Cases.

McMein was equally noted as a hostess and friend of such notables as Alexander Woollcott, Irving Berlin, Marc Connolly, Bea Lillie, Irene Castle, Richard Rodgers, Dorothy Parker, Jascha Heifetz and George Abbott, who visited at her studio or home. As young models, Kay Francis and Frederic March posed for her. Her biography, **Anything Goes** by Brian Gallagher, tells the full story of that heady period.

Eventually, she turned to privately commissioned portraiture and painted many of the country's prominent women. The Whitney Museum of American Art has established a memorial fund in her honor, which is used to purchase work by living American artists. She was elected into the Society of Illustrators Hall of Fame in 1984.

In January 1934, Neysa McMein was accorded the unusual honor of having a gallery of her past covers for *McCall's* magazine reproduced as a tenth anniversary tribute.

Harry Morse Meyers, story illustration for the *Ladies' Home Journal,* December 1920.

**HARRY
MORSE
MEYERS.**

HARRY MORSE MEYERS (1886-1961) was a collector of antique arms and armor which he displayed on two carved oak screens that had belonged to the curator of arms at the Tower of London. Since he illustrated many period stories, these authentic objects frequently served as props for his characters.

Meyers was from New Orleans, Louisiana; he attended Tulane University there, followed by classes at the Art Students League in New York, and further study with Harvey Dunn.

With a few years' interruption during World War I as an Army airplane pilot, he had a long and successful career as an illustrator for the Crowell-Collier publications, particularly *Collier's* magazine.

William Oberhardt, portrait of Charles Dana Gibson, painted from life for an Elgin Watch Company advertisement, 1925.

Early in his career, WILLIAM OBERHARDT, A. N. A. (1882-1958) found his greatest interest in delineating the human head. Over the years, he developed a remarkable facility for presenting the special qualities revealed by the sitter's character. An important factor in this ability came from his own warm personality which relaxed and charmed his subjects.

"Obie" would never draw from photographs, but always insisted on working directly from the model, earning added respect from his fellow-artists for his incisive likenesses.

His sitters comprised a veritable Who's Who. He said that most of them were people he would have paid willingly for the privilege of portraying. Among these famous subjects were Presidents Taft, Harding, and Hoover; Thomas Edison, Sergei Rachmaninoff, Luther Burbank, Ezio Pinza, Cardinal Spellman, Bernard Baruch, and Walter Lippmann. Oberhardt was chosen as the portraitist for *Time* magazine's first cover, on March 3, 1923.

During World War II. Oberhardt contributed by drawing a great number of portrait sketches of men from various armed services at numerous centers and hospitals.

RUSSELL PATTERSON (1896-1977) was very influential as an illustrator (in the 'twenties his flappers were as definitive as those of John Held Jr.), and also successful in many areas outside illustration.

Patterson was born in Omaha, Nebraska. The family moved to Canada, where he spent one year studying architecture at McGill University. When financial reverses terminated that study, Patterson tried various newspaper jobs, finally doing a comic strip in French, "Pierre et Pierrette," for *La Patrie* in Montreal.

He next went to Chicago and attended the Chicago art Institute and the Academy of Fine Arts. His early work was for department stores: Carson, Pirie, Scott & Company, and Marshall Field, where he became noted for his interior designs.

A year of painting landscapes in France followed. When he returned to America in 1921, the Jazz Age was just beginning. Patterson began to draw sexy coeds, and they were an immediate success when they appeared in *College Humor.* With his incorporation of their raccoon coats and flapping, unbuckled galoshes in his drawings, Patterson became a pacemaker in setting styles. He had a special flair for clothes, and his drawings were followed eagerly for what was right to wear.

Commissions for the theatre followed. Patterson did both the costumes and set designs for the Ziegfeld Follies of 1922 and a number of other Broadway shows, including George White's Scandals.

Patterson spent the 1930s in Hollywood doing set and costume designs for the movies, mostly elaborate musicals, similar to his Broadway shows.

In the late 'thirties, he returned to New York, again to the department store field. He designed coats for I. J. Fox, Christmas toy windows for Macy's, and resumed his advertising illustrations.

During World War II, he designed the Women's Army Corps uniforms, train interior; he drew a comic strip, and also designed hotel lobbies and restaurant interiors.

Russell Patterson, *"Gluttons for Punishment,"* Cover for *Life* magazine, Septemeber 28, 1928.

HERBERT PAUS (1880-1946) was a native of Minneapolis and got his first job as a cartooneer for the *St. Paul Pioneer Press.* Ambitious to become an illustrator, he enrolled in the Fine Arts School there, and later found employment in a Chicago art studio.

Eventually, he moved to New York where he became a freelance illustrator. Paus had a strong sense of design, which was ideally suited to posters. He was a member of the Government's committee on pictorial publicity during World War I, and painted many effective posters to support the war effort. This approach, combined with a striking use of vivid color, was carried over into his magazine illustrations and cover designs for such magazines as **Woman's Home Companion**, **American Magazine**, **The Youth's Companion**, and **Collier's**.

Among his many outstanding book illustrations were those for Maurice Maeterlinck's play "Betrothal" as told for children entitled *Tyltyl*.

Paus also painted for such advertisers as Hart, Schaffner, & Marx, Goodyear, General Motors, Certain-teed, and Victor Records, and from 1927 to 1931, was under exclusive contract to do all of the spectacular covers for **Popular Science Monthly**.

Herbert Paus, *Pouring molten steel at the Foundary.*
Cover illustration for **Popular Science Monthly**, February, 1930.
Collection of Jim Steranko.

James Preston, illustration for "Not in the Guidebook" by F. Scott Fitzgerald.
Published by the **Woman's Home Companion**, November, 1925.

May Preston, *"He created a Sensation..."* Published June, 1933. © Copyright June
1933, 1961 by the Meredith Corporation. All rights reserved.
Used with the permission of **The Ladies' Home Journal.**

JAMES MOORE PRESTON (1873-1962) studied at The
Pennsylvania Academy of the Fine Arts with fellow-students
Robert Henri, Frederic R. Gruger, William Glackens, George
Luks, John Sloan, and Everett Shinn, and then went to Paris to
complete his training. There he met May Wilson; they were
married in 1903 upon their return to the United States. The
success of their union can be seen in the similarity of styles,
reflecting their influence on each other. For many years both were
active contributors to nearly all of the major magazines.

James, a close friend of Glackens, was also an active painter,
exhibiting in the historic Armory Show in 1913, and participating
in the Pennsylvania Academy annuals, at the National Academy
of Design, and in other group shows. His work is represented in
the Metropolitan Museum of Art, the Whitney Museum of
American Art, the Wadsworth Athenaeum and the Barnes
Collection.

MAY WILSON PRESTON (1873-1949) came to New York to
attend the Art Students League after graduating from Oberlin.
This was followed by study in Paris with Whistler at the World's
Art Center. She first came to the master's notice when he
discovered black on her palette. "There is no such color . . . Scrape
it off!" Such was Whistler's prestige that other students eagerly
offered him their lace handkerchiefs for his use as paint rags, to be
treasured later as mementos.

May Wilson's first magazine illustrations were published by
Harper's Bazar as early as 1901. For the next thirty years she
illustrated stories for **McClure's, Scribner's,** and particularly **The
Saturday Evening Post,** including a number of serials by Mary
Roberts Rinehart. A prolific painter, her illustrations were airy and
witty, reflecting her own energy and good humor.

WILLIAM MEADE PRINCE (1893-1951) was born in Roanoke, Virginia, and grew up in Chapel Hill, North Carolina. He reportedly could not choose between West Point, or architecture at Georgia Institute of Technology, so he settled it by going North to study art at the New York School of Fine and Applied Arts.

After five years of advertising work in Chicago, he settled in Westport, Connecticut, where he could combine his illustration work for the magazines in New York with his interest in riding and maintaining fine arabian horses. When Westport eventually paved its streets and became too urban for riding, Prince returned to Chapel Hill, where he built his own studio and stables and continued to do illustration. He was particularly noted for his Dodge Brothers ads and his spirited interpretations of Roark Bradford's black stereotype stories for *Collier's* magazine.

For several years, Prince also taught illustration and figure drawing at the University of North Carolina and was head of the Art Department there from 1943-1946.

William Meade Prince, cover painting for *The Country Gentleman,* July, 1927. © 1927, 1955 by The Curtis Publishing Company.

Ellen Pyle, cover painting for *The Saturday Evening Post,* October 8, 1927. © 1927, 1955 by the Curtis Publishing Company.

ELLEN BERNARD THOMPSON (PYLE) (1876-1936) was one of the original ten students in Howard Pyle's illustration class at Drexel Institute to be invited by him to attend his summer school at Chadds Ford in 1898. Under his tutelege, she was soon able to obtain professional illustration assignments. Her first, with several other Pyle students, was to illustrate Paul Leicester Ford's novel *Janice Meredith* in 1899.

In 1904, she married Howard Pyle's younger brother, Walter, and interrupted her career to raise four children. After her husband's death in 1919, she returned to illustrating as a livelihood, finding a market in painting covers for *The Saturday Evening Post*. She rendered young people very sympathetically, often using as models her own children or youngsters she knew. Her paintings were done in a broad poster manner with strong color, which was very effective for cover design, and she continued with the *Post* for the rest of her life.

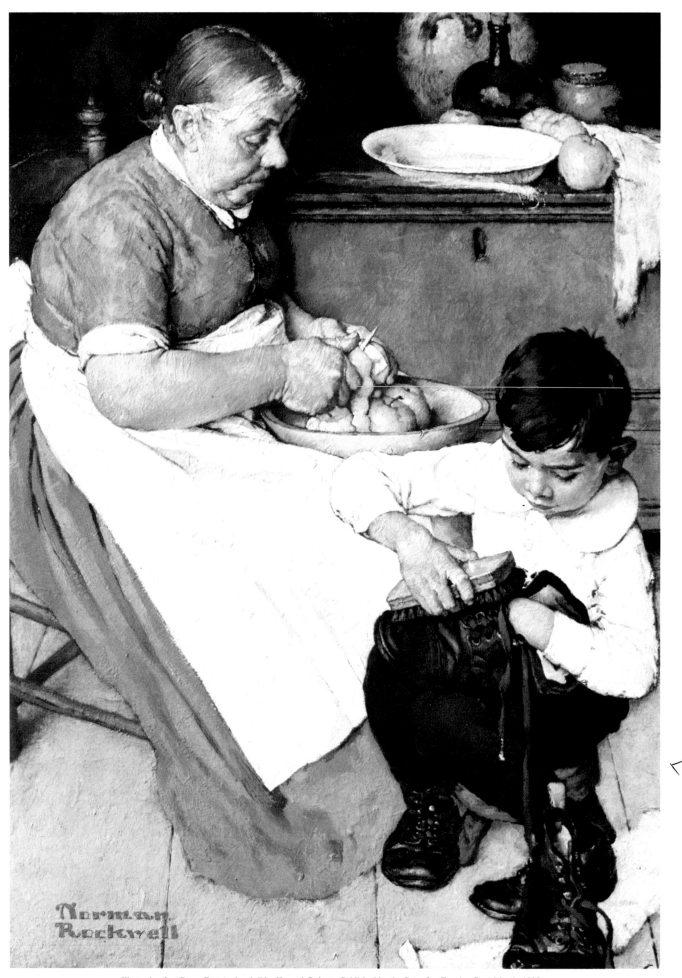

Illustration for "Down East Ambrosia," by Kenneth Roberts. Published by the *Saturday Evening Post,* March, 1938.
Printed by permission of the Norman Rockwell Family Trust. © 2000 the Norman Rockwell Family Trust.

Unpublished version of *Tom, Huck, and the Dead Cat,* from ***Tom Sawyer****.*
Collection of James Gurney

Rockwell was unfailingly loyal to ***The Saturday Evening Post*** from the publication of his first cover, May 20, 1916, up to his last in 1963.

Norman Rockwell

The pictures of NORMAN PERCEVAL ROCKWELL (1894-1978) were recognized and enjoyed by almost everybody in America. The cover of *The Saturday Evening Post* was his showcase for over forty years, giving him an audience larger than that of any other artist in history. Over the years, he depicted there a unique collection of Americana, a series of vignettes of remarkable warmth and humor. In addition, he painted a great number of pictures for story illustrations, advertising campaigns, posters, calendars, and books.

As his personal contribution during World War II, Rockwell painted the famous "Four Freedoms" posters, symbolizing for millions the war aims as described by President Franklin Roosevelt. One version of his "Freedom of Speech" painting is in the collection of the Metropolitan Museum of Art.

Rockwell left high school to attend classes at the National Academy of Design, and later studied under Thomas Fogarty and George Bridgman at the Art Students League in New York. His two greatest influences were the completely opposite titans Howard Pyle and J. C. Leyendecker.

His early illustrations were done for *St. Nicholas* magazine and other juvenile publications. He sold his first cover painting to the *Post* in 1916, and ended up doing over 300 more. Presidents Eisenhower, Kennedy, and Johnson sat for him for portraits, and he painted other world figures, including Nassar of Egypt and Nehru of India.

An important museum has been established in Stockbridge, Massachusetts, where he maintained his studio. Each year, tens of thousands visit the largest collection of his original paintings extant.

Part of the effort to save the foundering *Post* was its complete redesign including the covers in 1961. Here Rockwell depicts a young designer searching for a new logo.

A major retrospective, "Norman Rockwell: Pictures for the American People" originating at the High Museum in 1999, and culminating at the Solomon R. Guggenheim Museum in New York in 2001, made a major breakthrough for the artistic status of the artist as well as for the field of American illustration.

GRANT TYSON REYNARD, N. A. (1887-1968) attended the Chicago Art Institute and the Chicago Academy of Fine Arts, paying his way by doing odd jobs, including piano playing for sheet music sales, in his home town of Grand Island, Nebraska.

In 1912, his first professional position was as art editor of **Redbook** magazine, at that time located in Chicago. There he met and worked with many of the top writers and illustrators, and had his first opportunity to do his own illustrations.

After three years, Reynard decided to go East to study further with Harvey Dunn in Leonia, New Jersey, with the hope of working for more important magazines. Within a year, he had made it; his clients eventually included **The Saturday Evening Post, Harper's Bazaar, Cosmopolitan, Good Housekeeping** and **Collier's.** During the 1910s and 1920s, most of his illustrations were done in charcoal with a full range of values.

He began experimenting in other mediums for exhibition pictures, and gradually turned to an independent career as painter and etcher. Study with Mahonri Young and Harry Wickey, with a year of travel and sketching in Europe, furthered this ambition. Reynard's pictures and prints now hang in many major museums, including the Metropolitan Museum of art, the Addison Gallery of American Art, the Fogg Museum in Boston, the Newark Museum, and the Library of Congress. He also won a number of prizes.

Over the years, Reynard taught at various art schools and universities and lectured widely.

Grant Reynard, illustration for **The Saturday Evening Post,** January 12, 1918. *"I am not impressionable — but I was impressed by this girl, I must confess."* Collection of Susan E. Meyer.

J. Allen St. John, jacket illustration for **At the Earth's Core** by Edgar Rice Burroughs, 1922. Collection of Glynn Crain.

JAMES ALLEN ST. JOHN (1872-1957) dominated a special zone of illustration that was unfashionable for a serious illustrator in the 1920s. He is most closely identified with the fiction of Edgar Rice Burroughs and other early writers of fantasy and science fiction. Since that audience was primarily the Pulp magazine readers, the genteel subscribers to the slick family magazines were unaware of his work. St. John could have and occasionally did work for the more lucrative general magazines, but he obviously felt an enthusiastic rapport with the more bizarre and lurid covers of publications such as **Weird Tales, Fantastic Adventures, Blue Book,** and **Amazing Stories.** His "Tarzan" illustrations were published in book form as well as in the Pulps, and he also made many renderings in pen and ink or black and white halftone for book interiors.

St. John had a solid artistic background, beginning with studies at the Art Students League under H. Siddons Mowbray, William M. Chase and J. Carroll Beckwith, followed by the Academy Julian in Paris under J. P. Laurens. He later moved to Chicago where, in addition to his illustration output, he taught at the Chicago Art Institute and the American Academy of Art. **J. Allen St. John; An Illustrated Bibliography** by Darrell C. Richardson, was published in 1991. St. John was elected into the Society of Illustrators' Hall of Fame in 2000.

Tony Sarg, *The Mad Artists Ball,* cover design for **Vanity Fair**, November, 1923.

The interests of TONY SARG (1882-1942) were as diversified as his background. Sarg was born in Guatemala, and sent to school in Germany. With no formal art training, he did his first professional work in London for **The Sketch** magazine and also did advertising drawings.

In London, he became fascinated with marionette performances by the great Holden, and for months followed the troupe on their tour to learn the secrets of the craft.

When Sarg came to America in 1914, he successfully organized his own marionette workshop, and also experimented with early animated cartoons.

Among Sarg's first illustration assignments was one for Irvin Cobb's "Speaking of Operations" in **The Saturday Evening Post.** The humor of his drawings matched Cobb's delightfully. He eventually illustrated for a great number of publications and advertisers.

Sarg also wrote and illustrated several books for children, and he designed textiles, wallpapers, boxes, rugs, glass and pottery. As a result of his interest in puppets, Sarg created toys and invented the monster balloons for the annual Macy's parades on Thanksgiving Day in New York City.

JOHN E. SHERIDAN (1880-1948) was at his best as a poster and magazine cover artist, as exemplified in his designs for **The Ladies' Home Journal**, **The Saturday Evening Post**, **American Magazine**, **Collier's**, and in the posters he made for the Federal Committee of Public Information during World War I. He was also noted for his advertising illustrations for Hart, Schaffner & Marx and the Bosch Magneto Company.

Sheridan was born in Tomah, Wisconsin, and earned his tuition for Georgetown University in Washington, D.C. by painting posters for sports events. He also spent a year at the Colorossi School in Paris. He next became art editor of the **Washington Times**, and later helped produce the first Sunday supplement in color for the **San Francisco Chronicle.**

He was an active member of the Society of Illustrators, The Players club, the Dutch Treat Club, and he taught at the School of Visual Arts in New York from 1945-48.

John Sheridan, cover illustration for **The Saturday Evening Post,** June 3, 1939.
© 1939, 1967 by The Curtis Publishing Company.

Frank Street, publication and date unknown. Collection of Wall Drug, Wall, South Dakota.

FRANK STREET

FRANK STREET (1893-1944) came from Kansas City, Missouri, to study at the Art Students League in New York and at the Charles Chapman-Harvey Dunn School of Illustration in Leonia, New Jersey.

Dunn, who carried on the Pyle tradition, was the dominant influence in Street's work. Dunn also helped him to obtain his first illustration commission from Walter Dower, then art editor of *The Saturday Evening Post*. Street subsequently had a long career of illustration work in the *Post* and many other publications, including *The Ladies' Home Journal*, *Cosmopolitan*, *Collier's*, and *The American Legion Monthly* magazines.

Although he did not exhibit them formally, Street painted many landscapes and portraits between illustration commissions, and also conducted private classes in his own studio for the last five or six years of his life.

Earle G. Teale, *White Sixteen-valve 4' — The Runabout Body.*
An advertising illustration for the White Motor Company.

TEALE

EARLE GRANTHAM TEALE (1886-1919) was tragically killed while standing in the darkened interior of a garage when a driver coming in from the bright sunlight failed to see him in time.

At the time of his death, he was one of the country's foremost automobile artists, having painted a brilliant series of advertisements for the White Motor Car Company. Also memorable was an illustrated catalog for the Canadian Pacific Railway Company's Transatlantic Steamship Service, lavishly printed in full color. His style was decorative and influenced by both his admiration for Japanese prints and his interest in murals.

Teale had attended the Art Students League in New York and later studied architectural design at Stanford University as a preparation for mural painting. His death occurred when he was just reaching his prime as an artist, cutting off a career that deserves to have far greater influence and recognition.

On the Move, from a series, "Masterpieces of the Old West," reprinted by permission of and copyrighted by Brown and Bigelow, St. Paul, Minnesota.

DONALD TEAGUE

DONALD TEAGUE, N.A. (1897-1991) was respected by his fellow-illustrators as a thorough craftsman whose pictures were composed and painted with great professional competence.

Teague began a picture with many thumbnail sketches in black-and-white, followed by small full-color studies of the most promising approaches. After a composition evolved, models were posed for further sketching and photographing, for factual information. Photostats, reduced in scale from the rather large figure studies, were then projected and traced on watercolor paper, free from any corrections or erasures, ready to render in watercolor or gouache.

Research for authenticating every detail was highly important in his picture-making. Teague, who lived in California near the motion picture studios, had the advantage of being able to use their props for Westerns. He obtained cowboy actors, a stage coach complete with horses, and even used the Western Town movie sets as backdrops for his pictures. The Pacific Ocean was equally accessible for his sea illustrations. Air express made it possible for him to meet deadlines with publishers in the East.

Teague also worked under the pseudonym "Edwin Dawes." Because of rivalry between the two publications, Teague used his own name for *The Saturday Evening Post*, Dawes at *Collier's.*

Teague was born in Brooklyn, New York, studied at the Art Students League in New York under Bridgman and DuMond.

Troops storming a Group of Outlaws, date and place of publication unknown.

After serving in the Navy during World War I, he went to England and studied under Norman Wilkinson, P.R.I. Back in America, he found Dean Cornwell most helpful while he was getting started as an illustrator.

Besides his work for publications, Teague exhibited regularly. His prizes and awards, too numerous to list, included the Gold Medal of Honor from the American Watercolor Society in 1953; and the S.F.B. Morse Gold Medal from the National Academy in 1962. He is also represented in many museums and private collections, including the Virginia Museum of Fine Arts in Richmond; the Frye Museum in Seattle, Washington; and the Collection of the State of California in Sacramento.

Illustration for "Swag" by Charles Francis Coe in *The Saturday Evening Post*; ©1928, 1956 by The Curtis Publishing Company.

SAUL TEPPER (1899-1987) was born on the Lower East Side of New York City, and remained a New Yorker all his life.

As a youngster, Tepper was awarded a correspondence course from the Landon School of Art. He also studied at The Cooper Union, the Art Students League, and at the Grand Central School of Art, under Harvey Dunn.

Tepper first worked as a letterer in a fashion catalog studio before establishing himself as an illustrator. He eventually did an almost equal proportion of fiction and advertising assignments, for most of the magazines, and for many national accounts, such as Mobil Oil, Texaco, Packard, General Motors and Coca-Cola.

Among his many honors were the Harvard Award (1929), the Newspaper Award (1936), Annual Advertising Award (1940) and the Laskinlamb Institute Award (1943).

For many years, Tepper was also an active teacher and lecturer at Pratt Institute, The Cooper Union, the New York Art Directors Club and the Society of Illustrators.

Music was a parallel interest. Saul wrote many popular songs which were recorded by Nat "King" Cole, Ella Fitzgerald, Ezio Pinza, Glenn Miller, Harry James and others. He was a member of ASCAP and AGAC, and wrote sketches, lyrics and music for fifteen annual Society of Illustrators Shows. Tepper was a life member of the Society of Illustrators, and was elected to its Hall of Fame in 1980.

Leslie Thrasher

CHARLES LESLIE THRASHER (1889-1936) was made famous by signing on for a long-term contract to paint every single week's cover for *Liberty* magazine. It was a back-breaking commitment to work at such a pace and an even greater challenge to come up with enough original cover ideas. The latter problem was partially solved by settling on a continuing story line, which followed a couple's courtship, marriage and children. It was a popular series, later made into a movie called "For the Love of Lil." His marriage provided the ingredients for it, and he served as his own model for the hero. As the presentation was humorous and light, the artwork tended to be lightweight, below the standards of his earlier cover work for *The Saturday Evening Post, Collier's,* and his advertising illustrations for Cream of Wheat, Fisk Tires, and Spaulding.

Thrasher's career had an auspicious beginning. He studied at the Pennsylvania Academy of the Fine Arts and won a year's scholarship to attend the Ecole de Grande Chaumiere in Paris. After his return in 1910, he studied briefly with Howard Pyle, and developed a close friendship with fellow-student Douglas Duer. They both served overseas during World War I, where they were assigned to camouflage with the Fortieth Engineers.

He resumed his illustration career after returning to the U.S., working for various magazines such as *Redbook, Collier's, Popular Magazine* and *Everybody's*, prior to the *Liberty* contract.

Thrasher's career came to an early tragic end when his summer home burned and he developed a fatal pneumonia from smoke inhalation.

Leslie Thrasher, *Playing Hooky,* advertising illustration for Cream of Wheat, 1912. Courtesy Nabisco, Inc.

R. Van Buren

Born in Pueblo, Colorado, RAEBURN L. VAN BUREN (1891-1987) learned his craft in the best of training schools — as a newspaper sketch artist. In his case, he was fortunate to work on the *Kansas City Star* under an excellent art editor, H. Wood. Out of that same bull-pen came Robert Lambdin, L. L. Balcom and Loran Wilford, all of whom went on to have careers as illustrators in New York. Van Buren spent three-and-a-half years in Kansas City, and at the age of 21, felt he was ready for the big time.

His newspaper friends, already in New York, introduced him to a number of art editors, and he was soon working alongside them. After his first assignment for Pulp publisher Street & Smith, he went on to *The Saturday Evening Post, Liberty, Redbook, Cosmopolitan, Collier's, Esquire, The New Yorker,* and other magazines.

In 1937, the late Al Capp offered to collaborate with him on a comic strip and "Abbie an' Slats" was born, with Capp doing the writing and Van Buren the drawings. This kept Van Buren on a treadmill of deadlines for many years but built him a loyal and large following until the strip finally folded in 1971. Van Buren was named "Best Cartoonist" in 1958 and elected to the National Cartoonist Society Hall of Fame in 1979.

Raeburn van Buren, *Did I Hear Someone Knocking? Esquire,* January 1935.
By permission of Esquire magazine. © Hearst Communications, Inc. Also, Esquire is a trademark of Hearst Magazines Property, Inc. All Rights Reserved.
Collection of Charles Valauskas.

JOHN VASSOS (1898-1985) was born in Bulgaria of Greek parentage. His first artwork as a budding political cartoonist, was published in Constantinople, where his father was editor of a Greek newspaper. His too-liberal ideas got him into serious trouble with Turkish authorities, however, and he escaped the country aboard a British freighter.

World War I had just begun, and he had numerous close calls, including the torpedoing of his ship in the North Sea, but he made port in Boston and began his new life as an American. He studied nights at the Fenway Art School; one of his instructors was John Singer Sargent. This led to a job as assistant to stage designer Joseph Urban, and a series of assignments with the Boston Opera Company. He next branched out to designing advertising for opera stars for Columbia Records.

In 1924, he moved to New York, establishing his own design studio, and studying nights at the Art Students League under George Bridgman, John Sloan, and Louis Bouché. His professional assignments included designing window displays for department stores and murals for the lobbies of the Rialto and Rivoli theatres. Advertising accounts included Packard automobiles and the French Line; he also designed radio cabinets, fountain pens, juke boxes, and the first television set for RCA.

Vassos's entry into book illustration began with an assignment from a Greek dramatic society to illustrate a program for Oscar Wilde's "Salome." His creation of an early geometric Art Deco style had a powerful impact and led to several more books in a similar vein in stark black and white gouache; among them *Contempo*, *Ultimo*, *The Ballad of Reading Gaol*, and *Humanities*, with text by his wife, Ruth Vassos. The artist found another role in directing the Silvermine Guild of Art in Norwalk, Connecticut, raising its profile to that of a national institution. He also exhibited widely and won the "50 Best Books of the Year" award in 1952.

John Vassos, *Man returning to a devastated land;* 1931; unpublished.

EDGAR FRANKLIN WITTMACK (1894-1956) specialized in painting magazine covers. He had a strong poster style that was well adapted to the eye-arresting requirements of cover art.

For many years, he regularly painted the covers for *The Popular Science Monthly*, picturing the latest in technological advances, often working from blue prints or conceptual models. He did another long series of covers for *Nation's Business* as well as *Motor Magazine* and *Cities Service* trade publications. Between these assignments, he periodically painted topical covers for *The Saturday Evening Post, Collier's* and other national magazines.

Wittmack was a versatile advertising artist as well, adept at subjects as disparate as hardware and wildlife.

Edgar Franklin Wittmack, cover for *The Saturday Evening Post,* April 10, 1926.
© 1926, 1954 by The Curtis Publishing Co.

Loran Wilford, illustration for "The One I Knew Least of All" by Maude Adams. © Copyright 1926, 1954 by the Meredith Corporation. All rights reserved. Used with permission of *The Ladies' Home Journal*

I.F. Wilford

LORAN FREDERICK WILFORD (1892-1972) taught at the Ringling School of Art in Sarasota, Florida, prior to his teaching at the Grand Central School of Art in New York City. This followed a long career of painting for exhibition, and illustrating for newspapers and magazines.

Born in Wamego, Kansas, Wilford studied at the Kansas City Art Institute and was soon doing feature illustrations for the **Kansas City Star.**

Ambitious, he gravitated to the East for further study with Jonas Lie and George Pearce Ennis. Soon he began working for such publications as **Cosmopolitan, Everybody's, McCall's,** and **Hearst's International.** His early illustrations were done in dry brush; later he became much interested in watercolors which he began to exhibit.

Wilford went on to become an outstanding watercolorist, and won many honors for both his watercolors and oils. He painted several murals, and is represented in the permanent collections of the Toledo Museum of Fine Art, the High Museum in Atlanta, Georgia, and in many private collections.

C.D. Williams

CHARLES DAVID WILLIAMS (1875-1954) worked in pen-and-ink in the early part of his career; especially notable were his sensitive line drawings for Booth Tarkington's **Monsieur Beaucaire**. He later worked in charcoal and pastels with great control and subtlety in these difficult mediums.

Williams, who was from Pittsburgh, had had a brief career in the 1890s, as a professional lightweight boxer.

Gregarious and hard-working, he spent much of his time on behalf of the programs of the Society of Illustrators and served as its president from 1927 to 1929.

C. D. Williams, *All Good Things Come in Threes,* illustration for the cover of the *Associated Sunday Magazines,* May 12, 1912.

1930–1940

Constantin Alajálov
James Edward Allen
Harold N. Anderson
Boris Artzybasheff
Ernest Hamlin Baker
Lowell Leroy Balcom
McClelland Barclay
Cecil Calvert Beall
Harry Beckhoff
Frank C. Bensing
Earl Blossom
Vladimir Bobritsky (Bobri)
Hannes Bok
E. Melbourne Brindle
Elmore J. Brown
Paul Brown
Elmer Simms Campbell
Pruett A. Carter
Frederick Trench Chapman
Benton Clark
Matt Clark
Ralph Pallen Coleman
Grattan Condon
Dan Content
Mario Ruben Cooper
Bradshaw Crandell
William Galbraith Crawford
Douglass Crockwell
John Henry Crosman
Robert W. Crowther
Floyd Macmillan Davis
Gladys Rockmore Davis
Nick Eggenhofer
Fritz Eichenberg
Carl Oscar August Erickson (Eric)
John Russell Fulton
Theodore Geisel (Dr. Seuss)
George Giguere
Frank Godwin
Jules Gotlieb
Ruth Sigrid Grafstrom
Roy Frederic Heinrich
Wilmot Emerton Heitland
Clarence Peter Helck

David Hendrickson
Edwin Henry
E. Everett Henry
R. John Holmgren
George Howe
Frances Tipton Hunter
Elbert McGran Jackson
William James (Dufault)
Rockwell Kent
Joseph Francis Kernan
Steven R. Kidd
Walter Charles Klett
Clayton Knight
Larry B. Kritcher
John LaGatta
Charles Louis LaSalle
Manning DeVilleneuve Lee
Philip Lyford
Orison MacPherson
Ronald Norman McLeod
Frederic Kimball Mizen
Irving Nurick
Robert Patterson
George Petty
Garrett Price
William Reusswig
Martha Sawyers
Mead Schaeffer
Oscar Frederick Schmidt
James W. Schucker
Howard Scott
Henry J. Soulen
Roy Frederic Spreter
Herbert Morton Stoops
Katherine Sturges (Knight)
Haddon Hubbard Sundblom
Dan Sweeney
Harry Laverne Timmins
Rico Tomaso
Edmund F. Ward
William P. Welsh
James W. Williamson
Revere Wistehuff
Denys Wortman

Hannes Bok "Out of the Storm" by Wm. H. Hodgson.
Collection of Robert Lesser.

George Petty girl, 1939.
By permission of *Esquire* magazine. ©
Hearst Communications, Inc. *Esquire* is
a trademark of Hearst Magazines
Property, Inc. All Rights Reserved.

"Mopey Dick and the Duke", by Dennis Wortman.
United Features Syndicate.

THE DECADE 1930-1940

The Thirties was a grim decade embraced by the great Depression. Like the rest of the population, artists also felt its full effects; for some it finished their careers. A few star performers, like Norman Rockwell, Maxfield Parrish and John LaGatta, scarcely felt it, even in a shrinking market, but nearly everyone else did. Several popular magazines that had been bright stars in the 'twenties, such as *Vanity Fair,* the old *Life* magazine, *Smart Set,* and *Judge,* all quietly folded. As advertisers cut back their budgets, a vicious cycle was created; the amount of fiction purchased and published had to be greatly curtailed; the number of pages were cut back, and fees paid to contributors were greatly reduced. At least the surviving magazines were using illustrations consistently, though photography was making inroads, too.

Arthur William Brown, who had been one of the busiest and most successful illustrators in 1929, averaging a story a week, reported that he had but a single assignment in 1931. Gallery painters had it far worse. No one was buying art for their walls.

Their biggest salvation was the Government relief programs, beginning with the Works Progress Administration. Murals for Post Offices and government buildings were commissioned through the WPA. Although they were "make work" projects then, many still survive and are proudly admired.

Despite the hard times, there was also a creative determination to make do and get by. Barter became popular and enabled the exchange of pictures for dental work, farm produce, or auto repairs. Movies were an inexpensive escape from reality. Poster artists glamorized the stars in top hats and formal gowns, and audiences identified with them even though paying the admission price had to be budgeted.

One genre that thrived during this period was the Pulps. So named because they were printed on a cheap pulp paper stock, they could be sold at the giveaway price of a dime. The illustrations inside were done in dry-brush to avoid the cost of halftone engraving. The only outlay of consequence was for the cover, on coated stock, printed in full color. The success or failure of that issue depended on the ability of the artwork to outshout its neighbor on the newsstand. Subject matter was lurid — gangsters, gun molls, Western shoot-em-ups, and aviation battles were standard fare. Payment for the dry-brush drawings ranged from $10 to $25 for a double-spread, and the full color oil cover would pay $75-$150. This was a good training ground for young beginners like John Clymer, Tom Lovell, Emery Clarke, Walter Baumhofer, Amos Sewell, Robert G. Harris, and John Falter, who eventually graduated to the "slicks" (the standard magazines on coated paper). Some established artists also found security in working for the Pulps. John Newton Howitt, Robert Graef, Herbert Morton Stoops, and George and Jerome Rozen, made a secure, if less prestigious second career in the Pulps.

Interestingly, little pictorial evidence of the Depression appears in the national magazines. Like Hollywood, which focussed on escapist adventure and high society in films, the magazines also mostly ignored the effects of poverty and privation. Henry Raleigh pictured elegant couples in evening dress and his Maxwell House Coffee ads depict the affluence of the antebellum South. John LaGatta's lovers were obviously from Newport and Park Avenue.

Among the few depictions of the Depression during these years was in the cartoon series "Metropolitan Movies," featuring "Mrs. Rumple's Boarding House" and "Mopey Dick and the Duke," drawn by Dennis Wortman. This feature chronicled the daily lives of everyday people coping with their hardships through a prism of humor and irony; it was not published in a magazine, but by the *New York World-Telegram and Sun.*

Esquire magazine defied the hard times. Launched in 1933 as a men's fashion magazine, it soon found its niche by adding fiction and other departments, such as travel and sports. But the biggest boost to its initial success was the full-page Petty Girl with her white telephone and skimpy attire. Esquire paid its contributors very little but made up for it in the prestige of full-page, full-color reproductions, and artists like Gilbert Bundy, E. Simms Campbell, and Barbara Shermund enhanced their careers through regular appearances there. *The New Yorker* was also a haven of support for cartoonists and cover artists, if a quirky and unpredictable market, Garrett Price, Constantin Alajàlov, and particularly Peter Arno, were among their regulars. Ironically, *Fortune* magazine, launched in 1930, thrived in this decade. No one could throw away these opulent issues, each powerful poster-cover a paean to progress, based on T. M. Cleland's artistic vision.

The economy was gradually healing itself under the New Deal, but it was the impetus of the rearmament for America's involvement in World War II that ended the Depression itself and by the end of the decade, America was putting itself on a war footing, with new priorities. Illustration was again to have a major role in its contribution to that endeavor.

This Constantin Alajálov promotional illustration for the movie "Monkey Business" was done for Paramount Studios in 1931, when the Marx Brothers were then four: Harpo, Zeppo, Groucho, and Chico.

a l a j á l o v

CONSTANTIN ALAJÁLOV (1900-1987) sold his first cover to *The New Yorker* magazine in 1926, and continued to paint a long and colorful series of satirical vignettes of American life for both *The New Yorker* and *The Saturday Evening Post* until 1962.

Alajálov was born in the Russian town of Rostov-on-the-Don. The Revolution came when he was seventeen and a student at the University of Petrograd. He survived this period by working as a government artist, painting huge propaganda pictures and portraits, and in 1921, he made his way to Constantinople, which was an international refugee haven.

Although largely self-taught as an artist, Alajálov earned a precarious living by sketching portraits in bars or painting sidewalk advertisements for movie houses. He progressed to doing murals for night clubs, taking mostly food as payment. After two years of this, he saved enough to pay his passage to America.

Once here, Alajálov resumed painting murals, in Russian night clubs, and within three years had sold that first *New Yorker* cover. For the rest of his career, he continued to give us a candid and humorous look at our foibles.

J.E. ALLEN

JAMES EDWARD ALLEN (1894-1964) was a student and serious experimenter all his life. Born in Louisiana, Missouri, he attended the Art Academy in Chicago, the Art Students League, the Grand Central Art School and the Hans Hoffman School in New York. He also studied in Paris and London.

Among his instructors were Frank Stick, Joseph Pennell, Robert Brackman, Robert Philipp, William Auerbach-Levy, Arshile Gorky, Sigurd Skou and Harvey Dunn.

He began illustrating for the *People's Popular Monthly* in 1913. Assignments from nearly all of the major magazines followed. Most of his pictures were painted in oils, but he also produced lithographs and etchings which have been exhibited widely in the United States and abroad.

Allen was a member of the Salmagundi Club, the New Rochelle Art Association and the Society of Etchers in New York, the Chicago Society of Etchers, and the Philadelphia Society of Etchers . His work won many awards and is represented in several collections, including the Brooklyn Museum, the Cincinnati Museum, the Cleveland Museum of Art, the Seattle Art Museum, the Philadelphia Museum of Art and the Library of Congress.

J. B. Allen, illustration for "The Stone Growers" by Albert Payson Terhune; published by *The Saturday Evening Post*, November 5, 1921.

Harold Anderson, cover illustration for *Liberty* magazine, March 8, 1941.
© 2000 Liberty Library Corporation.

HAROLD ANDERSON

HAROLD ANDERSON (1894-1973) studied at the Fenway Art School in his native Boston. Among his instructors were Chase Emerson, Harold Brett, and Arthur Spear.

His first illustrations were made for *Boy's Life* in 1919 and were followed by work for most of the leading publications, many national advertising campaigns, and twenty-four-sheet billboard posters.

He won numerous poster awards and exhibited in Art Directors Club shows in 1937, 1940, 1942, 1946, 1950 and 1951. Anderson was a member of the Society of Illustrators, The Old Greenwich Art Society, the Artists Guild and the Westport Artists. He had a one-man show at the Society of Illustrators in 1942.

Artzybasheff

BORIS ARTZYBASHEFF (1899-1965) combined a spirit of fantasy with wry humor in his incomparable ability to give human qualities to machines; his meticulous rendering made his most imaginative creations entirely convincing. His designs were always carefully planned — there is not an accidental stroke in them — and he mastered every technical problem by thoughtful preliminary studies.

Artzybasheff was born in Kharkov, Russia, and was graduated from the Prince Tenisheff School in St. Petersburg. After the Revolution, he escaped the country on a freighter. When he arrived in America in 1919, he had only a few Turkish coins, the equivalent of 14 cents.

Befriended by a Russian Orthodox priest, he found work in an engraving shop doing lettering, borders and ornamental details. He first gained a reputation as an artist by illustrating over 40 books, several of which he also wrote or edited. Among the best known of these are his *Aesop's Fables*, *Seven Simeons*, and Balzac's *Droll Stories*. Advertising and magazine cover painting assignments followed. He was a regular contributor of incisive and penetrating cover portraits for *Time* magazine for 24 years, painting over 200 covers. His work was also well known abroad; he did commissions for firms overseas as well as many advertising campaigns for leading companies in the United States.

During World War II, Artzybasheff served as an expert adviser to the U. S. Department of State, Psychological Warfare Branch.

During his long career, he was the recipient of many awards, including the Newberry Medal, and citations from the American Institute of Graphic Arts. In 1998, Artzybasheff was posthumously elected into the Society of Illustrators' Hall of Fame.

Artzybasheff, *Radio Propoganda, Two Headed Monster*, from a series of anthropomorphic war machines published by *Life* magazine, 1941.

Ernest Hamlin Baker, cover portrait painting of General Omar Bradley, for *Time* magazine, May 1, 1944. © 1944 Time, Inc. From the Collection of the National Portrait Gallery, The Smithsonian Institution.

Ernest Hamlin Baker

ERNEST HAMLIN BAKER (1889-1975) was a self-taught artist who evolved his own personal, and painstakingly intricate approach, as typified by his cover designs for *Fortune* and other magazines, as well as the nearly 400 cover portraits he painted for *Time* magazine.

These portraits were painted from photographs of the subjects taken from all possible angles, with different light sources, studied minutely — even with a magnifying glass — to gain a knowledge of the whole face and head.

Baker then made a highly detailed preliminary pencil study of the "facial guide-map." Every wen, wart, indentation or vein was factually and honestly depicted. It was from a careful analysis of these "facts" and their relationship to each other, that a faithful likeness emerged, one that revealed character.

His painting process was equally detailed, beginning with a tracing from the pencil drawing on illustration board. The portrait was gradually built up with repeated strokes of diluted tempera color, allowing the drawing beneath to show through. Values were thus built up from light to dark with minute strokes, even for the large areas, each stroke successively blotted to remove any excess of color. This unique process, laborious as it was, gave the artist continuous control of the painting right up to the final stroke.

BALCOM

LOWELL LEROY "TONY" BALCOM (1887-1938) was born in Kansas City, Missouri, and got his start there. He studied privately with John D. Patrick and at the Kansas City Art Institute with Charles Wilimovsky. His first job was as an artist for the *Kansas City Star.* In the Army during World War I, his duties consisted largely of drawing and painting portraits of officers.

After the war, Balcom visited the Virgin Islands to paint in watercolors and oils. He made his first experiments there with linoleum cuts which he was later to develop as his preferred medium.

Balcom's first break came when he did a series of illustrations for the U.S. Shipping Board, which also provided him an opportunity to travel to the Orient and the Mediterranean. Subsequently, he did illustrations for numerous magazines such as *The American Legion* and *Hearst's International*, and for such advertisers as Exide Batteries and Bridgeport Brass.

He was a member of the Artists Guild in New York and was active in the Silvermine Guild in Norwalk, Connecticut, up to the time of his death.

L.L. Balcom, *The Sacred River,* linoleum cut illustration for "Why India Follows Gandhi," *The Forum,* May, 1931.

#

McCLELLAND BARCLAY (1891-1943) was commissioned a Lieutenant Commander, U.S.N.R., during World War II and contributed many posters, illustrations and officer portraits for the Navy before being reported missing in action, in the Pacific Theatre, aboard an L.S.T. which was torpedoed.

Before the war, Barclay was most noted for his ability to paint strikingly beautiful women, as best exemplified by his long running series for General Motors illustrating the slogan, "Body by Fisher." Some of his other advertising clients included Lever Brothers Co., Frigidaire, A&P, Eaton papers, Crane and Pike Company, Elgin Watches, and especially Humming Bird Hosiery. He also illustrated fiction for most of the large-circulation magazines.

Sculpture was another facet of the artist's career, and his McClelland Barclay Art Products Corporation produced a whole line of three-dimensional decorative products.

Born in St. Louis, Missouri, Barclay was a student of H. C. Ives, George Bridgman and Thomas Fogarty. He was a member of the Artists Guild, the Art Students League of New York, and the Society of Illustrators.

One of many metallic sculptures designed by Barclay and produced by the Dodge Company.

One of a series of illustrations for Humming Bird Hosiery, painted in 1932.

Our Fleet in Action, published in **Coronet** magazine.

CECIL CALVERT BEALL (1892-1967) traveled a long way from his birthplace of Saratoga, Wyoming. He studied at the Art Students League under George Bridgman and at Pratt Institute. His early illustrations were done in a bold poster style in watercolor marked by a strong pattern of light and shadow which was favored by a number of illustrators of the *Collier's* "school."

In 1936, Beall did a composite portrait of President Roosevelt for a *Collier's* cover which so pleased the President that he appointed Beall art director for the National Democratic Committee,

During World War II, Beall painted the portraits of a number of decorated heroes for covers of *Collier's* magazine. At the close of the war, Beall was one of the privileged few to witness the surrender ceremony aboard the U.S.S. Missouri. His painting of the event was made the official one by President Harry S. Truman.

Beall was a member of the Society of Illustrators and won their Award of Excellence in the 1961 exhibition. He also belonged to the American Watercolor Society, the Overseas Press Club, the Hudson Valley Art Association, and the Salmagundi Club. His pictures are included in many collections, including the Air Force Academy Museum in Colorado Springs, Colorado, and the Marine Museum at Quantico, Virginia.

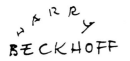

HARRY BECKHOFF (1901-1979) began his pictorial compositions with small sketches that were almost literally thumbnail in size. These tiny drawings contained all of the information needed for the final rendering — even down to facial expressions. He then pantographed the drawing, about five times larger, and inked in the outlines. The tonal or color areas were painted in with flat washes.

Beckhoff described his work as having been influenced by the French illustrators Martin, Brissaud and Marty. He also cited his teachers, George Bridgman, Dean Cornwell, and Harvey Dunn for their encouragement and training.

The Country Gentleman published his first magazine illustrations in 1929. Beckhoff subsequently worked for many of the other periodicals, but he was most closely associated with the wonderful Broadway characters he drew to illustrate Damon Runyon's famous stories which ran for many years in *Collier's*.

C. C. Beall, story illustration for *Collier's* magazine.

Typical compositional drawing at this exact size, before being enlarged.

Harry Beckhoff, illustration for "The Revolt of Horace Plum," *This Week* magazine, October 15, 1950. Collection of Howard Chaykin.

FRANK BENSING

FRANK C. BENSING (1893-1983) was born in Chicago, Illinois, and received his art training there at the Art Institute. Among his teachers were DeForrest Schook, Wellington Reynolds, Charles Schroeder and Walter Biggs.

Bensing's first illustrations were made in 1926 for *Redbook*, an association which continued for many years. He also worked for *McCall's*, *Country Gentleman*, *The Saturday Evening Post*, *American*, *Pictorial Review*, *The American Legion*, and *This Week* magazines.

Bensing paralleled his illustration for periodicals with exhibitions of his oils and watercolors at the National Academy of Design, the American Watercolor Society, Allied Artists and others. In later years, he turned increasingly to portraiture.

Bensing was a member of the Dutch Treat Club, the Artists and Writers club, the Allied Artists, the Salmagundi Club, the American Watercolor Society and the Society of Illustrators.

Frank Bensing, illustration for a murder mystery; date and place of publication not known. Collection of Terrence V. Flannery.

Earl Blossom, illustration for *Collier's* "Three on a Spare" by Philip Clark; July 26, 1941.

Earl Blossom

EARL BLOSSOM (1891-1970) had no formal art instruction, but received his training in the practical school of advertising. Some of his early work included drawings for men's fashions, newspaper illustration for the *Chicago American*, and a stint as a bull-pen artist in the Charles Daniel Frey studio in Chicago.

Many of the large advertising agencies were getting started in the 'twenties, and Blossom worked at one time or another for most of them. He also spent some time promoting the land boom in Florida; he wrote and illustrated full-page advertisements for Boca Raton real estate.

Blossom had known Pete Martin earlier in Chicago and under his art direction at *The Saturday Evening Post,* Blossom began to do fiction illustration. He was not entirely happy at the *Post,* however, where "everyone was supposed to imitate Arthur William Brown," and when Martin left the Post, Blossom switched to *Collier's* magazine.

William Chessman, who was art director at *Collier's,* encouraged Earl to develop his own humorous bent. Said Chessmen, "He is a masterful artist. You never have to tell him what do do. Just give him a good story and let him alone." Blossom responded with a wonderful blend of comedy and realism that became his specialty.

Bobri, illustration for the "Style and Beauty" section of *McCall's* magazine.

bobri

VLADIMIR BOBRITSKY "BOBRI" (1898-unknown) was a student at the Kharkov Imperial Art School in the Ukraine before the Russian Revolution and had begun to design sets for the Great Dramatic Theatre of Kharkov.

Swept up in the conflict, he fought in several armies on both sides and eventually, with a passport he forged himself, managed to escape to Constantinople.

Several years of varied art activities followed — including painting Greek icons and playing guitar in a gypsy chorus — before Bobri was able to come to America.

His experiences here were no less varied, ranging from the operation of a textile printing business, to art direction for Saks Fifth Avenue. His newspaper and magazine layouts represented a fresh departure. Bobri soon found himself with enough clients to embark on a freelance art career, largely for advertising illustration, and strongly influenced by his background of classical training and theatrical designing.

He continued his serious study of the guitar both as composer and performer; he was president of the Society of the Classic Guitar in New York, and served as editor and art director of the *Guitar Review*. He also illustrated many children's books.

HANNES BOK (1914-1964) was the self-designed name for WAYNE WOODARD. The alienated product of a divorced family, he struck out on his own to support himself and to become an artist. His passion was science fiction and fantasy. He made up for his lack of training by visiting museums, pouring over books, and studying the Pulp magazines. Being in the middle of the Depression, a difficult time even for professionals to find work, Bok was only able to sell his first artwork to *Fantasy* magazine in 1934 after many unsuccessful years.

Meanwhile, he had contacted the eminent Maxfield Parrish about his working methods, and began to follow them himself, including Parrish's use of the theory of "Dynamic Symmetry" in composing his pictures. Bok also tried Parrish's use of glazes to produce translucent color. Unfortunately, this was an extremely slow process with long drying time between layers of varnish which limited Bok's production of pictures.

Despite these handicaps, Bok eventually found recognition in his chosen field, and was published by *Weird Tales, Future Fiction, Startling Stories* and other Pulp magazines while continuing to be underpaid and struggling to survive. Like many pioneers in their fields, Bok came along too soon, unable to benefit from what has now become a huge interest in science fiction and fantasy subjects. The limited number of his works that have survived show him to have been an original, creative talent.

A Hannes Bok Treasury edited by Stephen D. Korshak was published in 1993.

Hannes Bok, " *The Sentry*", 1944. Originally created as a work of fine art, this was reproduced in a fanzine prior to the 12th World Science Fiction Convention. In that use, it illustrated a poem entitled "Come and Kill Me, Earthman!" by Richard Geis.

Melbourne Brindle, *Today's Clipper Ship,* illustration for the Commercial National Bank and Trust Company of New York.

Melbourne Brindle

Named for his birthplace in Australia, E. MELBOURNE BRINDLE (1906-1995) made a reputation for himself in the United States with his precise and fastidious illustrations.

With no formal training, Brindle progressed through a number of jobs in the San Francisco area, from show card writing to a department store's art department, to affiliation with a large advertising agency.

Becoming at home in every medium, he first developed a brilliant black and white technique which won him medals in the New York Art Directors Club's annual shows in 1934 and 1938.

Brindle began to do editorial illustration for **Woman's Home Companion** in 1940, followed by commissions from most of the other national magazines. He was especially expert in depicting antique automobiles, since he collected and restored them as a hobby. Brindle researched and fully illustrated with his own paintings **Twenty Silver Ghosts**, a beautiful book on historical Rolls-Royce automobiles, published by **McGraw Hill** in 1971.

Elmor Brown

ELMOR J. BROWN (1899-1968) illustrated Ernest Hemingway's first published short story, "A Matter of Color," in the **Tabula,** an annual for the Oak Park [Illinois] High School where both were students in 1916.

Brown went on to study at the Chicago Art Institute and the Art Students League in New York. Among his instructors were John Norton, George Bellows, Leopold Seyffert, Leon Kroll and Eugene Speicher.

His first major illustrations, done for **The Ladies' Home Journal** in 1931, were soon followed by work for most of the other national magazines. His work appeared most regularly in **Collier's** magazine, however, from 1933 to 1949.

Brown, a keen student of the technical problems of painting, once determined that to obtain Munsell's neutral #5 gray required .01 of an ounce of black and .3904 of an ounce of white! He worked from light to dark in accord with his own scientific analysis of the problems of painting.

Brown was a member of the Artists and Writers association and a life member of the Society of Illustrators.

Promotion illustration for "Morning Glory" (RKO Pictures) 1933, starring Katharine Hepburn (who won an Oscar), Douglas Fairbanks, Jr., and Adolphe Menjou.

Polo match, *Cosmopolitan* magazine.

Paul Brown

PAUL BROWN (1893-1958) began to draw horses at the age of six; they continued to be his favorite subject to the end of his life. During this time, he wrote thirty-three books of his own and illustrated over 100 more by other authors.

Brown's knowledge of horses was acquired through continuous study and sketching at polo matches and races until he became so familiar with them that he could draw them entirely without models. His specialty was painting horses in sports or in violent action.

He began drawing catalog and sporting illustrations for Brooks Brothers in 1920, continuing with them for nearly forty years. Brown also illustrated for many magazines, including *Cosmopolitan*, *Collier's*, *Spur*, *Polo*, *Harper's Bazaar*, *Liberty*, *The Elks*, and *The American Legion.*

ELMER SIMMS CAMPBELL (1906-1971) first appeared in print in his St. Louis high school weekly newspaper as a cartoonist. After a year of college, Simms switched to the Chicago Art Institute where he learned the fundamentals of drawing and painting. This led to a job with the Triad Studios, a midwest advertising art agency. After two years, he quit his job to try New York in 1929, in time for the onset of the Depression. He did find some work at the Munig studios, and began to submit cartoons to *College Humor, Judge* and *Life.*

It was Russell Patterson who gave him the key advice which started him on his road to fame. He advised Simms to specialize in pretty girls as he had done, advising him, "You can always sell a pretty girl!"

Thus, in the depth of the Depression in 1933, he was hired by the newly launched *Esquire* magazine to submit cartoons and his hallmark harem girls, in full page and full-color, soon became among the favorites with readers. He was also submitting idea gags to the magazine for other artists to render, finally deciding to try his own daily feature, "Cuties," for King Features Syndicate.

Campbell, who was of African-American descent, of necessity drew white characters for his market, but in this drawing, one of his most magnificent for *Esquire*, he makes a bold statement about racial roles in the caption: "Sorry buddy — you'll have to deliver them at the trade entrance"

He escaped the prevailing racial prejudice in America by moving to Switzerland for the last fourteen years of his life.

"The Stolen God" by Edison Marshall. *American Magazine*, February, 1936.

PRUETT CARTER

PRUETT A. CARTER (1891-1955) once described the role of the illustrator in this manner:

"The illustrator may be likened to the director of a motion picture, or a spoken stage-play. He must know his characters — their emotions and desires — he must set the stage, and direct the arrangement and action and conflict of drama. He must live the part of each actor. He must do the scenery, design the costumes and handle the lighting effects. His illustration must be deeper than a poster, for he must make his characters live and breathe and react to each other as the author intended."

For nearly 40 years, Carter fulfilled this role in his work for the leading magazines. Especially, he had the ability to paint women sympathetically; his heroines were noted for their gentle, patrician beauty. Walter Biggs had taught him the use of color, and Pruett used his palette with brilliance and taste.

Carter was born in Lexington, Missouri, and was reared on an Indian reservation in Wyoming where his father ran a trading post and his mother taught school. The family moved on to California so that Pruett could go to high school there. Upon graduation, Carter was encouraged in his art ambitions by James Swinnerton, the cartoonist, creator of "Little Jimmy."

Carter went to the Los Angeles Art School and got his first job on Hearst's *New York American*; he was later transferred to the *Atlanta Georgian*. As a step toward his ambition to become a magazine illustrator, Carter next became art editor for *Good Housekeeping* magazine, and eventually was able to assign one of the story manuscripts to himself. From then on, he worked as a freelance illustrator.

A vacation trip to California in 1930 became a permanent move. Taking along an assignment from Henry Quinan, art editor of *Woman's Home Companion*, Carter airmailed the pictures back. With the addition of long-distance telephone conferences, he found this to be a practical arrangement.

Carter taught many other illustrators, some at the Grand Central School of Art in New York, others at the Chouinard Art Institute in Los Angeles, where he headed the illustration department for several years. He was elected into the Society of Illustrators' Hall of Fame in 1988.

Illustration for a racing story, *American Magazine*, 1939. Collection of Houshyar Broukhim.

Breaking the Bronco, advertising illustration for Hickok Bar H. Belts, 1943. Collection of River Enterprises Inc.

BENTON CLARK (1895-1964) owed much, as have all subsequent painters of the Old West, to Frederic Remington and his authoritative recording of that period. Benton also greatly admired Harvey Dunn and Frank Hoffman for their work in the western genre.

The son of a harness maker in Coshocton, Ohio, Benton Clark knew horses, wagons, and all the details of harnessing horses. Since he specialized in historic subject matter, his knowledge of horses was invaluable.

Clark's own contribution is in dramatically synthesizing the era in a robust and colorful way. His illustrations make the past alive and convincing; the picture reproduced here epitomizes his work.

Benton was trained at the Art Institute of Chicago and the art school of the National Academy of Design in New York. His early work was in the art department for M-G-M in Culver City, California; for the Stevens-Sundblom Studio; and in the King Studio, both in Chicago.

He first illustrated for **Liberty** magazine in 1927, and subsequently for most of the other major magazines, including **The Saturday Evening Post**, **McCall's**, **Cosmopolitan**, **Blue Book**, and **Good Housekeeping.**

Delivery of a Guinea Hen, Illustration for ***The Saturday Evening Post,*** October 21, 1939. ©1939, 1967 by The Curtis Publishing Company.

MATT CLARK

Like his older brother Benton, MATT CLARK (1903-1972) was born in Coshocton, Ohio. He, too, attended the National Academy Art School in New York and was also an expert in depicting the Old West, particularly horses and their accoutrements, harnesses and buggies. For several years, the brothers shared a studio and used the same models, and their work looked very similar. Matt's subjects were in no way restricted to the Old West, however; he was equally at home with contemporary subjects, from the farm to urban society.

Although Benton worked almost exclusively in oils, Matt was noted for his masterful use of dry-brush, often combined with watercolor. This medium, because of the underlying black-ink drawing, reproduced exceptionally well, whether in full color or in black-and-white.

His first illustrations were published in ***College Humor*** in 1929; he added nearly all of the other magazines to his list of clients, including a long association with ***The Saturday Evening Post.***

FREDERICK TRENCH CHAPMAN (1887-1983) had a strong sense of line and pattern which logically led to his concentration in the field of book illustration. He was an acknowledged master of the figure in action and specialized in period costume subjects for which he could utilize his love of historical research.

Notable examples of this talent are seen in his illustrations for the **History of America**, published by D. C. Heath and Company; **Virginia History**, **Government**, **Geography** published by Charles Scribner's sons; plates drawn for **The Quarterly**: **The Company of Military Collectors & Historians**; and the many historical juvenile novels he illustrated for various publishers.

Chapman was a Californian who studied at the Art Students League of New York with George Bridgman. Some of his early artwork was done in collaboration with the Czech artist Vojtech Preissig, who was an expert printmaker and exponent of the use of the linoleum block.

For a number of years, Chapman illustrated for magazines such as **Everybody's**, **Harper's Bazaar**, **Collier's**, **Liberty** and **Woman's Home Companion**, but it was the success of his first book, **Voyages to Vinland**, published by Alfred A. Knopf in 1942, that led to his specialization as an illustrator of books.

One of the series of wood engravings in two colors executed for *Voyages to Vinland*.

RALPH PALLEN COLEMAN

Over his long career, RALPH PALLEN COLEMAN (1892-1968) illustrated stories by many famous authors including Somerset Maugham, Rex Beach, F. Scott Fitzgerald, Louis Bromfield and Clarence Budington Kelland; this work appeared in most of the major magazines.

Coleman, who was educated at the Philadelphia Museum School of Industrial art, sold his first illustration to **The Saturday Evening Post** in 1919. His work appeared regularly thereafter in the **Post** and other magazines for over twenty years. He also found time in his busy career to paint many portraits and a number of murals in churches in Jenkintown, Lancaster, and Montoursville, Pennsylvania, and in Wilmington, Delaware. In addition, he executed a series of paintings depicting the Life of Christ for the George Washington Memorial Park in White Marsh, Pennsylvania.

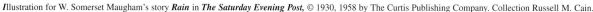

*I*llustration for W. Somerset Maugham's story **Rain** in **The Saturday Evening Post,** © 1930, 1958 by The Curtis Publishing Company. Collection Russell M. Cain.

Grattan Condon, illustration for "Cardigan" by Robert W. Chambers. *The American Boy-Youth's Companion*, serialized 1929-1930.

DAN CONTENT

The illustrations of DAN CONTENT (1902-1990) retain the strong stamp of his teacher, Dean Cornwell. A precocious student, Content also studied at Pratt Institute and the Art Students League of New York. He sold his first illustration at the age of twenty-one to *McCall's* magazine.

Stories of high adventure predominate among his illustrations for such magazines as *Cosmopolitan, Good Housekeeping, Liberty, The Ladies' Home Journal, Collier's,* and *Woman's Home Companion.*

Content taught at the Work Shop School of Art in 1947-48, and subsequently was affiliated with an advertising marketing firm in New York City.

GRATTAN CONDON

GRATTAN CONDON (1887-1966) is perhaps best known for his illustrations of stories of World War I, although he could draw other subjects equally well. Many of his illustrations were rendered in charcoal and have a freely drawn effect as though done directly at the scene; it is this quality that makes his war subjects so convincing. Among other leading publications, he was a regular contributor to *The Saturday Evening Post* and *The Ladies' Home Journal.*

Condon was born in Eugene, Oregon, and studied at both the Los Angeles School of Art and Design, and the Art Students League of Los Angeles; his teachers included Walter Biggs and Lewis Daniel.

An illustrator, painter and educator, Condon was a member of the Society of Illustrators and the Salmagundi Club in New York City.

Dan Content, *Couple on Veranda*, 1923. Collection of the Society of Illustrators Museum of American Illustration.

BRADSHAW CRANDELL (1896-1966) took over the *Cosmopolitan* cover when Harrison Fisher retired. For a period of twelve years, in the 'thirties and 'forties, he did a continuing series of beautiful girls' heads in pastel for their monthly covers. Many top Hollywood stars and young starlets of that time were his models.

Crandell was born in Glens Falls, New York, educated at Wesleyan University and at the Chicago Art Institute. He sold his first cover to *Judge* magazine in 1921, and from then on concentrated on cover designs for such other publications as *Collier's, Redbook, American, The Ladies' Home Journal* and *The Saturday Evening Post.*

In later years, he confined his work to portraiture, painted the governors of various states and many prominent society figures. He was a member of the Society of Illustrators, the Artists and Writers, and the Dutch Treat Club.

Bradshaw Crandall, Cover design in pastel, probably for *Cosmopolitan* magazine. The Charles Martinette Collection.

MARIO COOPER

MARIO RUBEN COOPER, N.A., A.W.S. (1905-1995) had several careers in the field of art, each pursued with great enthusiasm and marked by excellence.

Born in Mexico City of Mexican-American parentage, he was reared in Los Angeles and received his education there at the Otis Art Institute and Chouinard Art Institute. He later attended the Grand Central School of Art and Columbia University in New York. Among his teachers were Pruett Carter and Harvey Dunn, Dunn especially influenced his philosophy and point of view.

Cooper was at various times employed in an engraving house; as a visualizer for Batten, Barton, Durstine and Osborne; as art director for Lord and Taylor; and as an expert layout man and letterer; before finally obtaining his first commission for an illustration from *Collier's* magazine.

As an illustrator, Cooper was noted for the dramatic concepts of his pictures combined with a meticulous rendering, usually in colored inks on illustration board. His work appeared in many national magazines but was most closely identified with *Collier's* and other Crowell-Collier publications.

Cooper himself taught illustration at the Grand Central School of Art, Columbia University, the National Academy, the Art Students League, and the City College of New York.

He had also been an active watercolorist, President of the American Watercolor Society and the author of several books on watercolor painting techniques.

A parallel interest was sculpture. He studied under Oronzio Maldarelli and executed a number of commissions for churches and other institutions.

A long-time member of the Society of Illustrators and the National Sculpture Society, Cooper was also a past president of the Audubon Artists.

Two early Cooper illustrations from the 1930s, probably for *Collier's* magazine.
Collection of Dale Meyer Cooper.

W. Galbraith Crawford, *Lamb and Two Vixens*, (perhaps ***Harper's Bazaar***).

J. H. Crosman, illustration in watercolor. Perhaps in ***American Magazine***, 1930's.

Galbraith

WILLIAM GALBRAITH CRAWFORD (1894-unknown) was a prolific and facile draftsman who signed his work with his middle name. He was best known for the humor and drawings of his widely-syndicated panel cartoon, "Side Glances," which he drew for twenty-three years, but he had extensive prior experience as an illustrator for such publications as ***The Saturday Evening Post***, ***Vanity Fair***, ***The New Yorker***, ***Harper's Bazaar***, ***Cosmopolitan***, and ***The Delineator*** magazines.

Crawford was born in Salt Lake City, Utah, and attended Brigham Young University for two years. This was followed by instruction at the Art Students League in New York, the Los Angeles School of Art and Design and the University of Mexico. Among his teachers were Mahonri Young, Thomas Fogarty, Edward Dufner and Henry Wolf.

J. H. Crosman —

JOHN HENRY CROSMAN (1897-1970) began his career in illustration in the 'twenties as a brilliant performer in pen-and-ink. In the 'thirties, however, tastes in illustration changed considerably, and the pen-and-ink medium was no longer popular with the magazine-reading public. Crosman then successfully changed his technique, working occasionally in watercolor or wash, but usually with Russian charcoal.

For over twenty years, Crosman illustrated for most of the major publications, including ***Collier's***, ***Woman's Home Companion***, ***The Ladies' Home Journal***, ***The Saturday Evening Post***, ***American***, and ***Good Housekeeping***, but later confined his work to portraiture.

Born in Swampscott, Massachusetts, Crosman attended the Massachusetts Normal Art School in Boston, studying under Richard Andrew and Ernest Major. He also did some teaching and was a member of the Guild of Boston Artists.

Cover for *The Saturday Evening Post,* July 6, 1940. © 1940, 1968 by The Curtis Publishing Company.

The illustrations of DOUGLAS CROCKWELL (1904-1968) were often simply signed "Douglass" to avoid confusion with the signature of Norman Rockwell, particularly since their work was being published on the covers of *The Saturday Evening Post* during the same period. Necessary too, because Crockwell also worked very realistically, and like Rockwell, was particularly good with children.

Their backgrounds, however, were entirely different. Crockwell was born in Columbus, Ohio, and took his degree in Science at Washington University, followed by study at the Academy of Fine Arts in Chicago and the St. Louis School of Fine Arts. He received his first commission for a cover for *The Saturday Evening Post* in 1933, and this was followed by many more, as well as work for other periodicals and a long list of national advertisers.

During the 'thirties, he also completed Post Office murals in Vermont, New York State and Mississippi, and began to work on experimental animated films. The films, and inventing a "pan-stereo" viewing camera to produce them, occupied the rest of his life, although he also continued to do some twenty to forty illustrations a year.

His work won Art Directors Club medals in 1943, 1945 and 1946, and his films are in the Museum of Modern Art Film Library.

Advertising illustration for Lederle, a division of American Cyanamid Co.

Crowther, illustration for a story in **The Saturday Evening Post.**© 1937, 1965 by The Curtis Publishing Company.

ROBERT W. CROWTHER (1902-1978) worked in charcoal which he employed with sure control and strongly contrasted values. This insured good reproduction and made for strong, dramatic pictures.

Crowther was born in Philadelphia and attended both the Pennsylvania Museum School of Industrial Art and the Pennsylvania Academy of the Fine Arts, then also studied under Thornton Oakley. He himself taught at the Pennsylvania Museum School of Industrial Art from 1926-28.

His first illustrations appeared in **Lutheran Young Folks** magazine in 1924; eventually he worked for many major publications, including **The Saturday Evening Post**, **The Country Gentleman**, **Farm Journal**, **Liberty**, **Cosmopolitan**, **Pictorial Review**, **McCall's**, and **Good Housekeeping**.

N. EGGENHOFER

NICK EGGENHOFER (1897-1985) was born in Gauting, Bavaria. As a young boy, he was fascinated by stories of Buffalo Bill and other heroes of the American Wild West. He also greatly admired the drawings and paintings of Frederic Remington and Charles Russell which were reproduced in German publications.

By the time he arrived in the United States at the age of sixteen, he had decided to become a Western artist himself. He studied nights at Cooper Union and thoroughly immersed himself in the subject by making exact scale models of wagons, stagecoaches, harnesses and other authentic props.

In **Western Story**, a pulp magazine of Street & Smith, he found a ready and voracious market for all the drawings he could produce, for years. He also illustrated for other magazines, and many books to which his dry-brush black-and-white drawings were ideally suited. He wrote and illustrated **Wagons, Mules and Men**, published by Hastings House in 1961, and his autobiography, **Horses, Horses, Always Horses,** was published by Sage Publishing Company in 1981.

Eggenhofer made his home in Wyoming and painted Western subjects which have been exhibited widely in the West and at Kennedy Galleries in New York City.

One of the many pulp covers that Eggenhofer produced over the years for Street & Smith's **Western Story** magazine and other publications.

London Underground 1943, from **England at War,** April 3, 1944. Published by *Life* magazine.

FLOYD MACMILLAN DAVIS (1896-1966) gave much of the credit for the success of his pictures to the critical judgment of his wife, painter Gladys Rockmore Davis. Floyd's point of view, however, was uniquely his own. His visual world was peopled by a gallery of wonderful characters depicted with poetic realism and warm humor. The wealth of detail in his pictures would seem to have required much study from ,models or photos of them. In fact, Davis did not use any models at all but relied instead on his remarkably retentive memory and lively imagination.

In his early years, he produced a great deal of advertising illustration notable for the fragile beauty and lofty hauteur of the society types he drew.

In the 'thirties, Davis began to illustrate stories of humbler subjects. His pictures of southern rural and hill people for such authors as William Faulkner, Sigman Byrd, Glenn Allan and MacKinlay Kantor became immensely popular. He loved those assignments and filled the pictures not only with a fascinating cast of individuals, but added the special Davis touches, a cat crouched in the corner ready to leap out at a rival, a fly on an old man's head, a small lizard hiding behind a tree. None of these details intruded on the narrative itself; they were there for the perceptive viewer to discover. Readers responded enthusiastically; his pictures were admired as much as the stories themselves.

With the outbreak of World War II, Davis was selected as a correspondent-artist for the War Department and painted in various war theatres. Many of these distinguished paintings were reproduced by *Life* magazine as part of a pictorial record of the war, and were hung in the Pentagon building in Washington, D.C.

Over the years, Davis won several Art Directors Club medals and other awards, but more importantly, his work had the admiration of his whole profession. Floyd Davis was one of the great figures of American illustration.

Illustration for *Tomorrow* by William Faulkner, published by *The Saturday Evening Post,* November 23, 1940. ©1940, 1968 by The Curtis Publishing Company; Collection of the New Britain Museum of American Art.

The Story, reproduced as a cover for **McCall's**, homemaking section, 1945.

Gladys Rockmore Davis

GLADYS ROCKMORE DAVIS (1901-1967) was born in New York, but received her art training at the Art Institute of Chicago where she studied under John Norton. She enjoyed a very successful illustration career for several years.

The mutual influence she and her husband shared made their early work look very similar, although Floyd worked for more men's fashion accounts.

Gradually, as their children grew, she experimented with oil and pastel and began to paint more for exhibition. She won prizes at the Corcoran Gallery of Art, the Art Institute of Chicago, the Pennsylvania Academy of the Fine Arts, the National Academy of Design, the Virginia Museum of Fine Arts. Her work is represented in many collections, including the Toledo Museum of Art and the Encyclopedia Britannica Collection.

Fritz Eichenberg

FRITZ EICHENBERG (1901-1990) was primarily a graphic artist who worked in lithography, but his best medium was wood engraving. He was also a prolific book illustrator; his many publishers included the Limited Editions Club, Heritage Press and Random House. Among the classic titles he illustrated were **Richard III**, **Gulliver's Travels**, **Crime and Punishment**, **The Tales of Edgar Allen Poe**, **Wuthering Heights**, **Jane Eyre**, and the short stories of Wilkie Collins.

Eichenberg was born in Cologne, Germany, and was apprenticed to a lithographer at the age of sixteen. He also studied at the State Academy of Graphic Arts in Leipzig under the noted Hugo Sterner-Prag. He first worked as an artist-reporter for various newspapers and magazines. In 1933, he emigrated to the United States, and quickly found work illustrating books. He was active as a print maker and exhibited at the National Academy of Design, the Library of Congress, and the American Institute of Graphic Arts, winning many awards and purchase prizes. In 1944, he received the Joseph Pennell Memorial Medal in recognition of his contributions to the graphic arts.

Illustration for **Wuthering Heights** by Emily Brontë.
Random House Publishers, 1943.

This fashion illustration for the American Viscose Corporation was awarded the New York Art Directors Club Medal.

"Cancan at the Bal Tabarin," *Vogue* magazine, date unknown.

 CARL OSCAR AUGUST ERICKSON (ERIC) (1891-1958) dominated the field of fashion illustration for over thirty-five years. His virtuosity of line and tone was combined with innate elegance and taste. Eric's work looks deceptively effortless, but dozens of preliminary attempts often were discarded before a final direct and spontaneous effect was ready for his signature.

Eric's birthplace was Joliet, Illinois; his formal art training was limited to two years at the Chicago Academy of Fine Arts. This was followed by work for Marshall Field, Lord & Thomas, and other advertising accounts in Chicago until 1914, when he moved to New York City.

In New York, he continued with advertising illustration and made his first fashion drawings for the **Dry Goods Economist**. In 1920, Eric first trraveled to Paris where he felt in total rapport; for the next twenty years it was his second home. During that period, he illustrated for French publications and did society portraits. Beginning in 1923, he became a staff illustrator for **Vogue** magazine. In 1940, he returned to America, continuing his work for Condé Nast, and began illustrating for American rather than French advertisers.

Himself the personification of his elegant world, Eric wore a bowler and carried a walking stick, and he directly participated in the fashionable life of the international set. His drawings and paintings are authoritative because he knew his subjects and their world; his taste and beautiful draftsmanship reveal him to be an artist of permanent importance.

The Brooklyn Museum held a retrospective show of his drawings in 1959 shortly after his death.

A dress by Jean Patou delineated for **Vogue** magazine © March 15, 1933, 1961 by the Condé Nast Publications, Inc.

John Fulton, ***Blue Book*** illustration for ***Kiss of the Scorpion***, by Sax Rohmer, June, 1951.

JOHN RUSSELL FULTON (1896-) was a studio artist who did advertising illustrations for several years but is best remembered for his association with two periodicals, ***Redbook*** and ***Blue Book.***

His ***Redbook*** illustrations in oils were in the manner of Harvey Dunn, strong and well composed, but it was in ***Blue Book*** that he developed his own individual approach. ***Blue Book's*** masculine, swashbuckling subject matter gave Fulton an opportunity to use dramatic action and a much freer technique. He developed a dry-brush method of working black over white and vice-versa on a rough white ground which allowed good reproduction in 'line,' yet produced a rich halftone effect. Oftentimes he used a second color, also in line, to heighten the dramatic effect.

Fulton was born in Valley Center, Kansas, and grew up in Oklahoma Indian Territory with all of the youthful adventures of frontier life. He worked as a newspaper artist on the ***Wichita Beacon,*** the ***Kansas City Star*** and the ***Chicago Tribune*** before switching to advertising and editorial illustration.

Frank Godwin, *The Spirit of Philadelphia*, World War I poster design. Collection of Diane and Jordan Berman.

FRANK (FRANCIS) GODWIN (1889-1939) divided his career between cartooning and illustration, moving from one field to the other with basically the same approach. He first became a master of pen-and-ink. When the medium went out of vogue for illustration, he adapted it to comic strips, notably "Connie" and "Rusty Riley," but also many others, sometimes under other by-lines. To make his characters realistic and consistent, Godwin, who had also worked in the studio of sculptor Gutzon Borglum, modelled busts of them in clay so they became perpetual models he could turn to for variations in position and lighting.

Godwin, the son of the city editor of the ***Washington Star***, was born in Washington, D.C., and started his art career as an apprentice on that paper. Later study at the Art Students League and the helping hand of his mentor James Montgomery Flagg got him his first work in New York, mostly for the humor magazines. Over the years, his work appeared in ***Liberty***, ***Cosmopolitan***, ***Collier's***, and many other periodicals; he also did advertising illustrations for clients such as Prince Albert Tobacco, Texaco, and Coca-Cola.

The Cat in the Hat, published in 1957, is still a popular favorite children's book.

Typical **Flit** advertising illustration, 1930.

Dr. Seuss THEODOR SEUSS GEISEL, otherwise known as "Dr. Seuss" (1904-1991) was a master entertainer through three successive phases of popularity: first, his inimitable cartoons for the humor magazines, then his long-running association with the Flit insecticide advertising campaign with its single message "Quick, Henry, the Flit," and most of all through his hugely popular children's books, which he both authored and illustrated.

His first attempt at a book for children was rejected by twenty-eight publishers before Vanguard Press took a chance on it, and *I Saw it All Happen on Mulberry Street* became the first of more than forty subsequent books.

Geisel first found his metier as the editor-in-chief of the Dartmouth College humor magazine, the *Jack-O-Lantern*. After graduation and a sojourn in England and the Continent, he returned to the U.S. in 1927. He sold his first cartoon to *Judge* magazine and became a regular contributor ot it, as well as to *Life*, *College Humor*, *Vanity Fair*, and *Liberty* magazines.

Geisel's work won him many honors. He was awarded the Pulitzer Prize in 1984 and received several honorary doctorates and medals as well. A permanent collection of his original artwork is held in the University Library, University of California, San Diego.

GEORGE GIGUÈRE

Born in Boston, GEORGE E. GIGUÈRE was diverted from an intended career as a mechanical engraver when his high school drawing teacher hired him as an assistant in free-hand drawing. From then on, his ambition was to become an illustrator.

His first commission was to illustrate a James Oliver Curwood serial of the Frontier North. With its success, he went on to a long career. His work exhibited a strong influence of Harvey Dunn and was characterized by dramatic presentation and a good use of color. Giguère appeared in many periodicals in the 'teens, 'twenties and 'thirties, including *The Delineator*, *American*, *The Century*, *Liberty*, *Redbook*, *Every Week*, *Outdoor Life*, and *Science and Mechanics.* Among his advertising clients were Whitman Chocolates and Granger Rough Cut Tobacco.

Giguère was a long-time member of the New Rochelle Art Association and the Guild of Free Lance Artists. He also had a studio in Silver Lake, Connecticut.

Anthony visiting Cleopatra. Reproduced as a self-advertisement in *Advertising Arts and Crafts,* 1924. Collection of Jeffrey Rich.

Backstage, illustration for **This Week** magazine.

GOTLIEB

JULES GOTLIEB (1897-unknown) traveled in many out-of-the-way parts of the world, from North Africa to the jungles of Dutch Guiana, collecting background material for his illustrations. He also accumulated a library of over 2,000 volumes for reference in doing historical illustration for nearly every national magazine, including **Collier's**, **Cosmopolitan**, **Redbook**, **American**, **Woman's Home Companion**, **Liberty**, **This Week**, **The Ladies' Home Journal**, and for several books.

A native New Yorker, Gotlieb studied at the National Academy School of Fine Arts, the Pennsylvania Academy at Chester Springs and the Art Students League. Among his teachers were George Bridgman and Harvey Dunn. He later taught at the League himself from 1932 to 1934.

Grafstrom

RUTH SIGRID GRAFSTROM (1905-unknown) was born in Rock Island, Illinois, and studied at the Art Institute of Chicago and at the Colorossi Academy in Paris with Henri Morriset.

A fashion artist for **Vogue** magazine from 1930 to 1940 in the New York, Paris, and London offices, she had also done freelance advertising illustrations for Saks Fifth Avenue, the Matson Line and various fabric, cosmetic and clothing manufacturers.

This work led to fiction assignments for magazines such as **The Delineator**, **Cosmopolitan**, and **Woman's Home Companion**, involving fashionable people and backgrounds. Grafstrom's work was marked by sophistication and good drawing which won her many awards and citations in annual exhibitions of the New York Art Directors Club. She was also a member of the Society of Illustrators in New York.

Illustration for **Vogue** magazine, Feb. 15, 1933; © 1933, 1961 by The Condé Nast Publications Inc.

RFH

ROY FREDERIC HEINRICH (1881-1943) was best known for his series of Vermont historical illustrations, and had completed exactly 100 of them at the time of his death. The drawings, made with litho-crayon, are noted for their authenticity of detail and spirit, as well as originality of concept.

Heinrich was born in Indiana, and reared in New York State; he studied at the Connecticut League of Art Students under Charles Noel Flagg. His first work was for a small Sunday newspaper. In 1910, he moved to Detroit, to become one of the earliest automobile illustrators, and his clients included Graham-Paige, Packard, Ford, Chevrolet, Buick, Dodge, Chrysler and Cadillac. He also illustrated for many other advertising accounts.

Of all his assignments, however, Heinrich most enjoyed the pictures of early Vermont. These were exhibited widely in galleries in New York and New England, and shown in the Vermont building at the New York World's Fair in 1939-40. They were published in book form, of which several hundred thousand were furnished by the advertiser, the National Life Insurance Company, to fill requests from schools and individuals all over the country.

Roy Heinrich, "Learning to read from a Horn book"
Reproduced courtesy of National Life Insurance Company, Montpelier, Vermont.

W. E. Heitland, illustration for a ***Woman's Home Company*** story, "Penny Eyes," by Eleanor Hallowell Abbott.

W EMERTON HEITLAND

WILMOT EMERTON HEITLAND, N.A. (1893-1969) was a master watercolorist; his paintings of Barbados, particularly, rival the directness and vigor of Winslow Homer. His illustrations also had the same quality of strength, the watercolor reinforced by a bold outline, with emphasis on composition and rich color.

Heitland was born in Superior, Wisconsin, studied at the Pennsylvania Academy of the Fine Arts, won the Cresson traveling scholarship in 1913, and he attended the Colarossi School in Paris and the Art Students League in New York. His teachers included Arthur Covey, Harvey Dunn and Walter Biggs.

He first illustrated for ***Collier's*** in 1922. This was followed by work for ***Cosmopolitan, McCall's, Woman's Home Companion, The Delineator*** and other magazines. Both his illustrations and exhibition watercolors won many awards, and his work is represented in several museums, including the Brooklyn Museum, the Art Institute of Chicago, and the Philadelphia Museum of Art. He also taught at the Art Students League, the Pennsylvania Academy Summer School, and the Philadelphia Museum School of Art.

Pre-race practice —a wet track, 1964. The painting depicts 1938 Mercedes and Maserati cars at the site of the 1915 Pan-Pacific International Exposition in San Francisco which was also the site of the 1915 Vanderbilt Cup Race. Collection of J.W. Carpenter.

PETER HELCK

CLARENCE PETER HELCK, N.A. (1893-1988) spent his life painting a record of man's work. He made this basic theme a monumental one in his pictures, whether it be of a giant foundry, an open mine, or a dramatic moment in an automobile race.

Peter came by his love for automobiles as a boy when he saw some of the early racing competitions. He eventually came to know many of the drivers and their giant racing cars intimately. These later became the inspiration for his illustrated book, *The Checkered Flag,* published in 1961. He owned a number of old automobiles, including "Old 16," the famous Locomobile which won the Vanderbilt Cup race in 1908. The second of his two books, *Great Auto Races,* was published in 1976.

Helck studied at the Art Students League of New York, and privately with many distinguished teachers, including Sir Frank Brangwyn in England. In addition to complete artistic competence, he had great capacity for hard work, as evidenced by the preliminary, thinking stages of his pictures. The nature of his subject matter demanded thorough mechanical knowledge, including the parts that did not appear in the picture itself. His working drawings which precede the finished paintings were completely worked out even down to the placement of the bolts.

Helck's rate combination of artistry and factual know-how made him the dominant figure in this field for many years. He won many medals and awards in art director's exhibitions. He illustrated for almost every national magazine; his advertising clients were the industrial giants General Electric, Chevrolet, Mack Trucks, National Steel Corporation and numerous others.

During the 1920-1940 period, Helck traveled and painted extensively abroad. Subsequently, this work was given one-man shows in New York, and shown in major Fine Art annuals in the East and Midwest. Except for some favorable reviews and awards, however, the twenty-year effort to breach the barrier separating fine and commercial art proved unfulfilling. It was natural for him to resume full time the remunerative field of advertising and magazine illustration.

Advertising illustration for Alcoa aluminum, April 23, 1951.

D Hendrickson

DAVID HENDRICKSON (1896-1973) was born in St. Paul, Minnesota, and won a scholarship there to attend the St. Paul Institute of Art. He later studied at the Ecole des Beaux-Arts at Toulouse, France, the Grand Central School of Art, and the Art Students League of New York. Among his teachers were Harvey Dunn, Dean Cornwell and George Bridgman.

Beginning in 1913 with his first art job for the **St. Paul Dispatch and Pioneer Press,** Hendrickson had a long and varied career illustrating for periodicals, advertisers, and book pub-lishers, and he exhibited widely.

His special ability was in portraying the rural American scene, sympathetically, truthfully and without artifice. His direct, vigorous pictures are basically drawn in line, sometimes with washes of tone or color added.

He was a member of the Artists Guild, the Society of American Etchers and Graphic Artists, the Society of Illustrators, the Phillips Mill Artists in New Hope, Pennsylvania, and the Palo Alto Art Club in California, where he also taught from 1948 to 1951.

David Hendrickson, *Country Auction*, illustration for **The Country Gentleman,** 1941.

Edwin Henry

EDWIN HENRY was primarily an advertising illustrator, his career coinciding with the tremendous growth of advertising art in the 'twenties and 'thirties. As a partner in the Chicago advertising art service of Stevens, Sundblom and Henry, he did illustrations for many of the largest national accounts, including Studebaker, Packard, Procter & Gamble, Camel and Chesterfield cigarettes, Kohler of Kohler, Graybar Electric, Postum, Quaker Oats and others. He painted editorial illustrations for most of the major magazines as well, his work marked by sensitivity and a very effective use of color.

Henry was born in Mt. Sterling, Kentucky, and studied at the National Academy of Design in New York. He later taught illustration at the Studio School and at the American Academy in Chicago, as well as at the Grand Central School of Art in New York. He was a member of the Artists Guild and the Society of Illustrators.

Edwin Henry, magazine story illustration. Collection of the Society of Illustrators Museum of American Illustration.
J. Walter Thompson Company Purchase Fund.

Everett Henry, cover illustration for *The American Weekly,* 1951.

Everett Henry

E. EVERETT HENRY (1893-1961) was an advertising artist during much of his career, which began in the 'twenties, and he illustrated many advertising campaigns.

Henry brought to his work a thorough academic training through study at the Art Students League, the School of Fine and Applied Art, New York University and Columbia University. He also did some teaching at the School of Fine and Applied Art in New York.

In 1935, he painted murals for the Ford Company Building at the San Diego Fair. This led to many other mural commissions, several of which he executed in collaboration with Allen Saalburg and Louis Bouché. These included decorations for twelve club cars for the Pennsylvania Railroad, designs in the Westinghouse Building, the U. S. Government Building and the Building service center, all at the New York World's Fair in 1939-40. He also painted both murals and easel pictures for private collectors, and is represented in the permanent collection of the Whitney Museum.

HOLM GREN

The illustrations of R. JOHN HOLMGREN (1897-1963) were characterized by a fresh, youthful outlook and bright color. He managed, over a long span of years, to keep his fiction heroines looking contemporary, beginning with the pert flappers in his first cover illustrations for the old *Life* and *Judge* magazines in the 'twenties.

Holmgren was born in St. Paul, Minnesota, and studied at the St. Paul Art Institute before going to New York in 1919 to study at the Art Students League under C. O. Woodbury, George Bridgman, Robert Henri and Frederic R. Gruger.

His illustrations appeared in most of the national magazines and for many advertisers, including Chevrolet, Ford, Alcoa, White Rock and Cunard Lines.

A long-time member of the Society of Illustrators, Holmgren was its president from 1941 to 1944. He was also a member of the Dutch Treat Club, and the Artists and Writers club.

John Holmgren, illustration for *Click* magazine, 1957.

231

George Howe, illustration for "Sundown Jim" by Ernest Haycox, published in *Collier's* magazine, October 2, 1937.

G H

GEORGE HOWE, originally HAUTHALER, (1896-1941) was born in Salzburg, Austria. He ran away from home at the age of fourteen, visited the United States, then went to France, where he studied art for two years before returning to America to stay.

He had to work at all kinds of jobs, from dishwashing and chauffeuring to painting scenery for a motion picture studio, before realizing his ambition to illustrate for the magazines.

Howe painted almost exclusively with watercolor, treated in a flat, poster style, similar to that of Ludwig Hohlwein of Munich, Germany. For many years, his work was associated with the Crowell-Collier publications *Collier's*, *American Magazine*, and *Woman's Home Companion*, although he also illustrated for others, such as *Elks* and *Good Housekeeping*.

Like many other women illustrators, FRANCES TIPTON HUNTER (1896-1957) made children her specialty. Her own childhood was scarred by the death of her mother when she was only six years old, and she was raised by her aunt and uncle.

Her art talent appeared early in high school, and she graduated with honors from the Philadelphia Museum School of Industrial Arts. Further study at the Pennsylvania Academy of the Fine Arts and the Fleisher Art Memorial prepared her for her debut as an illustrator.

Hunter's early work appeared in the *Woman's Home Companion*, followed by illustrations for *Collier's*, *Liberty*, *Good Housekeeping*, and a long series of covers for *The Saturday Evening Post*. She also produced an extremely popular series of calendar paintings over a period of eleven years, and many advertising illustrations for products such as Listerine and Occident Flour. A book, *Frances Tipton Hunter's Paper Dolls*, was published in 1943 by the Whitman Publishing Company.

F. T. Hunter, advertising illustration for Pro-phy-lac-tic Brushes, 1930.

Illustration for *Midnight*, written and illustrated by Will James. Published by The American Boy-Youth's Companion, July, 1930.

WILL JAMES

Illustration for "The Breed of 'Em," written and illustrated by Will James in 1927. Published by *Redbook* magazine.

WILLIAM JAMES (1892-1942) was born in Great Falls, Montana, of French-Canadian parentage and christened JOSEPH ERNEST NEPHTALI DUFAULT.

The facts of his life were fictionalized in his later autobiography, *Lone Cowboy,* partly to cover up his early lawlessness which included a penitentiary sentence for rustling cattle and partly to account for his new persona. He took a new name, William Roderick James in 1910.

He drew almost compulsively throughout his nomadic years while becoming an expert rider and cowhand. Will James's introduction to illustration was quite by chance. Harold Von Schmidt was conducting a painting class at the California School of Fine Arts in San Francisco and advertised for a cowboy model. James, just then in the city with a shipment of cattle, answered it and was hired. During the course of posing sessions, Will brought in some of his own crude drawings, and Von Schmidt recognized in them an observation and knowledge of animal anatomy which showed great promise. Through the encouragement and criticism of both Von Schmidt and Maynard Dixon, James was able to sell his first drawings to *Sunset* magazine.

A year later, he sold a short story with his own illustrations to *Scribner's* magazine. The combination of true-to-life Western story and drawings was an immediate success, and was followed by several more. His first book appeared in 1924. He was awarded the Newbery medal by the American Library Association for his book *Smoky*. Both *Smoky* and *Lone Cowboy* were made into films. Altogether, he wrote and illustrated twenty books and many short stories.

E. M. Jackson, "The Eavesdropper," by Louis Bromfield, *Cosmopolitan,* March, 1934. Collection of Bruce Bent.

 As a child, ELBERT McGRAN JACKSON (1896-1962) showed early interest in drawing, and took Saturday morning lessons from the only art teacher in town, but went on to graduate as an architect from Georgia Tech.

He eventually realized that his real ambition was to be an illustrator and went back to study art at night. With the help of "arrived" illustrators, such as James Montgomery Flagg, he was able to sell his first pictures.

Jackson had a special flair for posing and painting women to make them seductively glamorous, and his architectural training made his picture settings a convincing background for them. Like most artists of that era, Jackson painted from the posed model, and that contributed much to the spontaneity of his technique. Although he was generally given manuscripts involving romance and high society, Jackson was able to do a wide variety of subjects from murder mysteries to masculine adventure. In addition to the stories he illustrated for many magazines, he also designed covers for publications such as *Collier's*, *The Ladies' Home Journal* and *The Saturday Evening Post*.

 STEVEN R. KIDD (1911-1987) illustrated for the Sunday fiction page of the New York News-Chicago Tribune coast-to-coast syndicate for over thirty years. Despite their transitory life, Kidd lavished on those illustrations the same artistry and design that distinguishes his work for magazine and book publishers.

Kidd's versatile pen line could be decorative or realistic, bold or delicate. Over the years,, he successfully coped with every possible pictorial subject and historical period, his conceptions always original and arresting.

Kidd was born in Chicago, Illinois, and attended the Chicago Art Institute there. Coming to New York, he studied at the Art Students League with George Bridgman and for ten years with Harvey Dunn at the Grand Central School of Art.

During World War II, he was an official Army war artist and covered the occupation of Korea for the Historical Section of the War Department. Many of these oil and watercolor paintings were hung in the Pentagon. He also painted illustrations for the Air Force Historical Museum.

Kidd was a member of the Society of Illustrators, taught for three years at the Newark School of Fine and Industrial Art in New Jersey, and for more than twenty years at the Art Students League in New York.

Illustration for the New York News Syndicate Co., Inc., 1937.

234

Neither Snow, nor Rain, nor Ice... painted in Greenland 1932, courtesy of Hammer Galleries, New York City.

Rockwell Kent

ROCKWELL KENT (1882-1971) won fame outside of illustration as an engraver, lithographer, mural painter, writer, lecturer and political activist.

As an illustrator, Kent was equally noted for his own books: **Wilderness**, **Voyaging**, **N. By E.**, **Salamina**, and **This is My Own**, as well as for those of others, such as **Candide**, **Moby Dick**, **Leaves of Grass**, and **Canterbury Tales**.

Kent also made a great many distinguished illustrations for advertisers, among them Marcus & Company, Jewelers; Steinway

& Sons; Rolls-Royce, and American Car and Foundry Company. Some of his advertising and humorous pictures were signed "Hogarth, Jr."

Born in Tarrytown Heights, New York, Kent studied art with Robert Henri, Abbott Thayer and William Merritt Chase. Much of his work was based on personal experiences in his travels to such remote areas as Greenland, Alaska, and Patagonia.

During his lifetime, Kent was a controversial political activist, and his open sympathies with leftist causes resulted in his being blacklisted during the McCarthy era. In retaliation, Kent refused his title of National Academician when elected.

A retrospective exhibition of Kent's work was shown at the Hammer Galleries in 1977, and he was elected to the Society of Illustrators' Hall of Fame in 1986. A major retrospective exhibition, "The Odyssey of Rockwell Kent" relating to the artist's sojourn in the wilderness, will travel to several museums in 2000 and 2001.

Captain Ahab from **Moby Dick,** published by Random House, 1930.

Fair Wind, woodcut print.

235

J – F
– KERNAN –

JOSEPH FRANCIS KERNAN (1878-1958) was a sportsman all of his life and the majority of his subjects featured, as he described it, "the human side of outdoor sports, hunting, fishing and dogs." These were ideal subjects for magazine covers and his work appeared on all of the major — and some minor — magazines, including *The Saturday Evening Post*, *Collier's*, *Liberty*, *The Country Gentleman*, *Capper's Farmer*, *The Elks*, *Outdoor Life*, and the *Associated Sunday Magazines*. His work was also commissioned for calendars and advertisers such as Fisk Tires, International Harvester and Pratt & Lambert.

Kernan was born in Brookline, Massachusetts, and studied at the Eric Pape School of Art in Boston. This was financed by playing professional baseball. He also taught for two years at the Pape School before launching his art career.

A major collection of some 450 of Kernan's illustrations spanning a career of over forty years is held in the collection of the Glenbow Museum in Calgary, Alberta, Canada.

J. F. Kernan, cover painting for *The Saturday Evening Post*, November 10, 1934.
©1934, 1962 by The Curtis Publishing Company.

Klett.

WALTER CHARLES KLETT (1897-1966) specialized in painting glamorous women for the reason, as he put it, that Rubens, Velasquez, or Botticelli preferred to paint beautiful females rather than ugly ones. He painted portraits of many celebrated women in the arts of his era, including Gladys Swarthout, Mrs. William Woodward, Mrs. Jansen Noyes, Alicia Markova, Vera Zorina and Bidu Sayao.

Klett had been a painter for both magazine illustration and for the galleries, and he brought a contemporary approach to each. His fiction illustrations appeared in most of the national magazines, and he designed and executed numerous campaigns for national advertisers. He also exhibited in many museums and galleries, including the Pennsylvania Academy, the Faragil Gallery, the Reinhardt Gallery, the Metropolitan Museum of Art, Grand Central Art Galleries, and at shows of the Art Directors Club of New York.

Born in St. Louis, Klett attended the St. Louis School of Fine Arts, Washington University, and made study trips to France, England, Italy, Switzerland and Germany. He was the author of a popular book, *Figure Painting*, published by Watson-Guptill, and taught portrait and figure painting for ten years at Pratt Institute in Brooklyn, New York.

Walter Klett, illustration for *Collier's* magazine, September 22, 1945.

236

Clayton Knight, cover illustration for *The American Boy,* April, 1931.

Kritcher

LARRY B. KRITCHER (1900-) was born in McKeesport, Pennsylvania. He studied at the Carnegie Institute of Technology in Pittsburgh and the Pennsylvania Academy of the Fine Arts in Philadelphia, where he was awarded a Cresson Scholarship to study and travel in Europe for two years.

Kritcher returned to America just in time for the 1929 crash and found that the illustration art market had disappeared with it. In 1932, he joined *The Saturday Evening Post* staff. This was valuable experience for gaining an insight into the requirements of illustration from the magazine's point of view; Kritcher's illustrations are always directly to the point, explicit and competent.

Clayton Knight

CLAYTON KNIGHT (1891-1969) brought a lifetime of knowledge and authority to his aviation illustrations. During World War I, he joined the U. S. Army Air Service which was attached to the Royal Flying Corps in France. He was shot down and taken prisoner by the Germans, and spent many months in hospitals recovering from his wounds.

After the war, Knight returned to an illustration career specializing in flying stories for books or magazine articles.

Prior to the United States' entry into World War II, Knight headed a committee which enabled American flyers to join the Canadian and Royal Air Force during the critical Battle of Britain. He himself was a combat historian for the 8th, 11th and 20th Air Forces, covering the Aleutians, Alaska, and the Pacific. He also attended the ceremony of Japan's surrender on the U.S.S. Missouri at the end of World War II.

Knight was born in Rochester, New York, and studied at the Art Institute of Chicago. Among his teachers were Robert Henri and George Bellows. He was married to Katherine Sturges, a well-known advertising artist; their son, Hillary Knight, is a famous illustrator of children's books.

Larry Kritcher, illustration for "The Man Who Blew the Whistle," March 28, 1959, *The Saturday Evening Post.* ©1959, 1997, by The Curtis Publishing Company.

CHARLES LOUIS LaSALLE (1894-1958) was a classmate of Harold Anderson and Arthur Fuller at the Fenway Art School in Boston. He and Anderson later had shared studios at the Beaux Arts Studio in New York and later in New Rochelle.

LaSalle, who was born "Lassell" in Wakefield, Massachusetts, first worked as a bull-pen artist in the Snow Advertising Agency in Boston. His early work, in emulation of F. R. Gruger and Henry Raleigh, was drawn in Wolff pencil. He later began to use charcoal and developed a mastery of the medium in his own style. His first magazine illustrations were for *Boys' Life,* and he was soon working for *The Saturday Evening Post, Collier's, Redbook* and others. Advertising clients included Ford, General Motors and General Electric.

After many productive years, he moved to Arizona where he followed a new career painting Western subjects for galleries and exhibitions until the time of his death.

Painted with the authority of the avid duck hunter that he was, LaSalle produced this subject for *Outdoor Life* magazine in February, 1950.

Exhibition painting, *Ballet Backstage.*

Cover Illustration for *The Saturday Evening Post,* June 24th, 1939.
©1939, 1967 by The Curtis Publishing Company.

JOHN LaGATTA (1894-1977) showed a full appreciation of the female figure in his illustrations. In even the most decorously dressed of his models, the clothes appeared to reveal the figure rather than to hide it. Millions of readers would have had it no other way.

Despite his emphasis on the figure, there is no overtone of suggestiveness in LaGatta's work. The women are painted in frank admiration of their beauty and he made them colorful, curvaceous, and vital.

LaGatta was born in Naples, Italy, but received his education in America, studying under Kenneth Hayes Miller and Frank Alvah Parsons at the New York School of Fine and Applied Art. His first work was in advertising and much of his early work shows the influence of Etienne Drian, the famous French illustrator.

As he developed his own personal style, LaGatta's work was in tremendous demand. He worked for nearly a decade to the limit of his capacities in supplying all the magazines that competed for his pictures. After the 'forties, LaGatta curtailed his output, but found a new career in teaching at the Art Center School in Los Angeles, California where he was a tough but his enthusiastic instructor. He was elected into the Society of Illustrators' Hall of Fame in 1984.

238

Cover for *The Saturday Evening Post,* July 8, 1933.© 1933, 1961 by the Curtis Publishing Company.

Manning Lee, "Ghosts of the Scarlet Fleet," by Rear Admiral E.R.G.R. Evans, *American Boy Youth's Companion,* January 1932.

M.de V. Lee

MANNING DeVILLENEUVE LEE's (1894-1980) art education was interrupted by two stints of Army duty. The first was on the Mexican border in Texas as a member of the Virginia Field Artillery in 1916. This was promptly followed by service in World War I, as a Lieutenant at the front in France with the anti-aircraft artillery.

Following the war, Lee resumed his studies at the Pennsylvania Academy of the Fine Arts, and won the Cresson Scholarship for travel in Europe in 1921. The following year, he won the Second Toppan Prize at the Pennsylvania Academy, and with this encouragement began his long career as a freelance illustrator.

Over the years, Lee illustrated for a great many magazines and advertisers, and for more than 200 books for 27 publishers. He also made film strips and designed several series of postage stamps for the Republics of Liberia, Indonesia and Guinea.

LYFORD

PHILIP LYFORD (1887-1950) painted one of the best known posters of World War I as an illustration for the poem, "In Flanders Fields." It was also used as a flyer for the fifth Victory Loan, and a reproduction of it, 150 feet high, was lighted in San Francisco Bay. The painting, made while he was a young artist in a Chicago studio, helped to burnish his own career; he became one of Chicago's top advertising illustrators, with major clients such as National Mazda Lamps and the Chevrolet Motor Company. He also illustrated for such publications as *Redbook*, *Collier's*, *College Humor*, *Country Gentleman* and *The Saturday Evening Post*.

Lyford was born in Worcester, Massachusetts, and studied for four years at the Boston Museum of Fine Arts under Frank Benson, Edmund C. Tarbell and Philip Hale.

Philip Lyford, *The Artist and his Model.* Collection of Daley Art Gallery.

MacPherson, illustration for "Mirthful Haven" by Booth Tarkington, May 31, 1930 in *The Saturday Evening Post*. © 1930, 1958 by the Curtis Publishing Company.

Orison MacPherson

ORISON MacPHERSON (1898-1966) spoke with the Scottish accent of his Pictou, Nova Scotia, birthplace. His art education was acquired partly at the Ontario Art School in Toronto, and at the Art Students League in New York under John Sloan. He learned most, however, from the helpful advice of his friends J. W. Schlaikjer, Franklin Booth, and the artist whose work he admired above all others, F. R. Gruger.

After the usual odd jobs to keep alive, MacPherson got his start as an assistant to the art director of *Hearst's International* magazine. Within a short time he obtained his first illustration assignment from *The Country Gentleman*, followed soon by others from *The Saturday Evening Post*, *Good Housekeeping*, and several Canadian publications, including *MacLean's* magazine and *Chatelaine*. He also did a long series of advertising illustrations for the Jones and Laughlin Steel Corporation.

RONALD McLEOD

RONALD NORMAN McLEOD (1897-1977) was born in St. Paul, Minnesota, and was educated at the University of Chicago. He never had formal art training but made up for it by arduous self-education and observation.

In the process, McLeod developed his bold poster style in transparent watercolor based, as were the other *Collier's* artists, on the poster renderings of the German artist Ludwig Hohlwien.

Beginning in 1928, McLeod illustrated for *Collier's* regularly for twenty years, and he also worked for many other periodicals including *American Magazine*, *Cosmopolitan*, and *Pictorial Review*. Over this same period, he did an immense amount of advertising and poster illustration, several times having his work included in *100 Best Posters of the Year*.

Ronald McLeod, cover illustration for *Collier's* magazine, November 3, 1934.

241

Frederic Mizen, Coca-Cola advertising illustration, 1922.

IRVING NURICK (1894-1963) took a trip to France in 1928 for a chance to study art and to make a change from the advertising drawing and layout work he had been doing in New York. He fell in love with Paris, and it became his second home.

His Paris paintings and sketches provided an entree into the field of magazine illustrations. Nurick's wife showed them to various editors in New York who were impressed and began sending him manuscripts.

Although Nurick set many of his pictures in Continental locations, he eventually became best known for his ability to depict teen-agers and sub-debs sympathetically. Young people responded with enthusiasm, and wrote him for suggestions about clothes and hair styling; Irving Nurick fan clubs came into existence as far away as New Zealand and Australia.

He also continued his painting for exhibition and had one-man shows in New York and Paris. For exhibitions at the National Academy of Design, he won the Ranger Prize in 1957 and the Samuel Finley Breese Morse Medal in 1960.

FREDERIC KIMBALL MIZEN (1888-1965) was a dominant figure in the billboard advertising field for several years, many of his paintings doubling as magazine advertisements. He also illustrated fiction for magazines such as **Cosmopolitan** and **The Saturday Evening Post**, but is probably best known for his long and distinguished series of advertising paintings for the Coca-Cola Company in newspapers, magazines and billboards.

A Chicagoan, Mizen attended Smith's Art Academy from 1904-06, and obtained his first employment with the Gunning System, a predecessor to General Outdoor Advertising. Meanwhile, he continued to study in evening classes at the Art Institute of Chicago under John Vanderpoel, DeForrest Shook and Walter Marshall Clute.

He later conducted his own school, the Mizen Academy of Art, for several years, but eventually restricted himself to portraiture.

Nurick, illustration for "First Love, Farewell," November 1936. © 1936, 1964 Meredith Corporation All rights reserved. Used with the permission of the Ladies' Home Journal.

ROBERT PATTERSON (1898-1981) was born in Chicago and attended the Chicago Art Institute. Among his teachers there and later were Harvey Dunn, Walt Louderback, Ralph Barton, Pierre Brissaud, and Carl Erickson.

Patterson began his professional career in Chicago, and for some time, directed the Patterson studios there with his brother Loran. In 1922, he came to New York and began doing fashion illustration.

Judge magazine sent him to France in 1924 to do a feature entitled "Betty Goes Abroad." When **Judge** failed in 1927, he managed to obtain a fashion illustration assignment from **Vogue** in Paris, where he stayed until 1934.

Upon his return to the United States, he began to do editorial illustrations for the major magazines, including **McCall's**, **Cosmopolitan**, **Good Housekeeping**, **The Ladies' Home Journal**, **Redbook**, **Collier's**, **Woman's Home Companion**, and **American Magazine**, as well as advertising assignments and book illustration.

Robert Patterson, Date and place of publication not known.

The name GEORGE PETTY (1894-1975) was almost synonymous with that of the fledgling *Esquire* magazine. His provocative drawings of immodest young women were an immediate sensation and had much to do with the early success of a new magazine launched in the middle of the Depression. The Petty Girl's most usual accompaniment was a white telephone, varied by other simple symbolic props for one-line gags.

Petty had begun as a Chicago commercial studio artist, adept with the airbrush. The Petty Girl was really a family enterprise with Mrs. Petty as the first model. Later, daughter Marjorie grew into the role, not only posing but also suggesting ideas for frothy subjects. Petty's son also posed for the occasional male figures that appeared.

After a disagreement with *Esquire*'s owner and publisher, Petty quit and took on assignments for other magazines, such as *True* and *The Saturday Home Magazine*. He was also active in movies and had many advertising accounts, including Jantzen, Orange Crush, Old Gold cigarettes, Quaker Hosiery, Gem Razor, and Bestform. His pictures were also re-used for calendars, and playing cards, and he created program covers for the Ice Capades. When not at his drawing board, Petty was off on hunting expeditions in Alaska or on safari in Africa.

An excellent biography simply entitled *Petty*, by Reid Stewart Austin, was published by Gramercy Books in 1997.

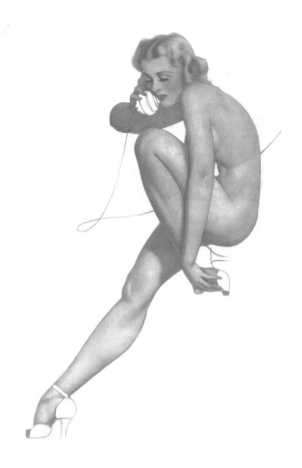

George Petty, *"I'm not posing for that account any longer. It seems I took the customer's mind entirely off the product."*
By permission of *Esquire* magazine. © Hearst Communications, Inc. *Esquire* is a trademark of Hearst Magazines Property, Inc. All Rights Reserved.

April 20, 1940 · THE · Price 15 cents
NEW YORKER

Garrett Price did over fifty covers for *The New Yorker*, spanning twenty-five years. Copyright © 1940, 1968, The New Yorker Magazine, Inc. Reprinted by permission.

Garrett Price

GARRETT PRICE (1896-1979) made it a lifetime habit to carry a small sketch pad with him. Many of his best picture ideas were generated from these on-the-spot notes, sometimes coming to life only years afterward.

Although Price had a long career as an illustrator, he was best known for the original humor and incisive renderings of his *New Yorker* covers.

Price was born in Bucyrus, Kansas, and attended the University of Wyoming and the Art Institute of Chicago. His earliest art job was in 1916 with the *Chicago Tribune*, where he first carried his sketchbook on assignments for news stories. Later, he made the transition to illustrating magazine stories for *College Humor*, the old *Life*, *Collier's*, *Scribner's*, and other major magazines. A collection of his work entitled *Drawing Room Only* was published by Coward-McCann, Inc. in 1946.

Garrett exhibited extensively, at the Metropolitan Museum of Art, the Pennsylvania Academy of the Fine Arts, the American Watercolor Society, the Chicago Art Institute, and others. He was an active member of the Society of Illustrators in New York, the Westport Artists, and the Mystic Art Association in Connecticut.

William Reusswig, illustration for "An Antidote for Spring" by Lorraine Stevens, *McCall's* magazine.

REUSSWIG

WILLIAM REUSSWIG (1902-1978) was a fine illustrator, and married to an equally fine one, Martha Sawyers (below). They traveled the world together and, in collaboration, wrote and illustrated two books about the Far East, published by Grosset & Dunlap in 1961 and 1964. They worked out of a New York apartment with two studios, where each could pursue their individual assignments.

William was born in Somerville, New Jersey; he studied at Amherst College and the Art Students League in New York. He was only twenty-three when he made his first illustrations for *Collier's*, and then illustrated for most national fiction magazines, including *Cosmopolitan*, *True*, *Redbook*, *The Saturday Evening Post*, *McCall's*, *The Country Gentleman*, *Sports Afield*, and *Outdoor Life*. Masculine subjects of adventure and sports were his special forté.

MARTHA SAWYERS

MARTHA SAWYERS (1902-1988) became an illustrator unintentionally. Her drawings and paintings of China and Indonesia were on exhibition at the Marie Sterner Gallery and happened to be seen by William Chessman, the art editor of *Collier's*. Chessman offered her a manuscript with an oriental setting, which she illustrated with the sensitivity and taste for which her work became famous.

Martha was from Cuero, Texas, and studied at the Art Students League. Throughout her career, she further lived and painted in Paris, Bali, Peking, Nepal, and in numerous other parts of the world.

During World War II, *Collier's* sent her as an artist-correspondent to the China-Burma-India area, and published numerous illustrated articles by her about the armed forces' personnel and the native populations. *Life* magazine published a series of her pastel portraits of Asian people in the British Merchant Navy. She also designed posters for China Relief. Martha brought special insight to her illustrations for the writers Mona Gardner and Pearl S. Buck. Sawyers was elected into the Hall of Fame of the Society of Illustrators in 1998.

Martha Sawyers, illustration for *Collier's* magazine.

Illustration for "The Lady and the Pirate" by Rafael Sabatini, *American Magazine,* May 1936. Collection of Walter and Louise Simonson.

Illustration for *Good Housekeeping* magazine.
Collection of Daniel and Renee Kaplan.

Mead Schaeffer

The work of MEAD SCHAEFFER (1898-1980) divides itself into two periods. The early one deals with romantic, swashbuckling and theatrical subjects. The second, although still strong and dramatic, is based on authentic, factual themes and is more reportorial.

Born in Freedom Plains, New York, he studied at Pratt Institute, and got advice from Harvey Dunn and Dean Cornwell. A brilliant student, he was illustrating for major magazines while still in his twenties and had begun a series of sixteen illustrated classics for Dodd, Mead, including **The Count of Monte Cristo, Les Miserables, Typee** and **Moby Dick.** Eventually, he wanted to deal with contemporary subjects that he could personally observe and learn about.

With this objective, Schaeffer began to paint covers for **The Saturday Evening Post,** which by 1940 was featuring themes of Americana. The **Post**'s artists traveled to various parts of the country to find regional material with national appeal. Schaeffer made an extended trip to the West with his friend and fellow-artist Norman Rockwell. From this and other trips, many fine covers resulted.

During World War II, Mead painted a notable series of **Post** covers of American soldiers representing various branches of the service. The paintings were done with the full approval and cooperation of United States military authorities, who provided all the facilities. In researching the pictures, Schaeffer rode aboard a submarine, a Coast Guard patrol boat and various aircraft. Later, under the sponsorship of the **Post,** the paintings were exhibited in more than ninety cities in the United States and Canada in promoting the war effort. They are now part of the permanent collection of the USAA, an association of military officers, former officers and their families, in San Antonio, Texas.

In other exhibitions, Schaeffer won the Salmagundi Club's Shaw Prize in 1930, and a Gold Medal at the Pennsylvania Academy of the Fine Arts in 1944.

O.F.Schmidt

OSCAR FREDERICK SCHMIDT (1892-1957) attended Pratt Institute in Brooklyn, and won a scholarship to the Art Students League where he studied under George Bridgman.

During World War I, he served in the artillery in France. Following his discharge, he went on an extended tour of the world, including North Africa and the Marquesas Islands, where he remained to carve a tombstone for the unmarked, weed-grown grave of Paul Gauguin.

Schmidt preferred to paint in gouache, which he handled with great competence in illustrations for magazines such as *Redbook, Liberty* and *The Saturday Evening Post.*

He exhibited often and was a member of the Salmagundi Club and the Society of Illustrators in New York.

Schucker

JAMES W. SCHUCKER (1903-1988) was born in Mt. Carmel, Illinois. He received his education at the Carnegie Institute of Technology, and the Art Institute of Chicago, and he studied with Harvey Dunn at the Grand Central School of Art.

His first editorial illustrations were for *Redbook* magazine; over the years, his work apeared in most of the national periodicals. He also did campaigns for advertisers Quaker State Motor Oil, Travelers Insurance Company, and Seagram Distillers Corporation, among others.

An active painter, Schucker received an honorable mention at the Watercolor International show at the Chicago Art Institute. He was a member of the Philadelphia Art Alliance, and taught at his own school in Quakertown, Pennsylvania.

Story illustration for *American Magazine*, 1936.

HOWARD SCOTT

HOWARD SCOTT (1902-1983) thought of his twenty-four-sheet poster designs as analogous to one-act plays. He set the scene, cast the characters, and directed the actors. The moral, or message, had to be immediately clear to the viewer, traveling 60-miles-per-hour along a highway.

Scott added to his work a sparkling opaque watercolor technique and an ability to obtain very realistic characterizations in a bold poster treatment.

As an artist, he was noted as a completely regulated and organized professional who kept his studio as neat and businesslike as a reception room.

Scott was long associated with Esso, Ford, Schlitz, Heinz, Servel refrigerators, and other national products, but also designed magazine covers, notably for **The Saturday Evening Post**.

Howard Scott, cover for **The Saturday Evening Post**, February 27, 1943.© 1943, 1971, by The Curtis Publishing Company.

H.J. Soulen

The work of HENRY J. SOULEN (1888-1965) is richly colored and strongly patterned. Each of his pictures is treated in a manner appropriate to the lack of pictorial depth of a mural painting, and equally, to a magazine cover. He was given a Peabody Award for his magazine cover designs.

Soulen was born in Milwaukee, Wisconsin. He attended the Chicago Academy of Fine Arts and later studied with Howard Pyle. For many years, his work appeared regularly in most of the quality magazines and usually in color — even when the use of color was restricted — because of the brilliance of his palette.

During World War II, he gave free art lessons at the Valley Forge Military Hospital, a rehabilitation center for veterans.

"The Lost Little Song of Chang Hao," published October, 1926. ©1926, 1954, by Meredith Corporation. All rights reserved. Used with permission of **The Ladies' Home Journal.**

Illustration for **The Saturday Evening Post.** Date of publication unknown.

Spreter (signature)

ROY FREDERIC SPRETER (1899-1967) was another of the gifted group of painters who made advertising art their special province.

Spreter's work was distinguished for the subtlety of his color and values and the good taste which his art conveyed to the advertiser's products. He was long associated with the campaigns of Camay, Campbell's Soup, and Bon Ami, and in demand as an artist for twenty-four-sheet billboards, which require sure control, since the reproductions enlarged the original art from eight to ten times.

His fiction illustration, equally colorful and artistic, was mostly for the women's monthly magazines, where his sensitive and beautiful heroines found much favor.

A Chicagoan, Spreter had brief training at the Art Institute there, but learned most from Joseph Chenoweth, Philip Lyford, Leopold Seyffert and other members of the Palette and Chisel Club. He was a member of the Art Directors Club and the Society of Illustrators in New York.

Roy Spreter, illustration for *Pictorial Review*. Collection of Timothy F. Marek.

This advertising illustration for McCallum Silk Hosiery in December, 1923, displays the artist's homage to Japanese art both in subject and in her linear treatment, with flattened color areas within a fan shape.

Katharine Sturges (signature)

The wife of aviation artist Clayton Knight, KATHERINE STURGES (KNIGHT) (1890-1979), was an accomplished illustrator in her own right. Born in Chicago, she attended the Art Institute there; she afterwards traveled to Japan to study asian art.

Her illustrations for an early children's book, *Little Pictures of Japan*, were inspired by the trip. Her work continued to reflect this Japanese influence throughout her career, which included greeting card design, illustrating other children's books, fashion drawing for *Harper's Bazaar,* and award-winning advertising illustrations for clients such as McCallum Hosiery, Stehli Silks, and Oneida Community Silver.

In 1956, Katherine designed a commemorative toile depicting the career of President Eisenhower, which was used in Blair House. She also designed for Spode china, as well as jewelry and fabrics for Macy's based on Peruvian motifs.

In the 'forties and 'fifties, she also collaborated with her husband on several aviation books.

Advertising illustration for New Departure Brakes, ca. 1940. Collection of Warren Peters.

HERBERT MORTON STOOPS (1888-1948) was closely identified with the adventure fiction of *Blue Book* magazine during his long career in illustration. Its wide variety of subject matter gave Stoops an opportunity to display his expert knowledge of military subjects, the Old West (particularly Indians), animals, and human figures in violent action. Many of his black-and-white dry-brush illustrations were attributed to his pen name, Jeremy Cannon. He also painted *Blue Book*'s monthly covers regularly for over 13 years. At the time of his death, he had painted the 17th of a series of covers depicting historical episodes in each of the 48 states.

A clergyman's son, Stoops was reared in Idaho, attended Utah State College, and worked as a staff artist for newspapers in San Francisco and Chicago. In 1917, he enlisted and served as a First Lieutenant with the Sixth Field Artillery of the First Division in France.

After the war, Stoops began his illustration career and his association with *Blue Book.* He did not confine himself to those pages alone; he illustrated for *Collier's, This Week, Cosmopolitan,* and many others, as well as painting for exhibition. His picture, "Anno Domini," won the Isador Medal at the National Academy Exhibition in 1940.

Stoops served as president of the Artists Guild in New York, was a member of the Salmagundi Club, the Society of Illustrators, The American Artists Professional League, and highly prized his honorary membership in the New York Association of Veterans of the French Foreign Legion.

An excellent compilation of Stoops's black and white work, *The Blue Book Illustrations of Herbert Morton Stoops,* by Colonel Charles Waterhouse USMCR, was published by Art Direction Book Company in 1999.

Illustration for *Pascu* by Konrad Bercovici, *Good Housekeeping* magazine July, 1932.

Advertising illustration for Procter & Gamble soap, January, 1929.

Color sketch for a Cashmere Bouquet soap advertisement, 1934.

First Night, illustration for Budweiser Beer, 1946.

SUNDBLOM

HADDON HUBBARD SUNDBLOM (1899-1976) dominated the art field in Chicago beginning in the 'twenties when he formed a studio partnership with Howard Stevens and Edwin Henry.

The studio, under the artistic direction and influence of Sundblom, attracted a great number of young artists who later, as alumni of the "Sundblom circle," went on to become name illustrators in their own right. Among those included in this book are Harry Anderson, Earl Blossom, Matt Clark, Edwin Henry, Walter Richards, James Schucker, Thornton Utz and Coby Whitmore. Sundblom acknowledged the influence on his own style of many painters, including John Singer Sargent, but primarily Anders Zorn. As amalgamated by Sundblom, it was a brilliant and colorful technique, combined with his own good taste and joie de vivre.

These qualities kept his work in steady demand for nearly forty years for both magazine stories and advertising campaigns which won for him many medals and citations. His style became a hallmark for advertisers, such as Coca-Cola, Procter & Gamble, Palmolive, Peet & Company and Maxwell House Coffee. For over twenty years, Sundblom painted an annual Santa Claus subject for Coca-Cola; its prominence on the back cover of many national magazines made it a famous feature. Sundblom used himself as the model in the later years.

Born in Muskegon, Michigan, Sundblom left school to work at the age of thirteen when his mother died. For many years, he attended school at night or took correspondence courses to complete his education. He also studied for four years at the Chicago Art Institute and for three-and-a-half years at the American Academy of Art. His art apprenticeship was served at the Charles Everett Johnson Studio in Chicago, and in 1925, the partnership of Stevens, Sundblom and Henry was launched.

In 1987, Sundblom was elected into the Society of Illustrators' Hall of Fame.

Dan Sweeney, story illustration for ***Collier's*** magazine. Collection of Ramon Moore.

Harry Timmins, *Bal Masque,* advertising illustration for Studebaker, 1929.

Dan Sweeney

DAN SWEENEY (1880-1958), a native of Sacramento, California, began his long career as a newspaper illustrator for the ***San Francisco Chronicle.***

Sweeney also painted posters for theatre lobbies which led to his doing travel posters. He began to specialize in this for various steamship lines and traveled around the world to many out-of-the-way places, to research unusual poster subjects. One of his most successful series of pictures was of pirate characters for the Grace Lines.

For many years, Sweeney was a steady contributor of fiction illustrations to ***Collier's*** magazine, particularly of sea and Western subjects rendered in wash or transparent watercolor.

Timmins

HARRY LAVERNE TIMMINS (1887-1963) was an extremely versatile illustrator who was at home in every medium including dry-brush and gouache, and covered a wide variety of subject matter over a long advertising and editorial art career.

His pictures appeared in ***The Ladies' Home Journal***, ***Woman's Home Companion***, ***Pictorial Review***, ***Cosmopolitan***, ***American Magazine***, ***This Week***, ***Collier's***, and in Canadian publications ***MacLeans***, the ***Toronto Star Weekly***, and others. These and his national advertising illustrations won numerous awards over the years.

Timmins was born in Wilsonville, Nebraska, and studied at the Art Institute of Chicago. He was a co-founder of the American Academy of Art there, where he also taught for several years in the 'twenties. In the last years of his life, he painted for galleries in Carmel, Hollywood, and San Francisco, California, and had several one-man shows.

He was a member of the Society of Illustrators, the American Federation of Arts, and the Palette and Chisel Club of Chicago.

EDMUND F. WARD (1892-1990) made his first illustrations for *The Saturday Evening Post* before he was twenty. His early pictures were large, generally with a dark tonality, serious, and painted in oils. By 1930, he changed to more humorous subjects and began to work in wash and watercolor. For many years he illustrated the Alexander Botts and Assistant District Attorney Doowinkle stories for the Post.

Ward was born in White Plains, New York, and studied at the Art Students League in the same class with Norman Rockwell, with whom he also shared an early studio. Among Ward's teachers were Edward Dufner, George Bridgman and Thomas Fogarty.

He spent his professional illustration career in White Plains, where he also painted a mural for the Federal Building. He was a long-time member of the Salmagundi Club, the Guild of Freelance Artists, and a member of the Society of Illustrators.

As a young man, RICO TOMASO (1898-1985) played piano in a small dance orchestra, wearing heavy, black woolen gloves as his trademark (but also to be able to hit harder on the keys to compete with the drummer). The drummer was Dean Cornwell, then just starting his illustration career.

Tomaso was encouraged in his art ambitions by a family friend, John T. McCutcheon, the famous cartoonist for the *Chicago Tribune*. He studied at the Chicago Art Institute under J. Wellington Reynolds. Later on, other teachers were Cornwell, Harvey Dunn, and Robert Henri. His work mostly resembled Cornwell's in concept and broad brush style. Tomaso was at his best illustrating mystery stories or those of high adventure in exotic locations, for example, the Albert Richard Wetjen stories of the South Australian Mounted Police for *The Saturday Evening Post*. He was also known for a series of vigorous, full-color portrait illustrations for Granger Pipe Tobacco.

For some years after the Grand Central School of Art was dispossessed from Grand Central Terminal, Tomaso carried on Harvey Dunn's illustration class in Mamaroneck, NY. He also painted for exhibition, was represented by the Grand Central Art Galleries and by Jean Bohne, Inc. in New York.

WELSH

WILLIAM P. WELSH (1889-unknown) developed his decorative painting approach through his study at the Julian and Delecluse Academies in Paris and at the Art Students League in New York.

Although Welsh did fiction illustration for numerous publications and advertisers, his poster style was best suited to the many magazine covers he painted, some of the best being those for *Woman's Home Companion.* He also did several murals, many portraits, exhibited internationally, and taught at the Chicago Art Institute. In 1945 and 1946, he made paintings in the Far East Theatre of Operations for the Historical Records of the United States Army Air Forces.

Among his numerous awards were First Prize at the International Watercolor Exhibition in 1921; First and Third Prizes, at the Poster Competition for Chicago's World's Fair; and medals from the New York Art Directors Club's annual exhibitions of advertising art.

Welsh was a member of the Tavern Club in Chicago, the Chicago Society of Arts, and the Society of Illustrators in New York City. He was elected a fellow to the British Royal Society of Arts in 1950, and to the International Institute of Arts and Letters in 1962.

William Welsh, cover for *Woman's Home Companion,* September, 1933.

James Williamson, the New Ford Convertible Cabriolet, 1930.

JAMES W. WILLIAMSON (1899-1984) made an immense number of advertising illustrations for such clients as Arrow Shirts, Clicquot Club Ginger Ale, Ford, Paul Jones, and Yardley, all treated with circumspect restraint.

In his editorial illustration, however, his sense of humor emerged and became his most engaging characteristic. Williamson distilled action and renderings down to their essentials, allowing the poses of the figures to tell the story.

Williamson was born in Omaha, Nebraska; he was a graduate of the 1923 class at Yale. A self-taught artist, he sold his first work to the old *Life* magazine while still in college. This was followed by sales to *Judge, Vanity Fair, The Delineator,* and nearly all of the rest of the major magazines, including *The Saturday Evening Post,* where his work appeared for over thirty years.

During those years, his work was exhibited regularly at Art Directors Club shows in New York and Los Angeles, winning many awards. Williamson also taught at the Art Students League for a year in 1933. He was elected into the Society of Illustrators Hall of Fame in 1984.

REVERE F. WISTEHUFF

REVERE F. WISTEHUFF (1900-1971) was one of the central group of cover artists in the New Rochelle art colony in the 1920s, '30s and '40s which included the Leyendeckers, Norman Rockwell and Walter Beach Humphrey. "Wisty" did covers for virtually all of the national magazines, including *The Saturday Evening Post, This Week, Liberty, Collier's*, and many secondary publications, such as the Canadian *MacLean's, The Country Guide, The New York Herald Tribune Magazine, Everybody's Weekly, Capper's Farmer, American Girl*, and *People's Home Journal*.

Among his many advertising accounts were the John Hancock Mutual Life Insurance Company, Western Union, Beck Beer and Gulf Oil. In most of his work, Wistehuff followed the same style and family-oriented subject matter that marked the approach of his good friend, Norman Rockwell.

Revere Wistehuff, cover for *Liberty* magazine, July 1, 1933. © 1933, 1961 Liberty Publishing Corporation. Reprinted by permission of Liberty Library Corporation. Collection of Ilene and Steven Berman.

Denys Wortman, "Mopey Dick and The Duke," reprinted by permission of the New York World-Telegram and Sun. © 1933, 1961 by the United Features Syndicate.

Wortman

DENYS WORTMAN, N.A. (1887-1958) was a social commentator of penetration and wit. He conveyed much good humor and sympathetic perception in his daily cartoon panel, "Metropolitan Movies." Although his drawings were predominantly concerned with New York characters: frowzy landladies, bums and hangers-on, the panel was syndicated in 45 newspapers as "Everyday Movies." The common touch and wealth of homely observation made it equally appreciated across the country. His characters, like "Mopey Dick and the Duke," managed to evoke smiles even through the somber period of the Depression.

Wortman was born in Saugerties, New York, and educated at the Stevens Institute of Technology, Rutgers University, and the New York School of Fine and Applied Art under Kenneth Hayes Miller. His first artwork was done for the *Herald Tribune,* and he illustrated for many magazines including *The New Yorker, The Saturday Evening Post,* and *Collier's,* but his longest association was with the *New York World-Telegram and Sun* newspaper.

Wortman was equally interested in serious painting. He exhibited at the Armory Show, the National Academy, the Macbeth Galleries, and the Society of Illustrators, where he served as president from 1936 to 1938.

His work is represented in the collections of the Metropolitan Museum of Art and the New York Public Library.

"Sublet this place for the summer? Gosh, I hate to think of somebody using my things."

1940–1950

Courtney Allen
Harry Anderson
Lyman Matthew Anderson
John Atherton
Warren Baumgartner
Walter M. Baumhofer
Lonie Bee
Rudolph Belarski
Geoffrey Biggs
Chesley Bonestell
Rene Bouché
Gilbert Bundy
Emery Clarke
John Clymer
Stevan Dohanos
Albert Dorne
John Philip Falter
Robert Fawcett
Fred Freeman
John Gannam
Edwin Georgi
Arthur Getz
John F. Gould
Hardie Gramatky
Hamilton Greene
Glen Grohe
John Groth
Lealand R. Gustavson
Robert George Harris
Raymond F. Houlihan
George Hughes
Earl Oliver Hurst

Robert F. Kuhn
Robert E. Lougheed
Tom Lovell
Fred Ludekens
John Alan Maxwell
Alfred Parker
Perry Peterson
John Pike
Henry Clarence Pitz
Ben Kimberly Prins
Ray Prohaska
Paul Rabut
Frank Joseph Reilly
Walter D. Richards
Robert Riggs
Nicholas F. Riley
Allen Saalburg
Leslie Saalburg
Richard Sargent
Barbara E. Schwinn
Amos Sewell
Ben Shahn
Edward Shenton
Noel Sickles
Benjamin Albert Stahl
Fredric Varady
Alberto Vargas
Harold Von Schmidt
Lynd Ward
Jack W. Welch
Jon Whitcomb
Mortimer Wilson, Jr.

Hamilton Greene *Blue Book.*

John Ganam Illustration. Collection of of Norma and John Hilt.

THE DECADE 1940-1950

If the preparation for war, and World War II itself, ended the Depression, it also brought strictures and shortages that kept a check on public access to new housing, automobiles and home appliances. Rubber for tires was cut off from import and gasoline was severely rationed. Magazine publishers were also limited to paper quotas that precluded circulation growth, and industry, converted to war production, ceased making civilian automobiles, refrigerators and vacuum cleaners.

In this environment, illustrators found various ways to participate in the war effort; some joined the armed services directly, serving from privates to commissioned officers, or were involved in creating war propaganda posters, instructional charts and pamphlets. Tom Lovell and John Clymer enlisted in the Marine Corps the same day with consecutive dog tag numbers and produced artwork for the Marines. Jon Whitcomb, John Falter and McClelland Barclay served with the Navy. (Barclay lost his life aboard a torpedoed LST in the Pacific.) Gilbert Bundy and Harold Von Schmidt were artist-war correspondents; *Stars and Stripes* and *Yank* were staffed with artists including Ed Vebell and Bill Mauldin. Hamilton Greene, representing *The American Legion* magazine in the European Theatre, was wounded by sniper fire.

On the home front, advertisers employed illustrators to portray their war-time products; aircraft, tanks and ships needed to be depicted in action. Magazine fiction — now catering more to a female audience — featured romantic content and the anticipation of returning husbands or lovers. Young men were invariably pictured in uniform. Al Parker found the right combination of elements of war-time fashions, inventive selection of props and eye-stopping page layouts to make him the most popular illustrator of the day, and by example, the founder of a whole Parker School of imitators that would continue to be an influence through the following decade. Illustrators who were not directly involved in the Service, through the New York Society of Illustrators and other organizations, regularly visited hospitals to make portrait drawings for wounded servicemen to send home, or improved morale by making impromptu decorations on plaster casts.

Following the war's end and demobilization, the country quickly returned to civilian status, with a boom in housing and industrial goods. Illustrators were in great demand for magazine publishers who were able to expand their numbers of pages and subscriber base as well as by manufacturers that had new products to advertise. Virtuoso illustrators like Robert Fawcett, John Gannam, John Falter, and Haddon Sundblom had full schedules and there was plenty of room for the many new emerging talents.

The era of Harvey Dunn's School of painting sumptuous oil on canvas was passing; most illustrators were now working in gouache at a smaller scale, but with more emphasis on detail.

The decade also saw the revitalization of the children's book genre as the Baby Boom burgeoned.

Courtney Allen, illustration for *The Saturday Evening Post*, "Gold from Crete" by C. S. Forester. © 1942, 1970 by The Curtis Publishing Company.

COURTNEY ALLEN

COURTNEY ALLEN (1896-1969) sold his first drawing to his home-town newspaper in Norfolk, Virginia, at the age of eleven. Thus encouraged, he decided on an art career. He later studied at the National Academy, the Corcoran School of Art in Washington, D.C., and with Charles W. Hawthorne in Provincetown, Massachusetts. His study was interrupted by fifteen months spent in the American Army during World War I: twelve months in France, eight of them at the Front in the Camouflage Section.

In the following years, Allen divided his time between illustrating for books and magazines, painting for exhibition, and from 1946-50, teaching at the Huguenot School of Art in New Rochelle, New York.

During World War II, he was a regular participant in sketching trips with other members of the New Rochelle Art Association to Halloran Hospital on Staten Island, making portrait drawings of convalescent servicemen.

He was an active member of the New Rochelle Art Association, where he won a Gold Medal for oil painting; he also exhibited and won other awards at the Hudson Valley Art Association, the Norfolk Museum of Arts and Sciences. the National Academy, the Allied Artists in New York, the Chrysler Art Museum, and the Provincetown Historical Museum.

Harry Anderson

HARRY ANDERSON, N.A. (1906-1996) became a watercolorist because of an allergy to oil paint. He adapted to gouache which he managed to blend on the brush like oils, and added the spontaneity of the water medium.

Anderson (no relation to other Andersons in this book) was born in Chicago, attended the University of Illinois, and graduated from Syracuse University in 1930. He had studios successively in New York, Chicago, Washington D.C., and finally in Ridgefield, Connecticut.

His illustrations appeared in most of the major magazines, and he painted a memorable series of calendar illustrations for Esso and Humble Oil. Anderson was commissioned by the Seventh Day Adventist Church to paint a series of Biblical murals; he also made a second series of large religious paintings for the Church of the Latter-Day Saints in Salt Lake City. By using a substitute for turpentine, he was able to paint them in oils and they have become his major legacy.

He also exhibited regularly, and as a member of the American Water Color Society, he won the Grumbacher Purchase Prize in the 1956 exhibition.

Harry Anderson, *A Way with Boys,* © November 1948, 1976 by The Meredith Corporation. All rights reserved. Used with the permission of *The Ladies' Home Journal*. Collection of Tom Browning.

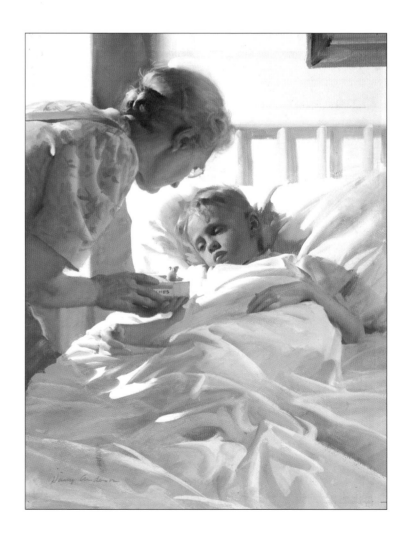

Lyman Anderson, "The Blue Cloak," illustration for **Woman's Home Companion**, 1940. Collection of the Society of Illustrators Museum of American Illustration.

LYMAN ANDERSON

LYMAN MATTHEW ANDERSON (1907-1993) got his big break when some spot illustrations he'd made for an insurance company advertisement were accepted for exhibition in the New York Art Directors Club's annual show. Unknown to the acceptance jury, the original paintings were very large and when hung, dominated the whole show. The pictures attracted much favorable attention and launched Lyman on the national scene as an illustrator.

Anderson had prepared himself well for the opportunity when it came. Born in Chicago, Illinois, he was a graduate of the Art Institute there, and attended the Grand Central School of Art in New York City. Among his teachers were Pruett Carter, Walter Biggs, Harvey Dunn, Naum Los and Wayman Adams. His early artwork included a great deal of illustration for Pulp magazines, as well as a syndicated comic strip for King Features.

During his career, his clients included such advertisers as Pepsi-Cola, Vitalis, the New York Life Insurance Company, and Pan-American airline, as well as magazines such as **Woman's Home Companion**, **The Saturday Evening Post**, **Cosmopolitan** and **American Magazine**. He was a long-time member of the Society of Illustrators and was an honorary life-member of the Joint Ethics Committee.

John Atherton painted this cover illustration in the tradition of John Peto and William Harnett for **True** magazine, September, 1951.
Courtesy of Michael Rosenfeld Gallery, N.Y.C.

Atherton

For JOHN ATHERTON (1900-1952) there was no line drawn between "fine" and "commercial" art. He painted pictures for advertisers, magazine covers, and galleries alike, all characterized by his strong sense of design, color, and good taste.

Atherton was born in Brainerd, Minnesota, and he studied at the College of the Pacific, and the California School of Fine Arts in San Francisco. He first worked in a number of West Coast art studios learning the basics of his craft. When he won a $500 first prize award in the annual exhibit of the Bohemian Club in 1929, it financed his move to New York.

There he began to do advertisements for General Motors, the Container Corporation of America, and Shell Oil, as well as covers for **Fortune**, **Holiday**, and **The Saturday Evening Post**.

His first one-man show was held in Manhattan in 1936; in the "Artists for Victory" show in 1943, his painting, *The Black Horse*, won the $3,000 fourth prize from among 14,000 entries. It is now in the collection of the Metropolitan Museum of Art in New York. His work is also represented at the Whitney Museum, the Museum of Modern Art, the Chicago Art Institute, the Pennsylvania Academy of the Fine Arts, the Albright-Knox Art Gallery in Buffalo, and the Wadsworth Atheneum in Hartford.

Atherton's great avocation was fishing. He tied flies of original design expertly, was a member of the Anglers' Club and author of a book, **The Fly and the Fish**. His death occurred while he was on a salmon fishing trip in New Brunswick, Canada.

Illustration for "Mrs. Benson" by Ernest Haycox, published in *Collier's* magazine, January 20, 1948.
Collection of Frank B. Milligan.

Pecos Bill (with his live rattlesnack hatband), cover for *Adventure* magazine.

Baumgartner

WARREN BAUMGARTNER, N.A. (1894-1963) was born in Oakville, Missouri, and came to a lifetime love of fishing from his boyhood in the Ozarks. In the years following, he studied at the Art Institute of Chicago under J. Wellington Reynolds, at the Grand Central School with Pruett Carter, and with Walter Biggs.

A very fine watercolorist, Baumgartner painted pictures for both magazine illustration and exhibition, winning numerous awards in both fields.

He was a member of the Society of Illustrators, the American Watercolor Society, the National Academy of Design, and the Salmagundi Club of New York.

Walter M Baumhofer

For years, WALTER MARTIN BAUMHOFER (1904-1987) painted cover designs for the Pulps, such as *Adventure* magazine, Street & Smith's magazines, and Popular Publications's titles. He developed a bold, dramatic approach for them that characterized his subsequent work.

He painted the first series of *Doc Savage* covers, and depicted a gallery of other western and detective characters. A versatile performer, Baumhofer also illustrated for publications as diverse as *The Ladies' Home Journal*, *Liberty*, *Collier's*, *Argosy*, *Esquire*, *Outdoor Life*, *Cosmopolitan*, *True*, *Woman's Day*, and *Sports Afield*.

Baumhofer studied at Pratt Institute in Brooklyn, New York, graduating in 1925, and was a long-time member of the Society of Illustrators.

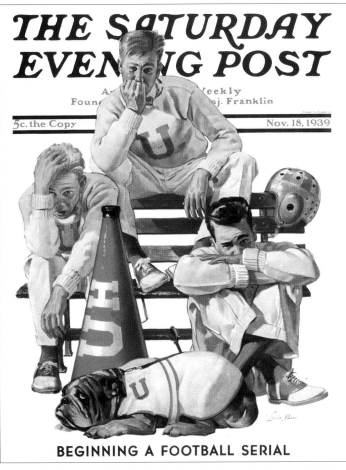

Loni Bee, cover illustration for *The Saturday Evening Post,* November 18, 1939. ©1939, 1967, by The Curtis Publishing Company.

LONIE BEE (1902-unknown) was born in Santa Rosa, California, and remained there, one of the few major illustrators based on the West Coast.

After training at the University of California and the California School of Fine Arts and Crafts, he appeared on the national scene with his spirited illustrations for the magazines *Collier's*, *American*, *Cosmopolitan*, *Woman's Home Companion*, *Woman's Day*, *Good Housekeeping* and *The Saturday Evening Post*; among these, he painted numerous covers. Over the years, he also did advertising illustrations and painted designs for twenty-four-sheet billboard posters, winning many awards and citations.

Subsequently, Bee turned to landscape painting and portraiture. He exhibited at the Society of Illustrators in New York, The Bohemian Club, and the Carmel Gallery in California.

One of Belarski's many paperback covers, this one for the digest-sized Phantom Books, of the early 1950s. Collection of Robert D. Portwood.

RUDOLPH BELARSKI (1900-1983) came from a poor family in DuPont, Pennsylvania, and went to work as a slate picker in a local coal mine instead of finishing grade school. One day he made a drawing on a whitewashed wall near the mine entrance that caught the eye of his foreman. This led to an assignment to make some safety posters for the mine and an inside office job. Despite the offer of the company to send him to engineering school, Rudy knew he wanted to be an artist. At nineteen, he left for New York and attended Pratt Institute, supporting himself by waiting on tables, sign painting, and teaching art in a settlement house. He also went back to grade school during the summers to make up for his missed education.

Belarski won several awards while at Pratt and as an outstanding student, he was invited to teach there after graduation. For his freelance assignments, he sought out camping, sports, and action stories, which reflected his personal interests. He soon became one of the most prolific and dynamic artists in the Pulps, excelling at detective, aviation, science-fiction, with heroes such as John Carter, and the Phantom Detective, always with compositions organized on the diagonal. As the Pulps waned, the paperbacks and men's magazines replaced them, and Belarski kept active with a wider diversity of subjects, including hunting and fishing for *Outdoor Life*. When he sought work at *The Saturday Evening Post,* art editor Ken Stuart advised him to stick with what he was doing so successfully and named him "the perfect paperback artist." At the conclusion of his freelance career, he became an instructor at the Famous Artists Schools in Westport, Connecticut.

GEOFFREY BIGGS

GEOFFREY BIGGS (1908-) was born in London, England, but
went through high school in America, and studied at the Grand
Central School of Art. Among his teachers were Arthur Woeffle,
Arshile Gorky and Harvey Dunn.

Biggs's highly detailed and realistic work was first published
in *Collier's*, where it attracted wide attention, and was soon
followed by commissions from most other periodicals, including
The Saturday Evening Post, *True*, *Liberty*, *Woman's Home
Companion*, *Coronet*, *Pic*, and *Good Housekeeping*, as well as
from many major and minor advertising agencies in New York.

In addition, Biggs found time to exhibit at the Society of
Illustrators and at the Midtown Galleries in New York.

Geoffrey Biggs, illustration for "Fight at Painted Rock," by Alan LeMay,
Collier's magazine May 6, 1939.

Bouché's advertising illustrations for Elizabeth Arden using a wet watercolor over a
soluble ink line became a distinctive hallmark of their corporate image in the 1940s.

RENÉ BOUCHÉ (1905-1963) was a superb draftsman who
learned his craft as a fashion illustrator for *Vogue* magazine,
beginning with the Paris edition in 1938. He was able to convey
the elegance of clothing and accessories with a spare, linear
drawing combined with a limited tone of conté pencil or wet-in-
wet watercolor. This elegance also brought him many advertising
clients, such as Elizabeth Arden, Saks Fifth Avenue, and Helena
Rubenstein. For several seasons, he drew major television
luminaries for CBS from life, including Jack Benny, Red Skelton,
Edward R. Murrow, Ed Sullivan and Danny Kaye, but he was
particularly esteemed for his glamorous treatment of famous
women socialites and movie stars, including Claire Booth Luce,
Mrs. William Paley, Gloria Swanson, Tammy Grimes, Julie
Harris, Jacqueline Kennedy, Joan Greenwood and Sophia Loren.

Bouché was born in Prague, Czechoslovakia, and began to
work as an advertising artist in Berlin. In 1933, he moved to Paris
for further art instruction, and was able to land a staff job with
Vogue.

An early conceptual painting of the construction of a manned satellite in orbit 500 miles above Earth. Bonestell Space art/ © Chesley Bonestell estate.

Chesley Bonestell

CHESLEY BONESTELL (1888-1986) was the artistic authority for the exploration of space, long before the NASA. His interest in astronomy was initiated in boyhood when he first viewed Saturn through a telescope.

Although he was a student of architecture at Columbia University and practiced that profession for several years, primarily as a designer and renderer, he came back to astronomy by way of the movies. His expertise with perspective had qualified him as a special effects matte-artist able to paint convincing backgrounds and led to his work with science-fiction films, such as *The War of the Worlds,* and *Destination Moon.*

His combination of science and imagination made him a natural for interpreting possibilities of space exploration, and his concepts were published by *Life, Coronet,* and *Scientific American.* In collaboration with Wernher von Braun, Bonestell created memorable illustrations foretelling the future possibilities of space travel in a series of articles published by *Collier's* magazine in 1952. Bonestell was also valuable to NASA in conceptualizing planetary geography.

The artist was honored by a Special Achievement Award at the World Science Fiction convention in 1974 and was inducted into the Society of Illustrators' Hall of Fame in 1997.

The lunar landscape bathed in the copper glow of an eclipse of the sun. Bonestell Space Art/ © Chesley Bonestell Estate.

263

GILBERT BUNDY (1911-1955) was born in Centralia, Illinois, the son of an oil company scout, and was brought up in a succession of oil boom towns in Oklahoma. He eventually finished high school in Winfield, Kansas, and went to work for a Kansas City engraving company.

In 1929, Bundy headed for a career in New York, and began to do cartoons for the old *Life* and *Judge* magazines.

In the early 1930s, he became associated with the fledgling *Esquire* magazine. His deftly drawn, risqué humor had much to do with the success of that magazine. It was also a valuable showcase for Bundy and led to his spectacular popularity as an illustrator for most of the major magazines and with many advertisers. These included campaigns for Cluett Peabody, Munsingwear and Sanka Coffee.

Bundy's pictures looked spontaneous but were the result of much careful preliminary study. He emulated the classic Chinese method of drawing from memory once he had made many prior studies from the model.

During World War II, Bundy covered the Pacific War

Gilbert Bundy, illustration for "Horse Play" by Parke Hanley, *This Week* magazine, May 12, 1935. Collection of Art Wood.

Theatre as a combat artist for King Features. He went through a series of harrowing actions, including Tarawa, Iwo Jima and Okinawa; he was the sole survivor of a direct hit on an amphtrack and spent a day and night in the water before being rescued.

Although he resumed his career in illustration after the war, Bundy never recovered from his experiences and took his own life in 1955.

EMERY CLARKE

EMERY CLARKE (1911-1990) was a multi-faceted, multi-talented artist whose art work ranged from magazine covers to comic strips to caricatures. When he wasn't wielding a brush, he was also a cook, an expert carpenter, a fine dancer, a guitar player and a high-ranked handball player. Other enthusiastic interests included camping and kayaking.

Emery was born in Kansas and studied at the Art Institute there by working his way and winning a scholarship. He later studied at the Pennsylvania Academy of the Fine Arts in Philadelphia. He rode his motorcycle to New York and his drawing samples impressed Street & Smith, which commissioned him to paint his first pulp cover in oils. He worked for several years thereafter as a pulp cover artist depicting "The Shadow" and other famous characters. His next target was *The Saturday Evening Post*, and he painted several covers for them, and story illustrations for other magazines such as *Look*, *This Week*, and *Liberty*.

During World War II, Clarke served in the U.S. Air Force assigned as an artist for training films at Canute Field in Illinois. He met fellow-artist Russell Stamm there and devised a comic strip, "The Invisible Scarlett O'Neil," which they continued for the next ten years. An adjunct of cartooning was his ability to make pithy caricatures, and his roster of "victims" included many corporate executives and politicians.

In the 1950s, Clarke was an instructor on the staff of the Famous Artists Schools in Westport, Connecticut.

Clarke's humor is clearly shown here as the small town visitor to the Chicago World's Fair describes its wonders to a mixed reception back home for *The Saturday Evening Post,* July 15, 1939. © 1939, 1967 by The Curtis Publishing Company.

Thunder Mountain, 1935. One of a series of paintings related to Northwest Indian life.

John Clymer

JOHN CLYMER (1907-1989) was born in Ellensburg, Washington. His art education was acquired at the Vancouver School of Fine Art, the Ontario College of Art in Port Hope, Canada, as well as at the Wilmington Society of Fine Arts in Delaware, and the Grand Central School of Art in New York. With this background, his loyalties had ever since been divided between the United States and Canada.

Clymer's first illustrations were made for Canadian publications, followed by American pulps, which lead to editorial assignments for most of the American magazines, numerous advertising campaigns, and an extensive series of paintings of historic episodes for the United States Marine Corps during World War II.

His paintings have been exhibited widely in both countries as well, with the North West Artists in Seattle, the Ontario Society of Artists, the Royal Canadian Academy in Toronto, Canada (where he was an Associate member), the National Academy in New York, the Salmagundi Club, the Society of Animal Artists, and the Hudson Valley Artists. Clymer was an exhibiting member of the Cowboy Artists and the National Academy of Western Art, winning numerous awards. His biography ***John Clymer, An Artist's Rendevous with the Frontier West*** was published by Northland Press in 1976. He was elected to the Society of Illustrators Hall of Fame in 1982.

Clymer posed his family for this ***Saturday Evening Post*** cover May 31, 1952. ©1952, 1980 by the Curtis Publishing Company. Collection of Diane and Jordan Berman.

265

Tea Party, cover for ***The Saturday Evening Post,*** January 31, 1953 ©1953, 1981 by the Curtis Publishing Company.
Collection of Ilene and Steven Berman.

Homecoming New York Harbor: Christmastime, 1944. By permission of **Esquire** magazine. © Hearst Communications, Inc. Also, **Esquire** is a trademark of Hearst Magazines Property, Inc. All Rights Reserved.

Stevan Dohanos

STEVAN DOHANOS (1907-1994) made his mark as a nationally famous cover artist for **The Saturday Evening Post** and chronicler of Americana, but he began at the bottom.

He studied nights at the Cleveland School of Art long enough to get a job as an apprentice letterer, and gradually developed a solid studio background. A hard worker, he simultaneously painted and printed woodcuts for national exhibitions.

In 1936, he painted an assignment for the Treasury Art Project in the Virgin Islands, and later, various mural commissions for federal buildings in Elkins, West Virginia; West Palm Beach, Florida; and Charlotte Amalie, Virgin Islands. His pictures are in the collections of the Cleveland Museum of Art, the Whitney Museum, the Pennsylvania Academy of the Fine Arts, Avery Memorial of Hartford, and the New Britain Museum of American Art.

His illustrations have appeared in almost all of the major magazines; he painted over 100 covers for **The Saturday Evening Post.** Twice a victim of tuberculosis himself, Dohanos contributed Christmas seal designs to the National Tuberculosis Association, and made many posters and designs for national and local charitable purposes. He designed well over forty stamps for the U.S. Postal service, and for several years he served on the Citizen Stamp Advisory Committee for the Postmaster General and as its Design Coordinator.

Dohanos was a member of the National Society of Mural Painters, the Artists and Writers club, the Dutch Treat Club. He served as President of the Society of Illustrators from 1961-63, was inducted into its Hall of Fame in 1971, and served as Honorary President from 1982 until his death.

Owl and Clock, 1962 one of Dohanos' many independent paintings. Collection of Mr. & Mrs. Sherman Small.

"The Strange Case of the Bottled Wife," *Esquire* magazine, February 1952.

ALBERT DORNE

ALBERT DORNE (1904-1965) was born and grew up on the Lower East Side of New York, and had to leave school in the eighth grade to go to work. In 1963, he fittingly received the Horatio Alger Award for Achievement from the American Schools and Colleges Association, Inc.

Through a combination of natural ability and strong drive, Dorne progressed successively from being an unpaid assistant to a commercial artist to one of New York's most successful advertising artists, while still in his early twenties. He went on to become a leading editorial illustrator, was elected president of the Society of Illustrators (1947-48), and in 1948 became the founder-director of the Famous Artists Schools in Westport, Connecticut.

These remarkably successful correspondence schools sprang originally from Dorne's interest in helping aspiring artists who continually came to him for advice.

Among his achievements, Dorne highly ranked his being co-founder of the Code of Ethics and Fair Practices of the Profession of Commercial Art and Illustration. In 1953, he was awarded the first Gold Medal for a "distinguished career" by the New York Art Directors Club. Adelphi College conferred on him an honorary Doctor of Fine Arts degree in 1958.

Illustration for "Beware Unfamiliar Spirits," published by *The Saturday Evening Post* © 1946, 1974 by The Curtis Publishing Company. The Sanford Low Collection of American Illustration, New Britain Museum of American Art.

East Meets West at Promontory Point, Utah, May 10, 1869. One of Falter's Bicentennial paintings for the 3M Corporation in 1976.

This moving cover for *The Saturday Evening Post* symbolized the concerns of all sweethearts, parents, or spouses for family members in service during World War II; published May 8, 1943. ©1943, 1971 by The Curtis Publishing Company.

JOHN FALTER

JOHN PHILIP FALTER (1910-1982) was born in Plattsmouth and reared in Falls City, Nebraska. He studied at the Kansas City Art Institute, the Art Students League in New York on a scholarship, and the Grand Central School of Art in New York. Among his teachers were Mahonri Young, George Wright and Monte Crews.

Falter began his career in illustration early, starting with the Pulps, and at 20, sold his first picture to *Liberty,* a "slick" paper magazine. Talented and prolific, he soon added most of the other major magazines, and many advertising agencies, to his roster of clients.

His most important pictures were painted for the covers of *The Saturday Evening Post,* and he produced more than 200 of them. Many were based on the experiences of his Nebraska boyhood, in small town and country settings. He also painted a notable series of detailed street scenes in cities across the United States. These grew out of a chance visit of a *Post* art editor to Falter's studio; there a picture of Gramercy Park caught his eye, which Falter had painted for pleasure.

John served in the Navy as a Chief Boatswain's Mate during World War II; later, he was commissioned a Lieutenant on special art assignments. Among other projects after the war, he illustrated over 40 books for *Reader's Digest* and completed many portrait commissions, including those of Admiral Halsey, Louis Armstrong, Olivia de Havilland, James Cagney, Mrs. Clark Clifford, and tenor John Charles Thomas. He later painted an outstanding series of historical subjects for the Bicentennial, commissioned by the 3M Company in 1976.

Falter was a member of the Society of Illustrators, the Players, and the Philadelphia Sketch Club. In 1976, he was elected to the Society of Illustrators' Hall of Fame. Although he did not often exhibit, his paintings are in several museums.

Born in London, ROBERT FAWCETT, A.N.A. (1903-1967) was given much encouragement in his early drawing efforts by his father, an amateur artist. Fawcett's family moved from England to Winnipeg, Canada, and later to New York City.

At nineteen, Fawcett returned to London, and for two years studied drawing under the rigorous discipline of the famous Slade School of London University. He came back to the United States in 1924, and began the long career in advertising and editorial illustration that brought him preeminence as "the illustrators' illustrator." Fawcett earned that reputation through his superb draftsmanship and mastery of composition, as shown in the Sherlock Holmes stories he illustrated for *Collier's* magazine, and also in "If the South Had Won the Civil War" for *Look* magazine.

In later years, he preferred to restrict his work to reportorial assignments, as, for example, his assignment to Oxford, Mississippi, for *Look* magazine. His book, ***On the Art of Drawing,*** was published in 1958.

Fawcett was twice president of the Westport Artists and also a member of the founding faculty of the Famous Artists Schools in Westport, Connecticut.

He was elected to the Hall of Fame of the Society of Illustrators in 1967. A second book based on Fawcett's drawings and teaching, ***Drawing the Nude***, was written by his colleague and friend Howard Munce, and published in 1980.

Artist and Model, ***Woman's Home Companion.*** Private collection.

Here Fawcett depicts the moment of truth as an aspiring illustrator shows his artwork to a jaded art director.
The Art Director- Partners in Production Advertising Howard Paper Mills Inc., circa 1951. Collection, Howard Chaykin

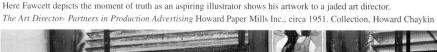

"The Adventure of the Red Widow" by Adrian Conan Doyle and John Dickson Carr, *Collier's* magazine, October 2, 1953.

Fred Freeman, one of the first serious editorial treatments of the cyborg concept. "Man Remade to Live in Space," *Life* magazine July 11, 1960.

Opening Night, Sept. 26, 1953. Arthur Getz © 1953, 1981 *The New Yorker* Magazine, Inc. Reprinted by permission. Collection of Bruce A. Block.

Fred Freeman From logging to layout work in a large department store, FRED FREEMAN (1906-1988) accumulated a diversity of experience which contributed greatly to his artistic development. He was a Naval Reserve Lietenant Commander during World War II, and skippered three different ships, taking part in actions at Guadalcanal, New Zealand, the Solomon Islands, Saipan, Guam, and the Aleutians. With this naval background, he was able to combine a technical knowledge with dramatic impact in his authoritative illustrations for the book *United States Submarine Operations in World War II*.

In his subsequent commercial career, Freeman continued to combine this intricacy of documentary detail with strongly composed artistry. The burgeoning developments of space-age technology had been a special province for Freeman who took on many major illustration assignments for publications such as *Collier's*, *This Week*, *Life*, *The Saturday Evening Post*, and *Reader's Digest.*

Arthur Getz, Campaign Train. Collection of Sarah Getz.

Getz Beginning July 23, 1938, ARTHUR GETZ (1913-1996) painted more covers for *The New Yorker* than any other artist, and was able to meet their indefinable requirements through creative artistry as well as prodigious hard work and perseverance. He always carried a sketch book with him and drew interesting bits and details for cover ideas wherever he went. Yet one could not go out and find the specific street corner or hotel that appeared on a particular cover. Getz synthesized those quintessential scenes out of his head, from a lifetime of observing New York and its suburbs.

His media was varied. Early covers were painted in encaustic; subsequently he used ink, watercolor, casein, or tempera, and mastered other mediums as well.

Getz was born in Passaic, New Jersey, and studied at Brooklyn's Pratt Institure, graduating in 1934 with honors. During World War II, he served in the Army as a surveyor in the Philippines.

In addition to his long *New Yorker* affiliation, Getz illustrated for other magazines, including *Esquire*, *The Nation*, *Cue*, *P.M.*, *The New Republic* and *Audubon*. He wrote and illustrated children's books, painted murals in Post Offices in Bronson, Michigan, and Lancaster, New York, and taught at the School of Visual Arts, the University of Connecticut, and the Washington Art Association in Washington, Connecticut.

Getz resided in a loft studio in Manhattan until 1969, when he moved to a farmhouse in Sharon, Connecticut, and he continued to work and paint there for the rest of his career.

A

C

D

A. "Girl with the Glow" by Harriet Frank, Jr., *The Saturday Evening Post*.
© 1955, 1983 by the Curtis Publishing Company.

B. *Redbook* story illustration February, 1952.

C. "Murder for a Million," date and place of publication unknown.

D. "The Man She Married," *Redbook,* April, 1958. Collection of Peter and Marie Myer

B

Georgi

EDWIN A. GEORGI (1896-1964) was studying civil engineering at Princeton when World War I broke out. He volunteered and served as a pilot in the U. S. Air Force.

After the war, Georgi took his first job doing paste-ups in an advertising agency art department, and began his practical training as an artist under his mentor, René Clarke.

His early illustrations were for advertisers. Over the years, he did series of advertisments for Hartford Fire Insurance, Crane Paper Co., Webster Cigars, The Italian Line, Ford Mercury, Brooks Brothers, Hockanum Woolens, and Yardley & Co.

Georgi's ability to depict beautiful women and sumptuous settings also brought him story manuscripts; he was soon illustrating for most of the national magazines, including **Woman's Home Companion**, **Redbook**, **McCall's**, **Cosmopolitan**, **The Ladies' Home Journal**, and **The Saturday Evening Post**. His later use of color was lavish and dramatic, a kind of pointillism layered in colored ink, watercolor, and gouache. This gave his pictures great impact on the printed page.

Nude at Mirror, illustration for **Cosmopolitan** magazine, January, 1946.
To his fellow illustrators, each new painting by Gannam was an inspiring event.

"Rule by Power," *Collier's*, September 18, 1937.

JOHN GANNAM

JOHN GANNAM, A.N.A. (1907-1965) was a totally absorbed, dedicated artist. He worked almost exclusively in watercolor, and was a lifelong student of the effects of light and color. Oftentimes a particular problem would preoccupy him for months as he tried out innumerable variations. He kept on until satisfied, finally, that he understood such effects as sunlight and underwater rocks on the surface of a mountain stream or the glow of a fire in the sky and its reflection on wet pavement as firemen fought a blaze. But the final product invariably looked quick and spontaneous.

Gannam worked at his paintings almost vertically, very freely, his brush loaded with water. He was after the broad, but exact effect, little concerned with details or with corrections which could be made later, if needed, with opaque paint.

He was born in Lebanon, grew up in Chicago, but was forced to leave school to work at 14 when his father died. He went through a succession of menial jobs until be eventually became a messenger boy in an engraving house. Here he first found a purpose for himself — to become an artist like the men who did

the layouts, lettering and drawings for engravings. Within a few years, through close observation and a stiff schedule of self-education, he reached his goal, working for studios in Chicago and Detroit.

The next step was New York and magazine illustration. He received his first manuscript from Henry Quinan of *Woman's Home Companion*, followed soon thereafter by work from most of the other national magazines. Gannam always sought fresh, unclichéd viewpoints which, with his excellent taste, kept him in constant demand by advertisers as well as publishers. His illustrations for campaigns of Pacific Mills, Ipana and St. Mary's Blankets are particularly memorable.

Gannam also exhibited his watercolors, and was an associate of the National Academy of Design. He was a member of the American Artists' Professional League, the American Watercolor Society, the Society of Illustrators, and on the faculty and board of directors of the Danbury Academy of Arts. In 1981, he was elected to the Society of Illustrators' Hall of Fame.

JOHN F. GOULD (1906-) estimated that he did about twelve thousand adventure and detective story illustrations for pulp magazines before tackling **The Saturday Evening Post**. To prepare himself for the **Post**, he spent a year-and-a-half picking a different story each week and re-doing the illustrations in his own way. A representative group of these, shown to the Post's art editor, won Gould his first commission.

Following that, he illustrated for **Redbook**, **Collier's**, **The Country Gentleman**, and numerous national advertising accounts.

Born in Worcester, Massachusetts, Gould studied at the Tiffany Foundation, and was graduated from Pratt Institute where he then taught for twenty-two years. He also taught at the Newark School of Fine and Industrial Art, as well as in classes at the Bethlehem Art Gallery near Newburgh, New York.

John Gould, illustration for "Happy the Bride" by David Lamson, July 3, 1943. Published by **The Saturday Evening Post,** ©1943, 1971 by The Curtis Publishing Company.

As a boy, HARDIE GRAMATKY N.A. (1907-1979) wanted to be a comic strip artist. He realized that ambition early, "ghosting" the "Ella Cinders" comic strip soon after completing his studies at Stanford University and at the Chouinard Art Institute in Los Angeles. This preparation led to a job in Walt Disney's studio, where for six years he worked his way up and finally became head animator.

In 1936, Gramatky came to New York to free-lance; some of his first assignments were reportorial paintings for **Fortune** magazine. He specialized in the watercolor medium, and his illustrations for fiction, editorials, and advertising appeared in virtually all the magazines.

As a result of painting tugboats, he became interested in doing a children's book, when he noticed one taking on a personality. His story, **Little Toot**, has been a perennial best seller ever since, was made into an animated film by Disney, was included in the CARE-UNESCO book program, and has been rated by the Library of Congress as one of the great children's books of all time. He subsequently wrote and illustrated many other books well-known in the children's book field.

Gramatky also painted and exhibited all over the world, winning top watercolor awards at the Chicago International in 1942, the National Academy in 1952, and the American Watercolor Society in 1962. His works are in the permanent collections of the Brooklyn Museum, the Springfield Museum of Art, the Toledo Museum, the New York Public Library, and in many other collections.

Hardie Gramatky, illustration for "Retreat from Moscow" by Quentin Reynolds in **Collier's** magazine.

276

HAMILTON GREENE

HAMILTON GREENE (1904-1966) produced a great quantity of competent illustrations, beginning with the Pulp magazines, and later on for the men's magazines *Argosy*, *True*, *Cavalier*, *Elks*, and for Dell publications.

Greene was appointed an overseas artist-correspondent for *The American Legion* magazine in 1944-45, and made many authentic, eyewitness drawings of fighting in the European theatre. While with a Ninth Army Patrol near Geilenkirchen, Germany, he was wounded in the stomach and lungs by sniper fire. According to an excerpt from a letter by the director of the Public Relations Division, Supreme Headquarters, A.E.F., "Mr. Greene was conspicuously forward in every operation in which he participated, and was well-known to the personnel of the units he accompanied because of his place in the forward assault where he sought opportunity to watch the reactions of the American soldiers in the attack..." In 1951, Greene again served as a war correspondent, in Korea for *Blue Book* magazine. A large collection of his war illustrations is in the U. S. Army Center of Military History in Washington, D.C.

Hamilton Greene, illustration for *Blue Book* magazine, "Holland Para-drop," September, 1949.

Glen Grohe, *Sieving the Baby*, advertising illustration for The Travelers Insurance Company in 1940.

grohe

GLEN GROHE (1912-1956) was born in Chicago and worked his way through the Art Institute and the American Academy of Art there. He obtained his first job with the Swan Studio in Chicago, and in 1937, went to New York, joining the staff of an advertising magazine, and later the Charles E. Cooper Studio.

He attracted the attention of magazine art editors through the originality and strong design of his advertising illustrations which he carried over into his work for periodicals including *The Saturday Evening Post*, *This Week*, *Cosmopolitan*, and *Good Housekeeping* magazines.

Among Grohe's many advertising clients were the Dow Chemical Company, Conoco, and the Travelers Insurance Company. During World War II, he served as a consultant in the Graphics Division of the O.E.M. and designed posters for the O.W.I.

Grohe was also interested in still and motion picture photography. He made a documentary film for the San Mateo County Recreational Department and had nearly finished a very imaginative film on the artwork of patients in a mental institution at the time of his death.

John Groth, illustration for Ian Fleming's "Tokyo, Swinging City of the Sensuous East," *True* magazine, July, 1963.

GUSTAVSON

LEALAND R. GUSTAVSON (1899-1966) was born in the Swedish community of Moline, Illinois. He studied nights for several years at the Chicago Art Institute while working in printing houses, advertising agencies and art services. After moving East, he resumed night classes, studying under Walter Biggs and Harvey Dunn.

Although he illustrated for *The Saturday Evening Post, Collier's, McCall's,* and many other periodicals, Gustavson was one of the mainstays of *Blue Book* magazine for many years and in his illustrations for the blood and thunder stories managed to "kill a staggering number of people in all the diabolical ways an author can dream up…"

Along with his interest in art, he was an ardent sportsman. For several years, he played tournament badminton throughout the East, holding a national championship title and several New England titles. He was equally interested in golf, both as a player and in illustrating the fine points of the game for books and magazine articles.

He exhibited widely and won many awards; he taught at the Chicago Art Institute and Ray Commercial Art School in Chicago. Gustavson was a member of the Salmagundi Club, the American Watercolor Society, and the Academic Artists Association.

Lealand Gustavson, illustration for one of the David Lamson stories in *The Saturday Evening Post* ©1941, 1969 by The Curtis Publishing Company.

John Groth

As an aspiring young illustrator, JOHN GROTH, A.N.A. (1908-1988) was advised by an artist friend to make a hundred drawings a day. John took the advice literally and kept up the practice for years. This driving pace trained him as an artist and shaped his free, expressionist style of drawing.

Impressed by the vigor of his work, *Esquire* magazine hired him as its first art director. He promptly assigned himself on travel junkets to draw and paint for the magazine in Mexico, Russia, France, England and Germany.

As an artist-correspondent for the *Chicago Sun* during World War II, he was present at the liberation of Paris and the surrender of Berlin. Groth became a friend of Ernest Hemingway in France, and out of this association came his assignment to illustrate Hemingway's *Men Without Women*. Hemingway also wrote the preface for Groth's own book of war drawings and experiences, *Studio: Europe*. He later covered the Korean War, and wrote and illustrated another book, *Studio: Asia*.

In the years between wars, Groth continued to travel, and carried out assignments for *Look, Fortune, Sports Illustrated, Town and Country*; he also illustrated several classics including *War and Peace* and *The Grapes of Wrath*.

Groth taught at the Art Students League and the National Academy of Design. His work is in the collections of the Museum of Modern Art, the Library of Congress, and the National Gallery of Art. He was also a member of the Society of Illustrators.

R. G. Harris, illustration for *McCall's* magazine, July, 1947.

From his boyhood in Kansas City, Missouri, ROBERT GEORGE HARRIS (1911-) always knew he wanted to be an artist. After study with Monte Crews at the Kansas City Art Institute, he went East via motorcycle, attended classes at both the Grand Central School of Art with Harvey Dunn and the Art Students League under George Bridgman.

His first published artwork was for Street & Smith's *Western Story* magazine covers before he graduated to the mainstream slick-paper magazines. In contrast to the violent Pulps, Harris became noted for his highly finished and sympathetic depictions of children and young love. This made him a natural choice for art editors of the women's magazines *The Ladies' Home Journal*, *Good Housekeeping*, and *McCall's*. His illustrations also appeared regularly in *The Saturday Evening Post* and *Cosmopolitan.* Many national advertising accounts followed.

At present Harris lives in Arizona where he has been painting portraits. He is a life member of the Society of Illustrators and an early member of the Phoenix Art Museum which has held a one-man show of his portraiture.

Ray Houlihan, illustration for "No Substitute for Victory," *Reader's Digest,* October, 1964.

RAYMOND F. HOULIHAN (1923-) started out by doing cartoons for his hometown newspaper in Worcester, Massachusetts. This short career as a cartoonist was interrupted by World War II.

Houlihan was assigned as a combat soldier to an armored division in Europe. There, during his spare time, he helped to start a battalion newspaper. Gradually his duties were shifted to allow him time for special map-making projects and to make sketchbook drawings of terrain and inhabitants. He believes that this training was extremely valuable in his artistic development.

After the war, he returned to the *Worcester Telegram*, but found himself increasingly interested in becoming an illustrator. Through the G.I. Bill, he was able to go to the Art Students League in New York, where he attended classes under Reginald Marsh, John Groth and Jon Corbino.

Soon afterward, he began to obtain work from *Blue Book*, *Pic*, *Coronet*, and then from many other magazines and book publishers. His pictures are all distinctly linear in nature — even when in halftone — and lend themselves ideally to the historical subjects he enjoys. Some of his most distinguished work has been in black-and-white for *American Heritage*.

Hughes —

A native New Yorker, GEORGE HUGHES (1907-) studied at the Art Students League and at the National Academy of Design. Some of his early work included fashion drawing, and there was a stint as a special designer in the automobile field in Detroit.

For many years, Hughes was one of the most prolific painters of *Saturday Evening Post* covers; in addition, he painted many editorial illustrations for the *Post* and other publications, including *McCall's*, *Woman's Day*, *American Magazine*, *Reader's Digest*, and *Cosmopolitan* magazines.

Hughes was one of the originators and masters of the "sit-com" magazine cover, and through his efforts, readers would spend minutes rather than seconds looking at the covers.

Also a painter, he exhibited at the Pennsylvania Academy of the Fine Arts, The Detroit Museum, and the Art Institute of Chicago. In recent years he restricted his work to portraiture.

George Hughes, *Company Arrives Early*, cover illustration for *The Saturday Evening Post*, November 23, 1957, ©1957, 1985, The Curtis Publishing Company. The Sanford Lowe Memorial Collection, The New Britain Museum of American Art.

Good humor was the most characteristic trait of EARL OLIVER HURST (1895-1958), as an individual and in his illustration.

Hurst's illustrations look very facile and as though dashed off, in keeping with their spirit of fun. Actually, they are very soundly based on thorough preliminary preparation. In fact, for some years, it was his practice to render two variations of the same concept, to see how much more freedom and excitement he could add to the first rendition.

He was born in Buffalo, New York, and attended the Albright Art School in Buffalo, the Cleveland School of Art, and the John Huntington School of Art. He further studied under Pruett Carter at the Grand Central School of Art, and with Boardman Robinson at the Art Students League in New York.

Hurst exhibited often and his work received many awards. He wrote and illustrated several juvenile books, and was a contributing editor for *American Artist* magazine, having a regular monthly column, "The Hurst Page," with information and interviews pertaining to commercial art and illustration.

Earl Oliver Hurst, cover for *Collier's*, May 25, 1940. Collection of Joe Haidar.

Reproduced in *The Animal Art of Bob Kuhn,* North Light, 1973. Collection of the artist.

KUHN

ROBERT F. KUHN (1920-   ) is more interested in drawing and painting animals than any other subject and always has been. As a boy, he sketched animals continuously, later frequenting zoos to draw them from life whenever possible. In his youth, Kuhn's idol and mentor was Paul Bransom, who offered him a great deal of personal encouragement and criticism.

Kuhn was born in Buffalo, New York, and studied at Pratt Institute in Brooklyn. Among the guest lecturers who especially influenced him there were Harold Von Schmidt and Paul Brown.

To further his study of animals under their natural conditions, Kuhn has traveled extensively in the wilderness areas of Newfoundland, Western Canada, Alaska, other parts of the United States, and for several months in Africa.

His first illustrations appeared in *Field & Stream*, followed by publication in *True*, *Outdoor Life*, *Reader's Digest*, and other magazines. He has also illustrated numerous books and painted for calendars and advertisements. His book, *The Animal Art of Bob Kuhn*, was published by North Light in 1973.

Kuhn has also exhibited his wildlife paintings, winning several awards, including First and Second prizes at the National Academy of Western Art annual shows, and First prize, purchase award, at the Wildlife Art Show. His pictures are included in the collections of the National Cowboy Hall of Fame; the Wildlife World Museum in Monument, Colorado; the Genesee County Museum of Rochester, New York; and in many private collections.

ROBERT E. LOUGHEED (1910-1982) was born on a farm in Ontario, Canada, and from childhood on, his subjects were animals, all kinds of animals, but particularly horses.

His first art training came through a correspondence course in commercial design which he worked at assiduously during the long Canadian winters. With this start, he got a job in the art department of an engraving and printing firm in Toronto; later he worked for the *Toronto Star Weekly* doing news illustrations.

From there, Lougheed headed for New York, supported himself by doing cover paintings for the Pulp magazines and studied at the Art Students League under Frank Vincent DuMond.

Lougheed then divided his time between illustrating for publishers such as *True*, *The National Geographic*, *Reader's Digest*, and Brown & Bigelow, and painting for exhibitions and galleries. He regularly painted animals in their natural habitats, traveling north of the Arctic Circle, throughout Canada, Alaska and other parts of the United States to observe them.

Lougheed was a member of the Animal Artists Society, the Salmagundi Club, the Cowboy Artists, and the National Academy of Western Art, where his art won many awards.

Golden Harvest, advertising illustration for Early Times Distillery Co., 1951

Wellman Zeppelin — Rescue at Sea, **True** magazine; Collection of Robert and Susan K. Horvath.

The transition to the upscale publications was an easy one for Lovell and he became an expert with romantic love story situations. This example was published by **Good Housekeeping** in December, 1958.

Lovell got his start as a professional illustrator while still in art class at Syracuse University. Beginning with black and white dry-brush interior illustrations for the Pulps, he soon gravitated to the color covers, and eventually did hundreds of westerns, gangsters, detective and mystery subjects as preparation for his entry into the slicks in 1936.

Blackfeet Wall, showing a confrontation with members of the Lewis and Clark expedition. ©1986 Tom Lovell. Collection of David Lovell.

Tom Lovell

TOM LOVELL (1901-1997) was an intense, serious artist who drove himself to the point of perfection in his documentary approach to illustration; no detail of research was too small to be verified. His settings were painted with a conviction based on many years of experience in painting from nature.

Lovell was born in New York City and was graduated with a B.F.A. from Syracuse University, where he studied with Hibbard V.B. Kline. While still in college, he did his first illustrations for the Pulp magazines, and continued on in this field to develop his technical facility.

With this solid apprenticeship, Lovell was a fully developed artist when he first appeared in the major national magazines in the late 1930s, and eventually worked for nearly all of them.

During World War II, Lovell served as a staff sergeant in the U.S. Marine Corps Reserve. Many of his paintings of Corps history are now in the permanent collection of the Marine Corps. Other institutions holding his work are The National Geographic Society, The Explorers Club of New York City, and the Permian Basin Petroleum Museum in Midland, Texas.

He was a member of the American Watercolor Society, the Society of Illustrators; he won a Gold Medal in their 1964 annual exhibition, and was elected into the Society of Illustrators Hall of Fame in 1974.

In the late 1960s, Lovell moved to Santa Fe, New Mexico, and he became a regular exhibitor in the annual shows of Western artists held in Arizona, Texas and Oklahoma. He was twice the recipient of the Prix de West awarded by the National Academy of Western Art and the Gold Medal in Oil from the National Cowboy Hall of Fame. A member of the Cowboy Artists of America in 1975, he also won silver and gold medals in their exhibitions.

A biography of the artist entitled **The Art of Tom Lovell, an Invitation to History** was published by the Greenwich Workshop, Inc. in 1993.

Fred Ludekens, The Eagle Looks to the Sun, advertising illustration for All-Year Club of Southern California, Ltd., 1943.

Fred Ludekens (signature)

FRED LUDEKENS (1900-1982) was born in Huoneme, a third-generation Californian. He grew up in Victoria, British Columbia, and during those years made several trips to Alaska. His only art training was a night class under Otis Shepard at the University of California extension.

Ludekens worked for the Foster and Kleiser outdoor advertising agency in San Francisco, then freelanced for a time, and later became art director for the San Francisco office of Lord and Thomas. This gave him an insight into advertising art from the business point of view, which helped him to eventually become one of the most successful illustrators in the country.

A commission to illustrate a book about his boyhood country, **Ghost Town,** led **The Saturday Evening Post** to assign him a western serial story. The success of these pictures thus launched his second career as an editorial illustrator, and he pursued both, later adding another top position as co-creative director of Foote, Cone and Belding. With Albert Dorne, he founded the Famous Artists School in Westport, Connecticut, and was Chairman of the Board of Directors prior to his death.

John Alan Maxwell

JOHN ALAN MAXWELL (1904-1983) was always drawn toward portraying historical subjects, partly as a result of his childhood exposure to talk of the Civil War, Robert E. Lee, J.E.B. Stuart, and other Southern heroes, at the home of his grandfather. His own romanticized slant on the antebellum period made him an ideal interpreter of the historical novels that were his specialty.

Maxwell was born in Roanoke, Virginia, and studied at the Corcoran School of Art and the Art Students League in New York. Among his teachers were George Bridgman, Frank Vincent DuMond, George Luks, and Joseph Pennell. As a student, he also assisted painter Victor White on a group of mural decorations. Maxwell himself painted a mural for the Hamilton Bank in Johnson City, Tennessee.

Over the years, his illustrations appeared in **The Golden Book**, **The New Yorker**, **The Saturday Evening Post**, **The Country Gentleman**, **Life**, **Esquire**, **Collier's**, **American Magazine**, **The Ladies' Home Journal**, **Woman's Home Companion**, and other national magazines. With the popularity of the historical novel, Maxwell also painted many period illustrations for book jackets of authors such as Conrad Richter, Pearl Buck, J. B. Priestley, Louis Bromfield and Thomas B. Costain.

John Alan Maxwell, illustration for **Collier's** magazine, February 8, 1947.

Perry Peterson in his Studio, an advertising illustration for Art Instruction, Inc.

The illustrations of PERRY PETERSON (1908-1958) were done with special flair and apparent spontaneity. Peterson took pride in creating this effect and worked hard in the preparatory stages to achieve it. Years of training in art studios gave him a complete technical command of the watercolor medium, which he used with strong three-dimensional effect.

Peterson was born in Minneapolis, Minnesota, and his first art education was through the Federal Schools' correspondence course, followed by brief attendance in the evening at the Chicago Art Institute. His early art jobs included catalogue illustration for Montgomery Ward in Chicago, automobile renderings in Detroit, and advertising drawings for the Byron Musser Studio in New York City.

Soon after his first illustrations for *Liberty* magazine were published in 1942, he received assignments for stories in **Good Housekeeping**, **Woman's Home Companion**, **Collier's**, **The Country Gentleman**, **The Saturday Evening Post**, and others, until his untimely death from burns suffered in an accidental fire in his New York studio.

JOHN PIKE, N.A. (1911-1979) was a lifelong student of the watercolor medium despite diversions at such varied jobs as theatrical design, jewelry making, and director of advertising for a Jamaican rum company.

Born in Winthrop, Massachusetts, Pike studied in Provincetown with Charles Hawthorne and Richard Miller. He next spent five years in Jamaica before returning to this country, where his one-man shows and illustrations for magazines made a full-time art career possible. He illustrated not only for many magazines, but also for advertising accounts, and he exhibited extensively.

In addition, Pike served in the Combat Art section, Corps of Engineers, heading a unit to record the United States occupation of Korea; he also made paintings for the United States Air Force Historical Foundation in France, Germany, Greenland, South America, Formosa and Japan.

Pike's work is represented in many collections, public and private; he won numerous prizes, including the "Watercolor U.S.A." Award, and the National Academy Hallgarten Prize. He was a member of the American Watercolor Society, the Philadelphia Watercolor Club, the Salmagundi Club, the Woodstock Art Association, Grand Central Art Galleries, the Society of Illustrators, and the National Academy of Design.

John Pike, illustration for "The Loveliest Island" by Pat Frank, *Collier's*, April 20, 1946.

Illustration for "Rebound" published in **The Saturday Evening Post,** © 1946, 1974 by The Curtis Publishing Company.

Parker painted some fifty mother-daughter covers for **The Ladies' Home Journal** between 1939 and 1951, eventually adding a little brother as well. ©1949, 1977 by The Meredith Corporation. All rights reserved. Used with permission of **The Ladies' Home Journal.** Collection of Tom and Judy Johnson.

Illustration for "The Sound and the Fury" by Sidney Carroll; **Cosmopolitan** , 1948.

"A Partner in Productive Advertising — the Artist." Illustration for Howard Paper Mills, St. Regis Paper Company.

The work of ALFRED PARKER (1906-1985) was so varied and inventive that it is difficult in this space to choose pictures that represent him fully or summarize his career.

From the time of his arrival in New York from St. Louis in the mid-'thirties, Parker's illustrations excited and beguiled public and publishers alike. As his popularity grew, so did the number of his imitators, and the Al Parker approach became the dominant one in the magazines. What set his work apart from his imitators, however, was not only his impeccable taste, but the originality of his thinking. Other artists were always one step behind him.

Among his innovations were the extreme close-up, the "candid" unposed look of his models, the use of unusual props, and a picture idea strong enough to serve as a "stopper" for the casual magazine reader. Each of his pictures was unique in composition and color. He used all mediums, and combinations of them, from children's crayons to acrylics. His versatility was such that he once illustrated an entire issue of *Cosmopolitan* magazine by himself using a different name and style for each story.

In 1939, Parker painted a cover for *The Ladies' Home Journal* in which a mother and her daughter were dressed alike. Its immense success created a demand for the long series that followed, and set a whole new style for mother-daughter fashions.

A jazz buff, Parker had played saxophone in a band on a Mississippi river boat and he participated in many combination jam-session-and-sketching-trips to service hospitals during World War II.

Over the years, he won more than twenty-five gold medals and awards of excellence in Art Directors Club and Society of Illustrators' shows. He was a past president of the Westport Artists and was elected to the Society of Illustrators Hall of Fame in 1965.

Parker moved to Carmel, California by 1961, and with the demise of many of the magazines, his output of illustrations was curtailed. He continued to do occasional assignments for publications such as *Sports Illustrated* and *Boys' Life*. One such commission was an outstanding series of paintings of the Grand Prix auto race of Europe for *Sports Illustrated.*

287

Henry C. Pitz

HENRY CLARENCE PITZ, A.N.A. (1895-1976) was an outstanding performer in several fields, including illustrating for magazines and books, teaching and lecturing, writing on art subjects, painting and exhibiting.

His talents appeared early; while still in high school in Philadelphia, he won a scholarship to study at the Philadelphia Museum School of Art, and then went on to the Spring Garden Institute. Among his teachers were Walter Everett and Maurice Bower.

Although Pitz experimented with, and worked in, almost every medium, he had a special affinity for line drawing and book illustration. He illustrated more than 160 books, as well as for a whole range of magazines from *The Saturday Evening Post* to *St. Nicholas*.

Among his many popular art books were: *Pen*, *Brush and Ink*, *The Practice of Illustration*, *Drawing Trees*, *Ink Drawing Techniques*, and *Illustrating Children's Books*.

Pitz exhibited nationally and internationally, winning awards too numerous to list here. His work is represented in many public collections, including the Library of Congress in Washington, D.C., and the Philadelphia Museum of Art.

Pitz served as director of the illustration course at the Philadelphia Museum College of Art, and was a visiting lecturer and instructor to many schools in that area. He was also a contributing editor of *American Artist* magazine.

Henry Pitz, illustration for "The Madness of Anthony Wayne," *St. Nicholas*, December, 1930.

Prins

BEN KIMBERLY PRINS (1904-1980) was born in Leiden, Holland, but was brought to the United States at the age of one. Reared in Brooklyn, he was a graduate of Pratt Institute, and also studied at the Art Students League and at the Grand Central School of Art. His teachers included Arthur Guptill, Ernest Watson, George Bridgman, and Dean Cornwell.

He began his career as an art director at Batten, Barton, Durstine & Osborn Inc., then worked at the Dorland International Agency, and at Lennen & Mitchell. By 1939, he was freelancing, and his drawings for an *Illustrated History of the Railroad* won him a Gold Medal at the Art Directors Club show in 1940.

Prins soon thereafter began illustrating for magazines such as *Collier's*, *Woman's Home Companion*, *Pictorial Review*, and *The Saturday Evening Post*, for which he also painted a number of covers.

He was a member of the Society of Illustrators, The Art Directors Club of New York and the Wilton Historical Society.

Ben Prins, *Leaving Southfield*, cover for *The Saturday Evening Post*, June 9, 1956. © 1956, 1984 by The Curtis Publishing Company.

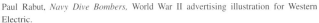

RAY PROHASKA (1901-1981) was born in Mulo, Yugoslavia, and came to America at the age of eight. He studied at the California School of Fine Arts in San Francisco, and followed this with several years of commercial work on the West Coast and in Chicago.

He came to New York in 1929, and obtained his first illustration manuscripts from *The Delineator* and *Woman's Home Companion*. Prohaska's modern style and careful characterizations soon won him a long list of other magazines as clients, and many advertising commissions as well.

Along with his illustration, he also painted for exhibition and won several prizes, including the Hallmark Award in 1949, the Audubon Medal in 1954, the John Marin Memorial Award in 1962, the M. Grumbacher First Prize in 1958, and the Society of Illustrators' Gold Medal in 1963.

Prohaska served as president of the Society of Illustrators in 1959-60. He taught at the Art Students League in 1961, followed by the post of Artist-in-Residence at Washington and Lee University in Lexington, Virginia. He also painted a large mural depicting the communications media for the Department of Journalism and Communications at the University.

His book, *A Basic Course in Design*, published by North Light Publications, remained in print for many years.

Ray Prohaska, illustration for *The Saturday Evening Post*, date of publication unknown.

Paul Rabut, *Navy Dive Bombers*, World War II advertising illustration for Western Electric.

PAUL RABUT

PAUL RABUT (1914-1983) characteristically immersed himself so thoroughly in research for his illustrations that he became an authority on the subject matter of his assignments. This led to his long-time interest in United States history, in logging, in Northwest Indian culture and artifacts, as well as other primitive art: Oceanic, pre-Columbian, and especially African wood-carvings and masks. He was a consultant for collectors and galleries on the subject of primitive art and had one of the finest private collections in the country.

Rabut attended the College of the City of New York, the art School of the National Academy of Design, the Grand Central Art School, and the Art Students League; his teachers included Jules Gotlieb, Harvey Dunn, Ivan Olinsky, and Lewis Daniel.

His first break came when one of his early story illustrations for *American Girl* magazine won the Art Directors Club Medal in their annual exhibition in 1942. This led directly to commissions from *The Saturday Evening Post* and other major magazines. Subsequently, he won several additional Art Directors Club awards for both editorial and advertising illustrations, and his work was selected for the State Department exhibition of advertising art, which traveled to Europe and South America in 1952. He exhibited widely and is represented in the permanent collection of the U. S. Medical Museum, Washington, D.C.

Frank Reilly, *Committee Examining the Recast Liberty Bell.*
Advertising illustration for Continental Distilling Corporation, 1948.

FRANK REILLY FRANK JOSEPH REILLY, A.N.A. (1906-1967) was a great teacher. In addition to the qualities which made him an outstanding illustrator, Reilly had a scientist's sense of order and analytical acumen combined with a missionary's enthusiasm for his subject. Reilly was Bridgman's successor at the Art Students League in New York and for over twenty-nine years, his classes were the largest there. He then founded his own school across the street, the Frank Reilly School of Art.

Frank received his own instruction at the League under George Bridgman and Frank Vincent DuMond. He later worked as Dean Cornwell's assistant on several mural projects, and it was

Cornwell who influenced him most, both as an artist and teacher.

Reilly illustrated for many editorial and advertising assignments. Outstanding were those for the Pennsylvania Railroad and the Continental Distilling Corporation. He also designed a 63-foot mosaic mural for the Bronx High School of Science.

He was an associate member of the National Academy of Design, a painter-member of the Art Commission of New York City, and a member of American Artists' Professional League, the Allied Artists, the Century Association, the National Society of Mural Painters, the Salmagundi Club, the Artists and Writers Guild, Art Students League, and the Society of Illustrators.

Walter Richards depicts John James Audubon painting bird specimens in his log cabin studio, ***Reader's Digest***, circa 1970.

Walter Richards

WALTER DuBOIS RICHARDS (1907-) worked in black-and-white for many years as an advertising artist; his illustrations are characterized by a mastery of values whether in monochrome or full color.

Richards was born in Penfield, Ohio, and was graduated from the Cleveland School of Art. He first worked in the famous Sundblom studio in Chicago, later for the Tranquillini studio in Cleveland, where he met and worked with Stevan Dohanos. Next, Richards moved to New York, where he joined the Charles E. Cooper studio and then freelanced as an illustrator for most of the magazines and many national advertisers.

Through the years, he continued to experiment and to paint for national and international shows in watercolor and print-making. He is a member of the American Watercolor Society, the National Academy of Design, the Society of Illusrators, the Connecticut Watercolor Society, Westport Artists, and the Fairfield Watercolor Group. His work has won many awards, including four consecutive first prizes in lithography at the Cleveland Museum of Art, 1935-38. His most recent one-man exhibit was held at the Connecticut Graphic Arts Center in 1999.

Nicholas Riley, illustration for "Adventure with Women" by Sophie Kerr; published by **Woman's Home Companion,** January, 1938.

Nicholas F. Riley

NICHOLAS F. RILEY (1900-1944) taught many hundreds of students of illustration in his years as a teacher at Pratt Institute. His thorough grasp of fundamentals and his gentle courtesy in presenting them won the respect of his classes and conveyed to many a lasting sense of idealism for the art of painting and illustration.

Riley was born in Brooklyn and was graduated from Pratt Institute himself. This was followed by two years of study with M. Scott in Paris. One of his portrait paintings was selected and hung in the Paris Grand Salon in 1925.

He began his teaching career at Pratt in 1927, soon after his return to America, and continued there until the time of his death. In the meantime, he also contributed many illustrations to **The Saturday Evening Post**, **Woman's Home Companion**, **Good Housekeeping**, **Redbook**, and other magazines.

He was a member of the Salmagundi Club, the Lotus Club and the Society of Illustrators.

Robert Riggs

ROBERT RIGGS, N.A. (1896-1970) was a painter and lithographer of monumental compositions, yet achieved his effects through meticulous means. In lithography, he worked from black to white, picking out detail with a scraper blade. For color, he used dry tempera mixed with mastic varnish and alcohol, a medium that dried immediately and allowed him to paint over successive layers if necessary.

Riggs was born in Decatur, Illinois, and studied for two years at James Milliken University in Illinois. He followed this with a year of study at the Art Students League in New York, terminated by two years in the Army during World War I. Following the Armistice, he stayed overseas for several months to study at the Académie Julian in Paris.

After his return to the United States, Riggs spent several years sketching for the N.W. Ayer & Son advertising agency, and produced many excellent advertising illustrations. Over the years, he was a consistent prize-winner in the annual Art Directors Club shows.

His simultaneous efforts in fine art contributed to his success in both fields. His favorite lithographic subjects were the circus and prize fighting; many of his prints are in museum collections, including the Brooklyn Museum, the Library of Congress and the Dallas Museum of Fine Arts.

Riggs collected a great many primitive artifacts during extended trips to Europe, North Africa, India, and Thailand, and part of his studio and living quarters housed a personal museum.

Robert Riggs, *The Hoop-la of the Steeplechase—Coney Island.*
Illustration for **Fortune** magazine, August, 1938.

291

Allen Saalburg

ALLEN RUSSELL SAALBERG (1899-unknown) was the younger brother of Leslie, and he had an equally distinguished illustration career. In addition, Allen had a strong career as a painter represented by the Kraushaar Gallery, exhibiting at the Whitney Museum of American Art, and painting murals for the New York World's Fair in 1939.

Allen studied at the Art Students League and gravitated to magazine cover and poster design, producing covers for *Fortune*, *The Saturday Evening Post*, *Good Housekeeping*, *House & Garden*, *Reader's Digest*, and *The Delineator*; he also produced posters for the Office of War Information and the U. S. Treasury during World War II. Saalberg had an impressive list of advertising clients which included Kohler and Kohler, DeBeers Consolidated Mines, Shell Oil Company, Penn Mutual Life Insurance Company, Pabst Brewing Company and Textron. *Fortune* magazine also commissioned him to make reportorial paintings of various industrial operations, which he usually rendered in dramatic opaque watercolors.

Allen Saalburg, cover painting for *Fortune* magazine, July, 1940.

Leslie Saalburg

LESLIE SAALBURG (1897-1974) was temperamentally of the old school. He admired the elegance of fine old interiors, correct attire, good manners and the fine craftsmanship of artisans unhurried by modern pressures of mass production.

Saalburg's work beautifully recreated this air of the genteel past in his renderings of spacious drawing rooms, restaurant interiors, and antique and classic automobiles.

In his approach to picture-making, Saalburg also preferred the classic method of sketching directly from the objects or settings, eschewing photography for facts unless absolutely necessary. His first sketches were, in effect, shorthand notes, adding details to indicate a section of paneling, a color of a fabric, or the design of a rug. These became the factual basis for a full-scale working drawing, in which the perspective was completely determined, and all details carefully constructed. This was then traced onto drawing paper for the final rendering. The scale of his illustrations was small, usually as near to the printed size as was practical, with the result that most of the richness of the original was retained in reproduction.

Saalburg had only three months of instruction at the Art Students League, but rebelled against it, preferring to learn to draw and paint by continuously practicing by himself. He also learned much through employment in various art studios until experienced enough to become a freelance illustrator. He was associated longest with *Esquire* magazine for which he painted several "portfolios" of special subjects, but he also worked for *Collier's*, *Vogue*, *Town and Country*, *Vanity Fair*, *Holiday*, and many publications abroad.

Leslie Saalburg, *The 21 Club, New York*, from "The World's Seven Greatest Bars." By permission of *Esquire* magazine.

In a Hurry, cover for **The Saturday Evening Post**, October 21, 1961. ©1961, 1989 by The Curtis Publishing Company. Collection of Diane and Jordan Berman.

DICK SARGENT

RICHARD SARGENT (1911-1978) did many cover paintings for **The Saturday Evening Post**. As in the example here, they are characterized by their good humor and insight into human frailties. He also illustrated for **Fortune**, **Woman's Day**, **American Magazine**, **Photoplay**, and **Collier's** magazines.

Sargent, who was born in Moline, Illinois, received his art education at the Corcoran School of Art and the Phillips Memorial Gallery in Washington, D.C. He also worked with Ben Shahn.

His pictures were exhibited in many parts of the United States, including New York City, Washington, D.C. and San Francisco, California, as well as abroad. He was a member of the Society of Illustrators in New York, and for many years, lived and painted in Spain.

schwinn

BARBARA E. SCHWINN (1907-), later Mrs. F. Bertram Jordan, wanted to be a fashion designer from the time she was twelve, when she first cut out and made her own dresses. To prepare for this, she studied at Parsons School of Design in New York and at its branch in Paris.

Her first work after graduation was making accessory and fashion drawings for department stores. In a short time, she was able to obtain top assignments from Lord & Taylor, Macy's, and Best & Co. This was followed by a period of drawing for continuity comic strips and later, cover designs and magazine illustrations for **Collier's**, **Cosmopolitan**, **American Magazine**, **The Saturday Evening Post**, and **The Ladies' Home Journal**. Many of her illustrations also appeared in European periodicals.

She later turned to portraiture, with an international clientele including Queen Sirikit of Thailand, Princess Grace of Monaco, Deborah Kerr, Conrad Hilton, and Maurice Pate, former Director of UNICEF. She also completed a painting of Princess Margaret of Britain, who had not previously posed for an American artist.

Illustration for "Come Back to Sorrento", **Collier's** magazine, January 12, 1952

Illustration for the story, "Tattletale Tape." It is interesting to note her reinvention of Coles Phillips's "Fadeaway" device here.

"River Singer," by Pete Martin, *The Saturday Evening Post*. © 1947, 1975 by The Curtis Publishing Company. Collection of Gary Blakeslee.

Cover, *The Saturday Evening Post*, October 3, 1953. ©1953, 1991 by The Curtis Publishing Company. The Charles Martignette Collection.

AMOS SEWELL

AMOS SEWELL (1901-1983) had a special empathy for children and also particularly enjoyed depicting homespun, rural subjects. These special gifts were ideally combined in the illustrations he made for a series of stories about Babe, Little Joe, Big Joe, and Uncle Pete by R. Ross Annett that ran for over twenty years in *The Saturday Evening Post.*

Sewell was born in San Francisco and studied nights at the California School of Fine Arts, working days in a bank. After some years of this, he decided to try his luck as an illustrator in the East. To get there, he shipped out as a working hand on a lumber boat going by way of the Panama Canal.

In New York, he studied at the Art Students League and at the Grand Central School of Art. Among his teachers were Guy Pène DuBois, Julian Levi and Harvey Dunn. At the same time, he began to draw black-and-white dry-brush illustrations for the Pulp magazines.

He illustrated his first major manuscript for *The Country Gentleman* in 1937; next came *The Saturday Evening Post,* for which he subsequently also painted many covers. This led to commissions from the other national magazines. Sewell also illustrated for many major advertisers, and his work won awards from the Art Directors Clubs of New York and Cleveland, were exhibited at the Society of Illustrators, and included in traveling exhibits both here and abroad.

"An Ornery Kind of Kid," by William Saroyan, story illustration for *The Saturday Evening Post.* © 1949, 1977 by the Curtis Publishing Company.

"Remember the Alamo" by Sigman Byrd illustrated by Sickles in a basic line technique with color washes added. Published by *The Saturday Evening Post.* ©1948, 1976 by The Curtis Publishing Company.

Noel Sickles

NOEL SICKLES (1911-1982) was a master in the use of line. His brush work was direct and spare, each stroke reduced to the most expressive minimum. Although he used color very effectively, it was usually subordinate to the drawing, often applied in thin washes over the basic black-and-white brush rendering.

Sickles's approach grew logically from his early career as a newspaper artist and cartoonist. He established a whole new style of cartooning in his adventure strip, "Scorchy Smith," by indicating full light and shade in his black-and-white drawings.

Seeking to develop further as an illustrator, Sickles abandoned the strip and began to accept advertising and editorial commissions. Among these was a notable series of World War II drawings for *Life* magazine. These resulted in his being placed under contract by both the War and Navy Departments in Washington to do similar illustrations for instruction in the Armed Services, where much of his work was classified.

After the war, Sickles resumed his freelance illustration career with special emphasis on his interest in American historical subjects. He made many outstanding illustrations for *The Saturday Evening Post*, *Life*, *This Week*, and the Reader's Digest Condensed Books.

Sickles was elected to the Society of Illustrators Hall of Fame in 1983.

Illustration for *Beloved,* a condensation of the book by Vina Delmar. Published by the Reader's Digest, 1956.

Inside Looking Out. Illustration for **Seventeen** magazine, 1953. Collection of The Butler Institute of American Art, Youngstown, Ohio.

Ben Shahn

BEN SHAHN (1898-1969) had a major impact on American painting and American illustration through his own work, and also by example through younger illustrators. Among his important protégés was David Stone Martin, who picked up on Shahn's "nervous" line while tracing off cartoons for murals as a Shahn assistant. Shahn was much more than a staccato line, however; it was his provocative content that made him a dominant name.

Born in Lithuania, he came to Brooklyn at the age of eight and was early apprenticed to a lithographer, finishing college and art school at night. His own struggle to work his way up led him to identify with the underdog and to support radical causes.

His early paintings of Sacco and Vanzetti, the Mooney series, posters for the CIO Political Action committee, and his powerful posters for the Farm Security Administration, all identified him as a political radical. Yet he could also be non-political, illustrating for publications as diverse as **Seventeen, Look,** and **Time**. In his later years, he became increasingly interested in Jewish themes, often combined with calligraphy. His paintings were exhibited widely, and he completed several murals following his early association with Diego Rivera on the controversial Rockefeller Center frescoes. Shahn's paintings are in the permanent collections of the Museum of Modern art, the Whitney Museum, the Wadsworth Atheneum and other museums.

Edward Shenton

EDWARD SHENTON (1895-1977) specialized in black-and-white illustration and managed to exploit a great variety of value and textures from the line medium. Although quite realistic, his drawings are also stylized and decorative as shown here.

Shenton was born in Pottstown, Pennsylvania, and studied at the Pennsylvania Museum School of Industrial Art and the Pennsylvania Academy of the Fine Arts, where his teachers included Thornton Oakley, George Harding, and Henry McCarter. He won the Lee Prize in 1922, and the Cresson Traveling Scholarships in 1923-24, which enabled him to study further in Paris.

Although Shenton's work appeared in many magazines, his line technique was ideally suited for books, and he illustrated for many publishers including Scribner's, Doubleday, Random House, Harcourt Brace, and W.W.Norton.

In addition, Shenton had an active career in editing and writing. One of his earliest jobs was as an editor for the Penn Publishing Company, and he also served as a part-time editor for Macrae Smith. His short stories appeared in **The Saturday Evening Post, Collier's, Scribner's** and **Cosmopolitan**, and he wrote and illustrated several books. His wife, Barbara Webster also wrote a number of books about Pennsylvania country life, which he illustrated charmingly.

His mural projects included a wall of the Chester County Court House in West Chester, Pennsylvania, and two large facing

Illustration for "The Bear" by William Faulkner, published by **The Saturday Evening Post** ©1942, 1970 by The Curtis Publishing Company.

panels in the Chapel of the War Memorial Cemetery at Saint-James in Brittany, France.

In addition to all of these assignments, Shenton also taught classes at the Moore College of Art in Philadelphia and at the Pennsylvania Academy of the Fine Arts.

Stahl could readily shift from the sacred to the profane in his subject matter, ranging from this sensitive Nativity painting to a luxurious brothel, below.

Stahl

As a boy, BENJAMIN ALBERT STAHL (1910-1987) was encouraged to become an artist by his grandmother who took him to visit the Chicago Art Institute and the Marshall Field Art Galleries. At seventeen, he got a job as an errand boy and apprentice in an art studio, and within five years had landed a job as an artist with one of the top studios in Chicago.

In 1937, **The Saturday Evening Post** editors saw one of his advertising paintings of a seascape and invited him to illustrate a sea story. This was the beginning of his career in illustration, in which he worked for nearly all of the magazines and for many national advertising campaigns.

Stahl's many other activities included a series of illustrations for the Bible, and a book he wrote and illustrated, **Blackbeard's Ghost,** published by Houghton, Mifflin, which was later made into a movie by the Disney Studios with Peter Ustinov as Blackbeard. Several years ago, Stahl built a Museum of the Cross in Sarasota, Florida. He designed the building and painted the mural-size Stations of the Cross around the museum walls. At the height of its fame, the entire collection of paintings was cut out of the frames and never recovered.

The artist also created an educational TV series on the art of painting called **Journey into Art with Ben Stahl**, consisting of twenty-six half-hours of painting demonstrations and lectures by the artist.

Stahl lived for protracted lengths of time abroad, including three years in southern Spain and several years in Mexico. This Mexican influence resulted in his renewed interest in the Old West and the resultant paintings were exhibited in the invitational Cowboy Hall of Fame shows and at the Settlers West Gallery.

Stahl taught at the Chicago Academy of Fine Arts and at the American Academy of Art in Chicago. He also was one of the founding faculty members of the Famous Artists Schools in Westport, Connecticut. In 1979, he was elected to the Society of Illustrators Hall of Fame.

Collection of David Stahl

297

Fight for the Cabin, **The Saturday Evening Post** ©1950, 1978, The Curtis Publishing Company, Illustration for "The Man from Texas" by Bill Gulick.

"Beneath the weight of their bodies, it snapped like a match," illustration for "Death Rides the Mesa," by Tom Gill, **American Magazine**, Sept. 1933.

Slayer in the Night, **The Saturday Evening Post** © 1943, 1971, The Curtis Publishing Company, Illustration for "Let the Young Men Smoke" by Richard Wormser.

298

Riding Down the Outposts, **The Saturday Evening Post** ©1950, 1978, The Curtis Publishing Company, Illustration for "The White Invader" by James Warner Bellah.

HAROLD VON SCHMIDT

HAROLD VON SCHMIDT (1893-1982) grew up in the West a generation after Remington and Russell, but had a close kinship with them and the Old West throughout his painting career. A native Californian, von Schmidt was orphaned at five and reared by his grandfather who had been a Forty-niner. His grandfather's stories, together with his own experiences as a construction worker, lumberjack, and cowhand gave him authoritative insight into the earlier era.

He studied at the San Francisco Art Institute and the California College of Arts and Crafts, also with Worth Ryder and Maynard Dixon. His first art job was as an art director for Foster & Kleiser, followed by illustrating for *Sunset* magazine.

In 1924, Von Schmidt came East to study further with Harvey Dunn. He always acknowledged the tremendous effect that Dunn's teaching had on his career. It was Dunn who taught him to paint the epic aspect of the text rather than the incidental, and he always kept to this high standard.

He was a member of the American Olympic Rugby Football team at Antwerp, Belgium, in 1920, and was an ardent athlete all his life; he also played baseball, hockey, and coached the local High School football team once he moved to Connecticut. Feeling that an artist should also be active in civic affairs, he served as a Selectman for the Town of Westport for eight years, and was on the Board of Finance, the Police Commission, and the Public Library Board.

During World War I, Von Schmidt designed posters for the U. S. Navy; during World War II, he was an invited artist-correspondent for the U. S. Air Force in the European Theatre of Operations, and artist-correspondent for King Features Syndicate in the Pacific Theatre of Operations.

Twelve of his paintings depicting the westward trek and the Gold Rush of 1849 were hung in the Governor's office in Sacramento, California; five Civil War paintings are in the permanent collection of the United States Military Academy at West Point, and many others are in important private collections.

Von Schmidt was a life trustee of the Artists Guild, New York; president of the Society of Illustrators from 1938-41; a member and officer of the American Indian Defense Association; president of the Westport Artists, 1950-51; and a founding member of the Famous Artists Schools in Westport, Connecticut. He was awarded the first Gold Medal by the trustees of the National Cowboy Hall of Fame in 1968, and was elected to the Society of Illustrators Hall of Fame in 1959. His biography was published by Northland Press in 1972.

299

Born Joaquin Alberto Vargas y Chavez, ALBERTO VARGAS (1896-1983) was a native of Arequipa, Peru, where his father was a professional photographer. After a few months of art training in Paris and his discovery of the nudes of Ingres and the sensual illustrations of the Austrian artist Raphael Kirchner, Vargas found his own direction. Simply put, it was to make drawings and paintings of "perfect" women, clothed or not. Rather than returning to Peru, he came to New York in 1916 where he found work in a variety of low-paying art jobs. Meanwhile, he made samples of his dream girls. These were shown to the theatrical producer Florenz Ziegfeld, and resulted in his twelve-year association with the "Ziegfeld Follies," drawing glamorized portraits of the show girls. This was followed in 1934 with similar contracts in Hollywood with Fox Studios and then Warner Brothers.

With the Depression still on and work becoming scarce, Vargas returned to New York and was signed up by *Esquire* magazine to replace the famous George Petty, then having a contract dispute with publisher David Smart. Vargas became an instant hit and Smart, determined to avoid another dispute with a prima-donna artist, induced the naïve Peruvian to sign a long-term contract that made him a virtual art slave, in which he even ceded the copyright of his name (Americanized by *Esquire* to "Varga"). A decade after the contract finally expired, Vargas found a haven with *Playboy*, and an amicable sixteen-year relationship which made Vargas famous with a new generation of readers. Over his lifetime, Vargas's pin-up pictures were reproduced in uncountable millions. During World War II, they were a favorite with GIs, and his pictures adorned innumerable footlockers, ships, and planes as well as playing cards and calendars.

An excellent biography of the artist by Reid Austin was published in 1978.

FREDRIC VARADY (1908-   ) was born in Budapest and attended the Royal Hungarian Academy of Art there. Upon graduation, he began to design movie posters, he worked on theatre set designs, and made fashion drawings.

He left Hungary in 1927 and worked at a succession of art jobs, from painting lampshades to murals in private houses in Istambul. He did fashion drawing and clothing design in Paris and in Berlin, before coming to the United States to establish himself as a freelance fashion artist.

Varady's dramatic flair for drawing and his meticulous rendering made a very favorable impression on magazine art editors, and he obtained his first manuscript to illustrate from *American Magazine* in 1939. This was soon followed by commissions from most of the major magazines, including *Cosmopolitan*, *Good Housekeeping*, *McCall's*, *Redbook*, *Today's Woman*, and *The Saturday Evening Post*.

Varady currently spends his time painting abstract art for exhibition and sale.

Here Varady presents a typical Bobby-Soxer of 1946. Cover for *Collier's* magazine.

Illustration for *The African Giant* by Stuart Cloete, published by Houghton Mifflin Co., 1955.

LYND WARD

LYND WARD, A.N.A. (1905-1985) first came to prominence as an artist for his novel told entirely in woodcut pictures, *God's Man*, published in 1929. He eventually produced five others, including *Mad Man's Drum*, *Song Without Words*, and *Vertigo*. (In 1974, these six novels were re-published in one volume by Harry Abrams, Inc., titled *Story Teller Without Words*.) These books established Ward as an original talent; magazine and book publishers kept him busy until his retirement in 1975.

Much of his work was done in woodcut prints, but to keep his outlook fresh, he experimented with lithography, pen or brush with ink, watercolors, oils, casein, and other media.

Ward had prepared for his career thoroughly, with four years at Columbia University studying theory of design, art history, and teaching methods. This was followed by a year as a special student at the State Academy for Graphic Arts in Leipzig, Germany, where his instructors were Hans Mueller, Alois Kolp and George Mathey.

He illustrated many of the classics for the Limited Editions and Heritage Book Clubs, and in collaboration with his wife and author May McNeer, produced some of his finest illustrations. A member of the Society of Illustrators and the Society of American Graphic Arts, he won many awards, including the Caldecott Medal, the John Taylor Arms Memorial Prize, the Library of Congress Award and the Limited Editions Club Silver Medal.

Welch

JACK WELCH (1905-1985) was a tall Texan from Cleburne. He went through public school in Temple, Texas, took the W. L. Evans correspondence course in cartooning, and did a short turn at Southern Methodist University illustrating yearbooks. This was enough to launch him as a newspaper artist; he worked for papers in Texas, California, Seattle, Chicago, Philadelphia, and New York.

The next logical step was as an advertising agency sketch man; he spent several years doing sketches and comprehensive drawings for advertising layouts. His sense of humor and feeling for freely rendered action made him a natural for drawing children, and he began to do the "finishes" for advertisers such as Keds, Jell-O, Pullman, and Traveler's Insurance.

These illustrations, in turn, brought his work to the attention of *The Saturday Evening Post* for which he created a number of memorable covers, then other magazines, including *Family Circle* and *Woman's Day*.

His work brought Welch several awards in annual shows at the New York Art Directors Club and for billboard advertising art.

Trying to Make Baby Smile. *The Saturday Evening Post* cover, February 19, 1949 © 1949, 1977 by The Curtis Publishing Company. Collection of Diane and Jordan Berman.

301

Collier's Cover, January 3, 1942.
Collection of William Gillis.

Advertising illustration for Community Silverplate, circa 1950.
Collection of Daley Art Gallery.

Illustration for "A Story to be Read in June," *Cosmopolitan*, June 1947.
Collection of Howard Chaykin.

JON WHITCOMB (1906-1988) made his name synonymous with pictures of young love, and glamorous, beautiful women. During World War II, a series of illustrations for advertisements he created on the theme "Back Home for Keeps" became a pin-up fad for women deprived of their husbands or sweethearts.

Jon was born in Weatherford, Oklahoma, and reared in Manitowoc, Wisconsin. He attended Ohio Wesleyan University and was graduated from Ohio State where he created pictures for the school publications and worked during the summer painting posters for a theatre in Cleveland.

This was excellent training ground, and although he had majored in English with an ambition to write, Jon switched to art classes. After graduation, he was able to obtain work in a series of studios designing travel and theatre posters, as well as general advertising illustrations.

In 1934, he moved on to New York to combine studio work with freelance illustration. His first illustrations were for *Collier's*, followed by *Good Housekeeping*, and then most of the the other national magazines in succession as Whitcomb's pretty girls began to attract enthusiastic readership.

His career was interrupted by World War II, when he was commissioned a Lieutenant, J.G. in the Navy. His assignments varied from mine-sweeping duty off the East Coast, to the Public Relations Department in Washington, to the Pacific as a combat artist with the invasions of Tinian, Saipan, and Peleliu. After hospitalization for tropical infections, he was discharged in 1943 and resumed his art career.

Whitcomb's writing ability became useful when he began to compose a monthly series of sketches and articles about motion picture stars for *Cosmopolitan*, called "On Location with Jon Whitcomb." He also wrote several short stories, two children's books about poodles: *Coco*, and *Pom Pom's Christmas*, and a book about feminine glamour, *All About Girls*.

French actress, Mylene Demongeau, portrayed for *Cosmopolitan* magazine.
The Charles Martignette Collection.

Artist and his Model, circa 1940; Collection of Diane and Jordan Berman.

Mortimer Wilson Jr.

From Lincoln, Nebraska, MORTIMER WILSON, Jr. (1906-1996) had a rich, sumptuous style of painting, based in part on his training as a portraitist. His father, conductor of the Atlanta Symphony and a composer, had wanted his son to follow a musical career, but both violin and piano were discarded when Mortimer showed a genuine interest in drawing and painting.

Wilson studied painting at the Art Students League in New York, continued studying on his own and painted a few portraits. He also became involved in summer theatre work as a director while teaching painting on the side.

The need to earn enough money to marry prodded him into trying story illustration. The combination of his drama experience with the painter's craft produced a fresh approach, and Wilson soon became a popular illustrator for **American Magazine**, **The Saturday Evening Post,** and **Woman's Home Companion,** as well as for advertisers such as Maxwell House Coffee and Woodbury Facial Soap.

In 1956, he moved to Arizona and exhibited his portraits, still lifes, and genre painting widely in the West.

1950–1960

James S. Avati

James Elliot Bama

Isa Barnett

James R. Bingham

Bruce Bomberger

Joseph Bowler

Ward Brackett

Austin Briggs

McCauley Conner

Bernard D'Andrea

Joseph De Mers

Gillette Elvgren

Stanley W. Galli

Denver Gillen

Louis S. Glanzman

Albert Gold

Robert Tompkins Handville

Albert Hirschfeld

Robert Jones

Morgan Kane

Harvey Kidder

Robert Lavin

James Lewicki

Michael Ludlow

David Stone Martin

Robert Theodore McCall

John R. McDermott

Franklin McMahon

Stanely Meltzoff

Al Muenchen

Paul Nonnast

George Edward Porter

Robert Riger

Kenneth Riley

Morton Roberts

Alexander Ross

John Scott

William Arthur Smith

Richard F. Stone

Tracy Sugarman

Robert A. Thom

Thornton Utz

M. Coburn Whitemore

Austin Briggs advertising illustration for *Time* magazine.

David Stone Martin, record album cover.

James Avati, *Tobacco Road* by Erskine Caldwell, published by Signet.

THE DECADE 1950-1960

By the beginning of this period, illustration was becoming big business. Manufacturers allocated big budgets to magazine advertising and ad agencies employed top illustrators to depict their products. More advertising meant more editorial funds for fiction and the illustrations to interpret it. In addition to the top freelancers, many art studios and art services were providing the supporting comprehensive sketches, layouts, and lettering. It was an expansive time. Cooper Studio alone had as many as seventy-five artists on staff who alternated editorial work with paintings for national advertisers.

Yet, this decade went from boom to calamity for illustrators.

The new television box was to become an integral fixture in every household. Through it, escapist fiction could be viewed without the effort of reading. Instead of an isolated cross-section of the action as presented by the illustrator in a magazine story, the televised fiction had action from beginning to end. This hot new medium began to usurp the role of many magazines including the biggest — *Collier's*, *The Saturday Evening Post*, and *Life* — as advertisers withdrew their budgeted money from periodicals to go to television.

The gradual but inexorable process was not recognized by most magazines until too late. Publishers blamed the illustrators for being too stodgy and losing the readers' interest. Many illustrators accepted this blame and tried to find more strident imagery or a more avant-garde approach. Whereas in the past, illustrators had complained about being pigeon-holed by subject and expected to keep within their established styles, now innovation was not only encouraged, but expected.

Many illustrators responded with enthusiasm. Al Parker deliberately made each illustration as different from another as possible, and worked in every medium from finger-paint and crayon to oil. He once illustrated a whole issue of *Cosmopolitan* magazine using a different pseudonym and painting style for each story. Austin Briggs pioneered the use of minimal outlines, simplified detail and candid-camera, stop-action poses. The new medium of acrylics permitted splashy washes of color that suggested forms rather than spelling them out. For their part, the magazines gave their art editors freer reign, with lavish use of color, full-page bleeds, and evocative fiction. Editors such as Otto Storch and Herbert Mayes at *McCall's* led the way. Illustrators were given double-spreads and encouraged to be as "arty" as possible. In their new guises, the magazines never looked better, and subscribers certainly got their money's worth.

Yet the readers and advertisers still deserted them, to the critical point that issues cost more to print than the income derived from them. Magazines with huge subscription lists hemorrhaged money with every issue and simply went bankrupt. Ironically, it was the smaller magazines with mostly newsstand sales that survived — by raising their prices just enough and counting on a core group of loyal readers to stay with them.

As their markets disappeared, illustrators had to look for new venues. Every form of printed material was sought out — annual reports, record covers, motion picture poster art, and books — especially paperback novels. This unlikely cover space, a mere 7 x 4$^1/_4$", was to become a savior for the careers of many illustrators as the paperback industry burgeoned into the next decade.

JAMES S. AVATI (1912-) is the best representative of a young group of illustrators who successfully faced the challenge of a declining illustration market in the traditional magazines in the late 'fifties by gravitating to the field of paperback cover art.

As a wartime outgrowth of the pulp magazines, the early paperback covers were especially lurid in concept. Although Avati did do some magazine illustration beginning in 1949 for *Collier's*, *American Magazine*, *McCall's*, *Atlantic Monthly*, and others, it was in the paperback field that he found his special niche and where he brought new distinction to that art.

Avati's approach was honest and unblinkingly realistic, in keeping with the gritty fiction that was becoming popular in books and movies, but he painted with an artistry that won readership for the books, and a score of imitators who tried to emulate the "Avati look." To keep his lead, Avati went through successive stylistic changes, and he long remained a major force in the field. This impact is the more remarkable for his having had no formal art training. He is a graduate of Princeton University, but self-taught in art. In the 'seventies, Avati started teaching in his own small school. He also has exhibited at the Society of Illustrators where his work has won several awards.

James Avati, cover illustration for *Sanctuary* by William Faulkner; published by Signet, 1954

Young Plains Indian 1979. Reproduced as book jacket illustration for *The Art of James Bama,* text by Elmer Kelton, published by The Greenwich Workshop, 1993.

JAMES ELLIOTT BAMA (1926-) currently lives and works in a Wyoming studio on his ranch, twenty miles from the nearest town. Having been born and lived in New York City for his first forty-two years, he prefers it that way.

Bama studied at the High School of Music and Art in New York and at the Art Students League under Frank Reilly. His early illustration work included many of the men's magazines, as well as *The Saturday Evening Post* and other major magazines, but his style matured through his many covers for paperback publishers. He also became affiliated with the New York Giants football team as their official artist, and worked for the Baseball Hall of Fame.

Through the Society of Illustrators, he traveled extensively on assignments for the U.S. Air Force; his art is respresented in the Air Force Academy collection.

The decision to move West and to paint western subjects grew out of a vacation trip to a friend's ranch. Once made, it resulted in a whole new painting career for Bama. His first showing was a complete success, and he has continued to build a clientele of collectors, which has given him freedom from publishers' deadlines and the opportunity to paint subjects of his choosing. Many of his western works are in museum collections such as the Whitney Museum of Western Art, The Calgary Foundation, the Klamath Falls (Oregon) Museum of Art, and the Cowboy Hall of Fame in Oklahoma. In 2000, he was inducted into the Society of Illustrators Hall of Fame.

B

ISA BARNETT (1924-   ) was born in Carbondale, Pennsylvania. He studied at the Philadelphia Museum School of Industrial Art and at the Barnes Foundation. Among his teachers were Henry Pitz, Robert Riggs, and later on with Robert Fawcett, who gave him special instruction.

His art career was postponed by World War II — he was a much-decorated United States paratrooper — but by 1946, he had sold his first illustration to *Argosy* magazine. This was soon followed by assignments from *The American Weekly*, *Life*, *True*, *The Saturday Evening Post*, *Cosmopolitan*, *Outdoor Life*, *American Heritage*, *This Week*, and many others.

Barnett has exhibited at the Art Alliance in Philadelphia, won Gold Medals at both Cleveland and Philadelphia Art Directors Club Shows.

He has also taught at the Philadelphia Museum School, the Moore Institute, and at the Philadelphia College of Art.

Lee's Surrender of the Army of Northern Virginia, **This Week** magazine, July 4, 1965. Here Barnett relied on an eyewitness sketch by Alfred Waud.

Bingham

JAMES R. BINGHAM (1917-1971) was born in Pittsburgh, Pennsylvania and studied at the Carnegie Institute of Technology. During World War II, he put in a stint animating Army Air Force films and received an appointment as a Naval officer attached to the Office of Research and Invention.

Following the war, the heroics and adventure in his life was confined to the usual subject matter of his illustrations, such as a long series of pictures for Erle Stanley Gardner's "Perry Mason" serials and other mystery stories in *The Saturday Evening Post*. He also illustrated the "Tugboat Annie" series for the same publication.

In addition to editorial work, Bingham did a great deal of advertising illustration for clients such as Philadelphia Whiskey, the Gulf Oil Corporation, Maxwell House Coffee, the Air Transport Association, the Caterpillar Tractor Company, and won numerous awards, including Art Directors Club Medals in New York, Philadelphia, Chicago, and Miami.

James Bingham illustrated this Perry Mason story for *The Saturday Evening Post*. © 1958, 1986 by The Curtis Publishing Company.

Bruce Bomberger

BRUCE BOMBERGER (1918-1980) was a native Californian who, except for a year in New York, made his career there as one of the "West Coast Artists." He had a varied background of experience, going from an art service, to the Lord & Thomas ad agency, to freelance, to a partnership in an art service, and finally back to freelance again.

A past president of the San Francisco Society of Illustrators, Bomberger did a wide variety of advertising illustration in addition to editorial drawings and paintings for *True*, *The Saturday Evening Post*, *Cosmopolitan*, *Good Housekeeping*, *This Week*, and other publications.

Outstanding among his pictures were the wildlife paintings he did for the Weyerhaeuser Timber Company advertising series.

Bruce Bomberger, illustration for **The Saturday Evening Post**, date of publication unknown.

Ward Brackett, *House at Sag Harbor*, cover **North Light Magazine**, July 1979.

Ward Brackett

WARD BRACKETT (1914-) is a sound painter who developed his abilities through many years as a studio artist. He was born in Milwaukee, Wisconsin, and studied at the Layton School of Art there. At the age of twenty, he was fortunate to be taken on at the Stevens, Sundblom and Stultz Studio in Chicago. From there, he went to the Grauman Studios in 1938 and to the Charles E. Cooper Studio in New York in 1940.

During World War II, Brackett was attached to the Quartermaster School where his duties involved producing a large volume of visual aids and training posters.

Following the war, he freelanced for the Crowell-Collier magazines, **Good Housekeeping**, **Parents**, **Redbook**, **Reader's Digest**, **Cosmopolitan**, and others.

In 1953, he traveled with a USO troupe to Japan and Korea, doing portrait sketches of Army and Marine personnel in hospitals and rest centers, and artillery emplacements. In 1964, he toured the U. S. Air Force bases in Spain with other illustrators to make reportorial drawings and paintings. Some of this work is represented in the Air Force Academy art collection.

Brackett returned to school in mid-career to study painting with Reuben Tam at the Brooklyn Museum. His time now is devoted almost entirely to painting, especially landscapes, with some figure work and portraiture. He currently exhibits in Naples and Sarasota, Florida (where he has a winter studio), and in Wilton and Southport, Connecticut, and is a member of the Silvermine Guild in Connecticut. His comprehensive instruction book, **When You Paint**, published by North Light, contains much of his personal philosophy and demonstrates his painting techniques. Brackett has also designed eight U. S. Postage stamps.

Illustration for "The Charms of Monique" by Francis Price, *The Saturday Evening Post*, March 28, 1959. ©1959, 1987 by The Curtis Publishing Company.

JOSEPH BOWLER (1928-   ) knew early in his career that he wanted to be an illustrator and accomplished it by making his first sale to *Cosmopolitan* magazine at the age of nineteen. He became one of the top performers, and for many years his romantic illustrations appeared regularly in *McCall's, Good Housekeeping, Redbook, The Ladies' Home Journal,* and other publications.

Born in Forest Hills, New York, Bowler studied at the Art Students League under Frank Reilly, Robert Hale and Howard Trafton. In 1948, he joined the staff of the Charles E. Cooper Studio, noted for developing talented young artists, and from there launched his illustration career.

Among his other activities, he has made recruiting posters for the Air Force and is represented in the permanent collection of the Air Force Academy in Colorado Springs. He has also appeared as a guest lecturer at Parsons School of Design in New York. In 1958, Bowler was almost completely paralyzed by polio, but through determination and long and intensive physiotherapy was eventually able to resume his career.

In recent years, Bowler has devoted himself almost exclusively to portraiture, working in his studio on Hilton Head Island, South Carolina; his sitters have included members of the Eisenhower and Kennedy families and other notables.

His work has won many awards in various annual exhibitions of the New York Art Directors Club and Society of Illustrators, and he was named Artist of the Year by the Artists Guild of New York. He was also elected into the Hall of Fame of the Society of Illustrators in 1992.

Grant and His Generals, one of the outstanding series of advertising illustrations for **TV Guide**, 1960. Reprinted courtesy of Triangle Publications, Inc.

AUSTIN BRIGGS (1909-1973) did some of his early illustrations for **Blue Book** magazine on the textured surface of white window shade cloth. It was his idea for obtaining a halftone effect for a magazine restricted to line reproductions.

Such resourcefulness and experimental enterprise characterized Briggs's entire career. Once he mastered a particular medium or method of working, he was never long satisfied. In the process, he left his many imitators behind and for over thirty years, kept his work fresh and contemporary.

Briggs was born in a private railway car on a siding near Humboldt, Minnesota. His father was an electrical engineer employed in installing telegraphic equipment, and his family traveled along. Austin grew up in Detroit, Michigan, and was awarded a scholarship to the Wicker Art School. After a brief stay there, followed by a semester at the City College of Detroit, he had an opportunity to become an assistant to an automobile illustrator, drawing the figures to set off the automobile.

Ambitious to do story illustration, he made some drawings for the **Dearborn Independent.** With these as samples, he tackled New York where he obtained work from **Collier's**, **McClure's**, and **Pictorial Review**. He also continued to study and enrolled in classes at the Art Students League under George Bridgman and Walter Jack Duncan.

This auspicious beginning was blighted by the Depression as the magazines retrenched. Briggs, who had not yet developed his own individual style, was expendable. For the next several years, he executed a variety of artwork, from movie posters to "ghosting" Alex Raymond's comic strip "Flash Gordon." He also began to do Pulp illustration for Don Kennicott of **Blue Book** magazine. **Blue Book** became a new training ground; the care that Briggs lavished on these assignments began to bring out in him a more individual point of view. He attracted the attention of **Redbook**, then **Cosmopolitan**, **The Saturday Evening Post**, and others. From that period on, Briggs became a dominant force in illustration. In 1969, he was elected to the Hall of Fame of the Society of Illustrators.

Illustration for "Sign that Boy!" by Garson Kanin, *McCall's* magazine, January 1962. Reprinted with permission.

Here Briggs boldly forces the reader to look at a murder victim in this illustration for *The Saturday Evening Post.* Collection of Brian Postman

Briggs' *Blue Book* training gave him an excellent grounding for mystery stories. Here he illustrates "Island Pursuit" for a *Saturday Evening Post* serial by William L. Worden; March 14, 1953. ©1953, 1981 by The Curtis Publishing Company.

311

Conner

McCAULEY ("MAC") CONNER (1913-) sold his first covers to **The Saturday Evening Post** while still an art student. He studied at the Philadelphia Museum School with Henry Pitz and at the Grand Central School of Art in New York under Harvey Dunn.

Service in the Navy interrupted his career for several years, after which he joined with William Neeley to form an art agency, Neeley Associates.

Conner has also had an active freelance career as an illustrator for the **Post**, **McCall's**, **Cosmopolitan**, **Redbook**, **Woman's Day**, **Argosy**, **Woman's Home Companion**, **The Ladies' Home Journal**, and other magazines. Currently he is doing paperback covers for Harlequin, Warner Books, Fawcett, Ballantine, and others. Recently, he has also turned to portraiture.

Conner is a member of the Society of Illustrators, and has exhibited at the Palm Beach Galleries and at the Country Art Gallery in Westbury, Long Island. His work won the Philadelphia Art Directors Award in 1959.

In this fifties illustration for **Collier's**, Mac Conner records the early days of television when the few owners of sets had to endure the invasion of curious neighbors and friends who would drop in for a look.

Illustrator, painter, and teacher, BERNARD D'ANDREA (1923-) has had an active career, always searching for new artistic horizons.

Born in Buffalo, New York, D'Andrea's illustration career started in 1950 in New York City, represented by the eminent Charles E. Cooper Studio, after four years as a U. S. Army artist. Launched on a long and successful career that has spanned the decades since, he appeared in a variety of national and international publications. Over the years, he has been the recipient of many awards and distinctive honors for his work.

Some recent assignments have been a series of paintings illustrating a major atlas and "People and Places of the Past," for the National Geographic Society of Washington, D.C.

In May, 1983, D'Andrea had a sold-out exhibition of landscape paintings at the Red Piano Gallery of Hilton Head Island in South Carolina. He has also had a major exhibition of landscape paintings at the Contemporary Gallery of the Hunter Museum of Chattanooga, Tennessee.

D'Andrea was married to the late Lorraine Fox, the Hall of Fame artist who died in 1976. He is now remarried to Jean Reist Stark, a prominent goldsmith, teacher and painter. In 1994, D'Andrea did a last illustration for **Good Housekeeping** magazine, and with his wife relocated from New Jersey to Hilton Head Island, South Carolina, where he is now fully involved in painting.

Bernard D'Andrea illustration for **Cosmopolitan**, also reproduced in **Illustrators '59**.

Joe De Mers

JOE DE MERS (1910-1984) specialized in that most transitory and ephemeral area of illustration, depicting modern American women. He depicted them, not as stereotypes, but as a diverse array of dazzling females — sweet, predatory or sophisticated. To dress them, he enlisted the fashion expertise of his wife, Janice, for styles that would not become dated in the six months between painting and publication.

De Mers was born in San Diego, California, and attended the Chouinard Art School in Los Angeles. Among his teachers were Pruett Carter, Lawrence Murphy, and later, Reuben Tam at the Brooklyn Museum Art School. De Mers spent about ten years as a production illustrator and designer for motion pictures, mostly for Warner Brothers Studios.

His first illustration assignment was for *Fortune* magazine in 1937, followed by assignments from *Esquire,* and then from most of the other major magazines in the United States and Europe. He was one of several illustrators who found a steady market for second rights to pictures for publishers in England and in Europe.

De Mers exhibited at the Museum of Modern Art, the Corcoran Museum of Art, the Los Angeles County Museum, various Art Directors Club shows, and at the Society of Illustrators in New York. He taught at the Chouinard Art School from 1934-37, and later at Parsons School of Design in New York. He was a resident of Hilton Head Island in South Carolina for several years and the proprietor of an art gallery there. In 1997, De Mers was elected into the Society of Illustrators Hall of Fame.

Illustration for "The Durable Fire", by Howard Swiggett. ca. 1957. © November 1957,1985 Meredith Corporation. All rights reserved. Used with the permission of *The Ladies' Home Journal.* Collection of Mitch and Mary Itkowitz.

Elvgren

GILLETTE ELVGREN (1914-1980) was an artist who helped to give pin-up art a good name — even respectability. His subjects were never overtly sexual but he presented momentary, accidental glimpses of flesh based on a humorous gag. This approach combined with his unmatched ability to paint beautiful young women gave his pin-up calendar a huge audience.

Elvgren was born in St. Paul, Minnesota; he studied at the Minneapolis Art Institute and the American Academy of Arts in Chicago. Although he graduated in the midst of the Depression, he landed a job with the Stevens, Gross Advertising Art agency in Chicago. He soon became a protégé of the great Haddon Sundblom and emulated his painting style, though his brushstrokes had more finesse. His obvious talents were employed by the Louis F. Dow calendar company in 1937 to do a series of pin-up paintings. These were so successful that they became the focus of his career. Brown & Bigelow lured him away with an offer of $1,000 per pin-up for twenty subjects per year, a very substantial income in 1944. This came in addition to his freelance advertising paintings for Coca-Cola, Schlitz Beer, and other clients. The relationship with Brown & Bigelow lasted nearly thirty years. In between the pin-ups, Elvgren also did "straight" story illustrations for *Cosmopolitan*, *Woman's Home Companion*, *McCall's*, and other magazines.

Some Help, ca. 1955. Reprinted by permission of and copyrighted by Brown & Bigelow, St. Paul, Minnesota. Collection of Pierre Boogaerts.

313

Otter Family on Weyerhauser Tree Farm, 1960. Courtesy of the Weyerhauser Company.

STANLEY W. GALLI (1912-) was born in San Francisco and spent seven of his formative years between high school and art school doing many odd jobs. The Depression was on, and he worked successively as a roustabout and ranch hand near Reno, Nevada, an apprentice in a Reno bakery, a longshoreman in San Francisco, and as a member of the Teamsters' Union, went through all the violence of a coastal strike.

Galli finally saved enough to enroll at the California School of Fine Arts in San Francisco (now the San Francisco Institute of Art). Hired out of school by a San Francisco art service, he became a partner in the firm just before World War II. He was then called into special service by the Navy Department to work at structuring educational programs and materials. After the war, he returned to his art service partnership but found the business aspects too demanding and decided to return to drawing and painting as a freelance illustrator.

He eventually received assignments from most major publications, including *The Saturday Evening Post*, *True* magazine, *McCall's*, *Today's Woman*, and the *Reader's Digest*.

Galli also played a key role in developing an advertising campaign for the Weyerhauser Company based on themes of conservation, making over fifty paintings himself and enlisting other artists to illustrate the wildlife scenes. On the same theme, Galli designed twenty-six stamps for the U. S. Postal Service, mostly commemoratives for wildlife conservation; several have won important prizes.

In 1981, Galli was elected to the Hall of Fame of the Society of Illustrators. His time is now divided between his studios in California and in Tuscany, Italy, where he spends several months each year. Recent painting projects have included the series "Ancient Italy Re-interpreted" and "Early Spanish Colonial California."

Denver Gillen, "Wizard's Wife" by Owen Cameron, *Collier's* magazine, June 22, 1946.

DENVER LAREDO GILLEN (1914-unknown) was born in Vancouver, British Columbia, Canada, the son of a sea captain.

Gillen had no intention of becoming an artist, until at seventeen, a protracted illness kept him in a hospital bed for several months. As therapy, the doctor, who was an amateur artist, interested his patient in drawing. When Denver was well again, he obtained a beginner's job in the art department of the Hudson's Bay Company. He also studied with Frederick Varley during this time and began to go on outdoor painting expeditions.

Later, he progressed from studios in Toronto and Chicago (including a stint for Montgomery Ward's art department making catalog drawings) to a variety of freelance assignments on every possible subject. In the process, he was evolving his own personal strongly linear style, and began to obtain manuscripts to illustrate from *Collier's*, *Esquire*, *True*, *Outdoor Life*, and many other magazines, including a long association with the *Reader's Digest*.

In addition to magazine and advertising assignments, Gillen continued to do independent paintings, exhibiting at the Toronto Museum, the Chicago Art Institute, the Society of Illustrators in New York, and the Oehlschlaeger Gallery in Chicago. He also completed a series of mural paintings for the Missouri Pacific Railroad.

Louis Glanzman, "The Strange Girl" by J. B. Priestley, *Collier's*, May 9, 1953.

LOUIS S. GLANZMAN (1922-) had no formal art training, but from childhood on, a strong urge to draw impelled him to train himself.

The Army gave Glanzman his first acquaintance with art on a professional level when he was attached to the *Air Force* magazine art department in New York. There he was able to fill in many of the gaps in his art background, and by the time of his discharge was ready for a career as a freelance illustrator.

True magazine bought his first pictures in 1948. Later, he sketched court trials for *Life* magazine and illustrated for *Collier's*, *The Saturday Evening Post*, *Cosmopolitan*, *Redbook*, ,and *Woman's Day*. During this same period, he illustrated many children's books along with advertising work. *Life* magazine assigned him subjects for their Civil War and Presidential series. For *Time* magazine, he painted over forty portraits of prominent people, as well as Neil Armstrong's landing on the moon. He has done many paintings for the National Parks Department, and *National Geographic* commissioned him for articles in their magazine and in several of their books.

He has won awards from the Society of Illustrators, the New York Art Directors Club, and the Salmagundi Club. His paintings are in many collections, including the Smithsonian Institution, the U.S. Air Force Historical Art Collection; the Museum of the City of New York, and the Civil War Museum at Fredricksburg, Virginia. His 1987 painting, "The Signing of the Constitution," was hung in Independence Hall in Philadelphia.

Albert Gold, *Hex Sign Painter,* illustration for **Sunday Bulletin** magazine, Philadelphia. ©1962, Bulletin Company.

Cf Handville

Born in Paterson, New Jersey, ROBERT TOMPKINS HANDVILLE, A.N.A. (1924-1993) studied at Pratt Institute and the Brooklyn Museum Art School under Reuben Tam. He was a member of the Society of Illustrators, the American Watercolor Society, and was elected to the National Academy as an associate in 1981.

Handville exhibited widely and won many awards, among them the Ranger Fund Purchase Prize, the 21st and 27th Annual New England exhibition awards for painting, the National Academy of Design's Speyer Prize in 1982, the American Watercolor Society's Mary Pleissner Memorial award in 1981, and the Mario Cooper Award in 1983.

The artist was the designer of the Yellowstone National Park Commemorative Postal stamp and The Alfred Verville Commemorative Air Mail Stamp.

Handville was a contributing artist-reporter for **Sports Illustrated**, and chairman of the Society of Illustrators' "Artists in the Parks" program for the National Park Service, Department of the Interior.

Collections and exhibitions include the Metropolitan Museum of Art's "200 Years of American Watercolor Paintings;" the National Portrait Gallery show "Champions, Heroes of American Sport," in 1981-82; the United Nations; The Butler Institute; the U.S. Air Force Historical Art Collection; Syracuse, Denver, and Oklahoma Universities' collections; as well as the Royal Society of Watercolour Painters, London, England, by invitation.

Robert Handville, Mohammed Ali vs. Joe Frasier, "The Slugger and the Boxer," Collection of the Society of Illustrators, Museum of American Illustration. Cover for **Sports Illustrated** magazine. Robert Handville for Sports Illustrated; ©1971, 1999, Time, Inc.

albert gold

In an age of specialization, ALBERT GOLD (1916-) is a rarity: the complete artist. He is a realist but does not try to see photographically; a painter-reporter for the printed page as well as for exhibition walls; a social commentator in his choice of subject; and a gifted teacher.

Gold was born in Philadelphia and attended the Philadelphia Museum College of Art, studying under Earl Horter and Henry Pitz. During World War II, he contributed to **Yank** magazine and spent three years as an artist-correspondent in Europe. The rigorous training of that on-the-spot selection and drawing has shaped his work since.

Much of his postwar commissioned work for publications such as **Ford Times**, **Argosy**, **What's New** (Abbott Laboratories), **Lincoln-Mercury Times**, **Holiday**, **The Lamp**, **Bulletin** magazine, and others, has been of a reportorial nature.

Gold has exhibited regularly in major shows, has won two Tiffany Foundation grants, also the Prix de Rome (1942), the Sesnan Gold Medal from the Pennsylvania Academy of the Fine Arts, and numerous other awards. His work is represented in many collections, including the Philadelphia Museum of Art, the Smithsonian, the Library of Congress in Washington, D.C., the New York Public Library, and the New Britain Museum of American Art.

During his career, he also found time to teach at the Philadelphia Museum College of Art and to serve as Associate Director of the Graphics Department.

ALBERT HIRSCHFELD (1903-) sits at his drawing board enthroned on an old-fashioned barber's chair and, at the age of 97, turns out caricatures of the notables of stage and screen for *The New York Times* theatre reviews. For those portrayed, it is a badge of honor and an envied status symbol. Hirschfeld can take outrageous liberties, but he never skewers his subjects; he is kind but unerringly perceptive in exaggerating his subject's features.

He was born in St. Louis, Missouri, and had a wide-ranging art education from the Art Students League and the School of the National Academy of New York, to the Académie Julian in Paris.

Undecided whether to be a painter or a cartoonist, he pursued both, but eventually the lure of the theatre won out, and he has covered virtually every aspect of it, from painter of motion picture posters in Hollywood, as a theatre correspondent for *The New York Herald Tribune*, doing covers for *TV Guide*, and making line drawings for almost every major magazine in addition to his regular stint for *The New York Times*. His preferred medium, best suited to newspaper reproduction, is pen and ink, but he also works in opaque watercolor when color is required. His incorporation of his daughter Nina's name in each picture is an open secret, well known to all his fans who search it out in each new caricature.

The artist is the subject of several books including *Hirschfeld's World* and *Show Business is No Business*, a film, *The Line King*, and innumerable magazine and newspaper articles. Among his many honors, he was a recipient of the Brooks Atkinson Award and elected into the New York Society of Illustrators Hall of Fame in 1986.

Al Hirschfeld, caricature of Carole Burnett, *TV Guide* cover, April 11, 1970. Collection of the Sigety Family.

ROBERT JONES (1926-) became an illustrator by way of cartooning. Born in Los Angeles, he was drawing animation for Warner Brothers while he was still in high school.

After high school, Jones became a gunner and aviation radio operator in the Navy. He next attended the University of Southern California for two years, followed by another two-and-a-half years at the Art Center School in Los Angeles.

He was still interested in humorous illustration when he joined the Charles E. Cooper Studio in New York, and his early fiction assignments in *The Saturday Evening Post* were on whimsical subjects. He has gradually expanded his range, and now illustrates a wide variety of subject matter for many national publications, including art for paperback book covers.

Robert Jones, illustration for "Island of Women" by Louis Paul, *The Saturday Evening Post*, October 21, 1961. © 1961, 1989, by The Curtis Publishing Company

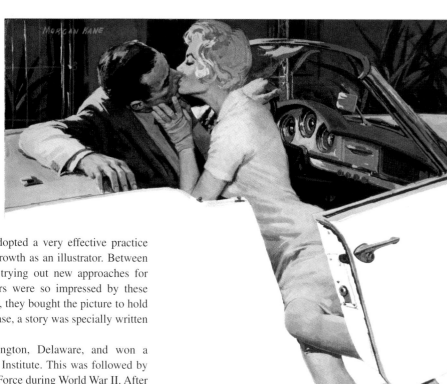

MORGAN KANE

MORGAN KANE (1916-) adopted a very effective practice which contributed much to his growth as an illustrator. Between assignments, he spent his time trying out new approaches for hypothetical stories. Art directors were so impressed by these samples that, in several instances, they bought the picture to hold for an appropriate story. In one case, a story was specially written to fit the picture.

Kane was born in Wilmington, Delaware, and won a scholarship to the Cleveland Art Institute. This was followed by three-and-a-half years in the Air Force during World War II. After the war, he got a job doing advertising illustrations in Chicago and obtained his first story manuscript for *Extension* magazine. In time, he illustrated for nearly all of the major periodicals.

Morgan is also an expert photographer and in the early 'sixties left illustration for full-time photography, though he resumed painting in the mid-seventies, having clients for advertising, paperback covers, and movie posters for Paramount Pictures, United Artists, Universal Studios and Warner Brothers.

Kane also paints and exhibits in several galleries in the West.

Morgan Kane, "Anything for Love" by William Fay, published by *The Saturday Evening Post*, ©1959, 1987 by The Curtis Publishing Company.

Harvey Kidder

Over a long career, HARVEY W. KIDDER (1918 -) developed the versatility to take on virtually any subject — from a blast furnace to an African safari — and to make it convincing. The diversity of his clients, which included *The Saturday Evening Post*, *True*, *Ford Times*, *Reader's Digest*, *Golf Digest*, *Argosy*, and *Lithopinion*, also gave him the impetus to produce such a variety of subjects.

Kidder was from Cambridge, Massachusetts, and studied art at the Child-Walker School of Design. His first commissions were for book illustrations from Houghton-Mifflin and Ginn and Company in Boston, which led to his subsequent career. Among other projects in which he has participated have been the National Park Service Art Program and the U.S. Air Force Art Program through his membership in the New York Society of Illustrators.

He has also produced over forty editions of lithographs for John Szoke Graphics and his work is exhibited in many galleries.

Harvey Kidder, "Fury at Furnace 4," *The Saturday Evening Post*, August 8, 1954; ©1954, 1982 by The Curtis Publishing Company.

Lavin

ROBERT LAVIN (1919-1997) ably combined drama and fact in his paintings of industrial and mechanical subjects. This made him a successful illustrator for such accounts as General Electric, National Steel and United Engineers, as well as fictional subjects involving construction, planes and ships for *The Saturday Evening Post*, *Reader's Digest*, *The American Weekly*, *Argosy*, *Newsweek*, and others.

Lavin was born in New York City and obtained his B.A. at the College of the City of New York. He also studied at the National Academy of Design art school under Ivan Olinsky.

As an active painter and exhibitor, he won second prize in the Long Island Annual art Show in 1962, and was a member of both the Society of Illustrators and the American Watercolor Society. He also taught at the College of the City of New York from 1957 to 1966.

In his later work, he specialized in industrial painting for corporate offices, publications, annual reports, and public relations.

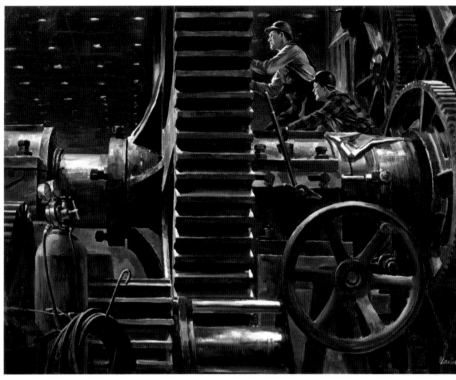

Robert Lavin, *"King-Size Machine for Heavy Industry"*, advertising illustration for United Engineers; published in *Fortune* magazine, 1964.

James Lewicki, cover design for the *American Druggist* magazine, August, 1951.

LEWICKI

JAMES LEWICKI (1917-1980) was a scholar as well as an artist; many of his painting projects came from ideas suggested by research. He was probably best known for his several major series for *Life* magazine, including "The Folklore of America," a five-part series consisting of sixty-six paintings, (later expanded into a book, *The Life Treasury of American Folklore*), the "Pageant of Life," on evolution, "The Origin of Christmas," "Christmas Legends," and others. His paintings are all distinguished by their originality of concept, their knowledge of the subject, and their brilliant color.

Lewicki was born in Buffalo, New York, and majored in art at the Buffalo Technical High School. He attended the Albright Art School there, won a scholarship to the Detroit Society of Arts and Crafts School, was graduated from Pratt Institute in 1939, and also studied at New York University.

His first assignment while still at Pratt was a book, *New York from Village to Metropolis*, published in 1939. From then on, Lewicki had commissions from many magazine and book publishers.

He also exhibited widely, won many awards, traveled extensively to do research, served as Chairman of the Fine Arts Committee of the Long Island Arts Center, and he taught design at the Evening School of Pratt Institute from 1946-52. He was Professor of Art and Chairman of the Visual Arts Department at C.W. Post College, Long Island, New York, at the time of his death.

MICHAEL LUDLOW (1921-) combines a light touch with the ability to depict beautiful young women. This made *Esquire* magazine a natural market, and he painted a great many female subjects for them. He has also completed more decorous subjects for *Family Circle*, *Good Housekeeping*, *Collier's*, *Woman's Home Companion*, *American Magazine*, *Today's Woman*, *Coronet*, *The Saturday Evening Post*, and others, as well as national advertising assignments.

Ludlow was born in Buffalo, New York, and attended classes in illustration, composition, and life drawing at the Art Students League under William C. McNulty.

His first illustrations were made for the Sunday supplement of the *New York Journal-American* in 1948, and he has been a prolific painter since.

DAVID STONE MARTIN (1913-1992) had no formal art training beyond high school in Chicago and began his career as a graphic designer. He designed many publications, becoming an expert calligrapher. Among his major projects were designs and murals for the "Century of Progress" Chicago World's Fair, and he worked variously as a supervisor of a Federal Arts project for the Elgin State Hospital in Illinois, an art director of the Tennessee Valley Authority for six years, and as an assistant to Ben Shahn, painting murals. He was artist-correspondent for Abbott Laboratories and for *Life* magazine during World War II. He also worked for the O.S.S. and was an art director in the Office of War Information in 1942-43. After the war, he followed a freelance career, participating in many advertising illustration projects for clients such as the Disc Company of America and CBS Television.

Martin used a calligraphic line that was widely imitated. No one else, however, matched his ability to present the essence and mood of a subject in his very personal way.

His advertising and editorial illustrations received a great many citations and awards, and examples of his work are included in numerous Art Directors Club Annuals.

He also found time to teach — at the Brooklyn Museum School of Art in 1948-49, and at the Workshop School of Advertising and Editorial Art in New York in 1950. In 2000, he was elected into the Society of Illustrators Hall of Fame.

David Stone Martin, *"Here comes the Bride...Remember?"* Advertising illustration for Security Mutual Life Insurance Company. This won an award for Distinctive Merit at the 34th Annual Exhibition, New York Art Directors Club, 1955.

Cygnus among the Asteroids, 1978. Concept art for Walt Disney.

McCall

ROBERT THEODORE McCALL (1919-) is from Columbus, Ohio. He studied at the Columbus Fine Arts School and at the Art Institute of Chicago. Following his military service, he worked as an illustrator with Bielefelt Studios in Chicago for three years and then joined the Charles E. Cooper studio in New York.

He is well qualified to do aviation and aerospace illustration; during World War II, he was an Army Air Corps bombardier instructor. After the war, he traveled around the world with special trips to Europe, Africa, the Far East, Japan, India, and the Middle East, as a guest of the U. S. Air Force for various documentary painting projects and contributions to the U.S.A.F. art collection in Washington, D.C. and Colorado Springs, Colorado.

In 1976, McCall completed a huge mural project for the Space Museum in Washington, D.C. In 1983 he finished another large mural painting, *The Prologue and the Promise*, at the Disney EPCOT Center in Florida. McCall has also served as a consultant on several movies, including **Star Trek**, and **The Black Hole**, for which he was given screen credit as art director.

Three of his books on space have been published: ***Our World in Space*** in 1973, ***A Vision of the Future — The Art of Robert McCall***, published by Abrams in 1982, and ***The Art of Robert McCall***, published by Bantam Doubleday in 1992.

McCall is a member of the Society of Illustrators in New York which elected him into its Hall of Fame in 1988.

Space Shuttle Docking, 1971.

John McDermott, *The St. Valentine's day Slaughter*, illustration for "Convict 852080" by Dave Magroff; *Argosy* magazine, June, 1958.

JOHN R. McDERMOTT (1919-1977) was born in Pueblo, Colorado. After finishing high school in Hollywood, he went to work for the Disney Studios as an animator. This ended at the outbreak of World War II, and McDermott became a Marine in the Pacific Theatre. During part of this time, he served as a combat artist and made drawings for the Corps' records of actions in the Solomons, Guadalcanal, Guam, and Okinawa.

At the end of the war, some of thse drawings were seen by *Blue Book*, and this began McDermott's illustration career, establishing him as expert in military subjects and depiction of action.

A few years later, with a group of his illustrator friends, McDermott made a home movie, "Dawn Patrol," as a parody on old World War I movies. The project inspired McDermott to work in cinema, and with his friends as volunteer actors, produced a memorable documentary film on the Civil War, "Pickett's Charge," which was shown twice in 1957 by CBS Television. In 1964, he received a Ford Fountation grant for further film experimentation and made a film of the Marines at the Battle of Belleau Wood in 1918, again with his group of amateur actors.

McDermott was the author of four novels; one, *The Rat Factory*, was an unsympathetic version of his Disney experiences. Another book, about a hapless illustrator "Brooks Wilson," was made into the movie *Loving*, starring George Segal and Eva Marie-Saint.

Franklin McMahon, illustration for "Fail-Safe" by Eugene Burdick and Harvey Wheeler, *The Saturday Evening Post* © 1962, 1990 by Curtis Publishing Company.

FRANKLIN McMAHON (1921-) is a Chicagoan by birth and education. He attended the Art Institute, the Harrison Commercial Art Institute, and the Institute of Design there. Among his many teachers were Francis Chapin, Paul Weighardt, E. W. Ball, Emerson Woeffler, and Richard Fillopowski.

A B-17 navigator during World War II, McMahon was shot down over Mannheim, Germany, and spent the last three months of the war in German P.O.W. Camps.

After the war, he re-established his studio in Chicago and began to do freelance illustration for advertising, magazines and books. In addition, he pursued an active career in fine art painting and has won many awards.

McMahon is essentially a reportorial artist with an especially strong sense of line. He has an innate feel for composition; he can begin a drawing at a given point without prior planning or blocking in, and carry it through to a finish. This gives his work a look of on-the-spot credibility which a more finished rendering based on photographic information would not provide. He does, in fact, work directly from his subjects whenever possible, and his assignments have taken him to many parts of the world for most of the leading publications. Many of his assignments, such as his coverage of the Ecumenical Council and Vatican II, have been self-generated and sold to the appropriate publications after completion. In recognition of McMahon's many talents, the Artists Guild of New York chose him as "Artist of the Year" in 1963.

Stanley Meltzoff, *World War I Troops Reviewing Damage*, **Saga** magazine, March, 1964.

Born in New York City, STANLEY MELTZOFF (1917 -) earned a B.S. from the College of the City of New York and an M.F.A. from the Institute of Fine Arts at New York University. His pre-war teaching was interrupted by four years in the Army during World War II, during which he eventually became art editor of **Stars and Stripes** in Africa and Italy. After the war, he resumed teaching, first at C.C.N.Y. and then at Pratt Institute, continuing his own painting and learning to be an illustrator.

His first major opportunity was an assignment to do covers for the reborn *Scientific American*, more than sixty of which he eventually painted. These were largely symbolic still lifes in the guise of realism. His most notable advertising assignments were of new chemical products for Rohm and Haas, and a long series of industrial subjects for United Engineers. He wasn't only a scientific artist, however, and illustrations and covers were made for **The Saturday Evening Post**, **Argosy**, **Field & Stream**, and above all, **Life**, as well as numerous paperback books. Subjects ranged in history from prehistoric mastodon hunts, ancient Greece, the American Civil War, and political history, to present-day steel-construction workers.

Having been a diver by avocation for most of his adult life, Meltzoff was assigned to paint fish underwater for art editor Dick Gangel at **Sports Illustrated**. Finding himself almost alone in this field, he became a specialized painter of submersive subjects for **Sports Illustrated** and later **National Geographic.** He has completed an extended series on ten big salt water game fish. In the process, his market gradually shifted to art galleries and large limited edition prints. Meltzoff was elected into the Hall of Fame of the Society of Illustrators in 1999.

Al Muenchen, illustration for "Flame Out" by Frank Harvey in **The Saturday Evening Post**, April 23, 1955; ©1955, 1983 by The Curtis Publishing Company.

AL MUENCHEN (1917-1975) was a versatile artist, who was equally at home illustrating fiction or advertising. His renderings were crisp and precise, which made for effective presentation of mechanical subjects, such as planes, automobiles and ships. These abilities were well combined in his striking illustrations for "The Guns of Navarone" (later made into a motion picture) for **The Saturday Evening Post**. They were equally useful for painting in Antarctica for the Air Force in recording the lives and work of personnel based there. These paintings are now part of the Air Force Permanent Art Collection.

Muenchen was born in Cincinnati, Ohio, and attended the Chicago Art Institute and the Carnegie Institute of Technology in Pittsburgh, Pennsylvania. He first worked for Pittsburgh Studios in 1937 and did a considerable amount of advertising illustration prior to his fiction assignments, which appeared in **The Saturday Evening Post**, **Cosmopolitan**, **Collier's**, **American Magazine**, **True**, and other magazines.

Muenchen was an active member of the Society of Illustrators, serving on the Exhibition committee and the Joint Ethics Committee.

Paul Nonnast, illustration for "The Mountain of Death" by Arthur Mayse in *The Saturday Evening Post*. ©1953, 1981 by The Curtis Publishing Company.

nonnast

PAUL NONNAST (1918-) chose an artist's career because of a heart condition in his youth, but he has been working at it strenuously ever since.

He was born in Carlisle, Pennsylvania, and was graduated from the Philadelphia Museum School of Art in 1940. Nonnast worked first for the McCandlish Lithograph Corporation and the *Philadelphia Record*, followed by freelance advertising for many national accounts, including Armco, Bell Telephone, Chevrolet, Masonite, Dole Pineapple, and United Air Lines.

The Saturday Evening Post gave him his first illustration assignment in 1947; he has since contributed to the *Post*, *Cosmopolitan*, *Field & Stream*, *Argosy*, *Reader's Digest*, and others.

Nonnast won two Gold Medals in Philadelphia Art Directors shows and served as head of the Advertising and Illustration department of the Moore Institute of Art in Philadelphia from 1943 to 1946.

A serious photographer as well, he has traveled widely in the United States, Canada, and Europe to take pictures.

George Porter, illustration for "In Vivo" by Mildred Savage, published by *Good Housekeeping*, 1964.

GEORGE EDWARD PORTER (1916-) was born in Perry, Florida. He studied at the Ringling School of Art in Sarasota and the Phoenix Art Institute in New York under a distinguished group of teachers, including Lucille Blanche, Thomas Fogarty, Sr., Franklin Booth, Lauros Phoenix, and later with Reuben Tam at the Brooklyn Museum.

During the war years of 1944-45, he did historical and combat art for the Fifth Air Force in the Far East and for the Navy. Under the auspices of Dr. Charles Mayo, and the American Red Cross, he had a one-man show in the hospital at NADZAB, a base in New Guinea.

Since the war, Porter has done both advertising and editorial illustrations appearing in *Good Housekeeping*, *McCall's*, *Redbook*, *The Saturday Evening Post*, *Woman's Day*, *Parents*, and *The Ladies' Home Journal*.

Porter is a member of the Society of Illustrators and has exhibited in its annual shows as well as at those of the Art Directors Clubs of New York and Baltimore.

The Robe Trade, painted in 1984. Private collection.

For several years Riley illustrated the popular *Horacio Hornblower* series by C. S. Forester for **The Saturday Evening Post**.

Ken Riley

The illustrations of KENNETH RILEY (1919-) are remarkable on many counts: strength of draftsmanship, effective composition, the color and quality of the painting, and the portrayal of mood. Riley's pictures reveal that he is clearly a master of all these, particularly in his use of color. He is at home with almost every subject and period; for instance, some of his finest pictures were painted for the historical Captain Hornblower stories by C. S. Forester in **The Saturday Evening Post**. His work has appeared in most of the national publications from **Reader's Digest** to **Life** magazine and in a variety of media from line to full color.

Born in Missouri, Riley studied under Thomas Hart Benton at the Kansas City Art Institute. Then he went to New York, where he studied under Frank Vincent DuMond at the Art Students League, and under Harvey Dunn at the Grand Central Art School. In his approach, Riley has successfully amalgamated the viewpoints of teachers whose methods differed radically and has added to these his own personal direction.

Currently he lives and works in Arizona, exhibiting in several western art galleries. He is a charter member of the National Academy of Western Art and a member of the Cowboy Artists of America. In 1993, he was honored with the Eiteljorg Museum Award and given a one-man retrospective show in 1993.

\   His paintings are included in the Phoenix Art Museum , West Pint Museum, The White House and the Custer Museum.

325

A Perfect Death, one of the series of paintings for *Life* magazine recording an historic era of the South and the origins of jazz as the Negro's contribution to American music; 1958. Morton Roberts for *Life* magazine © 1958, 1986, Time, Inc.

MORTON ROBERTS (1927-1964) crowded a full career into his very short life, but gave promise of much greater things to come. His command of technique was lush and full, and he applied it with equal facility to paintings for exhibition and those for publication in magazines. He was also a teacher of life drawing at Pratt Institute in Brooklyn.

Among his best-known pictures were those made for *Life* magazine of Rasputin for a history of Russia, memorable scenes from the opera "Rigoletto," and an outstanding series on the

"Story of Jazz." He also illustrated for many other publications, including *Collier's*, *True*, *Reader's Digest*, *Redbook*, and Bantam Books.

Roberts was born in Worcester, Massachusetts, and was graduated from the Yale School of Fine Arts. Among his many prizes were the Edwin Austin Abbey Fellowship from the National Academy of Design, the American Watercolor Society's Pratt Purchase Prize, and the First Altman Prize, also from the National Academy of Design.

Rigoletto with Dancers 1958; from a *Life* series on Verdi's opera, "Rigoletto." Morton Roberts for *Life* magazine ©1958, 1986, Time, Inc.

"The Man Who Wasn't There," *McCall's* magazine, April, 1957. Reprinted by permission of The McCall Publishing Company.

Born in Dunfermline, Scotland, ALEXANDER ROSS (1909-1990) came to the United States at the age of three. With early ambitions to be an industrial designer, he studied nights for two years under Robert Lepper at the Carnegie Institute of Technology in Pittsburgh, Pennsylvania.

Otherwise self-taught, Ross got a job in the Rayart Studios in Pittsburgh. From there he progressed to Pitt Studios, and then to the Charles E. Cooper Studio in New York. Two years later, he sold his first cover design to **Good Housekeeping** magazine. This was followed by a total of 130 cover paintings over the next twelve years. In the meantime, he was doing editorial illustrations for most of the other national magazines, including *Collier's*, *The Saturday Evening Post*, *The Ladies' Home Journal*, and *Cosmopolitan*. He illustrated several books, among them *Saints; Adventures in Courage* for Doubleday and Company.

Ross painted many experimental pictures in watercolor and in mixed media, exhibited regularly, and was a member of the American Watercolor Society and the Fairfield Watercolor Group.

His awards included the Ranger Fund purchase prize, the Saxe Foundation award, and the Connecticut Watercolor Society award. His work is represented in the U.S. Air Force Art Collection, the New Britain Museum of American Art, the Mattatuck Museum, the National Academy of Design, and in many private collections.

In 1953, he was awarded a Master of Arts honorary degree by Boston College.

"The Pursuit of Happiness," published by **The Saturday Evening Post**, date of publication unknown.

For a *Sports Illustrated* story, "Now the Playoffs," Riger illustrated the New York Giant power as Frank Gifford passes off to Chuck Conerly.

ROBERT RIGER

ROBERT RIGER (1924-1995) was a student of sports who expertly drew, painted, photographed, analyzed, and wrote about the outstanding performers.

Riger was born in New York City where he studied at the High School of Music and Art and at Pratt Institute. His early ambition was to become a teacher, but he switched to advertising design while at Pratt. After graduation, he worked as a layout artist for *The Saturday Evening Post*. This was followed by art and advertising agency work until he got the chance to combine his love of sports with drawing for the newly launched *Sports Illustrated* magazine.

He was one of the first illustrators to use a sequence of action drawings in revealing the key to championship form in baseball, boxing, football and other major sports. To research these, Riger had to become an expert photographer, taking endless shots in order to analyze and select the significant details for his drawings.

Riger also became associated with television coverage of outstanding sports events, combining drawing with personal commentary. His book, the *ABC Wide World of Sports*, featuring his drawings and photographs of some of these competitions, was published by the American Broadcasting Company in 1965. He also published a book in collaboration with Branch Rickey, *The American Diamond*.

John Scott

JOHN SCOTT (1907-1987) developed his strong, sound approach to illustration by the simple expedient of hard work.

His first art assignments were for the western Pulp magazines during the 'thirties until the outbreak of World War II.

During the war, Scott was overseas as a staff artist on *Yank* and covered the war in Europe as artist-correspondent.

After returning home, John began to work for the general magazines, such as *This Week*, *Woman's Day*, and the *Canadian* publications *Chatelaine* and *The Toronto Star*. He gradually gravitated to the men's magazines, including *True*, *The Elks*, *Argosy*, and *Sports Afield.* He particularly enjoyed the hunting and fishing assignments, which gave him an opportunity to go on location in the wilderness to write and paint. Similar assignments were carried out for the Winchester Arms Company and the Garcia Corporation. These led to a series of paintings on the early days of oil drilling in Texas for the Permian Basin Petroleum Museum in Midland. Several years were then spent painting very large (12 by 32 foot) murals for buildings in Washington, D.C. and in Salt Lake City for the Mormon Church. Up to the end of his career, Scott was concentrating entirely on gallery paintings of the early and contemporary American West.

John Scott, cover painting for *The Elks* magazine, March, 1962.

"He was everybody, grown a little taller," one of an outstanding sersies of historical personages painted for the John Hancock Mutual Life Insurance Company, in 1952.

WILLIAM ARTHUR SMITH, N.A. (1918-1989) made pictures for a broad spectrum of uses and in a great variety of media. To each picture, whether for exhibition or publication, he brought a distinctive and highly creative viewpoint.

Born in Toledo, Ohio, Smith studied at the University of Toledo, at the Grand Central Art School and the Art Students League in New York, l'Ecole des Beaux-Arts and l'Académie de la Grand Chaumiere in Paris, and with Theodore J. Keane in Toledo.

Smith's work is represented in many major collections, including the Metropolitan Museum of Art and the Los Angeles Museum; he exhibited in nearly every important museum in the United States. He also had one-man exhibitions in more than twenty principal cities of Europe and Asia.

Among his many prizes were the Grand Prize and Gold Medal of Honor of the American Watercolor Society (twice); the Society of American Graphics Artists' Award for Lithography; the Winslow Homer Memorial Prize; and the Society of Illustrators' Gold Medal Award for Advertising Illustration.

He taught at the Grand Central Art School and at Pratt Institute in Brooklyn; he lectured at many colleges in the United States and abroad, was president of the American Watercolor Society and president of the International Association of Art, the UNESCO-affiliated organization of painters, sculptors and graphic artists of seventy nations. Smith was posthumously elected into the Society of Illustrators Hall of Fame in 1981.

Tracy Sugerman, "A Life for a Vote" by John Hersey, published by *The Saturday Evening Post,* September 26, 1964. © 1964, 1992 by the Curtis Publishing Company.

Tracy Sugarman

TRACY SUGARMAN (1921-) initiated a personal assignment of reporting the student voter-registration efforts in Mississippi in 1964 and 1965. Feeling strongly about the issues and wanting to make a contribution as an artist in a reportorial series of drawings, he enlisted sponsorship of the project by the Columbia Broadcasting System and the United States Information Agency. The work was featured in a CBS TV Documentary, "How Beautiful on the Mountains," and in USIA publications throughout the world.

These sensitive line and wash drawings were made from on-the-spot observation, often under dangerous conditions, but honestly and without sensationalistm. The drawings were also used by *The New York Times Magazine*, and the *The Saturday Evening Post*, and are now a permanent archive of the Civil Rights Movement at Tougaloo College in Mississippi. Sugarman's book about his experiences in the South, *Stranger at the Gates*, was published by Hill and Wang in 1966.

In 1969, Sugarman helped create Rediscovery Productions, Inc., a prize-winning documentary film company, devoted to the exploration of social and political issues. He served as a writer and Art Director for more than thirty documentaries dealing with civil liberties, racism, ageism and health. Sugarman's drawings and paintings added emotional depth and variety to the story-telling. In recent years, he has painted murals for the pediatric units of the Norwalk Hospital in Connecticut, and the Elmhurst Hospital in Elmhurst, Queens. He is currently working on a mural for the AFL/CIO Housing Investment Trust in Washington, D.C. Since 1985, he has been commissioned by seven communities in Connecticut to make folios of watercolors featuring significant historic sites.

Tracy Sugarman was born in Syracuse, N.Y., and was graduated from Syracuse University College of Fine Arts in 1943. After serving in the U.S. Navy as an amphibious officer for the D-Day invasion, he began his career as an artist in New York City. He studied further with Reuben Tam at the Brooklyn Museum Art School and with David Stone Martin.

His illustrations have appeared in *Fortune*, *Collier's*, *Esquire*, *Woman's Home Companion*, *American Magazine*, *Parents*, *Boys' Life*, and *Gentlemen's Quarterly* magazines. His book illustrations have appeared for Simon and Schuster, Doubleday, Random House, Scott Foreman, and Hill and Wang.

In addition to membership in the Society of Illustrators, he has been President of the Westport Artists and of the Westport-Weston Association for the United Nations.

Richard Stone, "Edge of the Sea" by Lee Colgate, *Good Housekeeping*, 1961.

Dick Stone

RICHARD F. STONE (1925-) was born in New Jersey. He studied both at the New York Art Students League and at Yale University, where he earned a B.F.A. His paintings are assured and subtle, carefully simplified, always in good taste. He successfully combines the traditional accomplishments of good drawing and academic painting that holds its own with contemporary techniques.

Stone's illustrations have appeared in most of the major publications, including *The Saturday Evening Post*, *Reader's Digest*, *McCall's*, *Family Circle*, *Woman's Day*, *Argosy*, *Good Housekeeping*, *Sports Illustrated*, and *Cosmopolitan*. He was affiliated with Neeley Associates and has done work for many national advertisers, among them Southern Railway, Ford, Plymouth, Rambler, Four Roses, Opel, and Time, Inc.

Robert Thom, *James Lind, Conqueror of Scurvy,* one of the History of Medicine series; ©1958, 1961 Parke, Davis & Company.

ROBERT THOM

In 1948, ROBERT A. THOM (1915-1980) took on an assignment for a series of historical paintings for Parke, Davis & Company to illustrate the story of pharmacy. To make the forty paintings constituted a monumental, ten-year effort in research and consultation in order to insure the necessary accuracy of concept and detail.

This series was followed by another very demanding one of forty-five paintings to illustrate the history of medicine. These paintings were reproduced in magazine advertisements and later enlarged and distributed widely among druggists. The original paintings have been exhibited in every state of the Union, and most of Canada, and represent institutional and advertising art at its best. The two series won numerous awards.

Thom was born in Grand Rapids, Michigan, and had brief art training at the Institute of Fine Arts in Columbus, Ohio, and under Robert Brackman at Noank, Connecticut. He opened his own studio in Detroit, Michigan, and did commercial illustration for General Motors, Dodge Division of Chrysler Corporation, Bohm Aluminum and others prior to his Parke, Davis commissions. His career was tragically ended in an automobile accident.

Thornton Utz

THORNTON UTZ (1914-2000) liked to work out the poses of his figures with rapid, free sketches that clearly expressed the mood or mental attitude of his characters. Once this had been established, he then posed and photographed his models, as nearly as possible, in the predetermined positions. The photos furnished the details of folds and lighting which lent added factuality to his original poses.

He used this approach effectively for his humorous *Saturday Evening Post* covers as well as for the more serious fiction illustrations for *Cosmopolitan*, *McCall's*, *The Ladies' Home Journal*, *Redbook*, and *Good Housekeeping.*

Utz participated in the Society of Illustrators Air Force Art Program and received a citation from General Curtis LeMay for documenting the airlift of Hungarian refugees. Utz also received the Governor Bryant of Florida Award for his freedom posters.

He was born in Memphis, Tennessee, and studied under Burton Callicott in Memphis. He also attended the American Academy of Art in Chicago and later taught at the Chicago Art Institute. Utz eventually concentrated on paintings and commissioned portraiture, which included President Carter's family and Princess Grace of Monaco. He was a member of the Chicago Artists Guild and the American Artists Professional League. He later lived in Sarasota, Florida.

Thornton Utz, cover painting for *The Saturday Evening Post*, May 2, 1953. ©1953, 1981 by The Curtis Publishing Company.

"Old Enough for Love" by Jack Finney, May 1962. Reprinted by permission of the McCall Publishing Company.

Cover of *Cosmopolitan* magazine, November 1949.

M. COBURN WHITMORE (1913-1988) described his three primary interests as "racing cars, illustrating, and smart clothes on good-looking women." The racing cars were a hobby, but he was thoroughly professional in his illustrations of beautiful women. Probably no other illustrator was so inventive over so long a time in doing variations on the theme of "boy meets girl."

Whitmore was born in Dayton, Ohio, and attended the Dayton Art Institute there. Next, he went to Chicago as an apprentice in the studio of Haddon Sundblom and Edwin Henry, and attended the Chicago Art Institute nights. Following his apprenticeship, he worked for the *Chicago Herald Examiner* and the Charles Jensen studio in Cincinnati. Then he moved to New York, for a long association with the Charles E. Cooper Studio, and also began to get illustration assignments from the major magazines, including *McCall's*, *The Ladies' Home Journal*, *Redbook*, *Good Housekeeping*, *Cosmopolitan*, and *Woman's Day*. Many foreign publications purchased the second rights to publish his pictures abroad.

Whitmore exhibited at Art Directors' shows in New York, Philadelphia, Chicago, and Westchester county, winning many awards and citations. He was a member of the Society of Illustrators and was elected to its Hall of Fame in 1978.

"Target for Matrimony," by Steve McNeill. *The Saturday Evening Post*, © 1952, 1980. by The Curtis Publishing Company.

1960–1970

Robert K. Abbett

Thomas B. Allen

David Blossom

James Neil Boyle

Jerry W. Daniel

Reynold Brown

Paul Calle

Mia Carpenter

Seymour Chwast

Ted C. CoConis

Guy Deel

Jack Dumas

Naiad Einsel

Walter Einsel

Lorraine Fox

Marvin Friedman

Bernard Fuchs

Milton Glaser

Philip Harrison Hays

Robert Heindel

Mitchell Hooks

Gordon Johnson

Victor Kalin

Sanford Kossin

Mort Künstler

Arthur Lidov

Frank C. McCarthy

John McClelland

Robert E. McGinnis

Frank Mullins

Fred Otnes

Robert Peak

Bayre Phillips

Jack Potter

Richard M. Powers

Anthony Saris

Harvey Schmidt

Daniel Schwartz

Arthur Shilstone

Saul Steinberg

Shannon Stirnweis

Herbert Tauss

Howard A. Terpning

Edward T. Vebell

Robert Weaver

William H. Whittingham

Fritz Willis

Ben Wohlberg

Robert Peak movie poster for **Modesty Blaise.**

Bernie Fuchs, Martin Luther King, **Look** magazine.

Sanford Kossin, "Bay of Pigs," courtesy of **Life** magazine

THE DECADE 1960-1970

Although many of the magazines appeared to be healthy at the beginning of the decade, by the mid-sixties the traditional family magazine bases for illustration had shriveled as one after another of the major magazines died. *Liberty* was the first of the weeklies to go in 1950. Crowell-Collier, with its flagship, *Collier's,* succumbed in 1956. The mighty **Saturday Evening Post** was discontinued in 1969.

A few magazines were still hanging on as the decade ended. **Sports Illustrated,** with a strong niche, ran counter to the trend by switching from photography to art for featured stories, and sent Bob Peak on a shooting safari with the Shah of Iran, Bernie Fuchs to Spain for the bull fighting season, and Al Parker to Monte Carlo for the Grand Prix. Such reportorial assignments provided a healthy creative environment. The artists were free to interpret the events in a personal, behind-the-scenes way without direct editorial supervision. The artists and the magazine both benefitted. *Fortune* magazine also continued to leaven its pages with art drawn or painted on location. Photo-oriented magazines *Look* and *Life* also occasionally used the talents of illustrators to cover the Civil Rights movement, the attempted Cuban invasion and the escalating Vietnam War. These were exceptions, however, that did not compensate for the rapidly shrinking number of general magazines.

Paperback books were becoming a national fad, and their covers were the saviors for illustrators. The books had their genesis before the war, in inexpensive reprints of popular novels as pioneered by Penguin Books, Pocket Books, Bantam Books and other publishers. They had been helped by distribution of pocket sized books to the Armed Forces during World War II and growth was accelerated when paper stocks were no longer rationed after the war. Like the Pulps before them, they were sold as much by the art on the cover as by the name of the authors. Flagging sales could be rejuvenated by republishing the same

book with a new cover. Artwork had to be carefully designed within the small format and the cover subject needed to be symbolic of the whole book rather than depicting an incident in the story. Illustrators who could combine these requirements artistically found as much work as they could handle. James Avati, Stanley Meltzoff, James Bama, and others made the transition from "slicks" to paperbacks effortlessly and set the pace for a new generation of artists who only painted covers. Paperbacks offered all levels of quality and were, therefore, less limiting than the pulps had been. Many commissioned cover paintings were fine enough to compete with the art of Thomas Dewing and Renoir or other painters which were sometimes used to decorate an appropriate novel by experimental art directors. Other covers could be shamelessly exploitive of sex, whether representative of the contents or not. After publishers had run out of classics, novels were created just for paperback publication and certain genres, were sure sale. Some subjects, such as the Gothic Romances became formulaic; the covers depicted a beautiful heroine in mortal danger, trying to escape in the night. Behind her would be a castle or a decaying mansion with an eerie light in one window. Countless variations on this theme were painted. Westerns and detective stories had their own formulae.

Aside from paperbacks, and movie poster art, a new market for artists who could paint Western subjects evolved through the newly-formed "Cowboy Artists of America," then affiliated with the Cowboy Hall of Fame in Oklahoma City. With the dearth of original paintings by Frederic Remington or Charles Russell available, newly oil-rich Texans were looking for substitutes. Many illustrators, including John Clymer, Tom Lovell, and Robert Lougheed moved West and became very successful in painting historical and contemporary Western pictures for collectors through galleries and exhibition sales.

Luke, **North Light** cover, September/October 1974. Courtesy Robert K. Abbett.

ROBERT K. ABBETT (1926-) was born in Hammond, Indiana, He holds a B.S. from Purdue University and a B.A. from the University of Missouri. In addition, he studied nights at the Chicago Academy of Fine Art.

He started his professional career as a writer for a public relations agency in Chicago, but wanting to be an artist, apprenticed himself to the Stevens-Gross Studio. He next transferred to the Bielefeld Studios, and from Chicago went to New York with the Alexander Chaite Studios.

Abbett made his first magazine illustrations for **Extension** magazine in Chicago and began to take on more assignments in New York, eventually freelancing for such magazines as **True**, **Argosy**, **Redbook**, **This Week**, **Reader's Digest**, **Sports Afield**, and many paperback publishers, including Bantam Books, Dell, Signet, Fawcett, Ballantine and Pyramid Books.

Leaving illustration in the early 'seventies, Abbett devoted himself fully to painting outdoor scenes. Best known for his definitive work with sporting dogs, he has also made paintings for the stamp/print programs of several conservation groups. Portraiture includes actor James Stewart (for the Cowboy Hall of Fame) and Luther Burbank (for the Burbank Center for the Arts).

Abbett taught the techniques of editorial illustration at the Silvermine Guild in Norwalk, Connecticut from 1959-62. He has also conducted workshops in the Scottsdale Art School for several years. He is a past president of the Westport Artists and a member of the Society of Animal Artists.

THOMAS B. ALLEN (1928-) was born in Nashville, Tennessee, spent two years at Vanderbilt University and obtained a B.F.A. after another four years at the Art Institute of Chicago. He exhibits regularly, is represented in New York by the D'Arcy Gallery, and has won numerous awards, including the New York Art Directors Club Gold Medal and the Society of Illustrators Gold Medal. He also taught at the School of Visual Arts in New York from 1958-'64, Parsons School of Design from '74-'75, Syracuse University from '75-'78, University of Kansas from '82-'94, and since '95 at the Ringling School of Art & Design.

Long recognized as an innovator of American illustration for major magazines and corporations, Tom has involved himself in the world of children's literature since 1985. Five of his illustrated books have been chosen for anthologies of elementary school literature. They are: **In Coal Country**, **On Granddaddy's Farm**, which he also wrote, **Across the Wide Dark Sea**, **A Place called Freedom**, and **Blackberries in the Dark**.

In his paintings, too, Allen combines a feeling of old and new in his almost-Victorian style of dealing with contemporary subjects. As a result, his pictures are set apart from the usual printed material and gain increased attention for his reportorial subject matter for such venues as **Esquire**, **Sports Illustrated**, **McCall's**, **Life**, **Redbook**, **Playboy**, CBS, Signet Classics, and Harper & Row.

A two-year exhibition of his work called "The Journey of an American Illustrator" began at Nashville's Ryman Auditorium in 2000, accompanied by a book with the same title.

Tinker, Tailor, Soldier, Spy, featuring Alec Guinness, PBS
Copyright © by Thomas B. Allen, 1981.

DAVID BLOSSOM (1927-1995) was the son of illustrator Earl Blossom. (David's son Christopher is carrying on the family talent as a very able marine painter.) Blossom learned about illustration from watching his father at work. In addition, he studied for a year at the Yale School of Fine Arts and for two years of night school at the Art Students League under Reginald Marsh.

For the next fourteen years, he worked as an art director for the J. Walter Thompson advertising agency in New York.

With this thorough groundwork, David decided in 1961 to become a freelance illustrator. He started at the top by selling his first illustration to *The Saturday Evening Post*, followed by work for most of the other major magazines, including *McCall's*, *Good Housekeeping*, and *Reader's Digest.* He also illustrated for many national advertisers, such as Pan-American Airlines and the Pontiac Motor Division of General Motors.

Blossom exhibited regularly in the Society of Illustrators Annual Exhibitions, winning Awards of Excellence, and in 1972, he was given the Society's prestigious Hamilton King Award for the best illustration of the year by a member.

During the Bicentennial, he designed a series of postal cards commemorating famous events of the American Revolution for the United States Postal Service.

This advertising illustration for Pan American Airways won the Society of Illustrators Award for Excellence in 1962.

Ruby's Place, Twenty-six California Artists Watercolor Exhibition 1984.

JAMES NEIL BOYLE, (1931-) was born in Granum, Alberta, and raised in Fort Macleod, Alberta, Canada.

His formal education includes training at the Banff School of Fine Arts in Alberta, Canada, at Chouinard Art Institute, and at Art Center College of Design in Los Angeles. Boyle has taught at both art schools in Los Angeles and has held an associate professorship with the University of California at Long Beach and Northridge.

A commercial illustrator for over twenty years, his work appeared in *The Saturday Evening Post*, *Reader's Digest*, and *Good Housekeeping* magazines, as well as for the Rand Corporation, Walt Disney Productions, and the U. S. Postal Service. Four paintings were selected for the U. S. Bicentennial Commemorative Stamp Series.

Boyle has traveled to Southeast Asia, Europe, and the United States at the request of the U. S. Air Force Historical Program, adding over thirty documentary paintings to the permanent educational collection at the Smithsonian Institution and the Pentagon. In 1984, he completed a commission for Mt. Sinai Memorial Park in Glendale, California, which depicts the history of the Jew in America from 1655 to the present. It was converted into a mosaic masterwork 146 feet long by 38 feet high which covers the facade of the main mausoleum.

Boyle is the recipient of numerous art awards including the Lifetime Achievement Award from the Society of Illustrators of Los Angeles, and is a signature member of both the Oil Painters of America and the California Art Club.

Seventeen galleries throughout the United States and Canada are currently representing his work.

This version of the poster for **Curucu, Beast of the Amazon** was not used, since Universal decided it revealed the monster too clearly, and they opted for a pose of the beast in concealment. Collection of the Brown Family Trust.

As a poster artist for the motion picture industry, REYNOLD BROWN (1917-1991) was rarely allowed to sign his work. Certainly the general public, lured to the films by his melodramatic portrayals of monsters and catastrophes, had no idea who had painted the images. In the heady postwar years of the drive-in theatres, when producers competed to satisfy the vast, teen-age appetite for shocking subject matter, Brown was the utility man who could conjure up and paint anything, sometimes for films that did not yet have scripts. Among Brown's film credits were **The Creature from the Black Lagoon**, **This Island Earth**, **The Incredible Shrinking Man**, **The Attack of the 50-ft. Woman**, **The Revenge of the Creature**, **Monster on the Campus**, and **The Monolith Monsters.** Among his more "respectable" titles included **Ben Hur**, **How The West Was Won**, **Dr. Zhivago**, **Mutiny on the Bounty**, and **The Four Horsemen of the Apocalypse**, totalling over 250 campaigns from 1950 to the end of the '60s when he retired to paint for himself.

Brown was born in Los Angeles and studied at the Otis Art Institute. He first worked as an assistant to Hal Forrest, creator of the comic strip "Tailspin Tommy." During the war years, he was an indispensable artist for the North American Aircraft Company. After the war and a short sojourn East where he worked for paperback books and magazines such as **Boys' Life** and **Outdoor Life**, he returned to California and became a freelance artist for Universal-International, Allied Artists, and M-G-M. For several years, Brown was also an instructor at the Art Center College of Design in California.

A documentary film featuring Brown's career, entitled **The Man Who Created Bug-eyed Monsters**, was shown on the Public Broadcasting System in the 1990s.

The Mountain Men, a recent lithograph, is an extension of Calle's meticulous pencil technique.

FIRST MAN ON THE MOON — UNITED STATES — © USPS

PAUL CALLE (1928-) is probably best known for his skill with a pencil, his favorite medium; he is the author of **The Pencil**, published by North Light Publications, which has gone through multiple reprintings.

Born in New York City, Calle attended Pratt Institute and sold his first work to **Liberty** magazine at the age of nineteen. He went on to illustrate for **McCall's**, **The Saturday Evening Post**, **National Geographic**, **Fortune**, and many other magazines as well as national advertising accounts.

He was selected as an official artist of the National Aeronautics and Space Administration Fine Art Program, and he became involved with many of the NASA projects. As a related project, he designed the "First Man on the Moon" stamp for the U.S. Postal Service, one of thirteen stamps he has designed.

Involvement with the Department of Interior's Artist in the Parks program gave Calle the opportunity to travel throughout the West. This led to his interest in the history of the area and in drawing and painting the life of the early settlers. He now devotes full time to historical pictures. His works are in the collections of several western institutions, as well as the NASA Collection, the National Park Service, and the U. S. Department of the Interior. A retrospective exhibit of his work was held at the Gilcrease Museum in Tulsa, Oklahoma, in 1991.

Mia Carpenter

MIA CARPENTER (1933-) has an excellent sense of composition and design which she combines with the subtle sensitivity that distinguishes her work.

Mia is a Californian, from Los Angeles, and obtained her B.A. From the Art Center School there. Her first work was for **Seventeen** magazine in 1957, and she has since illustrated for **Redbook**, **The Ladies' Home Journal**, **Good Housekeeping**, **McCall's**, **Parents** magazine, and **The New York Times**. In addition, she has illustrated a book for Harper & Row and two textbooks on fashion design.

Carpenter's work has also been exhibited at the annual shows of the New York Society of Illustrators, and she was awarded a gold medal for advertising in **Illustrators '62**.

Carpenter has more recently worked as a sketch artist for entertainment advertising — particularly film — with clients including M-G-M/United, Paramount Pictures, and numerous agencies in the Hollywood area.

Mia Carpenter, one of a series of illustrations for Joseph Love, Inc. featuring children's fashions.

Seymour Chwast, poster illustration for the **I, Claudius**, PBS Television series, sponsored by Mobil Corporation in 1978.

S. CHWAST

The name of SEYMOUR CHWAST (1931-) immediately conjures up an association with the Push Pin Studios, of which he was a founding partner in 1954, along with Milton Glaser, Isadore Seltzer, and Paul Davis. Their Push Pin style has had a tremendous influence on graphic art — and illustration — in all the years since.

With an eclectic approach that borrows freely and irreverently from any source, Chwast adapts his drawing style to the individual client's requirements. Among his clients have been the most prominent corporations, and he has worked for virtually every magazine, including **Time**, **Newsweek**, **New York Magazine**, **Esquire**, and **The New York Times Magazine.** In addition, he has designed record covers, children's books, package designs and posters.

Chwast was born in New York City and studied at Cooper Union with Sidney Delevante. His first illustrations were for **Seventeen** magazine, which was a trendsetter in providing wider artistic freedom and encouragement to young illustrators.

In 1970, Chwast and Push Pin Studios were honored with a retrospective exhibition at the Louvre's Musée Des Arts Decoratifs, followed by showings in other major cities in Europe, Brazil, and Japan. His posters are in the collection of the Museum of Modern Art in New York and other museums worldwide.

He is in the Art Directors Hall of Fame, a recipient of the AIGA Medal, and currently director of the Push Pin Group.

TED C. CoCONIS (1927-), was born in Chicago, and studied at the Academy of Art there. Following his brief service in the military, he worked in an art studio in San Francisco. He accepted his first freelance commission in the early '50s and within ten years, moved to New York to establish himself as one of the country's top illustrators.

His work has appeared in publications from **Good Housekeeping** and **Ladies' Home Journal** to **Playboy** and **Cosmopolitan** and many books.

CoConis also produced award-winning movie posters for such classic films as **Fiddler on the Roof**, **The Man of La Mancha**, **The Prime of Miss Jean Brody**, **Dorian Grey**; others included the Jim Henson Muppet television specials. His work has also been used in advertisements for cruise ships, airlines, hotels, and tourist agencies.

He decided to concentrate on his own work while living in Paris and the Greek Islands for several years. On his return to the States, he left the Bay area for the small artist-colony/fishing-village of Cedar Key, Florida. Summers are spent in his studio on the coast of Maine.

His work has won numerous awards from the Society of Illustrators, The Art Directors' Clubs of New York and Los Angeles, and other associations. His work is in the collections of The Society of Illustrators Museum of American Illustration, The Bishop Museum, and the Boca Raton Museum of Art, as well as in several other corporate and private collections.

T. CoConis, illustration for "Do You Resent Your Children?" *Parents* magazine, August, 1966.

GUY DEEL (1933-) arrived at his interest in the American West through his own family background. His grandparents began ranching in Texas in the 1880s; his father was a Texas cowboy, and his mother cooked for the ranch hands.

Deel was born in the west Texas town of Tuxedo. He was awarded a scholarship at the Art Center College of Design and after graduation, had further training with Pruett Carter. He also studied sculpture at the Otis Art Institute.

His professional career, beginning with work as an animator and background artist for a film production studio, has also included freelance assignments from **Redbook**, **True**, **The Saturday Evening Post**, **Good Housekeeping**, **This Week**, **Westways**, **Reader's Digest**, and **Esquire** magazines. In addition, he has done paperback cover illustrations for leading western authors, such as Luke Short, Will Henry, Elmer Kelton, Clay Fisher, Lewis Patton, Gary McCarthy, and Louis L'Amour. A major project included four years' work at the EPCOT center at Disney World in Florida painting historical subjects of the Revolutionary War for the American Adventure Pavilion. Currently, he is coming full circle, concentrating on gallery paintings based on themes of the Old West and his family history.

Guy Deel, "Dream of a Strange Land" by Graham Greene, *The Saturday Evening Post,* January 19, 1963, ©1963, 1991 by The Curtis Publishing Company.

JackDumas

JACK DUMAS (1915-1998) was born in Seattle, Washington. Just out of high school, he joined Disney Studios as an animator. He soon went back to Seattle to attend the Cornish School of Allied Arts and the Seattle Academy of Art. He next moved to Los Angeles and worked for the *Los Angeles Examiner* editorial art department; then he joined a commercial art service with Ren Wicks, and also attended Los Angeles Art Center.

Following a five-year Army stint, he moved to San Francisco and came under the helpful influences of Maurice Logan, Willard Cox, Stan Galli, and Fred Ludekens.

His first editorial art published was a cover for *Argosy* magazine in 1956. This was soon followed by assignments for many magazine and advertising clients, most notably the Weyerhaeuser Company of Tacoma, Washington, which provided opportunities to paint wildlife in their forest habitat. He also illustrated for *Sports Afield* for over 20 years, as well as work for *Reader's Digest*, *Argosy*, *Outdoor Life*, and many Bantam book covers of Louis L'Amour and Luke Short westerns.

Enthusiasm for wildlife subjects naturally led to his doing gallery paintings of the same subject matter. His art helped to raise thousands of dollars for conservation projects; his paintings were included in the North American Wild Animal Art Exhibition and shown with the Society of Animal Artists of New York.

Jack Dumas, calendar illustration for Eddie Bauer, Inc., 1972-74.

Walter Einsel, "The Age of Information," for AT&T at EPCOT in 1983.

Naiad and Walter Einsel, ©USPS.

EINSEL WALTER EINSEL (1926-1998) was born in New York City. He attended the Art Students League and graduated from Parsons School of Design.

The New York Times Magazine gave him his initial illustration assignment. This was followed by commissions from *American Heritage*, *Life*, *Look*, *Time*, *The Saturday Evening Post*, *Gentlemen's Quarterly*, *Tennis Magazine*, *Golf Digest*, *Smithsonian* magazine, and other publications.

He created logos for Gilbey's Vodka, Hostell, and Merrill Lynch (the bull) as well as TV commercials for many clients.

His first three-dimensional art object was a valentine for Naiad; other such mementos became more complex, and movement was added by means of gears, ratchets, motors and springs. These became a part of his artistic repertoire and animated sculpture dominates his work. Clients have included Macy's, *Reader's Digest*, The U.S. Postal Service and AT&T, which commissioned Einsel to design an exhibition for its corporate participation in the EPCOT Center in Orlando, Florida. His exhibit involves fifty-five figures, most of which move in various ways and includes a twelve-foot ferris wheel and a fourteen-foot "Einsel Tower Phone Mobile." The Barnum Museum of Bridgeport houses several of his figures in their permanent exhibit.

NAIAD NAIAD EINSEL (1927-) was born in Philadelphia and graduated from the High School of Music and Art in New York City and Pratt Institute. As an art director in the promotion department at CBS, she met her future husband, Walter, then her counterpart at NBC. Their similar artistic tastes became even more alike as they worked alongside each other and soon they could collaborate at any stage of their assignments.

Naiad's first illustrations were for *Seventeen* magazine. Further commissions came from *The New York Times*, *Redbook*, *The Ladies' Home Journal*, *Collier's*, *Look*, *Parents*, *Woman's Day*, *Family Circle*, *Good Housekeeping*, *Smithsonian*, and other national magazines. Other work has included children's books, book jackets, record album covers, TV titles, package designs and movie posters. Together, she and Walter designed a four-panel block of commemorative stamps, "Progress in Electronics," in 1973 for the U. S. Postal Service. She also designed a Christmas stamp in 1981.

They have both exhibited their work at the Society of Illustrators, The American Institute of Graphic Arts, and the Art Directors Club of New York. They also taught together at Parsons School of Design and the Silvermine School of Art. Recently, they had been designing wind-driven sculpture and weathervanes.

lorraine fox

LORRAINE FOX (1925-1976) who became Mrs. Bernard D'Andrea, was as equally accomplished an illustrator as he. Born in Brooklyn, she studied at Pratt Institute and the Brooklyn Museum Art School under Reuben Tam.

Her early professional experience was acquired in the layout departments of various New York advertising agencies. In 1947, she did her first illustration for **Better Homes and Gardens**, followed by assignments for **Woman's Day**, **Seventeen**, **Good Housekeeping**, **Cosmopolitan**, **The Ladies' Home Journal**, **Redbook**, and **McCall's**.

She exhibited her work at the Society of Illustrators' annual shows, the New York and Philadelphia Art Directors Club exhibits, the Brooklyn Museum, the New York City Center Gallery, and at the Silvermine Guild New England Show, winning several Gold Medals and other awards.

Fox taught at the Parsons School of Design in New York and was a member of the faculty of the Famous Artists School in Westport, Connecticut. In 1979, she was posthumously elected into the Society of Illustrators Hall of Fame.

Lorraine Fox, illustration for "The Glow of Love' by Camilla Bittle.

FRIEDMAN

MARVIN FRIEDMAN (1930-) exhibits a thorough knowledge of drawing in rendering the most complex subject matter with a direct reportorial manner. His color is vibrant and exciting; his control of values impressive.

Friedman was born in Chester, Pennsylvania, and his solid training was acquired at the Philadelphia Museum School of Art where he studied under Henry C. Pitz and Ben Eisenstat.

His first published work was for small religious publications, followed by illustrating for **Good Housekeeping**, **Cosmopolitan**, **The Ladies' Home Journal**, **Playboy**, **Changing Times**, **This Week**, **Cavalier**, **Redbook**, **Ford Times**, **Boys' Life**, **Better Homes & Gardens**, and a long series for **Gourmet** magazine.

His advertising clients have included the Ford Motor Company and Sharp & Dohme Pharmaceuticals. In addition, Friedman has illustrated some thirty-five children's books.

Since 1980, he has devoted increasing time to painting. He recently won a major grant from the State of New Jersey to paint four large murals for the Burlington County Memorial Hospital. He regularly exhibits at the American Watercolor Society and other institutions, such as the Moore Institute of Philadelphia, the Society of Illustrators and the Philadelphia College of Art.

"This Time Tomorrow" by Ken W. Purdy, **Playboy** magazine.

Milton Glaser

MILTON GLASER (1929-) is a native of New York where he attended the High School of Music and Art, and Cooper Union Art School. Following graduation, he received a Fulbright scholarship which allowed him to study etching in Italy under Giorgio Morandi. Later, Glaser spent another period in Italy for an eight months' study of lithography.

In 1954 Glaser was a founder, and president, of the Push Pin Studios formed with several of his Cooper Union classmates. Glaser's work is characterized by directness, simplicity and originality. He uses any medium or style suggested by the picture problem — from primitive to avant garde — in his designs for book jackets, record album covers, advertisements and direct mail pieces, as well as for magazine illustrations. He started his own studio, Milton Glaser, Inc., in 1974. This led to his involvement with an increasingly wide diversity of projects ranging from the design of New York Magazine, of which he was a co-founder, to a 600 foot mural for the Federal Office Building in Indianapolis. Throughout his career he has had a major impact on contemporary illustration and design. His work has won numerous awards from Art Directors Clubs, the American Institute of Graphic Arts, the Society of Illustrators, and the Type Directors Club. In 1979 he was made Honorary Fellow of the Royal Society of Arts and his work is included in the Museum of Modern Art, the Victoria and Albert Museum, the Israel Museum and the Musée de l'affiche in Paris.

Glaser has taught at both the School of Visual Arts and at Cooper Union in New York City.

A. Poster for album ***Bob Dylan's Greatest Hits, Vol.1***, 1968. Milton Glaser, Inc.

B. Book illustration for Gogol's ***Tales of St. Petersburg,*** published by Olivetti, 1987.

C. "Verdi" poster for Exxon / PBS, 1985

As

B

C

343

"Love in San Francisco," *Good Housekeeping*, 1966.

Portrait of Tony Curtis for *TV Guide*, 1975.

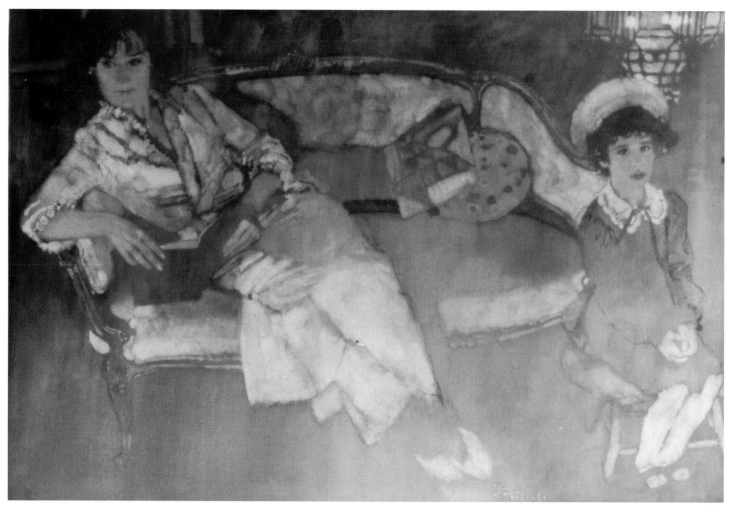

Patti and Sara; "Basic Instructions," *McCall's*, April, 1979.

Columbus, Mural for Royal Caribbean Lines, 1995.

American All Stars, Sports Illustrated, June, 1983.

BERNARD FUCHS (1932-) was named "Artist of the Year" in 1962 by the Artists Guild of New York, signalizing his position at the top of the illustrator's profession at the youthful age of thirty. He was also the youngest illustrator ever elected to the Society of Illustrators Hall of Fame, in 1975. His pictures for *McCall's*, *Redbook*, *Sports Illustrated*, *Cosmopolitan*, *TV Guide* and other magazines are probably more admired — and imitated — than those of any other current illustrator.

Fuchs is equally at home as a galery painter and has done official portraits of both Presidents Kennedy and Johnson. He met Kennedy just before the Cuban crisis and subsequently painted several pictures of the late President, two of which are in the Kennedy Library Collection. He has also painted portraits of many literary, political and theatrical celebrities.

Bernard was born in O'Fallon, Illinois, and attended the Washington University Art School in St. Louis. For five years after graduation, he worked for detroit advertising art studios. He then moved East to Westport, Connecticut, and began to do editorial magazine illustration.

He has had one-man shows in various parts of the country and participated in many group shows, including the United States Information Agency Graphics Exhibition in the Soviet Union. Since the Society's first annual national exhibition in 1959, the juries have selected his work for inclusion in every yearly show and have awarded his numerous gold and silver medals.

Phillip Harrison Hayes, illustration for *Cosmopolitan* magazine story, early 1960's.

In his work, PHILIP HARRISON HAYS (1932-) has always looked for innovative ways to interpret his illustration assignments. This may involve borrowing heavily from earlier eras, combining extracts from an old look with a contemporary point of view. The result is both novel and provocative and has won for him many awards from the Society of Illustrators, the National Society of Art Directors, the Art Directors Club of New York, and the American Institute of Graphic Arts, including Silver and Gold Medals.

He has illustrated for a wide range of magazines, from *Fortune* to *Rolling Stone*, and his advertising clients have included Alitalia, American Airlines, Coca-Cola, AVCO-Lycoming, and Columbia Records.

His work is represented in the Graphics collection of the Metropolitan Museum of Art and was included in the United States State Department exhibition of "Graphic Arts in America" on tour in many cities in Europe including the U.S.S.R.

Hays was born in Sherman, Texas, and grew up in Shreveport, Louisiana. He attended the Kansas City Art Institute, the Ringling School of Art in Sarasota, Florida, and the Art Center School in Los Angeles. He has taught illustration at the School of Visual Arts in New York City and for the last several years has been chairman of the illustration department of the Art Center College of Design in Pasadena, California.

ROBERT HEINDEL (1938-) has always made his pictures with no regard to their purpose as "art" or "illustration." This is the enviable position that he has earned by making each painting the best possible artistic solution to a picture problem, whether it is imposed by a magazine editor, advertiser, or self-assigned.

Born in Tolelo, Ohio, his art education was through a correspondence course with the Famous Artists Schools. Heindel was quickly able to land top accounts with magazines such as *The Saturday Evening Post*, *Fortune*, *Time*, *Sports Illustrated*, *Good Housekeeping*, *Redbook*, *Woman's Day*, and *The Ladies' Home Journal*, and with numerous advertisers. He also illustrated *The Grapes of Wrath* for The Franklin Library.

For the past two decades, Heindel has been inspired by both dance and dancers throughout his work, displaying his mastery in capturing the body in motion or repose. Heindel has accepted invitations to work with the Royal Ballet, the Birmingham Royal Ballet, the American Ballet Theatre, the San Francisco Ballet, the San Francisco Performing Arts Library, Les Ballets de Monte Carlo, the Scottish Ballet, the Maki Asami Ballet, the Matsuyama Ballet, and Noh and Kabuki theatres.

Heindel's work is featured in both public and private collections worldwide, including those of the National Portrait Gallery in London, and the Smithsonian Institution.

Robert Heindel, *Dancer with Red Hair* published as a serigraph for The Obsession with Dance Company.

Mitchell Hooks

The career of MITCHELL HOOKS (1923-), like that of many other artists of the post-World War II era, has been involved to a great extent with paintings for paperback book covers. His interpretations have a strong poster quality, in keeping with the need to hold their own on display with other competing titles on the bookstands, but also have a subtlety and sensitivity that attracts a closer and longer look.

In addition to his book designs for Avon, Bantam, Dell, Popular Library and Fawcett publications, Hooks has illustrated for *Cosmopolitan*, *The Saturday Evening Post*, *The Ladies' Home Journal*, *Redbook*, *McCall's*, *Woman's Day*, and other magazines.

Mitchell was born in Detroit, Michigan, and obtained his art education at the Cass Technical High School there. Later, he studied further with James Billmyer in New York. After the war, and Occupation duty as a Second Lieutenant in Germany, he returned to New York to begin his freelance illustration career.

In recent years, Hooks has become more diversified, dividing his work betweem magazines, movie posters, hardcover books, paperback covers, and advertising. Hardcover books include illustrations for the Franklin Library, Reader's Digest Books, and Coronado Publishers.

In 1999, he was elected to the Society of Illustrators Hall of Fame.

Mitchell Hooks illustration for "The Time of Evensong" by Donald J. Plantz, *The Saturday Evening Post*, August 5, 1961 © 1961, 1999 by the Curtis Publishing Co.

Cover for *The American Weekly*, February 17, 1957. Collection of Daniel Duke.

Gordon Johnson

GORDON A. JOHNSON (1924-1989) was an able all-around professional whose work was characterized by its clarity and directness. His self-confidence was a reflection of his sound tutelage by Dean Cornwell and Frank Reilly at the Art Students League in New York.

Born in Worcester, Massachusetts, he had studied earlier at the Vesper George School of Art. His first professional work was a cover for the *American Magazine* in 1954, and this was soon followed by covers for *Outdoor Life*, *The American Weekly*, *Boys' Life*, a series of maritime calendar paintings for Atlantic Insurance Company, 24-sheet billboard posters, and paperback covers for almost all the major publishers.

Johnson taught at the Paier Art School in Connecticut and his work is included in the permanent collections of the Baseball Hall of Fame, the U. S. Coast Guard Academy, and the U. S. Air Force Academy.

Victor Kalin [signature]

VICTOR KALIN (1919-1991) was so versatile that it is difficult to specify his style. Unlike many artists who develop a strong, easily identifiable technique, he was so interested in experimentation that his work looked continually new. In the competitive field of illustrating for paperback book covers, where the drive is always to look as new as possible, this was an ideal qualification.

Kalin was born in Belleville, Kansas, and was graduated with a B.F.A. From the University of Kansas. He also taught classes there in painting and drawing in 1941-42. During World War II he did artwork for the training manuals, three-dimensional assembly drawings, and also served as a field correspondent for *Yank* magazine.

His first illustrations were done for the **The American Weekly**, but for many years, the majority of his pictures were painted for paperback book covers. Other accounts included assignments for advertising, record album covers, and illustrations for hard cover publishers such as Reader's Digest Books and Holt, Rinehart and Winston.

Here Kalin found yet another variation on the perennial Gothic novel cover theme of the threatened, beautiful young woman at night, sighting a single lighted window in the tower of a deserted mansion.
Once Upon a Tombstone by Elizabeth Salter; published by Ace Publications.

Kossin [signature]

In his powerful series of pictures for *Life* magazine's re-creation of the Bay of Piggs invasion, SANFORD KOSSIN (1926-) strikingly demonstrated the role the illustrator can play in summarizing the total effect of war action in a way that the camera cannot. Each of his pictures highlights a major phase of the tragedy, from the initial landing to final overwhelming defeat.

Kossin, who was born in Los Angeles, studied there for four years at the Jepson Art Institute under Rico Lebrun and Herbert Jepson.

His first work after coming East in 1952 was for science fiction magazines. He also illustrated children's magazines before graduating to *Life*, *Good Housekeeping*, *Parents*, *Redbook*, and other national publications. As many of the magazines began to disappear or cut back on fiction in the 'sixties, Kossin became more involved with paperback art, including covers for Bantam Books, Ballantine, Pocket Books, and Berkley Books.

He has also returned to humor—his first love—in *Boys' Life*, *Reader's Digest*, and other publications, including over a dozen children's books. For ten years (though part time), Kossin has taught drawing at Parsons School of Design in New York City and two years at Pratt Institute in Brooklyn.

Kossin is a life member of the Society of Illustrators; his work has been represented in annual exhibitions there and at New York Art Directors Club shows.

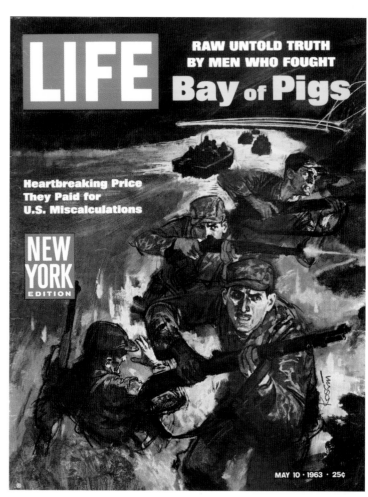

Life cover illustration for magazine article, "Bay of Pigs, We Who Tried," May 10, 1963; © 1963, 1991 Time, Inc.

The Review at Moss Neck, Fredericksburg, Virginia, January 20, 1863. ©1995 Mort Kunstler, Inc.

MORT KÜNSTLER (1931-) has never been swayed by the vagaries of style or technique. His approach is straightforward and painstaking. For him the challenge is in the picture concept and in solving all of the problems of research.

Work with *National Geographic* magazine early in his career taught him the importance of accuracy, and he goes to extreme lengths to verify the authenticity of his reference material. This has been a vital necessity for his many historical recreations and for corporate clients, such as the Rockwell International Corporation, which commissioned him to do a series of paintings on the space shuttle Columbia.

Künstler was born in New York City and attended Brooklyn College and U.C.L.A. before switching to Pratt Institute for the illustration course. His early work was for the men's magazines, and he has also been published in *The Saturday Evening Post*, *Reader's Digest*, and *Newsweek*. Most of his illustration has been involved with advertising, however, and his clients have included such major corporations as General Electric, Exxon, U.S. Steel, American Cyanamid, and Texaco.

Künstler has also been painting for exhibition; Hammer Galleries have given him nine one-man shows. In 1982, a commission from CBS-TV to do a painting for the mini-series, "The Blue and the Gray," initiated his interest in the Civil War. His painting, *The High Water Mark*, was unveiled at the Gettysburg National Military Park Museum in celebration of the 125th anniversary of the battle, and is considered the most accurate painting of the event. Since then, he has been concentrating on Civil War subject matter, and his pictures are included in many collections, among them the U.S. Air Force Museum, the Favell Museum, the U.S. Naval Academy, and the San Mateo County Historical Museum.

In 1986, more than 200 of Künstler's works were published in the book, *The American Spirit—the Paintings of Mort Kunstler*, with text by historian Henry Steele Commager. *Images of the Civil War, The Painting of Mort Künstler*, with text by Pulitzer Prize winning author James McPherson, was published in 1992. *Gettysburg—The Paintings of Mort Künstler*, also with text by James McPherson, was published by Turner Publishing as a companion piece to the epic feature film and mini-series *Gettysburg*. A one-hour television special, entitled *Images of the Civil War—The Paintings of Mort Künstler,* was shown on the A&E network in 1993.

The Life-giving Balancing Act. The artist created an extraordinary series of paintings interpreting *Life* magazine's articles on "The Human Body." Arthur Lidov for *Life* magazine. ©1962, 1990, Time, Inc.

Arthur Lidov

ARTHUR LIDOV (1917-1990) held a B.A. in Sociology from the University of Chicago but was self-taught in art. He also believed that illustration is the only kind of painting worth doing.

This conviction was also his own challenge which he capably met in commissions for a wide variety of magazines, including *Fortune*, *Collier's*, *The Saturday Evening Post*, *Redbook*, *Good Housekeeping*, *American Magazine*, *Cosmopolitan*, *American Mercury*, *The Sign*, *Life*, *Sports Illustrated*, *Field & Stream*, *Parents*, and *True*. Added to these clients were commissions from most of the major drug companies and several medical magazines.

Lidov's paintings have been exhibited at the Museum of Modern Art, the Art Institute of Chicago, the National Gallery, and others, as well as in Art Directors Club exhibits in New York, Chicago, Detroit, Milwaukee, and by the American Institute of Graphic Arts, winning numerous awards.

His work is included in the permanent collections of the University of Chicago, Harvard University, NASA, The Fogg Museum (Cambridge, Mass.) and the National Portrait Gallery in Washington, D.C.

J. McClelland

JOHN McCLELLAND (1919-) was born in Stone Mountain, Georgia, and attended the Alabama Polytechnic Institute, the Grand Central School of Art, and the Art Career School of New York City. He also studied with Jerry Farnsworth.

John is especially successful in painting children and was commissioned to paint a portrait of Mrs. John F. Kennedy with her children for *Good Housekeeping* magazine. He is affiliated with Portraits, Inc., and paints as much for exhibition as for publication. His work has won several first prizes and other awards at shows in New York, Boston, New Haven, Hartford, Atlanta, and at regional exhibits.

McClelland first illustrated for *Collier's* magazine in 1947 and has now worked for most of the national magazines, including *Woman's Day*, *Good Housekeeping*, *McCall's*, *Redbook*, *American Magazine*, *This Week*, *The American Weekly*, and *The Ladies' Home Journal.*

He taught at the Silvermine Guild of Artists in Norwalk, Connecticut, and for the past few years, has created paintings for a series of Limited Edition Collector's Plates and a group of porcelain figurines. He has won awards for the collector plates including the top awards in 1980 and '81 from the National Association of Limited Edition Dealers.

McClelland moved to Savannah, Georgia in 1986 and co-founded the Landings Art Association there. He continued to show in regional exhibits and has won several awards. He conducts occasional workshops and is currently represented by the Tucker Gallery in Savannah.

Susan, Howard Paper Mills, Inc., *Printer's Ink*.

350

In McCarthy's pictures, the setting plays as important a role as the action presented within it, and it is painted with equal fidelity.
Where the Ancient Ones Had Hunted, © Frank McCarthy.

FRANK C. McCARTHTY (1924-) is a master technician and strong colorist whose pictures are always exciting to look at. He is a New Yorker who studied at Pratt Institute and at the Art Students League under George Bridgman and Reginald Marsh. He developed his talent early and was in his mid-twenties when he began to obtain illustrating commissions from *American Magazine* and *Collier's*. These were soon followed by *Redbook*, *Argosy*, *True*, *Outdoor Life*, and others, as well as a great many paperback cover assignments for Bantam Books, Signet, Dell, Avon, and Popular Library. In addition, he has done illustration for Ballantine Beer, Goodyear, Warner Brothers, Columbia Pictures, United Artists, Twentieth-Century Fox, and other advertisers.

In 1972, after twenty-seven years as an illustrator in the East, his transition to painting historical westerns for galleries was completed and in 1974, McCarthy moved to Arizona. He was invited to join the Cowboy Artists of America in 1975, showing his work with such great illustrators as John Clymer, Bob Lougheed and Tom Lovell. He has won Certificates of Award by the Printing Industries of America for his limited edition prints published by Greenwich Workshop. Fine books have been published on his work, including the *Western Paintings of Frank C. McCarthy* in 1974, *Frank C. McCarthy, the Old West* in 1981, and *The Art of Frank C. McCarthy* in 1992.

Four retrospective shows of his paintings have been held: in the Museum of the Southwest of Midland, Texas; the R. W. Norton Art Gallery in Shreveport, Louisiana; The Thomas Gilcrease Museum in Tulsa, Oklahoma; and the Cowboy Artists of America Museum in Kerrville, Texas.

McCarthy was elected into the Society of Illustrators Hall of Fame in 1997.

War Party of the Beartooth, © Frank McCarthy. Photograph courtesy of Big Horn Gallery.

Poster illustration for Marlboro Grand Prix Racing, 1975.

In his work, JERRY W. McDANIEL (1935-) emphasizes the use of line, shape and texture as a foundation to create visual excitement. This approach has won him over 300 hundred citations and awards from the New York Art Directors Club, *Graphis* annuals, AIGA, the One Show, and the New York Society of Illustrators. His "Harlow Poster" (published in the previous edition of this book) is in the poster collection of the Metropolitan Museum of Art.

McDaniel was born on a farm in Vinton County, Ohio. He studied at The Columbus College of Art and Design, the New School, the Fashion Institute of Technology/SUNY, the School of Visual Arts, and the New York Institute of Technology.

In 1957, his first illustrations appeared in *Redbook* magazine and later *Good Housekeeping*, *Reader's Digest*, *Parents*, *The Ladies' Home Journal*, *Seventeen*, *Business Week*, and others. In 1962, he landed the Pan Am account and illustrated 52 consecutive weeks of full page advertisements in the *New York Times*. In 1965, he designed and illustrated the complete Zane Gray Western series for Simon and Schuster, and the S.S. Van Dine "Philo Vance" murder mysteries for Scribner's. Since 1970, McDaniel has illustrated Marlboro Sports promotions for Phillip Morris International.

He has been an active member of the Society of Illustrators, and is a founding member of the Graphic Artist Guild.

In 1995, McDaniel was elected chairman of the Advertising, Packaging, and Graphic Design Department at the Fashion Institute of Technology/SUNY. In 1996, he received the Distinguished Service Award from the International Broadcast Design Association for his contribution to art education.

FRANK MULLINS (1924-1978) used an impressionist's brush and color with very carefully controlled values to paint highly effective illustrations. In this advertising illustration for General Electric Automation Systems he realizes the drama of the operation in strong contrasts of reds, oranges, and yellows to heighten the action.

He varied his color to suit the mood, from boxing or golfing assignments for *Sports Illustrated* to fiction settings for The *Saturday Evening Post* or *Redbook*. His range of subjects was also diverse; he illustrated for *American Heritage*, *The Book of Knowledge*, J.P. Lippincott Co., and a series of several paintings and drawings reporting on oceanography as experienced aboard the "Chain" out of the Woods Hole Oceanographic Institute for Chemical and Engineering News.

Frank was also an active member of the Society of Illustrators in New York and exhibited in their annual shows.

Advertising illustration for General Electric Automation Systems

McGinnis' poster painting for ***Cotton Comes to Harlem*** is already a classic icon and was reproduced on the cover of a book, ***What It Is ...What It Was!***
...The Black Film Explosion of the '70s in Words and Pictures by Gerald Martinez, Diana Martinez and Andres Chavez (Miramax Books, 1998).

ROBERT E. McGINNIS (1926-) was born in Cincinnati, Ohio, and he studied both at Ohio State University, where he was a varsity football player, and the Central Academy of Commercial Art in Cincinnati. He is a fine draftsman and painter, particularly of women—Good or Bad—for paperback book covers. His females, while elegant and high-class, have a definite "come hither" attitude. This approach has kept McGinnis one of the busiest and most prolific painters for cover designs, totalling over 1,000, and he has worked for virtually every paperback publisher. In addition, he has illustrated for ***The Ladies' Home Journal***, ***The Saturday Evening Post***, ***True***, ***Woman's Home Companion***, ***Good Housekeeping***, ***Guideposts***, ***Argosy***, and other magazines. He also did the titles for the Hollywood movie, ***Hallelujah Trail*** and has designed posters for four James Bond movies, Jane Fonda's ***Barbarella***, Burt Reynolds's ***'Gator***, and others. His painting of John Wayne for ***The Searchers*** was made into a limited edition print by the Greenwich Workshop and was awarded a Silver Medal by the Society of Illustrators. For the past several years, McGinnis has been exhibiting Western paintings and nudes through the Husberg Gallery in Sedona, Arizona.

Where the Tracks Ran Out, A recent example of McGinnis' western paintings, shown at the Husberg Fine Arts Gallery.

FRED OTNES (1925-) is a native of Junction City, Kansas; he was educated at the American Academy and the Art Institute of Chicago.

His early illustrations, which were distinguished by expert draftsmanship, appeared in a wide variety of magazines, including *Town and Country*, *True*, *The Saturday Evening Post*, *Fortune*, *Redbook*, and the *Reader's Digest.* Subsequently, Otnes evolved a new approach to picture-making, incorporating collage, assemblage and printing techniques with his images. Gradually, these have taken over — he now works as much with the photostat camera, the engraver's vacuum frame, and a photo enlarger as with brush or paint.

The results are striking, provocative, and can be extremely complex, requiring the viewer to spend more time to read the picture message. This has made Otnes a particular favorite for advertisers, and among his clients have been General Motors, Exxon, Chevrolet, Ford, Chrysler, Dobbs Hats, Italian Lines, and the Tennessee Gas Transmission Company.

His work has also been exhibited extensively and has won well over 150 awards in Chicago, New York, Detroit, Cleveland and Minneapolis Art Directors' Club shows. He has been an exhibitor in many museums as well, including the Butler Institute of American Art, the Kansas City Art Institute, the University of California, and institutions in Korea, Japan, and Hawaii. He is a member of the Society of Illustrators and received their prestigious Hamilton King Award in 1974.

Fred Otnes, *314 and W,* 1997. Collage on board.

BARYÉ WINCHELL PHILLIPS (unknown -1968 or '69) habitually signed his work with just his first name, with an accent on the "e". He was known in the trade for his speed; he often had overnight deadlines and could regularly turn out four covers a week. He soon won the title "King of the Paperbacks" from his colleagues. As described by one of his art editors, Al Allard at Fawcett Publications, "He was good; he was fast; he had imagination; he always met deadlines. He also had the rare gift of being able to change his style." During his career, Phillips worked for almost all the paperback publishers, including Avon, Bantam, Dell, Signet, Pocket Books, Fawcett Gold Medal Books and several hard cover publishers.

Phillips worked as an illustrator of training manuals during World War II, and following a brief stint with the advertising department at Columbia Pictures after the end of the war, gravitated to painting paperback covers. He was an expert photographer, able to pose and shoot his own reference photos which contributed to his fast pace. Phillips took time out during the Korean War to serve as an artist-correspondent for the Army in Southwest Asia. Phillips subsequently served two terms in 1966 and 1967 as president of New York's Society of Illustrators.

Cover for *Take a Murder*, *Darling* from the Shell Scott series, Gold Medal Books.

One of a series of illustrations for Coca-Cola.
Courtesy of the Coca-Cola company, copyright owner.

Potter

JACK POTTER (1927-) prefers black-and-white to color, and his favorite line is black wax crayon or charcoal. He also insists that his drawing be only from life — that drawing from photographs is criminal! Although this point of view no longer has many protagonists, there is no question that Potter is an excellent draftsman who does not need to work from photographs and that his drawings are all the better for it. Certainly he has had a strong influence on the field of illustration, both as a practitioner and as a teacher. He taught for three years at the Art Center School in Los Angeles and later at the School of Visual Arts in New York.

Potter is a Californian. He studied in Los Angeles at the Art Center School and at the Jepson School under Rico Lebrun. He also feels a kinship with Vuillard, Toulouse-Lautrec, and the Post Impressionists.

His work has appeared in national magazines such as ***Cosmopolitan***, ***McCall's***, ***The Ladies' Home Journal***, ***Woman's Home Companion***, and for many national advertisers, including Coca-Cola, Northeast Airlines, and L.S. Ayres & Company.

powers

There was nothing orthodox about the work of RICHARD M. POWERS (1921-1996) whether for publication or for exhibition. He cut through directly to the picture-idea using as sparing a means as possible; he varied his approach to fit his subject.

As an illustrator, Powers did a number of children's books, cover designs for many of the classics of poetry and literature for Dell Publications, and a series on ***Major Cultures of the World*** for the World Publishing company. He also illustrated for ***Esquire***, ***The Saturday Evening Post***, ***Redbook***, ***Life***, and ***Natural History*** magazines.

In addition to 'straight' illustration, Powers executed some 400 science fiction/fantasy paintings over three decades and this is where his fame and ingenuity rests. In 1983, he was given the Frank R. Paul Award. Simultaneously, Doubleday produced a portfolio of sixteen of his surrealist paintings titled ***Space Time Warp***.

He was associated with the Rehn Gallery in New York and had twenty-four one-man shows. He was included in a New Talent exhibition at The Museum of Modern Art in 1952 and also exhibited at the Metropolitan Museum of Art, the Corcoran Gallery in Washington, D.C., the National Academy of Design ,and the Whitney Museum.

Powers was born in Chicago and studied at Loyola University, the Chicago Art Institute, and the University of Illinois. Later, he worked with Julian Levi at the New School for Social Research in New York, and studied with Jay Connaway in Maine and Vermont.

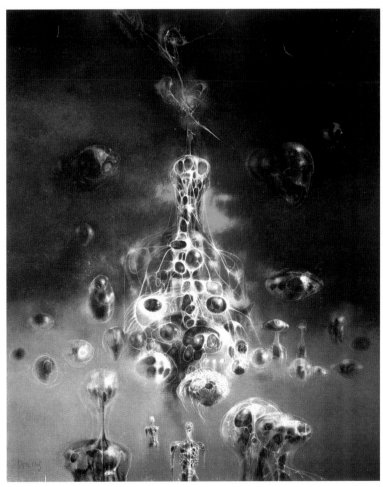

Gof-fFlar, Quasarquark of fFlar. From the ***Space Time Warp*** portfolio, ©1983 by Richard M. Powers.

355

Mother Teresa, cover illustration for **Time** magazine.

One of several versions of a movie poster for *Star Trek IV — The Search for Spock* ca. 1984 (this version was not published).

The paintings and drawing of ROBERT PEAK (1928-1992) look deceptively simple. To those who followed his work, it was apparent that the process of simplification gradually evolved over a period of years as a result of his deliberate effort to subordinate details to ideas. This emphasis on idea required a lot of preliminary thought and experimentation, but once determined, the actual rendering may have required only a few hours. Peak kept his outlook fresh by rejecting conventional solutions, always looking for new aspects of a subject, and preferred to work from life whenever possible.

Peak was born in Colorado and brought up in Kansas. Although he liked to draw, he first studied geology at the University of Wichita. With time out for Army service and his interest in art revived, he followed this up with two and a half years at the Art Center School in Los Angeles.

Moving East to become an illustrator, he found the first few years very difficult; it was after he stopped looking at the work of other illustrators and concentrated his efforts on developing his own point of view, that he began to attract the attention of the major publishers and advertisers.

His work regularly appeared in magazines such as **The Ladies' Home Journal**, **McCall's**, **Good Housekeeping**, **Parents**, **TV Guide**, and **Esquire;** he designed more than forty **Time** covers. Advertising accounts included French Lines, Columbia Records, Samsonite Luggage, Puritan Sportswear, 7-Up, and he executed paintings for more than 100 motion picture posters, including **Camelot**, **Apocalypse Now**, **My Fair Lady**, **Superman**, and **Star Trek.** Peak also completed designs for the U. S. Postal Service for a series of thirty postage stamps on sports themes for the Olympic Games.

Peak's work was shown regularly in Art Directors Club and Society of Illustrators exhibitions where he won many awards, including eight Gold Medals. He was named "Artist of the Year" by the Artists Guild of New York in 1961 and was elected into the Society of Illustrators Hall of Fame in 1977.

His untimely death cut short a new phase of his career in which he was exploring themes of the historical West.

For the 1984 Olympics, Peak was commissioned to do the entire series of 28 individual stamps by the U. S. Postal Service. © USPS 1983/1984.

TWA commissioned a series of mural paintings for the interior decor in their 747 jetliners in 1972.

Poster for the film *Camelot* reprinted courtesy of Warner Brothers, Seven Arts, and Bill Gold Advertising, Inc. Also reproduced in the **Society of Illustrators Twenty Year Award Winners** 1981, for a Gold Medal Award.

Anthony Saris, *Ma Rainey*, illustration for "History of Jazz/Part III," published by ***Show Business*** magazine, 1961.

Saris

ANTHONY SARIS (1923-) researches his pictorial subjects thoroughly before planning any layouts or compositions, preferring to keep completely receptive to any new ideas suggested in the course of his inquiry. Similarly, he does not make preliminary drawings, but having worked out the problems in his mind, makes his finished renderings while there is still a creative challenge to be met, rather than to redo an approved sketch. This method produces some occasional failures which must be redone, but Saris works rapidly — usually in pen and ink with tone or color added — so that the time factor is not unduly important. He spends much more time in research and planning than in the rendering itself.

Saris was born in Joliet, Illinois, but moved to New York City while a boy, and attended Pratt Institute, the Brooklyn Museum Art School, and the New School for Social Research. He himself taught at Pratt Institute beginning in 1956 and retired as adjunct professor in 1994.

He has illustrated for most of the major publications and many national advertisers including pharmaceuticals, and his work has won numerous awards in exhibitions for New York and Washington Art Directors Club shows, the Society of Illustrators, the Outdoor Advertising Show, and the American Institute of Graphic Arts.

Harvey Schmidt

Fresh from the University of Texas with a personal and unusual portfolio, HARVEY SCHMIDT (1929-) landed his first art job in New York for the graphics design department of NBC Television. There he had the opportunity to design and execute the title illustrations for national network shows, learning to eliminate superfluous details that would interfere with communicating his ideas. This directness characterizes all his work for freelance magazine and advertising assignments.

Schmidt was born in Dallas and spent his boyhood between drawing and teaching himself to play the piano by ear. At the University of Texas he continued to follow both art and music, and wrote a musical in collaboration with lyricist Tom Jones while still in school. In New York, the two again successfully collaborated on ***The Fantasticks***, the world's longest running musical, now in its fourth decade at the same Greenwich Village theatre where it opened in 1960.

His first Broadway musical score was for the David Merrick hit, ***110 in the Shade***; which was followed by another Merrick success ***I Do! I Do!*** directed by Gower Champion and starring Mary Martin and Robert Preston. Other film scores include a short art film with Tom Jones called ***A Texas Romance 1909***, for which he composed the music in addition to doing a section of paintings along with Robert Weaver, Elaine Morfogen and Robert Benton.

Although this division of talents tends to limit his output in art, he has continued to do picture reportorial assignments for clients such as ***Fortune*** magazine, Abbott Laboratories' ***What's New***, ***Sports Illustrated***, ***The Lamp*** — a Standard Oil of New Jersey publication, ***Esquire***, ***Life***, ***Harper's Bazaar***, and others, winning numerous top awards and medals from the Society of Illustrators' and Art Directors Clubs' annual exhibitions.

Harvey Schmidt, *The World's Largest Mobile Lane Machine,* illustration for "The Dynamic Force of the Energy Industries." ***Fortune*** magazine, October, 1962.

DANIEL BENNETT SCHWARTZ N.A. (1929-) was raised in New York City. After the High School of Music & Art, he attended the Art Students League, studying painting with Yasuo Kuniyoshi. From there, he studied at the Rhode Island School of Design, where he received his Bachelor of Fine Arts degree in 1949. He has had thirteen one-man shows and exhibited in group shows both here and abroad. He numbers among his awards two Louis Comfort Tiffany grants in painting and the 1992 Benjamin Altman Figure Painting Prize at the National Academy. In 1997, he was elected to membership in the National Academy. He has conducted a private class in painting and drawing for more than thirty years. He has also taught at Syracuse University, Parsons School of Design, and the School of Visual Art.

Believing that illustration can be an extension of an artist's serious preoccupations, Schwartz brought his painter's skills to the editorial pages of *Fortune*, *Sports Illustrated*, *Life*, *McCall's*, and *Esquire.* His subjects were diverse, from portraits of professional athletes and the personalities of the Paris "New Wave" in the fifties, to the emerging teen culture of the sixties, and in the seventies, to industrial America and reportage in

Illustration for "Centennial," ©1975 Meredith Corporation; all rights reserved. Used with permission of *The Ladies' Home Journal.*

Southeast Asia. He created the art for the 1981 Academy Award-winning documentary film, *Genocide*, and in the early eighties, designed a series of graphic posters for Mobil Masterpiece Theater. Over the years, he has been awarded eleven Society of Illustrators' Gold Medals, and honors, including the Hamilton King Award in 1978. He continues to paint, exhibit, and teach.

ARTHUR SHILSTONE, (1922-) is a native of New Jersey and received his art training at Pratt Institute in Brooklyn, New York. His first illustration commissions were magazine stories and articles, but slanted to sporting subjects. His many clients have included *Life*, *Sports Illustrated*, *The National Geographic*, *Smithsonian*, *Sports Afield*, *Gray's Sporting Journal*, and *Field & Stream*.

During this time, he also provided illustrations for corporate annual reports, including such clients as Exxon, U.S. Steel, AT&T, and NASA. The latter project included on-site reportage of launchings and landings of the space shuttle program. With the decline of magazines as a market, Shilstone turned to his primary interest, hunting and fishing subjects. He found a ready market for them in art galleries and now devotes himself entirely to outdoor subjects. He prefers the spontaneity of the watercolor medium and is an exhibiting member of the American Watercolor Society.

Illustration for "The Odessa File," Reader's Digest Association.

Robert Shore

ROBERT SHORE (1924-   ) has a painter's interest in texture, color and abstract design. His subjects are presented strongly, with a minimum of detail and have great impact on the printed page.

Born in New York City, Shore studied at the Cranbrook Academy of Art in Detroit, Michigan, and at the Art Students League in New York. He was awarded a Fulbright Fellowship in painting in 1952. His work has been exhibited at the Detroit Institute of Fine Arts, the Smithsonian Institution, the National Gallery, the National Academy, and at Cornell University.

Shore has illustrated for a long list of magazines, including *Seventeen*, *Redbook*, *Pageant*, *The Reporter*, *Park East*, *Esquire*, *Show Business*, and *Woman's Day*; for book publishers such as Macmillan Company, and Rinehart & Company; and for advertisers E.R. Squibb & Sons, and NBC.

Shore was awarded a Gold Medal at the Society of Illustrators in 1967. He has also been an instructor at the Henry Street Settlement, the Cooper Union, and at the School of Visual Arts in New York City.

Illustration for "A Vacationer's Guide to Country Fairs" by Mitchell Goodman, *Redbook* magazine, August, 1961.

STEINBERG

SAUL STEINBERG (1914-1999) was in a rarefied class of one. His work was more in the tradition of doodling than from any academic norm. He also set himself apart by his unorthodox thought processes and provided his viewers with a fascinating progression of variations on chosen themes. One of his preoccupations was the official document, such as a passport or a proclamation. He could produce a most plausible looking facsimile of such, complete with scrolls, seals and rubber stamps, but in an invented undecipherable language of his own.

Steinberg was born in Romania and obtained an architectural degree in Italy. With the beginning of World War II, he left Italy for Portugal (with his self-doctored passport) to escape certain internment as a foreign Jew. He eventually arrived in the U.S. in 1942.

He found a perfect milieu in *The New Yorker* covers, but he also painted cover designs and illustrations for *Vogue*, *Fortune*, *Look*, and *Town and Country*. He was the author of many books including *All In Line*, *The Art of Living*, and *The Labyrinth*. His pictures fell in a netherworld between illustration, cartoon, and fine art, but he exhibited internationally and is represented in many museum collections, including the Museum of Modern Art, The Metropolitan Museum, and the Whitney Museum of American Art, which gave him a retrospective exhibit in 1978.

In a pictorial commentary, "Our False-Front Culture," Steinberg depicts an Unidentified Flying Object as a cultural package traveling from one center to another. *Look Magazine*, January 9, 1968.

The career of SHANNON STIRNWEIS (1931-   ) has encompassed the whole range of the field from his beginnings as an advertising agency sketch artist to serving as President of the Society of Illustrators and as a Founding Trustee of the Graphic Artists Guild.

He was born in Portland, Oregon, and attended the University of Oregon for a year before studying at the Art Center School in Los Angeles under Reynold Brown, John LaGatta, Joseph Henninger, and Pruett Carter. After graduation in 1954, he served as an illustrator with the U.S. Army in Europe. Upon his return, he settled in New York to become a freelance illustrator following a four-year stint as an agency sketchman.

His first illustrations were done for *Sportsman's Magazine* in 1959, followed by work for *Field & Stream*, *Reader's Digest*, *Mechanix Illustrated*, *Money*, *Outdoor Life*, *Boys' Life*, and *Popular Mechanics*, as well as a long list of advertising clients, movie posters, and paperback covers for virtually all the publishers in New York.

Stirnweiss has also participated in several special assignments for various U. S. Government agencies, involving trips to the Berlin Wall, the Everglades, Alaska, and Arizona. More recently, he has been painting historical pictures of the Old West and exhibits in several galleries. His work is represented in many private and public collections, including the U.S. Air Force, the U.S. Army Historical Museum, the Department of the Interior, and Federal Savings Collections in California.

Shannon Stirnweiss, Vanishing Trail.

HERBERT TAUSS (1920-) Born in New York City, Tauss attended the High School of Industrial Art, and upon graduating, secured an apprenticeship at the Traeger Phillips Studio. His first illustrations were made in 1949 for *Pageant* magazine, following by work for other publications which included *American Weekly*, *Argosy*, *The Saturday Evening Post*, *Redbook*, *National Geographic*, *Parents*, and *McCall's* magazines.

He joined the Charles E. Cooper Studio in 1955 and when the illustration markets began to constrict in the early 1960s, he moved to England to work for the British market. He returned to the U.S. In the early 1970s and became prolific in the paperback market when, among other things, he illustrated an important series of historical novels, the *Kent Family Chronicles*, which sold over 40 million copies. He also illustrated several limited edition books for The Franklin Library. Tauss has taught at the School of Visual Arts, Pratt Institute, Marymount College in Tarrytown, New York, and is currently an adjunct professor of illustration at the Fashion Institute of Technology in New York City.

The Man who Stopped the Square Dance, *McCall's* magazine.

Inducted into the Illustrators Hall of Fame in 1996, Tauss has great drafting skills, versatility in a broad range of subjects and mediums, and an excellent sense of pictorial composition.

361

Council Of Chiefs, 1979. This is a typical example of Terpning's work as an observer and recorder of Native American life.

The range of Terpning's skills as an artist is vividly demonstrated by this earlier magazine story illustration of a contemporary bar scene, showing him to be equally at home with a sophisticated urban society

HOWARD A. TERPNING (1927-   ) was born in Oak Park, Illinois, and studied in Chicago at the American Academy of Art and the Chicago Academy of Fine Arts. After service in the Marines in World War II, he went to New York to do advertising, editorial and motion picture illustration. Among others, he designed posters for the films **The Guns of Navarone**, **Dr. Zhivago**, **Cleopatra**, and **The Sound of Music.**

His magazine clients have included **McCall's**, **Good Housekeeping**, **Reader's Digest**, **The Ladies' Home Journal**, **Field & Stream**, **Redbook**, **True**, and **Cosmopolitan**. Advertising clients have included Gold Label Cigars, BOAC, TWA, the Hat Corporation of America, and Pendleton Woolen Mills.

In 1977, Terpening moved to Arizona and became a member of the Cowboy Artists of America in 1979. He has won top awards in their annual exhibitions since, as well as two Prix de West Awards from the National Academy of Western Art. He had a one-man show at the Gilcrease Museum in 1985. In 1990, he won the Hubbard Art Award for Excellence. His work has also been exhibited in Beijing, China, and at the Grand Palais in Paris. His book, entitled **The Art of Howard Terpning**, published by Greenwich Workshop in 1992, is in its second printing.

Here, Weaver painted a portrait of Presidential candidate, Jack Kennedy, illustrating his emergence from the background of local politics to the rotunda of national statesmanship. "Kennedy's Last Chance to be President", by Richard H. Rovere, April, 1959. By permission of *Esquire* magazine, ©1959 Hearst Communications, Inc. Esquire is a trademark of Hearst Magazines Property, Inc. All Rights Reserved.

The Crane Company Under Repair. ***Fortune*** magazine, March, 1957. One of his earliest reportorial assignments Weaver emphasized shape and movement in his composition.

R Weaver

ROBERT WEAVER (1924-1994) had a strong conviction that the role of the illustrator should be a decidedly active one. He believed that the artist should make his contribution at the thinking stage as well as in painting the picture itself, whether for an advertising client or an editorial assignment. He helped to create a climate for this point of view by the many creative pictures he painted under this obligation to himself for *Fortune*, *Life*, *Look*, *Sports Illustrated*, *Cosmopolitan*, *McCall's*, *True*, *Seventeen*, *Town and Country*, *Playboy*, *New York Magazine*, and *Esquire*.

Born in Pittsburgh, he studied at the Carnegie Institute of Technology, the Art Students League in New York, and the Accademia delle Belle Arti in Venice.

Weaver exhibited at the D'Arcy Galleries, the American Institute of Graphic Arts, the Society of Illustrators, and at Art Directors Clubs in New York, Washington, and other cities. The Society of Illustrators elected him into their Hall of Fame in 1985, and he had many additional honors, including a retrospective show in 1977 at the School of Visual Arts Museum.

Weaver taught at the School of Visual Arts in New York for more than thirty-five years and was a visiting faculty member at Syracuse University.

Poster for the School of Visual Arts. Art Director: Silas H. Rhodes, Designer: William J. Kobasz, Illustrator: Robert Weaver, Copywriter: Dee Ito.

363

Ed Vebell, illustration for "The Exploit of Sam Magill," published in condensed form by **Reader's Digest**, March 1957, from book **Never a Shot in Anger** © 1956, 1984 by Duell, Sloan & Pearce, Inc.

EDWARD VEBELL (1921-) brings the same intensity to his art work as to his other major interest: fencing. He represented the United States on two Olympic fencing teams, on one World Championship team, and was ranked as one of the top epée men in the country.

Vebell is one of the top illustrators, too, a pro who can take on a difficult assignment, on virtually any subject, and do it quickly and competently. An expert photographer, he directs and takes his own reference pictures and has a large collection of costumes and props, such as guns, swords, and helmets. Because of his background, he does many illustrations of war and military subjects, as well as sports.

Vebell grew up in Chicago and attended art schools there. After a short time in his first art studio job, he was inducted into the Army. Vebell spent the war years on the staff of **Stars and Stripes** in Europe, served as illustrator-reporter in France and Italy, covering the taking of Monte Cassino. Following the war, he spent an additional two years in Paris as a freelance illustrator for French publications.

In 1947, he returned to the United States and to freelancing for American publications, which have included many of the major magazines such as **Life**, **Reader's Digest**, **Field & Stream**, and **Sports Illustrated.**

In recent years, he has become increasingly immersed in historical art and is a founding member of the Society of Historical Artists.

Vebell has designed fifteen stamps for the U.S. Postal Service and has also been active in the related field of First Day Covers.

William Whittingham, illustration for "The Glendale People" by John O'Hara, **The Saturday Evening Post**, March 2, 1963. ©1963, 1991, Curtis Publishing Company.

WILLIAM H. WHITTINGHAM (1932-) is typical of today's illustrator, approaching his picture-making from a painter's viewpoint and exploiting the latest pictorial trends in either field.

He was born in Detroit and studied at the University of Michigan as well as with Reuben Tam at the Brooklyn Museum. His work won a first prize at the New York City Center and has also been exhibited at the Society of Illustrators.

Whittingham has had his illustrations reproduced in many women's magazines in England as well as in **The Saturday Evening Post**, **Ski** magazine, **TV Guide**, **Parents** magazine, and by Bantam Books in this country.

Fritz Willis

FRITZ WILLIS (unknown - 1979) attended the Vesper George Art School and gravitated to the film industry in California. As a handsome young man, he landed some small roles as an actor, including a part in *Alice Adams* with Katherine Hepburn. Art was his prime interest, however, and he found work at Warner Brothers Studio in publicity and in making compositional set designs. He worked alongside another ambitious young artist, Joe DeMers, and they began to collaborate, often doing parts of the same drawing. They continued the practice after *Esquire* asked them to create a series of pin-ups for a new "Esquire Gallery" series to which both signed their names. The pin-ups were a great popular success, but eventually the two went their separate ways.

Willis went on to illustrate for *Collier's*, *Redbook*, *The Saturday Evening Post*, and for many advertisers, such as Pepsi Cola, Springmaid Cotton Mills, Gilbert Quality Papers, Max Factor, Crown Zellerbach, Rose Marie Reid, and the Ice Follies program covers. He did a fifteen-year series of calendars for Brown & Bigelow, including an "Artist's Sketchbook" pin-up series. Among his books were art instruction titles for Walter Foster publishers, such as *Art Shortcuts*, *Secrets to Still-life Painting*, and *Faces and Features*. He also wrote and illustrated a children's book, *Me, Too*.

Artist's Sketch Book calendar subject, July, 1963. Reprinted by permission of and © 1963 by Brown & Bigelow, St. Paul, Minnesota.

Ben Wohlberg, from *Illustrators 15*, published by Joseph T. Mendola, Ltd.

Ben D. Wohlberg

BEN WOHLBERG (1927-) had an early interest in architecture, which he studied for a year at Kansas State College. Classes in drawing stimulated him to shift his interest to art, and he transferred to the Chicago Academy of Fine Art and then on to the Art Center School in Los Angeles.

Wohlberg's paintings are large in scale, marked by bold color and strong composition, yet with subtle value changes and sensitivity of form. The majority of his work has been for *Redbook*, for which he did his first illustrations in 1960, but he has also painted for *Good Housekeeping*, *The Ladies' Home Journal*, *Woman's Day*, *McCall's*, and *Guideposts*. He has also painted paperback covers for Dell, Ballantine, Pinnacle, Fawcett, Popular, Tower, and New American Library, as well as hard cover book illustrations for Reader's Digest and The Franklin Library.

He exhibits with the American Watercolor Society and the annual shows of the Society of Illustrators, from which he won the Award of Excellence in 1962.

Portraiture was a natural transition from illustrating in 1987. He also does abstract painting, showing in galleries in New York and Block Island, where he lives and works.

365

1970–1980

Raymond Ameijide
John Berkey
William Charmatz
Alan E. Cober
John Collier
Clifford Ara Condak
Jeffrey W. Cornell
Robert Crofut
Robert M. Cunningham
Ken Dallison
Jack Davis
Paul Davis
Diane Dillon
Leo Dillon
Mark English
Randall Enos
Bart Forbes
Frank Frazetta
Gerry Gersten
Paul Giovanopoulos
Alex Gnidziejko
Edward Gorey
David Grove
H. Tom Hall
Roger Hane
Richard Hess
Brad Holland
Stanley R. Hunter
Doug Johnson
David McCall Johnston
Jeffrey Jones
David Levine

Malcolm Liepke
Victor Livoti
Robert Maguire
Allan Mardon
Mara McAfee
Gerald McConnell
Wilson McLean
Wendell Minor
James McMullan
Patrick Nagel
Robert Andrew Parker
David J. Passalacqua
Jerry Pinkney
Don Ivan Punchatz
Charles Santore
Isadore Seltzer
Maurice Sendak
Thomas Sgouros
Jim Sharpe
Burt Silverman
Hodges Soileau
James J. Spanfeller
Richard Sparks
Walt Spitzmiller
Benjamin F. Stahl
Gilbert L. Stone
Ross Barron Storey
Murray Tinkelman
Jack Neal Unruh
Don Weller
Robert M. Ziering
Stanley Zuckerberg

Brad Holland, op-ed illustration *The New York Times*

Space Trek by John Berkey

Sorcerer, *Eerie* magazine, © Frank Frazetta

THE DECADE 1970-1980

The 1970s were a period in which the magazine audiences fragmented, or dried up, the great art directors retired, and the profession became largely anonymous. In this difficult time, illustrators had to find new clients, breaking away from their traditional bases of periodicals.

The Space Program had attracted many artists like Robert McCall, Paul Calle and others who documented the successive launches from Cape Kennedy, as well as those who imagined a future of intergalactic exploration, like Chesley Bonestell and John Berkey. These talents were also employed in the production of movies such as *Star Wars* and *2001*, in conceptualizing the space ships and plotting the flow of the action.

A parallel field, with its genesis in the novels of pulp writers evolved into the "Sword and Sorcery" paperback books with artwork to illustrate them by Frank Frazetta, Jeff Jones, and many other artists. Comic books had evolved from the staid Superman drawings to expert draftsmanship and imaginative compositions. They furnished a market for artists who could draw heavily-muscled and otherwise-endowed figures in violent action and foreshortened perspectives. Underground comics exerted an unexpected influence on posters, animation, and fringe publications.

Op-Ed pages of the newspapers, like *The New York Times* encouraged creative interpretations for editorials, and artists like Brad Holland, Edward Gorey, and Marshall Arisman made it a highly visible niche for themselves.

The specialty magazines, which were replacing the old national publications, continued to proliferate until the total magazine market became even larger than it had ever been. The main difference was the now much lower visibility to the artists, whose work would be seen only by the readers of that magazine or book, with an audience of thousands rather than millions. The magazines no longer provided the same kind of national showcase that had made Norman Rockwell, J. C. Leyendecker, or Charles Dana Gibson so famous.

Some artists created their own audience and were more likely to be known through their "prints." This became a big market for illustrators who sought out collectors of specialized subjects such as westerns, wild life, sports, or the Civil War. Through printers and distributors like The Greenwich Workshop and Mill Pond Press, large reproductions were produced by offset lithography and sold in signed and limited editions.

Courtrooms had long provided employment for artists who could sketch the proceedings rapidly and accurately, since television and cameras were barred from most trials. For famous trials, networks increasingly featured the drawings of the artists who captured the drama. Obversely, TV also created work for illustrators willing to do story boards for shooting scripts used for filing of commercials.

Meanwhile, the paperbacks continued to be a major market for cover art. *Sports Illustrated* was still using the talents of many artists; *TV Guide* covers featured portraits of star performers by artists such as Richard Amsel, Robert Peak, Bernie Fuchs and Mark English. *The Reader's Digest* commissioned art for its covers and for many interior stories and articles as well as their condensed books.

The illustration field rarely looks backward, but the 1970s were a time of rediscovery of roots, in many ways. Artists were raiding the libraries and borrowing styles and motifs from their Golden Age heroes. Also, it was the time that several museums were establishing collections, or were dusting off their Howard Pyles, as old originals were seen to have new value.

For a profession that had seemed to have no future, this decade required established illustrators to readjust; some found self-renewal or rediscovery, others were blazing new trails that would open up in the following decade.

 RAYMOND AMEIJIDE
(1924-2000) was appro-
priately described as a "rainbow snipper." Certainly he used all
the colors of the rainbow in the felt cloth or paper he employed as
his medium. All the shapes had to be carefully designed, cut out
and assembled to make his bas-relief constructions. For felt
sculptures each piece was glued to a stiff paper to give it the
required rigidity and ability to be shaped. Then, either paper or
felt was bent or curved to suggest the various forms in the
assemblage. Behind each sculpture is an intricate glued
framework that holds each piece in precisely the correct position.
Ameijide's designs were carefully planned to convey the idea like
a telegram, in a happy marriage of medium and message.

He was born in Newark, New Jersey; the family name comes
from northern Spain in Galicia. He graduated with a B.F.A. from
Pratt Institute. His first employment was in the Ross Art Studio in
1949. As a freelancer, he illustrated for clients such as *Fortune*,
Vista, *Discover*, *Money*, *National Geographic*, Harcourt Brace,
Ginn and Company, Exxon, IBM, RCA, and Pfizer.

Ameijide won many awards for his work as exhibited at the
New York Art Directors Club and the Society of Illustrators. He
also won the Hamilton King Award from the Society in 1970.

Raymond Ameijide, felt sculpture for ABC-TV.

 Produced in his studio in a small
town in Minnesota, the art of JOHN
BERKEY (1932-) looks more as
though it might come off the drawing board of a team of NASA
engineers a hundred years hence. And it seems likely that some of
the spacecraft in the future will look the way he depicts them. No
matter how much mechanical detail Berkey introduces in his
futuristic vehicles, he is less interested in the nuts and bolts than
in the concepts. The effect is perfect, but on closer examination,
the detail is not real; rather, he conjures up a vision and makes it
convincingly believable. The artist is a dedicated craftsman who
works in casein and acrylic and grinds his own pigments.

Berkey was born in Edgley, North Dakota, and got his artistic
start by producing calendar art for Brown & Bigelow in St. Paul,
Minnesota. The many kinds of subject matter required, and the
need to work quickly, gave him an excellent training. He has since
attracted a wide variety of editorial and advertising clients,
including *National Geographic*, *Time*, *Life*, *Omni*, *Discover*,
Sports Afield, *TV Guide*, The Franklin Library, U. S. Steel, IBM,
Texaco, Otis-Sperry, Paramount, and 20th Century Fox.

Among his movie poster art projects have been *King Kong*,
Star Wars, and *The Towering Inferno.*

An excellent collection of his work is included in his book,
Painted Space, published in 1991.

John Berkey, *The Visitors*, 1990.

Charmatz

BILL CHARMATZ (1925-) brought a fresh expressionistic style in his illustrations that art directors welcomed for its unconventional brash look. Charmatz eschews detail in favor of the spirit of his subject matter, boldly stated both in form and color. His work has appeared in virtually every publication, ranging from **Fortune** to **Playboy**, and including **Harper's Bazaar**, **Esquire**, **Seventeen Collier's**, **Sports Illustrated**, **Look**, **The Saturday Evening Post**, and **The Ladies' Home Journal**. He has also served many advertising clients, such as Nestle's Coffee and Texaco.

Charmatz was born in New York City and attended the High School of Industrial Arts, studying under Henry Woll and Helmut Krone. He has himself taught at the School of Visual Arts in new York. He has illustrated several children's books including **Endearments**, **The Cat's Whiskers**, **The Little Duster**, and **Horse Bus Stop**.

Bill Charmatz, exhibition poster, Society of Illustrators Gallery, 1978.

Cober

ALAN E. COBER (1935-1998) was named "Artist of the Year" in 1965 by the Artists Guild in recognition of his original sense of design and expressive use of line. Although Cober's work was largely linear, he so freely and effectively used it with halftone or color it was not "line" work in the traditional sense.

Cober was born in New York City. He had begun the study of law at the University of Vermont before deciding to become an artist. After attending the School of Visual Arts in New York and the Pratt Institute Graphic Center, and another two years attached to the art unit in the Special Warfare School at Fort Bragg, he was able to begin freelancing. Eventually, he worked for all the major magazines, many Fortune 500 advertising accounts, and illustrated more than twenty-five children's books.

Recognition for his work was legion; he received numerous Gold and Silver Medals from the Art Directors Club of New York, the Society of Publication Designers, and the Society of Illustrators, which also honored him with the Hamilton King Award in 1969. Alan was president of the Illustrators' Workshop from 1975-1993.

Memorable projects included painting a 31-foot mural of George Washington for the Smithsonian Institution and making life-size portraits of all the circus members (animals included!) for the Ringling Museum. He did a series of visual essays on Sing Sing prison and the death chamber, as well as on mental patients at the Willowbrook State School on Staten Island.

Portraits of Antonio, Janice and Prince Paul.
Published by **Lithopinion**, Spring, 1975.

John Collier's advertising illustration for Arton Associates was awarded a Gold Medal by the Society of Illustrators in 1976.

JOHN COLLIER (1948-) has been a consistent award winner whenever his work is exhibited. His credits include many Certificates of Excellence, five Gold and seven Silver Medals from annual exhibitions at the Society of Illustrators, and the Champion Paper International Corporation Award. This recognition is well-deserved approbation for an artist whose works are as appropriate for the gallery walls as for his many editorial and advertising clients.

Collier was born in Dallas, Texas, and received his art training from his father, Carroll Collier. He attended college in Kansas and Texas, and began his art career as an assistant art director in an advertising agency in Dallas. A job as staff artist in Minneapolis followed. Since then, he has freelanced from Houston to New York to Lawrence, Kansas, where he presently lives. Among his clients have been *Newsweek*, *Time*, *TV Guide*, *The New York Times*, *Sports Illustrated*, *Redbook*, *Playboy*, and *Good Housekeeping* magazines; advertisers such as Mobil, Exxon, Shell, TWA, Swiss Air, CBS, and H. J. Heinz.

Collier has also found time for teaching at Pratt Institute and the Fashion Institute of Technology in New York, the Hallmark Corporation in Kansas City, and is currently teaching part-time at the University of Kansas.

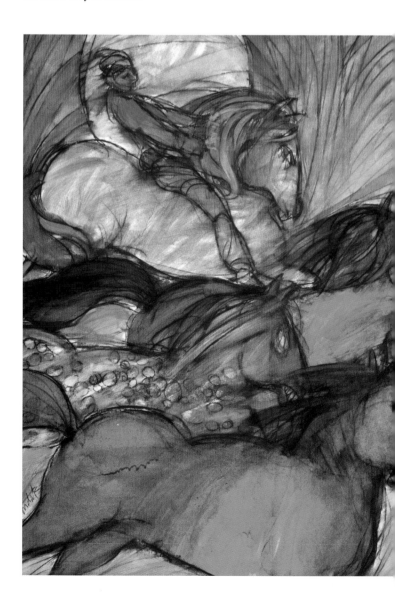

CLIFFORD ARA CONDAK (1930-1985) began attending art classes at Pratt Institute and the Museum of Modern Art School while still in high school. Born in Haverhill, Massachusetts, Condak won two art scholarships, and was a graduate of the Institute of Applied Arts and Sciences of the State University of New York, having majored in advertising art.

During two years' service with the U.S. Army in Austria, he studied painting at the Salzburg Museum. Upon returning to the U.S., he attended classes at the Art Students League under Howard Trafton, and later, studied at the New School in New York with Alexy Brodovitch.

Meanwhile, he was working in various advertising agencies as an illustrator-designer. In 1958, after a year's leave for further study in Florence, Italy, he began his freelance career. His first illustrations were done for *Gentleman's Quarterly* and *Nugget* magazine, followed by work for *Escapade*, *Esquire*, *Seventeen*, *Playboy*, *Sports Illustrated*, New American Library, Ballantine Books, and various advertisers.

For several years, Condak exhibited his paintings and had numerous one-man shows. He also taught at the School of Visual Arts, Pratt Institute, and Parsons School of Design.

Clifford Condak, almost guaranteed to be something.........

Robert Crofut, illustration for "Come Spring" by Charlotte Hinger, *Reader's Digest* 1986.

JWfonell

Like many contemporary illustrators, JEFFREY W. CORNELL (1945-) has learned to be adaptable in his work to the diversity of his clients. These have ranged from the classics, as represented by his illustrations for The Franklin Library and numerous paperback publications — including the complete works of Isaac Bashevis Singer — to annual corporation reports.

Cornell is a veteran of four years in the U.S. Air Force, and attended the Paier School of Art, where he studied under John Massimino. A meeting with guest lecturers Bernard Fuchs, Robert Heindel, and Mark English convinced him to switch to the illustration course.

His first work was for "gothic" paperback covers; subsequent clients have included *Good Housekeeping* magazine, *Redbook*, *Golf Magazine*, *Reader's Digest*, The American Stock Exchange, Bell Telephone, NBC-TV, RCA Records and Video Disks, Texaco, General Electric, and the Carnegie Corporation of New York. He also designed two commemorative stamps for the U.S. Postal Service to honor the Special Olympic Games in 1979 and 1985.

In 1994, Cornell moved to Florida to concentrate more on painting and drawing for exhibition and is represented by several galleries in the U.S. and in England.

CROFUT

Although ROBERT JOEL CROFUT (1951-) received a good liberal arts education from Tufts University and the Boston Museum School of Fine Arts, he credits illustrator Harry Anderson with the guidance to get successfully started as an artist.

His first commission was a paperback cover from Tower Books, and he has since done paintings for many other publishers including Signet, Berkeley, the Easton Press, the Franklin Library, and American Heritage, as well as magazines such as *Outdoor Life*, *Field & Stream*, *Guideposts*, *Seventeen*, and *Reader's Digest*. Advertising clients include M-G-M, NBC-TV, and Exxon.

Crofut has received many Citations of Merit in the Society of Illustrators Annual exhibitions, and is represented in the Sanford Low Collection of American Illustration at the New Britain Museum of American Art.

Jeffrey Cornell, *Palma*, 1985.

Baseball Spring Training, **Lithopinion**, 1975.

ROBERT M. CUNNINGHAM (1924-) was born in Kansas and attended the University of Kansas, the Kansas City Art Institute, and the Art Students League, studying with Kuniyoshi, Bosa and Corbino.

His illustrations have appeared in many of America's leading magazines, and his work has been seen at the Society of Illustrators, the New York Art Directors Club, **Communications Arts**, the American Institute of Graphic Arts, **Graphis** annuals, **Art Direction**, the "Century of American Illustration" exhibition at the Brooklyn Museum in 1972, the American Federation of Arts exhibition "Graphic Arts of the 20th Century" at the Smithsonian Institution in 1967-69, the "200 Years of American Illustration" exhibition at the New-York Historical Society Museum in 1976-77, and "Twenty Years of Award Winners" there in 1981. He has had two group shows in '90-'91 and a one-man show, "Eleuthera Paintings and Drawings," in 1991 at Lustrare Gallery, in New York City.

Most of his work was for corporate clients, such as DuPont, General Electric, Mobil, **Sports Illustrated**, Alfa Romeo, AT&T, IBM, American Express, American Airlines, Exxon, ABC-TV, New York Racing Assn., Manufacturers Hanover Trust Co., Bankers Trust, Eastern Airlines, New York Times, NBC-TV, New York Telephone, Alcoa, Panasonic, Chevrolet, Mead Paper, Monsanto, and National Westminster Bank USA.

Among his awards received: Gold Medals from the Society of Illustrators in 1966-67, 1978 and 1980; Silver Medals in 1983, 1985 and 1987; the Hamilton King Award in 1983, and election to the Society of Illustrators Hall of Fame in 1988.

He taught at Pratt Institute 1975-76, is a member of both the Graphic Artists Guild and the Society of Illustrators. He was also the designer of the 1980 Summer and Winter Olympic stamps for the U.S. Postal Service.

Comprehensive sketch, Bahamas fisherman with net, 1990; Old fisherman with net, Governor's Harbour, Eleuthera, Bahamas.

372

Ken Dallison

Ken Dallison, *Lincoln Beachey, America's Greatest Stunt Pilot of his Day,* ***The Heroic Age of American Flight*** for The Scott Calendar, 1974.

KEN DALLISON (1933-) was born in Middlesex, England, where he attended the Twickenham School of Art. Moving to Canada, he obtained his first illustration assignments from *Liberty* magazine (Canada) and CBC-TV Studios in 1955. He subsequently moved to Long Island, New York, and has illustrated for many American publications including ***Sports Illustrated***, ***Esquire***, ***Redbook***, ***Car and Driver,*** and ***Flying***.

Although Dallison has painted general subject matter for many advertisers and publishers, his special forté is the depiction of automobiles, and he does them all, from antique racing cars to the newest experimental models; clients include the majority of top auto manufacturers world-wide.

His work has been exhibited at the Society of Illustrators and at Art Directors Clubs in New York, Detroit, Pittsburgh, Toronto, Montreal, and London, England.

A member of the Society of Illustrators and the Graphic Artists Guild, Dallison currently lives in Mississauga, Ontario, Canada.

JACK DAVIS (1926-) is a phenomenal draftsman in the tradition of T. S. Sullivant, who can "do it straight," but finds more challenge and satisfaction in caricature and exaggeration.

Davis was born in Atlanta and studied art at the University of Georgia under the G.I. Bill following three years in the Navy.

After moving to New York in 1951 and studying at the Art Students League at night, he made his first entry into the art field as an inker for a comic strip, "The Saint." He was soon heavily involved in comic art of every description, and became one of its top practitioners for *Mad* magazine, *Trump*, *Playboy*, and many other publications.

Davis subsequently went on to the more lucrative advertising art market where his humor, combined with an ability to draw anything and to meet almost impossible deadlines, has made him very successful. He has also done covers for *Time* magazine, totaling thirty-six to date. Other work has included animation and artwork for television, movie posters and newspaper advertisements, covers for RCA Records, Topps Baseball cards, and three children's books for Random House.

Jack Davis, The cast of *M*A*S*H*, cover design for ***TV Guide***

373

Paul Davis

A native of Centahoma, Oklahoma, PAUL DAVIS (1938-) came East and attended the School of Visual Arts on a scholarship. There he studied under a distinguished roster of teachers: Philip Hays, Robert Weaver, Thomas Allen, Robert Shore, Howard Simon, George Tscherny, and Burt Hasen

His first illustrations were published in *Playboy* in 1959, and he has since appeared in *Life, Time, Look, Sports Illustrated, Evergreen Review, Harper's, Horizon, McCall's, Show, Esquire, Mirabella, Worth, Money,* and other magazines. He has also designed record covers, book jackets, and advertising illustration. Recent clients have been Unite!, Disney, Lincoln Center, Bernstein Real Estate, and Manhattan Plaza.

Davis has exhibited in many international poster shows and had one-man shows in museums of modern art in Kamakura, Gunma and Kyoto, Japan in 1975-76, and at the Centre Georges Pompidou in Paris in 1977. His work is also represented in galleries in Tokyo and Rome.

Books devoted to his work include E. P. Dutton's *Paul Davis Posters and Paintings* and *The Arcadia Seasonal Mural and Cookbook* published by Harry Abrams, Inc., which features a fold-out reproduction of the 70-foot wraparound mural he created for New York's acclaimed Arcadia restaurant.

In 1990, Davis received an honorary Doctor of Fine Arts degree from the School of Visual Arts, the 1990 Medal from the American Institute of Graphic Arts, and he was the first recipient of a special Drama Desk award in 1987 for his outstanding theater posters.

Paul Davis, poster for the *Three Penny Opera* with Raul Julia (New York Shakespeare Festival, 1976)

E N O S

RANDALL ENOS (1936-) is a satirist in the guise of a primitive, and he uses the linoleum block medium with the sleight of hand of a magician to conceal the sophistication of his renditions. Enos may use a block like a rubber stamp, for instance, creating a whole crowd out of a single figure; he also prints with many different inks on varieties of colored papers and cuts and pastes freely.

Enos was born in New Bedford, Massachusetts, and attended the Boston Museum School of Fine Arts where he studied painting and graphics. After a stint as an instructor in the cartoon course at the Famous Artists School, he began to do freelance illustration, first for *Cavalcade* magazine, then *Playboy, Esquire, Holiday, Fortune, National Lampoon, The New York Times, The Wall Street Journal, Time, Newsweek, Barron's, Forbes,* and many other publications. He has also worked in animated film, designing for clients such as IBM, Olivetti, Xerox, Burlington (the famous crisscross animated signature is his design) and also some film titles, such as those for *The Russians are Coming*.

Enos taught at Parsons School of Design for several years. His work has been exhibited in annual shows at the Society of Illustrators, the Society of Publication Designers, and Art Directors Club shows, winning many awards and a Cannes TV Festival Award for Animation in 1964.

Randall Enos, "Diary of a Movie Extra," for *The Boston Globe*, June, 1983.

Illustration from *Ashanti to Zulu, African Traditions*, by Margaret Musgrove, published by Dial, 1976. The illustrations won the Caldecott Award for the artists.

L+D DILLON

LEO and DIANE DILLON (1933-   ) were both born in March of the same year but hail from opposite coasts and different races. They began their collaboration while studying together at Parsons School of Design and the School of Visual Arts, and were married in 1957. To preclude professional jealousy, they have fused their two artistic personalities into a single and singular career, pushing each other's standards and trusting each other's input to forge a "combined artist," where each contributor critiques and takes over the other's work.

In addition to drawing and painting, the rigor of print-making techniques is evident in their work for *The Saturday Evening Post,* Caedmon records, Ballantine, Fawcett, and Time-Life.

The Dillons have employed varied styles and techniques to express the most appropriate feeling or effect for the subject at hand. This search for perfection has earned them the Hamilton King Award from the Society of Illustrators in 1976, the Caldecott Medal for Children's Book Illustration in both 1976 and 1977, the Hugo Award for Science Fiction and Fantasy in 1971, plus Honorary Doctorates from Parsons School of Design in 1991. In 1997, they were inducted into the Society of Illustrators Hall of Fame. Together they have taught at the School of Visual Arts in New York and exhibited variously in many galleries and museums around the country. A collection of their work is represented in *The Art of Leo and Diane Dillon* published by Ballantine Books in 1981.

Exhibition poster for a one-man exhibition by Mark English at the Jack O'Grady Gallery in 1979, awarded a Gold Medal by the Society of Illustrators, in 1981.

MARK ENGLISH (1933-) has evolved in his work through several stages and painting styles, but each has been distinguished by his use of subtle changes in color and value while emphasizing the overall pattern of shapes and sense of mystery.

English was born in Hubbard, Texas. He attended the University of Texas before serving in the U.S. Army. Upon discharge, he enrolled in the Art Center School in Los Angeles where he studied with John LaGatta and Joseph Henninger. Even before graduation, he landed a job on the staff of a major Detroit advertising agency. He later worked as an illustrator on major automobile accounts.

After considerable studio and advertising experience, he obtained his first fiction illustration assignment from *The Saturday Evening Post*. Since then, he has contributed to many other publications, including *Redbook*, *Parents*, *The Ladies' Home Journal*, *Good Housekeeping*, and *Sports Illustrated*.

English has made the transition to painting for exhibition. To that end, he became artist-in-residence at Hallmark Cards in Kansas City, conducting teaching sessions for the staff artists. He has been a member of The Illustrators Workshop, a distinguished teaching group of professional illustrators and later joined The Illustration Academy with his son.

His work has been exhibited widely and has won awards from the Society of Illustrators and the Art Directors Clubs of Pittsburgh and Detroit. His paintings are also shown at the Eleanor Ettinger Gallery in New York, the Maxwell Gallery in San Francisco, and several other galleries. English was named Artist of the Year in 1969 by the Artists Guild in New York and was elected into the Society of Illustrators Hall of Fame in 1983.

Bart Forbes, advertising illustration, Cutter Bill Western World, 1981.

Born in Altus, Oklahoma, BART FORBES (1939) was the son of Air Force parents and relocated several times while growing up. He graduated from the University of North Carolina with a B.A. in 1961. After serving in the Army, he did graduate study at the Art Center School in Los Angeles; one of his instructors there was John LaGatta.

After about six years as an advertising illustrator in Dallas, he received his first editorial assignment from *The American Way*. He has since worked for many national magazines, including *McCall's*, *Time*, *The Saturday Review*, *TV Guide*, *Money*, *Seventeen*, and *Redbook*, as well as for Doubleday Books and various paperback publishers. Advertising clients included RCA, Exxon, Eastern Airlines, American Express, and Sony.

Forbes made theme paintings for a variety of PGA and Seniors golf tournaments. He has also painted official posters for the Boston Marathon, the America's Cup, the Indianapolis 500, as well as the 1992 and 1996 Olympic Games. He has also designed over 20 commemorative postage stamps for the U.S. Postal Service, including the 1988 Olympics stamps.

A member of the Society of Illustrators and the American Institute of Graphic Arts, he has won many awards in their exhibits. Former President Jimmy Carter had seven Forbes paintings in his White House collection, and the artist is represented in the collections of George Bush, the Ronald Reagan Presidential Library, and the Smithsonian Institution.

GERRY GERSTEN (1927-) is a product of the Cooper Union Art School and in 1986, he was granted the Augustus St. Gaudens Award for outstanding professional achievement in art by his Alma Mater. He has also done many effective caricatures of founder Peter Cooper on the school's behalf.

Having been born in New York City and attended the High School of Music and Art, he received a thorough grounding in the fundamentals of drawing, and they are his greatest strength. Much of his work is drawn in pencil on tracing paper, then dry-mounted on illustration board, at which point, washes or color may be added when appropriate.

Gersten is a particularly effective caricaturist. As he describes his approach, "When I get an assignment to do a character, I try to make him as universally 'readable' as I can. I try to create a symbol, so that the viewer can feel that he knows this person, perhaps he has met him somewhere..."

Gersten's humor and irreverence have kept him busy for clients such as *Boys' Life*, *The Ladies' Home Journal*, *Playboy*, *Newsweek*, *McCall's*, *Harper's*, *Time*, *Life*, *Sports Illustrated*, *Scholastic* and many other publications, as well as various advertising accounts, such as American Express, Exxon, Mobil Oil, and Times-Mirror.

He is a member of the Society of Illustrators, the Graphic Artists Guild, and the Society of Publication Designers.

Gerry Gersten, Jocko Smithers, *Town Sheriff; Politics and People,* published by Scholastic, 1977.

"A Princess of Mars," published in *The Frank Frazetta Calendar 1977*.Credit: ©1977 Frank Frazetta.

FRANK FRAZETTA (1928-) is an artistic phenomenon who has created a cult following for his fantasy paintings. His ingredients include a mixture of sex, violence, melodramatic action, exaggerated anatomy and exotic, impossible settings—and he makes it all work. Paperback publishers vied for his services; his illustrated calendars and posters have sold in the tens of thousands to avid fans. Very few Frazetta paintings have been marketed; instead, poster reproductions must serve for those who would collect his work.

Frazetta was born in Brooklyn and had dual talents in drawing and athletics from childhood. He won the Most Valuable Player award and batted .487 in his Parade Grounds Baseball League and received several offers to play professional baseball. At the same time, he had been selling comic book drawings beginning in his second year of high school, and the promising young artist had received an invitation from Walt Disney Studios to come to Hollywood. Frazetta decided to stay in Brooklyn to be near the Dodgers, but he reasoned that an artist's career could be a longer one than a ball player's.

The comic book field was an excellent training ground, particularly in forcing the use of imagination, and Frazetta flourished in it. For a while he had his own strip, "Johnny Comet"; he worked as an assistant to Al Capp on the "Li'l Abner" strip for several years; and drew for *Mad* magazine and *Playboy*. He also designed several movie posters.

It was the chance to do a series of Ace paperback covers for a new edition of Edgar Rice Burroughs stories that started him on his present course. They were enormously successful and led to many commissions for "sword and sorcery" titles, including the Conan series by Robert E. Howard.

Frazetta's covers had much to do with the success of this genre, and a whole school of fantasy artists has followed his lead. Meanwhile, Frazetta has been able to create his own market through publishing ventures which distribute his signed reproductions, posters and annual calendars, freeing him to choose his own subjects and to paint them at his own volition.

In 1998 Frazetta was honored by his election into the Society of Illustrators Hall of Fame.

Paul Giovanopoulos, *Mona Lisa*, variations on a theme. Exhibited at The Butler Institute of American Art, 1996.

Giovanopoulos

Born in Macedonia, Greece, PAUL GIOVANOPOULOS (1939-) came to the United States as a teenager, knowing no English. This difficult situation served to nurture his visual senses; after graduating from high school with honors, he went on to a two-year scholarship at New York University's School of Fine Arts. He continued his studies under Robert Weaver at the School of Visual Arts and graduated in 1961.

Giovanopoulos then embarked on a career in painting, which earned him the John Armstrong Challoner Foundation Fellowship to live and work abroad for two years. Upon his return to the U.S. in 1965, he had several successful one-man shows at the Lacarda Gallery in New York City. Although Giovanopoulos had dabbled in illustration since his college years, it was the death of his father in 1967, thrusting him into the role of family breadwinner, that began his career in commercial art.

Soon, Giovanopoulos' talent and originality was recognized by such publications as *Playboy*, *New York*, *Fortune*, *Time*, and *Esquire* magazines, as well as national advertisers and book publishers. His work garnered many awards, among them a Gold Medal from the Society of Illustrators, and two New York Times Ten Best Illustrated Children's Book citations. He also found time to teach at the School of Visual Arts, Parsons School of Design, and Pratt Institute.

In 1986, Giovanopoulos returned to his first love, painting, and has enjoyed success through a series of one-man shows in New York, Florida and Chicago. A retrospective of his work recently inaugurated the contemporary branch of the Butler Institute of American Art in Ohio.

ALEX GNIDZIEJKO (1943-) follows a careful, logical process in planning and painting his pictures. Without artifice or ostentation, he conveys a sense of dignity and strength in his work. In 1975, he received a Gold Medal from the Society of Illustrators and was awarded a Creativity Certificate of Distinction from *Art Direction* magazine in 1979. In 1980 he received advertising's Andy Award as well as an Award of Excellence from *Communication Arts* magazine.

A student at Pratt Institute and the School of Visual Arts, he first illustrated for *Playboy* magazine in 1966. He has since worked for many magazines and advertisers, including NBC, *Time*, *Sports Illustrated*, *New York* magazine, *McCall's*, *Mobil Oil Corporation*, *Penthouse*, *Good Housekeeping*, *Esquire*, *National Geographic*, Holiday Inns, and Lenox China.

Gnidziejko also paints for exhibition and has shown at the New Jersey Watercolor Society, the Rizzoli Gallery in New York, and the Landsman Gallery in New Jersey.

Alex Gnidziejko illustration for "The Life of Lucky Luciano" for *Penthouse*, 1974.

379

Edward Gorey, Fan design: injured dog brought into drawing room. Date and place of publication unknown.

EDWARD ST. JOHN GOREY (1925-2000) needs a special artistic category of his own. His drawings were almost staid and very reserved, in a manner reverting back to Victorian illustrators. Yet, there is also a bizarre, ghoulish bite in them and the combination is delightfully unsettling. His macabre outlook has been displayed to millions of television watchers of "Mystery!" on Public Television which has long been introduced by Gorey's animation of mock-dastardly deeds. Otherwise, the Gorey audience must look for his work in small editions of books written and published by himself or by venturesome editors who have taken a chance on them despite the lack of a marketing categery. Among some of the titles have been *The Gashleycrumb Tinies* (1963), *The Glorious Nosebleed* (1975), *The Gilded Bat* (1966), and *The Loathsome Couple* (1977).

From his birthplace in Chicago, Gorey went to Harvard, but his art was mostly self-taught. After service in the Army, he worked for the art department at Doubleday and Company. It took some time to find acceptance for his own book ideas, but eventually he published over seventy-five titles and had to turn down many of the projects that were offered to him. He preferred to work in pen and ink, occasionally embellished with muted watercolor. It is very probable that his anachronistic drawings and deadpan humor will have a lasting appeal to future generations.

DAVID GROVE (1940-) developed an interesting variation of the Coles Phillips "fadeaway" technique by melding background and foreground colors and values. This demands much preliminary planning for the final result to look so spontaneous.

Grove was born in Washington, D.C. and attended the Syracuse University School of Art. In 1964, he took a year off to travel in Europe but stayed on in Paris for several years as a freelancer. Following another stint in London with Artist Partners Ltd., he returned to the States — to San Francisco — and the west coast has been his home base since. There he works for a wide range of clients, such as *Car and Driver*, *The Saturday Review*, Bantam Books, Ballantine Books, Dell Publishing Company, Standard Oil, the U.S. Navy, the Atlantic Richfield Co., Western Airlines, NFL Properties, Inc., Pendleton Woolen Mills, CBS, the Bank of America, and Walt Disney Productions.

Grove has also taught at the Academy of Arts College in San Francisco and is a member of both the San Francisco and New York Society of Illustrators and the Graphic Artists Guild.

David Grove, *Captain Blood* by Raphael Sabatini, Bantam Books.
Here Grove is carrying on the tradition of Dean Cornwell and Mead Schaeffer who illustrated the Captain Blood stories two generations earlier.

Hall

H. TOM HALL (1932-) grew up in Prospect Park, Pennsylvania, and studied at the Tyler School of Fine Art and the Philadelphia College of Art. His teachers were Henry C. Pitz, Joseph Krush, Benjamin Eisenstat, and Albert Gold, and he was inspired by the work of Ben Stahl and Robert Fawcett.

While stationed in Japan with the U.S. Army, he wrote a children's book, which was published by Knopf upon his return to civilian life. This became his first assignment and the start of twelve years working in the children's book and magazine field.

In 1970, armed with a new portfolio, Tom shifted to adult book and magazine illustration. His first two paperback covers were John Steinbeck novels for Bantam. He went on to illustrate the covers for all the Thomas Costain books and many romance covers, such as **Shanna** and **The Thornbirds.** He also illustrated the **87th Precinct** series by Edward McBain and **The Spanish Bit Saga** series by Goldsmith.

Hall did book and magazine illustrations for **National Geographic** and enjoyed traveling to Honduras and Peru for background research. He has worked for Avon, Bantam, Ballantine, Warner, New American Library, Fawcett, **Reader's Digest**, and many other publications.

H. Tom Hall, **The Money Man** by Thomas B. Costain; published by Avon Books.

ROGER HANE (1938-1974) crowded a distinguished illustrating career into a short life span. Tragically, he was robbed and beaten to death in New York's Central Park at the age of thirty-six. Just three weeks earlier he had been voted "Artist of the Year" by the New York Artists Guild.

He was born in Bradford, Pennsylvania, and was graduated from the Philadelphia Museum School of Art in 1961. Moving to New York, he quickly established himself as a strong new talent; his carefully rendered surrealist/fantasy concepts found him many clients, including **Fortune**, **New York** magazine, **Redbook**, **The Lamp**, **Look**, **Vista,** and **Playboy**. Simon and Schuster published his covers for the Carlos Castenada books, **Journey to Ixtlan**, **The Teachings of Don Juan**, and **A Separate Reality**, which were perhaps his best-known pictures. He also worked for other paperback publishers, such as Avon Books, E.P. Dutton Company, and Collier Books. Advertising clients included Formica, Sylvania Bulbs, DeBeers Diamonds, and Merck, Sharp & Dohme, Inc. He also designed a number of record album covers for RCA, Columbia Records, and Philadelphia International Records.

Roger Hane, **Accounting for Murder**, published by Avon Books.

R·Hess RICHARD HESS (1934-1991) came to illustration by a circuitous route. One of his first jobs was as a designer of paint-by-number sets for the Palmer Paint Company in Detroit. Born in Royal Oak, Michigan, he early showed art talent but lacked formal training. After a short stay at Michigan State and evening classes at the local Society of Arts & Crafts, he was able to land an advertising agency job. This was his art training ground. Through a succession of agency posts in Detroit, Philadelphia, and New York, he learned to handle typography, design in an allotted space, and to handle various mediums.

A natural primitive, Hess did not tamper with his style and it was the strength of his ideas that made him a successful, creative art director, designer and illustrator with a host of clients, such as *Vista* magazine, which he also art-directed, Random House, *Playboy*, *Esquire*, *Newsweek*, *New York* magazine, American Airlines, Western Union, CBS, *The New York Times*, U.S. Plywood, Champion Papers, Xerox, Westvaco and many others. His work received gold and silver medals and merit awards from Art Directors Clubs in New York, Detroit, Philadelphia, Chicago, Houston, Los Angeles, and San Francisco; he won additional awards from the American Institute of Graphic Arts, the Society of Illustrators, and other organizations.

Richard Hess, *Charles Ives*, record album cover painting, CBS Records.

Hunter Like many other artists, STANLEY R. HUNTER (1939-1999), got his professional start in Detroit as an automobile illustrator. For about ten years, he painted the accompanying backgrounds and figures, as well as some cars, for various agencies and studios.

He was born in Lansing, Michigan, and after high school attended the Society of Arts and Crafts in Detroit where he studied with Nick Beauholis and where his training landed him his first studio job.

In 1974, he moved East and worked for many periodicals, including *Newsweek*, *TV Guide*, *Reader's Digest*, *Life*, *Look*, *The Ladies' Home Journal*, *National Geographic*, and book publishers such as Doubleday and the Franklin Library.

Hunter's work won many Awards of Excellence, a Gold Medal in a Detroit art show, and a Silver Medal from the Society of Illustrators.

Stanley Hunter, cover for *An Excess of Love* by Cathy Cash Spellman.

Illustration for "Uncle Don" by Shel Silverstein, *Playboy*, © 1987 Brad Holland.

HollAND

BRAD HOLLAND (1943-) appears to be endlessly inventive in powerfully portraying the foibles of humanity. Using an unorthodox symbology, he shocks and surprises while forcing the viewer into unavoidable recognition of the underlying truth in his pictorial commentary. His talents have been ideally suited to the Op-ed pages of *The New York Times*, which has commissioned and published some of his best work since 1971.

Holland was born in Fremont, Ohio; he grew up there and in Fort Smith, Arkansas. He was submitting cartoons to magazines while still in high school; he moved to Chicago after graduation and found his first employment in a tattoo parlor and later, some small illustration jobs. Moving to Kansas City in 1964, he worked briefly for Hallmark cards and formed the Asylum Press "to print eccentric projects with friends."

In 1967, he moved to New York City and began to contribute drawings regularly to *Playboy* magazine. He also worked for the underground press: *New York Free Press*, *The East Village Other*, *Review*, and other publications, such as *Redbook*.

His work has won many awards including Gold Medals from the Society of Illustrators, the New York Art Directors Club, and the Society of Publication Designers. He has also exhibited in the Musée des Beaux Arts in Bordeaux and at the Louvre in Paris. A book with drawings and text by Holland titled *Human Scandals* was published by Thomas Y. Crowell Company in 1977.

Editorial page illustration for "Bipartisan Consensus? A Mirage," in *The New York Times*, June 13, 1983.

383

Cover painting for *Nine Princes in Amber,* by Roger Zelazny; Avon books. This painting is clearly an homage to N. C. Wyeth. © 1990 Jeffrey Jones. Collection of Robert Wiener.

JOHNSON, DOUG (1940-) was born and educated in Toronto, Canada, attending the Ontario College of Art.

Johnson has created illustration and design for packaging, recordings, advertising, and magazines for over thirty years, and he has been a principal and partner in Dodger Productions, whose Broadway shows have garnered over fifty-six Tony awards as well as international Doras and Oliviers, for plays including Leonard Bernstein's *Candide* in 1974 to *Footloose* in 1998.

He has taught and lectured extensively throughout the U.S., Canada and Japan, including sojourns at the School of Visual Arts in New York, the Ontario College of Art and Design in Toronto, the graduate program at Syracuse University, and the Yale School of Drama.

He has been honored by a great many design and illustration awards, with Gold Medals from the Society of Illustrators and the New York Art Directors Club, among others. He was awarded the Hamilton King Award from the Society of Illustrators in 1995 and the Lifetime Achievement Award from *Air Power* magazine in 1999.

From Atlanta, Georgia, JEFFREY JONES (1944-) was initially a geology student at Georgia State College, but his childhood interest in drawing reasserted itself and he switched to art. His early role models were Howard Pyle and the Brandywine School as well as Frank Frazetta and Gustav Klimt. His early training came from the Famous Artists School correspondence course and from many instruction books, including George Bridgman's anatomy texts.

Jones was especially attracted to fantasy themes and he found early work for *Creepy* magazine. Moving to New York brought him in contact with the paperback field and he quickly made it his milieu. Painting large oils and amalgamating the styles of his influences, he painted many fantasy/science fiction and "sword and sorcery" covers for publishers such as Avon, Belmont, Tower, the Warren illustrated magazines, and for publisher Donald Grant. He created his own utterly unique cartoon art feature, "Idyl" for the *National Lampoon* beginning in 1971.

For the past several years, he has left commercial assignments for more personal paintings which harken back to the romantic era of the past century.

Doug Johnson, poster illustration for the musical *Big River*, 1985.

David McCall Johnston

DAVID McCALL JOHNSTON (1940-) is a Midwesterner, born in South Bend, Indiana. After completing his studies with honors at the Art Center College of Design in California where he studied with Joseph Henninger and John LaGatta, he returned to the Midwest for his first art job as a studio artist at Art Staff in Detroit, Michigan, in 1964. Eventually, he became a partner in his own Detroit firm, Designers and Partners.

Now a freelance illustrator, he has worked for a wide variety of clients, including Signet, Prentice-Hall, Ballantine Books, Green Willow Press, Bantam, Harper and Row, K-mart Corporation, the Berringer Wine Company, the Mount Rushmore National Monument Society, the Franklin Mint and the Franklin Library. Johnston has also created designs for Steuben Glass, with some pieces collected by museums.

He regularly exhibits his work, which has been included in annual shows of the Art Directors Club of Detroit, winning both Gold and Silver Medals, and the Society of Illustrators in New York.

Johnston, one of four original paintings commissioned to commemorate the novels of Jules Verne by the Jules Verne Museum, in Nantes, France.

McAfee

The art of MARA McAFEE (1934-1984) was almost an anachronistic throwback to the era of Norman Rockwell. Furthermore, she was a very capable artist who could paint as realistically as he did. There the resemblance ended, however. Like the *National Lampoon*, with which her work was most closely associated, her outlook was irreverent, and instead of glorifying the past, she ridiculed the present.

McAfee was born in Los Angeles and went to school at the Chouinard Art School there, before moving East to study at the Art Students League under Frank Mason. Her first illustrations were done for *Playboy* and in addition to *Ms.* magazine, *New York*, *Esquire*, *Redbook*, *Oui*, *Viva*, and other magazines, she also painted paperback covers for publishers such as Pocket Books, Bantam, and Fawcett.

She was an accomplished portraitist as well, represented by Portraits, Inc., and exhibited her paintings in a number of galleries in addition to annual shows at the Society of Illustrators. Her work won many awards from the New York Art Directors Club, the American Institute of Graphic Arts, the Society of Publication Designers, and others.

A book, *The Art of Mara McAfee*, was published in 1981 by Simon and Schuster.

Mara McAfee, cover design for the *National Lampoon*, August, 1978.

Let us Prey, a variation on the famous Thomas Nast theme (see page 21)
Published September 20, 1973, *The New York Review of Books*.

This caricature of Philip Roth for *The New Yorker* magazine
won a Gold Medal for Levine in 1996.

If anyone deserves the mantle of political cartoon Thomas Nast, it is surely DAVID LEVINE (1926-), who wields perhaps the sharpest satiric pen today.

Levine studied at the Tyler School of Art in Philadelphia, and for a year with Hans Hofmann in New York, although his influences run from Will Eisner and Harold Foster to Edouard Vuillard and Thomas Eakins.

He began by freelancing for *Esquire* in 1958 and since the early 'sixties has become a mainstay at the *New York Review of Books*, where he has caricatured a virtual encyclopedia of great literary, artistic, and political figures. One of the most notorious of these depicted Lyndon Johnson displaying his appendectomy scar which Levine gave the shape of Vietnam. He escalated from there to lambaste Richard Nixon on the covers of *Time* and *Newsweek*.

Several books of his drawings have been issued, most recently *The Arts of David Levine* published by Alfred A. Knopf in 1978. The Forum Gallery in New York exhibits his pen-and-inks as well as his non-illustrative work: very sensitive portraits, beach scenes, and cityscapes in watercolor.

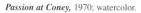

Passion at Coney, 1970; watercolor.

One of the most traditionally painterly of current illustrators, MALCOLM "Skip" LIEPKE (1954-) has had no formal schooling in art. "In constantly striving to become a better artist," he says, "my teachers have been Velasquez, Whistler, Sargent, Chase, and many others in the great museums around the country." Liepke was born in Minneapolis, Minnesota, and did not complete college.

Since 1976, when he made drawings that appeared in titles for the ABC-TV show *Rich Man*, *Poor Man*, he has gone to the top of the profession with covers for *Time*, *Forbes*, *Newsweek*, and *Fortune* magazines. In addition, his illustration clients include the Franklin Library, *Reader's Digest*, *McCall's*, *Good Housekeeping*, and *The Ladies' Home Journal.*

He has accumulated impressive awards, a Gold Medal from the Allied Artists, a Purchase Award from the National Academy of Design, and from the Society of Illustrators, a Gold Medal, Norman Rockwell Award, and Past Chairmen's Special Award.

Malcolm Liepke, *Rolling Stone* magazine, Portrait of Spike Lee

He has exhibited frequently at the National Academy, American Watercolor Society, Allied Artists, the National Arts Club, the Salmagundi Club, and is represented in collections at the Smithsonian Institution, and the Brooklyn Museum, and has taught at the School of Visual Arts in New York. He is currently represented by the Eleanor Ettinger Gallery in New York City.

Victor Livoti

VICTOR LIVOTI (unknown) is probably illustration's best kept secret. (He keeps his date of birth a secret, too.) Known only to a few friends in the profession, he does not sign his work, nor does he exhibit it. Yet, to insiders, he is the consummate paperback artist, having painted several hundreds of covers for a distinguished array of authors and nearly all of the publishers, including Bantam, Harlequin, Signet, Fawcett, Zebra, Ballantine, Berkeley, Avon and Dell.

He has worked for too many advertising agencies to list and received several awards for his outdoor advertising subjects. His work is characterized by strong contrasts and a full range of values and color that give them the necessary visual impact.

Born in New York City, Livoti had a year at Georgia Tech and studied art at the National Academy school; he also took classes at the Art Students League.

Victor Livoti, book cover for *The People Eaters*, by Hollis Alpert, Dell publishers.

ROBERT A. MAGUIRE (1921-   ) whose family name is McGuire, was one of the many students of Frank Reilly who gravitated to the paperback book cover market. He has had a long career in that field, beginning in 1949 with Avon Books, and over the years has painted for virtually every other publisher, including Pocket Books, Harper Books, Fawcett, Bantam, Ballantine, Ace, Signet, Dell, Berkley, Monarch, Hillman, and Lion Books. His work is marked by its versatility and consistent high quality which is particularly effective with romantic subjects.

Maguire also paints for exhibition and is represented by O'Brien's Gallery in Scottsdale, Arizona. He is a member of the Society of Illustrators in New York and the American Artists Professional League.

Robert Maguire, *Dangerous Yesterdays*, Dell publishers.

ALLAN MARDON (1931-   ) grew up in the town of Sarnia, Ontario and went to the Ontario College of Art, the Edinburgh School in Scotland, and the Slade School in London. After returning to Canada, he set up a studio in Toronto and began to freelance. Putting together a portfolio of his work, he called on *Sports Illustrated* and landed his first assignment in the U. S. After a lot of flights between Toronto and New York, he moved to Connecticut, and has developed a large clientele since. Among them are *McCall's* magazine, *The Ladies' Home Journal*, *Redbook*, *Time*, and *National Geographic*. Other clients include many large corporations, such as Gulf & Western, Exxon, American Express, Mohawk Paper, Lightolier, and numerous pharmaceutical accounts.

Mardon's crisply rendered work is usually in mixed media, reinforced by pen line which reveals the sure draftsmanship of his Slade School training; he has won several awards from Art Directors Clubs in New York and Boston and an award of merit from the Society of Illustrators.

Allan Mardon, *The Arts*, montage for poster illustration.

GERALD McConnell (signature)

Born in East Orange, New Jersey, GERALD McCONNELL (1931-) studied at the Art Students League with Frank Reilly and simultaneously apprenticed under Dean Cornwell. It is not easy to pinpoint an influence on his work, however, since it covers such a range of stylistic approaches and applications.

Starting with Pocket Books in 1953, McConnell painted western covers for most of the major paperback publishers. When he began making assemblages in 1967, an entirely different (and better paying) group of clients became patrons. And when he won the Hamilton King Award in 1981, it was for his ultra-rendered pencil drawing of Grand Central Terminal. Other awards included "Best in Show" of the Real Show in 1979, a Silver Medal from the Society of Illustrators in 1997, and numerous certificates from Art Directors Clubs. He has also exhibited his work in the U.S. Air Force Museum in Dayton, the NASA Museum, and the National Parks Department in Washington.

McConnell has long been a backbone of the Society of Illustrators, serving on the Board of Directors or the Executive Committee consecutively for the last thirty-six years. A founding member of the Graphic Artists Guild, he served on its Board of Directors and Executive Committee for over twenty years.

Along with Mark Borow, McConnell founded PropArt in 1982, a company that creates sets and props for print ads and television commercials. More recently, McConnell has been concentrating on his publishing ventures. To date, his company Madison Square Press has published over one hundred titles dealing with the applied and fine arts.

Gerald McConnell, **Grand Central Station,** a tour-de-force rendering in pencil and wash. Published by The Society of Illustrators, 1980.

WILSON McLEAN:

WILSON McLEAN (1937-) was born in Glasgow, Scotland, moved to London at the age of ten. With no art training, he landed his first job designing magazine layouts. This led him to try freelancing in Copenhagen, but he found London to be better and returned to freelance there until making the big decision to move to America in 1966.

The decision was well-timed. His carefully designed, meticulously rendered compositions found immediate acceptance and have had a strong influence in the field. He has illustrated for virtually all the major magazines, including **Esquire, Sports Illustrated, Time, McCall's, Redbook, New York, Intellectual Digest, Saturday Review, Playboy, Oui, Penthouse,** as well as for a number of advertising clients.

McLean has taught at the School of Visual Arts, the Savannah College of Art, Kent State University, and Syracuse University. He has been a regular participant in the New York Art Directors Club shows, and in the annual exhibitions of the Society of Illustrators, where he has received several awards. In 1980, he was also the recipient of the Society's Hamilton King Award. He has been included in many group shows and is represented in collections of the Smithsonian Institution and the Air and Space Museum in Washington, D.C.

Wilson McLean, advertising illustration for Visa card, 1990.

LINCOLN CENTER THEATER AT THE VIVIAN BEAUMONT

James McMullan

JAMES McMULLAN (1934-) comes from a missionary family and was born in Tsingtao, China. His boyhood was divided between China, India, and Canada, followed by service in the U.S. Army. He graduated from Pratt Institute in Brooklyn and began an art career that has been marked by great diversity of clientele and use, but consistent in the intensity of his artistic outlook.

Among his activities has been work for TV animation, record jackets, posters, book covers, magazines, and advertisements. McMullan was associated with the Push Pin Studios from 1965 to 1968 and has since formed his own organization, Visible Studio, Inc. He has designed a number of theatrical posters for Alexander H. Cohen and in conjunction with Robert Blechman created an animated Christmas film for Public Television in 1977.

McMullan has also been director and vice-president of the AIGA and was one of the founders of the Illustrators Guild. A member of the Society of Illustrators, he received their Gold and Silver Medals in 1981 and their Hamilton King Award in 1988. In 1998, he received the Herschel Levit Award for lifetime achievement from Pratt Institute. A book of his work, ***Revealing Illustrations***, was published in 1981 by Watson-Guptill.

In 1990, McMullan completed a sixty-foot mural, "Rehearsal Chairs" at the Vivian Beaumont and Mitzi Newhouse Theaters at Lincoln Center, and in 1995, he was given the Joan Cullman Award for his creative contribution to Lincoln Center Theater.

James McMullan, poster for the revival of Cole Porter's ***Anything Goes*** in 1987. This design won the Andy award from the Advertising Club of New York.

W. Minor

WENDELL MINOR (1944 -) was born in Aurora, Illinois, and is a graduate of the Ringling School of Art and Design in Florida, where he studied under Loran Wilford. He has illustrated over 2000 book jackets and 17 childrens' books since his first assignment from Harcourt Brace in 1969. Among his many publishers have been Doubleday, Random House, Simon & Schuster, Houghton-Mifflin and Harper-Collins as well as magazines such as ***Good Housekeeping***, ***McCall's***, ***Atlantic Monthly***, and ***The Ladies' Home Journal***.

Minor has received some 250 awards from major competitions, including four Gold Medals from the Art Directors Club of New York and the Society of Illustrators of Los Angeles and New York. He taught at the School of Visual Arts from 1975 to 1986 and served as president of Society of Illustrators in New York from 1989 -1991.

Minor has had numerous solo exhibitions, and his work can be found in the permanent collections of the Illinois State Museum, the Muskegon Museum of Art, the Mattatuck Museum in Connecticut, NASA, the Arizona Historical Society, the Library of Congress, the Museum of American Illustration, and others.

Perhaps his best remembered cover, this design for ***The Illustrated Man*** by Ray Bradbury was published by Doubleday. © 1975 by Wendell Minor.

Wendell Minor: Art For the Written Word, a retrospective of twenty-five years of Minor's book cover art, was published in September 1995 by Harcourt Brace and Company, with an introduction by Pulitzer Prize-winning author David McCullough.

Patrick Nagel, illustration for "Playboy After Hours," July, 1982. Copyright © 1982 by *Playboy*, reprinted with permission.

PATRICK NAGEL (1945-1984) crammed a very successful career into his brief thirty-eight years. He got his big break through an early assignment for *Playboy* magazine which led to his becoming a regular contributor and having an increasingly more important role with the magazine. His assignment was a remarkably open one: to paint anything and as much as he wanted each month. His "Nagel Girls" quickly became a reader's favorite. His style was deceptively simple, carefully designed with a reliance on line and flat color. While sensual, his pictures were always in good taste and lent themselves perfectly to posters and prints. Many of these were exhibited and released in seriagraphed limited editions.

His record album cover design for Duran Duran in 1983 was reputed to be the best known cover in the world.

Nagel was from Dayton, Ohio, but moved to California where he studied art at the Chouinard Art Institute and received a B.F A. from California State University, Fullerton. He taught at Art Center College while developing a career as a freelance illustrator and painter. Following his connection with *Playboy*, he branched out to many other clients, including Universal Studios, M-G-M, IBM, United Artists, *Psychology Today*, and *Harper's* magazine. His work is in the Collections of the Smithsonian Institution, the Library of Congress, and the Musée des Arts Decoratifs and the Musée de L'Affiche in France.

ROBERT ANDREW PARKER (1927-) has had multiple careers in the gallery world and on the printed page, as well as in film. Some of his watercolors of battle scenes done for his son were published by *Esquire* magazine and led to commissions from other magazines, including *Fortune* — which sent him on several major reportorial assignments around the world — *The Lamp* magazine, *Playboy*, *Sports Illustrated*, and *New York* magazine.

The movie projects included doing all of the artwork for the Vincent Van Gogh biography *Lust for Life*, comprising those in the studio and others "in progress," as though painted by Kirk Douglas. His own watercolors accompanied two films on the poetry of Wilfred Owen and that of Keith Douglas.

Parker was born in Norfolk, Virginia, and studied at the Art Institute of Chicago. Following a stint in the Army Air Force as a flight engineer on a B-25 bomber, he won a scholarship to the Skowhegan School of Painting and Sculpture in Maine, studying under Jack Levine and Henry Varnum Poor.

He exhibited with Young American Printmakers in 1952 and worked at Atelier 17 in New York in 1952 and 1953. The following year, he had a successful one-man show at the Roko Gallery, including a purchase by the Museum of Modern Art. Since then, he has appeared in many exhibitions, and received numerous awards. His work is included in public collections at the Whitney Museum, the Metropolitan Museum, the Brooklyn Museum, and the Los Angeles County Museum.

Parker also taught at Rhode Island School of Design, the School of Visual Arts, and Parsons School of Design in New York.

Robert Andrew Parker, illustration for Vladimir Nabokov's "Ada," April, 1969. Copyright © 1969, 1997, by *Playboy*. Reprinted with permission.

Passalaqua

Much of the work of DAVID J. PASSALACQUA (1936-)
conveys a feeling of intensity and energy, like the artist himself.
His work is also very diverse, including line drawings, pastels,
markers, watercolor, collage, and assemblage. His clients, too, are
diverse, including most of the national magazines, such as *The
Ladies' Home Journal*, *The Saturday Evening Post*, and *Sports
Illustrated*, many paperback book publishers, among them
Bantam Books, and a long list of advertising accounts —
Celanese Corporation, Standard Oil, Dayton-Hudson, Universal
Studios, and Warner Communications.

His drawings are represented in the Boston Museum of Fine
Arts, the Singer Collection, the Don Padilla Collection, the
Celanese Corporation, and numerous private collections.

Passalacqua was born in San Francisco and studied at the
Chouinard Art Institute in Los Angeles as a Disney Scholarship
student. He also attended the Otis Art School and the County Art
Institute.

In addition to his active illustration career, he currently
teaches drawing and illustration at Parsons School of Design,
Pratt Institute, and Syracuse University. He has lectured at
universities and art schools across the country and abroad.

Advertising illustration for United Engineers, 1969. © David J. Passalaqua

Jerry Pinkney

Born in Philadelphia, JERRY PINKNEY (1939-), studied at the
Philadelphia Museum College of Art. In 1960, he moved to
Boston and obtained his first work in a design studio as a
designer-illustrator. Later he became one of the founders of
Kaleidoscope Studio, leaving after two years to freelance. During
this time, he was actively involved in design work for the Boston
National Center for Afro-American Artists and served as the
visiting critic of the Rhode Island School of Design.

Since 1971, he has been located in Croton-on-Hudson, New
York, and handles a wide range of assignments for clients which
have included *Seventeen*, *American Home* magazine, *Woman's
Day*, *Essence*, *Boy's Life*, *Scouting*, Dial publications, Harper
and Row, Dell publications, Coward, McCann and Geoghegan,
Seagram Distillers, S.D. Warren Paper Company, and others.

His work has received Gold, Silver, and Bronze Medals from
Art Directors Club shows in various cities. He has garnered other
awards from the Society of Illustrators, the Council on Interracial
Books, and The New York Times' Outstanding Book of the Year
in 1975. Pinkney's work has also been exhibited in the Boston
Museum of Fine Arts; the Black Artist exhibition in New York and
Boston, in 1971; the Studio Museum, in Harlem, New York; and
at North Florida State University.

Pinkney, illustration for Seagram's Black Historical Calendar, January, 1977.

Escape from the Poppy Field, from L. Frank Baum's **The Wizard of Oz**, Random House, 1991.

Charles Santore

CHARLES SANTORE (1935-) has that ideal combination for an illustrator: a good solid base of the traditional fundamentals of picture making, along with a very contemporary outlook. A good designer, his pictures are dramatic and arresting.

santore is from Philadelphia and attended the Philadelphia College of Art, studying under Henry Pitz and Albert Gold. His first assignment was for the Armstrong Cork company in 1958, and he has gradually added a long list of clients which include many of the top advertising agencies in New York and Philadelphia, as well as **Redbook**, **The Ladies' Home Journal**, **The Saturday Evening Post**, **Reader's Digest**, **Time**, **Life**, **Newsweek**, **Penthouse**, **Playboy**, **TV Guide**, **Esquire**, and other magazines.

Santore has received three gold medals at the Philadelphia Art Directors Club Show, Awards of Excellence from the Society of Publication Designers, and the Society of Illustrators. In 1972, he received the Society of Illustrators' Hamilton King Award. He had a one-man show at the Tyler School of Art/Temple University, and his work can be found in the collections of the Free Library of Philadelphia, Museum of Modern Art in New York, as well as in many private collections.

Advertising illustration for Pfizer Pharmaceuticals to depict vertigo, symbolized by Alice in Wonderland's fall into the rabbit hole, 1974.

Avon Book cover for *America the Raped* by Gene Marine, © 1970 Don Ivan Punchatz.

DON IVAN PUNCHATZ (1936-) was born in Hillside, N.J., and after high school, received a full scholarship to the School of Visual Arts in New York. His most influential teachers there were Burne Hogarth and Robert Gill. While continuing evening classes at SVA, he began working at an advertising agency and later at an animation studio.

Drafted by the Army in 1959, he was assigned to do medical illustration and training films. Following his discharge, he spent a five-year stint as an art director in Pittsburgh. After moving to Texas in the late '60s, he founded Sketchpad Studio. At the same time, he began teaching illustration at Texas Christian University and has done so for the last thirty years. He has also been a guest instructor for Syracuse University's Independent Masters Program since the mid-eighties.

Among his clients have been *Boys' Life*, *Time*, *Newsweek*, *Playboy*, *Penthouse*, *Esquire*, *Omni*, *National Lampoon*, *New York Magazine*, *Rolling Stone*, Dell, Avon, Fawcett, Simon & Schuster, Berkley Books, New American Library, U.S. Steel, General Electric, Johnson & Johnson, and Budweiser.

Punchatz has received numerous professional awards from Art Directors Clubs, the Society of Illustrators, the Society of Publication Designers, and other graphics societies.

His work is included in the permanent collections of the National Portrait Gallery, the Dallas Museum, the George Eastman House, and many private collections.

ISADORE SELTZER (1930-) credits the Push Pin Studio as his professional training ground. Certainly his work has the "Push Pin look" but with his own unpredictable variations of it.

He was born in St. Louis and attended school at Chouinard in Los Angeles for two years interrupted by Army service, and was graduated after another two years at the Art Center School. Following school, he found a few freelance jobs doing shoe ads and record album covers, but it wasn't until he moved to New York and joined the Push Pin staff in 1960 that he began to hit his stride. After four-and-a-half years, he was invited to join the stable of artists represented by Harvey Kahn, beginning an association of over twenty years. During that time, his work has appeared in *The Saturday Evening Post*, *Time*, *Newsweek*, *Esquire*, *The Ladies' Home Journal*, *Redbook*, *McCall's*, and *Playboy*, and for many advertising accounts. He has also designed several movie posters, including *The Hotel New Hampshire*, a Woody Allen film, and a four-months' long project doing all of the tattoos for the movie *Tattoo*.

Seltzer does not exhibit but does paintings, watercolors, and woodcuts for himself. He also teaches, both at Parsons School of Design and at Syracuse University.

Seltzer, illustration for "Out of Character" by Garson Kanin, *The Saturday Evening Post*, October 20, 1962. ©1962, 1990 by The Curtis Publishing Company.

"I Hate the Queen" from Sendak's own story **Hector Protector**, published by Harper & Row © Maurice Sendak, 1965, 1993

Maurice Sendak [signature]

For more than forty years, the books MAURICE SENDAK (1928-) has written and illustrated have nurtured children and adults alike and have challenged established ideas about what children's literature is and should be. **The New York Times** has recognized that Sendak's work "has brought a new dimension to the American children's book and has helped to change how people visualize childhood."

Sendak was the winner of the 1964 Caldecott Medal for **Where the Wild Things Are** and in 1970, he became the first American illustrator to receive the international Hans Christian Anderson Award, given in recognition of his entire body of work. In 1983, he received the Laura Ingalls Wilder Award from the American Library Association, also given for his entire body of work.

Beginning in 1952, with **A Hole is to Dig** by Ruth Krauss, Sendak's illustrations have enhanced many texts by other writers, including the **Little Bear** books by Else Holmelund Minarik, children's books by Isaac Bashevis Singer and Randall Jarrell, and **The Juniper Tree and Other Tales from Grimm**. **Dear Mili**, Sendak's interpretation of a newly discovered tale by Wilhelm Grimm, was published to great acclaim in 1988.

Among others, Sendak has both written and illustrated **The Nutshell Library** in 1962, **Higglety Pigglety Pop!** in 1967, **In The Night Kitchen**, in 1970, and **Outside Over There** in 1981.

Since 1980, Sendak has designed the sets and costumes for highly regarded productions of Mozart's **The Magic Flute** and **Idomeneo**, Janacek's **The Cunning Little Vixen**, Prokofiev's **The Love for Three Oranges**, and Tchaikovsky's **The Nutcracker**.

In 1990, Sendak founded The Night Kitchen, a national

Poster, "Freedom to Read," © 1991 by Maurice Sendak.

theater company devoted to the development of quality productions for children. In 1997, Sendak received the National Medal of Arts from President Clinton.

Max stalks "Wild Things" from **Where the Wild Things Are**, story and pictures by Maurice Sendak; © 1963, 1991 by Maurice Sendak; By permission of Harper Collins Publishers.

THOMAS SGOUROS (1927-   ) describes himself as "teacher/illustrator/artist," and he has worked at it full time. He served as chief critic in the European Honors Program for the Rhode Island School of Design in Rome, Italy. He has been associated with the Illustration Department of RISD in various capacities since 1962, graduating from there with a B.F.A. in 1950. Following school, he freelanced for several years in Boston, New York, and Providence, his work published by *Time*, *Life*, *Reader's Digest*, *Yankee*, *Ford Times*, Ginn & Company, Random House, Brown University Press, and for many advertising accounts, including TWA, Ford Motor Company, U.S. Steel, and Coca-Cola. His work, exhibited at the Society of Illustrators and Art Directors Club shows in New York, Boston, Providence, and Denver, has won many Gold and Silver Medals, as well as numerous merit awards.

Simultaneously, Sgouros has been painting for exhibition regularly; he has had several one-man shows, and is a member of the Boston Society of Watercolor Painters, and the American Watercolor Society. His work is represented in the Cleveland Museum of Fine Arts, the Jacksonville Museum of Fine Arts, the Anchorage Museum of Fine Arts in Alaska; the Rhode Island School of Design Museum of Fine Arts, and in many private collections.

Thomas Sgouros, advertisement for the American Iron and Steel Institute in *Steelways* magazine in 1962.

William Conrad of "Cannon"; TV Guide Cover.

JIM SHARPE (1936-) is a native of Vernon, Texas, and attended Texas Tech in Lubbock as an advertising design major. He then entered the Navy and served as a jet fighter pilot for four years. Returning to school, he enrolled in the Art Center School in Los Angeles and was graduated with honors in 1964.

His first positions were in art direction and studio illustration in Detroit. In 1968, he moved to the New York area to begin his freelance career. Early work included many paperback covers for Bantam, Dell, Fawcett, Warner, Signet, Ballantine, and others. Advertising agencies also commissioned his work for the 3M Company, U.S. Steel, Armstrong Tires, General Electric, and many other corporations. He painted over twenty covers for *Time* magazine between 1970 and 1979; has painted more than a dozen covers for *TV Guide*, two for *Newsweek*, and other covers for *Golf Digest*, *True*, and *Field and Stream*, as well as editorial illustration for *Woman's Day*, *Scouting*, *Reader's Digest*, *Popular Mechanics*, *Cosmopolitan*, *Boys' Life*, and others. He has also made paintings for the National Parks Association and worked with the producers and directors of the ABC Television News program *20/20* making illustrations for the major theme of a story which could not be recorded in film. One such was on Howard Hughes, another on "The Death of Elvis Presley." He has also designed twelve commemorative postage stamps for U.S. Postal Service for the Performing Arts Series, and a design featuring the late Dr. Ralph Bunche.

Burt Silverman, Portrait of Anwar Sadat to accompany his article, "In Search of Identity," for *Time* magazine, 1978. Collection of the Society of Illustrators Museum of American Illustration.

BURT SILVERMAN, N.A. (1928-) like many other current illustrators, paints both for the printed page and gallery exhibition. He has had twenty-seven one-man shows in galleries in New York, Philadelphia, Houston, Washington, and Boston, and won more than thirty awards and prizes from annual exhibitions of the National Academy of Design and the American Watercolor Society, as well as various other regional and national exhibitions.

Born in Brooklyn, he attended the High School of Music and Art and the Art Students League, where he studied with Louis Bouché and Reginald Marsh. He also earned a B.A. at Columbia University in 1949. His first work was published by *Sports Illustrated* in 1959, and he has added a long roster of other periodicals since, including *Time*, *Life*, *Fortune*, *Esquire*, *The New Yorker*, *New York*, *Redbook*, *McCall's*, *Newsweek*, *Discover*, *People*, and *Psychology Today*.

In 1990, he was elected to the Hall of Fame of the Society of Illustrators, and the Museum of American Illustration awarded him the Geismann Memorial Invitational Retrospective Exhibition. A collection of ninety of his drawings created for Bill Moyer's PBS series on the "Constitutional Convention of 1787-Report from Philadelphia" was published by Random House in 1987. He was elected to the Pastel Society of America Hall of Fame in 1991, and in November 1998, was honored by the American Society of Portrait Artists with the Annual John Singer Sargent Award for Distinction in Portraiture.

Of French Cajun ancestry from Eunice, Louisiana, HODGES SOILEAU (1943-) received his education at the University of Southern Louisiana. He began his art career as a freelance artist in the Houston/Dallas area from 1969 to 1978. After establishing himself on the East Coast, his clients have included *Reader's Digest*, *The Ladies' Home Journal*, *Seventeen*, *Fortune*, *World Tennis*, and *Better Homes & Gardens*, as well as book publishers such as the Franklin Library, Bantam, Ballantine, New American Library, Avon, and Easton Press. His corporate clients have included the Unicover Corporation, Air Canada, NBC-TV, and Exxon.

Soileau is a member of the Society of Illustrators in New York and his work is often included in their annual shows. He has also been shown at the Master Eagle Galleries in New York and at Sacred Heart University in Fairfield, Connecticut.

Hodges Soileau. frontispiece for *The Analects of Confucius,* published by Easton Press, 1976.

James Spanfeller, illustration for John Luke Associates, 1989.

The art of JAMES J. SPANFELLER (1930-) appears to have more kinship with the European illustrators Harry Clarke and Kay Nielsen than to have any American influence. He has their same fascination with the macabre and intricate, distorted detail. The result both disquiets and intrigues the viewer.

Spanfeller has had a thoroughly American background, however. He was born in Philadelphia and attended both the Philadelphia College of Art and the Pennsylvania Academy of the Fine Arts. His first illustrated book, *Where Did You Go? Out. What Did You Do? Nothing* by Robert Paul Smith, was on the best seller list for more than a year. He has since worked for many other book publishers, including Ballantine Books, Harper & Row, Time-Life, and Random House. He supplied the jacket art for Frederick Exleef's *A Fan's Notes* and Jack Kerouac's *Visions of Gerard*. Magazine appearances include *Seventeen*, *Playboy*, *The Ladies' Home Journal*, *McCall's*, *Redbook*, *House Beautiful*, *Charm*, *Columbia*, *Avant-Garde*, and others.

He was named the Artists Guild's "Artist of the Year" in 1964; he received the Herald-Tribune Children's Book Award in 1965; and he won Gold and Silver Medals from the Society of Publication Designers. He teaches at Parsons School of Design and is an active member of the Society of Illustrators.

R-SPARKS

RICHARD SPARKS (1944-) started out aiming to be an architect and received his degree in architecture from the Texas A.& M. University. Realizing that he really wanted to be an artist, he enrolled in the Art Center School of Design in Los Angeles where he studied under Harry Carmean, Donald Puttman, and Joseph Henninger. There he met and married his wife Barbara, also an illustrator. They freelanced in Amsterdam, Holland, for three years before returning to the States and the New York art market.

Sparks found acceptance quickly, and his work has been published by *Time* magazine (twenty-five covers), *Fortune*, *Sports Illustrated*, *Esquire*, *Forbes*, *Redbook*, *The Ladies' Home Journal*, *Psychology Today*, *McCall's*, *New York*, *Reader's Digest*, *Cosmopolitan*, *Boy's Life*, *Family Circle*, *Woman's Day*, and other periodicals. He completed seven U. S. postage stamp designs for the Great Americans Series. His portrait painting for a *Time* cover of Mstislav Rostropovich was placed in the National Portrait Gallery in Washington, D.C. Other paintings are in the Franklin D. Roosevelt Library and the Academy of Art College in San Francisco. Sparks has received a Gold Medal and an Award of Excellence for his work exhibited at the Society of Illustrators. Other honors and national recognition have come from the American Institute of Graphic Arts, *Graphis*, *Print* magazine, *Art Direction* magazine and *Communication Arts Annual.*

Richard Sparks, Chinese Empress, *Reader's Digest*

WALT SPITZMILLER (1944-) is from St. Louis, Missouri, and was graduated from Washington University there with a B.F.A. in 1969. His first freelance artwork was for advertising agencies, and he supplemented his income with part-time teaching at St. Louis Junior College and Washington University.

McCall's magazine gave him his first editorial job, and Spitzmiller, who now lives in Connecticut, has since gravitated to sports subjects. He has done over thirty-five assignments for *Sports Illustrated* and works regularly for publications such as *Golf*, *Golf Digest*, *Sports Afield*, *Outdoor Life*, Playboy books, The Franklin Library, and *Signature* magazine. He has collaborated with Carlo Fassi on *The World of Figure Skating* published by Charles Scribner & Sons, worked on projects for the United States Football League, and for the 1984 Olympics.

He has had several one-man shows and won awards from Art Directors Clubs across the country; he has exhibited many times at the Society of Illustrators. One of his paintings is included in the Rodeo Museum in Colorado Springs, and others are held in the private collections of Jack Nicklaus, Tom Watson, Lee Trevino, and Sam Snead, in addition to the Baseball Hall of Fame, the Smithsonian Institution, and the Museum of American Illustration at the Society of Illustrators in New York.

Walt Spitzmiller, *Willie Stargell, 1988 inductee*, **National Baseball Hall of Fame & Museum Yearbook**; ©1988 National Baseball Hall of Fame and Museum, Inc.

B.F. STAHL

BENJAMIN F. STAHL (1932-) has always scrupulously avoided trading on his famous illustrator father's name, rarely signing his work and for years using a pseudonym. In developing his own style and identity, Stahl's work is marked by its combination of strength and sensitivity. He depicts young people particularly well and has won American Institute of Graphic Arts awards for Children's Book Illustration in 1977 and '79; his work was included in Outstanding Science Books for Children (National Science Teachers Association, 1976).

His art has been commissioned by most of the major publishers, including Houghton-Mifflin; Little, Brown; Putnam; Coward, McCann and Geoghegan; Random House, Scribner's, The Franklin Library; the Limited Editions Book Club; Bantam Books, *Reader's Digest*; Warner Publishing Company; and Holt, Rinehart, and Winston.

Stahl was born in Chicago and grew up with illustration, never having a formal art training. He is nevertheless an excellent teacher; for various periods between 1955 and '70 he taught at the Famous Artists Schools, Bridgeport University, and at the Ringling School of Art in Sarasota, Florida. He currently works from his studio on Prince Edward Island in Canada.

Ben F. Stahl, cover for *Child of the Holocaust*, Bantam Books.

Gilbert Stone, cover design, *The Empty Face*, Richard Marck publishers.

GILBERT L. STONE (1940-1984) made an illustration career out of presenting a unique, sidewise-compressed vision of the world. The optical illusion conferred itself to the picture content as well, adding an element of mystery and forcing the viewer to interpret its meaning. The effect was intriguing and very successful in attracting the attention of the reader.

Stone was born in Brooklyn and went to the High School of Art and Design. He attended Parsons School of Design on a scholarship, then furthered his education at New York University, graduating with honors. In the years following, he was active as a media artist, exhibited regularly and taught at the School of Visual Arts for many years. His published work appeared in *Playboy*, *McCall's*, *Redbook*, *The Ladies' Home Journal*, *Esquire*, *Oui*, *Sports Illustrated*, and *New York* magazine. He won many awards when exhibited in Art Directors Club shows, and three Gold Medals at the Society of Illustrators Annual Exhibitions.

Concurrent to his honors for published work, Stone had three one-man shows and participated in six group shows in New York. His pictures are in many collecions, including the Brooklyn Museum, the Joseph Hirshorn Collection, and the Smithsonian Institution, as well as in several corporate and private collections.

ROSS BARRON STOREY (1940-) has been an active illustrator since the age of twenty.

Born in Dallas, Texas, he studied the Famous Artists Course and attended the Art Center School in Los Angeles. Storey's first illustrations for publication were for the Sunday magazine of the *New York Journal-American*, followed by *This Week* magazine, *Woman's Day*, *Children's Digest*, *Time*, *National Geographic*, *Saturday Review*, and work for various paperback publishers, including Avon, Fawcett, and Pocket Books.

He has executed numerous advertising illustration assignments and received awards for his work from Art Directors Clubs in New York, Los Angeles, Denver, and Dallas, as well as a Gold Medal from the Society of Illustrators in 1976.

Storey has taught at Pratt Institute and the School of Visual Arts in New York. His studio is now located in San Francisco.

Barron Storey, illustration for *Road and Track* magazine, 1980.

Murray Tinkelman, story illustration, "Of the Flea, A Modern Bestiary," *Lithopinion* #26, 1972.

Barrell Pacer from **Rodeo Drawings of Murraty Tinkelman**, Art Direction Book Co., 1982.

MURRAY TINKELMAN (1933-) has had a major impact on contemporary illustration both by the example of his work and through the enthusiasm of his teaching and lectures.

Born in Brooklyn, Tinkelman was graduated from the New York High School of Industrial Art and served in the Army. He returned to study at the Cooper Union art school for two years, then switched to the Brooklyn Museum Art School on the Max Beckman scholarship to study under Reuben Tam. Taken on by the Charles Cooper Studio, Tinkelman quickly made a name for himself.

When the studio dissolved in 1964, he became a freelancer and has since worked for a wide range of clients, including **The Saturday Evening Post**, **Playboy**, **Boy's Life**, **The Ladies' Home Journal**, **Good Housekeeping**, **American Heritage**, **Family Circle**, and **Field & Stream**. He has done twenty-five children's books for publishers such as Harper & Row; Coward, McCann, and Geoghegan; Macmillan; and Knopf; as well as a large number of fantasy book covers for Ballantine Books by H.P. Lovecraft, and western covers for Pocket Books by Zane Grey. He has often appeared on the Op-Ed page of **The New York Times**.

All this is in addition to an almost full-time career as a teacher. He served on the illustration faculty of Parsons School of Design for many years; at present he is a professor of art at the College of Visual and Performing Arts at Syracuse University. In addition to serving on the undergraduate faculty, he also chairs the Masters of Arts graduate program in illustration.

He was selected as "Artist of the Year" in 1970 by the Artists Guild in New York and has been awarded numerous Gold and Silver Medals by the Society of Illustrators, the Art Directors Club of New York, and the Society of Publication Designers. His book, **The Illustrations of Murray Tinkelman**, was published in 1980, and **Rodeo Drawings of Murray Tinkelman** in 1983, both by Art Direction Book Company.

Active in the Society of Illustrators Air Force Art Program, he has gone on numerous trips to document the activities of Air Force training. Tinkelman has also served as chairman of the Permanent Collection Committee at the Society of Illustrators and is currently chairman of their Hall of Fame committee. His most recent honor was the Distinguished Educator in the Arts award from the Society in 1999.

Jack Unruh, Portrait of Blues artist Muddy Waters published by *Rolling Stone*, 1989.

The art of JACK NEAL UNRUH (1935-) has evolved considerably during his career, becoming increasingly linear and disciplined in drawing with more emphasis on texture and pattern.

The son of an Air Force father, Unruh was born in Pretty Prairie, Kansas, and moved often during his childhood. He was graduated with a B.F.A. from Washington University in St. Louis, Missouri, having studied under Bob Cassel. He then started a studio with a partner in Dallas, Texas, but was called to active military service during the Berlin Crisis in 1961-'62. Upon his return, he started to freelance as an illustrator with a Dallas group called Portfolio. Since 1981 he has been on his own.

During these years, his work has appeared in many magazines, including *Redbook*, *Seventeen*, *Sports Illustrated*, *Quest*, *Boys' Life*, *Oui*, *Outdoor Life*, and *National Geographic.* He has also illustrated the annual reports for LTV, Dresser Industries, Borg Warner, Triton Oil, and others, as well as advertising illustrations for American Airlines, Braniff, NBC, Hyatt Hotels, ITT, Kimberly Clark, Exxon, and 20th Century Fox.

Unruh is a member of the Society of Illustrators, the Dallas Illustrators, and the Dallas Society of Visual Communications. He has also taught drawing and illustration at East Texas State University. He was chosen for the Hamilton King award in 1998.

The illustrations of DON WELLER (1937-) are like the performances of a juggler; he successfully keeps all of the elements of his pictures — form, color, chapes, and a bit of spatter — all in the air. He also uses distortion with good effect; there are a lot of accidentals and surprises in his pictures that make them effective.

Weller is a West Coast illustrator; he was born in Colfax, Washington, and earned his B.A. at Washington State University. His first published work was a cartoon for *Western Horseman* magazine. He has gradually added a long list of publications as clients, such as *Time*, *TV Guide*, *Sports Illustrated*, *Boys' Life*, *Westways*, *Seventeen*, *Emergency Medicine*, *Road and Track*, *Communications Arts*, *Bon Appetit*, and *Idea* magazine.

Weller does many posters for sports and entertainment clients, including a long running series for the Hollywood Bowl. He did a series of five sports stamps for the U. S. Postal Service in 1995 and a flag for Summit County, Utah, where he now resides, in 1996. He has illustrated many books, including three for children: *The Phantom of the Opera*, *Professor Fergus Fahrenheit and His Wonderful Weather Machine*, and *The Magic Bat*.

His work has been exhibited in many shows on both coasts, and he has won Gold and Silver Medals from the Art Directors Clubs of New York and Los Angeles, various merit awards and the Society of Illustrators of Los Angeles' Lifetime Achievement Award in 1982.

Don Weller, cover painting for *Westways*, May, 1974.

ROBERT M. ZIERING (1933-   ) is a specialist in an expressive line that effectively conveys the feeling of shape and motion, along with the multiple imagery he often uses to invoke the animation of his subjects. More recently, he has been working in pastel and mixed media.

Ziering was born in Brooklyn, New York. He attended the High School of Music and Art before going on to the New York University School of Education and the School of Visual Arts in New York City.

His first professional illustration was done for **Coronet** magazine and has been followed by commissions from **Time**, **Life**, **Esquire**, **Runner**, **Redbook**, **Print** magazine, **The Chicago Tribune**, **McCall's**, **National Geographic**, **The Saturday Review**, and other publications, as well as advertisers such as TV Guide, Barton's Chocolates, Arista Records, NBC, Mobil Oil, the New York City Opera, and IBM.

Ziering's works appear regularly in the exhibitions at the Society of Illustrators, the Art Directors Club of New York, the AIGA, and have also been exhibited at the Butler Institute of American Art, the Carroll Reece Museum, East Tennessee State University, the Museum of Modern Art, the Alonzo Gallery in New York, and Heritage Arts in New Jersey. In addition, he has taught at the School of Visual Arts and a senior portfolio class at Pratt Institute in Brooklyn.

Robert Ziering, *Twilight of the Gorilla,* cover illustration of brochure for his one-man exhibition at the Central Park Zoo Wildlife Gallery, 1994.

STANLEY ZUCKERBERG (1919-1995) was a New York City native and went to local art schools: Pratt Institute in Brooklyn, and the Art Students League. He launched his illustration career in 1940 at the time of the emergence of the paperback book cover market, and after some experience in the Pulps and a stint with Classics Illustrated Comics, he painted his first cover for Bantam Books in 1949. He had found his right metier and went on to produce over 300 covers for the major publishers, including Dell, Fawcett, Avon, Ballantine, Signet, Popular Library, and Pocket Books.

By 1965, Zuckerberg decided to restrict his work to painting for exhibition and began a long association with Grand Central Galleries, painting his favorite Long Island harbor and beach scenes.

Stanley Zuckerberg, paperback book cover for **The Heller**, by William E. Henning, Bantam Books, 1957.

1980-1990

Richard Amsel
Marshall Arisman
Christopher Blossom
Michael David Brown
Anthony Chen
Kinuko Y. Craft
Linda Crockett
Etienne Delessert
Vincent DiFate
C. Michael Dudash
Elaine Duillo
Peter M. Fiore
Gervasio Gallardo
Hector Garrido
Robert Guisti
Glenn Harrington
Robert Hunt
Roger Kastel

Gary Kelley
Howard Koslow
Birney Lettick
Francis Livingston
Dennis Luzak
Daniel M. Maffia
Sergio Martinez
Marvin Mattelson
Ann Meisel
Barbara Nessim
Mel Odom
George Stavrinos
Drew Struzan
John Thompson
Richard Tomlinson
Chuck Wilkinson
Bruce Wolfe

Richard Amsel - *TV Guide* cover November 12, 1983.

Elaine Duillo - ***Born to Love***, Warner Books, 1984.

Gary Kelley - ***Glamour Magazine.***

THE DECADE 1980-1990

With many restless, younger illustrators appearing on the scene, impatient with their more staid brethren, a segment of illustration began to take on a new look. These "New Illustrators" deliberately turned their backs on the accepted norms of drawing and painting, following the lead of punk rock. There was much to rebel against. Many illustration jobs were repetitive, of uninteresting subjects, drawn small because of tight deadlines, and required rendering photographs. Alternatively rejecting old ideas and yet borrowing heavily from a cross-cultural melange of imagery ranging from Op-Art and Dada, Andy Warhol to Paul Klee, Dali, Krazy Kat, and the Underground Comics of Robert Crumb, these artists produced irreverent images motivated to shock and ensnare the viewer. Many found their first acceptance through appearances on record album covers, posters, T-shirts, coffee mugs, shopping bags and other non-traditional venues. Although the movement seemed rudderless, it began to take on a characteristic look and to find an audience in anti-establishment publications such as **The Village Voice**, **Mother Jones**, and **Raw**. "Ugly" was in, realism was bad, color was hyped with day-glo and magic markers. Distortion became an effective parody of reality. Like its counterpart in the Dada movement of post-World War I, by ridicule, it forced a new aesthetic into being. While still a fringe group in the Seventies, it continued to expand its influence and would evolve further into the Nineties.

Meanwhile, mainstream illustration was also undergoing changes; it, too, was borrowing from the past. The Twenties idiom of simplified poster shapes known as Art Deco or Moderne style became modern again. Artists rediscovered J. C. Leyendecker, Tamara de Lempicka, Leon Bakst, and A. M. Cassandre. Even the illustration style of Hugh Lofting's "Doctor Doolittle" was not safe from exploitation, and as usual, the current leaders, such as Bernie Fuchs and Bob Peak, had a long trail of followers.

Paperback publishing still required realistic artwork, though ironically, it was increasingly dominated by fantasy titles. Cover art was one of the last preserves of traditional drawing and painting, and many illustrators found it a steady and supportive market. The field was losing its cutting edge though, and became almost a backwater, increasingly reliant on safe clichés, photographically rendered, with the most popular author's names buttressed by die cutouts and embossed lettering that crowded out the art.

The beginnings of computer-produced art were also edging into print. Experimentation made converts of many of those willing to try it; to younger artists it became a natural extension of the eye and hand. Like the New Illustration, it was to contribute its own influence to the volatile mix of the eighties.

·AMSEL·

RICHARD AMSEL (1947-1985) had a brilliant but tragically short career that flamed out with AIDS. Within that brief time, he reached the top of the profession that he had entered while still an illustration student at the Philadelphia College of Art in 1969.

His chosen field was in advertising and movie posters, a highly competitive one in which he regularly won the big movie accounts over more seasoned professionals. Among his spectacular poster designs were those commissioned for **Raiders of the Lost Ark**, **Chinatown**, **The Dark Crystal**, and **The Sting**. The latter was done in the style of J. C. Leyendecker; with **Nijinsky**, he emulated the Russian Leon Bakst, and for other assignments he created homages to Rolf Armstrong and Coles Phillips. **TV Guide** commissioned him to do over forty covers, depicting a lengthy roster of stars and celebrities, including John Travolta, Lucille Ball, Katharine Hepburn, Elvis Presley, Vivien Leigh, the Duke and Duchess of Windsor, and Clark Gable. Amsel also illustrated fiction for magazines such as **McCall's**, and designed record album covers.

He received numerous awards from both the Society of Illustrators in Los Angeles and New York, a Golden Key Award from the **Hollywood Reporter**, and a Grammy Award.

To settle his estate, Christie's auction house held a one-man sale of his movie poster art in 1987, which elicited avid bidding by many private collectors.

Richard Amsel, poster design for **The Shootist**. This was John Wayne's last film.

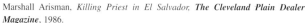

Marshall Arisman, *Killing Priest in El Salvador*, **The Cleveland Plain Dealer Magazine**, 1986.

MARSHALL ARISMAN (1938-   ) is a strong force in the illustration field both as a performer and as a teacher. He also exhibits in New York galleries, and although he was trained at Pratt Institute and chairs the Masters program at the School of Visual Arts, his most apparent influence is the Irish painter Francis Bacon. To extend that viewpoint, Arisman renders a persona with a combination of metallic flesh and feral eyes, that is unnerving and foreboding. This ominous viewpoint finds its perfect application to the distopian Op-ed piece or in muck-raking journalism.

Arisman has been regularly published, by **Omni** magazine, **The Nation**, **Time**, and **The New York Times**. He received the Hamilton King Award in 1997 for "Best Illustration of the Year" from the Society of Illustrators in New York. The artist has an international following, with one-man exhibits in Japan, Korea, and in China where he recently showed a series of sculpture, drawings, and paintings of sacred monkeys.

Arisman's work has been accessioned by the Brooklyn Museum, the National Museum of American Art, and the Smithsonian Institution, as well as by several corporate and private collections.

Christopher Blossom

CHRISTOPHER BLOSSOM (1956-) is the son and grandson of the distinguished artists in this book, David Blossom and Earl Blossom. Each of them has had a great artistic competence, yet have all been very different. Christopher was taught by his father and studied at Parsons School of Design under Sanford Kossin, James Spanfeller, and David Passalacqua.

His direction in art, however, was triggered by his first work in the industrial design studio of Robert Bourke. There he learned to read blueprints of boats and to analyze their structure from the inside out. This, coupled with his ardent love of sailing, led him into the highly specialized area of painting historical ships and sailing craft.

He won a Gold Medal Scholarship from the Society of Illustrators at the age of twenty and also became a charter member of the American Society of Marine Artists. He has since become a dominant talent in this field, attracting commissions from

Christopher Blossom commission by Avon Books.

publishers and private collectors alike. His works have been exhibited at the Peabody Essex Museum, the Mystic Seaport Museum, the Colorado History Museum, and the Gilcrease Museum, and he has participated in the U. S. Naval Art Program.

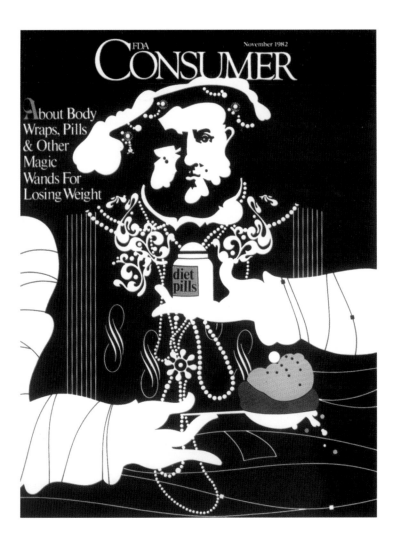

Michael David Brown

MICHAEL DAVID BROWN (1944-) is a strong designer, many of whose works build on an underpinning of black and white. His color is often more of an accent than part of the structure. As such, his artwork has a poster-like quality of great impact, ideal for magazine or book covers.

The artist was born in Fullerton, California, and studied at Colorado State College and the Colorado Institute of Art. Establishing his own graphic design firm, he has built a wide variety of advertising and graphic design clients which have included *Sports Illustrated, Fortune, Newsweek, Outlook, Review, FDA Consumer, Art Expo CAL,* and he has made four stamp designs for the United States Postal Service.

His other roles include teacher — he is adjunct professor at the Maryland Institute College of Art — lecturer, and exhibitor. He is also an active member of the American Watercolor Society, the Society of Illustrators in New York, and Art Directors Clubs in Washington, D.C. and New York City.

Michael David Brown, cover design for *FDA Consumer,* November, 1982.

407

ANTHONY "TONY" CHEN (1929-1994) was born in Jamaica, but his parents were Chinese. From childhood he began to draw naturally and was fully encouraged by his nurturing family. Coming to the U.S., he attended Pratt Institute. He was greatly influenced by Richard Lindner, one of his teachers. Other influences were Julius Bissier, Paul Klee, Franz Kline, and Piet Mondrian.

His own style was timeless. He was particularly expert with animals, and his renderings in oils or watercolors, while modern, also reflected the ancient Chinese values of clarity and simplicity. Chen's clients included the Bronx Zoo, the National Federation of Wildlife, UNICEF, and *Reader's Digest*. He illustrated over forty books for children, among them a *Children's Illustrated Bible* for Doubleday; *There's a Train going by my Window*; *The Little Raccoon*; and *Wart Hogs.* He won awards from the AIGA, the Art Directors Club in New York, the Children's Book Showcase, and the Educational Press Association of America, as well as the Society of Illustrators in New York.

Tony Chen, *Jaguars* for *Wild Animals*. Collection of Alvin Schwartzman.

Born in Japan, KINUKO Y. CRAFT (1940-) had an early proclivity to draw and paint. After obtaining a B.F.A. from the Kanazawa Municipal College of Fine and Industrial Art, she came to the U.S. and attended the Art Institute of Chicago. She first worked for several art services in Chicago, but was soon able to embark on her own as a freelancer. She has not lacked for clients since, with an ever-expanding variety of assignments. Her attention to detail and jewel-like renditions have a kinship with Western painters of the Renaissance as well as having an oriental overtone that uniquely identifies her handiwork.

Her clients have been remarkably diverse, ranging from magazines such as *Playboy* to *National Geographic,* to *Time, Newsweek, U.S. News & World Report,* and *Forbes Magazine*.

Advertising assignments have been commissioned by AT&T, Clairol, Citibank, Seagram's, Colgate, and ITT. She created a series of posters for the Washington Opera and the Dallas Opera, and has illustrated several children's books for William Morrow, including *The Twelve Dancing Princesses, Baba Yaga, Vasilisa the Brave,* and *Pegasus*. Two books she illustrated were written by her daughter, Marie Charlotte Craft.

Her services also are in demand as a guest lecturer, teacher at summer workshops, and as a judge at exhibitions. She herself exhibits regularly and has won many awards in exhibitions at both the Society of Illustrators in Los Angeles and New York, which also honored her with the Hamilton King Award in 1987. *Step-by-Step Graphics* published a detailed article on her artwork in 1989.

Kinuko Craft, book cover for *The Book of Atrix Wolfe*, published by Berkley Books.

LindaCrockett

LINDA CROCKETT (1948-) focuses on the picture idea — and the mood — with less attention to detail than to the conception. As a result, her pictures express the spontaneity of a momentary event that gives them a feeling of reality and authority.

Born in Slater, South Carolina, she has been on the move ever since, having lived in New York, Nashville, Key West, the Chesapeake Bay area, Ohio, and abroad in England, Scotland, Amsterdam, and Paris. Along the way, she has been involved in every conceivable aspect of an art career, from designing gift wrap and wallpaper to costume design (with her own private label), pasteup, art direction, and freelance illustrator. She has studied at the Cleveland Institute of Art, Cooper School of Art, Cleveland State University, and Macomb County Community College. Her first illustration was done for American Greetings.

Among her clients have been magazines such as *Yankee*, *Sports Illustrated*, *Working Mother*, *Seventeen*, *Greenpeace*, *Family Circle*, and *Cricket*, as well as a long list of book publishers, including Houghton-Mifflin; Dodd, Mead and Co.; Ginn; Viking-Penguin; Simon & Schuster; and Avon. Along the way, she has had several one-woman shows, and won many awards for her work.

Linda Crockett, "Ringside Seat for Life" by Pete Hammill, 1981, published by *The Cleveland Plain Dealer*. This painting was awarded a Gold Medal by the Society of Illustrators in New York, and is now part of their permanent collection.

ETIENNE DELESSERT (1941-) is a natural story teller. Born in Switzerland, he is self-taught and allows the story to set the style. He can present both fanciful and serious topics, ranging from AIDS and terminal illness to animated cartoon characters. He has over eighty illustrated children's books to his credit. Among the titles are *The Endless Party*, *Dance*, *Ashes, Ashes* and *A Long, Long Song*. His media are varied; he is at home with animated films, posters, books, institutional advertising, newspapers, and magazines, including *The New York Times Magazine* and the *Atlantic Monthly*. Delessert's clientele is an international one, and he has also had one-man shows in Italy, Switzerland, Paris, Canada, and the U.S. In 1995, his one-man retrospective was mounted at the Musée des Arts Décoratifs in the Louvre.

The Society of Illustrators has awarded him several Gold and Silver Medals as well as the prestigious Hamilton King Award in 1996.

The Seven Dwarfs by Ettiene Delessert, published by Creative Editions, 2000. Also reproduced as a poster design, *Inventing Visual Mythology*, for an exhibition of the artist's work at the Museum of the School of Visual Arts, 1999.

409

Vincent DiFate, *Star Fire* by Paul Preuss, published by Tor Books, 1987.

VINCENT DI FATE (1945-) is one of the major illustrators of futuristic themes. *People Magazine* has described him as "one of the top illustrators of science fiction." In his thirty-year career, DiFate has produced more than three thousand works for such diverse clients as IBM, *Reader's Digest*, *National Geographic*, CBS, and the National Aeronautics and Space Administration.

The artist was born in Yonkers, New York, and was graduated from the New York-Phoenix Art School, which he attended on scholarship. He worked as a photoengraver, taught elementary school art, and worked in animated films before turning to freelance illustration in 1969. He has since received many awards, including the Frank R. Paul Award for Outstanding Achievement in Science Fiction Illustration, the prestigious Hugo Award (Science Fiction Achievement Award) for Best Professional Artist in 1979 and has had one-man shows in North America, Europe and Japan. His work is included in the Smithsonian's National Air and Space Museum, and at NASA.

A book of his paintings entitled *Di Fate's Catalog of Science Fiction Hardware* was published in 1980. He was commissioned by NASA to create the official painting of the international space station "Freedom," in 1987, and is the author and editor of the book, *Infinite Worlds: The Fantastic Visions of Science Fiction Art*, an historical overview.

Di Fate is an Adjunct Professor at the Fashion Institute of Technology in New York City, where he teaches a course in science fiction illustration. He served as President of the Society of Illustrators (1995-97) and was a founding member and a past president of the Association of Science Fiction/Fantasy Artists.

C. M. DUDASH ✝

C. MICHAEL DUDASH (1952-) is a Minnesotan, born in Kankato. He majored in art at Macalester College in St. Paul and at the Minneapolis College of Art and Design. He began his art career as a staff illustrator for the McGraw-Hill publications *Postgraduate Medicine* and *Sports Medicine* in Minneapolis. Now freelancing from Vermont, his work has encompassed over one thousand paintings and assignments since 1978, including movie posters, advertising, book and magazine illustrations, as well as designs for the U. S. Postal Service and the United Nations. He has also marketed his original oils, limited edition prints, and posters. Dudash has been featured in *Step-by-Step Graphics, American Artist,* and *The Artist's Magazine*.

He has won numerous awards from both the Society of Illustrators in New York and Los Angeles. He has taught illustration at the Vermont Community College and participated in workshops in Los Angeles and Dallas.

Michael Dudash, *Interrogating Viet Cong Prisoners, TV Guide.*

Elaine Duillo, cover illustration for **Keeper of the Dream** by Penelope Williamson, Dell Publishing, 1992.

Elaine

ELAINE DUILLO (1928-   ) has long dominated the look of paperback romance book covers, setting the style of this artform with a high standard for other artists to follow. This has been across the field, since her covers have been commissioned by virtually all of the major paperback publishers including Bantam Books, Avon, Dell, Ballantine, Berkley, Warner, Harlequin, New American Library, Jove Books, Pyramid, Penguin USA, Fawcett, and others. Her assignments have also included hard-cover book art for Doubleday, Random House, Grosset & Dunlop, and St. Martin's Press.

Duillo is a New Yorker, born in Brooklyn, and attended the High School of Music and Art in Manhattan. This was followed by training at Pratt Institute where she studied with Charles Mazoujian. Her first professional work was commissioned by **Seventeen** magazine, and she also illustrated for **Good Housekeeping** before entering the specialized paperback field.

She is often called upon to lecture about her work and over the past fifteen years, has taught at Syracuse University and at several Long Island colleges. Her work has been exhibited regularly, and she was named "Illustrator of the Year" in 1986 by **Romantic Times**.

P. Fiore

PETER M. FIORE (1955-   ) is a versatile professional whose work has won over thirty-five major awards. His adaptability has allowed him to attract a wide variety of clients including **Time, TV Guide, McCall's, The Ladies' Home Journal, Redbook, Reader's Digest,** and advertisers Price Waterhouse, AT&T, Xerox, IBM, Geigy Pharmaceuticals, NBC, CBS, WOR, American Express, Canon, Texaco, Exxon, Pepsi Cola, Union Pacific Corporation, Union Carbide, Nikon, Pan-Am, the U.S. Air Force, the U.S. Army, and International Paper.

Fiore was born in Teaneck, New Jersey, and studied at both Pratt Institute and the Art Students League. Among his teachers were David Passalacqua, Gerry Contreras, Robert Cunningham, and John Collier. His career was launched by an assignment from **McCall's** magazine in 1976, and he has been busy ever since. He taught at Pratt from 1978 to 1984, and at the School of Visual Arts from 1992 to the present. A long-time member and medal-winner of the Society of Illustrators, he served as its President from 1993 to 1995.

Peter Fiore, album cover for the Cannonball Adderley Quintet, CBS Records, 1986.

411

Gallardo

GERVASIO GALLARDO (1934-   ) brought a new flavor to illustration that has made him a strong influence in American paperback cover and advertising art. He was born in Barcelona, Spain, and received his art education there. He gravitated to advertising art and broadened his horizons by working in Munich and Paris. He first came to New York in 1963 and freelanced both as a commercial illustrator and as an exhibiting artist.

His work, reminiscent of Henri Rousseau and René Magritte in its surreal treatment of people and places, lends itself well to both fields. Gallardo adds an element of humor to the fantasy that makes his work particularly popular with magazine and book publishers on both sides of the Atlantic. He has worked periodically in the U.S., Paris, and Spain. Among his many book titles were *A Fine and Private Place*, *The Last Unicorn*, *Khaled*, and *Great Short Novels of Adult Fantasy Books 1* and *2*.

Gallardo uses any medium that will best express his subject, often mixing several in the same picture. His work has won many medals and awards both here and abroad.

Gervasio Gallardo, advertising illustration for Laboratories Roussel, May, 1984.

H. GARRIDO

HECTOR GARRIDO (1927-   ) is a native of Argentina and he attended Il Perugino Art School for three years, followed by another four years at the National Academy of Fine Arts in Buenos Aires.

His first professional artwork was in advertising illustration. Following his immigration to the United States in 1957, he worked for the McCann Erickson advertising agency for ten years designing 24-sheet posters for Esso Oil and many other clients. He also painted poster subjects for movie advertising, including the movie *Oliver!*, and plate designs for the Bradford Exchange.

He then gravitated to the paperback field and for several years painted covers for a majority of those publishers, including Dell, Fawcett, Avon, and Pocket Books. He later began to illustrate for *The Catholic Magazine* and other religious publications. This shift of clientèle gave him the opportunity to paint Biblical subject matter with a wider artistic latitude. Currently, he is fully booked through his affiliation with publisher Quadriga Recordata.

Hector Garrido, paperback cover for *The Pilgrimage* by Zenna Henderson, Avon Books.

ROBERT GIUSTI (1937-) was born in Zurich, Switzerland, the son of the famous designer and illustrator George Giusti. After immigrating with his family to the United States, Robert received his formal training at the Tyler School of Fine Arts and the Cranbrook Academy of Art.

His first illustration commission was from *The American Girl* in 1956, and he has worked steadily since for a long list of magazine clients including *McCall's*, *Fortune*, *Redbook*, *Time*, *Penthouse*, *Playboy*, and *Idea*, as well as advertising assignments ranging from the Cincinnati Zoo to Pirelli, British Airways, Tri-Star Pictures, Atlantic Records, and the U.S. Postal Service.

Giusti has also worked from the art director's side, at Cunningham and Walsh in 1961, and for Random House from 1962 to 1973. He also taught the illustration portfolio class at the School of Visual Arts from 1972 to 1980.

The variety and quality of his work has won him repeated awards at the Society of Illustrators, the Art Directors Club, and the Advertising Club, all in New York. He has been featured in *Communication Arts* magazine, *Studio* magazine, and *Print*, as well as in publications in Brazil and Japan.

Robert Giusti, illustration for the Cincinnati Zoo, 1986 .

GLENN HARRINGTON (1959-) paints in the classic tradition with a sensuous appreciation of color, form, and the human figure. This made him an ideal candidate to interpret a series of Bantam Classic books including *Wuthering Heights*, *Anna Karenina*, *A Room With a View*, *Pride and Prejudice*, *Mansfield Park*, and *Shakespeare's Plays and Sonnets*, for Sterling Publishers. He also has the versatility to do a wide range of subjects, from his first assignment in 1979 for *Heavy Metal* magazine to *The New Yorker*, with a children's book, a Maria Callas poster, work for *Golf* magazine, and the *New York Times Magazine* in between.

Harrington is a New Yorker and has a B.F.A. from Pratt Institute in Brooklyn. He exhibits his work regularly, participating in shows in the Kirin Art Space in Tokyo and Osaka; the Norman Rockwell Museum in Stockbridge, Massachusetts; the United States Golf Association in Far Hills, New Jersey; and the Society of Illustrators in New York. Harrington also has lectured at his alma mater and at the School of Visual Arts in New York.

Anna Karenina, cover illustration by Harrington for Bantam Books.

ROBERT HUNT (1952-) received a B.A. in art history from the University of California and a Masters degree in illustration from the Academy of Art in San Francisco. His work reflects this classical training, but with a contemporary take.

Hunt has created illustrations for a wide variety of corporate clients, including the American Red Cross, AT&T, British Petroleum, Bank of America, CBS Records, Chevron, Disney, Fisher Audio, Federal Express, Levi Strauss, Lucasfilm/Industrial Light and Magic, M-G-M, Paramount, Pendleton Woolen Mills, and Universal Studios.

Publishing clients have included Avon Books, Ballantine Books, Bantam Books, *Bicycling Magazine*, the Book-of-the-Month Club, Dell Publishing, Dial Books, Doubleday, *Field & Stream*, *Good Housekeeping*, Penguin Putnam, *Reader's Digest*, Thomas Nelson, and many others.

His personal project documenting the reconstruction of the San Francisco Bay Bridge following the October 1989 earthquake brought his work to national attention. Recent projects include a documentary series on the Tour de France, the motion logo for the Dreamworks SKG film studio, and a mural in the Commonwealth Brewery in Rockefeller Center, New York City.

Hunt's work has received numerous awards, including eleven Gold and Silver Medals from the San Francisco Society of Illustrators. A large exhibition of his work was held in 1996 at the Museum of American Illustration in New York.

Robert Hunt is a member of the Society of Illustrators in New York, and is a past president of the San Francisco Society of Illustrators.

One of a series of paintings documenting the reconstruction of the San Francisco Bay Bridge, with an article by Robert Hunt, published by *Communication Arts*, 1990.

ROGER KASTEL (1913-) is the embodiment of the ideal paperback cover artist. His pictures convey the story succinctly and directly, but also have a substance of detail to support the image that intrigues the viewer to read the book.

Born in White Plains, New York, Kastel attended the Art Students League, studying under Robert Beverly Hale, Edwin and Sidney Dickinson, and Frank Reilly, who influenced him most.

He first illustrated for *Argosy* in the early '60s and other magazines, such as *Good Housekeeping,* but was drawn to the paperback field early on. He has since worked for all of the major publishers, including Avon, Bantam, Dell, Fawcett, Signet, Penguin, and Pocket Books.

Kastel has had a parallel career in painting for galleries, both East and West. Among them, are the J.N. Bartfield Gallery in New York, and the Wadell and Husberg Galleries in the West. He is a member of the Kent Art Association, the Artists Fellowship, and the Society of Illustrators in New York.

Kastel's painting for *Jaws* is one of the best known of Hollywood images; it was published by Bantam Books in 1974 and widely utilized by Universal Studios to advertise Peter Benchley's story.

HOWARD KOSLOW (1924-) is a native New Yorker, born in Brooklyn. He was awarded an Art League scholarship to Pratt Institute, graduating in 1944. He then served as an apprentice to Jean Carlu, the French poster artist, in his New York City studio. Seeking more training, Koslow went to the Cranbrook Academy of Art in Bloomfield Hills, Michigan, and furthered his studies at the School of Visual Arts in New York.

Beginning in 1946, his first artwork was in advertising, and he worked for many major accounts, including Bethlehem Steel, Goodyear Corporation, TWA, General Electric, and Babcock and Wilcox. Interspersed were commissions from many publishers, such as *National Geographic*, Pocket Books, Avon Books, *Reader's Digest*, Random House, and *Popular Mechanics*, as well as twenty volumes on Jacques Cousteau. Another regular account was the U.S. Postal Service, for which he has designed over forty stamps. In addition, he has designed hundreds of stamps and cachets for the Republic of the Marshall Islands.

For the Unicover Corporation, Koslow completed a two-and-a-half year project of 105 montage paintings depicting "The Greatest Military Heroes of America." The paintings were exhibited at the Society of Illustrators in New York in 1986.

He has been a participant in the U.S. Air Force Art Program contributing many paintings to the Air Force Permanent Collection. Paintings commissioned by NASA are on exhibition at the National Air and Space Museum, Washington, D.C. and at the NASA Art Gallery in the Kennedy Space Center. He has also been commissioned by the National Park Service and the U.S. Coast Guard to create paintings for their historical art collections.

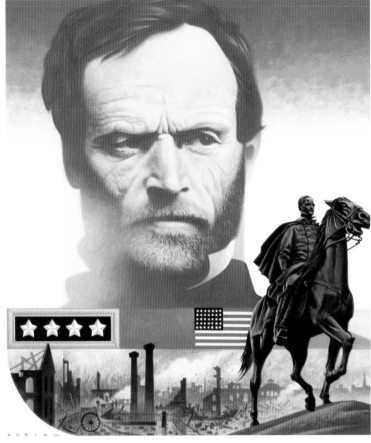

Howard Koslow, *William T. Sherman — Civil War,* cachet illustration. © Copyright 1984 Unicover Corporation.

BIRNEY LETTICK (1919-1986) was a consummate craftsman. A native of New Haven, Connecticut, he attended the Yale University Art School and studied with Joseph Albers. He learned anatomy by dissecting cadavers and all the other fundamentals involved in a painter's classic education. His abilities won him the Tiffany Scholarship as one of the ten most promising art students in the country.

His art career, delayed by four war years in Europe, soon revived. He found advertising clients for national ads and cover work for *Time* magazine, *Collier's*, *Reader's Digest*, *National Lampoon*, *Newsweek*, and *National Geographic*, as well as movie poster ads for *Star Trek*, *The Champ*, *Sergeant Pepper's Lonely Hearts Club Band*, *The Goodbye Girl*, *Rooster Cogburn*, *The Odessa File*, *The Front Page*, *Rocky II*, *Heaven Can Wait*, and many others. His paintings were exhibited by the Graham Gallery in New York, and he taught at the New Haven Art Workshop from 1955 to 1970. Just prior to his death, he had lectured to art school students in Japan at the Tokyo Designers Gakium College and related schools in Nagoya, Osaka, and Kyushu, Japan.

Lettick painted many still-lifes for exhibition. Here he humorously presents *The Fatal Gift.*

415

Illustration for *Scenario* magazine, pastel on paper. This was awarded a Gold Medal for Editorial Illustration by the Society of Illustrators in 1996.

GARY KELLEY (1945-　) is a Midwesterner, born in Algana, Iowa. He obtained his B.A. in art from the University of Northern Iowa and has continued to maintain his studio in Iowa. Yet his work has had a major national and international impact, winning awards in New York, Los Angeles, Tokyo, Italy, and Paris. To date, he has won 23 medals from the Society of Illustrators as well as the distinguished Hamilton King Award.

Beginning with his first commission from *Better Homes and Gardens* in 1970, he has added a large roster of clients, including *Rolling Stone*, *Playboy*, *Atlantic Monthly*, *Time*, *Entertainment Weekly*, and *Los Angeles* magazine, as well as poster designs and many advertising assignments.

As Kelley's style has evolved, he has incorporated many influences, notably the work of Tamara de Lempicka and Edwin Dickinson, but made them his own. His great strength is in design: his concepts are powerfully focussed and abetted by dramatic use of color.

Kelley is a popular teacher and has been involved with the Syracuse University graduate art program; he also taught at the Illustration Academy in Kansas City and at the Hartford Art School in Connecticut.

[signature: Livingston]

FRANCIS LIVINGSTON (1953-) paints for publication as well as exhibition, and often his work for one arena works as well as for the other. He particularly likes to paint contemporary street scenes with the interplay of people and buildings.

Francis is a Coloradan, born in Cortez, and he attended the Rocky Mountain School of Art in Denver. He also studied at the San Francisco Academy of Art College. Currently, he works out of Idaho. Thanks to overnight postal delivery, he can function far from the usual urban publishing centers.

Harcourt Brace first published his work in 1979, and his subsequent appearances have included *Hemispheres* magazine, *Southwest Art*, and *The Artist's Magazine*. His corporate clients have included Bank of America, Chevron, Gallo, Hewlett-Packard, Sheraton Hotels, Crown Zellerbach, MasterCard, and Coca-Cola.

His paintings are shown through Thomas R. Reynolds Fine Art of San Francisco. A member of both the Society of Illustrators in New York and Los Angeles, he has won Gold, Silver, and Best in Show Awards from each. Livingston's teaching activities have included a decade at the Academy of Art College (1981-91), and more recently, at Boise State University.

Francis Livingston, *Sue and Artie*, published by Marcel Shurman Cards.

[signature: Dennis Luzak]

DENNIS M. LUZAK (1939-1995) was educated at the Art Institute of Chicago, the University of Chicago, and the University of Notre Dame, where he received his Bachelor of Fine Arts degree in 1961.

He began his career at Ford Motor Company as a conceptual designer in a special projects studio under the auspices of Lee Iacocca. He concluded his experience at Ford as senior designer of the Thunderbird studio.

In 1967, he returned to Chicago and began his career as an illustrator. He soon garnered a long list of clients which included *McCall's* magazine, *Good Housekeeping*, *The Ladies' Home Journal*, *Redbook*, *Playboy*, *Fortune*, *Newsweek*, *Time*, and *Forbes*, as well as corporate advertisers such as Ford, General Motors, Chrysler, Xerox, Eli Lilly, Universal Studios, Paramount Pictures, Warner Communications, and several commissions from the U. S. Postal Service.

Luzak had a parallel career as a portrait painter whose subjects included Rose Kennedy, Lee Iacocca, and Joe Louis; his portrait of Babe Ruth hangs in the Baseball Hall of Fame, and a painting commissioned by NASA is in the Air and Space Museum of the Smithsonian Institution.

For three years, he taught at the Paier College of Art in New Haven, Connecticut and exhibited in several regional and group shows, winning "Best of Show" in the 1988 Connecticut Annual.

Dennis Luzak, *Dancers at Rehearsal*.

THE BOOK OF EBENEZER LE PAGE

a novel by G. B. Edwards

with an introduction by John Fowles

DANIEL MAFFIA (1937-) whose birthplace was Nevers, France, came to America and studied at Parsons School of Design in New York. Among his teachers there was Howard Baer. He landed his first professional assignment from *Esquire* magazine in 1968.

Maffia has subsequently added a long list of prestigious clients to his roster, including *Time*, *Rolling Stone*, *New York* magazine, *Newsweek*, *Sports Illustrated*, *Fortune*, and numerous book publishers. He taught at Sarah Lawrence in 1963. He also paints and exhibits, participating in shows in the U.S. as well as in England and France.

The Book of Ebenezer Le Page, by G.B. Edwards, Alfred E. Knopf Inc. Publisher. For this illustration, Maffia was awarded a Silver Medal in *Illustrators 24* in 1983 by the Society of Illustrators in New York.

SERGIO MARTINEZ (1937-) has had an international career in Mexico, and the United States, as well as in Europe. Born in Orizaba, Mexico, he received his art training at the Academia de la Grande Chaumiere, in Paris. His first artwork was commissioned by the Librairie Hachette in Paris in 1973, and he soon branched out to illustrating for book and advertising clients in France, Switzerland, Spain, England, Central and South America, and Mexico where he presently lives. Much of his current artwork is for the BBC and many American publishers, including Signet, New American Library, Disney Press, the *Reader's Digest*, and Elfin Light Press. His work has also been widely exhibited in Europe and Mexico City with several appearances in the annual exhibitions of the Society of Illustrators.

Although trained classically to use the standard mediums, Martinez has evolved a personal technique that is his hallmark and which enables him to attain a glowing luminosity. The originals are rendered on a transparent vellum in wax crayons and colored pencil, working on both the front and underside, dissolving the charcoal pencil or crayon into tone by means of Turpenoid. The effect is similar to a Maxfield Parrish glaze but by entirely different means. His working method is detailed in a *Step-by-Step Graphics* cover story, in the January/February 1996 issue.

David Copperfield, cover illustration by Martinez for the BBC-Bantam audio tape.

MARVIN MATTELSON (1947-) works in a photo-realistic mode that is very appropriate for cover illustration and for advertising clients. To this clarity, however, he often brings an element of unreality, rendered with the same degree of believable conviction — unsettling and arresting to the casual viewer.

Mattelson was born in Philadelphia and is a graduate of the Philadelphia College of Art. After a brief foray into cartooning, he found his current style and a long list of clients. His cover art has been commissioned by *Time*, *Life*, *Atlantic Monthly*, *National Lampoon*, and *Psychology Today*, and for many advertising accounts.

He has taught at the School of Visual Arts for several years, and his pictures have been regularly exhibited in annual shows at the Society of Illustrators in New York.

Marvin Mattelson, illustration for MTV, 1991.

ANN MEISEL (1947-) is a New Yorker by birth and inclination, but she received her art education at the Philadelphia College of Art, graduating with a BFA in 1969. Her influential teachers there were Albert Gold and Jack Freas. Even before graduation, she was published by *Cosmopolitan* magazine, *Ingenue,* and *Reader's Digest.* She moved to London in 1972, and for several years worked for British and European publishers and advertisers. With her return to the U.S. in 1981, she has had a varied list of clients, including *TV Guide*, ABC-TV, Simon & Shuster, Oleg Cassini, Penguin, *Prevention*, Random House, Radio City Music Hall, Avon, Grosset & Dunlop, and various advertising agencies.

Her work has been published and exhibited in the Society of Illustrators Annuals Shows in New York, the Association of Illustrators in London, and in *European Illustration*. She has also lectured at the School of Visual Arts in New York, at Syracuse University, and at the Royal College in London.

Ann Meisel, greeting card design for Paper Moon Graphics, 1982.

BARBARA NESSIM (1939-) represents part of the advance guard of the "New Illustrators." As early as the '70s, she was exploring a fresh, visual vernacular in avant-garde publications, and as an early investigator of computer-generated art, she helped to develop its idiom.

Nessim is a New Yorker, born in the Bronx, and received her art training at the High School of Art and Design and at Pratt Institute in Brooklyn. Among her influential teachers were Robert Weaver, Bob Gill, Jacob Landau, Walter Murch, Fritz Eichenberg and Richard Lindner. Getting started was difficult; her first illustrations were accepted only by a girlie publication, but she gradually found work from *Show* magazine, *New York Magazine*, *Mademoiselle*, *Rolling Stone*, and *Ms.*

She then discovered the computer and explored its latent potential — which evoked a freedom to experiment that has progressively shaped her commercial work. It has also led to a busy Fine Art career that has won her many awards in the U.S. and abroad. She is currently Chairperson of the Illustration Department at Parsons School of Design in Manhattan. In between, she has exhibited, lectured and written about illustration and the use of computer technology for which she is an ardent advocate. Her work is included in the Whitney Museum of American Art; the Smithsonian Institution; Arizona State University; several corporate, and many private collections. She has also curated annual New York Digital Salon exhibitions at the School of Visual Arts Museum.

Barbara Nessim, "Woman and Madness," published by *Ms.* magazine, July, 1972

MEL ODOM (1950-) counts among his awards "Illustrator of the Year" from *Playboy* magazine, which he has added to numerous honors from the Society of Illustrators and the Graphic Artists Guild in New York.

Born in Richmond, Virginia, he studied at Virginia Commonwealth and Leeds Metropolitan Universities, specializing in graphics and fashion illustration. He sold his first work to *Viva* magazine in 1975, followed by *Blue Boy*, *Playboy*, *Rolling Stone*, *Omni*, *Time*, and *The New York Times* magazines.

A recent activity has been his design of a best-selling doll, "Gene Marshall, Girl Star," based on the movie star prototypes of the 1940s and 1950s, along with his illustrated book about her, published by Hyperion. This has become virtually a full-time project with nationwide department store and TV appearances. Annual new models are in the works, to be distributed by Ashton-Drake Galleries.

Portrait of Freddy Mercury by Odom. Cover painting for Carol Publishing Group.

8·STAVRINOS·O

The artwork of GEORGE STAVRINOS (1948-1990) was characterized by its strong draftsmanship, and as a fashion artist, he created an arresting new look that set the pace for his contemporaries and still continues to be an influence.

Born in Somerville, Massachusetts, he was a graduate of the Rhode Island School of Design and in 1969, was granted a year's independent study in Rome. Upon his return, he first worked with the Push Pin studios and soon had work commissioned by Bergdorf Goodman, the New York City Opera, *The New York Times*, and magazines such as *Redbook*, *Gentlemen's Quarterly, and Cosmopolitan*.

Stavrinos concurrently exhibited in galleries in Manhattan, Los Angeles, San Francisco, Providence, Chicago, London, Paris and Tokyo. He also taught at the Fashion Institute of Technology in New York in the 1980's, and at Tokyo's Designers Gakium College in 1984.

Letters — a design for Fantasy Graphics, Inc. ©1978 by George Stavrinos.

DREW STRUZAN (1947-   ) has staked out the movie poster territory through his many years of specializing in this very competitive area. He has accumulated a long list of credits of art for films ranging from the *Indiana Jones* trilogies to *E.T.*, *The Flintstones*, *Star Wars*, *Hook*, the *Muppet* movies, *Beauty and the Beast*, *The Lost World*, *Back to the Future*, and many others.

He is a graduate of the Art Center College of Design where he studied with Lorser Feitelsen. His first clients were from the record industry, and he created album covers for artists such as Liberace, Alice Cooper, and Tony Orlando and Dawn. The shift to motion picture art came through a collaboration with Charles White III to do a poster for the first re-release of *Star Wars*. Twenty years later, he has also completed poster art for *Star Wars: Episode I — The Phantom Menace*.

Struzan was honored with a one-man show of his poster art in 1999 at the Norman Rockwell Museum at Stockbridge, Massachusetts, and at the Society of Illustrators in New York.

Drew Struzan, *Indiana Jones and the Temple of Doom*, © Copyright and ™, Lucasfilm Ltd. 1984. Used under authorization; All rights reserved.

Richard Tomlinson, United States Courthouse in Brooklyn, Federal Judge Jack B. Weinstein; Manville Trust personal injury settlement hearing; shown on the CNBC Business News channel, July 9, 1990.

TOMLINSON

RICHARD TOMLINSON (1933-) did not start out intending to be a courtroom artist. Born in Akron, Ohio, he studied at the Art Center School in Los Angeles and at the School of Visual Arts in New York. His first illustration was published by *Esquire* magazine in 1958, but it was in 1970, when he was hired as a television reporter by Metromedia Television News, that his real career was launched.

Television journalism needed reporters who could draw accurately and quickly, particularly to cover court trials where cameras were prohibited. It was a challenge to draw likenesses of the personalities in the trials or hearings, who were continually moving about during the proceedings, and to meet the daily deadline.

After fifteen years on staff, Tomlinson began to freelance, covering events for Fox, CNBC Business News, WNBC, WABC, WWOR, 47WNJU, WXTV News and *New York Newsday*. His pictures were also published by *Fortune*, the United Nations, *Show Business Magazine*, and various advertising accounts.

Meanwhile, his work has been shown in the Norfolk Museum of Arts and Sciences XXIII American Drawing Biennial, AIGA, Rutgers University Law Library, Syracuse University Lowe Art Gallery, and many others.

Thompson

JOHN M. THOMPSON (1940-) was born in Three Rivers, Michigan, and completed his B.F.A. from Miami University in Ohio. His first art job was with Foote, Cone and Belding in Chicago. In 1974, he was given a cover assignment for *Goal* magazine, the publication for the National Hockey League, and his freelance career was launched. This was followed by a long series of clients, including *Time*, *Playboy*, *Forbes*, *National Geographic*, *Scholastic*, *Guide Post*, *Field & Stream*, *Esquire*, and several book publishers. His work has won numerous Gold, Silver and Bronze Awards in exhibitions at both the New York and Los Angeles Society of Illustrators. He has also exhibited at the Zimmerli-Voorheis Museum, the Wycoff Gallery, the Pentagon Gallery, and the U. S. Air Force Gallery.

Thompson has taught at Syracuse University in the U.S. from 1994 to 1998, and at Syracuse University in Florence, Italy, in 1998 and 1999. About the work pictured here the artist states "*True North* is part of a series of paintings I have done dealing with the lives and history of African-Americans. I feel fortunate that I have had the opportunity to contribute my vision to the words I have been given."

John M. Thompson, *True North* cover illustration for Scholastic, Inc. This won a Gold Medal in the Book category in *Illustrators 40*.

Born in Detroit, Michigan, CHUCK WILKINSON (1932-) is a product of the art instruction at Cass Tech High School and Pratt Institute in Brooklyn. He first illustrated for *The Ladies' Home Journal* in 1967, followed by manuscripts from *McCall's*, *The New York Times*, and *Good Housekeeping* magazines. He also designs covers for book publishers, such as Bantam Books, Harper's, and Simon & Shuster, and he has created poster art for Mobil Masterpiece Theatre and designed six New York City bus posters.

Wilkinson taught at the Center for Creative Studies from 1973-1993.

He had a retrospective exhibit at the Howland Center in Beacon, New York, in 1997, and also exhibits at the New York Art Directors Club, The Detroit Athletic Club, and the Society of Illustrators in New York.

Chuck Wilkinson, poster design for *Love for Lydia*, Public Television, Mobil Masterpiece Theatre, 1986.

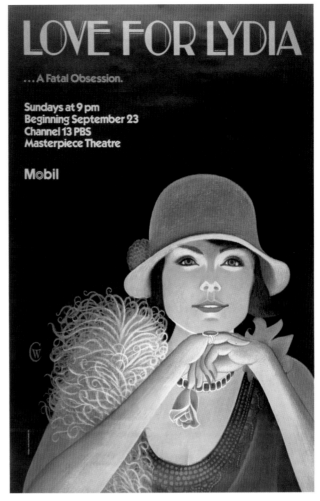

A native Californian, BRUCE WOLFE (1941-) studied art at San José State University and at the Art Institute of San Francisco. He also studied portrait painting with Bettina Steinke and sculpture with Bruno Lucchesi.

Wolfe worked as an art director at Foote, Cone and Belding advertising for ten years. While there, he had a show of his portraits, and in 1968, completed a bronze sculpture of Kurt H. Adler for the San Francisco Opera House.

In 1972, he began his career as a freelance artist. He has since shown his work in many graphics exhibitions, and been the recipient of many awards, including a Clio for best illustration in print, and the Gold Award from the Society of Illustrators in San Francisco.

Recent projects have included a bronze portrait of former Secretary of State George P. Shultz for the Hoover Institute, an oil portrait of Supreme Court Justice Anthony Kennedy, and a bronze portrait of Dr. Frank Soloman at the St. Mary's Medical Center in San Francisco.

Some of the artist's illustration clients have included Anheuser-Busch, Boeing, Chevron, Cisco, Del Monte, Hewlett-Packard, Kellogg's, Lucas Films, Macy's, Millpond Press, NASA, Nestlé's, *Playboy*, *Reader's Digest*, Time-Life Books, The Sierra Club, Sony, Southern Pacific, and Stanford University.

Wolfe taught at the Academy of Art in San Francisco in 1990, and at the California College of Arts and Crafts in 1999.

Bruce Wolfe, *Astronaut McCandless in Space*, Smithsonian National Air and Space Museum

423

1990–2000

Brian Ajhar
Wayne Douglas Barlowe
Guy Billout
Thomas Blackshear II
Braldt Bralds
Leslie Carbarga
Joseph Ciardello
Robert Dacey
Michael J. Deas
Peter de Sève
Henrik Drescher
Jack Endewelt
Max Ginsberg
Robert Grossman
James Gurney
Anita Kunz
William Low
Steven Lyons

Greg Manchess
Heide Oberheide
Rafal Olbinski
Tim O'Brien
Christopher Fox Payne
George Pratt
Timothy C. Raglin
Robert Risko
Arnold Roth
Bill Sienkiewicz
Art Spiegelman
Chris Spollen
Mark D. Summers
Nancy Stahl
Stevan H. Stroud
Simms Taback
Chris van Allsburg

Joseph Ciardello, Bluesman, 1999.

Enemy Ace by George Pratt combines realism with creative contemporary composition.

Steven Lyons harnesses the computer's magic.

THE DECADE 1990-2000

Even through great technological upheavals in printing over the past one hundred and fifty years, and through vagaries of fashion that have changed the look of illustration every decade, the basic process of illustrating a text is something Felix Darley would still — mostly — recognize. But with all the change that is occuring, in another ten years he might not.

Television had stolen the fiction magazines' audience and illustration's former position as pace-setter for popular culture was usurped. As magazines fragmented and multiplied, illustration's role became more incidental and decorative.

The advent of the computer is rocking the field more radically, and illustrators have been facing the dreaded paradigm-shift in multiple ways, each magnifying the next.

The image-processing ability of computers has turned photography into a nearly plastic medium — one can alter, add, or remove items that the lens captures — enabling the photographer to encroach onto the illustrators' territory. *Wired* magazine has pioneered the photographically-based but thoroughly massaged illustrations that can articulate an editorial message.

Many illustrators in the '90s produce professional pictures without traditional art training. Indeed, many can not draw. The illustrator is becoming more of a stage director with an array of effects at hand, and for those artists, the computer is a gift of freedom. The plasticity of on-screen images is a boon, and many illustrators use the computer as an editing tool, even if the finished art is produced by hand. Conversely, many artists have been downgraded to image-processors.

Recycling already-published images inexpensively through huge image banks is changing the financial foundation of the field. The proliferation of stock houses has led to wider exposure for some artists, but caused a corresponding drop-off in new illustration. It's even worse when the use is unauthorized. The focal battleground over copyright today is music and movies, but illustrators have had their work sliced and diced, modified, exerpted, morphed, and downloaded free of charge for years. The small industry built upon Saul Steinberg's single *New Yorker* cover of the westward view from Manhattan is an extreme example. The illustrator's hard-won victories, such as the ability to retain copyright to their creations, are hollow when the artists have to beg not to have their images freely posted across the Web.

On top of that, the artist's original art work may soon have no significance. When an image is produced digitally, manipulated on screen, and e-mailed to the publisher, with no physical entity, it has no intrinsic value as a work of art.

This is especially true of those artists who are marginalized from the creative process and are treated as a rendering tool. They are increasingly replaced by a novice armed with Photoshop and Kai's Power Tools, so the bread-and-butter work is vanishing.

That has rarely been a problem for the illustrators selected here, for they have generally been assertive in their contribution to an entire picture concept, and able to art-direct themselves. At bottom, it is the ideas that matter most, and the challenge of the artist is to express them by the best means available.

But as print itself becomes a marginalized medium, the illustrator has had to explore little-charted territory as outlets for his talents. As early as the 1960s, illustrators had to profoundly adapt and were venturing into model and game box art, concert posters, or record album covers. Then came trading cards, graphic novels, action figurines, and the World Wide Web. Now some of the best illustration never gets seen, as it is movie or animation concept art, or electronic game character design. Is this even illustration at all? Is it becoming a service industry when an artist is hired by the hour for his ideas, rather than by the canvas? Hard to say. When an illustrator's idea can evolve a children's book, a video game, trading cards, advertising, and a movie spin-off, it may not be recognizeable as illustration, but it is these media jugglers who will be the most successful of Darley's descendents.

Does this mean that traditionally drawn or painted pictures will become obsolete? Probably not; as "hand-produced" art becomes less the norm it may become more valued. The two approaches are not incompatible, and those who can combine their skills with computer technology may carry the art of illustration into an exciting role in the twenty-first century.

BRIAN AJHAR (1957-) has a free and fluid style of drawing coupled with humor that looks uninhibited and easy. It is based on a strong knowledge of the figure, however, and the ability to draw without slavish reliance on photographs.

Ajhar was born in Easton, Pennsylvania, and gained a B.F.A. at Parsons School of Design in New York. Among his distinguished teachers were David Passalacqua, Robert Shore, John Gundelfinger, J. C. Suarès, Stewart Shedelsky, William Klutz, and Burne Hogarth.

His first published work was for *Horizon* magazine in 1980, and he has kept busy since with clients ranging from *Time*, *Newsweek*, *The New York Times*, *Sports Illustrated*, *New York*, and *TV Guide*, to *Rolling Stone*, *Golf*, *Forbes*, *Worth*, *Smart Money*, and *The Wall Street Journal*, as well as a long list of advertisers.

Brian also finds time to exhibit his work and to teach. He has taught at the University of the Arts in Philadelphia, was a visiting professor at Syracuse University, and has lectured at the Rhode Island School of Design, the School of Visual Arts and at Parsons.

Brian Ajhar, cover illustration for *Storyworks* magazine, published by Scholastic, October, 1995.

WAYNE DOUGLAS BARLOWE (1958-) Born in Glen Cove, New York, to well-known natural history artists Sy and Dorothea Barlowe, Wayne attended the Art Students League and The Cooper Union in New York City. He apprenticed in the Exhibition Department of the American Museum of Natural History. During this period, Barlowe collaborated with his parents on his first professional book assignment, the *Instant Nature Guide to Insects* (Grossett & Dunlop).

In 1979, his first self-generated book, *Barlowe's Guide to Extraterrestrials*, was published by Workman Publishing. The *Guide*, which Barlowe conceived, illustrated, and co-authored, was nominated for the American Book Award and the science fiction community's prestigious Hugo. It was chosen Best Illustrated Book of 1979 by the Locus Poll, and a Best Book for Young People by the American Library Association. The *Guide*, considered by many to be a contemporary classic science fiction work, has sold 270,000 copies to date.

Subsequent books have included *Expedition*, *An Alphabet of Dinosaurs*, *Barlowe's Guide to Fantasy*, *The Alien Life of Wayne Barlow*, and *Barlowe's Inferno*. Interspersed have been over 300 book and magazine covers for almost every major publisher including *Life*, *Time*, and *Newsweek*.

His artwork has been seen on television on Walter Cronkite's "Universe" and Connie Chung's "Saturday Night" as well as on the Discovery Channel. An interview with Barlowe appeared on

Wayne Barlowe, *Wildseed* by Octavia Butler, cover for Warner Books, 1987.

the Sci-Fi Channel's "Inside Space" program. Portfolios and interviews in print have appeared in *TV Guide*, *Starlog*, *Realms of Fantasy*, *Science Fiction Age*, *Starburst*, and *Filmfax of 1998*. He also contributed alien creature and character designs for the animated 20th Century Fox release, *Planet Ice*, and other concept art.

Guy Billout

GUY BILLOUT (1941-) is from Decize, France, and received his art training at École des Arts Appliqués de Beaune in Burgundy. He worked as a designer in various advertising agencies in Paris before coming to New York in 1969.

His published work has a clarity and precision somewhat related to the style of the Belgian artist Hergé, but this clarity serves to mislead the viewer by concealing a visual deceit that is at complete odds with the first impression. It is this playfulness that makes his work so compelling and enjoyable to readers, and equally so to the audience for the seven children's books he has written and illustrated.

He first illustrated for **Redbook** in 1969, and since 1982, he has had a regular feature in the **Atlantic Monthly**. He has also illustrated for many of the other major magazines, including **Vogue**, **New York**, **New Republic**, **Rolling Stone**, **Time**, **Life**, **Newsweek**, **Seventeen**, **McCall's**, **The New Yorker**, **Le Monde**, and **The New York Times.**

Billout has received Gold and Silver Medals in exhibitions as well as the Hamilton King Award from the Society of Illustrators in New York. He has also been teaching at the Parsons School of Design since 1985.

Guy Billout, *Squid & Spider; a Look at the Animal Kingdom*, Prentice Hall, 1981.

Thomas Blackshear II

THOMAS BLACKSHEAR II (1955-) went to work for Hallmark Cards in Kansas City for one year after his 1977 graduation from the American Academy of Art in Chicago. While there, he met Mark English, and became his apprentice for several months. In 1980, he worked as head illustrator for the Godbold/Richter Studio. He became a freelancer in 1982 and has been self-employed ever since.

Known for his dramatic lighting and sensitivity to mood, Blackshear has produced illustrations for postage stamps, posters, collector's plates, magazines, greeting cards, calendars, books, and advertising. His clients range from Disney to **National Geographic**. He has illustrated 20 U.S. postage stamps, as well as a commemorative stamp book entitled **I Have a Dream**. Seventeen of the original paintings from the publication were exhibited at the Smithsonian Institution and subsequently toured the country.

The artist has illustrated three collector's plate series, including **Star Wars. The Wizard of Oz** and **Star Trek.** One of Blackshear's more successful ventures involved the creation of the popular African-American figurine line, **Ebony Visions!**

He has received many awards, including two Gold Awards in the 1990 Illustrators West Show, a Gold Medal from the Society of Illustrators in New York in 1988, two Silver Awards in the San Francisco Society of Illustrators 1989 show, and the Plate of the Year Achievement Award in 1990.

Blackshear has taught at the San Francisco Academy of Art College and lectured at numerous workshops throughout this country and in Sweden.

Thomas Blackshear, *Intimacy*, design for the Greenwich Workshop, 1995.

427

© Braldt Bralds.

Born in Hoogkerk, Holland, BRALDT BRALDS (1951-) came to New York in 1980 for a two-months' stay to try to find work as an artist. He had developed his training through a series of advertising and studio jobs in Europe and hoped he was sufficiently prepared. Fortunately, he was; he found the right agent who introduced him to the first of many subsequent clients. By 1984, he had won the Hamilton King Award for finest illustration of the year by the Society of Illustrators in New York. He has subsequently won many other awards and medals and had numerous one-man shows.

Bralds' work is marked by an extreme attention to detail, which he carefully modulates to serve the overall picture concepts. Surprisingly, he accomplishes the fine detail in oils, rather than in acrylics or opaque watercolor. His list of clients includes *Time*, the *Atlantic Monthly*, *Libelle*, *Newsweek*, *Rolling Stone*, *National Geographic*, Random House, and Doubleday & Company. Despite his busy schedule, he also found time to teach at the School of Visual Arts in New York City from 1983 to 1986.

Braldt Bralds, *Autonomous Vehicles*, Annual Report illustration for Charles Stark Draper Laboratories, Inc. 1989.

LESLIE CABARGA (1954-) has had an art career that is difficult to categorize. He began to work in his father's studio at twelve, cutting color separation overlays; by fourteen his first underground comics were being published by the New York underground newspapers. By twenty-one, he had begun an eclectic art career as an illustrator, cover designer, creator of type fonts, CD covers, letterheads, and author of many books relating to the graphic arts. His client list is equally wide ranging from *Time*, *Fortune*, *Business Week*, *Esquire*, *Rolling Stone*, *GQ*, *Playboy*, and *National Lampoon*, to CBS/Sony Music, Atlantic Records, RCA Records, Sony America, Nintendo, Pepsi Cola, American Express, Cinemax, HBO, Nickelodeon, MTV, and Tri-Star Entertainment.

Among his many books have been *Dynamic Black and White Illustration*, *1900-2000*, published by Art Direction Books in 1993; *A Treasury of German Trademarks; Art Deco Advertising*, and *The Lettering and Graphic Design of F. G. Cooper*, published in 1997, and several books of Clip Art of the 1920s-1950s. Among his many type fonts are "Cabarga Cursiva", "The Magneto Family", "Kobalt Bold", "Art Deco", "Raceway Script" and "Bad Typ."

Poland's Lech Walesa: Shaking Up Communism, Cover design for *Time* magazine, December 29, 1980, by Cabarga.

Ciardiello.

JOSEPH CIARDIELLO (1953-) is a native of Staten Island and attended the High School of Art and Design in New York. This was followed by study at Parsons School of Design. Among his teachers were James Spanfeller, Murray Tinkelman, and Maurice Sendak.

His first illustration assignments were those for *Scholastic*, *Crawdaddy*, and *Penthouse*. He has subsequently been published by *Playboy*, *Time*, *Sports Illustrated*, *The Atlantic Monthly*, the *Washington Post*, *The New Yorker*, and *The Wall Street Journal*. Included among his commercial clients are Exxon, Quest, the Franklin Library, American Express, Ziff-Davis, and Capitol Records.

Ciardiello has participated in numerous group shows including "200 Years of American Illustration," "Art for Survival" in 1990, and those hosted by the Society of Publication Designers, the Graphic Artists Guild, the Society of Illustrators of New York, and "Eye on America: Editorial Illustration in the 1990's" at the Norman Rockwell Museum in September, 1999.

Joseph Ciardiello, illustration for Rachel Carson's "Sounding the Alarm on Pollution," *Boys' Life* magazine, August, 1994.

ROBERT DACEY (1946-) is a graduate of Florida State University and the Art Center School of Design. Among his influential teachers were John Asaro and Richard Huebner. He himself enjoys teaching, and has served as part of the professional adjunct faculty at Sacred Heart University in Bridgeport, Connecticut, and has been associated with the Syracuse University advanced degree program; he is presently Chair of the Department of Visual Communications.

He has a long list of clients, including *Redbook*, *The Ladies' Home Journal*, Easton Press, *Golf Digest*, *Playboy*, and *Reader's Digest*, as well as advertising accounts for Mobil Oil, American Airlines, the U.S. Postal Service, The White House, Rockefeller Center, CBS, NBC, RCA, and ABC.

A Gold Medal recipient from the Society of Illustrators in New York, Dacey has received over three dozen Certificates of Merit from their Annual Shows. His work has hung in national and international museums and galleries including: The Tokyo Invitational Show, the Baseball Hall of Fame and Museum, the Indianapolis Museum of Modern Art, the Greenwich Workshop Galleries, the Second Street Gallery, and the New Britain Museum of American Art. In addition to writing articles on illustration, watercolor, and drawing for national publications, Dacey has been invited to lecture and present seminars and workshops throughout the United States.

Robert Dacey, "The List," published by *The Ladies' Home Journal*. ©1981 by The Meredith Publishing Corporation.

M · J · D E A S

MICHAEL J. DEAS (1956-) is a committed realist. With a thorough training and a B.F.A. from Pratt Institute, he can paint in the academic tradition. In a time when such ability is in short supply, he has found a ready market for his beautifully rendered subjects. Perhaps his most seen image is his spectacular painting of the symbol for the Columbia Pictures logo, even though the film audience is unaware of the artist who painted it. Also reaching a huge public was his James Dean Commemorative postage stamp for the U. S. Postal Service in 1996.

Much of his work has been commissioned as book covers and other illustrations for Random House, Harper Collins, *Reader's Digest*, *The Wall Street Journal*, and Scholastic. His artwork has also been featured in *Graphis* and *Communication Arts*, and exhibited at the New York Art Directors Club, the New Orleans Museum of Contemporary Art, the Norman Rockwell Museum in Stockbridge, and the Society of Illustrators in New York, where his work has been awarded four Golds and one Silver medal.

Deas taught at the School of Visual Arts from 1984 to 1988.

Michael Deas, *The Empty Summer* by Caryl Brooks. Published by Scholastic, Inc. 1993.

PETER DE SÈVE (1959-) works in an idiom that is a happy blending between old and new. His artistic heroes include A. B. Frost, Heinrich Kley and Winsor McCay, and while those influences are embedded in his work, there are also references to D. C. Comics, *Creepy*, *Eerie* and even the drawing style of Frank Frazetta. DeSève's subjects, however, are very contemporary— particularly his delightful covers for *The New Yorker*, and it is the application of style to his ideas that distinguishes him as an artist. His talents in this direction have taken him to the West Coast for assignments for Dreamworks and Disney Studios to conceptualize animation characters in a free-wheeling series of drawings. Films worked on have included *The Hunchback of Notre Dame*, *A Bug's Life*, and *Prince of Egypt*.

While DeSéve also has many magazine clients, including *Time, Newsweek, The New York Times Book Review*, and *Forbes* magazines, he enjoys the challenge of working in other areas as well. Recent projects have included poster designs for *Candide* and *A Funny Thing Happened on the Way to the Forum*.

Cover for *The New Yorker*, January 24, 1994. Copyright © 1994 Peter DeSéve.

HENRIK DRESCHER (1955-) was born in Denmark, and he has been on the move ever since, ranging from Boston where he attended the Museum School for a semester before dropping out, to Mexico, California, New Zealand, and other points where only his art representatives know where to find him. This indirect communication with art clients suits him best, and the use of faxes and Federal Express allows him to work anywhere without direct contact with clients or art directors. Since about half of his projects are books anyway — he has produced and illustrated more than fifteen titles — he can work with less of the distracting interruptions of short-term deadlines.

Drescher's self-selected influences are endless and diverse. He likes old Sears catalogs, Edward Gorey, Milton Glaser, postage stamps, Ralph Steadman, fetish drawings, Frida Kahlo, and myriad others.

His first published work was commissioned on the strength of his notebook drawings and each subsequent commission has been fulfilled somewhat unpredictably both to his clients and himself. Though hardly the leader of a movement, Drescher is one of the inventors of the New Illustration. Certainly his work keeps looking new. Among his many clients have been *Time*; Harcourt Brace & Co.; CBS Records; Hyperion Books for children; Peat, Marwick; *Entertainment Weekly*; *The Progressive*; and *Psychology Today*.

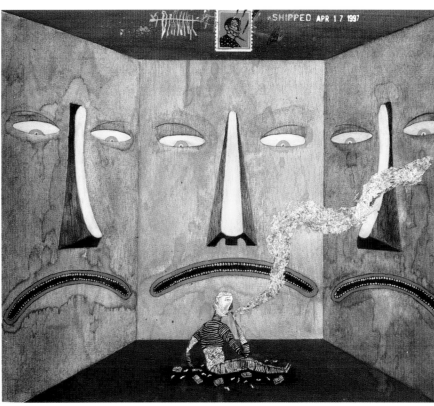

Henrik Drescher, *Smoker's Guilt*, illustration for **Hippocrates**, 1990.

JACK ENDEWELT

JACK ENDEWELT (1935-) developed a fascination with airplanes as a small boy growing up during World War II. His interest in drawing, coupled with that fascination with aircraft, developed his artistic skills and has remained with him as a professional illustrator.

Endewelt was born in New York City and graduated with a B.F.A. degree from the School of Visual Arts. There, his teachers were among the best: Robert Weaver, Jack Potter, and Howard Simon. His first published work was for a Time/Life promotion in 1961, and he has had an eclectic clientele since, ranging from *Dude*, *Gent*, and *Pageant*, to Dell Publications, Avon Books, Collier MacMillan, *Reader's Digest*, Silver Burdett, *The Ladies' Home Journal*, and *Parents* magazine. Like many of today's illustrators, he also exhibits his artwork in solo and group shows. Among exhibitors have been Helio Gallery, Alan Stone Gallery, Zoma, Diana Gordon Gallery, Vorpal, Cornwall Gallery, the American Watercolor Society, and the Society of Illustrators.

He began teaching in 1968 and has been Chairman of the Illustration Department at the School of Visual Arts since 1987.

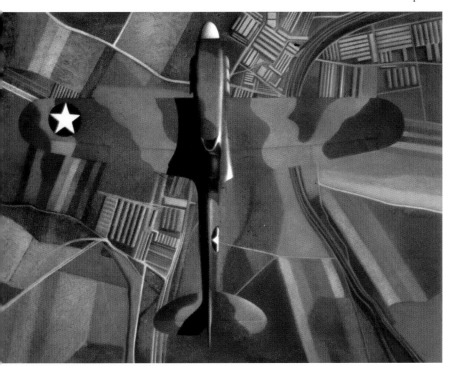

This painting graphically displays the effectiveness of camouflage, and reflects Endewelt's continued interest in aircraft and won him a Silver Medal from the Society of Illustrators in 1995.

MAX GINSBURG (1931-   ) was born in Paris, France, and his earliest training was from his painter father, Abraham Ginsburg. Following his move to the States, he attended the La Guardia High School of Music and Art in New York City. He subsequently earned degrees in art at Syracuse University and City University of New York.

He has since had a dual career in painting for publication as well as for exhibition, winning awards in both areas.

As an illustrator, his clients have included *The New York Times Magazine*, *Newsweek*, *Fortune*, *New York* magazine, *Playboy*, *Premiere* magazine, and *TV Guide*. He has also painted covers or book jackets for many publishers, such as Bantam; Warner Books; Harlequin Books; Avon; Delacort; Dell; Pocket Books; Scholastic Books; St. Martin's Press; Lothrop, Lee & Shepard; and Little, Brown & Co.

His paintings have been exhibited in the Museum of the City of New York, the Heritage Foundation Museum of Norfolk, Virginia, and at Allied Artists, ACA Gallery and the National Academy of Design.

For several years, he was an instructor of painting at the High School of Art & Design in New York; Ginsberg has taught at the School of Visual Art from 1985 to the present.

Max Ginsburg, cover painting for *The Friends* by Rosa Guy. Published by Bantam Books in 1981. Collection of the Sanford Low Memorial Collection, New Britain Museum of American Art.

ROBERT GROSSMAN

ROBERT GROSSMAN (1940-   ) had the advantage of growing up in his father's New York City design studio where he absorbed the mechanics of drawing and using the airbrush early on. Further encouraged to pursue art as a career, he attended Saturday morning art classes at the Museum of Modern Art, followed by study at the Yale School of Art under Joseph Albers. His predelictions ran to humor, however. He made cartoons for the *Yale Record*, and their parody issue, *The Yew Norker*, served as his sample for an interview and his first job at *The New Yorker*.

He soon found his professional focus through drawing comic strips in line for *Monocle* magazine, and eventually used the airbrush to give his work three-dimensionality. This was an ideal medium for caricature which has played a large role in his subsequent assignments for *Time*, *The Nation*, *Esquire*, *Newsweek*, *New York* magazine, *Institutional Investor*, *Forbes Magazine*, *Rolling Stone*, and many other publications. He has also adapted his work to commercial films rendered in animation and in stop-motion photography, winning several awards and an Academy Award nomination in 1978.

Grossman currently teaches in the graduate program at Syracuse University.

Robert Grossman, cover illustration for *Mother Jones* magazine, January, 1983.

The above painting created for The Greenwich Workshop became a precursor for the Dinotopia story. © James Gurney 1992.

JAMES GURNEY JAMES GURNEY (1958-) is as much a story-teller as an artist. His interest in science — he has a B.A. in anthropology — led him to serious study of archeology and the conjecture of a time when humans and dinosaurs might have lived together in harmony. Thus, his illustrated creation of *Dinotopia: A Land Apart From Time*. Copiously illustrated, the book proved a popular juvenile best-seller and has been followed by a subsequent volume, *Dinotopia: The World Beneath*, both published by Turner Publishing.

Gurney was born in Glendale, California, and studied at the University of California at Berkeley, where he won Phi Beta Kappa honors, as well as at the Art Center College of Design in Pasadena. His first professional artwork was as a background painter for the animated film, *Fire and Ice*. He subsequently illustrated over seventy science fiction and fantasy paperback book covers over a period of more than ten years. He also completed picture assignments for *National Geographic*. In 1988, he designed a postal card commemorating the "Settling of Ohio, Northwest Territory, 1788" and produced "The World of Dinosaurs," a commemorative panel of fifteen stamps in 1997 for the U. S. Postal Service. The artist's work was featured in *Step-by-Step Graphics* in 1990. Gurney is a member of the Author's Guild and the Society of Vertebrate Paleontology.

K ANITA KUNZ (1956-) who works out of Toronto, Canada, is representative of today's international illustrator with clients in the U.S., Canada, Germany, Sweden, South Africa, Portugal, Japan, France, and Great Britain. She is a graduate of the Ontario College of Art where she studied under Doug Johnson, and launched her career with a series of advertising illustrations for Del Monte.

Advertising clients have kept her busy ever since, but she prefers the editorial assignments which give her more opportunity for gritty, personal interpretation, her greatest strength. She has produced cover art for many magazines including *Rolling Stone*, *The New Yorker*, *Sports Illustrated*, *Time*, *Newsweek*, the *Atlantic Monthly*, and *The New York Times Magazine*. She has also illustrated more than fifty book jackets.

Kunz frequently teaches lectures and workshops. Her summer workshops are conducted at the Illustration Academy in Kansas, and at the Masters of Art degree program at Syracuse University. She has been honored with many awards and medals ,and her critically acclaimed paintings and scuptures have appeared in galleries world-wide. In 1997, she received the Les Usherwood Lifetime Achievement Award from the Advertising and Design Club of Canada. Her works are in the permanent collections at the Library of Congress and Musée Militaire de France in Paris, and nine of her *Time* magazine cover paintings are in the permanent collection at the National Portrait Gallery.

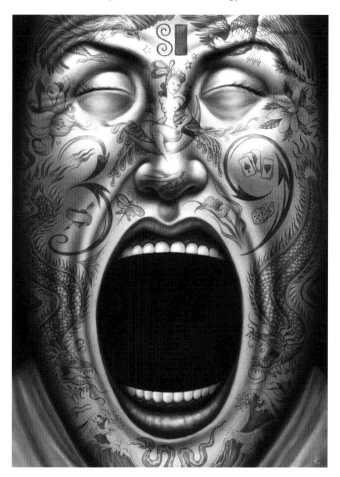

Poster design, *Call for Entries*, The Society of Illustrators, for which Anita Kunz was awarded a Silver Medal, 1996.

William Low

WILLIAM LOW (1959-) is a New Yorker, born in the Bronx. Showing his art talent early, he attended the High School of Art and Design, followed by study at Parsons School of Design, graduating with a B.F.A. in 1981. Among his influential teachers were Max Ginsburg and David Passalacqua. His natural inclination has been to paint his surroundings, and he has recorded many of the unique aspects of New York, taking advantage of dramatic lighting conditions.

William made his first illustration for the **New York Daily News** in 1982, and has since been commissioned assignments from clients such as **The New York Times**, **Gourmet** magazine, Holt, Rinehart & Winston, Bridgewater Books, Harper and Row Publishers, and **Philadelphia** magazine. He also finds time to teach: currently at the Maryland Institute College of Art, previously at the School of Visual Arts, and at the Fashion Institute of Technology. He is a member of the Graphic Artists Guild and the Society of Illustrators in New York, where he also had a one-man show.

William Low, *Media Decision Makers*, **The New York Times** Marketing Research Department.

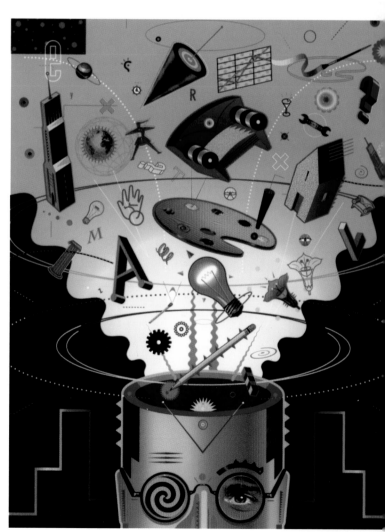

Originally from the Boston area, STEVEN LYONS (1956-) pursued his artistic career in the academic world of Fine Art printmaking, studying at the University of New Hampshire with Sigmund Abeles. In the mid-'80s, he embraced the Macintosh computer and began a voyage of discovery into the realm of digital illustration. In so doing, he has pointed the way for others to follow into the richly exploitable terrain of the pixel. His first illustration was published in **Los Angeles Weekly**.

His work has since decorated the pages of many juried annuals, including **American Illustration**, **Communication Arts** and **Print**'s regional Design Annual. He has created images for many of the high-tech giants, including IBM, Intel, Sun, and Apple. His subsequent editorial illustrations have appeared in **Newsweek**, **The Washington Post**, **Rolling Stone**, and **The Wall Street Journal**.

Steven Lyons, cover design, Society of Illustrators Digital Show, 1996.

Both images are from "Pursuing Justice in the Arctic" by Lawrence Millman. Published by *Smithsonian* magazine, May, 1998.

GREGORY MANCHESS (1955-) is from Fort Thomas, Kentucky. Although he did attend the Minneapolis College of Art and Design, he is largely self-taught. His role models are the illustrators of earlier generations, such as Saul Tepper and Dean Cornwell. He has successfully amalgamated this classic approach with his own contemporary sensibilities and has found a very receptive market in publications such as *Omni* magazine, *National Geographic*, *Smithsonian*, *Newsweek*, *Reader's Digest*, *Atlantic Monthly*, *TV Guide*, *Scientific American*, and for several paperbook publishers, including Bantam Books, Random House, Penguin, and Dial Books. It has also brought him Gold and Silver Medals from the Society of Illustrators' shows and their Hamilton King Award in 1999. Manchess has exhibited at the Ettinger Gallery in New York and periodically lectures at various art schools.

Heidi Oberheide, cover illustration for *Emma* by Charlotte Brontë. Bantam Books.

Oberheide

For HEIDI OBERHEIDE (1957-), the paperback covers have provided an ideal mode of art. She can paint realistically, focussing on the figures, but often they allow her to use landscape settings, her next favorite choice of subject.

Oberheide is from the Midwest. Born in Kansas, she attended high school in Indiana and graduated with a B.F.A. cum laude from Pratt Institute in Brooklyn, New York. There she found her focus through her teacher, Charles Gehm, himself a successful bookcover painter, and was able to land her first cover assignment even before graduating from college. She has since painted for Avon, Bantam, Berkley, Dell, Fawcett, Harlequin, the New American Library, Warner Books, Tyndale, Pocket Books, and others. Concurrently, she exhibits her paintings, lectures, and has taught at Pratt Institute and the School of Visual Arts.

Olbinski

RAFAL OLBINSKI (1945-) first came to illustration as a painter. The art director of *Omni* magazine saw this picture reproduced at an exhibition of his work at the Nathan Gallery in SoHo and adapted it for an article in the publication. The picture had been dedicated by the artist to his daughter to commemorate her sixth birthday, so it had a double significance.

In fact, Olbinski's work is characteristically marked by multiple significances. His pictures are not what they first seem to be and invite a double-take from the viewer. His ultra-realistic treatment also contributes to the effectiveness of the illusions.

Rafal was born in Kielce, Poland, and attended the Architecture Department of the Warsaw Polytechnical Institute. After emigrating to the U.S. in 1981, he launched his career as a designer, painter, and illustrator. He quickly made a name for himself in each category, with magazine clients such as *Time*, *Newsweek*, *Der Spiegel*, *Atlantic Monthly*, *Playboy*, *The New York Times*, and many poster assignments which have won him numerous awards including an International Oscar for "The World's Most Memorable Poster," Prix Savignac.

Olbinski's paintings have also received their share of awards, and he has had over thirty one-man shows in Poland, France, Austria, Belgium, Japan, Chile, Germany, and the United States. Additionally, his works are held in the collections of the Smithsonian Institution, the Library of Congress, the National Arts Club in New York, and various corporate and private collections.

Olbinski illustration for story by John Harrison, *Omni* Magazine, November, 1994.

He has been an active teacher with classes at the Tyler School of Art, from 1985-88, and at the School of Visual Arts from 1985 to the present.

O'BRIEN

Tim O'Brien, illustration for **Slam**, by Walter Dean Myers, Scholastic Books, 1997.

TIM O'BRIEN (1964-) was born in New Haven, Connecticut, within a short commute to the Paier College of Art where he studied under Ken Davies, Howard Munce, and Leonard Everett Fisher. Thus prepared, he was able to quickly find clients for his work, beginning with Avon Books in 1987, and soon followed by **Time**, the **Atlantic Monthly**, **Entertainment Weekly**, **New York** magazine, **Reader's Digest**, **Money**, **The New Yorker**, **Sports Illustrated**, and **Dial**, as well as Scholastic, Harper Collins, Ballantine Books, and many others. O'Brien's work is skillfully rendered and highly detailed, often combined with a symbolism pertinent to the subject.

His work has been featured in **Communication Arts**, **Print** magazine, and the Society of Publication Designers' and Society of Illustrators' annuals since 1987. He is currently House and Education Chair at the Society. He has taught at the University of the Arts in Philadelphia in 1989-91, and at the Paier College of Art in 1996-97.

GEORGE PRATT (1960-) is too young to remember World War II, let alone World War I, yet his illustrated novel, **Enemy Ace: War Idyl**, created for DC Comics/Warner Books in 1990 is so authentic in spirit that it has become required reading at the Military Academy at West Point. Most unusual in the format, story, and pictures, it is told from the German viewpoint and points to the brotherhood of soldiers on both sides. A subsequent book, **No Man's Land**, published in 1992 by Tundra Publishing Ltd., is equally compelling and convincing. It holds its own with the work of those artists who were there, including Harvey Dunn and Major John Thomason. Other subjects have included **The Great War**, **The Holocaust**, and **The Blues**.

A native of Beaumont, Texas, George studied at Pratt Institute in Brooklyn and later taught there. His work has been published in **Epic Illustrated**, **Eagle Magazine**, and **Heavy Metal**, as well as by Bantam Books, Ariel Books, Kipling Press, and he has executed comic book cover paintings for D.C. Comics. He has also exhibited his gallery paintings in Houston and New York. More recently, he has become involved with documentary film-making on blues music (he plays guitar himself), and on a story of the eight artist-war correspondents, who covered action at the front with the A.E.F. in 1917, including Harvey Dunn, Wallace Morgan, Harry Townsend, and George Harding.

George Pratt, speaking for Von Hammer: " *In a dogfight, indecision can be fatal...*" from **Enemy Ace: War Idyl**, DC Comics Inc. © 1990.

Book, *The Far Side of Paradise*

Nancy Reagan receiving Donald Regen's head, ***Regardie's*** *magazine, 1989.*

CHRISTOPHER FOX PAYNE (1954-) is a major contemporary talent with a wide ranging ability to cover subjects seriously as well as irreverently. His natural inclination is to humor and caricature, but with a highly realistic rendition which makes his exaggeration convincingly real. Payne is a native of Cincinnati and has returned there after sojourns to studios in Akron, Chicago, and Dallas. With a B.F.A. from Miami University and post-graduate study with the famous Illustrators Group in 1976, he was well prepared to launch his successful career with clients which have included *The Dallas Times Herald, Time* magazine, *Boys' Life, Mad,* the *Atlantic Monthly, GQ, Esquire, Penthouse, Yankee, Rolling Stone, Kiplinger, Money* magazine, and *The New Yorker.*

He has garnered numerous awards for his work, including Gold and Silver Medals from the Society of Illustrators as well as their Hamilton King Award in 1995; he has exhibited at the Cincinnati Art Museum and the Norman Rockwell Museum at Stockbridge, Massachusetts. Payne has also taught at various times at East Texas State, Miami University, Columbus College of Art and Design, the Illustration Academy in Kansas City, Missouri, and at Syracuse University's Graduate Program.

Book, *Appointment in Sumarra.*

T·R

TIMOTHY C. RAGLIN (1954-) is a Midwesterner from Independence, Kansas, and studied at the Washington University School of Fine Arts in St. Louis, Missouri.

Making his way to the New York marketplace, he first illustrated for **The New York Times** in 1979, followed by assignments from **The Saturday Review**, **Rolling Stone**, **Sports Illustrated**, **Quest**, **Money**, **Newsweek**, **Sesame Street**, and **The Smithsonian**. In the 1980s, he produced artwork for several excellent children's videos including **The Elephant's Child** and **Pecos Bill**, and the humor of his work is ideally suited for children's books. He recently illustrated **Uncle Mugsy and the Terrible Twins of Christmas** published by Madison Square Press, featuring his own characters. Raglin has been included in Society of Illustrators exhibitions, participated in the Humor Show, and won a Silver Medal for one of the **Uncle Mugsy** illustrations in 1997.

The True Death of Luther Burbank, © 1979 Tim Raglin.

Risko

ROBERT RISKO (1956-) could be described as a totemic caricaturist. A caricature's reduction of details to the subject's most telling features that summarize character can devolve into ridicule. Risko does not skewer his victims; he exaggerates their features and makes them grand. His specialty is show business celebrities, and he has treated a long list of them, from Woody Allen, Bill Cosby, Diana Ross, Joan Rivers, to Elizabeth Taylor with Richard Burton, as well as Jesse Jackson, Presidents Bush and Clinton, along with their spouses, and other political figures.

Risko is from Pittsburgh and received his art training at Kent State University. His first art assignment was for Andy Warhol's **Interview** magazine in 1978, and he became a regular contributor to **Vanity Fair** from its inception in 1982. Other publications have included **Time**, **Vogue**, **Rolling Stone**, **Playboy**, **The New Yorker**, **Madison Avenue**, and **Newsweek**.

Risko taught at Parsons School of Design periodically in the 1990's, and his artwork has been exhibited in Hong Kong as well as at both the Society of Illustrators in Los Angeles and New York.

Diana Ross in Blue, prototype for projected **Vanity Fair** cover, ©1981 Risko.

439

ARNOLD ROTH (1929-) was born in Philadelphia and attended the Philadelphia Museum School of the Industrial Arts. He has since played the dual roles of cartoonist and illustrator, doing just about everything possible in both camps. A past president of the National Cartoonists Society and member of the Association of American Editorial Cartoonists, he has also done animation and created his own comic strip, "Poor Arnold's Almanac," which ran from 1959-61 and 1989-90.

His illustrations have been published by a long, long list of magazines from 1951 on, including *TV Guide*, *Esquire*, *The Saturday Evening Post*, *National Lampoon*, *Psychology Today*, *Horizon*, *New Republic*, *The New Yorker*, *Look*, *Town and Country*, *Newsweek*, *Sports Illustrated*, *Rolling Stone*, *People*, *Mother Jones*, and *New Woman*.

Roth is a member of Art Directors Clubs in New York, Chicago, Philadelphia, San Francisco and Washington, D.C., the Society of Publication Designers, and the Society of Illustrators. He was awarded the Ruben (named for Rube Goldberg) in 1984 by the National Cartoonists Society and, like Rube, he is an entertaining after-dinner speaker.

Originally published as a cover for *The New Yorker*, November 16, 1992. Copyright © 1992 Arnold Roth.

BILL SIENKIEWICZ (1958-) is an admirer of the past great illustrators, but he is entirely contemporary in his own artwork. Within the comic book field, he has continually pushed against its limiting conventions, experimenting with distortions of lighting unconventional mediums and shapes as well as in off-balance compositions, to challenge and intrigue the reader.

The "graphic novels" that grew out of comic books have given him a wider latitude for this approach, and he has produced several titles, including *Stray Toasters*, described by *Entertainment Weekly* as "An eerie, non-linear tale involving some hellacious household appliances;" *Elektra: Assassin* in collaboration with Frank Miller; *Slow Dancer* for *Epic* magazine; *Big Numbers*; and *Shadow Play*. His *Sketch Book*, published by Fantagraphics Books in 1990, provides a unique look at his creative process.

Sienkiewicz has also been involved with non-comic book artwork, including the film *Unforgiven* and an animated series, *Where in the World is Carmen San Diego?* which brought him two Emmy nominations. Another recent project has been *Voodoo Child: The Illustrated Legend of Jimi Hendrix* published by Penguin.

Bill Sienkiewicz, Stray Toasters Model Three. Published by Epic Comics, 1891,1991.

art spiegelman

ART SPIEGELMAN (1948-) does not fit into the usual categories as an artist. A child of the '60s, he was part of the youth rebellion, the drug culture, and a college dropout. He was also the son of concentration camp parents whose experiences he would draw upon in a powerful indictment of the Nazi atrocities through his picture-novel, *Maus*. It made *The New York Times* best-seller list and has become a classic of its genre, winning him a special Pulitzer Prize.

From childhood, he was obsessed with the cartoon strip as an art form, and he has pushed it in many creative directions, through his own work and in collaboration with others. An early avenue was through the publicaton of a short-lived quarterly underground slick, titled *Arcade*, co-produced with Bill Griffith.

Later, in New York, Spiegelman again attempted a counter-cultural magazine, *Raw*, which found a receptive audience. The publication accepted few limits, but "to be a provocative comic publication for adults, indecent, bawdy, somewhat obscene, harsh and unfair."

In 1993, Spiegelman became a contributor of covers for *The New Yorker*, matching editor Tina Brown's efforts to shake up its staid image with deliberately provocative themes. Not everyone was amused, but readership increased. Even after Brown's departure, Spiegelman has continued to contribute his abrasive societal commentaries for the covers thereby helping to keep *The New Yorker* at the cutting edge.

This prophetic cover of September 13, 1993 appeared long before Littleton. Copyright © 1993 Art Spiegelman. Originally published by *The New Yorker*.

Chris Spollen

CHRIS SPOLLEN (1952-) has embraced the computer and all the help it can give him in creating the images he seeks. He finds the computer a demanding servant, however, and requires the diligence of keeping abreast of new software and technological advances. While no panacea, it has given him more and faster options and he is able to serve a growing number of clients which have included *Science Digest*, *Quest*, *Emergency Medicine*, *Boys' Life*, *Motor Boating*, and *Sailing*, *Medical Economics*, Ziff-Davis and Scholastic, as well as many advertising clients, such as General Motors, AT&T, Bell Labs, and Citibank.

A freelance illustrator and designer since 1975, he studied at the High School of Art and Design and Parsons School of Design in New York. As a pioneer in the digital world, he has been interviewed by *Byte*, *How*, *MacWorld*, and *Step-by-Step Graphics* magazines, and he lectures frequently.

He has taught at the Syracuse University Master Program, the Fashion Institute of Technology and Parsons School of Design Continuing Education Summer Program. He was co-chairman of the Society of Illustrators' first Digital Show in 1997 and is "constantly searching for innovations in both style and technique."

Chris Spollen, *Commerce and Technology* produced entirely via computer.

Moby Dick by Herman Melville; published by Barnes & Noble, 1996.

Yale New Haven Health, 1998.

Portrait of James Joyce from *Time* magazine's 100th issue. © Time, Inc. 1999

MARK D. SUMMERS (1955-) takes the illustrator's art back a century by enlisting the wood engravers' craft to the scratchboard medium. He gives it a thoroughly contemporary flavor, however, in the power of his imagery. Although he works for many other clients, his style has almost become the corporate image for Barnes & Noble bookstores through his portraits of literary figures.

Summers was born in Burlington, Ontario; he studied at the Ontario College of Art in Toronto, and with Will Davis. His first work was for the *Burlington Post* newspaper in 1977, followed by commissions from *Time*, *The New York Times Book Review*, the *Atlantic Monthly*, *Sports Illustrated*, *Entertainment Weekly*, and other publications.

His illustrations for Melville's *Moby Dick* won him his first Gold Medal from the Society of Illustrators and he has won several medals and other citations since from the Society and from *Communication Arts*.

NANCY STAHL

NANCY STAHL (1949-) has reinvented herself several times in her career in keeping up with digital technology in this fast-changing decade. In fact, she holds an edge over many of her computer art contemporaries — she can also draw and paint traditionally.

A native of Long Island, New York, she studied at the Art Center School in Los Angeles, as well as at Parsons School of Design and the School of Visual Arts in New York. Among her influential teachers were Seymour Chwast and Barry Zaid.

Her first illustration assignments were for Ginn textbook publishers in 1972. Her many subsequent clients have included *McCall's*, *The New York Times*, *Sports Illustrated*, *Esquire*, *Chicago Times*, *Forbes*, the *Atlantic Monthly*, *Time*, *Premiere*, *Travel and Leisure*, *Der Spiegel*, and the German *Esquire*. Stahl's work has been featured in *Step-by-Step Graphics* and *Communication Arts*.

She has exhibited her work at the Lustrare Gallery in New York, and is a member of the Graphic Artists Guild and the Society of Illustrators in New York. She also participated in the Syracuse Independent Study Program and taught at the School of Visual Arts.

Nancy Stahl, *Airshow*, for Houghton Brageau, won Gold Award from *Studio*, a Canadian magazine, 1989.

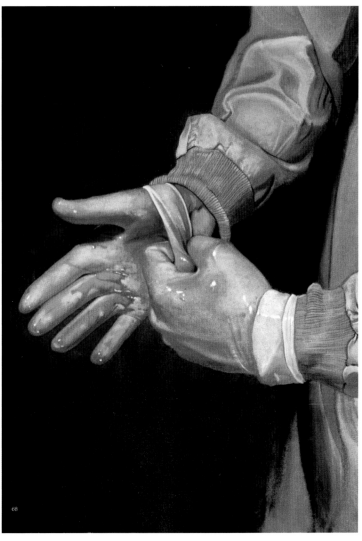

STEVEN H. STROUD (1947-) is a versatile illustrator who can adapt his work to a diversity of subjects ranging from Steven King novels to Pepsi Cola. A native of Chicago, he holds a degree in painting from Drake University and one in illustration from the Art Center College of Design.

After serving in the Navy as a photographer and graphic artist, he began freelancing in 1978. He has since worked for virtually all of the major New York publishers, including Bantam, Berkley, Cahner's Publishing, Dell, Doubleday, Fawcett, The Franklin Library, Harcourt Brace Jovanovich, New American Library, *Playboy*, Putnam, Random House, the *Reader's Digest*, Simon and Schuster, Scholastic, and Viking/Penguin.

Stroud's corporate clients include Eastern Airlines, the Danbury Mint, the U. S. Department of Defense, Hyatt Hotels, Nabisco, Seagram's, UPS, and Wells Fargo.

He recently served as President of the Society of Illustrators and has been a chairman of the Society's Annual Exhibitions. He has received numerous awards from the Society and various local and national design organizations including *Print*, The New Jersey Art Directors Club, and *Rx*.

Stroud has taught at Sacred Heart University, Paier College of Art, Norwich University's Master of Fine Arts program, and was the Tomlinson Fellow in the Visual Arts at Tabor Academy in Marion, Massachusetts.

Steven Stroud, *What Are Your Odds for Getting AIDS from Patients?* cover for *Emergency Medicine*, September, 1987.

There Was an Old Lady Who Swallowed a Fly. Viking Children's Books, 1997; illustrated and adapted by Simms Taback.

SIMMS TABACK (1932-) grew up in the Bronx, attended the High School of Music and Art, and graduated from The Cooper Union. Since then, he has worked as a graphic designer, advertising agency art director, and partner in a design/illustration studio. As a freelance illustrator, he has been a regular contributor to numerous magazines and has designed and published his own line of greeting cards. His work has won citations from many of the major arts organizations, including the Society of Illustrators, the New York Art Directors Club, the AIGA, and was awarded four Louies from the Greeting Card Association.

Taback has illustrated some thirty-five books for children. He was selected twice for a *New York Times* Best Illustrated Book Award, and *There Was an Old Lady Who Swallowed a Fly* was chosen to receive the Parents' Choice Gold Award, the Parenting Magic Reading Award and the Caldecott Silver Medal for 1998. The Caldecott committee described it as "A tour-de-force in innovative book illustration and design." His book, *Joseph Had a Little Overcoat*, was awarded a Caldecott Gold Medal in 2000.

Taback has taught illustration and design at the School of Visual Arts and at Syracuse University. He served as President of both the Illustrator's Guild and the Graphic Artists Guild, which bestowed on him its Lifetime Achievement Award in 1998.

Like some of the greatest masters, CHRIS VAN ALLSBURG (1949-) illustrates his own writing. His books combine those abilities, drawing upon an original inner vision. His books, he claims, are not for children but "for the kid in me." Nonetheless, children love his books as do critics. He has garnered two Caldecott Medals, a National Book Award, and seven medals from the Society of Illustrators, and his books have set sales records rivalling those of Dr. Seuss. His book *The Polar Express* was on *The New York Times'* best-seller list for two years after its publication. Among his book titles are *The Garden of Abdul Gasazi*, *The Wreck of the Zephyr*, *Two Bad Ants*, and *The Stranger*.

His interest in sculpture is reflected in his drawings for an alphabet book, *The Z was Zapped*. In fact, most of his illustrations have a three-dimensional sculpted quality that give them a quiet feeling of monumentality.

Van Allsburg was born in Grand Rapids, Michigan, and studied at the University of Michigan and at the Rhode Island School of Design, where he later taught from 1979 to 1989. In 1979, he embarked on his book career with Houghton Mifflin, which has since published several more of his books. He has also done book jacket and editorial work for Viking and other publishers.

Chris van Allsburg, calendar illustration, pen & ink and scratchboard, 1991.

BIBLIOGRAPHY

Abbott, Charles D., *Howard Pyle, A Chronicle*, New York & London: Harper & Brothers, 1925.

Advertising Arts & Crafts, Volumes I & II, New York & Chicago, Lee and Kirby Inc., 1924.

Allen, Douglas, *Frederic Remington and the Spanish-American War*, New York: Crown Publishers, Inc., 1971.

Allen, Douglas and Allen, Douglas Jr., *N.C. Wyeth; The Collected Paintings, Illustrations and Murals*, New York: Crown Publishers, Inc., 1972.

American Art by American Artists, New York: P.F. Collier & Son, 1914.

The American Historical Scene as depicted by Stanley Arthurs, Philadelphia:University of Pennsylvania Press, 1935.

Amstutz, Walter, editor, *Who's Who in Graphic Art*, Zurich, Switzerland: Amstutz & Herdeg Graphics Press 1962.

Annual of Advertising and Editorial Art and Design, New York; The New York Art Directors Club Yearbook, 1921 and annually thereafter.

Annuals of American Illustration published for the Society of Illustrators, New York: Hastings House, Madison Square Press, Roto Vision, Watson-Guptill, 1959-2000.

Anthony, A.V.S., Life and Character, drawings by W. T. Smedley, A.N.A., Harper & Brothers publishers, 1899

Armitage, Shelley, *John Held, Jr., Illustrator of the Jazz Age*, Syracuse, N.Y:Syracuse University Press, 1987.

___ *Kewpies and Beyond — The World of Rose O'Neill*, 1994, University Press of Mississippi.

Austin, Reid Stewart, *Petty, The Classic Pin-up Art of George Petty*, New York: Gramercy Books, 1997.

Ballinger, James K., *Frederic Remington*, National Museum of American Art, Smithsonian Institution, Harry N. Abrams, Inc., New York, 1989.

Bama, James and Ballantine, Ian, *The Western Art of James Bama*, New York: Charles Scribner's Sons and Peacock Press/Bantam Books, 1975.

Baragwanath, John, *A Good Time was Had*, New York: Appleton-Century-Crofts, Inc., 1962.

Barney, Maginel Wright, *The Valley of the God-Almighty Joneses*, New York: Appleton-Century, 1965.

Barton, Phyllis S., *William Frederick Foster, A.N.A. Portrait of a Painter*, Los Angeles, CA: Richlaine Publishing, 1987.

Beam, Philip C., *Winslow Homer's Magazine Engravings*, New York: Harper & Row, Publishers, 1979.

___ *Winslow Homer at Prout's Neck*, Little Brown and Co., 1966.

Beckett, Dr. James, *The Sports Art of Bart Forbes*, Dallas, TX: Beckett Publications, 1998.

Bell, Wm. Gardner, *Will James, The Life & Works of a Lone Cowboy*, Northland Press, 1987.

Benson, Frances M., *Essays on American Art & Artists: The Moran Family*, New York: Eastern Art League, 1896.

Berkey, John, *Painted Space*, Pittsburgh, PA: Friedlander Pub. Group, 1991.

Best, James J., *American Popular Illustration*, Westport, CT: Greenwood Press, 1984.

Bimson, Walter Reed, *The West and Walter Bimson*, Tucson, AZ: University of Arizona Museum of Art, 1971.

Biographical Sketches of American Artists, 5th Edition, Lansing, Michigan: Michigan State Library, 1924.

Birmingham, *Vision of the West: The Art of Will Crawford*, Birmingham Museum of Art, 1986.

Bloch, Maurice E., and others, *The American Personality; The Artist Illustrator of Life in the United States 1860-1930*, Los Angeles, California: The Grunwald Center for the Graphic Arts, University of California, 1976.

Bogart, Michele H., *Artists, Advertising and the Borders of Art*, University of Chicago Press, 1995.

Bolton, Theodore, *American Book Illustrators*, New York: R.R. Bowker Company, 1938.

Bossert, Jill, *Pro Illustration-Editorial*, New York: Pub. for Society of Illustrators by Rotovision, 1996.

___ *Pro Illustration-Advertising*, New York: Pub. for Society of Illustrators by Rotovision, 1997.

___ *Children's Book Illustration, Step by Step Techniques*, New York: Pub. for Society of Illustrators by Rotovision, 1998.

Broder, Patricia Janis, *Dean Cornwell: Dean of Illustrators*, New York: Balance House, Ltd., 1978.

Buechner, Thomas S., *Norman Rockwell, Artist and Illustrator*, New York: Harry N. Abrams, Inc., 1970.

Burnside, Wesley M., *Maynard Dixon, Artist of the West*, Brigham Young University Press, 1974.

Butterfield, Roger, *The Saturday Evening Post Treasury*, New York: Simon & Schuster, Inc., 1954.

Cabarga, Leslie, *Dynamic Black & White Illustration*, New York: Art Direction Books, 1993.

Calkins, Earnest Elmo, *Franklin Booth*, New York: Robert Frank, publisher, 1925.

___ and others, *A Book of Notable Illustrators*, 1926.

Cameron, Duncan F., *A Century of American Illustration*, The Brooklyn Museum, 1972.

Canemaker, John, *Winsor McCay-His Life and Art*, New York: Abbeville Press, 1987.

Carroll, John M., *Eggenhofer: The Pulp Years*, Fort Collins, CO: The Old Army Press, 1975.

Carter, Alice A., *The Red Rose Girls*, New York: Harry N. Abrams, Inc., 2000.

Carter, Denny, *Henry Farny*, Watson Guptill Publications, 1978.

Casteras, Susan P., *Pocket Cathedrals, Pre Raphaelite Book Illustrations*, Yale Center for British Art, 1991.

Charles, Milton, *The Art of Mara McAfee*, Pocket Books, 1981.

Churchill, Allen, *The Liberty Years 1924 1950*, Prentice Hall Inc., 1969.

Clark, Eliot, *History of the National Academy of Design 1825-1953*, New York: Columbia University Press, 1954.

Cohn, Jan, *Covers of the Saturday Evening Post*, Viking Penguin, USA, 1995.

Coke, Van Deren, *Taos and Santa Fe*, University of New Mexico Press, 1963.

Commager, Henry Steele, *The American Spirit, The Paintings of Mort Künstler*, Harry N. Abrams, 1986.

Cornebise, Alfred Emile, *Art from the Trenches, America's Uniformed Artists in World War I*, Texas A&M University Press, 1991.

Collins, Max Allan & Elvgren, Drake, *Elvgren, His Life & Art*, Portland, OR:Collectors Press, Inc., 1998.

Cortissoz, Royal, *The Works of Edwin Howland Blashfield*, New York: Charles Scribner's Sons, 1937.

Creative Artists, 1940, New York: Sackett & Wilhelms Lithographing Corporation.

Dalziel, George & Edward, *The Brothers Dalziel, A Record of Fifty Years' Work, 1840 1890*, London: Dalziel & Co., Ltd.

Daver, Manek, *David Stone Martin —Jazz Graphics*, Tokyo, Japan: Graphic-shga Pub. Co., Ltd., 1991.

Davis, Paul, *Faces*, New York City: Friendly Press, Inc., 1985.

Delessert, Etienne, *Les Quatre Saisons*, Musee Olympique Lausanne, Bertelsmann UFA, 1998.

Dell, John Edward, Editor, *Visions of Adventure*, N.C. Wyeth and the Brandywine Artists, Watson Guptill Publications, 2000.

DeShazo, Edith, *Everett Shinn 1876-1953*, New York: Clarkson N. Potter, Inc., 1974.

Di Fate, Vincent, *Infinite Worlds*, New York: The Wonderland Press, 1997.

Dippie, Brian W. Ed., *Charles M. Russell, Word Painter*; *Letters 1887-1926*; Amon Carter Museum. New York: Harry N. Abrams, Inc., 1993.

Downey, Fairfax, *Portrait of an Era as Drawn by C.D. Gibson*, New York and London: Charles Scribner's Sons, 1936.

Dunn, Harvey, *An Evening in the Classroom*, Privately printed at the instigation of Mario Cooper, 1934.

Dyal, Donald, Hastedt, Catherine A., Smith, Steven F., editors, *American Book & Magazine Illustrators to 1920*, Dictionary of Literary Biography, Vol. 188; 1998.

Dykes, Jeff C., *Fifty Great Western Illustrators; A Bibliographic Checklist*, Arizona: Northland Press, 1975.

Eastman, Max, *Journalism Versus Art*, Alfred A. Knopf, 1916.

Eggenhofer, Nick, *Horses, Horses, Always Horses, the life and Art of Nick Eggenhofer*, Cody, Wyoming: Sage Publishing Co., Inc., 1981.

Eiteljorg, Harrison, *Treasures of the American West*, New York: Balance House, 1981.

Ellis, Richard Williamson, *Book Illustration; A Survey of its History and Development*, Kingsport, Tennessee: The Kingsport Press, 1952.

Elzea, Rowland, and Hawkes, Elizabeth H., editors, *A Small School of Art: The Students of Howard Pyle*, Wilmington, Delaware: Delaware Art Museum, 1980.

Elzea, Rowland, *The Golden Age of American Illustration 1880-1914*, The Wilmington Society of the Fine Arts, 1972.

___ *American Illustration*, Delaware Art Museum, 1991.

Ermoyan, Arpi, *Famous American Illustrators*, Published for the Society of Illustrators by Rotovision, S.A., 1997.

Erté, *Things I Remember*, Quadrangle/The N.Y. Times Book Co., Sevenarts Ltd.,1975.

Essays on American Art and Artists, Eastern Art League, 1896.

Falk, Peter Hastings, editor in chief, ***Who Was Who in American Art 1564-1975***, in three volumes, Sound View Press, 1999.

Fawcett, Robert, ***On the Art of Drawing***, New York: Watson-Guptill Publications, Inc., 1958.

Fenner, Arnie and Cathy, editors, ***Legacy, Frank Frazetta***, Underwood Books, 1999.

___ ***Icon, Frank Frazetta, A Retrospective by the Grand Master of Fantastic Art***, 1998.

Ferber, Linda and Brown, Robin, ***A Century of American Illustration***, New York: The Brooklyn Museum, 1972.

Fielding, Mantle, ***Dictionary of American Painters, Sculptors & Engravers***, Flushing, New York: Paul A. Stroock, publisher, 1960.

Fischer, Katrina Sigsbee, ***Anton Otto Fischer; Marine Artist***, Brighton, Sussex, England: Teredo Books, Ltd., 1977.

Flagg, James Montgomery, ***Roses and Buckshot***, New York: G.P. Putnam's Sons, 1946.

Forbes, Edwin, ***Life Studies of the Great Army***, pub. By Edwin Forbes, 1876.

Frost, A.B. ***A Book of Drawings***, New York: P.F. Collier & Son, 1904.

Galbraith, John Kenneth, ***No Known Survivors, David Levine's Political Plank***, Boston: 1970.

Gallagher, Brian, ***Anything Goes, The Jazz Age Adventures of Neysa McMein***, Times Books, 1987.

Gallatin, Albert Eugene, ***Art and the Great War***, New York: E.P. Dutton & Co., 1919.

The Gibson Book, A collection of the published works of Charles Dana Gibson in two volumes, New York: Charles Scribner's Sons, R.H. Russell, 1907.

Glackens, Ira, ***William Glackens and the Ashcan Group***, New York: Crown Publishers, Inc., 1957.

Goodrich, Lloyd, ***The Graphic Art of Winslow Homer***, Smithsonian Institution Press, 1968.

Gomes, Rosalie, ***Black & White, Being the Early illustrations of Maxfield Parrish***, Brooklyn, NY: Thumbtack Books, Inc., 1982.

Gorey, Edward, ***Edward Gorey Amphigorey*** Also, pub. by Congdon & Weed, Inc. 1983.

Graphic Artists Guild Directory 1981-1982, New York: Annuals Publishing Company.

Grossman, Julian, ***Echo of a Distant Drum: Winslow Homer and the Civil War***, Harry N. Abrams, Inc., 1974.

Guitar, Mary Ann, ***22 Famous Painters and Illustrators Tell How They Work***, New York: David McKay Company, Inc., 1964

Guptill, Artrhur L., ***Drawing with Pen and Ink***, New York: The Pencil Points Press, Inc., 1928.

___ ***Norman Rockwell—Illustrator***, New York: Watson-Guptill Publications, Inc., 1946.

Hagerty, Donald J., ***Desert Dreams: The Art & Life of Maynard Dixon***, Gibbs-Smith Publisher, 1993.

Halsey, Ashley Jr., ***Illustrating for The Saturday Evening Post***, Boston: Arlington House, 1951.

Hamill, Alfred E., ***T. M. Cleland***, The Pinson Printers, 1929.

Hardy, David A., ***Visions of Space-Artists Journey through the Cosmos***, Gallery Books, W.H. Smith Publishers, Inc., 1990.

Harmsen, Dorothy, ***Harmsen's Western Americana***, Flagstaff, Arizona: Northland Press, 1971.

Harrison, Hank, ***The Art of Jack Davis***, Stabur Press, Inc., 1987.

Harrison Fisher's American Beauties, Indianapolis: The Bobbs Merrill Company, 1909.

Hassrick, Peter H., ***Artists of the American Frontier, The Way West***, New York: Promontory Press, a div. Of L.D.A.P. Inc.,1988.

___ ***Frederic Remington***, New York: Harry N. Abrams, Inc., 1973.

___ ***Western Painting Today***, New York: Watson-Guptill Publications, 1975.

Hawkes, Elizabeth & Allyn, Nancy E., ***William Glackens, A Catalogue of his Book and Magazine Illustrations***, Delaware Art Museum, 1987.

Hawkes, Elizabeth H., ***John Sloan's Illustrations in Magazines and Books***, Delaware Art Museum, 1993

Hedgepeth, Don & Reed, Walt, ***The Art of Tom Lovell, An Invitation to History***, Trumbull, CT: The Greenwich Workshop, Inc., 1993.

Helck, Peter, ***The Checkered Flag***, New York: Charles Scribner's Sons, 1961.

___ ***Great Auto Races***, New York: Harry N. Abrams, Inc., 1975.

Held, John Jr., Weinhardt, Carl, Connelly, Marc, and Hayes, Bartlett H. Jr., ***The Most of John Held***, Jr., Brattleboro, Vermont: The Stephen Greene Press, 1972.

Held, John Jr., ***The Works of John Held***, Jr., New York: Ives Washburn, publisher, 1931.

Heller, Steven, ***Seymour Chwast, The Left Handed Designer***, New York: Harry N. Abrams, Inc., 1985.

Heller, Steven and Chwast, Seymour, ***Jackets Required, An Illustrated History of American Book Jacket Design 1920-1950***. San Francisco, CA: Chronicle Books, 1995.

Heller, Steven, Editor, ***Innovators of American Illustration***, New York: Van Nostrand Reinhold Company, 1986.

Henning, Fritz, ***American Realist - Stevan Dohanos***, Westport, CT: North Light Publishers, 1980.

Hirschfeld, Al, ***Hirschfeld's World***, New York: published by Harry N. Abrams Inc. 1981.

___ ***The American Theatre as Seen by Hirschfeld***, George Braziller Inc. Publisher, 1961.

Hodgson, Pat, ***The War Illustrators***, New York: MacMillan Publishers, 1977.

Hogarth, Paul, ***Arthur Boyd Houghton***, 1981 by Paul Hogarth.

Holme, Bryan, ***The Journal of the Century***, compiled by Holme with the editors of Viking Press and the Ladies' Home Journal by Viking Penguin Inc., 1976.

Holme, Charles, editor, ***Modern Pen Drawings: European and American***, Special Winter Number of "The Studio" 1900 1901, London, Paris, New York, 1901.

Homer, William Innes, ***Thomas Eakins, His Life & Art***, New York: Abbeville Press, 1992.

Horn, Maurice, editor, ***The World Encyclopedia of Cartoons***, New York and London: Chelsea House Publishers, 1980.

___ editor, ***The World Encyclopedia of Comics***, New York: Chelsea House Publishers, 1976.

Hornung, Clarence P., editor, ***Will Bradley; His Graphic Art***, New York: Dover Publications, Inc., 1974.

Hornung, Clarence P. And Johnson, Fridolf, ***200 Years of American Graphic Art***. New York: George Braziller, 1976.

Horwitt, Nathan G., ***A Book of Notable American Illustrators***, Walker Engraving Co., 1926.

Hutchinson, William Henry, ***The World, The Work and The West of W.H.D. Koerner***, University of Oaklahoma Press, 1978.

Hydeman, Sid, ***How to Illustrate for Money***, New York and London: Harper & Brothers, 1936.

Hyland, Douglas K.S., and Brokaw, Howard P., ***Howard Pyle and the Wyeths: Four Generations of American Imagination***, Tennessee: Memphis Brooks Museum of Art, 1983.

Ingersoll, R. Sturgis, ***Henry McCarter***, privately printed at Riverside Press, 1944.

Janello, Amy and Jones, Brennon, ***The American Magazine***, New York: Harry N. Abrams Inc., Publishers, 1991.

Johnson, Fridolf, ***The Illustrations of Rockwell Kent***, with the collaboration of John F.H. Gorton, Director, the Rockwell Kent Legacies, New York: Dover Publications Inc., 1976.

___ editor, ***Treasury of American Pen & Ink Illustration 1881-1938***, New York: Dover Publications, Inc., 1982.

Johnson, Merle, compiler, ***Howard Pyle's Book of The American Spirit***, New York and London: Harper & Brothers, 1923.

___ Compiler, ***Howard Pyle's Book of Pirates***, New York and London: Harper & Brothers, 1921.

Jones, Jeff, ***Idyl***, Introduction by Eric Kimball, Blue Star, 1975.

___***Yesterday's Lily***, (Four separate copyrights, 1980).

Karolevitz, Robert F., ***Where Your Heart is … The Story of Harvey Dunn***, Aberdeen SD: North Plains Press, 1970.

Kellner, Bruce, ***The Last Dandy***, Ralph Barton 1891-1931, University of Missouri Press, 1991.

Kelton, Elmer, ***The Art of Frank C. McCarthy***, New York: The Greenwich Workshop Inc., publisher Wm. Morrow & Co., Inc., 1992.

___ ***The Art of Howard Terpning***, Bantam Books, 1992.

Kent, Norman, editor, ***The Book of Edward A Wilson***, New York: The Heritage Press, 1948.

Kery, Patricia Frantz, ***Great Magazine Covers of the World***, New York: Abbeville Press, 1982.

Knight, Clayton, ***Pilot's Luck***, Philadelphia: David McKay Company, 1929.

Korshak, Stephen D. editor, ***A Hannes Bok Treasury***, Underwood-Miller, 1993.

Landgren, Marchal E., ***Years of Art, The Story of the Art Students League of New York***, New York: Robert M. McBride & Company, 1940.

Lanes, Selma G., ***The Art of Maurice Sendak***, New York: Abradale Press, Harry N. Abrams, Inc., 1980.

Larson, Judy L., ***American Illustration 1890-1925***, Calgary, Alberta, Canada: Glenbow Museum, Glenbow Alberta Institute, 1986.

Lesser, Robert, ***Original Cover Paintings for the Great American Pulp Magazines***, New York: Gramercy Books, a division of Random House Value Pub. Inc., 1997

Lettick, Birney, *Vision*, (special issue) Tokyo Designers Gakuin College, 1987.

Low, Will H., *A Painter's Progress — The Scammon Lectures*, New York: Charles Scribner's Sons, 1910.

Lucas, E.V., *Life and Work of Edwin Austin Abbey*, R.A., in two volumes, New York: Charles Scribner's Sons, London: Methuen and Company, Ltd., 1921.

Ludwig, Coy, *Maxfield Parrish*, New York: Watson-Guptill Publications, 1973.

Lyon, Peter, *Success Story: The Life and Times of S.S. McClure*, New York: Charles Scribner's Sons, 1963.

McCall, Robert and Asimov, Isaac, *Our World in Space*, Greenwich, CT: New York Graphic Society, Ltd., 1974.

McConnell, Gerald, editor, *Twenty Years of Award Winners*, published for the Society of Illustrators, New York: Hastings House, 1981.

McCracken, Harold, *The Charles M. Russell Book*, Garden City, New York: Doubleday and Company, 1957.

___ *The Frederic Remington Book*, Garden City, New York: Doubleday and Company, 1966.

McElroy, Guy C., *Facing History - The Black Image in American Art 1710-1940*, San Francisco, CA: Bedford Art, Publishers, 1990.

McMullan, James, *Revealing Illustrations, The Art of James McMullan*, New York: Watson-Guptill Publications, 1981.

McMullan, Jim, *This Face You Got, The Art of the Illustrator*, Journey Editions, Charles E. Tuttle Co. Inc., 1994 .

Mahoney, Bertha E., Latimer, Louise P. And Folmsbee, Beulah, editors and compilers, *Illustrators of Children's Books 1744-1945*, Boston: The Horn Book, 1947.

Mahoney-Miller, Bertha, Viguers, Ruth Hill, Dalphin, Marcia, editors and compilers, *Illustrators of Children's Books 1946-1956*, Boston: The Horn Book, 1958.

Mallett, Daniel Trowbridge, *Mallett's Index of Artists*, New York: R.R. Bowker Company, 1935. Supplement published in 1940.

Margolin, Victor, *American Poster Renaissance*, New York: Watson Guptill, 1975.

Marling, Karal Ann, *Norman Rockwell*, Harry N. Abrams, Inc., Publishers in association with The National Museum of American Art, Smithsonian Institution, 1997.

Marshall, Francis, *Magazine Illustration*, New York: the Viking Press, Inc., London: The Studio Ltd., 1959.

Martignette, Charles G. and Meisel, Louis K., *The Great American Pinup*, Koln, Germany: Taschen, 1996.

___ *Gil Elvgren All his Glamorous American Pin-ups*, Benedikt Taschen verlag GmbH., 1999.

Martinez, Gerald and Diana, *What it is...What It was! The Black Film Explosion of the '70s*, Hyperion, Miramax Books, 1998.

Meglin, Nick, *The Art of Humorous Illustration*, New York: Watson-Guptill Publications, 1973.

Meyer, Claudia, *Donald Teague, A Life in Color*, Bozeman, MT: Nygard Publishing Company, 1988.

Meyer, Susan E., *America's Great Illustrators*, New York: Harry N. Abrams, Inc., 1978.

___ *James Montgomery Flagg*, New York: Watson-Guptill Publications, 1974.

___ *Norman Rockwell's People*, New York: Harry N. Abrams, Inc., 1981.

___ *Treasury of Children's Book Illustrators*, New York: Harry N. Abrams, Inc., 1983.

Michaelis, David, *N. C. Wyeth, A Biography*, New York: Alfred A. Knopf, 1998.

Millie, Elena G., *Nagel - The Art of Patrick Nagel*, 1987 Treville.

Minor, Wendell, *Art for the Written Word, 25 years of Book Cover Art*, Harcourt Brace & Co., 1995.

Mitnick, Barbara J., *Jean Léon Gerome Ferris, 1863-1930*: American Painter Historian, Laurel, MI: *The Lauren Rogers Museum of Art*, 1985.

Moffatt, Laurie Norton, *Norman Rockwell — A Definitive Catalogue* (in two volumes), Stockbridge, MA: The Norman Rockwell Museum at Stockbridge, 1986.

Moline, Mary, *Norman Rockwell Encyclopedia*, Indianapolis: The Curtis Publishing Co., 1979.

Morse, John D., editor; *Ben Shahn*, New York: Praeger Publishers, 1972.

Morse, Willard S. and Brincklé, Gertrude, compilers, *Howard Pyle—A Record of his Illustrations and Writings*, Wilmington, Delaware: The Wilmington Society of the Fine Arts, 1921.

Moskowitz, Sam, *Explorers of the Infinite, Shapers of Science Fiction*, Cleveland: The World Publishing Company, 1963.

___ *Virgil Finlay, An Appreciation*, West Kingston, RI: Donald M. Grant, Publisher.

Muir, Percy, *Victorian Illustrated Books*, B. T. Batsford Ltd., 1971.

Munce, Howard, *The Animal Art of Bob Kuhn*, Westport, Connecticut: North Light Publishers, 1973.

Munce, Howard and Fawcett, Robert, *Drawing the Nude*, New York: Watson Guptill Publications, 1980.

Murrell, William, *A History of American Graphic Humor*, New York: The Macmillan Company, 1938.

Nelson-Cave, Wendy, *Broadway Theatre Posters*, New York: Brompton Books Corp., Smithmark Publishers Inc., 1993.

Nudelman, Edward D., *Jessie Willcox Smith, American Illustrator*, Gretna, LA: Pelican Publishing Company, 1990.

___ *Jessie Willcox Smith: A Bibliography*, Gretna, LA: Pelican Publishing Company, 1989.

Oaklander, Christine I., *John Wolcott Adams — American Life and History*, Chadds Ford, PA:Brandywine River Museum Exhibition, 1998.

Official Directory, American illustrators and Advertising Artists, Washington, D.C.: American Federation of Arts, publisher, 1949.

Okrent, Daniel, *Fortune, The Art of Covering Business*, Historical Essay, Salt Lake City, UT: Pub. by Gibbs Smith, publisher, 1999.

O'Neill, William, Editor; *Echoes of Revolt: The Masses 1911-1917*, Quadrangle Books, Inc., 1966.

O'Rourke, P.J. and Charles, Milton, *The Art of Mara McAfee*, New York: Pocket Books, 1981.

Packer, William, *The Art of Vogue Covers*, New York: Harmony Books, 1980.

Paine, Albert Bigelow, *Thomas Nast, His Period and His Pictures*, New York & London: Harper & Brothers, 1904.

Paul, Rodman W., editor, *A Victorian Gentlewoman in the Far West, Reminiscences of Mary Hallock Foote*, Henry E. Huntington Library & Art Gallery, 1972.

Pennell, Joseph, *The Adventures of an Illustrator*, Boston: Little, Brown and Company, 1925.

___ *Modern Illustration*, London and New York: George Bell & Sons, 1895.

___ *Pen Drawing and Pen Draughtsmen*, New York: The Macmillan Company, 1889.

Perceptions and Evocations, The Art of Elihu Vedder, National Collection of Fine Arts, Smithsonian Institution Press, 1979.

Perlman, Bernard, B., *F. R. Gruger and His Circle; The Golden Age of Illustration*, Westport, Connecticut: North Light Publishers, 1978.

___ *The Immortal Eight*, Westport, Connecticut: North Light Publishers, 1979.

Petaja, Emil, *Showcase of Fantasy Art, - The Hannes Bok Memorial*, preface by Ray Bradbury, SISU Publishers, 1974.

Peters, Harry T., *Currier & Ives, Printmakers to the American People*, Doubleday, Doran & Company, Inc., 1929.

Pitz, Henry C., *The Brandywine Tradition*, New York: Weathervane Books, 1968.

___ *Howard Pyle*, New York: Bramhall House, 1965.

___ *Illustrating Children's Books*, New York: Watson-Guptill Publications, Inc., 1963.

___ *Ink Drawing Techniques*, New York: Watson-Guptill Publications, Inc., 1957.

___ *The Practice of Illustration*, New York: Watson-Guptill Publications, Inc., 1947.

___ *A Treasury of American Book Illustration*, New York and London: American Studio Books and Watson-Guptill Publications, Inc., 1947.

___ *200 Years of American Illustration*, New York: Random House, Inc., 1977.

Porter, Fairfield, *Thomas Eakins*, New York: George Brailler, Inc., 1959.

Pratt, George, *No Man's Land*, Northampton, MA: Tundra Pub. Ltd., 1992.

___ *Enemy Ace War Idyll*, New York: DC Comics, Inc., 1990.

Preiss, Byron, Editor, *The Art of Leo & Diane Dillon*, Byron Preiss Visual Publications, 1981.

Price, Charles Matlock, *Posters*, New York: George W. Bricka, 1913.

Price, Garrett, *Drawing Room Only — A Book of Cartoons*, Promenade (Robert L. Johnson Magazines, Inc.), 1946.

Rae, William E., editor, *A Treasury of Outdoor Life*, New York: 1975, 1982 by Times Mirror Magazines, Inc.

Rawls, Walton, *Wake Up, America! World War I and The American Poster*, Cross River Press, Ltd., 1988.

Ray, Frederic E., *Alfred R. Waud, Civil War Artist*, New York: The Viking Press, 1974.

Rebello, Stephen and Allen Richard, *Reel Art: Great Posters from the*

Golden Age of the Silver Screen, New York: Abbeville Press, 1988.

Reed, Henry M., *The A.B. Frost Book*, Rutland, Vermont: Charles E. Tuttle Co., 1967.

Reed, Walt, *Great American Illustrators*, New York: Abbeville Press, 1979.

___ *Harold Von Schmidt Draws and Paints the Old West*, Flagstaff, Arizona: Northland Press, 1972.

___ *John Clymer; An Artist's Rendezvous with the Frontier West*, Flagstaff, Arizona: Northland Press, 1976.

___ compiler, *The Magic Pen of Joseph Clement Coll*, Westport, Connecticut: North Light Publishers, 1978.

Reed, Walt and Roger, *The Illustrator in America 1880-1980*, New York: Madison Square Press for the Society of Illustrators, 1984.

Reid, Aileen, *Theatre Posters*, New York: pub. by Smithmark Publishers Inc., Brompton Books Corp., 1993.

Reid, Forrest, *Illustrators of the Sixties*, London: Faber & Gwyer Lord, 1928.

Renner, Frederic G., *Charles M. Russell*, New York: Harry N. Abrams, Inc., 1966.

Richardson, Darrell C., *J. Allen St. John — An Illustrated Bibliography*, Memphis, TN: Mid America Publishers, Inc., 1991.

Robinson, Frank, *Science Fiction of the 20th Century - An Illustrated History*, Portland, OR: Collectors Press, 1999.

Robinson, Frank M. And Davidson, Lawrence, *Pulp Culture: The Art of Fiction Magazines*, Portland, OR: Collectors Press Inc., 1998 .

Robinson, Julian, *The Fine Art of Fashion, an Illustrated History*, Julian Robinson, National Library of Australia.

___ *The Golden Age of Style*, London: ORBIS Pub., Ltd., 1976.

Rockwell, Norman, *Rockwell on Rockwell, How I Make a Picture*, Westport, CT: Watson Guptill Publications in cooperation with Famous Artists School, 1979.

Rockwell, Norman, as told to Thomas Rockwell, *My Adventures as an Illustrator*, New York: Doubleday & Co., Inc., 1960.

Rodman, Selden, *Portrait of the Artist as an American, Ben Shahn: A Biography with Pictures*, New York: Harper & Brothers publishers, 1951.

Rosenberg, Harold, *Saul Steinberg*, New York: Alfred A. Knopf in association with the Whitney Museum of American Art,, 1978.

Ross, Clifford and Wilkin, Karen, *The World of Edward Gorey*, New York: Harry N. Abrams, Inc., 1996

Rottensteiner, Franz, *The Science Fiction Book: An Illustrated History*, New York: The Seabury Press, 1975.

Rubenstein, Charlotte Streifer, *American Women Artists*, Boston: G.K. Hall & Co., New York: Avon Books, 1982.

Ruggles, Rowena Godding, *The One Rose: Mother of the Immortal Kewpies*, 1st ed. 1964; 2nd ed. 1972.

Samuels, Peggy and Harold, *Contemporary Western Artists*, Houston, Texas: Southwest Arts Publishing, 1982.

___ *The Illustrated Biographical Encyclopedia of Artists of the American West*, Garden City, New York: Doubleday & Co., Inc., 1976.

___ *Frederic Remington, A Biography*, New York: Doubleday, 1982.

Schau, Michael, *"All-American Girl," The Art of Coles Phillips*, New York: Watson Guptill Publications, 1975.

___ *J. C. Leyendecker*, New York: Watson Guptill Publications, 1974.

Schimmel, Julie, *The Art & Life of W. Herbert Dunton*, Starck Museum of Art, University of Texas Press, 1984.

Schmidt, Dorey, editor, *The America Magazine 1890-1940*, Delaware Art Museum, 1979.

___ *....Illustrated by Darley*, 1978.

___ *City Life Illustrated 1890-1940* (Sloan, Glackens, Luks, Shinn), Delaware Art Museum, 1980.

Schnessel, S. Michael, *Jessie Wilcox Smith*, New York: Thomas Y. Crowell, Toronto: Fitzheary & Whiteside Ltd., 1977.

Schoonover, Cortlandt, *Frank Schoonover, Illustrator of the North American Frontier*, New York: Watson-Guptill Publications, 1976.

Schreuders, Piet, *Paperbacks: USA*, San Diego, California: Blue Dolphin Enterprises, Inc., 1981.

Scott, David, *John Sloan*, New York: Watson-Guptill Publications, 1975.

Sears, Stephen W. Editor, *American Heritage Century Collection of Civil War Art*, New York: American Heritage Publishing Co., Inc., 1974.

Simon, Howard, *500 Years of Art in Illustration*, New York: World Publishing Co., 1942.

Skinner, Tina, *Harrison Fisher— Defining the American Beauty*, Schiffer Publishing, 1999.

Soria, Regina, *Perceptions and Evocations — The Art of Elihu Vedder*, Washington, D.C.: The Smithsonian Institution, 1979.

Steinberg, Saul, *The Art of Living*, New York: Harper and Brothers Publishers, 1949.

___ *The Labyrinth*, New York: Harper and Brothers Publishers, 1954.

Steine, Kent and Taraba, Frederic B., *The J.C. Leyendecker Collection: American Illustrators Poster Book*, Portland, Oregon: Collector's Press, 1996.

Stick, David, editor, *An Artist's Catch — Watercolors by Frank Stick*, Chapel Hill, North Carolina: University of North Carolina Press, 1981.

Stivers, David, *The NABISCO Brands Collection of Cream of Wheat Advertising Art*, A Collectors Showcase Library Publications, 1986.

Stoltz, Dr. Donald, Stoltz, Marshall L. And Earle, William F., *The Advertising World of Norman Rockwell*, New York: Madison Square Press, 1984.

Suares, Jean-Claude, editor, *Art of the Times*, New York: Universe Books, 1973.

Taback, Simms, *The New Illustration*, Pub. for the Society of Illustrators by Madison Square Press, 1985.

Taft, Robert, *Artists and Illustrators of the Old West 1850-1900*, New York: Charles Scribner's Sons, 1953.

Tarrant, Dorothy and John,, *A Community of Artists — Westport — Weston,* 1985.

Ten Eyck Gardner, Albert, *Winslow Homer American Artist: His World and His Work*, Clarkson N. Potter, Inc., 1961.

Thirty Favorite Paintings by Leading American Artists, New York: P.F. Collier & Son, 1908.

Thorpe, James, *English Illustration: The Nineties*, New York: reissued by Hacker Art Books, Inc., 1975.

Time Magazine editors, *The Face of History: Time Magazine Covers*, 1923-1991.

Tinkelman, Murray and Kagan, Daniel, editor, *The Illustrations of Murray Tinkelman*, New York: Art Direction Book Company.

Traxel, David, *An American Saga: The Life and Times of Rockwell Kent*, New York: Harper & Row, Publishers, 1980.

Updike, John, *The Complete Book of Covers from The New Yorker 1925-1989*, The New Yorker Magazine, Inc., 1989.

Vanity Fair Book, The John Day Company, 1931, Condé Nast Publications, Inc., 1930-31.

Varga— The Esquire Years, A Catalogue Raisonné, foreword by Kurt Vonnegut, Toronto: St. James Press, Ltd., 1987.

Vargas, Alberto and Austin, Reid, *Vargas*, foreword by Hugh Hefner, 1978.

Waterhouse, Col. Charles USMCR, *Illustrations in Black and White and Gray by Steven R. Kidd*, Glenbrook, Connecticut: Art Direction Book Company, 2000.

___ *The Blue Book Illustrations of Herbert Morton Stoops*, Glenbrook, Connecticut: Art Direction Book Company, 1998.

Watson, Ernest W., *Forty Illustrators and How They Work*, New York: Watson Guptill Publications, Inc., 1946.

Weinberg, Robert, *A Biographical Dictionary of Science Fiction and Fantasy Artists*, New York, Westport, Connecticut, London: Greenwood Press, 1988.

Welch, Naomi, Zeigler, Kim, editor, *The Complete Works of Harrison Fisher, Illustrator*, 1999.

Wenzell, A.B., *The Passing Show*, New York: P.F.Collier & Son, 1903.

White, Peter, Asst. Curator and Spalding, Jeffrey J., Curator of Art, *Charles Livingston Bull*, Glenbow-Alberta Institute, 1979.

Whiting, John D., *Practical Illustration, A Guide for Artists*, New York and London: Harper & Brothers, 1920.

Who's Who in American Art, Washington, D.C.: American Federation of Arts, publisher, New York and London: R.R. Bowker Co., 1936 to present.

Wood, Christopher, *The Pre-Raphaelites*, New York: The Viking Press and Christopher Wood Ltd., 1981.

Wortman, Denys, *Mopey Dick and the Duke*, New York: Fairchild Publications, 1952.

Wyeth, N.C. and Wyeth, Betsy James, editor, *The Wyeths*, Boston: Gambit, 1971.

The Year's Art/The Quarterly Illustrator, New York: Harry C. Jones, publisher, 1893, 1894, 1895.

Yost, Karl and Renner, Frederic Renner, *A Bibliography of the Published Works by Charles M. Russell*, Lincoln, Nebraska: University of Nebraska Press, 1971.

Young, Mahoric Sharp, *The Eight, The Realist Revolt in American Painting*, New York: Watson-Guptil Publications, 1978.

Zurier, Rebecca, *Art for the Masses*, Philadelphia: Temple University, 1988.

INDEX

Artists biographies numbered in red, other references in black.